D1711551

The Library of Southern Civilization
Lewis P. Simpson, Editor

The Civil War Diary of Clara Solomon

The Civil War Diary of Clara Solomon

*Growing Up
in New Orleans,
1861–1862*

Edited, with an Introduction, by

Elliott Ashkenazi

Louisiana State University Press
Baton Rouge and London

Designer: Glynnis Phoebe
Typeface: Cochin
Typesetter: Moran Printing, Inc.
Printer and binder: Thomson–Shore, Inc.

Library of Congress Cataloging-in-Publication Data
  Solomon, Clara.
      The Civil War diary of Clara Solomon :   growing up in New Orleans,
    1861–1862 /   edited, with an introduction, by Elliott Ashkenazi.
          p.   cm.
      Includes index.
      ISBN 0-8071-1968-7 (alk. paper)
      1. Solomon, Clara — Diaries.   2. New Orleans (La.) — History — Civil
  War, 1861–1865 — Personal narratives.   3. United States — History —
  Civil War, 1861–1865 — Personal narratives, Confederate.   4. Girls —
  Louisiana — New Orleans — Diaries.   5. Jewish girls — Louisiana — New
  Orleans — Diaries.   I. Ashkenazi, Elliott.   II. Title.
  F374.S65A3   1995
  976.3'3505'092 — dc20
      [B]   94-48820
                                                                                CIP
                                                                                 AC

Unless otherwise noted, illustrations are from the collection of Alice Dale Cohan and are used with her permission.

To my wife, Sandra Isaacs,
who has watched Clara grow and mature
while making sure Erica and Jennifer did the same.

Contents

Illustrations

Acknowledgments

I first looked at the Clara Solomon diaries, which are in the Louisiana and Lower Mississippi Valley Collection at Louisiana State University in Baton Rouge, some time ago while doing research for a study of Louisiana's nineteenth-century Jewish community. I expressed interest in editing the diaries for publication. Stone Miller, then director of archives, was kind enough to have the diaries put on microfilm for me so that I could edit them at a place closer to home. His support and encouragement helped make this edition of Clara's diaries possible. Stone's untimely passing was a loss to me and to all who had the pleasure to know and work with him.

During the 1930s someone working for the federal Works Progress Administration made a typescript of the diaries. While helpful, the typescript had enough errors to convince me to transcribe from the microfilm. Responsibility for the delay in bringing this job to fruition is entirely my own. Background information relating to the Jewish community in which Clara lived and wrote can be found in my *Business of Jews in Louisiana, 1840–1875* (Tuscaloosa, 1988).

I am indebted to Patricia Ann Fenerty of New Orleans for her efforts in applying her considerable genealogical talents to uncover information on Clara and her family subsequent to the period of her diaries. She added extensively to the small amount of material I was able to uncover myself during occasional trips to Louisiana. I also wish to thank Mr. E. Spencer Lazarus, Jr., of New Orleans, a grandson of Clara's sister Sallie (Sarah), who very kindly shared the substantial body of genealogical information he and his family possess. I am extremely grateful to his cousin Alice Dale Cohan of New York, who has guarded the family's pictorial heritage and who has kindly permitted the inclusion of some invaluable photographs of a truly remarkable American family in the edition. The Jewish community of New Orleans has been and continues to be a rich source of crucial information on the history of our country's nineteenth-century Jewish community.

Throughout the publishing process the editorial staff at Louisiana State University Press has performed in a professional and sensitive manner. Margaret Dalrymple, who had oversight of the manuscript in the early stages, and John Easterly, who followed through in the editorial phases, deserve particular commendation. I am especially pleased that Louisiana State University Press agreed to publish a manuscript as lengthy as this one, indicating to me their own appreciation of the importance of the diaries. As a result, many of us will now be able to join Clara Solomon in the New Orleans of 1861 and 1862.

Introduction

The diary of Clara Solomon begins in June 1861 and ends in July 1862. Even then, there is a three-month period within this time frame during which Clara did not keep her diary. She apparently could not obtain a new diary book in which to record her observations. Hence the hiatus. Clara is sixteen when we first meet her, and she celebrates one birthday before her diary ends. The surviving diary, therefore, covers a short period of time in the life of a young girl in New Orleans. The period, however, is a fascinating and important one, from the early days of the Civil War through several months of Union occupation of the city.

This diary is one of many dating from the years of the Civil War. We have accounts from soldiers detailing the events of battles in various places throughout the country.[1] We have accounts of merchants, both American and European, traveling through the country when conditions allowed. We also have diaries of young girls and women in the South, describing for the most part the difficulties wives and daughters faced as their lives on plantations suffered from the effects of the war. Some of these are memoirs rather than diaries in the proper sense of the word.[2] Valuable for many

1. Among the more recently published of this kind are: Francis W. Dawson, *Reminiscences of Confederate Service 1861–1865*, ed. Bell I. Wiley, (Baton Rouge, 1993); Silas T. Grisamore, *The Civil War Reminiscences of Major Silas T. Grisamore, C.S.A.*, ed. Arthur W. Bergeron, Jr. (Baton Rouge, 1992); William J. Seymour, *The Civil War Memoirs of Captain William J. Seymour: Reminiscences of a Louisiana Tiger*, ed. Terry L. Jones (Baton Rouge, 1991); Edward Porter Alexander, *Fighting for the Confederacy: The Personal Recollections of General Edward Porter Alexander*, ed. Gary W. Gallagher (Chapel Hill, 1989); and Charles B. Haydon, *For Country Cause & Leader: The Civil War Journal of Charles B. Haydon*, ed. Stephen W. Sears (New York, 1993).

2. Some memoirs and diaries that have recently appeared are: Pauline deCaradeuc Heyward, *A Confederate Lady Comes of Age: The Journal of Pauline deCaradeuc Heyward*, ed. Mary D. Robinson (Columbia,

reasons, the writings of women about their Civil War experiences have taken on additional interest because of the current emphasis on women's history. Indeed, many of the changes in the status of women in the economy and in the wider social structure of the postbellum period in America are now regarded at least in part as the result of the liberating effects of the Civil War on women. They needed to fill in for their absent spouses, and, in the case of southern women, unfortunately had the opportunity to confront the enemy directly.[3]

I have had, as any editor of a nineteenth-century diary would, to face the question of how to treat errors in the manuscript. Many of these occurred from instances in which Clara wrote words faster or slower than they appeared in her head, a trait common to anyone who writes with a pen or pencil as frequently as Clara did. Others were routine spelling errors. In both these cases I have changed the text without showing the corrections, in order to make it flow smoothly and without needless interruption. In a few special situations, and where Clara's handwriting has not been clear, I have inserted question marks or additional wording in brackets to cover some misspellings and omissions. My overall method, however, has been to change the text without comment in numerous situations

1992); Cornelia Peake McDonald, *A Woman's Civil War: A Diary of Cornelia Peake McDonald, with Reminiscences of the War, from March 1862*, ed. Minrose C. Gwin (Madison, Wisc., 1992); Ida Fowler Morgan, *The Civil War Diary of Sarah Ida Fowler Morgan*, ed. Charles East (Athens, Ga., 1991); Belle Edmonson, *A Lost Heroine of the Confederacy: The Diaries and Letters of Belle Edmonson*, ed. Loretta Galbraith (Jackson, Miss., 1991); Keziah Goodwyn Hopkins Brevard, *A Plantation Mistress on the Eve of the Civil War [Keziah Goodwyn Hopkins] Brevard's Diary, 1860–1861*, ed. John Hammond Moore (Columbia, S.C., 1992); Emma Holmes, *The Diary of Miss Emma Holmes: 1861–66*, ed. John F. Marszalek (Baton Rouge, 1979). The diary of Julia Le Grand, covering a similar period in New Orleans, is helpful for comparative, and other, purposes. Julia Le Grand, *The Journal of Julia Le Grand: New Orleans, 1862–63*, eds. Kate M. Rowland and Mrs. Morris L. Croxall (Richmond, 1911). Further records of women include Kate Stone, *The Journal of Kate Stone, 1861–1868*, ed. John Q. Anderson (Baton Rouge, 1955); Katherine M. Jones, *Heroines of Dixie: Confederate Women Tell Their Story of the War* (Indianapolis, 1955); Sarah A. Brock Putnam, *Richmond During the War: Four Years of Personal Observation by a Richmond Lady* (New York, 1867); Mary Chesnut, *Mary Chesnut's Civil War*, ed. C. Vann Woodward (New Haven, 1981); and Susie King Taylor, *A Black Woman's Civil War Memoirs*, ed. Patricia W. Romero (New York, 1988).

3. The arguments that southern women gained new feelings of independence and strength by displaying opposition to northern occupation forces and by taking on new work roles because of the necessities of war and defeat, are explored in George C. Rable, *Civil Wars: Women and the Crisis of Southern Nationalism* (Urbana, Ill., 1989), and Catherine Clinton and Nina Silber, eds., *Divided Houses: Gender and the Civil War* (New York, 1993). Other scholars focus on the vacuum that southern women filled on the plantation, where slaves had to be controlled in the absence of the master. Drew Gilpin Faust, "Trying to Do a Man's Business: Slavery, Violence and Gender in the American Civil War," *Gender and History*, IV (1992), 197–214, presents evidence to support the view that women did not take well to this authoritarian, violent role.

that would otherwise call for an explicit, unnecessary, and potentially confusing, explanation of Clara's words. My explanatory comments are in brackets in the text; the parentheses are as Clara wrote them in the original.

The writings of Clara Solomon are contemporaneous with the events, not recollections from a later period, and they give us insight into segments of southern society not normally passed on to us in the form of diaries. Clara is an urbanite, born and raised in a mercantile family in New Orleans, and she writes as a native daughter of the city. She is Jewish, and she offers us a glimpse of a vibrant element in the New Orleans commercial and social structure that has gone underrepresented in the published diaries thus far available to us.

Clara and her family have deep roots in the South and are staunch supporters of the Confederate cause, as are almost all of the people introduced to us in her writings. She is the second of six surviving daughters of Solomon and Emma Solomon (the diary speaks of seven sisters, but Clara must include Dell, a daughter of Lucy, the domestic slave and certainly a household member). A son had died at birth, and another daughter had died at age three from a congenital affliction. Clara's father, already forty-six years old in 1861, serves the Confederacy not as a fighting soldier but as a sutler, or supplier of clothing and equipment to the troops in Virginia engaged in the many battles there. He is therefore away during most of the period covered by the diary. His family on Hercules Street (later to be called Rampart) eagerly awaits letters and money from him.

Clara's Jewish heritage calls for some explanation. The Solomons are Jews of Sephardic background, with ancestry in England and perhaps the British West Indies, as they made their way across the Atlantic Ocean to South Carolina and then Louisiana. Sephardic Jews distinguish themselves from "Ashkenazic" Jews through ritual and points of origin. The ritual followed by Sephardic Jews goes back to the religious practices of Jews on the Iberian Peninsula before the expulsion of Jews from that area in 1492, and to the customs of Jews living in the Middle East. The ritual followed by Ashkenazic Jews relates to practices of Jews living in Central and Eastern Europe. The prayer books of the two groups differ in some respects, although the majority of the prayers are the same. Practices regarding the ritual slaughter of animals for food also differ, as do customs regarding permissible foods and holiday observance. Hebrew pronunciation is different for the two groups. Jews from both backgrounds lived together in many places around the globe, particularly in Holland and England, as Sephardic Jews moved away from Spain and Portugal centuries ago. It is from this general background that the Solomons come.

Both of Clara's parents, Emma and Solomon Solomon, were natives of South Carolina, members of an elite group among American Jews in the nineteenth century.[4] Sephardic Jews in America, never a large group numerically, held important political and economic positions from colonial days in America. The pillars of the early Jewish communities along the East Coast, from Newport to New York, Charleston, and Savannah, were generally Sephardic Jews. Increases in immigration of Ashkenazic Jews from France and the German states during the mid-nineteenth century made the Solomons of New Orleans and the rest of the Sephardic community a decided minority. But, as will appear in the diary, Clara could and did regard herself and her friends as part of a "haute bourgeoisie" among American Jews, particularly in the South, who were reasonably successful financially, mixed well with the general white southern population, intermarried regularly, and adopted many southern customs, including slave ownership, but still retained a Jewish identity.

The Solomons were members of the Dispersed of Judah Congregation, the principal Sephardic congregation of New Orleans, and attended regularly in the days before the disruptions of secession and war. Although organized earlier, the congregation first had a regular place of worship in 1847, in a former Episcopal church at the corner of Bourbon and Canal streets bought for its members by Judah Touro, the enigmatic philanthropist of Sephardic background who had attachments to both Newport, Rhode Island, and New Orleans. The congregation soon built its own synagogue on Carondelet Street before Touro's death in 1854, and with his help. This is the location at which the Solomons attended services. A beautiful building in the best Greek Revival style, it passed on to the Knights of Columbus in 1881, when the Sephardic congregation moved, and was ultimately demolished later in that decade. Southern patriots, the Sephardic Jews were among the casualties of the war and Reconstruction. By the end of the 1870s they could no longer maintain their independent Sephardic

4. There is evidence that Emma's maiden name was also Solomon, and that Emma's parents married in Charleston in 1805. See Brent H. Holcomb, *Marriage and Death Notices from the "Charleston Times,"* *1800–1821* (Baltimore, 1979), 117; *The Daily Picayune* of New Orleans, 1 December 1841. The Solomons were also part of a larger group of Americans who left the Charleston area in the 1840s for the West, as the growth of cotton spread from the eastern seaboard and the nearby uplands to the Southwest. See Alfred G. Smith, Jr., *Economic Readjustment of an Old Cotton State: South Carolina, 1820–1860* (Columbia, S.C., 1958). For information on the Jewish residents of New Orleans with ties to Charleston and smaller towns in South Carolina, see W. E. Myers, *The Israelites of . . . Louisiana* (New Orleans, 1905).

congregation in New Orleans, and had to merge with one of the more flourishing Ashkenazic synagogues, Congregation Gates of Mercy, filled with descendants of immigrants from central Europe, if not the immigrant generation itself.

While the Jews of New Orleans in 1861 were often recent immigrants from Europe and not comfortable with English, Clara was born in New Orleans to English-speaking parents. Her command of English, and her handwriting, were in every respect superb. Clara used her diary not only to record events. Her diary added another dimension to her life, one in which she was free to comment on people and events without fear of contradiction or embarrassment. It also gave to romantic Clara a vehicle for expression of a vivid and robust imagination, almost a world of fantasy regarding her feelings for others. She used her diary sometimes as a poet or writer of fiction would use their modes of expression.[5]

Clara's older sister, Alice, was a teacher at one of the public elementary girls' schools in New Orleans. In antebellum times the city's school system had been considered progressive in that it supported several elementary schools and two high schools, one for each sex, in addition to a normal school for training teachers. Union occupation forces were not sure what to do with the school system. General Benjamin F. Butler, the first head of the occupation authorities, soon realized that the schools continued to disseminate what he regarded as Confederate propaganda. He therefore reorganized the school system during the summer of 1862, and when school reopened in September the teachers had to swear an oath of loyalty to the United States and teach a pro-Union curriculum. It is not likely that Alice continued to teach in the public system on that basis.[6]

There are several themes to Clara's diary, which for the reader may be regarded as analytical tools for following the narrative. Clara writes as a native of New Orleans, the largest city in the Confederacy, about the progress of the war from the perspective of a southern partisan. She expresses the optimism shared by many during the early days of the war, then the increasing doubts as military victory eludes her people and the death toll mounts, and finally the frustration and despair of living under military

5. Both Clara and Alice kept diaries before those reproduced here, and probably after, but none of these has surfaced. We have some of Clara's diaries still available only because Louisiana State University was able to buy the manuscripts in 1939 from a book dealer, Charles Heartman, then living in Hattiesburg, Mississippi. How he acquired them is a mystery. In addition to keeping a diary and teaching, Alice contributed poetry to the local newspapers under the pseudonym "Sylvia Dale" after the war.

6. See R. C. Reinders, *End of an Era* (New Orleans, 1964).

occupation. She discusses the battles in Virginia, from Bull Run to Shiloh, the mobilization of residents of New Orleans, the politics of the Confederate war machine, and the horror felt as friends lose loved ones.

The optimism of the early phase of the war dissipated when the war did not end as quickly as Clara and her friends had anticipated. The Battle of Shiloh, on April 6–7, 1862, approximately one year after the outbreak of fighting, brought the realities of the war home to New Orleans in explicit and gruesome terms. Many soldiers from Louisiana fought in that bloody battle. The news reports were confusing and contradictory, but the army trains that came into New Orleans nonstop for two weeks carrying the wounded and dead ended the confusion and uncertainty. The slaughter was there for everyone to see.

Before Clara and others had time to absorb the tragedy of Shiloh, the Confederate government of the city of New Orleans (there was no other authority available) surrendered to Union military officials after a brief but fierce naval battle in the harbor. Clara then writes as a civilian living under military occupation. The press, which Clara and her sister Alice read voraciously, became a censored one, printing only what the occupation government wished it to print. Rumors were everywhere. Facts were hard to come by, but the worst indignity was the presence of the enemy in the streets and squares, and in the city's beautiful buildings. The demoralization of the true believers contrasts with the more practical acceptance of occupation by most of the community that needed, above all, to make ends meet. Union forces encountered verbal jeers throughout the occupation period from schoolchildren and adults (mostly women) despite prohibitions against such behavior. The jeers, at first a poor substitute for the humility of the peaceful surrender felt by the city's inhabitants, became an important element in boosting the morale of the citizens.[7]

There is also Clara's personal side. During the academic year Clara devotes much of her diary to recounting events at her school, the Louisiana Normal School, which trained girls to be teachers. She is somewhat serious about her studies, but school is for Clara primarily a social unit within which friendships are made and lost, often as a result of unyielding reliance

7. Gerald M. Capers, in his *Occupied City: New Orleans Under the Federals, 1862–1865* (Lexington, Ky., 1965), covers this period. Some scholars believe that the civilian population feigned cooperation with the occupying forces to protect their families and receive favors from the corrupt Butler administration. Bell I. Wiley, "Southern Reaction to Federal Invasion," *Journal of Southern History,* XVI (1950), 491–510. Whatever the motive, there was little serious resistance by the city's residents to occupation.

on rules of etiquette that loom large in the way Clara and her peers conduct their lives. One recurrent topic of discussion is who issued the last invitation to whom for a visit home after school.

Clara stands out at school by always being absent on Saturdays, as her mother compels her to observe the Jewish Sabbath. Clara herself would like to go to school on Saturdays, as she has to catch up every week, but she follows her mother's dictates. What is absent from Clara's diary is any indication that her Jewish identification and observance resulted in any negative feelings about her from her schoolmates. The girls deal with each other on an equal footing. If anything, Clara herself expresses condescension toward other Jews (some her father's creditors) whom she considers to be uncouth or "nouveaux riche." At school Clara and other Jewish students mix easily with the Christian population. Their American heritage, decidedly southern, gives them a comfortable place in the world of New Orleans.[8]

All the troubles and sorrows of the war mirror themselves in the lives of the girls at the Normal School. In the early days the girls do their patriotic duty by singing and performing benefits for the soldiers. "Bonnie Blue Flag" and, later, "Dixie" fill the school's halls. Girls begin to leave school, however, as their fathers go to war and families have to move away to find less expensive living arrangements. Clara wonders just how many girls will return to school after the summer vacation of 1861. Many in fact do not come back, and as the war drags on through the winter and the following spring, the exodus continues. Clara does not report any direct talk of war casualties among the girls, nor does she tell us of any formal ceremonies at school, but everyone knows when a classmate loses a father or brother or friend in the fighting. Classes became perfunctory ex-

8. The most overt case of anti-Semitic rhetoric mentioned in Clara's diary concerns her cousin Samuel Myers, who had criticized the *Daily True Delta* during his legal representation of Captain Bueter, provost-marshal of one of the regiments. The court recorder, a military person, ordered Myers imprisoned for contempt for his language. The newspaper commented on Myers's behavior on its editorial page in the following manner: "It will be seen that a Jack-leg lawyer-one of those 'Shysters' that hang like barnacles around recorders' courts—named, we believe, Myers, made quite an extraordinary splurge in the Recorder's Court of the First District yesterday, in abusing the True Delta. It was in the defense of some fellow named Bueter. Major Stith, who was acting recorder on the occasion, believing, we presume, and probably correctly, that no one about the True Delta Office had an extra pair of boots to spoil by an application of them to the posteriors of the said 'shyster' ordered his commitment for his undignified and ungentlemanly language. The 'shyster' Myers, subsequently apologized and was permitted to go. If 'shyster' Myers kicks up any more such didos [antics], we will go to the expense of buying an extra pair of double soled boots, notwithstanding the present high price of leather, for the express purpose of kicking him all around town." See *The Daily True Delta,* 30 March 1862.

ercises after the arrival of occupation forces. The number of students declined at an even greater rate. No one knew how long the school would remain open. General Butler issued order after order in his capacity as head of the occupation government, and the students and staff waited each day for him to act. But Butler let the 1861–62 school year run out without interference, and postponed any changes to the next academic year.

As resident of a neighborhood, Clara exhibits the same comfortable attitude that she does at school, even though the Hercules (Rampart) Street address is a new one for the Solomon family. (Their previous home was not far away.) There are the neighbors, the Viennes, the Mazareaus, and the Jarreaus, with whom Clara and Alice spend some time. The war, of course, makes all relationships tenuous. Adolphe Mazareau had been elected sheriff of New Orleans under the Confederate government and was charged with anti-Union behavior when Union occupation began. General Butler brought charges against Mazareau and was ready to send him to a prison in the North. However, Butler released him as arbitrarily as he had had him arrested.

Clara's most important role is as a dependent family member who yearns for her father's return, whose bad moods are equaled only by those of her mother, and who weaves an imaginary life of romance that only her revered sister Alice can penetrate. She writes of household chores, paying visits and receiving visitors, spending idle time with big sister Alice, and maintaining a difficult relationship with her mother, Emma, while her father is gone to earn a living. Visits to and from friends and relatives occupy a great deal of the family's time. The Nathans, also from South Carolina and members of the same synagogue, are their closest friends, at least until they, like many other city residents, move to another section of New Orleans to save money. The Nathans, while still neighbors, are constant visitors or hosts to various Solomons, and their boarder, Jacob Eisner, a recent Jewish immigrant who works in a dry goods store, is usually included. Most visitors to the Solomons are Jews, members of the Sephardic community and often members of the Dispersed of Judah Congregation. Some are relatives, like cousin Sam Myers, an attorney; others are friends, like Gus Leovy, a journalist, and Leopold Rosenfield, a clerk with Eisner in Bernard Dryer & Co.

Clara's life is a restricted one by modern standards, even before the arrival of occupation forces. When not going to school in the afternoons she helps around the house, particularly as baby-sitter for her youngest sisters, Rosa and Josephine (Josie.) This task usually fell to the family's

Irish domestic, Ellen Deegan, who was meant to come on a daily basis but often failed to appear.[9] The heavy household work is done by Lucy, the Solomons' domestic slave, whose position in the household becomes more and more problematic as Union authority extends into New Orleans and other sections of the Deep South.[10]

The highlights of Clara's daily life occur when she, usually in the company of her sister Alice, leaves the house other than for school. These outings may be shopping expeditions, normally unsuccessful, or occasional walks through the neighborhood to pay unannounced social calls, visits to the wealthy (and, to Clara, arrogant) Harris family in the French Quarter, or to the family of their cousin Joseph Solomon on the outskirts of town. Clara on these occasions is like a bird let out of its cage. She marvels at the hustle and bustle of Canal Street and its trolley, so different from the quiet of her own residential section. She describes every detail of her journeys, from the agonizing decisions over how to spend ten cents to the faces of passengers on the trolley cars. Clara and her family devote much time to either paying visits to friends and relatives or receiving them. In an age without telephones and other electronic means of communication, personal contact provided, along with correspondence, the dominant form of social interaction. The routine of the Solomon family was in line with the social habits of the general population of the city, as were the shopping expeditions and occasional visits to the military camps in and around the city before occupation.[11]

Clara writes vividly of the progressive shortage of food and merchandise in the city's stores as the war continues. In antebellum times New Orleans was a great exporter of the region's cash crops, cotton and sugar; it was also an importer of consumer and durable goods for its own population and the inhabitants of other areas reached by the Mississippi River network. Items for personal consumption, and those needed by the agricultural sector to make a crop and maintain the plantations and

9. New Orleans households had the largest number of white servants among southern cities in antebellum times. The typical white domestic servant was an immigrant, usually, like Ellen Deegan, an Irish girl. See Daniel E. Sutherland, *Americans and Their Servants* (Baton Rouge, 1981).

10. Clara, like many Confederate sympathizers, believed that slaves who took advantage of the opportunity to leave "well-intentioned" owners were beneath contempt. We have evidence from the Census that Lucy remained with the Solomon family into the postbellum period. Clara's younger sister Sallie, then a high-school senior, refers to "our faithful servant Lucy" in her own diary covering 1869. I am indebted to E. Spencer Lazarus, Jr., of New Orleans for permission to cite this and other references to the Diary of Sallie Solomon.

11. See Bennett H. Wall, ed., *Louisiana: A History* (Arlington Heights, Ill., 1984), 171.

farms, came for the most part from the North. Soon after the fighting began, the merchants of New Orleans lost their chief sources of supply for manufactured goods. Merchandise from northern ports reached the stores again after Union forces occupied New Orleans, but food products were still scarce when Clara's diary came to an end, in July 1862.[12]

Clara gives a personal account of the currency problems faced by the new government of the Confederacy. Even when there were commodities to buy, daily commercial transactions for household goods suffered for lack of change in the stores. The Confederate government was not able to institute a currency program to meet the needs of its citizens. Coins presented the greatest difficulty, for they did not remain in circulation long. The government's inability to support a currency prompted many individuals to issue what in effect was private money, called "shinplasters," that circulated for limited purposes in limited geographic areas with only the reputation of the issuer behind it. Currency questions, which depended to a great extent on the civilian population's confidence in a Confederate victory, plagued the Union occupation forces as well. General Butler sought to eliminate Confederate currency from circulation, but did not have an easy time of it. Even after the day that Butler decreed to be the last on which Confederate currency would be accepted, Clara tells us that such currency continued in circulation among the city's residents in some stores in certain sections of the city.

The antebellum South had suffered from a chronic shortage of cash even in the best of times. The mercantile community of New Orleans generally lived on credit, on both the giving and receiving ends. Personal consumption as well as business matters rested on credit extensions throughout the economic chain. The grocer and the dry goods merchant extended credit, like others. The Solomons had built up a sizable debt before the war with one of the city's clothiers, Davis & Jackson, under circumstances that Clara implies were less than ordinary. She regards Davis as the family's savior. Perhaps Solomon's business had soured. Whatever the original reason for the debt, the outbreak of war and the ensuing disruptions put creditors in an awkward position. They could not easily collect debts owed them from those whose present and future incomes were drastically reduced when they joined the Confederate military forces. As the war continued, and prospects for a Confederate victory diminished, Confederate

---

12. Direct trade with Europe, especially with England and France, did exist, but on a smaller scale. This trade had to overcome the naval blockade of southern ports that became effective a few months after fighting started.

money decreased in value, making debt repayment unattractive to creditors in any event. The general reduction in commercial activity in the city, as well as the uncertainties created by the new forms of currency, placed further obstacles in the way of debt collection.[13]

The Solomons' major creditor visited Emma more than once during the course of the diary, but only to request, very politely, partial payments. In any event, there would not be much legal recourse for a creditor against someone like Solomon, a civilian working to supply the troops. When Emma received money from her husband, much of it did go to Davis. Repayment by Emma not only reduced the Solomons' debt; it renewed their credit line so the family could once again make purchases throughout the city with nothing more than a promise of payment. Davis in turn paid the Solomons' bills, not with cash but with a draft Davis drew on someone who owed Davis money. Credit was the currency.

The Solomon family did what it could to earn some of its own money by sewing clothing for the troops, as subcontractors of friends who held the government contracts to supply the items. The sewing was as much a patriotic gesture as a cash provider. Very small amounts of money came to the Solomons in this way. Otherwise, the Solomons waited for funds to come from the father in Virginia. Alice's salary as a teacher, amounting to six hundred dollars a year, was a cushion, but on at least one occasion before Solomon left for Virginia he got to the school before his daughter and took the fifty dollars, a month's wage for Alice, to use himself.

The occupation period depressed and frustrated the people of New Orleans. Every decision made by General Butler and his occupation authorities was calculated to humiliate the city's residents, all of whom he regarded as enemies of war and potential spies. As Clara tells it, and historians agree, Butler angered everyone from the start when he executed by hanging a gambler named Mumford who tore apart a Union flag flying over the federal Mint. By the same token, however, the hanging helped stifle further expressions of rebellious sentiment.

There was no armed opposition to the occupation government. Those who wanted to express their outrage at Butler's behavior did so in different ways. Women demonstrated by spitting on Union soldiers and verbally insulting them. Clara's schoolmates adopted the practice of wearing black clothes and Confederate armbands to express their feelings, but

13. In rural areas, about which Clara did not have much information, land remained an adequate collateral for debt repayment and new loans, many of which stipulated that the creditor would wait until the end of hostilities to press for payment under the terms of the mortgage.

Clara considered the idea too morbid. The Union soldiers did not take kindly to such treatment, thinking that they ought to be appreciated as liberators.

General Butler responded to these disruptions by passing his famous "Woman Order," punishing expressions of anti-Union attitudes with imprisonment. A prominent friend of the Solomon family, Eugenia Levy Phillips, was among those sent to Ship Island Prison for violation of this order. She was charged with having spoken critically of Union soldiers.[14] Butler generated resentment in so many ways that he was recalled from New Orleans before the end of 1862. There were many allegations of corruption, especially about favors given by Butler to his brother. Butler also insulted the representatives of England and France and other foreign governments during his tenure.

Butler, called "the Beast" by generations of southerners, faced an issue that Clara, living in the city, can only allude to, that of the position of the slave population under the occupation government. Large numbers of slaves left their plantations hoping for protection by the Union army in Louisiana. The task of feeding and protecting all of them was too much for the occupation administration, and Butler hoped to have his troops return the runaways to their owners. On this point he faced the opposition of his own subordinates, who decided by themselves that one of the aims of the war was to end slavery, before Abraham Lincoln himself had publicly come to that conclusion.

Returning slaves to their plantations proved impractical as well as undesirable. Instead, the Union forces took over many of the abandoned plantations, leased them to northerners and hired freed slaves to work the plantations for wages as contract labor in order to save the crops and solve the problem of the runaways. The army troops in Louisiana then became instruments for the enforcement of the labor contracts to make sure the freedmen worked as required. We have only a shadow of this issue in the Solomon family, as they deal with Lucy, their domestic slave, when the end of slavery begins to become a reality.[15]

Beneath the sometimes rambling recitation by Clara of the daily events

14. Eugenia Levy was married to a well-known Jewish lawyer in New Orleans, Philip Phillips. He was not able to be of much help to his wife on this occasion, although she did leave prison after a shorter term than expected. Some of her diary has survived, and is in the manuscript collections of the Library of Congress in Washington, D.C.

15. See Armistead L. Robinson, "'Worser dan Jeff Davis': The Coming of Free Labor During the Civil War, 1861–1865," in Thavolia Glymph, ed., *Essays on the PostBellum Economy* (College Station, Tex., 1985).

in her family, with her friends, and in the wider New Orleans community, is a picture of urban life in the early days of the Confederacy through the frustrations and despair of surrender and occupation by enemy forces. The Solomons, apart from their father, stay in New Orleans throughout the period covered by the diary, although many of their friends leave. Of the families who do not leave for Europe or South America, some go to rural retreats to wait out the war, while others move near the areas of fighting in Virginia to be near their husbands. The Solomons are too large a family to move easily. Clara expresses the feelings of all the children when she writes that, born and raised in New Orleans, she would have difficulty leaving friends, relatives, and familiar surroundings. On one occasion, Solomon Solomon expressed his wish to take the whole family west when the war ended with the profits he was making in his sutlering business. The girls were not happy with the idea; in any event, their father never had the opportunity to try to realize this dream.

One feels in the daily narrative the increasing helplessness of those who lived in New Orleans even before occupation. The city's stores were short of food and other daily requirements soon after war began. The Solomons substituted parched and ground rye for coffee by November 1861; they took to drinking beer because of an ice shortage. Clara did not despair; she ached at the horrors the war produced as the months passed. These were mild compared to the events to come on the battlefields. Daily life improved in New Orleans as an occupied city, with more merchandise in the stores, but the inhabitants paid a dear price under General Benjamin Butler and General Nathaniel Banks after him. The battles continued in other areas; the fall of Vicksburg, Mississippi, in July 1863 had serious consequences for those in New Orleans, putting the Union in full control of the lower Mississippi River. We don't have Clara's comments on the events following July 1862, the end of her diary as we have it, but we can easily imagine the agony she felt.

Clara's diary of her life in New Orleans says much about the Jewish community in the city and the society in which Jews functioned. She, her older sister Alice, and her parents regard themselves as integral members of southern society and committed to the cause of the Confederacy. The cover sheet to the first book of Clara's diary that has survived contains a poignant statement of where Clara places herself in the South. She signs her name, "Miss Clara Solomon, New Orleans, La., C.S.A." The Sephardic Jewish community to which the Solomons belong has been intertwined with American history since colonial times. During the eighteenth and the first half of the nineteenth centuries, southern cities like Charleston and New Orleans were important centers of Sephardic life; Sephardic Jews had regular commercial and personal contact with the other principal Sephardic communities of the Northeast. Clara and her Jewish friends and relations thought of themselves as thoroughly American, but when the time came to choose sides, the Solomons were of a decidedly southern stripe. We therefore read of the paradoxical preparations to celebrate the Fourth of July, the founding of our nation, in the Confederacy in 1861.

There were of course many Jews with central European backgrounds in the New Orleans Jewish community of 1861, as there were in the rural sections of Louisiana, and the Solomons counted some of them among their friends. By the time of the Civil War, substantial numbers of Jews from the Alsace-Lorraine sections of France, bordering on the Rhine River, and from the German states on the eastern side of the Rhine had migrated to New Orleans and the Louisiana countryside. The French and German Jews, whose immigration in the 1840s and 1850s made the Louisiana Jewish population the largest in the South, also reaped the benefits of a growing economy and had some success themselves in coexisting with the local population. The Solomons, as Sephardic Jews, had a longer American heritage, grew up with the English language, and possessed a traditional ability to assimilate and yet maintain some religious identification.

Clara's father had been a merchant before the war, and many of the Jewish personalities that grace the pages of the diary are businessmen, working as aspiring clerks or as successful individual entrepreneurs. Two of the former who visit the Solomon home regularly are Jacob Eisner and Leopold Rosenfield. The Marks and Miller families, whose sons go off to war, are established city merchants. At the same time, the American roots of the Sephardic community and the benefits accruing in the way of education are evident in the numerous professional men in the Solomons' circle. Cousin Sam Myers is an attorney, as is Philip Phillips, whose wife Eugenia is mentioned above.

We meet other professional men, like cousin Joseph Solomon, who runs, as does Sam Myers, for the Confederate legislature. The connections of the Sephardic community with the Confederate government, of course, go all the way to the top in the person of Judah Benjamin, President Jefferson Davis's trusted cabinet minister. Benjamin, whose family came to America from England via the West Indies, spent his antebellum years as a lawyer in New Orleans with his cousin Hyam Hyams, the father of Clara's most idealized young woman, "Judo," known more commonly as Judith Hyams. Hyams was lieutenant governor of Louisiana before the war, while Benjamin went to Washington as a senator from Louisiana. These successful attorneys were also plantation owners, in the best southern tradition. As such, they were slaveowners on a larger scale than were urban families like the Solomons, who owned one domestic slave.

The Solomons also count newspaper publishers and reporters among their close Jewish friends. Durant da Ponte is a publisher as well as a writer; he goes off to the Virginia battlefields to send back firsthand reports of the fighting.[16] Gus Leovy (Levy) also writes for a newspaper. The Solomons' circle, then, is a mix of merchants and professionals. Living in New Orleans, Clara does not have much to say about the rural interests of her urban circle, but many have such interests. We hear of city friends (usually the women whose husbands go to war) leaving for country spas or their own rural retreats to await the outcome of the war. Many families who have secure economic foundations in New Orleans either started in the country or acquired country stores and plantations through their business dealings or as investments.

With such complete identification with the mores of southern society, the Solomons and the rest of the Sephardic community in New Orleans nonetheless maintain their synagogue and celebrate the major religious holidays. Clara does not attend services very often, nor does her mother, but Alice goes on a regular basis with their neighbor Sarah Nathan. The whole family is involved with celebration of the New Year, the Day of Atonement (Yom Kippur), and the Spring festival of Passover. It is fair to say that the Solomons were more concerned with Sabbath observance in both ritual and prayer than most American Jews of a century later. Clara writes of the difficulties in finding matzah for Passover, and seats for the major holidays that were usually reserved by a payment from her father who was unable to do so during these years. Synagogue records show that Solomon Solomon was an active participant in congregational matters both before and after the war.

Issues concerning Jewish survival in the South, however, give us a different perspective on the Solomons. The ease with which the Solomons and other Jews in their circle mixed with the southern population at this

16. A relative of Lorenzo da Ponte, Mozart's principal librettist, he also became a sister-in-law to Clara some twenty years later when he married her sister Rosa, four years old at the time of the diary. Da Ponte's first wife had died.

watershed in American history had serious negative implications. Hindsight tells us that their community blended so freely with the Christian population around them that many of Clara's generation gave up their Judaism. Assuming that group survival is of some benefit to Jews, there were too many interfaith marriages among the Solomons' circle for the Sephardic Jewish population of mid-nineteenth-century New Orleans to continue as an entity. The marriages that Clara reports, and there were several, were generally between Jews and non-Jews. To bring the issue close to home, Clara's own cousin Emilie, daughter of Joseph and Caroline Solomon (née Barnett), married out of her faith. As discussed in the Afterword, Clara's second marriage, but not her first, was to a non-Jew.

Such marriages did not automatically result in a total alienation from the organized Jewish community. Judith Hyams, for one, continues to appear at synagogue services after her marriage to Horatio Sprigg, performed in the city's principal Episcopal church. However, the long-term implications for survival of the Jewish community were not favorable. We do know that of the Solomon girls, Alice, Clara, Sarah, and Rosa married within their faith. The ultimate absorption of the Sephardic congregation by an Ashkenazic one in 1881 must be connected at least in part with a decline in the size of the Sephardic community because of intermarriages. When its congregation, Dispersed of Judah, gave up its own place of worship and merged with a congregation of French and German Jews, there were about fifty families left from the Sephardic group who joined the merged entity.

The course of events after the end of Clara's diary entries gives a tragic tone to all that Clara writes and does, as it does to all Civil War diaries. Southern diaries are permeated with a sense of tragedy in which forces more powerful than the individual shape the lives of all concerned. Clara emphasizes the right of the former southern states to control their own political destiny, as any Confederate partisan would, and she shows no interest in contradictory arguments. The family dentist, an avowed abolitionist, will visit the Solomon home only if no one talks politics. The only other person she knows personally who questions Confederate beliefs is a recent immigrant from Europe, and Clara dismisses his attitudes because of his background. She seems to build a wall around herself and her loved ones as the war continues, protecting the myths of Confederate life in the face of encroaching realities. She is, after all, but a child hanging on at all costs to the things she values the most, her family and friends.

1

The Solomon Girls:
June 15–July 3, 1861

Saturday, June 15th, 1861

10³/₄ A.M. At last, have I commenced my "new" book. How long it has been in expectation, I need not say. But I did really think that this moment would never arise, viz. the one in which I should first pencil the page of "da Ponte's gift".

But, notwithstanding, my presentiments, which are scarcely ever realized, either good or bad, it has arrived. I will say, that "the better the day, I hope will be the better the day". There's one mistake to begin with!! Shall I make my speech as a matter of preface to my Philomen?[1] No! for eccentricity, I won't! But I will merely offer up this prayer, "May I finish the book, and may every page breathe the spirit of contentment and happiness!!" What more could I want? May it be granted. *This book is far superior to the other in appearance and texture.* May it also be so in chirography [penmanship] and composition. I will not commence with the narration of the morning or in fact, of the past week, but will proceed with my feeble description of "our Camp". I was last in the Cars. We were anxiously awaiting the termination of our journey. But what suspense and torture racked our brains; we knew that they had gone, that *our* Camp was deserted. No familiar faces would greet us, no individual rejoiced at our arrival. How sad it is that people generally picture the dark side of the picture, disregarding its light and cheerful aspect. But were we not justifiable? Did we not see in the *Crescent* that "Maj. Wheat's first special battalion" was to leave Camp Moore on Saturday, June 15th, 1861, for the seat of war. Could we be gay or hopeful? But hush! we are nearing Tangipaho! The whistle is sounding! we are at the depot! "What hope, what joy our

---

1. Clara's name for her diary, personified as a friend.

bosom's swell!!!" Quickly my head is thrust out of the window in search
of one familiar, well beloved form. The report! It is seen!! A moment more
and we are with it. Our fears are ended. They have not gone! But *one* received the "kiss salute". How tantalizing!! He was glad to see us! Sufficient!
We slowly wind our way to the Hotel. We remain there a few moments
and then proceed to the seat of the action, "The Camp", accompanied by
Capt. White and his wife. Capt. Miller and I had a little spat, and on our
arrival at the Tent, we were not reconciled. There he said to me "Clara I've
something to show you". I thought I would speak, so I asked "What is it?"
He went to his trunk, took out his notes, and showed me the record that
he made of the "Love" that I gave him. He was *very* affectionate, and we
then became friends. We then dined, first at our own table and then at
Capt. Whites; the last was a very fine affair, having all the "delicacies of
the season", together with "condensed milk", which captivated both Alice
and me. We then returned to our tent, dear Obed[2] went to sleep, and we
had a lot of fun with him. We saw Pa: he had not gone to the City. I was
glad to see him. In the course of time, we went to the "Sutler's quarters".[3]
Got some nice things, and, as it looked threatening, we repaired to our own
quarters. It rained and after performing minor duties, we proceeded home
to the Hotel; went by the path of the Rail Road; Alice walking with dear
Obed. Arrived in good order, ate a hearty supper by ourselves and then
retired to the parlor. I forgot to mention our dear "blind man"; he was one
of the first to greet us; well, Alice occupied till bed-time, conversing with
him and a Dr. Greenwood, whom she was introduced to by him. And me!
Fanny,[4] Mrs. Miller and myself were sitting by the gentleman, keeping
watch over him. He was lying on the green bench, his head in Fanny's lap,
and she trying to soothe his temples to rest. If *she* succeeded, I know not.
Presently Fanny deserted her post, Mrs. M. went to see to her children,
and I was left alone. He was as kind and affectionate as the most fastidious taste could demand. His pain disappeared and he grew rather collo-
quial. Our *constitutions* demanded rest, and thoughts of sleep engaged our
attention. $9^1/_2$ was fixed upon as the appointed time, and at that moment
we ascended the steps, and were in the upper part of hotel at Tangipaho
for the first time in our existence. We found the room quite pleasant and

2. Obed Miller, son of Captain Obed Miller, with whom Clara spoke earlier. The Millers were
family friends.
3. The camp store, run by the quartermaster, with whom Clara's father worked until he left for
the Virginia front.
4. Fanny Miller.

commodious; Fanny was in bed, and looked very pretty. We divested ourselves of our garments and each went to his respective couch. Alice and Mrs. Miller, Fan. and I, Obed and Jennie.[5] The beds were rather agreeable; we did not get to sleep for some time, and had a few nocturnal visitors — The other two were awake much longer than I, conversing on *every* imaginable topic. Morning came. We arose, dressed and were down stairs at 6 o'clock. The Capt. welcomed us; Mrs. M. soon made her appearance, and we then went to breakfast at the Camp. We learned from him that the dear Major [Major Wheat] had arrived the previous night, and imparted to them the joyful, the sad, intelligence that they were to take their departure on the following Thursday. This of course was sufficient to dampen our spirits, and at times to cast a universal gloom over us. But they are glad to go; they are impatient! The Capt. was particularly blue. *How* I pitied him. When we arrived in our quarters, the first object that attracted our attention was our "handsome Major". He greeted us very cordially and then we prepared to breakfast; enjoyed it very much. Loitered about, went to Mrs. White's bower[6]; we then became acquainted with a dear specimen of humanity, bearing the cognomen of "Allen Dickinson". He was making out his pay-roll, and we had a lot of fun, making fun of every one, much to his amusement. I liked him so much, and he was so handsome, so *very* handsome. The sky became clouded, the drops began to fall, we found shelter in our "tent", from which we did not depart. We were not lonesome, but should it not rained, it would have been more pleasant. We were writing to Obed. Partook freely of Champagne, and I of real pain; but through the aid of the "log" and Mrs. White's ginger I was soon reduced to a state of quietude. It was now raining very hard; Capt. Miller, Mrs. White and I formed a company.

Somehow or other the idea got possession of me, that *they* [Clara's parents] were up to the Hotel, and therefore I was not very astonished when Mr. Hitchcock[7] confirmed my suspicions; he also told us that they had sent a conveyance for us, and that they were going up in the "four o'clock train". We were very much grieved to hear this; the vehicle at last came, but it was *such* a looking thing, that we refused to go into it; and it was also raining very hard. We were frightened that we would get a scolding. How we felt!! knowing that every moment brought us nearer to the termination of our

5. Jennie was the youngest of Captain and Mrs. Miller's three children. The Solomon girls were in the care of Mrs. Miller for this trip.

6. In medieval times, a lady's private apartment.

7. Solomon Solomon's business associate in the sutlering business.

long expected visit. Pa had been robbed considerably by some unprincipled wretches who probably had some spite against him. It was atrocious,
and they should be, if possible, detected and punished.

As evening approached there were hurried steps to and fro, packing,
etc. as Capt. and Major were both going to town with us. The Major was
very busy, but he had no feminine hand to share or lessen his toil; Capt.
was not in a like predicament, as the skillful hands of dear Mrs. Miller were
very active. We are all ready, waiting for the Capt! He turns! We simultaneously utter "there he is". In a few moments we were on our way with
the Major and Capt. as escorts, and agreeable ones were they. They all
went on in front, Miller and I bringing up the rear; this was at *his* request. We had a delightful walk, nothing *ever* seemed shorter. Both were
sad, at the idea of our to be parting. I say *both*. I *was, he said* he was. I was
right to believe him. He asked me not to forget him; as if I *could;* asked and
told me a thousand things which I never can forget, notwithstanding which,
I now have reason to doubt his sincerity of what he spoke. I should far
rather preferred to have remained in "blissful ignorance". He asked me
to endeavor to get a seat by him in the cars. I told him that I would. He
spoke so sweet, and seemed so earnest, that I almost credited what he said,
and thought that he was in earnest. He may have been at that time, for I
consider him just that fickle. Oh! he is so jealous and suspicious. God,
watch over and protect him. I supplicate you, I entreat you. He said that
he would think of me. Dare I indulge the hope? May he. For it is sweet
to know that there is some one who, when away, is cognizant of your existence. He is such a dear man. I—. No! I won't say that, it is too foolish.
We were the best of friends when we parted at the Hotel. I saw Mrs. Chafin;
she looked very pretty. Having some duties to perform, we went up stairs,
then came down and went to supper. But I was too excited, although every
thing was very enticing, to partake. Miller was by me. The idea of leaving
Tangipaho and its dear ones, was *too much!* I could not revive my drooping spirits; we would leave it, probably never again to behold it; and if
we did, where might be the *ones*, which had rendered this visit so pleasant.
Echo answers, "Where". Victims to the barbarous vandals of the North.
God forbid. I again renewed my promise to him, and then I left him at
the table. Equipped ourselves, took one farewell look at the now familiar
objects, and then to the depot, did we go. Capt. Miller entrusted me to the
care of Lt. Dickinson; we became quite intimate, and I liked him right well.
The engine is steaming along! It is now at Tangipaho! A crowd, a rush, a

clasping of hands, an embrace, anxiety and I am in the cars!! With much difficulty we are seated, I meanwhile, using all the dexterity and artfulness of which I am mistress, to procure *suitable* seats. I thought that the best move would be to obtain "Obed", but I now am aware of my short-sightedness. Dear little Dick came, gave a parting salute, expressed a desire for me to accompany him to Virginia, how foolish, as if I believed him, and then we parted, "it may be for years, and it may be forever". I felt very depressed, but *anticipated* a nice, long ride with "somebody". The Major and Alice were in front of me, Fanny, *by herself,* was behind and the others in some manner or other were disposed of. The cars have started. I look around for *him:* he comes! he will sit by *me!* No! he goes! he is with Fanny! But it is only for the time. I see he does not move. I ask him if he is not going to sit by me; he says "you do not want me". Probably he thinks so; how far, how *very* far is he from the right. I knew not what to make of him. I know now; 'twas one of his mad, or probably *jealous* freaks. Jealous, it may have been, not because he particularly cared, but because he thought he was not liked as much as he should have been. Maybe I did something to offend him, but whether I did or not his conduct was inexplicable and the ride home was far, far from to be pleasant, for I was *so* worried. Fanny B.[8] came and sat by me, I went to sleep, and the Capt. also. I woke a few moments previous to our arrival in the City. *Ma* walked with "Obed". Major and "Old man Foley's son" accompanied us home. The Major did not tell us "goodbye", as he promised to our *last* visit to "Camp Moore". Silently I disrobed, my mind full of conflicting doubts, and myself *rather* peevish. I went to bed, but *not* to sleep; I had too much to think of, too many conjectures to form, too many mysteries to solve. I knew how monotonous and every day like my life would be: *more so now than ever!!* Could I help feeling a little discontented? No!!! I could not realize that our visit was ended. Yes, ended. "Obed" promised to come up the following day: he was to leave on Tuesday! When might we see him again? Why did he not sit by me? *This* was the all-absorbing question. Did he not want to? or, did he think that I took little Obed as an excuse to get rid of *him?* How careful should persons be before they *allow* themselves to get angry. My motive was the best. *He may one day see this.* A happy thought. The following day was Monday. I awoke very late, peevish, cross, and in a crying mood. I was sick, both in *mind* and *body.* The day passed. Afternoon came. We dressed early, waited for him. He did not come until late. I had given him

8. Fanny Burbank, neighbor and friend of the Solomon girls.

up. I went down. He had on his uniform, and looked so handsome! He asked me if I was mad with him, last night. I told him "No". What did he mean. Oh, I am foolish to record this. Were I to do the same to *every* thing he said, I could fill a volume. He stayed as usual, but a few moments, scarcely shook hands, said that he would "try to be up" to-morrow, and went, leaving nothing but his dear, dear memory behind.

Alice and I were *expecting* the dear Major, and yet both *knew* that he would not come. At about 7 we walked around Caliope St. Some signs of commotion, but no familiar faces. Deceitful man! I don't believe he had an idea of coming. I *may* do him injustice. I know not *what* may have prevented him. And so we became resigned and considered our parting at the gate the final one: not forever! No not!! I shall *never* forget him. "Bright be the skies above him, friend of my early days". I wonder if he will *ever* think of us. If he does, 'twill be with no regretful feelings at parting with us. The following day, Tuesday, Capt. Miller called in the morning. I knew not why *then,* but I afterwards found that he came *especially* to ask us to see him off in the afternoon. I was not there but Alice told me that he scarcely said a thing about it. I felt *so* sad all day, thinking that we were so soon to part. Afternoon came, we were dressed *waiting for him;* the bell rang, and of course we thought that it must be him. But it was Mrs. Miller and Fanny. They were going to the "depot" and stopped for us. We donned our bonnets and mantillas and soon we were on our way. Fanny looked very pretty and we all were very, very sad.

We did not see him for some time after we arrived, as he was very busy with his men. We heard him! Alice and I stayed in the background, waiting to see if he would ask for us. Presently we heard, in the well known voice, the words, "Where are the Miss Solomons"? He saw us, came to us, greeted us cordially. He looked so sorrowful. His looks could not have been deceiving, he felt so; and doubly did I. His mother was there, to bid her son "Good bye" and wish him "God speed". It was tearful to behold. And then, he came to us. I looked at him. *Could* I keep the tears from falling. And yet I knew, I hoped that I would see him again. He said "Clara, good bye, if I have ever done anything to offend you, forgive me". I nodded assent. He asked me to forgive him! Did he feel himself guilty. He may have referred to some trivial act of his, wherein he thought he may have given offense. The whistle sounded, a hasty adieu to *all,* a *last* one to Ma; he jumped on the train, said "Ma, to morrow night, 12 o'clock, Girls, God bless you", and *he was off*. He waved his hat to the last, we turned away, feeling lone and desolate. And so we saw him off, saw the last of him for many a day. The world is made of partings, and they are the saddest things in life. I hate to say "good bye". And he had really gone. Each previous visit we thought would be the last, and now this, this was *the* one. It is singular how great a liking and how unaccountable a one, *we* took to this man. He said that we would hear from him. I hope that he will fulfil his promise. He had his ticket, "*which would take him to Virginia*". God bless him, may he return home safe and victorious, and may the "Old Dominion Guards" win gloriously the first laurels.[9] I returned home *very* downhearted; ma was not very amiable, and the evening, which gave a promise of being very dull, was lightened by the presence of Cousin Sam.[10] We made an agreement with him to take a ride the next afternoon in the new "Cars". He made a promise to come and dine with us. Precisely at *19 minutes past two* did he appear. We had a very nice dinner; started about 5. We were unable to take our ride, as there was too great a crowd, and resolved to try another time. Went to Vincents. Enjoyed the cream very much. Met aunt Clara, Sarah and Hester Hyams, who is here on a visit: stopped a little while. Sarah has grown very tall and pretty.[11] First cousins! Who would have believed it to have witnessed the salutation. I would like to be intimate. In the night Gus came; we went to get "Ice Cream". I hate him — although he *is* our *style*. I gave Cousin [Gus] a letter to mail to Lizzie Mix. Thursday, I have already recorded. I neglected to state that "Our dear Battalion" left to day. May God watch over them. In the afternoon detestable Eisner came and stayed about *three hours*. He is a perfect nuisance.[12] Cousin Sam came, but did not stay long. We were expecting Pa, but he did not come. Friday, we were also expecting him, and Ma was very uneasy. We stayed up at night, thinking surely that he would come. At last 12. o'clock came. We heard the whistle, the omnibuses rattle along. Waited patiently till about 12½, starting at every sound, thinking that every vehicle contained

9. The Old Dominion Guards were a newly formed Louisiana unit that went to fight at Manassas and Bull Run in the early days of the war, when optimism flourished in the South.

10. Samuel Myers, while not always a friend of the local judges, was in fact a prominent attorney in the city. He ran unsuccessfully for a seat in the state's Confederate legislature. Clara and her family were part of an extended Sephardic network, related to many of the other Sephardic families in Louisiana.

11. The Hyams family from Alexandria, La., were also of Sephardic origin and also strong Confederate supporters. Henry Hyams held important positions within the state's Confederate government.

12. Jacob Eisner boarded with the Nathan family and clerked in a popular variety store, Bernard A. Dryer & Co., in the French Quarter.

our "precious burden". But — he did not come, and we went to bed alarmed and in a great mystery concerning him. Ma therefore made up her mind to go up after him the following morning. It came. Ma and Alice were up, contrary to my predictions, bright and early. They went to the depot, anticipating going if they could obtain a permit. I eat breakfast, was just about my self, when I imagined I heard some one say "Alice". I looked around and *there was Ma and Alice* returned from their wild goose chase. They could *not* obtain the permit. I, am ashamed to acknowledge it, was glad, as I envied them. Alice and I passed the day, partly in writing, thinking of course, that Pa would be in at 12. He did not make his appearance, and we were very *much* worried. We thought it very strange that he had not written a line since he had left. Well, in the afternoon, Alice and I were sitting in the front room, in rather a not very nice condition to receive a visit, when I saw a form on the gallery, it was a uniform. I said to Alice, "It is nothing but a common soldier, don't be frightened". My only thought was news from Pa. She went to the door, asked him to come in; he complied; introduced himself as Mr. Hill, of Sargent and Hill.[13] He had come to see if pa was not in the city, as he had promised to come and see him immediately on his arrival in the city. He was not very prepossessing in appearance, but became very agreeable while conversing. I liked him so much, and before he left I thought him very handsome. He said that he had seen Pa, Thursday, saw the Battalion leave. We felt much relieved. Oh! Pa would be to night! We did not stay up and he did not come.

Monday, June 17th, 1861

The first Monday's journal that I have ever recorded in "big Philomen"!! How many will I record before its existence is terminated? To day was a most beautiful day; not warm at all. The sun is now shining as brightly as it ever did before, in all the romances, day previous to marriages and marriage ones. I love the sun — but how much more do I love the soft, mild radiance of the moon's light. I, cruel as ever, have stole away from Josie,[14] and left her to Alice's or anybody elses protection. I looked for Pa at 12,

13. Sargent, Hill & Co. were downtown New Orleans grocers.
14. Clara's youngest sister, one year old, who was in Clara's charge when Ellen Deegan, the Irish maid, was not around.

but he did not come. We have ceased to be uneasy since the receipt of a letter on Sat., assuring us of his safety and inability to return at present. I was glad for Ma, but for myself, I know not why, I was not uneasy; I know how dilatory the "dearest man on earth" is. Alice sent home a letter from school to day, which had been handed to her by Belle Grant.[15] It was from Pa. Belle had been up to Tangipaho and had seen him.[16] She and Louisa [Grant] accompanied Charles, who left yesterday for Vir. They are, of course, very sad. She said that Pa was looking so well. The handsome fellow, don't he always! He had on a *colored shirt*. She saw our "blind man". He was bothering Pa with his slate. Poor dear fellow, I *love him*. We were just in the act of dining, when Josh came in with a letter; it was from Pa! How uncle Naty came by it is a mystery *now*.[17] We opened it and a X [ten] dollar bill rolled out. It was very acceptable. He "thought that we would want some change". He said that he would be "home" to night. We will sit up for him. I hope that he will come. He told us that he had again been robbed; it is too bad, too bad.

Yesterday afternoon Cousin Sam came up. I did not see him. He brought a letter apiece for Ma, Alice and myself. Ma's was from Aunt Sarah; there was no news, merely a letter inquiring about ma's long silence. Alice's was from Solly: I have not yet read it. Mine was from *Lizzie Hillman*. I was rather astonished at the receipt of it. I was glad to see that she had not forgotten me. I wonder if any feelings of affection or love prompted her to write. I shall answer it as soon as convenient. I like her very well. In the night he came again. He proposed a walk. We went. And the mean wretch passed right by the Ice cream saloon, and never invited us to participate, and there I was starving. He said, "Lets cross over to go home", and then, I made up my mind to ask him, but Miss Alice would not listen to such a thing, and therefore, I was obliged to trudge home, without anything or any prospect of getting anything. He left immediately on our arrival home. We did not go to bed till 12½. Disappointed. 9¼. I did not dress until late. Alice and I took a ramble this afternoon. A short while after we came in Mrs. Miller's three children came to tell us that she had returned. There's a lot of news we have in store for us. We will go to see her shortly.

15. Alice taught at a nearby public school, the Webster School, from which she herself had graduated. Her salary was $600 per year.

16. Whenever possible, those at military camp looked for someone to deliver letters personally, even from Camp Moore, a trolley's ride from New Orleans.

17. Josh was the young son of neighbors Samuel and Sarah Nathan, whose father Clara calls "Uncle Naty."

The bell just rung. It is — Miss Sarah[18] and Uncle Naty. Horror of horrors! The gas, the gas!! It is over with, she is informed. The rubicon is passed!!! Yesterday, I combed Alice's hair back; she looked *beautiful.* She is perfectly beautiful. I love her, my idolized, my precious sister. What a treasure she is, what *would* I do if she was to get married and leave me! *What,* would I do.

Tuesday, June 18th, 1861

6³/₄ A.M. The first lines that I have ever pencilled to Philomen at A.M.!! I arose this morning laboring under the erroneous impression that it was later than it really was, but I don't care. I have been reading the paper, and thinking that I ought to answer Lizzie's letter. I don't believe that I ever stated that we have given up our "dear old Delta", and now take the Crescent; I don't think that it will last long, as we feel very much attached to our former friend, and besides we will have no opportunity of perusing "D's" and "J's" letters, which are at all times peculiarly interesting.[19] It is exactly typical of the human race. Longing for a thing, and then, when it is in our possession undervaluing or casting it away. By the by, I wonder how "Durant" is! I have scarcely bestowed a single thought on him, since his departure. I wonder if in his journal, if he has ever kept any, I would see the same thing of us? I have not the slightest idea that I wouldn't. And that man's promises! Why, I regard them as "trifles light as air". The world, the *greater* part, I mean is composed of *such stuff.* Baker, I think, accompanied him on his *voyage.* The "old longlegged shameface"!! I wonder what has become of him. He dares not come! for appalling visions of ice cream, Canal St, etc. rise before his mind. It frets me, if I should never see him. Miss Sarah did not stay very long last night. She had been to Mrs. Ellis, and gave us the unpleasant (?) news that we were soon to lose her. Louis having lost his situation, she was going up to live with her sister. Some fun in store, for Miss Ludie. Just to think! she never came to see us. I *hope* there

---

18. Clara followed the southern custom of referring to a married woman as "Miss—", followed by their first name. It causes some confusion to historians.

19. The *Crescent* and the *Delta* were competing dailies. The Solomons looked for the newspaper most partial to the Confederate cause. Clara and sister Alice, fifteen and seventeen, respectively, devoured the papers on a daily basis. "D" [da Ponte] had left for Virginia to report on the fighting there.

will be a time, when she will be glad, if we were to *allow* her to visit us. Miss Sarah gave Ma an account of her girl's leave. Maggie, you know is gone, and she is now living with Olivia Marks. Miss Sarah has a colored woman; she will miss Maggie.[20] Pa *did come again last night*. I don't know when to expect him. The best way is not to *at all*. Our dear Battalion! I wonder if they are *yet* in Virginia! Does "Miller" ever send a thought to us? I doubt it; he has forgotten us long ere *this*. *That is his disposition*. New scenes and faces continually please him, and cause him to forget those that he has left behind. Alice has just gone away angry because I sort of refused to braid her hair. I don't care. If she had got up early I would have, with pleasure.

Wednesday, June 19th, 1861

6³/₄ A.M. I have just opened the door for Ellen. I am so glad that she has come, for if she did not I would miss her very much.[21] Alice, bless her, is reclining on the sofa, in her night-robe writing in Felicie [the name given to Alice's diary]. I really do declare that the girl's *whole* life is wrapt up in that book. I wish that I could write, in both senses, as well as she. She has just now said "I wish Pa would come and buy me a new book". She uses them out like "fun". I *knew* that the man was going to leave the "True Delta"; so I patiently awaited to see what she would say to it. She came in, saw the paper on the sofa, said, "I wonder if the man brought 'my dear Delta'; bless him"!! She took up the paper, and the expression of horror which her physiognomy underwent, I leave *you*, Philomen, to imagine. "The wretch! He must be crazy"!!! To morrow, please God, we will again introduce to our "bed and board", our "Daily Delta".[22] I love "*D*" and J's letters. Pa did not come last night. We *scarcely* expected him, as yesterday morning about 10 o'c. as Ma and I were sitting at our work, we heard some one ascend the steps; the bell was rung; Ellen went to the door, I recognized "Mr. Murphy"! I saw a letter in his hand, I instantly grasped

20. Irish domestics, like Maggie, were on salary and were among the first luxuries to go when wage earners gave up their jobs for the military. Black domestics, many of them slaves, could be retained for a longer time. Their status was confusing, to say the least, as the war progressed. Olivia Marks was about twenty-three, a close family friend and wife of Theodore Marks.

21. Ellen Deegan came on a daily basis to the Solomon home.

22. A competing newspaper, *The Daily True Delta*, appeared, hoping to replace *The Daily Delta*. The *True Delta* was an antiwar paper, of no interest to the Solomon girls.

it, and in a moment saw that it was from my beloved Father. He stated that he could not leave, as he had been elected candidate for Sutler of the 7th Regiment, and as he had *some* hopes, he was desirous of waiting to know the decision. I hope to God it may be favorable. God knows he is deserving of some good luck; for a *better* man *never* lived; as good *may* have. And he thought that "without doubt", he would leave for home *last* evening. But we knew how *much* confidence to place in it, so we did not expect him, nor do I to day. How *much* will we miss him when he really *goes*. God only knows.

The letter, I suppose, was handed to Mr. Murphy to deliver. I think him *so good looking*. It is the most singular thing in the world, but *he* is another man, to whom Alice and I both took a decided fancy. Each expressed our opinions, unawares of each other's. But as Alice says, "Enough, Clara, he is *married*, has *red hair*, and fair *complexion*". I concur in saying "Enough". We will both like the *same* man, I know it, I know it. And in a few years *to come*, there will be one grand "heart struggle" and "life struggle". Alice says "I will not have to suffer, as *he* will always fancy *me*". Little sarcastic devil! She knows better. Well does she.

Ma, bless her, and myself had a little quarrel. As usual, it was ma's fault, solely and undeniably. I think *so*, but of course, ma don't. She thinks I am so *awful* bad, the worst one, and all such things. I wonder if I *am*. I don't think as bad as ma thinks I am. I know the sequel. She don't like me!!! But her, God knows how I love her. Ma, at times, treats me meanly, but, it is her opinion, that I am, "without doubt", the worst thing in the world. I don't believe that I am. It is singular how people don't know me. Ma *always* commences *every* fuss. Yesterday, for the first time, we had "Okra Soup". It was delicious.

Alice and I made up our minds, to go in the afternoon to see Mrs. Slimmer. So about $5^1/_4$, we jumped into the 'bus, and rode down to Canal St. The streets were alive with handsome men, women and children. Our walk from Canal St was very pleasant. The cars have not yet ceased to be a novelty, as they are always crowded.[23] They are astonishing in what rapid succession they follow one another. I hope soon to indulge in a ride. Sad to say, when we arrived at Mrs. Slimmer's, we found that she was out: "just our luck" said we as we wended our steps homeward: spent 15 cts and decided to stop at Sue's. We met Dibbie. She looked very pretty. It was quite

23. Trolley cars recently had come to downtown New Orleans, of which Canal Street was the hub.

late when we got to Sue's. Saw her and Shepard; both looked remarkably well; no sign of an *increase*.[24] I am sorry for her; but there is plenty of time. She said that she would be up to see us soon; we promised to spend the evening with her. Deo Volentes [God willing], we will. Arrived home safe. We were eating supper, when Cousin Sam came. He looked excruciatingly clean. There was quite an argument, respecting different members of the family, which ruffled the gent's temper. I was asleep when he left, but I think that he was restored to his usually *good* temper.

8¹/₂ P.M. Oh! the mosquitoes are devouring me. Alice is sitting by me writing and complaining of the aforesaid wretches. We have just come from supper; fare; black-berries, bread, fresh butter. Ellen is here, conversing about dresses, etc. to ma. It may seem strange to you, that in *these* times, the Solomons should have "fresh butter".[25] Knowing that you must have some curiosity on the subject, I will inform you how we came by it. To day, about 12¹/₂, while we were on the qui-vive [lookout] for Pa, we heard the gate creak. Ma and I of course were startled, thinking that it was the "stray sheep". We looked, and saw that it was a colored gent, with something in his hand. We thought that it was pa's availables, which had preceded him. I went to the door, and was handed a can of fresh butter, which the individual said had been ordered to leave here. I saw in a moment that it was from Pa, and learned from him that Pa was not on the train, so we gave up expecting him. The butter is very delicious and acceptable. Ma has sent out some. This afternoon, I heard the bell ring. I did not inquire at the time who it was, but I learned a few moments ago that it was *dear* Mr. Hill. I am sorry that I did not see him. I suppose you know Philomen, that Alice and I have determined not to marry any dark haired, dark eyed devil. Let's see. I was dressing this afternoon, when I heard a "gentle tapping at the parlor door". I looked over the gallery and I thought that it looked like Mr. Murphy. I came down and found that it was a letter from Pa. He said that he would in all probability be home to night. We will sit up. Miss Sarah & Uncle Naty have just come in. After we dressed, Alice and I went round to Mrs. Miller. She was not home; we returned immediately. A short while after we walked around the corner, and as the Prothro's steps looked very inviting, Alice and I enjoyed a short sitting on them, indulging copiously in the moonlight, and talking of "Our Battalion", or at least some members of it.[26] Miss Sarah has gone.

24. Pregnancy.
25. The war was a few months old, but many food items were already scarce.
26. Clara refers to the battalion of volunteers led by the family's friend, Captain Obed Miller, called the Old Dominion Guards. See *The Daily Delta*, 22 June 1861.

This afternoon, I commenced a letter to Lizzie. When will I finish it? At supper, I told Alice to drink out of a certain tumbler, and see if it reminded her of anything. Instantly Ma said, "I suppose when Miller kissed them". I just wonder how Ma knew. It was that too, and an exact representation is it. I will always drink out of it. Maybe Mrs. Miller has a letter from Obed!

Thursday, June 20th, 1861

4.50 A.M. Oh! how often have I wished that I was gifted with the art of composing well! of writing agreeably and pleasantly. You, my friend know how vain has been my wish. It is very warm, and I have just snatched these few moments; literally snatched them. I have been sewing.[27] I have yet to finish it, comb Alice's hair, dress Rosa, dress myself and I suppose, divers other things—Ma did not feel very well to day; she is now sewing. I have been quite enraged to day, because Ellen had the *impudence* to leave that *whole* dress for Ma to make; as if we didn't have enough to do. *Real impudence.* And because that Nathans[28] came last night just to get a drink. He is disgusting. And then to say that he wishes Pa would get the appointment and then he would be clerk. Indeed he shouldn't. He has neglected Pa greatly. And *she* to make preserves and not to send Ma a *bit.* Typical of the world!! They may be glad yet to *court* our Society. With the Ellises or Markses, it would be different. She told us that David and Theodore were both going— The first named gent's wife, so she says, does not care a bit. Strange, passing strange. Olivia I suppose will incline to the same opinion.[29]

6³/₄. I am sitting on a chair in the rear of the yard, having just completed my toilet. Dell has just tripped down the stairs, robed in a new barège. Poor little thing! She is happy while in the street. Nelly has been amusing me with snatches of different tunes. She is a smart little thing. I hear Rosa's

27. Women with sewing machines sewed clothing, generally undergarments, for the troops. They advertised their willingness to do so in the papers. See *The Daily Delta*, 2 November 1861. The Solomons and the Nathans received cloth from a government contractor who kept most of the government payments for himself.

28. Sarah and Samuel Nathan were neighbors and, like the Solomons, former residents of Charleston, South Carolina. They belonged to the same synagogue as the Solomons.

29. David Ellis and Theodore Marks were about to join the Army.

exclamations over the blackberries, so I conclude that Ma is fixing their supper. It is delightfully cool where I am sitting: I can *almost* imagine myself out of the dusty, noisy, unpleasant city. The scenes before me are certainly romantic. I am bounded on the North by a clear, blue sky, on the South, by the flagstones, on the East, by a *beautiful moon*, and *cistern*, on the West, by the clothes line and clothes. Alice and I have had a little misunderstanding about her hair; all her own fault; she to blame. Gracious knows, I am perfectly willing at all times to do it. Fanny would not lend me her shoes, I have no dress to put on, so I am a prisoner. This day we received a letter from Pa. There had been a fuss, previous to mustering in, which had been the cause of his delay. He writes that he will be home to night. I hardly *dare* to expect him. I hope that he will bring the eggs and peaches. With what avidity do Ma and I *tear open* his dear, welcome letters. "He comes to night", "how slow the hours linger". Ma, bless her is playing the piano. How I do wish for Pa to succeed for her sake; she is the best, dearest woman in the world. We were talking this afternoon about her going on with Pa; how I wish she could. I finished Lizzie's letter; probably I will give it to James to mail, if I go to morrow to Dr Dostie.[30] The man brought the detestable True Delta this morning, but I exchanged it for the "Dear Delta", with a boy. One of "D's" [da Ponte's] letters graced it. I hope that he will not be gone long, in order that he may speak in times to Mr. James. — Later 10 o'clock. Cousin Sam and Dr Taney have just gone. I have heard so much of him, and have had a great desire to see him. I like him very much, but every now and then thoughts of how I heard he treated his wife would steal over me. It may not have been true, and yet Dibbie told me. He is a dear little fellow, and I think quite handsome. Enough, he has light hair, and has been married. Oh! I am so mad; I don't know what to do. It seems that I am *always* provoked about something or other. I am enraged, enraged. And Ma, she *always* takes sides *against* me. It is about Miss Alice's hair; she told an atrocious *lie* against me. Atrocious, atrocious!! Oh! I could cry, cry to think of the wickedness in this world — The sinfulness!! I wonder if people *do* forget, or do they *really testify to a*

---

30. Dr. Anthony P. Dostie, a dentist with a political flair, had moved to New Orleans in 1852 from New York state. A popular dentist, Dostie also spoke up loudly against secession, calling it treason. He refused to take the oath of allegiance to the Confederacy after fighting began, and left New Orleans for Chicago in August 1861. He became a valued speaker in the North, describing the intolerance in New Orleans for any pro-Union sentiment. Dostie returned to New Orleans in August 1862, after Union troops occupied the city. See Emily Hazen Reed, *Life of A. P. Dostie; Or, The Conflict in New Orleans* (New York, 1868). He died there in the riots of July 1866 that began over the question of black suffrage.

falsehood. I have gained a victory, a glorious one!! I have governed my temper!!! And a struggle, a *great* one was it. I am nervous *yet* from the effects of it. The mosquitoes are so troublesome. We intend waiting up for Pa; but I don't think that he will come. Good Night.

Friday, June 21st, 1861

7¹/₂ PM. It is rather late, but I have not had a previous opportunity to write. "Long at expected, at length arrived". My dear, dear Father came to day. He looks so very well and handsome. We did not look for him, so it was rather unexpected. He brought a basket of very fine peaches, some eggs and a few other articles. He told us all the news, talking incessantly for I don't know how many hours. He brought a fine sword, which he has taken down to Hyde & Goodrich to dispose of.[31] I hope that he may realize something by the sale of it. He told us that the dear Major *intended* calling but could not really find the time. I am glad to hear it. Oh! it would take me *hours*, to record *all* he told us. Oh! I was so *delighted* to see him. We plagued him considerably about *Mrs. Chafin.* I will speak to you more anon.

Mrs. Ellis is now here; also Ellen, Mollie Blood, Laura Blood, and Mollie Jones.

Saturday, June 22nd, 1861

1³/₄ P.M. A hot, sultry day! Alice and I are in the front room, on one of the tête a têtes, holding communion with our books; I have just been relieved by a shower of tears occasioned by the perusal, for about the hundredth time of "Ernest Linwood". How I did sympathize with the lovely Gabriella. How many living representatives are there of her darling Husband. For instance our dear friend O.P. [Miller]. It is the most beautiful book, that I have ever read. It is, in fact, a book of poetry. How at some times,

31. Hyde & Goodrich, a popular jewelry store located in the prestigious Touro Building on Canal Street, closed its doors in November 1861, probably because of difficulties created by the war. Postwar successors ran a general store with the same name well into the 1870s.

did I envy the angelic heroine. What fearful responsibilities did she assume, when she swore to love, honor and obey that *man*. I can safely pronounce it an injurious book for young girls to peruse. Fanny is now reclining on *the mattress*. Oh! *now* for a pleasant house; for it certainly is hot! Oh! for a delightful, life-inspiring bath! What do poor people live for in Summer? I hastened my toilette this morning, as business of importance required it. I found Alice at the "rendezvous". She of course, had the Delta. She directed my attention to a paragraph, the heading of which was "Disgraceful". The substance of it was showing the hospitality (?) of the people of Chattanooga. They compelled them to pay for everything that they wanted. The men were even compelled to pay for bathing! It was outrageous; and unprecedented during the late troubles. What was my astonishment to read that it had been written by an officer of *Major Wheat's Battalion*. What memories do these words awaken! There was something else relative to the "First especial Battalion of Louisiana Volunteers". It stated that it was composed of a fine set of men, stated the respective Companies and Captains. Paid a eulogy to Maj. Wheat, styling him as the "Veteran of many fields". God bless, and preserve him. They expect soon to be at "Manassas", and will probably be the first in the *great* battle which is to come.[32] Under so efficient a commander they can *but* render a good account of themselves. Lieut. Hanna is authorized to receive additions to go immediately to Virginia.

Pa, I think, has serious ideas of not returning; some of them, as he said that "Miller may be a dead man, in less than a week", and "he hoped Wheat would not be killed".

3 o'clock. Pa has just come in, and says that he heard talk of a serious battle, with *great loss on our side;* and it is thought that the Washington Artillery[33] is in it. God grant, that it may be not as bad as expected. I am

32. Clara, like others, thought that the War Between the States would be settled after a small number of major confrontations. The first battle of Bull Run, thought of as quite large at the time, would be dwarfed by battles in the years to come. See Peter Davis & H. John Cooper, *First Bull Run, 1861* (London, 1971); William C. Davis, *Battle at Bull Run* (Garden City, N.Y., 1977).

33. The most famous of the Louisiana military units, the Washington Artillery Battalion was organized in 1840 and served in the Mexican War of 1846. Composed of sons of wealthy families, its soldiers stayed together at their own expense afterward. The battalion joined Lee's Army of Northern Virginia and fought in over sixty battles during the Civil War. Its ranks included members of New Orleans's Jewish community. The battalion left New Orleans for Virginia with much fanfare, its own cooks, and several "servants." William Miller Owen, *In Camp and Battle with the Washington Artillery of New Orleans* (Boston, 1885); Leonard V. Huber, *New Orleans: A Pictorial History* (New York, 1971), 59–60. Historians have questioned the military effectiveness of the unit, but the residents of New Orleans in 1861 had no such doubts.

anxious to see the papers. To return to my previous account. It seemed so strange and agreeable to have Pa at breakfast. I don't believe I knew before, how much I loved him. The eggs were a failure. *Chickens* are at a discount. Alice and I did not attend Synagogue. We were busy, fixing up our things.[34] There's dinner. 4 o'clock. It is over, and quite a sumptuous repast it was; but better than all, dearest Father presided over it. He was somewhat displeased with Alice and me for giggling. But—we could not help it. By one of the children something was said which recalled immediately a circumstance which Mrs. White related, respecting her mother's absent-*mindedness*. Pa saw in it nothing ludicrous at all. I told him that he must make all due allowance for the follies of "youth". Good natured, as he *always* is, he yielded. At dinner we thought of *two weeks ago;* condensed milk, etc. Two weeks! How we wondered where they would be. I suppose that Mrs. Miller has a letter from "Obed". We have not been to see her; I don't think that we will, yet-a-while. Ma or Pa, is not particularly pleased with her. I wonder if *he* will send us any letters. Oh! I suppose he is a real *"gasser"*.

The day has been quite long. Because I have been idle, I suppose. Alice and I are no longer belligerent. I made concessions, notwithstanding I was the injured party. We took a walk and, on the strength of it, invested in 5 cts Sugar Almonds; but they, being "not all our fancy painted", we exchanged them for "jelly cake". "Dr Taney" awfully grum. I never see a more grum personage in all my life. Alice says "he looks like he was jealous". I say "a la" "Ernest Linwood". Jealous? of what? why, *his* "Gabriella"!!!! Pa came home early. He proposed Ice Cream, Ma *vetoed* it. By the by, that reminds me of Gus! We'll never see *him*, again.[35] Pa invested in some Sardines and Ginger and we had a very nice supper. Retired very sleepy. Mrs. Nathans [Nathan] does not know of Pa's arrival; nor, I suppose does she care. Oh! I am so worried! I hope there will not be a destructive battle. God guard *"our* Battalion". How selfish!! Alice is just residing on the mattress, by Ma, reading out of the Crescent. I am desirous of seeing it, as there is a letter from one member of Major Wheat's Battalion. I wonder whom it is from! They are noticed considerably. I have got Sal. [Sallie, sometimes Sarah] to dress. I have yet a little incident to relate,

34. Clara, more than her older sister Alice, used whatever excuse she could find to avoid attending synagogue on Saturday mornings. Their neighbors the Nathans attended regularly and would ask the two oldest Solomon girls to join them. Clara did attend on the major holidays.

35. Gus Leovy, a family friend, was a reporter with *The Daily Delta*, no doubt on his way to the Virginia battlefront. The edition of 22 April 1862 has an article by him.

which occurred to day. Alice and I are no longer belligerent. Oh! I made a beefsteak, I mentioned it previously. I hope that we will go to the Bayou to morrow.

Monday, June 24th, 1861

4$^1/_2$ P.M. Oh! it is so excessively warm, that I can scarcely write. I know not where to go. But do not be of the opinion that it is warm *all* about, for I suppose that you are aware by this time, that this is *one* of the hottest houses of the City; and it is really tantalizing to see how the Vienne's trees are yielding to the influence of the Southern Breeze, a luxury of which *we* are deprived.[36] Pa is lying on the mattress in the entry; Dell is "making wind" for him and ergo, it is quite a "tableau vivant" [lively scene]. He communicated the sad intelligence, that he had put his name down to go Thursday. We will miss himself and his protection, for I think it quite unsafe to leave a parcel of females in a house without, in these times, a male. We know no one whom we can get to remain with us, and if we did, we have no accomodations; but I suppose that is "a horse of another color". God will protect the "grass widows". Ma is out there sewing. Alice is sitting at her table, conversing with Baby [a friend] for whom she received a letter on Saturday[37] — The romantic incident which I have not yet related. Well, to be brief, it is merely that Mr. James Rosser, Mrs. Prothro's brother, brought the letter, at Baby's request; she found out, by some means or other, that they were our neighbors. He is very handsome and quite captivated *Ma*. I suppose it is useless for Alice to write as Pa says that the mail will be suspended between New Orleans and the watering places; as yesterday a boat was fired into, and obliged to put back; fortunately the enemy were not close enough or they would have sunk the boat. No more, of course, will run. It is a sad pity as there will be *no* mode of conveyance, without great danger; so that families will be compelled to be separated for an indefinite space of time. We have not a sufficient force to op-

36. F. A. Vienne, a cotton broker, lived across from the Solomons on Hercules Street, now known as Rampart. See Gardner's *New Orleans Directory for 1860* (New Orleans, 1859). Street names in the city underwent several changes during the nineteenth century, making it difficult to keep track of locations.

37. Letters came to Alice's school for redelivery to the recipient. The school's address was a safe, reliable one in a city in which services were already breaking down.

pose them. Oh! This state of affairs! Oh! Philomen I have slighted you, by not informing you of the death of "Stephen A. Douglas"!! A subscription is being raised north for his family, as he left them almost *destitute.* I dislike to hear of the death of a great man, even if I *don't* admire him. Ma has requested me to do something for her. More anon.

6$\frac{1}{2}$ Back Stairs. Alice and I are in this location being desirous of obtaining some air; the children are all dressed and out; there are no fears of any visitors, so we can enjoy our "otium cum dignitate".[38] To proceed with my former journal. I did not feel very well, to day, and did not accomplish much in the sewing line. We have so much to do! Ma is continually exclaiming, "Sally and Rosa have not a single dress to wear". But with fixing and patching up old things, they manage to *get along.* Pa came at 3. Had "Okra soup"; very nice. He brought home the Evening's paper, from which we gleamed some news. I can't expect a letter from Lizzie Mix. I am sorry. Pa mailed my own to Lizzie H!!! *At last!!* I intended to go to school this afternoon, but Alice informed me that there was none. I had so confused a dream last night about the Grants, Cousin Sam and Durant da Ponte — !!! Alice told me that Miss Dentzel looked *real* pretty — How singular! Persons, whom at first sight we consider *very* homely, after acquaintance we consider them *very good looking.* We have not yet been to see Mrs. Miller.

Tuesday, June 25th, 1861

7 A.M. Having just partially waded through the columns of the Daily Delta, I relinquished all claims to it, gave it to Alice, determining to devote this leisure time to you, my friend. The paper has somewhat extensive news; numerous letters from "D" and "J", and as usual, very interesting ones. What nice times they are having. In one of "J's" letters reference is made to his traveling companions, Mr. D. da P. and Mr. M.A.B. They are enjoying themselves!! George Ellis alias Paragon has commenced publication in his establishment. My Pa is lying on the sofa, Rosa, Josie [Josephine] and Ellen [the Irish domestic] are by the door, Alice is getting her hair dressed, and the other members have not yet arisen. As it was quite late yesterday afternoon, before Alice and I finished writing, I thought it use-

---

38. Latin phrase meaning the girls were enjoying their "leisure with dignity." I imagine Clara refers to not having to dress for visitors.

less to dress, so donned merely my volante [robe]. The duty of sharing out the Black Berries, in consequence of Ma's absence, devolved upon me. A few moments, after I had been by the door, Mrs. Miller came. I was surprised to see her. She communicated as usual an amount of news. Said she had received two letters from "Obed"; she made no mention of any thing that he said for us. I wonder if he did. Probably he did and she would not tell us. I intend asking her. Can she be jealous? Ludicrous! She stayed rather long. Ma, as displeased, as ever with her. She constituted the talk at the supper table. I wonder when the D.L.S. will be home.

I have changed my location; it is now on the "kitchen steps", surrounded by the white and black juveniles — It is cool. I suppose that you missed me Sunday, and wish me to give an account of her whereabouts. Well, here it is. We made up our minds to go to the Bayou.[39] So the 11 o'clock omnibus conveyed Alice, Clara and Sol. Solomon to Canal St. We then took the new Cars, for the first time, which deposited us at the corner of Broad, and some other street. The cars are too warm, and the motion is *sickening* slow. 4$^1/_2$ P.M. Pa saw us to the corner, and we arrived there safe. We thought it singular that Cousin Caroline did not come to meet us, but we saw in a moment that she was sick.[40] Emily was not home, but she was sent for, and arrived in a few moments. She had on a very pretty dress, and looked very pretty.[41] It was about 11$^3/_4$. They asked if we would have

39. As used by Clara, the term "Bayou" refers not to the swampy lowlands of rural Louisiana but to the Bayou Road in New Orleans, where cousin Joseph Solomon and his family lived. Today in the heart of the city, Joseph Solomon's home was on its outskirts in 1861, a combination bus and trolley ride away from Clara's "uptown" address.

40. Joseph's wife Caroline, (née Barnett), came from a successful mercantile family in New Orleans. Her father Maurice did well as an auctioneer of various items, including slaves. Maurice attained respectability rapidly, and a relative, probably his son, became a notary, an important position within the Napoleonic legal system of Louisiana. Caroline contributed the funds for their house on Broad Street, acquired shortly after their marriage in 1840 from her sister's husband, Solomon (Simon) Audler. The Broad Street house became a famous example of Victorian New Orleans architecture in its area (Faubourg Gueno). Originally a small Creole cottage, the Solomons incorporated it into a larger structure during their occupancy between 1842 and 1877. Caroline added to the property as well, at least once in 1850, when she bought three adjoining lots. For years the most important of the surviving buildings in the Bayou Road neighborhood, the Solomon residence succumbed recently to the wrecker's ball after numerous attempts to raise funds to save it from that fate. See Roulhac Toledano & Mary Louisa Christovich, *New Orleans Architecture, Volume VI: Faubourg Tremé and the Bayou Road* (Gretna, La.,1980), 40, 152. Caroline's sister Helene Audler and her family were neighbors and substantial landowners along the Bayou Road. In October 1850 the Audlers' daughter Marie married Francois Bauduc, a non-Jew, in the Audlers' Broad Street home. While Marie's dowry amounted to some furniture and cash, Bauduc gave his father-in-law several slaves as a wedding gift. A. Barnett, notary, Vol. 3, Act 493, 19 October 1850.

41. Emily [Emilie] was Joseph Solomon's sole surviving child, a son Edgar having died a few

something to eat, but did not offer; of course, we refused. That is no way to do.[42] Luckily, I was not hungry. We passed a pleasant day. Playing the piano, talking, laughing, *sighing*, etc. The plum season had passed; but I did not care, as I am not particularly addicted to the fruit. In fact, I may say, that I like them least of any. Grandpa came in before dinner; he claimed a kiss on the plea of relationship. He is a dear old man; I love him. How often have I wished for a Grandpa! — I expressed it to him, and he kindly offering himself, I willingly accepted him — [43]

Cousin Jo seemed astonished to see us.[44] Dined about 3½. Nothing extra, although I ate very heartily, too much so for my comfort. Went in the garden, attempted to get some figs. Succeeded. Lounged about, awaiting the arrival of Ma and Pa. Cousin C. [Caroline] combed Emily's beautiful hair, into the most lovely curls. I wish I had them. "Thou shalt not covet"!!! The old man amused us. Emily was very earnest and pressing with her invitation for us to come and stay some time with her, but I can't say the same of her mère. It depends upon them whether we will go or not. If they want us, they will come up and see us, ergo, "Time" alone can decide our going. As it is I have not "*the most remote* idea" of it.

Cousin Jo frets a great deal. It was, indeed, a sad loss.[45] Ma came, remained some time, and then left. Emily's parting remark was, "the best of friends must part". Of course, the cars were crowded, so what did we do, but get into the cars, ride down to the Bayou Bridge, and up again. It would have been the only possible means, by which we could have got home, that is for an hour or so. The ride was very pleasant, but very

months earlier, in January 1861. *The New Orleans Bee*, 12 January 1861. The *Bee* was a bilingual paper in New Orleans, published in separate French and English editions. Emilie, younger than Clara, eventually married out of her faith, becoming the wife of William Alcée Ker. She died in 1923, and is buried in St. Louis Cemetery in New Orleans, a Catholic cemetery.

42. The oldest Solomon girls and their peers placed great importance on matters of formal etiquette.

43. Although Clara's father Solomon Solomon was about forty-six and her mother thirty-six at this time, neither had a living father. Nor is there any mention of a grandmother in the diary. The grandfather here referred to was on Caroline's side, Joseph's father having already died.

44. Joseph was the son of Aaron and Rebecca Solomon, Clara's uncle or great-uncle who had died in 1851. Like Clara's parents, Joseph was born in South Carolina. His family moved to New Orleans when he was twelve, in 1826. He married well and held a number of positions tied to political patronage in antebellum New Orleans. In 1857, for example, he was a court recorder and justice of the peace. In the first Confederate elections he ran successfully for a seat in the Confederate Congress. He managed to hold onto patronage positions in the early days of Reconstruction, serving as a port warden.

45. The loss of his son Edgar the previous January, age seven.

crowded. The impoliteness of some men, is shameful. They will sit and see a lady standing, and not offer their seat, and one, upon being *asked*, refused. There was one lady standing, so we took compassion on her and made room for her on our side. She was very thankful. We commenced a conversation. I happened to mention dear Wheat's name, and she told me that she was intimately acquainted with him. She knew all the officers of the Battalion and their companies. She had something to say about all of them. She was very pretty and lively. Pa was acquainted with her Father; "his name is 'Moore' on the Hercules St his mother feeds his children".[46] Let them pass on. We eat supper when we got home and then, quite fatigued, went to bed—So ended our visit to the Bayou Road. $6^1/_2$. It is raining. I have no more time to write. I must go and dress my Rosa. $8^1/_4$ P.M. Supper was just over a few moments ago. Fare, Black berries, cornbread, ginger: very nice. Pa is asleep on the sofa. Josie is squalling—No notable event occurred to day, which would serve to keep it from the waters of Lethe [the river of forgetfulness], to which they are all most consigned. We were favored with some refreshing showers, of which we were very much in need. It continued all the afternoon, and has not yet ceased. It has succeeded in a banishment, somewhat, of the mosquitoes—Jourdan sent Ma up the plums, and to morrow, please God, we will make preserves. We intend to send Mrs. Nathan some, as a hit to her, for not sending us any; unprecedented meanness. The man promised to bring me some figs to morrow. I hope that he may. Pa brought home some peaches and Maple Sugar. Both very nice. Alice's book is "out". Pa neglected to bring her up one, but [?] forgot it. She is therefore unable to write. Alice came home from School, and held up a picture before me, and asked me who it was: immediately I said "Steth". It was indeed, a correct likeness. The mouth is perfect. I forgot to tell you that Sally & Rosa, had their hair shaved: Rosa a lä Soldier; the height of the dear's ambition—

Alice and I were looking out for Pa, when the omnibus passed, and some one who was sitting with his back to us, with a cap on, we took to be Pa. We stood at the window and waited for him, but as he did not come, we laughed at the absurdity of the idea, but as we were laughing, we saw Pa come in the *gate*, really with a soldier cap on; it is very pretty and becoming. It is a Lieutenant's. I wish that he would get his uniform or the synonym "soldier clothes"—I am very tired, so adieu!!!

46. The Solomons' street.

Wednesday, June 26th, 1861

7¼. (A.M.) Pa has just come in from market, with his dear soldier cap on. I was rather lazy this morn. I see by the paper that "Mr. Baker, the private secretary of his Honor, Mayor Monroe, has returned to the City". I suppose he would have liked to remain with "your Mr. da P." He might have written one letter; probably he *could* not. His first visit will be to Judo's.[47] Lovely angelic being! It is sacrilege that I should write *thy* name, in connection with *any* ones. Pa received a letter yesterday from Mr. Hitchcock, the gentleman, *whose acquaintance, we had the pleasure of making, that day a month ago.* There was no news: he said he had written before, but they were never received. He asked Pa to try and raise $250!!! Preposterous!! Sad to say "the butter is *out*" !!! It paid us rather a long visit. The Exhibition of the Normal School, takes place on Saturday —

5¾ (P.M.). Nothing happened to day, with the exception of the excitement, consequent upon the making of the "preserves". They are very nice — *Ma* wonders if they will keep, Alice suggests if we don't eat them. I omitted to annex the P.M. Also the A.M. this morning. A very nice dinner — Pa home. He forgot to bring Alice's book, consequently she is not now writing but ringing on the Piano. He promised to bring it up this afternoon. I doubt it. "D's" letter was excellent to day. It was teeming with him. A superabundance of *large* words, for our benefit, I presume. In one part of it I just imagined that I saw him, with his head resting upon his hands, studying about the rain. I have just witnessed the departure of "Zulma". Viennes and Jarreaus, *very* thick.[48]

47. Clara saw Judith at synagogue and considered her an outstanding beauty. Like other Sephardic Jews, Henry Hyams's family came to the United States from England, in the 1790s. His father Samuel married Miriam Levy soon after his arrival. Living first in South Carolina, they moved to rural Louisiana after Miriam died, having given birth to five sons and a daughter. Samuel Hyams's sister was the grandmother of Judah Benjamin, the most famous of the Confederacy's Jews. Cousins Judah Benjamin and Henry Hyams followed similar educational and social paths. They studied law together, married non-Jews, and pursued political as well as legal and agricultural careers. Henry Hyams was a state senator in Louisiana in the 1850s and lieutenant governor of the state between 1859 and 1864. Both Hyams and Benjamin were substantial landowners and slaveholders before the Civil War. Henry Hyams may not have been particularly concerned about the maintenance of Jewish tradition in his family (he married Laura Smith of Donaldsonville, and his daughter Judith was about to marry a non-Jew), but he did serve as an officer of several Jewish charities in New Orleans, most notably the Association for the Relief of Jewish Widows and Orphans.

48. Clara's neighbors on Hercules Street, the Viennes and the Jarreaus, were respected merchants and active in Confederate city politics.

Thursday, June 27th, 1861

7$\frac{1}{2}$. A.M. Just escaped from the noise and confusion of the upper regions, and with breathless anxiety descended to the lower regions to ascertain if Ellen had come. In a moment it was decided. She had. I was very glad, as in her absence, the disagreeable duty of nursing devolves upon *me*. Lucy [their domestic slave] does not feel very well. I don't know what's the matter — Yesterday afternoon, while we were dressing, the bell rang and some one came up and said that it was Mrs. Stevens. We thought that it was Miss Sarah hoaxing us, but we found out that it was Mrs. L.A. Levy. Ma hastened down, but I was unsuccessful, as she had gone, by the time I made my appearance. I was sorry. Ma gave her some preserves and bread. She was delighted. She said that probably Emma would come and spend the day, either Saturday or Sunday, and that she would send Ma some Cucumbers. She is a nice lady. I almost, I mean "always liked her". She went over to Mrs. Ellis to join Sarah [Nathan] and Leah Marks. After her departure Ma tumblered up some preserves for us to take to Miss Sarah; committed the speech to memory, and, with all due ceremony presented them. It was as follows: "Miss Sarah, you must excuse the quantity, but Ma couldn't make any without sending you a taste"; or something to that effect. Josh said they were better than his Ma's. We can never forget her not sending us any of hers. Saw Mrs. Miller, but did not salute. Miss Sarah walked a few squares with us. When we got home Pa was there; *of course*, he did not have the book; plea; forgetfulness — Had a nice supper and retired early.

2$\frac{3}{4}$ P.M. I have just helped ma bottle up the remaining preserves. Alice has just come in, with the exclamation, "Clara, Miss Dentzel looked beautiful". She brought home her valuables, as to morrow is the "*last day*". It does not seem like it, the time has passed so quickly. I can scarcely believe it, and I *hear* so little about it. To morrow there will be many partings: partings to which there will be no reunions. 6$\frac{3}{4}$. P.M. Alice and I are sitting up on the back steps; Ma has gone out; Pa, I believe, has accompanied her. Well, Philomen here's a piece of intelligence. Dear Pa brought Alice's book; it is a beautiful one, and as she says herself "too good for the purpose for which it is intended". May she enjoy every page, may each one be written with a light and happy heart; may she, during its life, enjoy perfect happiness, as unalloyed as mortals *e'er* enjoy. The earnest wishes of Clara. He brought several others, one of which I claim, also a pencil. I am very well satisfied with my book, for the present — Little "Jennie Miller" has just gone. She said that "she must go to Grandma's to get something to eat", whereupon Ma gave her something—Poor children! They are half starved. Pa says they have nothing to eat. I should think it very bad management. Jennie said she had *some* dinner, but not *much*. I am very sorry for them.

"J's" letter was excellent; "D's" not so very good—I always think to day is Friday. It is after 7 and not *yet* dark.

Friday, June 28th, 1861

5½. P.M. Oh! Philomen, what do you think! That Ellen did not come to day! Gradually it dawned upon my perception that such would be the case. The little Irish — — —, well, I won't be profane, but I am angry enough to be. That is always the way; be too good and give too many liberties, and you know the consequences. Like dogs, the better you are to them, the worse they are to you. She is just playing sick—Ma is determined not to send after her—She is right—It was all explained—[49] I combed Alice's hair, and I think displayed great strength by yielding. But—it is all over. I succeeded very well, dressed myself and prepared for the task of minding Josie, who is very cross, but I suppose the child is sick. It happened so the last time, that she stayed away. Pa came down soon, relieved me while I fixed the table; Ma came down, breakfast was served, and I went up stairs to make Alice some "bow-catchers"—Alice complained of a *little stiff neck*—Thought nothing of it, and she went to School. I hastened to wash my breakfast things, as I had promised A. to pay her a visit, this being the "last day". I, of course, was longer than usual, at them, and then prepared to do "my rooms". Ma helped me, and I got through rather speedily; but just at this crisis Josie commenced crying, and I had serious objections to going, as she required constant minding, and it would devolve upon Ma; but at her suggestion I equipped myself. Put on my dress, like Alice's, both of which have faded in the back, and it is said that they will wash white; they would *then* be pretty. Gracefully threw the blue veil over my head and departed. Arrived there, and found Jo. seated on the platform, and she

49. The manuscript federal Census of 1860 for New Orleans often reported Irish domestics as members of household. In the Solomon home, the Irish maid did not live in, yet she and her family had an important claim on the Solomons, as will later appear. Jewish families mentioned in the Census records employed young Irish maids even when the family's personal property amounted to less than $500.

saluted me with "Don't Clara look like a young lady"!!!! Nettie was also there. Miss Jo. did not look well at all. She looked real ugly. We sat on the platform and had a nice talk, all about Ed, how he loved her, what he did, what she did, what he thought, what she thought, and *all* sorts of things—I suppose she loves him, as much as ever. She is not "*off*"!! How she would like to be—She left to go to Mrs. Merrifield, but returned shortly—She said that she was coming soon to spend the morning. Please God, we will go to spend the evening with us [wording?]—Show Pa off to the Calders—I saw Belle Grant. Poor thing! How she suffers—She has not heard from Charles. I hope that all yet will be well with them. They are an afflicted family. Louisa [Grant] was there—I saw Miss Dentzel; don't think her so *very* ugly. Jo., Allie and I went to see Miss Cavidaly, and at our request, she favored us with some songs.[50] The girls sing very "sweetly and Prettily". We then left her room, saw the other teachers, bade a final adieu, and then prepared to depart. There were no parties going on, with the exception of something, it can't be called a party, in Belle's room. I partook. The poor children, I suppose were of the same opinion as I, that they did not get "enough for their money". Alice was complaining of her neck. Miss Cavidaly said that I "grew taller every time when she saw me". I told her it was natural—She said that I "looked blooming". I added "as usual". I didn't mean it. Would that I had, for then I would be a little more contented—Self-appreciation is greatly to be prized, and I think it is the organ in which I am most deficient. I tell Alice that, and she says "Do you not ever look in the glass and think 'how nice I look'". I told her "no". "Nonsense", says she. I *may* have, but then it was a *very* transitory emotion, vanishing almost immediately at its birth. But—I am branching from my subject. Miss Tobin in her quick, old-maidish manner, which we imitate so correctly, said that "we looked so much alike, she could scarcely tell the difference".[51] Extravagant—Belle returned Rutledge, but Susie did not Nemesis. I think it so mean—I borrow books and don't return them, but I don't like persons to do so to me!!![52] Scarcely any of the children evinced any sensibilities, that is in the shape of "tears" at parting. Miss Dentzel tried to make them cry, but was unsuccessful. Maggie Myers was the only one, whom I saw with "tears in her eyes". The others regarded it as a "blessed deliverance"—Saw Lucy Edwards, whom I consider quite homely. Some

---

50. Miss L. A. Cavidaly was principal of the Webster School for Girls, where Alice teaches.

51. Miss Tobin teaches with Alice. Neither Alice nor Clara suffered from hostility or slight from their schoolmates or staff because of their religion.

52. A shortage of books led to borrowing as a matter of course.

of the "old girls" were there — Fanny *should* have been one of that number. But — she is the "dunce". She knows it — I disremembered the last vacation and wondered why I was not at school. Saw Mrs. Matthews, and promised her to attend the Exhibition, the following day. I did not like the idea of going home, as I knew that Josie was very cross, but I wanted to relieve ma, but, to quote Charles Hurley "spirit is willing, but physical strength is weak" — Alice was not lively at all — Told Belle that we would come and see, and hoping that she would soon get a letter, told her "good bye". And thus terminated my visit — When I arrived home, found things *just* as I expected — Partook of a slight refreshment and then of Josie. Alice's neck paining. At 2 o'clock, Pa came with a nice basket of figs, or rather a basket of nice figs — Eat dinner not very peacefully. Fooled about, did not dress.

Saturday June 29th, 1861

2¼. P.M. Oh! Philomen, what a disappointment, what a disappointment. We intended to go to the Exhibition of the Normal School, but Alice's neck being not better, we were unable. I did not care very much, but I know that Alice did as she had promised Mrs. Matthews — But, I should like to have gone. We were gone to wear our new dresses, leave at 9. o'clock etc. Had all our arrangements made, never thinking what obstacles may have been thrown in our way to have prevented our going. Pa doctored her neck last night with cold water, and we had every hope of her recovery by morning, but — "Man proposes, but God disposes". Is it all for the best? I got up early and perused Rutledge for about the hundreth time, and I wish it was not in my possession, read the paper, found no interesting communication, with the exception of "D's" letter, dated from Norfolk. We had a very nice breakfast, and would you believe it, I really cried, because *I had no appetite*!! Just to think of it! Pa proposed taking me, with Josie, to Carrolton — It vexed me to think that while Pa was away and we had nothing nice, I was so ravenous, and *now*, while we have plenty nice things — Boo hoooooo!!

Alice said that she would not live with me *alone* for $50,000 a year. And why? Because every little thing frets me. At present it is *the veins in my hand and the loss of my appetite* — Two *lamentable* circumstances. Oh! my appetite! I entreat, I beseech, I implore you not to *entirely* desert me, return again to me and I will welcome you as a dearly beloved friend, whom I have not seen for years. A nice piece of roast for déjeuner, and no appetite!!! I *know* I am a silly girl—And the veins in my hands! *They* will be my companions for life. At Alice's request I went down to get Alice's salary—Rode down and was told that "The teachers did not receive their salary to day". *Next* Saturday, which was the first in the month. So, I had to trot up here. Of course, all were surprised as they were confident of receiving it. The omnibus has stopped. It is Pa.

5¼ . . . Just before dinner as I was reclining on the sofa, a mysterious boy made his appearance, an unusual commotion was seen and heard, Pa accompanied him to the pantry, strange proceedings! I remarked "Pa they have come at last for the 'gas metre'". He with a doleful countenance replied "I suppose so, but I will settle it next week". The boy came out, lit the gas in the burners, did something in the street, and went leaving us all horrified. But I smelt a rat. I thought that dear Pa had complied with our oft-repeated request and had had the "gas turned on". He appeared bewildered, but after I thought I detected a smile. He wants to surprise us. I am certain *now*, that all is right, as Ma and I have *already* tried it. Woman's curiosity—And I am sure that to night, the gas light will illumine our parlors. If it be so, I am thankful—Ma was absent during the transpiration of the above events, but some how or other she was made cognizant of them. We have almost got use to the *one* candle. I hope that the bill will never be allowed to run up again. In great doubt and mystery, we proceeded to dine. I could eat scarcely a thing—Bought some figs for the evening meal. Ma promised me some "bitters".

Oh! it is so warm. A few moments ago, I sharpened my new pencil. It is of the make of Myer Phineas, and very excellent. To my dear Father am I indebted—God bless him, and may he return safe to us. Ellen came to day. Little Josephine is not quite well—I remarked to Alice that I was writing this book for the benefit of my "*child*"! I don't mean for her to derive benefit but merely to give her an insight into her mother's history. If I could only write like Alice. She expresses her most simplest thoughts in beautiful language, thus beautifying them, is concise, diffuse, just as her fancy or taste dictates. Oh! she is blessed. Is beautiful and smart and good. What more can be desired, or is requisite? And then she writes so beautiful a hand. Oh! Philomen, my miserable hand writing is a constant source of annoyance to me. I blush for your sake and for mine— Will I ever improve? If an ardent desire, and continual practice can make me, then I surely will—But I know I won't. And I am so great an admirer of it — God grant that I may — I must go and dress — It is after 6 . . .

8³/₄. Philomen, would you really believe it, I am pencilling these lines by gas light, yes, by gas light!!!!!!! The first time for many a month —

Well, you must know, Pa wanted to keep it a secret from us all; just after dark Louisa Grant came in, for the purpose of giving Pa a letter to take to Charles, as she thought that he was to leave to-morrow — We went to the gate to see her out, and while out there, I noticed that the front door was shut, and looking up, a blaze of light was visible through the shade. We said "good bye", and were embarrassed at going in as we, with the exception of Fanny, knew what was "up". We went in, and of course, uttered numerous exclamations, F's being the only sincere ones. Three were lit & the rooms looked like old times. Pa made numerous excuses, saying the "man forgot to turn it off", and a thousand other things. But I knew all the while. I thought Alice did not know, and she thought that I did not, until we were dressing, when all parties confessed. She telling that after dinner she tried the back room one, and it lighting, she was naturally satisfied — Pa was under the impression that we were *really* astonished until Sally, little mischief, said, "Pa, Clara lit the gas in her room this afternoon". *Pa was petrified.* His ejaculation was "you don't say so"!! I was rather chagrined as I thought that the delusion may as well have been kept up — And it was useless to undeceive him, as the surprise afforded him some pleasure. But it was *all* over. The "cat was out of the bag". I was sort of angry with Sally, as I had requested her not to mention it, but I suppose it had slipped her memory — Then *Rosa* came out with what *"sister Sallie"* had done, and then it came out that we all knew about it. We then marched in grand procession to supper, enjoying meanwhile our gas and food. We told Pa that it was unnatural, after he had spent all his money to educate us for us to turn out a "pack of fools" — His dear self laughed. *They* enjoyed a good, hearty supper. My appetite — I went and sat on the lumber [porch] with Ma. Came in, conversed about "Jo and Ed". Amused ourselves *of course*. Louisa gave grand accounts of the Exhibition. They had a great surprise in the shape of a party. Concocted unbeknown to many of the girls. It was very fine. I regretted very much not being able to attend — She said that Miss Bride sang so beautifully. I did not know that she was so gifted. Of course she pleased Mr. Lusher — [53] Louisa superintended the "Ice Cream" department — I suppose there will be [an] account in the paper —

53. Superintendent of the Louisiana Normal School.

Sunday, June 30th, 1861

4³/₄ . . . P.M. It is very warm. Ma and Pa are on the back steps. This, I suppose, is the last Sunday for many a day, that we will enjoy his dear, dear society — And how very, very angry, with myself, was I this morning.

At breakfast, I was undecided whether I would eat anything, and when Pa asked me if I would have a piece of liver, I was in rather a listless mood, and without answering — I handed my plate. Pa thinking this disrespectful, became angry and said that if I wanted any, I should ask for it.

He, kind, good, and forgiving as he always is, *asked me.* "I don't want any". Immediately after I was sorry for it. But — what could I do? I was vexed to think that Pa should have got angry, when the offense was totally unintentional. The little appetite I had, went and I ate nothing — Dear Ma brought me out some mush-melon and said there were some shrimps in the safe for me.[54] *Every body is too good for me.* The marketing was sent home before breakfast. I instantly devoured the "True Delta", being unsuccessful in finding any reading matter in the "Delta" — Was quite pleased with the former journal; in which were excellent burlesques on "D's" and "J's" letters of the Delta. I hope that they will not notice them — I dreamt of the first named gent. last night. Dream — very confused. I wonder why Gus has not been! If I were a man, I would not show myself so weak. He is afraid to come, lest it will cost him something. But he need have no alarms. And Cousin Sam, is he mad? And Eisner; is he mad? I think that it is his time this afternoon —

6³/₄ . . . I have just got over the *task* of dressing, and am now deposited on the sofa, by Alice, both scribbling — I don't feel very gay: I know not why. I braided Alice's hair before dinner, and I am now admiring my handiwork; although it did not exactly please me. Dressed Sallie, in her little new dress, which looked very sweet, Fanny did the same to Rosa, in her new white dress, and they are now to Miss Sarah's. Fanny has just come down, prepared to go there. I never saw such a girl — She cares nothing for personal appearances. Alice has just said "I wonder when will be her awakening" — I hope not for a *long, long* while — Alice expressed a desire to see the D.L.S.!! "'Tis said that absence *conquers* love, but Oh! believe it not".

---

54. Observant Jews will not eat shrimp, but the Solomons did. They also rode buses and trolleys and handled money on the Sabbath, activities which were and are forbidden to observant Jews.

Monday, July 1st, 1861

$6^1/_4$. A.M. I was just in the act of putting June, when glancing at Alice's book, I saw that it would be wrong. And I can scarcely realize that it is July. Yes, vacation has come. The months of April, May and June have flown so *very* rapidly. How truly 'tis that "we take no note of time, but by its loss". I do not expect to pass the summer, very pleasantly, but, if we all remain in health and if we receive frequent communications from Pa, *I shall be contented* — We intend, please God, to do lots of sewing, improve ourselves wonderfully and "a thousand other things, of which we never dream". God give us health and strength to carry them all out.

The morning is very fine and beautiful — Now for an Ernest Linwood, Marion Baker or William Rogers — No one came yesterday afternoon. About dark, Alice and I were walking up and down, manufacturing a beau ideal, at whose shrine we were both to worship, when looking towards the corner, I espied a form, no thrilling or bloody romance, which suggested to me the idea of "Gus Leovy" — I imparted the suggestion to my "walking companion", who said, "no, it ain't he". But, it was he — We stood up by the gate, and learned from him that he was on his way to tea, and did not intend to stop. He asked us to go and get ice cream, but we did not like the circumstances under which, the invitation was made, so we politely declined. He said that we were haughty, proud and ceremonious. He requested the pleasure of our company around the square, but we also begged exemption — He was quite indignant — After what Alice had told me in the afternoon about the offered kiss, etc., I did not expect that he would come again: and I am certain that the visit was unintentional. He said that he would forego the pleasures of tea, provided we would accept. We told him, "another time", and he remained for about an hour and a half. I was *very* tired — He told us that Mrs. da Ponte, left this afternoon, for some sort of "springs". Gus, of course, is unconsolable. Jenkins will be back soon; of Mr. da Ponte's whereabouts he is ignorant — He related an amusing anecdote, about the "milk", which Mr. da P. desired to be kept a profound secret: if I *ever* see him, I shall plague him about it. And would you believe it, he told us that Mrs. Julia Murray was a divorced woman. Did you ever hear the like? I was astounded, as I had always been told she was a widow — She must be very wicked. I don't like her *now*. I wonder if she and Mr. da P. are as good friends. They are both *very* bad. I did not think it *so* bad, while under the impression that she was a widow, but to be a *married woman* and act so, is disgraceful — $4^1/_2$. P.M. . . . Nothing *much* has transpired since last I held converse with you—In consequence of the great event of scrubbing the rooms, Lucy was absolved from the "up stairs" work: consequently we were all necessitated to take shares. The disagreeable job of mending the bar, devolved upon me, and with no good grace did I perform it—Everything, however, was accomplished, and notwithstanding this was the first day of vacation, Ma was no more, I may say not quite as, lenient as usual. I did no sewing of any account. Alice did some sewing which displeased ma, and there was then a, little "fuss". Ma made allusions to her awkwardness, which annoyed Alice considerably. I at the time was "on the machine"; and being rather slow, Ma became angry with *me, unjustly*. I was glad at this slight disagreement, as it convinced me that I was not as bad as I thought. Previously, I told Alice, that if she stayed home all day, she would quarrel as much as *I*. Ma determined not to give us any more sewing, but cooled down immediately, and *to my disappointment* handed me a petticoat body. I dispatched it quickly and then—lounged.

Pa did not go to market, consequently we did not expect him home to dinner. We were just partaking of mushmelon and Corn Pudding, when the gentleman made his appearance. Brought home the Evening Papers; no news with the exception of "J's" letter. Alice gave me a little encouragement to day! Looking over my book, here and there, she would say "Oh! Clara, what a pretty 'H' or 'M', etc." Oh! Philomen *do* you think that I will *ever* improve?[55]

Tuesday, July 2nd, 1861

$6^1/_4$. A.M. It was a great hardship for me to rise this morning. I suppose because I did not retire rather early. I have just scanned the paper, not a particle of news. Lucy has just thrown in the Picayune, obtained from Prothro's. Yesterday afternoon, Alice, Ma and myself went round to Mrs. de Castro, to try to obtain some scholars for a widow lady, Mrs. Smith, who proposes keeping a vacation School. She was not home, and Alice then went round to Mrs. Henriques.[56] We did not accompany her. Came

55. Clara continually criticized her penmanship. It is in fact quite easy to read her diaries.
56. De Castro and Henriques (sometimes Henriquez) are classic Sephardic surnames. Jacob Henriques is listed in the 1860 federal census as a bookkeeper and a recent arrival to New Orleans. Born on the island of St. Thomas in the West Indies, Henriques married a young Jewish woman from

immediately home, and while stopping at the corner, to change some money, I saw on the other square Sarah Hinckley and her beau. They went into a little house next to Coste and the vain idea seized possession of me, that she might have been coming to see me. But I suppose they have forgotten all about Clara Solomon. Sarah is shortly to be married. How quickly has the time passed since she told me. I should like her to have come. Found Pa sitting on the steps, and just seeing the white pantaloons, and not expecting to see Pa, the thought immediately occurred "It is Mr. da Ponte"! I am right anxious to behold his physiognomy—I walked with "Nelly Giradeau" and Sally to meet Alice. We met. Mrs. H. promised to send her two children, but unfortunately Mrs. D. had just put hers "out". They both expect an increase—Unfortunate beings—Alice is very much pleased with the family. I like them too—I owe Zippora [eldest child of the Henriques; the name is Hebrew for "bird"] a visit! Will I ever pay it?!! Received yesterday a telegraph from Mr. Hitchcock. Pa's expense of it was $5.45. He thought a great deal of it unnecessary—Sargent and Hill [wholesale grocers] have not the required articles—He says that he can sell to 5000 men! He tells Pa to come immediately to Columbia Hotel, Richmond. I do not know when he proposes leaving—Oh! Philomen, Gus told us that *"Judo" was to be married last night*—I wonder if it is true. The really lucky gentleman's name is Sprigg. It is a courtship of long standing, as some time since, I heard she was engaged. I cannot believe it. [57] It made me low spirited, and, foolish girl, I could not think or speak of it. She is the realization of all my dreams of a lovely woman. I am envious only of *him*, to think what a prize he will possess. I cannot think him handsome. I wonder if it is true—

Poor Mr. da Ponte. He will not witness her nuptials. Oh! what a lovely angelic being! Think of her beautiful neck and arms. Reflect. She is ignorant that on the face of the earth, there breathes a being by my name. She is foolish to get married. While a girl she was the admired of admirers—But a married belle is detestable. Don't I love her! Last night at the supper table, Pa asked us if we would not like to go and see "Judo's" house. Now it was just what Alice and I were wishing for, so we immediately assented and with the greatest imaginable pleasure—Pa said that he would

one of the Dutch islands, either Curaçao or Aruba. Five of their six children were born in the islands, the youngest in New Orleans. At the time Clara wrote, the oldest Henriques daughter was about Clara's age. Jacob died in New Orleans in 1891, age 77.

57. "Judo," Judith Hyams, married Horatio Sprigg in a ceremony performed by the Rector of Christ Episcopal Church, Reverend William Leacock, a known and respected minister in New Orleans. Sprigg was a planter from the northern parish of Rapides, where the Hyams family also owned land.

seriously object to walking, so proposed riding down in the 'bus. Ma, of course objected, thinking it extravagant and foolish, to go so long a way merely to see a *house*. Alice and I being very anxious, donned our mantillas and gloves, stood by the gate waiting very patiently for the vehicle. Strange to say, we saw numerous ones going up, but none going down. We knew not what to make of it and gradually it dawned upon us, that they had stopped for the night—As Pa would not walk, our disappointment was great. Dear "Judo"! she was ignorant that a girlish heart was beating for her, alone, and that earnest prayers ascended from it, for her future welfare and happiness. May her life flow calmly on; may he, who I hope, hope is *her* choice, *always* be the realization of her hopes. I hope that nothing but love, pure love prompted her marriage—Then she can but be happy. My prayers will be answered. After all it may not be true. *I hope not, for I am envious of Mr. Sprigg.* Indeed, anyhow I would be envious to think that his name had been so closely connected with *hers.* The husband of "Judo Hyams"! What does it *not* express!! Whatever *may* be her faults her perfect beauty, in my eyes, atone for them.

To console us Pa proposed a spree round to Mr. Nathan's. Accepted— Fannie was quite indignant, I know not why as she was asked to accompany us. She vowed she would go up stairs, without looking up or putting out the gas. She was true to it. Found them up on the gallery, prepared for bed. They came down. Alice indulged in an occasional nap. Partook of some cucumbers, not very nice. I don't believe I told you, that Ma had put up some.

Uncle Naty has left Mr. McCracken! The mean Yankee! He wished to reduce his salary *one half!!!* As though a man of family could live on $62.50 a month. It is one of the most unreasonable things, of which I have ever heard. He refused it. The mean thing then offered $80. But Uncle Naty, independent and spunky refused to take it, alleging that if he had offered it first, he would have accepted it. He is aware, he says, of the motives which induced him to make the last-named, *generous* proposal. It will be a rather difficult matter for him to procure another situation. Miss Sarah, I presume, will fret. Arrived home about 11. Retired. *Something wonderful.*

5¼. P.M. It has been raining the greater part of the day, and it is now cloudy. It rained yesterday, consequently it will rain all the week. "I was standing by the window, it was the very same", etc, watching for Pa. I saw him and ran to open the door. I saw that some one was with him and how I ran. It proved to be Uncle Naty—He had come to dine with us. He dispatched word to his spouse, and then proceeded to devour our meal. I suppose that Miss Sarah was angry. Our little "Orderly Sergeant" [Rosa] was dining with her, so we had an exchange. The dinner was not very nice, but he seemed to enjoy it.—Dear, dear Pa, informed us when he came home that he had the "appointment" for the "Polish Regiment". I am so glad. I suppose that he is certain.[58]

8³/₄. I thank God for it. I think that Pa offered Mr. Hill an interest, and he refused. Pa received to day a letter from "Dexter", I am ignorant of its contents. I suppose that "Uncle Naty" will have something to do in it— Return good for evil. We have done supper. Pa has just entered.

Wednesday, July 3d, 1861

6³/₄. A.M. The rain is fast falling. It is the first rainy morning, with which we have been visited for a long while.

I am sorry, as there is a "picnic" being held at the "City Park" (wherever that is), the proceeds to be distributed among the destitute families of the volunteers; in consequence of which, it will be thinly attended—[59] To-morrow is the "glorious Fourth", which we as usual celebrate.[60] Who *ever* knew it not to rain on "Picnics and Fourths of July"? Three days, or at least, two days of the vacation have gone—How quickly!

I told Fannie, that if she would get up early, I would play ever so many

58. The "Polish Regiment," so called because its commander was Colonel V. Sulakowski, became Louisiana's First Regiment. The colonel formed the regiment at the same time Solomon received his appointment. Organized hastily and with little regard for the background of its men, the Polish Regiment fought well in Virginia after a hesitant start.

59. The "Picnic," a fund-raising event as Clara said, had in fact been going on all week and, according to the newspaper, had been successful. See *The Daily Delta*, 4 July 1861. The park was some distance from the Solomons' home, but not very far from the home of Joseph Solomon. The City of New Orleans bought the land for the park from the McDonough family, one of the state's wealthiest, in 1854, but let its 160 acres decay once the Civil War began. Today City Park is an integral part of New Orleans and home to the New Orleans Museum of Art. See the *Historic Souvenir–New Orleans*, published in 1895 and on deposit at the Hill Memorial Library, Louisiana Collection, Louisiana State University, Baton Rouge.

60. The question was whether secession meant forgoing celebration of the *nation's* Declaration of Independence from Britain. The negative answer adopted by the Confederacy and its strongest supporters says much about the limited extent to which proponents of secession felt they were giving up allegiance to the United States.

games of "buric" with her. She said "Why gracious, it would kill me in less than a month". At dinner yesterday, the milk-man came, was impertinent to Pa, and had it not been for our interposition there would have been quite a skirmish. It is an awful thing to see a man under the influence of temper. I have great alarms for Pa while he is away as he is very hasty and he is very easily provoked; particularly with an *Irishman* — He gave Pa, a dollar too much change — Pa told him to leave; he said he would when *he felt like it.* That was enough to incense him. He ran in, I thought, for his pistol. But, had I known it was for the *poker,* with all the heroism of the women of '76, *I would have gone and got it for him.* Oh! Philomen, I am *so* foolish. Every time I talk to you, I am more and more convinced of it. Sometimes I can scarcely express myself. *One* of the *greatest* gifts is that of language. "A little learning is a dangerous thing". Exactly my case. I am possessed of sufficient knowledge to be aware of my ignorance. A very critical position.

I am one third through my book; at that rate I will, according to a course of reasoning, be through in *six weeks.* That is going a little too fast. Previous to Pa's departure I absconded a picayune[61] from his vest pocket. I had the pleasure yesterday, for the first time of beholding a "five cent postage stamp". $5\frac{1}{4}$ .... Little Josie is not well at all. She has been droopy all day — I think she is teething. I hope to God, she will be better to-morrow. Dr Ball was here. He prescribed some pills. Pa was desirous of getting a partner; this morning he had hopes of Mr. Converse, but on his arrival at dinner, he said that he refused. The "Yankee" declined having anything to do with it — Pa is somewhat perplexed, as *he* cannot accept it, if he is not fortunate enough to get some one to go in with. He says it is a most difficult matter, as their stocks are low, and no prospect of replenishing them. I hope he may be successful. Sargent and Hill received a dispatch from Mr. Hitchcock. Of course, they paid no heed to it. We thought it would be expedient for *him* to be here, but Pa says he could do no more than he. They probably can effect purchases at some other city.

It rained a good deal to day. I hope that it will be clear to morrow. Pa sent home an enormous quantity of figs to day. I was very much surprised to hear that their cost was *35 cents!* I guessed $1.50. Considerable disparity — I am so worried about Josie. Bless her —

I am expecting a letter from Lizzie. Why don't she write? Maybe she don't intend to.

---

61. A coin of little value, five cents, carried over in Louisiana from colonial Spanish currency.

Quite a catastrophe happened at Miss Sarah's the other day, when our little O.S. [Orderly Sergeant] spent with her. Some rudeness on the part of Josh [Nathan] occasioned Rosa [age 4] to tilt the what not: the things fell, and the damage, I hear is quite serious — I suppose the matter will be investigated —

2

Pa Readies for War:
July 4–July 29, 1861

Thursday, July 4th, 1861

6³/₄. A.M. . . . My dearest Philomen! Glancing over the paper this morning,
my eye was attracted to the notice of marriage. Imagine my consternation,
while I read "On Wednesday, 3d inst, by the Rev. Dr Leacock, *Horatio M.
Sprigg,* of Parish of Rapides, to *Judith Anne Hyams,* of this City". Is it possible. Think of the lovely being whose arms Horatio encircled last night —
I wonder if she loves him. If so, he should be perfectly happy. It was a bad
day, but towards evening, it cleared off beautifully. I presume she was married at night —

Imagine a being like that arrayed in her bridal robes. *I* can't. I have previously written of her. I am furthermore permitted [prohibited?] from
speaking or thinking of her. God bless her — Wicked girl I am! I will be
cross all day —

6¹/₄ P.M. Marvellous to relate, it has been a most beautiful day. "The gay
sun was shining and nature was decked in her provident array". This
was unusual as it invariably rains on the Fourth of July. Yes, to day is the
"fourth". I have not heard much demonstrations — Although there were
many provisions made for its proper celebration. But I must attribute it to
our vicinity. I remember the last Fourth. *"Ain't you glad its so forth of
July"*? I wonder when *he* will be back!

Oh! I did hear some demonstrations. They were the firing off of a pack
of crackers by the children and Josh (who spent the day with us). As I expected I have been rather ill humored to day. Thinking of Judo, of her, her
and only her. I wonder where she now is. Probably in *his* arms. I don't suppose that we will ever know of her whereabouts. Oh! I am so foolish! I
love her so much, and yet I do not know her. It is for her beauty. I suppose
Marion Baker was at the nuptials.[1] About 2¹/₂, I laid on Sallie's bed, and

1. Baker was secretary to New Orleans Mayor John Monroe and a friend of Henry Hyams and
others in Clara's circle.

unconsciously fell into a sleep. I was mystified when I awoke. I heard the clatter of plates, and immediately remembered the circumstances under which I went to sleep. I arose, went down to dinner. Very nice—Had a watermelon this afternoon, for the first time. $8^3/_4$. I was just then interrupted by the entrance of Cousin Sam, his child, Fannie and his "crazy sister". Poor thing, I am so sorry for her, but, of course, we could not restrain the laughter. Our attempts to draw her into a conversation were unsuccessful. I don't suppose she is unhappy— Little Fannie is a sweet little child. I wish that she were mine—Indeed does she regard him as "more than brother and less than God". If some one loved *me* as *he* does her. But she is very delicate. I consider her very pretty. Cousin Sam looked very well. I thought that he had deserted us. They left about dark; Alice and I walked round the square and determined to go to Miss Sarah's, on consideration that we heard no unusual commotion before approaching. Went, thought we heard signs, and turned to come home. I turned back and saw Leopold. I was sorry we did not go, but I thought that Harris would be there. Alice and I were talking of Durant [da Ponte]. We are desirous of seeing him. Maybe he won't be back for a long while. I wish it was time for him. It is astonishing how much you like a person when they have been absent for some length of time. I don't suppose that Cousin Sam will ever go to Mrs. Nathans—As Alice and I were out by the door, Mrs. Hertz and her three children passed by. They stopped. *Mapheena!* A good sort of a poor woman—Talked of her poor Hertz—Last night we were at the supper table, when the bell rang. Various conjectures and bets were made, which Alice compared to a "gaming table". Some said Cousin Sam, some, Gus, some, Mrs. Nathan. *I* heard a fumbling in the room, and for a moment, the foolish thought arose, that it may be Mr. da Ponte. It was "Uncle Naty" and his spouse. They brought a cucumber and partook of some preserves and again repeated that they were better than hers. Impudence—I did not tell you the mean trick that she did. The argument was, that when she got the remaining shirts of Mr. Harris, that she would divide with Ma.

There's Gus! Conclusion, please God, to morrow. Good night.

Friday, July 5th, 1861

5¹/₂. P.M. Philomen, scold me for being so indolent, but I did not arise from my couch till about 7¹/₂. Oh! *who* would slumber in his bed, when darkness from his couch has fled? I awoke early and went into Ma's delightful bed. Had an excellent breakfast, which I did not much enjoy. I did not do much work to day: we are yet busy on the chemises; being not yet completed. The other day *we* did, that is three people and a machine! three pairs of chemise sleeves!!!! But, I suppose, they are progressing. Dear Ma tucked mine very pretty. Nothing of importance to day. Ma rather uneasy at the beating of her right eye.

I don't believe that I am as superstitious. Pa came home, and brought a blackberry boy; of course, purchased some — Also, two letters of recommendation from Mr. W.P. Coleman; one to Col. Sulakowski, and the other to Capt. McGinis. He intends going to Camp Pulaski and proposed taking Ma and Josie. The proposition was accepted, and please God, they will go Sunday. Dined rather late. At my request Pa gave me "fifty cents". He brought home the Evening Papers. No letters. There was a report yesterday, that 30,000 men had crossed the Potomac. To day, it was contradicted. Federal Congress met yesterday — Ignorant as yet of the results — Gus told us that there was great commotion in town last night — There were some fears of a *servile insurrection*. It was false — [2] He stayed until 11 ¹/₂.!! Entirely too late. In fact he came too late. All persuasions were useless; he would not come in the back room, where the light was. He is not ashamed of himself — He is right good looking. Mrs da Ponte has gone. Assuredly he was to see her off. He received an introduction to Charlotte. *Says* he was not particularly impressed — Don't believe him. Asked us to lend him a Music book. He would not come and get it and I was glad of a pretext not to lend it. He has not returned "Will he find her". *Mollie Hart has* it. I am now going to braid Alice's hair. Au *river!!!* [3]

2. Those loyal to the Confederacy probably feared a slave revolt more than the Union troops at this stage.

3. A play on the proper French valediction, "au revoir."

Saturday, July 6th, 1861

12¹/₂. P.M. . . . . . It commenced raining about 10 o'clock, and has not yet ceased. We had a most powerful shower. Fortunately we did not go out as we intended—We proposed going to Synagogue, after which to go and get "Alice's money". Previous to Pa's departure, he said that it would rain, but subsequently the sun made his reappearance, and we had partially made up our minds to depart, but we loitered about until it, luckily, became too late. About a half of an hour afterwards the rain began to fall. Miss Sarah attended. I suppose she was sorry. Alice and I are out in the entry, sitting on the "famed mattress", scribbling.⁴ It seems to me so strange, that the "fourth of July", should have been the *only* pretty day of the week. Alice made a very pretty simile, said a whole lot of pretty words, respecting it; but *me,* poor me, well *you* know well enough what I mean. I suppose I resemble Rosa, "in having many thoughts, but being unable to express them". Some consolation, anyhow—*I am a fool.* I fixed up a little, up stairs and of course was '*very tired*'. I had just arisen from the bed, when Alice came tripping up the stairs. She had in her hand a paper, containing the picture of the *"immortal Ellsworth".*

He is quite a fine looking young man, of about 23! Although not in favor of the manner in which he lost his life, I can but admire his heroism. He thought *he* was acting right when he transplanted the "Confederate flag". Do we not admire Jackson? 'Tis true, the Northerners are raging an unholy and unrighteous war against us, but do they not think that they have Justice on their side. We know they haven't. Does that cure them of their fanaticism— We laud the *truly* heroic Jackson, they, Ellsworth. It is natural—⁵ He resembles very much our "cake-shop man"—She took a seat by me on the sofa, I knew nothing, I only knew that something was the matter. She said, "Clara, I am in a predicament, I know not how to act", and with that she drew from her pocket *five ten dollar bills!!!* I was petrified! Demanded an explanation. She gave it.

4. Another Sabbath prohibition for the observant, writing, was ignored in the Solomon household.

5. Clara is here referring to Ephraim Ellsworth, a Union colonel whose unit was part of a large force that crossed the Potomac and occupied Alexandria, Virginia, toward the end of June. While marching through Alexandria, Ellsworth saw a Confederate flag flying over a hotel. Enraged, he dismounted, took two men with him, climbed to the rooftop and took down the flag. The hotel owner, James Jackson, equally enraged, shot and killed Ellsworth and in turn died at the hand of one of the men accompanying Ellsworth. See Gary W. Gallagher, ed., *Fighting for the Confederacy. The Personal Recollections of General Edward Porter Alexander* (Chapel Hill, 1989), 32–33.

Pa had given it to her in the morning, informing her that *he had drawn her salary the past week.* It was his particular request that Ma should not know it. It will be complied with. Ma had said that she bet he had drawn it. And it all has gone. Fifty dollars in five days!!! It astonishes me where he got it from to pay back. We are *obliged* to practice some deceit. We intended going down for it, but as it is now raining, we know not what to do. It is useless that Ma should know. In the course of time she *may.* Pa has just spent it in market. I suppose it has cost him some uneasiness, as it is no easy matter to obtain $50.

I hope that the enterprise in which he is about to enlist may prove successful, for surely *none deserves* success *more* than he. Ma is now making some plum preserves. I hope that they will be as nice as the previous ones. I am in expectation of some figs. We had so nice a breakfast, as many delicious figs as we could conveniently hide. I bet as large a quantity as "Jo Solomon" [cousin Joseph] had on his table.

I do believe that since our last visit, not a meal has passed, but they have constituted most of the subject. Dinner, breakfast and supper. If they had given us such a dish of figs as we had at breakfast, they would have considered us under lasting obligations. Mean, mean people! From the oldest to the youngest "Requiscat in pace" [May they rest in peace] — If Pa were only rich! *Who* would fare better than we? No one!! He is too, too good — We can never get 'husbands' as good in every respect. Taking him as a criterion we consequently place our standard too exalted. Could I ever endure a stingy husband! If I had my choice I should prefer an indifferent Father — Our husbands would therefore appear to better advantage, whereas they can *never* equal our Father — *Will we ever have any!* *That* must be the first consideration — And Pa's hand! Was anything ever more exquisite — "I love him, I love him, etc." It has now stopped raining, and Alice is in a dilemma: ma wants her to go for her money. She has discovered some blots in her book which annoys her greatly — You too, are, in some places, soiled. You deserve a good scolding. To day is three weeks since first I made your acquaintance — I wonder what your *Father* [Mr. da Ponte, who bought the notebook for Clara] would say to you, could he see you. Fear not, he will inquire for you. When will he return?

Will my Papa be home to dinner? Philomen, I write so horrible. I wish that I could improve. How great a room is there. I hear a noise. It sounds like the bottling of preserves — anon. I was mistaken. Pa has come. He pretended as though he got it and brought it up. It is now safely in Ma's possession — "Oh! what a tangled net we weave, when first we practice to de-

ceive". There seems to be a strange fatality connected with our new or-
gandies. Four or five times we have intended to wear them — I am desirous
of seeing ourselves in them — They are so pretty. To morrow, please God,
is the day for the excursion. I hope it will benefit Josie — If they go, I
will be uneasy until they return — I am very much in want of a pair of shoes.
I will probably obtain them this afternoon — Important event. Lucy cut
my nails this morning —

I have yet to speak of the events of last night. In the afternoon, I braided
Alice's hair, walked round the square, spent 5 cents — About 8½, a visit to
Miss Sarah. The beautiful Heavens fixed our admiring gaze. It was a most
beautiful night. The stars seemed never so brilliant before — I did not tell
you how beautiful a comet nightly graces the Heavens. It is a beautiful
sight, and many say it is a sign of war — It has been visible for three or four
nights past — About this time last year there was also one. If it should come
in collision with our *little* Earth! What would be the result??? Traced
Scorpio, the Dipper and thoughts of the persons and circumstances under which they were shown to us. Found Mr. Elburger there [at the Nathans].
Alice as sleepy as ever. Quite an amusing incident occurred. Mr. E. standing up before Alice, his hand extended in the act of saying "good-night",
and she — asleep. It provoked our mirth.[6] Departed about 11 — Arrived
home, undressed, got into bed, and was *asleep* in *less than a half of an hour.*
I here refer to my "oldest sister" — whom, after retiring, I am unable to draw
into a conversation.

Sunday, July 7th, 1861

9¾. A.M. . . . Breakfast is over, the house is cleaned up, Ellen has gone to
Sunday School, and we are in a state of comparative quietude — It is more
noisy and the children are far more unmanageable than when Ma is home.
So you see that *they* have gone. And *what* a haste and confusion was attendant on it. Lucy, very thoughtless and silly, did not wake ma up, till *six*
o'clock. Then Ma's hair was to be combed, Ma, Josie and herself and Pa to
be dressed, breakfast to be eaten in the short space of ½ *hour.* They almost
gave up the thought, thinking it useless, but by great manoeuvres they suc-

6. Whether at home or on a visit, the practice of falling asleep in the company of others did
not arouse anyone's animosity. Periodic napping was the order of the day.

ceeded, and I hope are now nearing Amite — They left at five minutes to seven, the train leaves at seven — I suppose they were not "too late". We are now acting in the capacity of housekeepers, which, with the children so troublesome, I do not at all like — Josh [Nathan] has just now made his appearance. He, certainly will augment the disturbance — There was just such a haste as there always is in this house.

Ma looked very well, considering. Pa was saying, "It is no use, you will see us back again". Ma went in first, as she would be unable to make as rapid pace as Pa.

Tears came into my eyes as I parted from my dear Mother. How could I endure a long separation — Dell and Rosa were obstinate, Nelly committed a nuisance, and in fact, Dell and Nelly have so far been the worst. We will have no cooking, and were just thinking that if Cousin Jo or Durant were to come in, we could have a very nice *lunch* — Bought some cream-cheeses and figs — Pa thought of staying to night, but Ma would not consent: particularly as we could get no one to stay with us. Oh! what a row the children are making. It is enough to take a person's wits away.

I hope that Ma will enjoy herself and return safe. Pa did look *so* handsome. Oh! I am *so* proud of him. My mother, too. No one will believe that we are their children. Ma is generally taken for our sister, and a better looking one at that — When a girl, she was beautiful — Last afternoon was very cloudy and a heavy rain was momentarily expected. Ma was busy with the preserves, which are very nice — Saw Pa safely deposited in the omnibus, discoursed about the easy and rapid manner individuals of the male sex could prepare themselves to go down town — How much longer would it take us, how inferior would we look, and how less noticeable be than he.

Alice had a little Confederate (of course) flag, which at Alice's suggestion, I neatly arranged as a pendant to the gas fixtures — It is but a *very* miniature one, and yet I love it. I placed it there with my own hands, and in the invasion of the city, dare any Federalist lay his polluted hand upon it, then will be reenacted the tragedy of the "Marshall House". Yes, with my own hands, will I slay him.[7] There it floats, yielding gracefully to every breath of air. "Forever may it wave over the land of the free and the home of the brave" — We were just on the eve of dressing, when three little visitors of Alice's were announced. This, somewhat retarded our progress. Ma cut the cake; it was very nice. We were somewhat startled at Pa's voice & when he called us, I was still more so when he called us. He

7. Clara refers again to the recent shootings in Alexandria, Virginia.

said "Charley Dreux is dead; he was shot in the head in a skirmish"!!! I was horrified. He was so fine, intelligent and well-liked, man. I immediately thought of his young wife and child, whom he left. How she grieved and mourned at his departure — and what horrible news would she soon be made aware of. He held a position as Colonel, which is an exalted one for so young a man —

I thought that it probably some error, but to day's paper sadly affirms it — He is the first of the Louisianian Officers who has paid the penalty of his life. He is very brave. The skirmish occurred at Newport News. The loss on the Confederate side was three killed; that of the enemy is yet unknown. It will indeed be to his wife, a terrible affliction. And think how many more, valuable lives will be terminated before the cruel war is at an end.

In the agony of her grief will she exclaim, "Why was *he* not spared"! Will this be selfishness? It does seem hard, that he, so worthy, should be singled out from many as unworthy — And tis said that officers stand the least chance of being killed. But stop, we are quarrelling with Divine Providence. "*He* doeth all things well".

How many heart-rending tales like this, have we yet to hear. When first he received his wound, and felt that it must be fatal, instantaneously, thoughts of his dear wife and child must have crossed his mind, and with their names last on his lips, he was ushered into eternity — How painful will be the duty of the one who will unfold to her a tale, which will blight her young life, crush her dearest hopes, and perhaps, forever cast a gloom over her future — Who knows what a day may bring forth — And as Alice says, "tears start into my eyes as I think that I may one day take up the paper and see recorded the death of any of 'Our Battalion' [presumably the Old Dominion Guards].' God preserve them" — Can *all* similar prayers be granted — Received a telegraph from Mr. Hitchcock, yesterday — Pa was obliged to pay $5.70!! This is the third or fourth one. I think that Mr. H is *very* inconsiderate. He says that he could sell the greatest quantity, that he can procure all, except shelf goods. I hope that Pa may be successful in making his arrangements. Time is being lost, every day. Last night, Pa was lying in the sofa in the front room, we were sitting around him, the gas was brilliant, and he said, "Children, if I am successful, you may consider *California* your destination"!! He seems intent upon it. We told him that we would have no regrets at leaving this place, merely, but because it *was* our native place; but we would object to going so far. I asked him if we would ever return — He said if we did, it would be with our Husbands, as he would never—I seriously incline to the opinion that I will not either, for if I go, I never will be separated from them. I should like the trip, with the prospect of returning, but I should not like to remain there always.

I know, I would long for my native land, though no *ties* of importance bind me to it. I told Pa, "imagining things to take a change, before how long will we be there"? He said "Before next spring". Nous verrons!!! Miss Sarah was here last night. She told us that "Beauty" had gone home to Washington—[8] God bless her. One of the many persons whom I dearly love. She has been staying with Flora Levy. How she will miss her. Selfish me! I am glad that she has gone.

1½. Josh has gone, Rosa and Nellie and Fannie are asleep, con. [consequently] the house is peaceful. Little Jennie Miller passed. We told her to tell her mother to come around this afternoon. Alice has requested me to stop and read the paper with her—No one will come this afternoon. Peter is mad—There is no denying it. I suppose we have insulted him, for Ma says "We drive every body away".

Monday, July 8th, 1861

7¼. A.M. . . . They are all home safe and sound. And I am heartily glad that it is over, for in the absence of the heads of the family nothing goes right— The day seemed short, very, and Dell was the most unruly member. She will pay the penalty. Josh amused us with his military drilling and indeed his idea is excellent.

Dinner passed very well; after I braided Alice's hair. Was not successful this time. Don't believe I ever will be again.

Being very much fatigued from the events of the day, we concluded to dress slowly—While I was in about the last stage, the bell rang—I thought it was "poor Peter"—

It proved to be the petite Henriqueses and De Castros. They are very nice children and pretty. Some other little visitors came and Fannie said "It looked like a party"—

We came down and previous to their exit, Fanny Burbank and her sister Clara came in. I was much astonished, as I thought she had forgotten

8. Washington, Louisiana.

about us. She seems like a girl who does not readily make acquaintances or who is not easily attracted towards anyone. She is a sweet girl and right pretty. I like her very much —

We will positively go and see her.

She is so industrious and of great assistance to her mother, who is in delicate health. While she was here, Miss Sarah came. She did not stay long. As Fanny was going, Cousin Sam *came*. We thought it a good opportunity, so insisted upon Fanny's spending the evening. She acquiesced — I did not see much of her, having family duties to engross my attention —

I gave Cousin Sam a cucumber. Pronounced it "fine". About 9 o'c Fanny went. Cousin Sam and I accompanied her. The walk *seemed* short and *was* pleasant — The comet was visible in all its beauty and grandeur — Deposited them safe home, was presented to Mrs. Burbank. Said "Goodbye" and proceeded homewards. Fanny told us that Mrs. Miller received a letter from Capt., in which he sent his love to the Miss Solomons. I wonder if when we see her, she will tell us. I don't think so, for every woman has a "dash of jealousy" as well as "coquetry" in her nature — Fannie has *one* of the prettiest hands that it was ever my *good luck* to behold. I —. No. Remember "thou shalt not covet". How did mine suffer by the comparison — I greatly prefer a large *white* hand, to a small *dark* one: mine is a type of the latter — As we were coming home our conversation took of a doleful nature. It treated of Death, eternity, etc. I became quite excited — On Clio St, a delicious fragrance greeted us, our handkerchiefs being immediately brought in contact with our nasal organs. We were sitting in the front room, listening at every step, when I announced the "Strangers". "Thank God, they are safe".

Cousin Sam instantly vamoosed! I can attribute his sudden exit, to naught, save probably, a *sickness arising from the eating of the cucumber* — They had some fish, which was quickly cooked, but more quickly eaten —

They all had a pleasant time, Ma, naturally, being at times uneasy — Josie had been very good, and Ma would not have known *what* to have done, had it not been for Lucy. I was so tired, and we told Ma, that unless in a great emergency she *should* not go again. Told us all that she had seen and heard. Then required us to guess, whom she had met in the cars. A lady who gave her some lunch and who sent her love to us. We guessed lots, but *not* the right one. Alice and I went up to put dear little Sallie, who is the best child in the world, to bed, when Pa came sneaking up stairs and told us that it was *Mrs. Collins*.

She knew us at Gainesville and was very fond of us all — It was 9 or 10 years ago—As if we could have guessed it—He then said he would go down the back stairs "*unbeknownst*" to Ma. When we would guess she would then be astonished—You have a slight idea of his love of fun. He has promised that on his next trip, please God, Alice and I shall accompany him—Ate a hearty supper, and with great pleasure retired, being heartily tired out—It was about 11½. Regretted I had not longer to sleep—Anticipated a good night's rest.

6¾... I cannot believe that it is Monday. I don't know why—Yesterday did not seem like Sunday. Ma is in a very bad humor and I hurried my toilette to descend and hold communion with *you*. I am very warm as I have on a barége, *all* my muslins being in the wash. Unfortunate state of existence. Flora McFlimsey, what *would* you say!!!!

The day has been very quiet, until a few moments ago. I declare it is enough to provoke Ma; so many girls, and none the least assistance to her. Will we ever learn to do for ourselves? Got up rather late this morning— The fig boy did not come, so we had breakfast minus figs. Mrs. Deegan was here. I heard her remark to Ellen [Mrs. Deegan's daughter] "What a pretty man, Mr. Solomon is; what fine features he has"—Did not do much sewing to day. Ma was entertaining us with the details of her trip. Mrs. Collins has been residing on a plantation and is now going up to Louisville to spend a couple of months. She said that she had often wished for one of us, while there. She promised faithfully to come and see us on her return to our city.

I love her. She is the only person with whom I ever was a favorite. Ought I not to love her? She is very desirous of seeing me. Ma told her that she looked like me; she said there was always a resemblance. She said that she saw in a paper an account of the graduation of Miss Clara Solomon, and she knew it *must* be *me*. I hope that I will see her.

Tuesday, July 9th, 1861

6½. A.M. . . . . I don't know how, but I cannot make up my mind to get up early—

Ellen has not come. I don't suppose that she will. I hope so. Yesterday afternoon, Ma continued in an excebrably [execrably] bad humor. It was my misfortune to have to remain at home. Alice and Fannie went out to take a little walk — During their absence, I amused myself by holding Josie, playing with Sallie and Rosa. Ma, silent. I lit the gas, took my children on my lap when they entered, and immediately after them, came Pa — They had been around to Mrs. Miller. She had received a letter from him, and said that on a previous time she had forgotten to tell us that he sent his love. In the latest one he sent his love "to all, *but particularly to Clara*". I am delighted to think he has not forgotten us. But "particularly to Clara", what can that mean. I think I see through it. I may be mistaken though. Ma still unaccountably peevish. Cousin Sam and Dr Taney honor us. Shortly afterwards Miss Sarah and her husband came. It was the first meeting between Cousin Sam and her since they have become "belligerents". She treated him very cool — I like the "cake shop man" very well — He looks to be very passionate — He is rather good looking, and he and Cousin are *very* intimate. I declare once he made me blush. Miss Sarah eat something, Cousin Sam wouldn't, but said he would be around to day. Dr Taney said that he was passing around in his buggy, and seeing the door open, he leaned his head forward to "see what could be seen". The result was a form reclining on the sofa. He did not exactly know who it was. He went right down and told his "wife", alias Cousin Sam. I wished for Gus to come. And again, I did not, for there was no light in the front room, and you know that is the ruse to which we resort in order to see him plainly — But I think that if he should see any illumination or company he would not come in. He can't be bashful. Dr T. told Alice that she had a beautiful hand. Talking of hands, I called his attention to the veins in my own. I told how great a source of annoyance it was to me. He said that I was foolish and that he thought it *pretty*. It is awful, awful!! They left about $10^{1}/_{2}$. Ma made the acquaintance of Mr. Hardy, the gentleman who so interested himself in Pa, by endeavoring to make agreements for purchasing goods. Ma represents him as quite handsome and very polite. Maybe he will come & see us. I have no great desire — I imagine I see him. *He has a red neck!!* He intends accompanying Pa to Virginia as assistant —

Ma also had the pleasure of a chat with the Lieutenant Governor, *Judo's Father!!*[9] All eyes were directed towards him, and I suppose Ma thought it quite a distinction. On their arrival at the Hotel at Amite all anxiously came out on the gallery, inquiring if "the Governor was aboard" — I should think that he ought to command respect, for being the Father of *Judo*, even did he not occupy so elevated a position.

9. Henry Hyams.

5¼. P.M. . . . At 5½, we are to have the watermelon! Ecstatic happiness! Had Okra Soup and thought that Cousin Sam would be here to enjoy it with us. Josh has just come in; his dear little eyes are red from crying for, the death, or at least, killing of his little dog. A child's grief. Pa was round there before he came home to dinner, and told us that the dog had gone *mad*. He was willing to shoot it — They will miss it: but should be satisfied that it had done no damage — Pa is now to Miss Sarah and sent Josh around here. I saw by the paper yesterday the death of Dr Purnell by the accidental discharge of a gun in his pocket. It is indeed a "sad casualty". I sympathize with his young wife. It occurred up on his plantation at East Feliciana. How often have Alice and I admired him for his handsome and gentlemanly appearance. He was a young man of extraordinary talent, and one who commanded universal respect. "In the midst of life, we are in death". There is no end to the distressing accidents which occur around us —

Alice and I have just had a run. I heard some one open the gate. I looked out and saw that it was Mr. Wilcox. We ran. Dell went to the door. He inquired for Pa, she told him he was out, and he left — [10]

9¼. . . As I sit on the rocking chair writing, a delicious breeze is wafted to me, through the open door. Alice and I are "booking" it. Pa wanted to know the other afternoon "*If people who kept books were at them all the time*". And indeed we *do* devote a lot of time to you. Many a leisure moment would we have did we not consider the duty we owe to you. Pa is saying "filling up those books with nonsense". Alice has just been writing in her beautiful book, but two weeks and it is one half through — Ellen will not be here early to morrow.

The day has not been very tranquil — Ma marked our chemises — She made a mistake by putting my name on Fanny's, and Fanny's on mine — She remedied mine very nicely. The water-melon was delicious — Ma went out this afternoon to Rosenbergs. She did not get any shoes as he had none and said they were very dear and scarce. I have been so particular about getting them, that I suppose I will after all, get none. Ma bought a very pretty dress for herself.

10. Wilcox hoped to receive money on an overdue account for household items.

Wednesday, July 10th, 1861

5³/₄ P.M. . . . I have been suffering all day from a severe headache and have scarcely yet recovered. I expect an unwelcome visitor — I suppose it is accountable to that.

It is very cloudy and pleasant, that is cool. We had a very hard rain to day — Alas to day a week ago, Judo's wedding day —

Alice suggested that probably to day was her reception day. We have been engaged to day in making preserves and sewing on Ma's pretty, cheap dress. We have not made much progress in the latter — The former turned out splendid. They are delicious and we all predict that there will not be many left for the *winter.* The figs are almost all whole. I love them dearly. Ma purposes please God, making some more at a later day, also some peaches. A little tumbler full is put aside for Miss Sarah, but as it is now raining, they will not be conveyed to her this afternoon — Uncle Naty is still out of situation [work]. Josh speaking the other day happened to say "My father, why he hasn't got money enough to send to market". It occasions Miss Sarah some uneasiness — I don't presume that Pa will take him. Miss Sarah is determined that he shall not go away from her.

She declares that the moment he does she will get a divorce, go on to Charleston [where Sarah's mother still lives] and never look at him again — *Nous verrons* — Ellen did not come to day. We miss her a great deal. I am momentarily in expectation of having Josie deposited in my lap — I hope that she will come tomorrow — As I look out of the window, I see "Red Head" standing by his door. How can *any* girl love *him.* He has such a supercilious, disagreeable look. Surely he is *one* of the *few* persons in the *world,* whom *I* think are incapable of loving — Truly from the time of Desdemona to the present day, we never hear of a marriage, but we say " 'tis strange, passing strange". I dislike him because I once read a story, in which I imagine the disagreeable hero resembling *him.* His wife is quite pretty — It was an *elopement.* To day is the anniversary of our dear little Eveline's birthday — She would have been 10 years old. Tis better for her that she were dead, and yet I wish that she was living. A little angel![11] A few moments

11. Eveline was one of two Solomon children who were dead. Eveline lived for about two years, apparently with some congenital affliction. Eleven months before Eveline was born, in 1850, Emma Solomon gave birth to a boy, Chapman, who lived only three days. The boy was probably named after his grandfather Chapman, who died in 1849, age seventy-five. See Microfilm No. 1292082, Burial Records of Hebrew Cemetery, Mormon Genealogical Library, Salt Lake City, Utah. The film contains information deposited at the Louisiana State Museum, New Orleans.

ago, I heard the whistle of *the* train. How I wish that I was on it. Dear Pa has promised us, the next visit. I am in anticipation of it — Alice is not by me, I don't know why she remains up stairs so long. There she is now.

> "She spreads a charm through every scene,
> She mocks the cares of Life,
> She leans her trusting heart on mine,
> My own, endearing *wife*".

8³/₄. . . It is raining very hard. We have just finished supper. Ma is preparing to sew, Pa is lying asleep on the sofa, and your humble writer is so sleepy that she can only with difficulty manage to keep her eyes open. The Evening paper contained an account of a great battle in Missouri, with the loss of 300 to 1,000 Federalists.

It makes no mention of our loss. It is the opinion that important operations will not commence until the cool weather sets in.[12] There was a beautiful piece of poetry by James Randall on the lamented Charles H. Dreux. His body has not yet arrived. He will have an immense funeral, if that will be any consolation to his bereaved family — Alice and I have been considering about going to see Charlotte — Since Mrs. da Ponte's departure, she and her mother are staying at her house — Oh! I should like so much to see her. We have several visits to pay —

Thurʃday, July 11th, 1861

7. P.M. Well Philomen, here is your daily and almost only visitor — "Shades of evening have not yet closed o'er us". The day has been one of the most beautiful that I ever saw. It has been more like a mellow, autumn one, than that of July. After the tremendous shower of last night, it became quite cool. I am now enjoying the beautiful, soft tones of an organ at "Red Heads" expense. This morning Fannie went to change the corsets and shoes. I have not been successful in obtaining the last named articles. She procured a

12. The government of Missouri, a slave state, joined neither the Confederacy nor the Union. The state was itself split into its own internal civil war. Residents of Missouri joined both armies, the majority going to the Union forces. From the Union's point of view, it was important to begin military action early to keep Missouri from joining the Confederacy. This policy was successful.

perfect pair of corsets—She then went to Miss Sarah's, remained there, till 12, returned home, lunched with us. She [Miss Sarah] sent us some of her preserved plums!!! She must have known that she ought to have sent some. To make preserves and not send Ma any—She sent them saying that "they were so bad, she was ashamed to send any". Then why did she send them at all? Her conscience must have told her that it was wrong— Ma sent her some figs. She pronounced them excellent. Ellen came to day, so there was not much to do. She spent the day with Mrs. Samuels. When Pa came home to dinner, he brought a box of "Condensed Milk"—What recollections did it recall! How vividly arose to my mind the circumstances under which I had first "seen, tasted and liked it". How in imagination, did I see, form after form that sat at that memorable table. From the depths of my heart, ascended "God bless them".[13]

Pa heard that Mr. Hitchcock had a contract for furnishing clothes to the soldiers, which he expected would realize a fortune. He is anxiously waiting a letter, but it is to be presumed that he [Pa] has an interest in it. It will be very unfair and ungenerous if he hasn't as it is mainly owing to Pa that he has it. But hush, the thought is foolish. I hope that it may reach their highest expectations. I wonder when Pa is going.

$9^1/_4$. . . The mosquitoes are very bad and I am very sleepy. Alice, my twin sister, is by me writing. Pa is lying on the sofa, and Ma is preparing to go to bed. It is not as pleasant as it was to day.

Ma and Fanny went to Miss Sarah's. Ma had on her new dress—She and the dress, both looked beautiful. Alice would not accompany her as she said "Ma would look too nice". I braided her hair; not very nice. It has never been as good as the first time. I could not write much, as "*suppering*" all the children devolved upon me. I don't much admire it—

There have been no letters of "D's" [Da Ponte's] in the paper recently; several of "J's". I dreamed of the former gent. last night—

Pa threw in my lap to night a letter from Lizzie Hillman. It was a long time coming. It is very short and contains nothing of any importance.

Two or three times I was going to tell you of the mean trick of which Miss Sarah was guilty, as we thought, and as many times have been interrupted. When she and Ma made the shirts for Mr. Harris, it was understood that when she got the others, Ma would, of course, have a share. The other day Uncle Naty told us that she had finished the others. Ma, naturally became incensed, as she had said nothing to her about it. So made

13. Clara recalled her day at Camp Moore, before the volunteers left for Virginia.

up her mind to ask her about it — She embraced the opportunity yesterday, and strange to say, Miss Sarah *denied ever having them* — She said that "Sammy" told her that he told ma, but he was mistaken.

Then why did she wait to be questioned about? Why did she not inform Ma of the mistake? We can scarcely credit it. She also made shirts for Leopold. Why not tell Ma?

Friday, July 12th, 1861

7¹/₄. A.M. . . Ma and Alice have set apart this day, for their shopping expedition.

5¹/₄ P.M. . . Pa went out before breakfast and owing to his absence, we did not open the "Condensed Milk". Have not done much sewing to day — Mending, etc. Pa did not go to market, so dinner not tempting.

No letter from Mr. Hitchcock. Regard it as very strange. Wonder what can be the matter. If he had not written to his wife, it would not appear so unaccountable: but surely had he any spare time, he should have devoted it to Pa. Hope that we soon may be posted. His intentions are pure. Pa intends going to see Mrs. Hitchcock —

Pa mailed Belle Grant's letter — I wonder if Baby has received Alice's letter. I hope that she will answer it. I would so much like to see her. The day has been fine — Ma and Alice changed their minds and did not go out. Deferred until Monday, please God.

Pa put an advertisement in the Delta to day to this effect. Wanted. A person to take an interest in the Sutlership of a Regiment — I hope that he may be successful — [14] Alice and I were reading over some of her past Journal. It was amusing. I declare that I never saw her look so beautiful as she has this afternoon — In my opinion she is perfect in character and appearance — If no one else has this opinion, which I know is not so, she has the satisfaction of being thought so by one, unprejudiced, individual. She shan't see this. Then if I refuse to let her see it, after she asks, she will be angry. I do think that she gets prettier every day. If some one only had that opinion for me — But I — I am ugly, decidedly ugly — Not a pretty thing — But Ma gave me a long lecture, the other day about murmuring. Alice has just

14. The advertisement stated that interviews would be arranged through the newspaper. See *The Daily Delta,* 12 July 1861.

come up, and as I expected asked to see it. *She shan't.* It will make her too vain.

Saturday, July 13th, 1861

7¼. A.M. . . . I have been up some time, but I must confess that I have been too lazy to write, or to come down in plain terms, I have been fascinated with "Rutledge", which I have read nearly through for the *second time.* There also was quite an amount of matter in the paper to digest. The remains of poor Charles Dreux are expected to day. The Mayor has proposed to have the expenses of the funeral defrayed by the City, "of which, while living, he was so bright an ornament". There will be a immense crowd in attendance — His death has cast a universal gloom over the community. The morning is very fine. Alice and I purpose going to Synagogue. I would rather not. John promised to bring some figs, he has not yet done it. I doubt if he will.

6½ P.M. . . . We did not dress yesterday until late and I am sure that the afternoons are much shorter than formerly. About dark, Pa came home, he showed us some letters, which in the dim twilight all, except me, were unable to read the superscription. I recognized "B.H". There were three. Light was immediately brought on the subject, as we were very anxious to peruse them. They proved to be offers of partnership. The places of appointment were designated. Pa will go, and I hope make agreeable arrangements. After *that* excitement subsided, Pa, in as calm tones as possible, informed us that Mes. Hill and Hardy would honor us during the evening —[15] To Alice and me this was startling news — I was very desirous of seeing Mr. Hardy. Supped early, momentarily expecting, we hear steps, the bell is rung, and *they* are ushered in — I looked *particularly* ugly. No individual introductions, and I was perplexed to hear Pa address the one whom I thought Mr. Hill, by the appellation Hardy, and vica-versa. It was perfectly unaccountable. I looked at Alice, and she at me, both thinking it "in a high degree mysterious". I then arrived at the conclusion that Mr. Hill must be Mr. Hardy — But I was perfectly non-plussed —

Oh, I like Mr. Hardy so very, very much. He is very prepossessing, both

15. Hill and Hardy were New Orleans businessmen who might supply needed merchandise to Solomon and Hitchcock to sell in Virginia.

in manners and appearance. I should style him "handsome["]. I so much like the manner in which he expressed himself regarding the relation of husband and wife. Mr. Hill, I did not like so much. He undeniably, has the smallest, whitest and prettiest, hand, that ever graced a male body, and I may add with impunity, few female ones. Of course, we traced resemblances between them and a dozen other persons of our acquaintances — They left rather late. I hope that they will come again; but Mr. Hardy leaves Monday for Virginia. Oh! *I love him* — After their departure all was explained — Pa made himself so agreeable — *Could* any one require better company than he — Oh! I wish that I had not seen that hand. My veins, as troublesome as ever. Would that they would desert me! Poor Charles Dreux's remains arrived this morning, in the morning's train.

I saw the procession, saw the car which contained the lifeless form of a once brave and noble man. There was an immense concourse, but I suppose nothing to be compared to what it will be when it arrives at the City Hall, which is its destination.

His disconsolate wife, bereaved parents, brothers and sisters, have many sympathizing friends. His funeral takes place on Monday. Due notice will be given of the ceremonies. Alice went to synagogue this morning. I did not accompany her. I did not feel like it. At one time it looked so cloudy, that I thought it would rain — Wrote to Lizzie. I have not yet finished it — Alice returned about 12$^1/_2$. Said there were very few in attendance —

She related quite a romantic incident which occurred. Rebecca Harris bought some figs from a woman, she stole a silver knife, they recovered it, and the woman proved to be the property of Mr. Joe. Solomon —

Rebecca of course was very much alarmed about the loss of the knife, and while the search was being instituted, Mr. H. came in. She told him about it, he said "Oh! my child, what carelessness"!! He laid a trap and recovered their property.

To think of those mean people serving out figs by the picayune's worth — Not the ones to send a person a present of any. As Pa says it is no use to cultivate the acquaintance of *such* people. I did John injustice, for he did bring the figs and Ma has been busily engaged in preserving them — They are excellent — When Pa came home at dinner, he had several other communications. Said he had attended to those of the previous day, had rejected all with the exception of Mr. Trask. And he has made no definite arrangements with him. He has a capital of $5,000 — Pa's objections to the others were inadequate funds. Mr. Trask was up here about 5. I don't know the result of the interview. Pa said that he had bought two boxes of peaches, one to eat, and one to preserve—They looked very nice. I have not yet tasted them.

To day is dear Sallie's birthday—She is *eight years old*. May she live to enjoy many more, and may she on all of them, have as much *cause* for happiness—She is my darling child—Strong indeed must be the counter charm that can rival hers—

Sunday, July 14th, 1861

$7^1/_4$. A.M. . . I have forgotten the temptations offered to me in the shape of a Picayune and Delta, to pay my devoirs [obligation] to you, miss. I must do them in a short space, as I am getting tired. Yesterday afternoon Ma, Fannie, and a little basket of peaches, went round to Miss Sarah's. Pa came home about dark, took Sallie and Rosa and joined them. He showed us his papers, which he had got from Col. Sulakowski. They were the papers of his Sutlership. Miss Sarah promised to come round but didn't. While at supper, Gus came. "With eager haste, we dispatched the necessary". There was nothing new. He asked us to walk down town, we refused, and nothing would do but a walk round the square—Went rather far, and was rather tired. He told us that Mr. Jenkins was expected home in a day or two, Mr. da Ponte would take his place and consequently would not return for some time. Said Charlotte had gone to spend some time with her sister Emma. That Mrs. Leovy had gone, and that they very much enjoyed "Bachelors Hall". I don't think that they agree very well together. For my part I am not particularly fascinated. He is too sarcastic. I told him that I could write, a great deal better than I could speak. He remarked "Oh! how beautifully must you write ["]. He is an adept in the art of flattery—He left in his usual abrupt manner.

Monday, July 15th, 1861

7 o'clock A.M. Alice and I were sitting at the open window, prepared to give to you, our morning salutations, when the cry of "here's the daily Crescent", greeted our ears. In a moment we were the possessor of one. Scanned its pages and said that it "was enough for the money". The papers are full of "Charley Dreux". His last letter to his wife appeared. It is teeming with love to her and devotion to his Country—Alice says if she were in her place, she would not give it to the rude gaze of the world. I maintain that it is not the less precious to her on that account.

How he loves her! His funeral takes place to day. It will be one of the most impressive ceremonies ever witnessed, and one of the longest, similar parades. Pa has promised to take us to see it. Yesterday Ma preserved her peaches. They are fine; as Miss Sarah says, "Ma should take out a patent".

There was no sewing and the day passed tranquilly. We had distinguished visitors, in the shape of the little "Vienne boys", who came to sell, for pins, their baskets, etc. We purchased a quantity. Rosa has made quite a conquest in the shape of the heart of one—

I braided Alice's hair; very good. In the afternoon dear Peter came. So he was not angry. He noticed that there was some change in the manner in which Alice's hair was combed. Julius had left Dryer's, and was Lieutenant of the "McClellan Guards". All the salaries of the house were reduced, but Mr. Eisner wisely concluded not to leave—We were rather long in dressing, as we put on our new Dresses. They looked beautiful. I love mine. They have been finished for some time. I wish I "*had three like 'em*"—After Mr. E. [Eisner] left, we went round to Miss Sarah's. She admired our robes—No one was there. Josh brought her some of our preserves. She liked them. Stayed some time and she said she would come round, and if Mr. Elburger came, she would bring him.

About 8½ they came. We gave them supper, but none eat. Mr. E. [Elburger] is a very intelligent, well informed man, full of information.

He expressed *strong* union sentiments. He said that Lincoln was *our* President, and if not we then were "Rebels", thus endorsing Lincoln's words. His interests are with the North, and had better be guarded in his speech.[16]

They left quite late. While to Miss Sarah's some one passed whom I thought I recognized. A moment's reflection convinced me that it was the supposed bridal couple of the cars. Strange that we should ever see them again.

16. Clara's admonition was a serious one. Elburger was not alone among New Orleans residents in his support for Lincoln; others regarded secession as a mistake. The Confederate government of New Orleans became less tolerant of those who opposed the aims of the Confederacy, as the dentist Dostie, mentioned above, discovered.

3¹/₄ P.M. Of course, as is always the case in this house, it is very late. I am dressed, and Ma is not ready. The funeral leaves at 3¹/₂. I never [knew] what it was to be in time—It was arranged to leave at 2¹/₂!! But no such regularity. I bet that the City Hotel, to which we purpose going is now crowded. We came down in our old dresses, and Pa made us go up stairs and put on "the ones we had on yesterday".

They are preparing to start. Goodbye! I'll see you shortly. I hope.

Tuesday, July 16th, 1861

7 A.M. Yesterday for breakfast, Ma opened the "Condensed Milk"—I do not think that it is all their fancy painted. We did scarcely any sewing. Ma was fixing her preserves, when she found that the buckskin, which she had over her nicest bottle of figs, had been completely gnawed away by the rats. She declares that she will not eat them. It is a shame. About 1¹/₂, we went to dress. Eat dinner, and you are aware how late it was. Did not wait for the Omnibus, so walked down. The streets were crowded and had the appearance of a general holiday. We deemed it useless to think of going to the City Hotel. We first went to the Veranda Hotel, but as it was crowded and as we thought unsafe, we left. Proceeded down Camp, amidst the greatest jam, and Pa concluded to try at the War Office. Were successful and obtained excellent places, and concluded that we had come just the right time. It was quite a distinction as not many were allowed up there, and it is quite a distinguished place. I was not quite satisfied as I wanted to be further down town, but in the course of time became so: but I suppose it was chiefly owing to the lady whom I sat next to. She was a French lady, and I think beautiful. She was *very* passionate, I could see in a moment, it was visible in every movement of that mouth, in every flash of that bright eye. She was a most beautiful form, and her pretty head was supported upon as lovely a *neck* as ever graced a Venus—She seemed very proud and conscious of her charms. She was acquainted with a very nice man, a perfect gentleman, at least as far as his politeness extended to me. From her conversation, I ascertained that she was an intimate friend of Mrs. Dreux. She said that she had just returned from accompanying her to the City Hall to see what could be seen of her lamented husband—She was terribly excited. Poor thing, I pity her from the bottom of my heart. The procession

was advertised to leave at 3, but it did not until after 5. It was a splendid turnout, as fine as I ever saw. His family have a right to be proud of the ovation, which was paid him. There was an immense crowd. The hearse was beautifully decorated, and a very sad feature in the sad affair was that of his horse, draped in mourning, walking slowly behind the car which contained the remains of his beloved master.

He appeared as though aware of the solemnity of the occasion, and the event which he was celebrating. The stirrups, which he had so often mounted were thrown off. It was about an hour passing. We returned home very tired. Saw plenty people that I knew. And I now have arrived at the conclusion that the ovation made was too great, and the expenditures, considering the present state of affairs, were too great—Yes, let him be buried with military honors, accompanied by the escort which bore him home! But why all that excitement—Were we to do it for every Col. or Capt. that in the coming contest, may lose his life, the City would constantly be in a state of grand funeral processions.

Pa says it could have been no more "fuss" had it been George Washington. But it is all over, and Charles Didier Dreux's body is forever hid from mortal eye—Many as costly and noble a life will be sacrificed ere the termination of this war. And many a *day* will elapse before that "consummation so devoutly to be wished". It will be a bloody conflict and will result either in an entire subjugation by the North or a brilliant achievement of the Confed. States—Lincoln's call for 400,000 men and $400,000,000 will be granted. Can we resist them without money? As the Delta says "We send forth our sons, will we withhold our money"? They think it advisable to levy a "direct tax"—*Edward Everett* delivered a speech in N.Y. in which he spoke of "the justice of the cause of the North, and of the murderous and suicidal war which the South was waging". Yes, this is the man, who was so ably supported here. But his value is naught. In the words of the Delta, "The time for idle threats and bravado is over. We are in the midst of a great conflict, from which we can not back out if we would. We must conquer or perish. There is no alternative, for who thinks of submission? Who thinks of bending his neck to the yoke which Northern despotism would put upon it"?[17]

17. Edward Everett, a Whig politician and vice-presidential candidate of the Constitutional Union Party with John Bell as presidential candidate in 1860, argued that slavery might remain in the South but not be introduced in new western territories. Bell and Everett received some of the southern popular vote in that election.

Wednesday, July 17th, 1861

4¹/₄. P.M. We have just done dinner and it is the second meal since Pa's return at which he has not been present. At dinner Ma said that she "wished she did not love that man to distraction" — Nothing of note happened to day. Got up early, read the paper, digested one of "D's" [da Ponte's] letters. Did little sewing, Ma as usual talking of our laziness. Found that the detestable rats had again encroached upon our preserves. As they are useless, Ma intends sending Lucy out to sell them. I am so sorry that it happened as ma may never be so successful in making them again.

6¹/₂. P.M. Alice and I were up stairs dressing, when the bell was rung very authoritavely — Who could it be ! We saw a letter handed to Ma and heard that it was Mr. Prothro — We drew our inferences — It was from Baby. A very short letter, but entreating Alice to come over this Summer. I hope that she may. There is no danger between the two places — She said that Mrs. Stockton was not well, having had a miscarriage. I want to see Baby so bad. Miss Sarah and Josh are here. The latter is drilling — Ma did not go out to day. Last night, Ma got angry and she and Pa went to Miss Sarah's. Leopold was there. Nothing of import —

Thursday, July 18th, 1861

6¹/₄. P.M. The afternoon is cloudy and we have been threatened with rain all day. I overslept myself otherwise I should have had a previous interview with you. I have not been in a very good humor to day. This morning Alice came to me and said "Guess who is married. A girl whom you used to go to school with and who sang beautifully". I guessed various ones, and after she left the thought struck me that it was Olivia Leovy. I was right. She was married to Mr. N. J. Thaxton on the 16th instant. She is a beautiful girl — I hope that she may be happy. Pa received a letter from Mr. Hitchcock — He said that he had written often — Affairs prosperous. He had succeeded in obtaining the services of Mr. Gribble, which he considers invaluable. Pa brought home a paraphene candle. He stopped to Miss Sarah's. She was going to discharge her servant for want of sufficient funds to pay, as Pa says "her rent". Josh had been quite sick, the Dr was called in last night. Yesterday Miss Sarah promised to come back, but I

suppose that was the reason she didn't — Uncle Naty said that if "Mr. Harris
was like anybody, in his present circumstances, he would assist him" —
Ellen has just told me that she passed Lizzie Hillman's and saw her and
Maggie by the door. She is mean not to send me word of her arrival. To
day I read the funeral oration by Lieut. Col. Adolphus Olivier to Lieut.
Col. Dreux. It was very pretty and must [have] struck home to many hearts,
probably awakening in them emotions which will lead them on to deeds
of glory. Our troops have suffered a signal defeat in Western Virginia, and
the loss of the esteemed Gen. Garnett.[18] He was a great acusition [acqui-
sition] to our army. It is a sad state of affairs, and we may expect soon to
hear of a great vi — —. In whose favor it will be decided is known only by
him above — Before retiring last night, Pa, Ma, Alice and myself had
quite a dissertation on the state of the Country. It is pitiful — Lucy went out
with the preserves. Sold only one bottle, consequently realized 50 cents —

Friday, July 19th, 1861

6¹/₄. P.M. At my post! Oh! Philomen, I am so sorry, but we will soon have
to part. Your pages are numbered, and my fear is that your successor will
be your inferior.

I dislike to ask your grandpa for an equal, so what shall I do — Even if
your donor was here, I should feel a delicacy — Nous verrons [We shall
see] — Good news! July 18th General Beauregard achieved a great victory to day. At daybreak, this morning the enemy appeared in force at Bull's
Run. They attempted to cross the stream, when a severe battle ensued,
three miles N.W. Manassas Junction. General B. commanded in person.
The battle was at its height at 2 and continued until 5, the enemy having
retreated 3 times, they retired with considerable loss. The Washington
Artillery of N.O. did great execution — Maybe *"our batallion"* distinguished
themselves — or at least were engaged[19] — It rained a little to day — Alice

18. Robert Selden Garnett, a Virginian and one of many West Point graduates in Confederate
uniform. He and most of the men under his command died about a week earlier at Rich Mountain
in the new state of West Virginia. Garnett led his men straight into Union fire. See Gallagher, ed.,
Recollections of General Edward Porter Alexander, 37, 48–9.

19. Clara refers to the battle at Blackburn's Ford, a crossing of Bull Run Creek. It was a pre-
liminary skirmish to the much larger battle on 21 July that would involve about 28,000 Union soldiers and 32,000 from the Confederate Army. Confederate forces repulsed an attack by the enemy

wrote to Baby. Mr. Rosser called this morning, while Alice was in deshabille, and told her that he was going to-morrow and would take anything
to Baby. Alice was embarrassed at being caught, so we proposed to fix
up to-morrow when he came — Ma and Alice did not go out to day. Delays
are dangerous. *Last* Friday it was proposed to go Monday — As Lucy
was going down to the Poydras Market Ma suggested that probably
Jourdan could sell the "figs" — He said that he thought he could and said
to bring some more to day — Not much sewing to day. Made an underbody
for Alice and some other little things. The machine has been useless as it
has the greatest kind of fits. It would not sew *at all.* It needs repairing. We
all endeavored to remedy it, but failed. Ma bought some nice buttermilk.
I love it. When Pa came home he brought some nuts, I suppose from Mr.
Hill's. I wonder if he will ever come again. Pa has not yet made arrangements for his Polish Brigade. He finds it *very* difficult. Has been to *every*
grocery store in the City. Mr. Trask appointed a day to meet Pa and Pa has
not seen him since. He must have backed out. Regard him as "Trash". I
hope Pa will not have to give it up. I am confident, were Mr. Hitchcock
here, he could make arrangements. Pa says not.

Saturday, July 20th, 1861

$7^1/_4$. A.M. . . . I have been up some time, but too lazy to write. Contrary to our
expectations Mr. Rosser did not come, but, meeting Lucy in the street, requested her to bring the package. Alice sent the preserves. And so we were
cheated out of a sight of the handsome "James Rosser". Yesterday afternoon Alice and I went to the drugstore to pay the residue of the Cocoaine.
Being unable to change $10, we could not accomplish our purpose. Mr.
Israel changed it and we came home.[20] Ma had gone to Miss Sarah's. About

---

and were able to force the Union soldiers to retreat. The Union army lost more men than the Confederates,
about 2,700 versus 1,900, but the Confederate units failed to follow up by chasing the retreating Federal
soldiers. The commanding Union officer, General McDowell, and his Confederate counterpart, General
Beauregard, had been West Point classmates, and both used the same textbook tactics. See Richard
E. Beringer et al., *Why the South Lost the Civil War (Athens, Ga., 1986),* 111–17; and Gallagher, ed.,
Recollections of General Edward Porter Alexander, 41–7. Alexander claimed that the efforts of the Washington
Artillery were much exaggerated. Peter Davis & John Cooper, *First Bull Run, 1861,* (London, 1971),
and William C. Davis, *Battle at Bull Run,* (Garden City, N.Y., 1977) cover the entire episode.
    20. "Cocoaine" was a legal medicine in Louisiana in the mid-nineteenth century. Made from

dark Ma came. Had promised to go back. Pa brought a box of sardines, and we eat supper. Afterwards went to Miss S. I forgot to say that when Ma came home she brought an "extra" of the Delta containing an account of the battle — It was the first specimen of the kind that I had ever seen. It is very small, a miniature programe. One killed and several wounded — among whom was our friend Capt. Eshleman.[21] He received a slight wound in his leg and is in a fair way of recovery. I wonder if Charlotte [his wife] cares. The 7th Regiment, Charles Hurley's, was engaged. I wonder if he is wounded. Poor Belle, she must have fits. The report was 500 Fed. killed — Pa says it will be reduced to *100 killed, wounded,* and *missing.*[22] We found Miss Sarah upstairs with Josh, so we went up. While he was going to sleep, we went on the front gallery, talked of matters and things in general. She [Sarah Nathan] has no servant at all and consequently has everything to do. I wish that Uncle Naty could get a place — He says that he has made an engagement with Mr. Quirk *to make coffins.*[23] We were sitting there some time when we heard Mr. Elburger's voice. Wishing to be entertained we proceeded down stairs. He was as funny as usual, and as usual in his society our risibilities were excited. I do love to hear him talk. He said he would come to see us soon. Got home about 11. o'clock. Heard that Mr. Leovy had called. 6³/₄ A.M. Alice and I are sitting on the sofa, Pa is by us reading to us, extracts from the "Knickerbocker", a Northern paper presented to Pa by Mr. Hill, with the remark "to present it to your daughter, as probably she has not yet received a copy." There were many fine letters, and although not in the right cause, I could appreciate them.[24] Pa did not come to dinner. As Pa had promised to pay in some degree, the "baker", and according to appointment he was here at 8¹/₂ — It is shameful to allow the baker's bill to run up to such a height! $50!! He is very lenient and says that he will come *once more.* I hope that Pa will be able to pacify him.

---

the same leaf as the proscribed cocaine, the medicine was used for headaches. The Solomons purchased the cocoaine on a previous day but could only pay part of the cost because the druggist did not have coins for change.

21. B. F. Eshleman, although born in Pennsylvania, served almost the entire war in the Confederate Army. One of several Jewish members of the Washington Artillery, he went to Manassas as Captain of its 4th Company, a company he formed. Although seriously wounded in the leg at Bull Run, Eshleman remained in service, rising to the rank of lieutenant colonel of artillery by 1864. Confederate Service Records, Washington Artillery, RG 109, National Archives.

22. At Bull Run, the number of casualties were much greater than first reported.

23. John D. G. Quirk was an undertaker in downtown New Orleans, a business with unusually favorable prospects during wartime.

24. The *Knickerbocker* was a well-known New York newspaper.

About 5. Pa came, bringing with him the said "Knickerbocker" and some nuts. Fannie is bent on Pa's going to Tangipaho and taking her, and she has it planned that tomorrow, Ma, Pa, and she will go on a pleasant little trip. I am almost confident that they will go—

Sunday, July 21st, 1861

$10\frac{1}{4}$ A.M. . . They have really gone! Fannie, Ma, and Pa! The remainder are home, under the jurisdiction of Alice and myself. It seems like a dream — There was not as much haste as was attendant on their last trip, but not a bit too much time. We all breakfasted about $6\frac{3}{4}$, and in consequence it seems a great deal later than it really is. Josie is asleep. Ellen has gone to Sunday School, and the children are comparatively quiet. Dell, so far, has conducted herself admirably — "Experience once bought is better than twice taught." One whipping from Ma is worth *all* the menaces.

They are nearing their destination, but really I do not know the programme; something about Amite, Col. Sulakowski, etc; I hope that they will enjoy themselves. Pa said "Don't be frightened, if we ain't home to night." But that is impossible — I am rather hungry — This morning when Pa sent down for the paper, the report was "no paper". It was strange as Ma said that she had been awake and had not heard the carrier. We set the children watching for the "news-boys". About $7\frac{1}{2}$ "caught" one, but he did not have "our Delta". He said that it was not out, consequently no copies distributed among them. We were never so anxious to see it. Alice said "Maybe Mr. da Ponte is dead," or else "it was so excellent a copy, that they are all sold". While Alice and I were disposing of the "breakfast things" the children came running in, "The paper man has brought the paper". We ran out, desirous of learning the cause of its tardiness, but he had gone. "Too late. Too late." I have just glanced over it. A letter from Mrs. C.F. Windle, which I have not read, President Davis' message, ditto. Previous to the receipt of the Delta, we purchased the True Delta. It is no account. I suppose the people in the cars, will "jump at conclusions" respecting the non-appearance of the Delta, as it cannot possibly be aboard. I hear Pa, "Well it has bursted at last; I am not astonished; it's no more than I expected", etc., etc.

We sent Lucy to market. Tomatoes stew for dinner. I wonder if Ma will see the "blind man". Alice forgot to send any message — Maybe Ma will have thought enough to deliver some, notwithstanding. There is a very slim probability of Alice and me taking our long wished for trip as Pa says he will be "at the seat of war in 72 hours". I think *that* doubtful —

I wish we could go — Yesterday afternoon, after Pa had finished reading, Alice and I made up our minds to go round and see Mrs. Miller, determining if the house was shut and there were no signs of life that we would not stop. It was the case, and we concluded to go to Miss Sarah's.

Found her alone and busy — Uncle Naty came in shortly and said that he had concluded his arrangement with Mr. Quirk *the undertaker.* It is but a temporary situation, but Miss Sarah is not pleased at all. It is far preferable to idleness. She had made some "preserved figs"; she gave us some to taste and to take home to Ma. Just as we were leaving Mr. Elburger came in. Uncle Naty accompanied us home and remained some time. We promised Miss Sarah to come back, so after supper, with ma and Pa (as escorts) we fulfilled our promise.

I was very, very sleepy — Returned home and was in bed in a few moments.

3¹/₄... Dinner just over — very nice and enjoyed it very much. Everything quiet. Children good, particularly dear, angel little Josie. How soon could she be taught or at least teach herself to forget her mother. The only casualty, so far, was the breakage of a tumbler by Sallie — Rosa, the rebel, took a fine sleep and is now excellent. The clouds are threatening. We will have rain.

Monday, July 22nd, 1861

2¹/₂ P.M. Quite an unusual time for me to write, but as there is "nothing doing" I thought I would seize the opportunity — Ma and Fannie arrived safe last night. We heard them at the gate and also heard a strange voice. They entered, but Pa was not of the number. He had come as far as Amite with ma, and promised to be home the following morning (this one). He left Ma under the charge of Mr. Forbes, who escorted her to the door. Pa wished to see Col. Sulakowski.

Ma had not spent the day pleasantly at all — The dear old place is *perfectly deserted.* Ma and Fannie were very hungry. They could not relish anything at the Hotel, and in fact there was nothing to relish. Mrs. Wheat had died the previous day and was it any wonder that Ma turned in disgust from everything?[25] They willingly partook of our humble fare. They described the trip on the cars as very pleasant. I scarcely expected Ma home and had it not been for Josie, she would not have returned. I was exhausted when I got in bed. Fannie was my companion. We had come to the conclusion this morning that Pa would not return today and were just agreeing as to what could cause his detention when Sallie exclaimed "Pa's coming"—Too premature. We were glad to see him. We had a talk , he took a nap, and then found that he was minus "shirt and pantaloons"—What was to be done! Send to Miss Sarah and borrow, and forthwith Ellen is dispatched. She returned with a shirt and Uncle Naty's *Sunday-go-to-meeting pantaloons*. Pa wore them and looked quite distingué, in fact, I never saw him look nicer. He lunched with us. About 1 o'c it began to rain, and as Pa was going out, Ma advised him not to wear the pantaloons—Pa wore them, knowing no danger would accrue. Miss Sarah was good to send them—6³/₄. . . . Alice and I had made up our minds to go to Mrs. Miller, but just having had a little quarrel, I don't think that we will—Pa was home to dinner. A visit from the baker—Ma has alarmed us just now. She has a very small, strange looking sore in her side. She imputes it to the heavy hoof [falling]. I hope to God, 'tis nothing more. I have had a toothache all day and had it not rained, I should have gone to Dr Dostie's—Alice is not by me; it seems like a part of myself away. I was awakened this morning by Alice, saying, "Clara, what do you think, Gen. Beauregard is killed". It immediately recalled me to my senses and I asked her by what means she had learned it. She said she was awakened by the cries of the newsboys— She went down, obtained a paper, and the bad news was not confirmed. But there was an account of a "Great Battle" near Manassas Junction. It commenced at 4 this morn, was general at 12, and continued until 7, when the Federalists retired, leaving us in possession of the field. The battle was terrific and ended with *immense slaughter on both* sides!! Enemy's loss said to be 7,000, Con. 3,000—Gen Beauregard had a horse killed from under him (Alice must have misunderstood the boys) and one of the commanders of the Washington Artillery was killed.[26]

25. Mother of Major Bob [Roberdeau] Wheat. Major Wheat's father, a general at the outbreak of war, organized the First Louisiana Volunteer Battalion, made up primarily of veterans of the Mexican War of 1846.

26. The reports were of the First Battle of Bull Run. The battle was the largest confrontation of troops to date, but losses on the Union side were greatly exaggerated in the Confederate accounts. Early reports stated that Major Bob Wheat had died in battle, although in fact he was alive but wounded.

Tuesday, July 23rd, 1861

7 o'clock A.M. When I awoke this morning under the impression that it was very *early* when Alice astonished me by the information that it was near 7. I had some recollection of feeling a cold sensation at night and pulling up the covers. I found the windows and doors shut and Alice said that it blew a perfect gale last night. I did not hear a bit of it — It is as cold as an October morning. Yesterday evening's paper contained a confirmation of our victory. We lost 3 Generals, and 1 Colonel.[27] The extra which contained dispatches from Washington to Louisville says that the victory is ours, but with a great loss. Yesterday afternoon, Alice and I in hopes of hearing some news, and being anxious about dear Capt. Miller, went round to see Mrs. M. But as usual she was out. I wonder if "our Battalion" was in the fight. Capt. M. [Miller] with his rashness and intrepidity will be the first to fall. Went round to miss Sarah's — Encountered Aristocracy alias Mrs. Harris. Miss Sarah asked us to come and spend the day with her to-morrow. To day is dear little Rosa's birthday. She is four years old. She is a beautiful, lovable child. She has *demanded* birth-day party from Pa. I suppose she will get it —

Wednesday, July 24th, 1861

$6^3/_4$ A.M. . . It is a beautiful morning: very cool. Pa predicts fine weather — Yesterday morning I got in the bus, went to Dr D's, made an appointment for to-morrow, walked up, went to Miss Sarah's with the intention of spending the day. I found her doctoring Josh, as he had had an awful spell of coughing. She said she was so glad to see me, — but was astonished that I had made up my mind to come. She sewed a little on her machine, finished a petticoat and was about commencing another, when some visitors were announced. And she sewed no more. Uncle Naty came home soon, and very impatiently waited for dinner — He is very dissatisfied with the "coffin business", and I think that he will but stay the week out. Miss Sarah urges him to leave immediately, she told him not to go back yesterday af-

27. Reports of the loss of three generals were inaccurate. General Edmund Kirby Smith, though wounded, survived and became one of the Confederate heroes of Bull Run. See Steven E. Woodworth, *Jefferson Davis and His Generals* (Lawrence, Kans., 1990), 126.

ternoon — But he was heedless — A ride to the Bayou Bridge was proposed, so about $5^{1}/_{2}$, we started. Had no difficulty in getting seats and had a delightful ride. Canal is now *the* street, all the others are mostly deserted — There was a quantity of persons down there. Open carriages with pretty girls; some on horseback, some walking, and of course making a "splendid display". The cars are a great improvement to that portion of the city. We had a pleasant ride home, just the right time. It must be nice in these beautiful nights to go down in the 8 o'c car — Uncle Naty said that Ma, Alice and Pa had just left with the promise to come back. After supper, we waited and about $9^{1}/_{4}$ they came. It was current that Harry Isaacson was killed, but of course, in to day's paper, contradicted by a telegraph from him to his brother.[28] He is now with his *family* in Virginia, Richmond, for "they do say" that he has an heir. Can we believe it? She conveyed to me the *very* sad intelligence that "Our Battalion" were engaged, had suffered severely and dear, dear Major Wheat, and *others* were wounded!! I read it myself to day; I am *so, so* anxious to hear more. Dear, affectionate, tender Major Wheat, surrounded by rough though they may be attentive, soldiers. He who so willingly resign himself into woman's gentle hands. I wish I were there to administer to his wants. But we must hope that he will soon be himself again and ready for action. I hope "O.P." [Miller] is O.K. I am sorry that we know them. The little pleasure we experienced by our visit to the Camp was dearly bought. "Alas! by some degree of woe we every bliss must gain". The loss is now reduced to 200 killed, 1000 wounded. What exaggerated reports. No commander of Wash. Art. killed.[29] Ma and Alice paid several visits yesterday; viz. to Mrs. L.A. Levy, Octavia Harby and Mrs. E.L. Hens — Found no tacks in the stores, consequently made no purchases — Ma intended to go down town to day — Josephine was not home. Found Miss Calder, and family, quite distressed as their brother was a member of the "Continentals" and a fearful havoc is said to have been made in it. It is indeed a wise proceeding to suppress all names, until they can give them to the public with undoubted certainty.

Great excitement, all anxious to know their sacrifices. Pa brought Rosa home some cake, a fruit cake, which is not yet eaten, and funds to get "Ice Cream". While at Miss S. Mr. Elburger came. As usual Alice and I went to sleep. Miss Josephine had been away from "her Ed" for a week. She

28. Isaacson had formed his own unit as a captain in the Washington Artillery. He resigned his commission in August 1861. Erroneous reports were common.

29. The number of casualties, at first artificially high for Union forces, were then artificially low for the Confederate side.

spent it with Mrs. Burnett. Wonders never cease — The speech which Dr. Breckinridge delivered in senate, was published yesterday. It is a noble effort and clears that honorable gentleman from the imputation of being disloyal to the South. He ran a great risk in thus expressing himself — Vive Breckinridge!![30]

8½ P.M. . . . . Fannie and I are "two old maids" sitting in here alone. Fannie is reading the "Lost Heiress" (for you must know she has taken to novel reading.)[31] We are awaiting the arrival of *the* family, — for allow me to tell you that all, with the exception of your humble servant and her above-named sister went on a journey in the new cars, to the Bayou Bridge. I am momentarily awaiting them, although they have scarcely had time — They all looked pretty: every one. Oh! the house is so quiet. Alice did not want to go as she had said it looked too "babyish". Here they are!!!

Thursday, July 25th, 1861

6½ A.M. . . . . Before we came down, pa came in and pointed to something in the paper. Alice and I glanced and saw 'twas about "Maj. Wheat's Batallion". "Battle of Manassas: Louisiana's sacrifice upon the altar of liberty.. Maj. Wheat's Batallion — *Only 100 out of 400 escaped unhurt.* Lieut. Dickinson wounded: The Tigers in Virginia! They threw down their rifles but are still O.K." —

Dear Dickinson was wounded by a Minia ball in his thigh. He is well attended at Richmond — I hope it is nothing serious. The Tigers becoming dissatisfied with their Mississippi Rifles without bayonets, when ordered to charge, threw away their rifles and charged with their knives, as the enemy say, like demons and put all to flight before them: I think we should have heard had any others been wounded. Obed came around yesterday morning to see what Pa thought about his Father [Captain Obed Miller] — I had intended to go to Mrs. Miller's, but just as they were start-

30. John C. Breckinridge, vice president under Buchanan, 1857–61, and senator from Kentucky in the July 1861 special session, opposed Lincoln's war measures and sought to have Kentucky side with the Confederacy. When Kentucky chose to side with the Union in September 1861, Breckinridge joined the Confederate Army with the rank of brigadier general. Breckinridge, from a border state, agreed that slavery was legal and secession proper, but he did not think the time chosen to secede was a wise one. He would have continued negotiations with the federal government.

31. Fannie was fourteen.

ing, Miss Sarah came in. She staid until dark. Josh looked very bad—Alice says that, please God, she will go out this afternoon—Some fat in the store caught fire, and the children raised a general alarm. I thought the house was on fire—Alice, that "some boiling water was over one of the children"— Pa sent home a box of peaches, sack of sweet and Irish potatoes and a sack of Onions—

2³/₄ P.M. .... I returned from Dr D's. about ¹/₂ an hour ago. He did not accomplish much and I am to go to-morrow 12 o'clock. Fannie accompanied me—We rode down and up, spent a picayune [a 5¢ coin], consequently my expenditures were 25 cts!

F. was much disappointed in Judo's house.[32] Dr D. is so kind. I told him when Pa made some money he must send in his bill, and it would be "all right"— He said "It was all right now". He said my teeth were in a *very* bad condition— I appreciate highly his kindness—I asked him to call. He said he would if I promised *not to talk politics*. I did. Probably he will come Saturday Evening—I have vowed faithfully to perform my duty to my teeth. God aid me in it. Arrived home about 2¹/₂. It rained slightly while in the 'bus—Fannie was quite pleased with her trip; had I not been detained so long, I would have treated her to a ride in the new cars—There is no "*ðimunition*" in the size of my veins. I thought that when a certain visitor would appear, that they would disappear—But, alas!

Friday, July 26th, 1861

6³/₄ A.M. ..... Oh! Philomen, how heavy, heavy a heart have I had since last I saw you—When Pa came home to dinner, he told us that he thought dear Major Wheat's wound was mortal and that his dear life was despaired of!! Imagine my sorrow—Alice and I cried in unison, and had it been a relative my grief could not have been more. Every little incident of the Camp, in which he figured rose before us, the circumstances under which we first made his acquaintance, altho' we knew him for but a short time still we learned to love and respect him—He was a genial, warm-hearted friend, a jolly companion, generous, an affectionate son and universally beloved by all—No one that knows him, but would sadly regret to hear of the death

---

32. Judith Hyams Sprigg's house, visible from the trolley.

of Bob Wheat—"While there is life there is hope", and we must trust in God. There were no telegraphs this morning; how anxiously did I await, for I thought it would be tidings either of his death or recovery. He went away so cheerful, so hopeful, and then to be one among the first to be wounded. Mrs. Miller told us that Mr. Pilcher had received a telegraph telling him to come to Virginia and bring Mrs. Wheat (????????). I fear that for if his wound were not serious, his mother would not be sent for. Pray to God, may our hopes be granted, and may we soon secure tidings of our beloved Major's speedy recovery. Pa also told us that poor Capt. Eshelman's life is doubtful, if amputation of his leg does not ensue. It is sad. No news about our Lieut. Dickinson—When it does come, may it be favorable—Oh! what a barbarous war; it has no parallel in the history of unenlightened ages. Will the Northern Vandals ever awake from their lethargy—

Alice and I intended to go out, but it was too late and it looked cloudy, so it was again deferred until another time—After we were dressed we went to Mrs. Miller's. Found her as much distressed. Poor thing, she deserves pity. I think it strange that she has not heard from him. She thought of going on. Ladies are daily leaving. The other day 30 left—They are very much in want of nurses.

Just think the two persons, for whom we care most in the war, we should hear, in the very first battle, of *one* being seriously wounded, and—*nothing* of the other. All confirmed is better than suspense. Mrs. M. says she is prepared for the worst. How many, many bleeding and broken hearts are there—After we left her we went to Miss Sarah—Josh was not very well— She told us that on the battle field, Harry Isaacson was informed of the serious illness of his wife. He obtained a furlough, and when he arrived from utter exhaustion, suspense and fear, he was taken very sick. His wife lost her child and they are both very ill—In her situation she should not have gone on—It was very imprudent. But I suppose she cared more for the life of her husband than child. Leopold came in, Ma and Pa after him; we left, promising to come back. Had a nice supper. Ma took Miss Sarah a piece of fish, but Alice and I did not accompany them as we thought "Mr. Consequential" [Leopold] would attribute our visit to him.

Saturday, July 27th, 1861

6:20 A.M. I am writing now in my bonnet and shawl, or else, prepared to go out. Quite an unseasonable time, ain't it? And I suppose you wish an explanation of my conduct. Well, Ma bought me a dress yesterday, found that it was not enough for a flounce, and I am going down to Laroussini to match it and I heartily wish that I was not going. But I want a flounce! "A flounce, a flounce, a kingdom for a flounce"![33] Ma and Alice went out shopping yesterday—After they went, I prepared myself to go, but not shopping—I rode down and arrived at Dr D's in season. He attended to me without delay— Plugged one miserable tooth which hurt me severely. He impressed upon my mind the necessity of taking extraordinarily good care of my teeth, they being of a very soft nature. If the strictest attention and constant care will preserve them, they *shall* be preserved. Ma said that she would stop for me, as she was going home. After Dr D. finished, I waited for them, and in a few moments they came. Ma brought me a cake. We had a few moments' talk with him, and then left. I made no engagement for a few days. Rode up. Now that it is only 5 cents, it is dearer than before. Got home about $2^1/_2$.

Alice had a quantity of grapes, and she *made* me guess who was the generous donor—After giving me every clue, *except* the name, I guessed the right person, Mr. Wilcox—They were fine. Alice bought a box of "Cascarilla"[34]—Pa came shortly after—I had given him strict injunctions to bring me your "successor", but as he came in, I saw that I was doomed to be disappointed.[35] Pa said that coming up Julia St, on a door step, he saw a little boy, whom, from his resemblance to Mr. Hitchcock [Solomon's partner, now in Virginia], he thought might be his son. He asked his name and his suspicions were confirmed. He told Pa that his mother had received a telegraph, and Pa said he would go down in the afternoon to see what it amounted to—After dinner the goods which Ma had purchased in the day came up.[36] They all gave satisfaction with the exception of one. There were 2 dresses for F. and me, one for Alice and Ma, one for Dell, pocket handkerchief for me, and muslin for scarfs, for Alice and me. I wish that they were done—I think that scarfs are beautiful—particularly on graceful figures—Pa defrayed part of the expense of

33. A flounce is a frilly piece of fabric to attach to one edge of the dress.
34. The bark of a West Indian shrub, used to make incense or a tonic.
35. Clara hoped for a new notebook for her diary.
36. Home delivery by the storekeeper was the norm.

the bill. After eating figs, peaches, grapes, etc. I went upstairs to dress for Alice and I had so far progressed in our intention to pay 'those visits', as to go up stairs with the idea of dressing. Put on my organdy, wishing that my scarf was on me.

After I was dressed, I eat a piece of splendid watermelon. We left home at six, also the young lady of the opposite mansion, alias Mimi Vienne, did the same. She, whom we so often wished to know, walked behind us for 2 or 3 squares. I then found that she was walking very rapidly and that it was her intention to get in front of us, in order that we could obtain a good view of her. I endeavored not to let her, but spite of all she did. She certainly did look very handsome. She is a beautiful girl—Alice and I had quite an argument, respecting the impressions received by our olfactory nerves; I think it was wrong. Mimi is very haughty. I suppose she would think it a condescension to visit a person, who lived in a smaller house than her own. I wish I knew her.[37]

We went to see Belle Grant. They were all out—Then went to Mrs. Hens—Alice returned Miss Calder her umbrella. Miss Jo was not well, but no signs of an increase—She told us how poor Susie [?] Randolph fretted about her husband. I think it was loutish for him to go and leave her. She is in very bad health. She, who was so strong and healthy previous to her marriage. She has a beautiful child—She had better remained single—We told her what we heard about Mrs. Isaacson. She said that whatever happened to her would be a just retribution, for a woman, who had so good a husband and could not appreciate him, deserved to lose him. They say that he is a devoted husband, but she is not a loving, faithful wife. Miss Jo obtained the greater part of her knowledge from Mrs. Hite with whom she has lately become friendly. Mrs. H. and Mrs. I. once so very intimate are now enemies, and I think it very uncharitable the manner in which Mrs. H. speaks of her. For the sake of their old friendship she should be silent. I suppose what she says is veritable, as no one had a better opportunity of knowing—I always thought Emma Hite a sweet girl—The acquaintanceship between her and Mrs. Hens is very sudden—Miss J. is a little bothered at the thought that "Ed" may have to go away yet. But he says that he would not serve under Major Walton. He has become very unpopular, chiefly owing to his tyranny and partiality.[38] Miss J. dressed,

37. The Solomons had been at their current residence for a short time, and had not been introduced to the Viennes, a family across the street.

38. James Walton, soon to be made colonel, had been commander of the Washington Artillery since 1857. See Gallagher, ed., *Recollections of General Edward Porter Alexander,* 168, 177–78; Owen, *The Washington Artillery.*

I may *truthfully* say, "in the twinkling of an eye"; she walked to Prytania St with us, we saw her safely in the cars, as she was going to see Susie Randolph. Miss Jo. promised to come and spend one morning the early part of next week. She promised faithfully. As we were coming home we stopped at Fanny Burbank. She was out and Alice left her card. After we had gone a little ways the thought occurred to Alice that probably she had left Ma's, so we turned back and found that it was really so. A. tore off the initials and left the aristocratic name of "Solomon". We stopped to Mrs. Miller. Found her more composed. She thinks that dear Capt. ordered a telegraph to be sent, but through some one's negligence it was never done. "No news is good news". She had just seen Pa; he was going down to Mrs. Hitchcock, and promised to stop and tell her what he heard. There is nothing about our beloved Major. I hope to God, that he is better. God bless him, — and restore him to us. When we got in I did not recognize Mrs. Pierson — I was astonished to see her — Miss Jo. was just telling us that her ma was coming and coming, but something always prevented her. Ma got supper ready and Pa had just come in when F. Burbank and her brother came. Then I was dumbfounded — How soon she returned our visit! She said that she was coming next week to spend the morning. I like her very well, and shall be happy to have her come — She declined the invitation to supper, her brother and George Pierson, who had come for his mother did likewise. Uncle Naty came; we gave him some peaches (he said that's what he came for) and he went. He said that he and 'his wife' would come back. For supper we had fish, preserves and figs — Alice stayed with F. and when I was done I took her place, and she went to supper. After we were done Uncle N. and Miss S. came. Uncle N. eat something but Miss S. could not as she was suffering with her tooth. Mrs. P. left about 9½. She asked Alice and me to come and spend the day with her. Probably we shall. Fanny B. left later, and the others (later still). Miss S. promised to come and spend the day with us to day.

Sunday, July 28th, 1861

6¼ A.M. About 11 o'clock yesterday Miss S. and Josh came. We spent the day very pleasantly and would have spent it much more so, had not Josh, as usual, been *so* bad. But poor child he was sick — And I think Miss

S. is excusable for indulging him a little, but now he is past redemption. He is one of the worst specimens that were ever known. The older he grows, the worse he gets.[39] We had a nice lunch. Uncle Naty came to dinner and, as well as all, enjoyed it. Pa did not bring our books. I saw him get out of the omnibus with a bundle. I hastened down stairs and it proved to be some tea. I suppose there is no chance to day. About $5^1/_2$, we had the watermelon. Then went up to dress. Lucy combed Miss S.'s hair. She was very much pleased with it. About $6^1/_2$ Miss Calder came, Alice was not dressed. With all possible haste, she completed her toilet, and went down — I dressed about 7. and when I got down she was gone. She intends going away soon. I suppose that was the reason she came — It was her first visit. She is a very nice girl — She told Alice that Godery's was out, so about dark, A. and I went up to the book store to see if we could be fortunate enough to get it. Up on Hercules St I saw Lizzie Hillman and Maggie coming along. As Lizzie had treated me meanly in not sending one word of her arrival, I did not know how to act. I passed Mag. and recognized Lizzie, with a stiff bow. Now thought I here is an estrangement for ever. After it was done, Alice said that maybe I had done wrong. But it was done, and could not be undone. How I would have longed to embrace her, and tell her how happy, how *very* happy I was to see her. But pride stepped in and bade me pass on —

Went to the store and they did not have it [the book], but promised to get one for us. As we were coming home, whom should we see, but the above named ladies. We then stopped and saluted. She said that she intended to call. But what of that, she didn't! She said that she did not expect such ceremony from school girls — She had been up to see L. Campbell, Mrs. Shaw, and I think that she could as easily have come to see me, living as I do, so close. We parted with no understanding. I did not ask her to come and see me, nor she me. And we parted, "it may be for years, and it may be for ever". I am sorry for I love her. We may make it up again — She looked beautiful — I wish she loved me — When we came home, Miss S. had gone. Ma had gone to walk a little ways with her, so A. and I walked out and met her at the corner — Ma did not feel very well. I suppose Josh made her sick. Pa came home soon. He was drilling Rosa, also himself — Ma sent Uncle N. some supper by Ellen. Pa and I went round a few moments after. Ma said to be home soon. As we were going I saw Mrs. Miller on her steps and asked Pa to go over — We went. She had heard nothing

39. Clara had known Josh Nathan for some time already, even though her family only recently came to the Nathans' neighborhood.

of *him*. She had heard from Mr. Sykes, who accompanied Joshua Reynolds' remains here, that Wheat was mortally wounded, Gardner and Carey killed, 4 Tigers left. Mr. Eastman killed. She had not heard of Miller. I don't know if this is authentic as Pa says he is a great "gasser"—Mrs. M. seems distressed. Poor Reynolds is to be buried to day. His remains arrived yesterday by the R.R. Went to Miss S's—Josh was not well—She is determined to take him to the Dr this morning.

Uncle N. was not home and she was also uneasy about him—I could not leave her by her self. We were up stairs, Pa down stairs asleep—Josh was sleeping very quietly. About $7\frac{1}{2}$ Uncle N. came—He said that he was waiting for his money, and after all, got $5!! Mr. Quirk agreed to give him $12. a week!!! He thinks it better to get that, than nothing. He says: "that will get him something to eat anyhow". He eat his supper—I eat a fig—Poor Miss Sarah is so worried about Josh. She says that she knows it will end in Consumption.[40] Can she expect anything else! Poor little thing! He is to be pitied. Got home; found all in bed. Told A. what Mrs. M. had told me. There is no news to day. Bought a True Delta. As devoid as Delta; nothing of dear Major [Wheat]. Emma Levy said she would come to spend the day. Ma was not very well, last night. It is Eisner's time to day—I have not seen Cousin S. [Sam Myers] for so long—Dr Taney will never come again. Alice is my authority—$9\frac{1}{4}$ A.M. . . . Breakfast is over. I am so tired; Ma does not feel very well.

Monday, July 29th, 1861

$6\frac{3}{4}$ A.M. Ma complaining yesterday; Alice and I insisted upon sending for the Dr. Ma objected, but we "carried the day". He came and thank God, said it was just a little boil—Ma has a general cold. She was not well all day, but the Dr said that it was not attributable to the boil—We all became alarmed when the intelligence was brought to us of the death of a lady on our square from a carbuncle on her side. The foolish thought that probably Ma was getting one seized possession of us. But happily our fears were groundless. The Dr prescribed some cooling medicine. Ma felt better through the day. About 10, Emma Levy came. She has grown very

---

40. Tuberculosis, at the time an incurable disease.

much and is very pretty — Pa lunched with us; nice things. Fanny and I were angry — Had a very nice dinner, which Emma enjoyed — particularly the dessert, alias, peaches — Pa did not go out after lunch. After dinner, we had a watermelon. I then dressed — Then I came down and found Cousin Sam there. Talked on various subjects, which I have not space to communicate, my honored friend — Pa did not bring my book. And now, companion of most 2 months, we must part. Your existence is at an end. When your successor is may I be as happy as I now am.

[There are no entries from July 30 through September 8, 1861.]

3

Blockade:
September 9–September 23, 1861

Monday, September 9th, 1861

$6^1/_4$ A.M. . . Here we meet again, and I suppose you do not recognize yourself, but remember that "Dress does not make the man", and that you are
nothing more to me than my "dear Philomen". I hope that we may be months
together; we are fast friends, bound by ties which can never be unlinked.
'Twould be unreasonable were I to wish that no sombre shades would ever
cloud our horizon — For was not "man made to mourn"? It is impossible
for us to gaze into that "dim, unseen, future" — Who knows what you may
be called upon to hear; how one day, I may be in the height of joy, the next
in the depths of despair — But, through all the "ups and downs" of life I
expect to find you, the same, unchanging friendship. And now I will commence, but not before expressing the hope, that when your life is ended,
I can safely say, "There is not a line, which dying, I should wish to
blot" —, and also that the chirography[1] and diction may well accord with
your fine appearance. Offer your thanks to your absent donor![2]

Yesterday, while at dinner, the bell rang and "who *could* it be, at such a
rainy time." Ma conjectured Mr. N. with a letter, and ran to ascertain: F.
followed, and presently they came in, both faces betraying something unusual. "Guess who it is". A thousand beings flitted across my mind. In one
breath they exclaimed "The blind man".[3] I was *mute* with astonishment —

1. Penmanship.
2. There are no diary entries for over a month because no one gave Clara a new notebook. Neither
parent was interested in Clara's diary keeping, but her sister Alice, who kept a diary and earned a
salary, could have spent the 25¢ for Clara. The parents, however, controlled Alice's income. Clara's
notebooks had to come from outside the home, on more than one occasion from Durant da Ponte, but
he was often at the Virginia front sending reports home. The stores stocked only a few notebooks.
3. During the visit to the army camp described by Clara at the very beginning of the diary, she
and Alice were intrigued by a "blind man" they met, who was apparently deaf and without speech but
not blind.

Alice and I ran from the table, and prepared ourselves to greet our 'accomplished friend'. I bade the children cease their noise, forgetful that *all* was silence to him. In a few moments, I was before him — He produced his slate, and we carried on a few moments conversation. He inquired for "Miss Solomon", and in a short while she saluted him — The children gazed in open-mouthed astonishment at the voiceless man before them; and to confound them more, we said all imaginable extravagant things, and were supplicated, entreated by them "to hush", for "the man was only *fooling:* he *could* hear". It seemed as though their wonderment increased instead of subsided, by the eager manner in which they observed every action. As I gazed upon him, I was unconsciously thrown into a train of thought — How things do come to pass. Little did we dream, that the comical looking man, seated opposite to us at the "Tangipaho" table, would ever enter the portals of our door. He informed us that he had been in the City for a week and was learning the Photographic art at Mr. Clarks. He will remain here for a few weeks and then intends going to Va., where he will practice his profession. We wished him success in all his undertakings, for which he thanked us. It will not at all be lucrative, but I suppose he does it with a view also to pleasure. He says he is heartily sick of Tangipaho, for in fact, he never liked the "strait place"; his business is still conducted there. We requested him to favor us with *his* photograph, and he promised to comply. I asked him numerous questions, and thought if there was a record of all our conversations, to how little would it amount, and how visibly would we see the many hours wasted. He is very obliging and seems never to be wearied. To my inquiry, "If he were born a mute", he replied, "no, I lost my hearing at the age of four, by sleeping in the open air, in my grandfather's garden" — How wonderful then that he should also have lost his speech. Fearing that it may have been a delicate and painful subject, I discarded it, though I was very anxious to be informed of *all* the particulars. Josh came in, and his mouth was extended to an extraordinary size, when he looked upon the strange spectacle before him, the first one of the kind, that he had ever witnessed. The children will forget themselves, and act as they did in the presence of *all* gentlemen. It must be very convenient. A. and he conversed the greater portion of the time, for I became tired, and indeed it is very wearisome. They wrote "the biggest pack of foolishness", and A. was thoughtful enough to get pencil and paper, and when he wished to tear it, we objected and told him "we desired to keep it as a memento" — "It is not worth the reading", said he. I asked him if he had ever been in love — He replied that "he was now, and that Miss S. was the lady" — But all this was *just fun.* I asked if he attended

Church. He pointed to his ear. "But you could go to pray"—"I always read my bible". It may be seldom that he is fortunate enough to find attentive conversers, and he is not to be blamed, if he is tenacious of them when found. He was not in a very fine costume, and I think that common respect should have prompted him to have presented a better appearance. I have seen him when in "dress costume", and it is decidedly a great improvement. This one circumstance marred in a *great* degree the pleasure of his visit— He said he would see us again. He made a *very* long visit of about two hours. How much better do we find our lot to be when compared with that of others. I thought of all the pleasures from which he was debarred, and how little we, who were possessed of them, value them—"No mother's voice falls on his ear", he never heard the pealing of the Church bells, the merry laughter of joyous brothers and sisters ne'er gladdened his lonely heart. There is no power like that of words. When he receives the warm sympathy and condolence of friends, though it come direct from the heart, it is transmitted through a double medium and thus its effect is weakened— Does he ever rebel against his lot? It was ordained by *him*, and as all things are, for some wise purpose, that he, so intelligent, should be almost entirely cut off from all intercourse with his fellow beings. He is doubtless resigned to his fate— Though deprived of *some* blessings, he should be thankful of *those* with which he is endowed. Were his mind not cultivated, he would be but one degree above the brute creation—

Oh! I should like to write to him unrestrainedly! After taking A.'s address for about the fourth time, he rose to depart, and we both were glad, as the novelty had ceased, and a feeling of fatigue crept over us. He shook hands, and with an expressive smile and nod of the head was gone—How totally unprepared are we for some events which happen. While looking at you, I little *dreamed* that our first subject of conversation would be about— "The *Blind* man of Tangipaho". About 5 he left, and A. and I went up to dress, for I must tell you that I was in my volante—[4] We *heard* Cousin S. down stairs, but he had gone before we descended. I was very negligé in my toilet, as I did not feel well, and knew that "no one would come", and being deprived of the pleasure of a visit to Miss S's., the Harrises being there, and it would consequently be very unpleasant.

A. read to ma the conversation. About dark, Alice and I took a short walk, and thoughts *naturally* turned to the "absent Parent", and he became the subject of our conversation. With all youthful ardor and hope, we are already anticipating his happy return—How pleasant, could he

4. Literally "light" or "rapid," here used to refer to a dressing gown.

only spend with us the "Christmas holydays". What a joyful, joyful re-union —

The sun will cease to hope, to picture a radiant future. We then invoked God's blessings on him, and supplicated him to shield him from all harm, and restore to the bosom of his family, the "dearest and best of fathers". The lateness of the hour, warned us that it was time to "go in" — Eat supper. I feasted on the "Sunday Delta", A. on Saturday's, and then we were seated, till bed time should come. "Will it be this way, in the winter"? No acquaintances, no Pa! To bed early, and no diversion.

But, if we are all blessed with health, and good tidings are wafted to us of *him,* will we be lonely? Will we murmur? Away, away! "Sufficient unto the day, is the evil thereof". Cousin S. promised to come back, but *of course,* did not. We retired about 9, and could scarcely realize that before Pa's departure we never supped before 9 or retired before 11!!

Truly, did Alice remark, "Clara, *those* were some of the happiest moments of our lives". And yet were they not tinged with a deep sadness. While charmed by the music of his voice, and enthralled by the magic of his conversation, *could* we restrain the thought "How soon will we have to part" — After taking my medicine, and bidding "good night", to those I love, I resigned myself in *reality* to the arms of *Morpheus,*[5] but in *imagination* to the arms of some one else.

What a long, long week has the past been — 'Tis but 7 days ago, since School reopened, when with a heavy heart and weeping eyes, I saw them "one by one depart", and now with a heart, of not much less weight, do I herald in the following morning, for that "grim monster", the "Normal School", stares me in the face, and I have made up my mind to go this afternoon — The past days have been replete with incidents. The unexpected appearance and sudden departure of the "Captain" [Miller], the intervening events, and the visit of yesterday. When the present week will be the past, I may have some things more important to recapitulate.

4³/₄ P.M. . . . "We are sitting together on the new front sofa". A's. duties for the day are over, and we are now enjoying these few leisure moments. There seems to be a fatality attending my attendance of the "L.N.S". The rain altered my plans — we were visited by a heavy rain, and the streets are now impassable. Will it ever stop raining? I doubt it — Time assuages all grief. Alice and I have become reconciled to the separation, and now love each other, (if possible), the more. Ma's finances are in no better a state, and she has had an attack of the "blues" — I kept her company, but, I, in fact, felt

5. The Greek god of dreams.

sick, so there was some excuse. We did but little sewing, but talked a great deal. Principally of beaux, prospects of marriage, and other *foolish* subjects — Rosa complained of being lonesome, and expressed the desire to pay Miss S. a visit. Ma complied with it, and she went, accompanied by Dell. The rain detained her, and she came over after dinner. Ma's means unabled her to furnish a good dinner, and it was by no means "epicurean" — But we don't care for that — Let us reflect on the many nice ones, we *have* enjoyed. But what are we to do for money? The house, was, as usual in a flood, and it was always my impression, that the object of it was "to shelter you from the outward storm", etc., etc. But every one is liable to mistake. By a transmission of umbrella and shoes, the children arrived home in good order. A. said that she could not summon courage to broach the delicate subject to Miss C. Her fellow-laboress could devise no means, by which to obtain their dues, so they are compelled "to make the best of it". "What can't be cured *must* be endured". Josie has not been very well. She is cutting teeth. It is not raining, but cloudy and dismal. I wonder what pa is now doing. Maybe in the act of breaking a seal of a "letter from home". "Would I were with him". He may, in all probability, be seated, "otium cum dignitate", around a "camp fire" (what happiness), luxuriating in a fine cigar, and conversing with his comrades — We are in daily expectation of a "messenger of love" —

I have the same complaint to make to you, as I had to your predecessor — *My bad chirography.* I *try* to improve. *Why* can't I? I never expect to, and yet, how earnest is my desire. My hand-writing is one of which I am positively *ashamed*. Last night I dreamed of Liz. Mix. why don't she write? Oh? I feel so low-spirited. "Trifles, light as air", *always* affect *me* —

Tuesday, September 10th, 1861

6¹/₂ A.M. . . . After leaving you, yesterday, Alice and I, went up to dress. I was under the impression that Ma had gone to Miss S's, but as I came down, I was greeted by "Where's Clara", and some very acceptable cream and pound cake was handed to me. It was of "Col. Elsworth's" manufacture, and we were desirous of knowing how they had been obtained, as Ma had no funds. Ma would not enlighten us, but on the contrary mystified us, by displaying a large amount of money — I shall inquire into it to day.

A. and I took our walks on our "flags" [flagstones], and doubtless we imagine that we are promenading around the grounds of a noble mansion. Our conversation naturally turned upon "Love", its ennobling and refining influence, its universality and its different effects upon different natures. There is no one who has never felt this passion. No one has passed through this life, without enshrining in his heart *one* female form around which bright hopes of the future clustered—It comes alike to the refined and elegant *man*, the coarse and uneducated menial. It is a natural craving. "Give me love, give me love", without it I cannot exist.

Angelic "Judo", beloved "Beauty", dear "Mr. Rutledge", all claimed a share. Blessings rest upon them. As we passed our gas light suddenly illuminated our faces, and we "went in".

Found Ma very provoked with Lucy, whom she had again found in the act of falsifying [lying], and combined with this she was very insolent.[6] Mrs. N. came in, and all was quiet. She brought the first volume of the "Lady of the Isle", which she highly recommends. Doubtless I will read it.

She had already eaten of "bread and molasses", and refused to partake of "ours". Why ain't one party rich? Mrs. N. found that Ma had no money and was quite indignant to think that Ma did not send over to borrow some, maintaining that delicacy on *her* part, prevented her from sending it, unasked. Ma told her that she *had* intended to, but feared that she just had sufficient for her own wants. "You know", said she, "*whatever I did have, I would share it* with you". Mr. N. came over, and in his hand the 2nd Volume of the "Lady of the Isle", which he had been feasting on at home. We allowed him the privilege of reading by our "light". He is fascinated with the book. I was suffering with *Rheumatism*, and did not take part in the conversation— They left about 10.

9 3/4 A.M.. . . I have completed my household duties, and am now prepared to sew. The sun is shining— *12 1/4 P.M.*. . . Sun still visible. I wish that it would rain.

4.20. P.M.. . . A few moments after A. came from school Josh came bounding in the front door, with uplifted hands, and a half of dozen voices exclaimed, "A letter"; yes, a letter. The "messenger of love", after a journey of six days, arrived safely and was welcomed joyfully, at its destination. J. was also the bearer of another letter; the superscription (Mr. Laurie Solomon) unknown to us, but the writing seemed that of Baby's. We hesitated a few moments before opening it, but finally concluded to do so, not imagining

6. At this stage of hostilities, before Union troops entered New Orleans and before Lincoln issued his Emancipation Proclamation, Lucy's position in the household was at best awkward.

what the contents *could* be. It was a few lines from "Mollie Harner" (who be she), informing the above named gent. of her change of residence. That was of *very* little import to *us*, and as it is of a back date, and *can't* be of *any* importance to *any* one, we have determined to take no further note of it, but consign it to the winds.

If "Mr. Laurie Solomon" is anxious to see "Miss Mollie Harner", he will accomplish his purpose without *our* intervention, and if he has not the desire, the letter may prompt it, the visit may prove disastrous, and then upon whom will the blame rest? The writing was very much like Baby's, and I should certainly have pronounced it to be hers. We thrust it aside and directed our attention to the other letter. It was dated the 4th, and written in reply to the lines ma wrote in Alices of the 22nd. He says that they are in the midst of splendid weather, and that he is enjoying fine health; he states that his eyes have become very weak, since his arrival, and that he reads with difficulty. He dares to suggest the probability of being compelled to use spectacles! He knows how we rebelled against the idea! I hope that he will not.

He saw Mr. Whiting, who informed him that Mrs. Hitchcock & child had arrived with him in the City [Richmond]. Pa called on her at the Hotel. She was very desirous of seeing her husband, who was at Manassas. She requested Pa to tender to Ma her kindest regards and her regrets that she was unable to return her visit, previous to her departure. It was her intention, but the bad weather prevented her from paying any farewell visits. The week before her departure was one of constant rain. She had met with quite an adventure. An enemy of Mr. W's had informed the authorities that he was an Abolitionist and spy.[7] The party was arrested. Mrs. H. denied the accusation, stated that her husband was connected with the Confederate Army; the permission was granted her to proceed, but her Father would be detained, and an investigation into the circumstance be made by the Vigilance Committee. Of course she decided to remain with him — Their trunks were searched, but no evidences were found of his disloyalty. He was acquitted, and received a pass allowing him to continue his journey — Apologies were made to them for their disagreeable detention — The notion of the authorities was justifiable, as they are compelled to be very careful. Pa writes that Capt. Miller is in the City. It was his intention to return to this City, he having obtained a furlough of 30 days, and as his wife wrote him that one of the children was sick, but receiving

7. Mr. W. [Mr. Whiting] was Mrs. Hitchcock's father. The fear of northern spies was considerable, and justifiably so. In this case, however, old enemies tried to get even for imagined or real wrongs.

a dispatch that he was better, and as a great battle is thought to be soon at hand, it has naturally altered his plans, and he will return to Manassas — He is quite well, but still suffers from his leg. He looks remarkably well. The Hotel, at which Pa is now stopping, is very well kept, though not a first class one.

He is a favorite with the clerks. He has a fine, commodious room, capable of holding two beds, and although the house is crowded, they place none with him, but he is allowed to enjoy it by himself. Where is he not a favorite? On Capt. M's arrival, Pa offered him the accomodations his room could afford, and he accepted them, no doubt being very well pleased. He requests Pa to send *his* love to *his* wife and children. What impudence! Not a word of remembrance to *us*. It is positively outrageous.

Pa writes as follows, "The table is very well kept and I know you would enjoy it, and enjoy it you should, if it were in my power". Don't we know that! The house in question is the "Columbian".[8] Pa is yet undecided how he will act in regard to the "Polish Regiment". What a wavering point.[9] He says that Major Wheat is very sick at the Springs. It is attributable to his great improvidence. Pa says "The wound may kill him yet, and if it does through spreeing [spreading], it will *serve him right*". I suppose that he thinks having endured so much, his capacities of endurance are unlimited. The telegraph of Saturday, stating his recovery, is of later date, consequently there is no foundation for uneasiness. I hope that in future he will be more prudent.

Pa's remarks, that the City is crowded with officers, (and as he is acquainted with many) and dissipation and frolicking is the order of the day (and night). He is invited to participate, but respectfully declines the honor of their company — He says "It don't suit me at my time of life, so I quietly yield to others, and am in my room by 8, 9, or 10 o'clock".[10]

Pa states that he wrote to "Sam Myers, esq." a few days previous & requested him to call up and tell us, but as he did not, it could not have come to hand. Pa ought to have made some mention of my "little serap" [angel]. These were the principal items contained in the letter, and after devouring it, we proceeded to do likewise to the dinner. Susie Brown re-

8. The Columbian Hotel, Richmond.

9. The regiment had gone to Manassas, but Solomon had some doubt about acting as sutler for it in Virginia. Hitchcock and Solomon discovered that there was enough business to do without formal sutlership arrangements.

10. Richmond became the capital of the Confederacy as soon as Virginia voted to secede from the Union. As such, Richmond attracted officers who had, or hoped to have, government positions. Richmond was also the supply center for the Manassas war zone.

turned our "Nemesis", and I was glad to welcome the "stray sheep" — A. also brought with her from School, "Evelina". Miss Calder had obtained it some time ago from the Library, and when she sent it back, A. wrote a line to Mr. Curr, requesting him to transfer it to her, which he did. I have always had a great desire to read it, from the many encomiums which Ma (who read it years ago) has passed upon it. I suppose I will read it and no doubt be pleased. Accompanying Alice's lunch to day was a little piece of paper, upon which I wrote, "*Judo, Dentzel*". This *note*, though unintelligible to others, I knew *she* would understand. We thought that as Miss Dentzel knew every thing, she probably was acquainted with the whereabouts of "judo" — and as we are desirous of being informed upon the subject, A. determined to ask her, so I wrote her the note, to remind her of her duty.

But A. did not have an opportunity so we are to day, no wiser, but live in hopes that we will be soon. Some news. Not a drop of rain! It was predicted that we would have rain during the first quarter of the moon, and as it is now in its second, I suppose the weather will be clear. It will seem strange to have no rain, and it has visited us daily for the past six weeks. To day, I pointed a band for Sally. We do not accomplish much work for two persons and a machine. There was quite a change in our "bill of fare" to day. Breakfast — "Fried beefsteak" — I did not go to school, as it is Tuesday and Mrs. Shaw, is not there. Tomorrow I must go. How I dread it. If I could only stay home. That little "If" —

At this *very* moment the "Capt." may be in the arms of his *beloved* wife. He has been three days on his journey —

I did not feel very well to day. Still suffering from a *cold*. Several times, since we have been writing, the bell has been rung, and the idea seized possession of us, that it may have been the "Blind man", and as we did not feel like being interrupted or *bothered*, the ejaculations which escaped our lips, and the expression which stole over our faces, were anything *but* pleasant. Our surmises were incorrect for it proved to be persons in search of information. Belle told Alice that their house is to rent, and they are going to move. It is a great sacrifice, but in the present state of affairs, it is advisable for them to do it. Mrs. Byrne is also going to move.

Wednesday, September 11th, 1861

4¹/₄ P.M. . . . Yesterday afternoon Alice and I went over to Miss S. and found Ma over there. She congratulated us upon having no rain, and hoped that the weather would continue fine. In the hopes expressed upon this subject, she is not alone. Mr. N. came before dark, inquired about Pa, and we informed him of the principal items of the letter, one of which, by the by, I neglected to state to you. Pa writes, "The troops will be paid off next Saturday (7th)". I suppose there is money on the way for us.[11] Miss S. had been employed during the day in manufacturing drawers for the soldiers. Mr. Elburger obtained them for her from the establishment of Mr. Wolf, who has an enormous quantity on hand, having received an order for 600 dozen. Miss S. completed six, and is to be remunerated with the exorbitant sum of $1.25 per dozen. It will afford employment for many indigent women, and they have numerous applicants. If the war has deprived *some* of the means of obtaining a livelihood, it has, on the contrary, bettered the condition of many. Miss S. asked us to stay, but we declined and she promised to come over, which she did about 8 o'clock. Mr. N. succeeded in unraveling the mysteries of a "towel stand", which had perplexed wiser heads than his. We cheered him on his success —

They left about 9. We stayed on the gallery admiring the clear, beautiful moon, around which not a shadow was resting.

Maybe Pa was looking *then* at *that* moon, and in realms of fancy was with the "loved ones". Performed our respective duties in the "closing up of the house", and then, well you know what else. The day has been quite fine, and no event transpired to render it more memorable than any other one. There was quite an abatement in sewing — I tried my powers on the machine, but did not accomplish wonders —

Josie was quite cross. The unvaried fare at lunch. I spilt salt at breakfast, but was not *unusually* mad. The children came home from school. I reasoned with ma that it was useless for me to go to school this afternoon and proposed that A. and I would go down town and purchase some articles, of which we are in great need. She told me that Belle told her that Mrs. Pagand had remarked the previous evening, that as the school was already full, all those who had been absent, without a good excuse, would be stricken from the roll, and called the roll, and requested those who knew anything of the absentees, to inform her. On the calling of my name Louisa

11. On payday the store would be busy and Solomon would end up with cash to send home.

G. rose and said that I had been detained by indisposition. I tender to her my sincere thanks. Of course the excuse was accepted. I was very much alarmed while A. was telling me, as I feared she had bad news to communicate, and with breathless anxiety I exclaimed "Am I stricken from the roll"? On receiving her answer, I breathed freer. I shall go to-morrow. It must be done, then why hesitate? Mrs. Deegan was here to day, and Ma suggested the probability of her obtaining some of its "drawers", so wrote a few lines of recommendation and directed her to Mr. Wolf's. She promised to return and tell us the result. It will be a mere pittance as she will be compelled to do all with her hand, but she has no work, and "anything is better than nothing".[12] Poor woman! I wish that I could assist her. She is a worthy object for charity. How little now would render her happy.

8 1/4 P.M. .... Here are Alice and I, like two "old maids" with their pet birds, devoting to you, ladies, our time and attention. I have quite a little adventure to relate. A. and I concluded to go out. While dressing the clouds began to gather, and the general appearance was threatening, but we thought that it *could* not rain, so proceeded with our toilet. The object of our expedition was to purchase some "Cocoaine", which is awfully needed by the "whole family". After receiving funds from Ma, and injunctions to "turn back" if it rained, the "two Miss Solomons" emerged from their gate. We had not gone far ere the thunder was heard; but we paid no heed to it, thinking that it was but a passing wind and would soon "blow over". We ventured on, but while at the corner of St. Joseph and Apollo Sts, the drops began to fall, and we retracted our steps to the corner of Bacchus and Triton Walk. Remained there some time under shelter, and amused ourselves by making close observations of some pretty girls, the occupants of the noble looking mansion, opposite. They seemed to be amusing themselves on their gallery and doubtless were happy. How sad to think, of the many pretty girls in the world, whom we will never know.

The loveliest thing in nature, is a group of "pretty females". Bless them all. "How blessed are the beautiful". The rain ceased in some degree, and with strides, somewhat resembling those of "Abe" when he made his escape from Baltimore,[13] we directed our steps homeward, arrived in triple quick time, and with a grand exposé of limbs, etc., made an "inglorious retreat" into the back gate. Ma's first inquiry "Are you wet"? was answered

12. Mrs. Bridget Deegan, mother of the Solomons' maid Ellen, had to sew by hand and could earn much less.

13. Clara refers to Lincoln sneaking through Baltimore on the eve of his inauguration earlier in the year.

negatively, for the rain had stopped. I immediately commenced disrobing, being insufferably *hot*, from the recent exercise — F. consented to relieve me by arranging some of my things and I soon felt very comfortable. It cleared off so pretty that we almost regretted discontinuing our journey — Another day and no "Cocoaine" — We so seldom make up our minds to go out, and when we did you perceived, I hope, how we were thwarted in our attempt — About dark, A. and I, went to the cake shop, invested in 5 cts. cake, and walked up to Thalia St to enjoy them. As we passed the "Old houses", the thoughts which arose, found utterance on our lips — One and all of the "dear friends", claimed our attention and we felt how "Blessings brighten as they take their flight".[14]

When we got home, Ma was to Mrs. N's., and A., F. and I promenaded on our "flags", discussed school, the girls, etc. Ma and S. are now to Miss S's. I am in a perfect heat, I suppose caused by that large cup of tea, I swallowed at supper. It was Pa's cup. Did not that assurance make it doubly sweeter? Ma and S. have just come in. Leopold was over there. He has been to Pascagoula for the past few days. He received a letter from Julius. He has been sick and since his departure has expended quite a little fortune in medicines — If there is any tune for which he now has a partiality, it must be "Home again".[15]

Mr. N. has given up his situation at Mr. Quirk's [the coffinmaker].

The work is very hard, and the remuneration being not only very slight, but also uncertain. I wonder what he will now do.

The mosquitoes are as tormenting as "Gus", I have had a regular battle with them, and will now leave the field to them —

Ma has just gone up. Her "chicks" must follow. Good night.

Thursday, September 12th, 1861

$4^1/_4$ P.M. . . . .I come to you for a few moments preparatory to going to dress, for Alice and I are going to make another attempt to go out, and as the

14. Thalia Street is about two blocks away, crossing Dryades. Clara and Alice walked through their old neighborhood, recalling what were certainly better times.

15. Pascagoula is on the Gulf of Mexico, near Mississippi's eastern border with Alabama. Julius, presumably a relative of Leopold, lived there. Port cities or towns on the Gulf were natural trading points and logical locations for merchants, Jewish or otherwise.

afternoon is fine, there is no chance of a similar adventure. Oh! I am so hot. How I dislike to dress. Au revoir for a time.

Friday, September 13th, 1861

6¼ A.M. . . . . I was so fatigued last night that I was unable to detail to you the events of the day, and hoping that I have not incurred your displeasure I now proceed.

I did not rise yesterday, as soon as usual, as I had nothing to write, and "Evelina", or "Lady of the Isle", possesses no particular attractions for me. When at breakfast something was said about my not attending school, ma remonstrated and said that I *must*. I was very sorry, but I thought that ma would relent, but anyhow it rather depressed my spirits as I did not want to go. The day was a dreamy, beautiful one, but very hot. The work gave out, and I lay idly on the floor, talking with ma, and summoning up all my ailments, which, she says, are imaginary. If I were *really* sick no one would believe it. Ma said that I reminded her of Miss Jo. & Charlotte. But, in fact, I have not felt well these past few days. I complained of being hungry and Ma generously gave me 5 cts. to dispose of as I wished— I invested in Ginger cake. I wrote A. a note, to remind her to fulfil the promise of many days, of bringing home Ellen's books. As she intends to teach her, E. is very anxious, and with so many around capable of instructing her, it is shameful that she should grow up in ignorance. She is a very quick child, and no doubt, will learn readily. She would like so much to attend School. Is she not envious of those children that do? She is a well disposed child, and ma has often remarked that were it in her power, she would adopt her as her own. She is an affectionate, dutiful daughter.

About 2 o'clock, Mr. N. came in, and in his hand a "letter"—We eagerly seized it, and as eagerly opened, and as eagerly read it. It was directed to "Miss Alice Solomon", and bore post mark of Richmond, Sept., 9th!! How great was our surprise—It had been so short a time on its journey. Three days!, when we consider 7 to be the average time. It was dated Sept. 7th and addressed to "My beloved children Alice and Clara"—He apologizes for this address by saying that he did the previous one in the same manner, and this was a continuation of the description of his journey.

Ma says that this is a very broad hint and I shall take it, and write. Probably he thinks A. will be offended at not receiving an individual reply. He then tells us of the pleasure occasioned by the receipt of the "kind letter", and the liberty he took in showing it to some parties, whose acquaintance he has lately made, all of whom expressed the sentiment that should they ever visit the South, if Pa would honor them by an introduction — Pa told them that he would grant the favor. He gives us a most pleasing description of his journey, through some of the loveliest and most picturesque regions of the Country — Places, which after luxuriating in their lovely scenery, and in admiring the noble works of nature and art, he was loth to leave. Places, which for miles around, the eye could rest entranced — [16] They surely must have been worthy of this notice, for on such subjects, Pa is no enthusiast. With the consideration which is a part of himself, and which has so endeared him to our hearts, he constantly wished that we were with him — He gives us the pleasing intelligence of his continued good health, which is very cheering, but strange to say he makes no mention of William. When I write, I shall inquire into it.

I desire no lengthy eulogy on his merits, but merely a passing notice, as he *must* be of invaluable service. He acknowledges the receipt of Ma's favor of the 2nd. He has resigned the Sutlership of the Polish Regiment, and accepted that of a Mississippian. He uses a rather strong expression in regard to the Wheat Batallion, and says that it is not *yet* paid off, but "will, this week". He regrets his inability to remit "funds", being aware that we are in great need of them. Capt. Miller sends his kind regards to all. I suppose that it was neglect on Pa's part, in not conveying to us the remembrance in the last letter. It dispelled all my evil thoughts of him. Pa wrote "I did not get your letter in time for Mr. da P. (excuse me, "Capt."), but will attend to it". He refers to his daguerreotype which A. requested him to send by that gent. He writes "There is every prospect of a big battle soon". With what anxiety and trepidation did I conclude it, and then found *no* mention of *my little* note. Was it an oversight? or more probably it dropped out, and its contents were lost to him. I was very much disappointed, as I was certain that he would grant my request. The letter though unexpected was welcome, and when we had finished its perusal, I deposited it in its envelope, and placed it in a position, where it could not fail to arrest A's. attention on her return from school. She came in with a listless air. She sees the missive, the listlessness turns to animation, her eyes brighten,

16. It is likely that he made the trip in search of merchandise wanted by the troops.

and she exclaims "a letter from Pa", and for some time after was buried in its contents. I watched her and saw the smile on her face as she read the part about the "parties", which you are already recognisant of. We were then summoned to dinner. "Potato Pone", and "molasses candy" the order of the day.[17] A. observed the affinity between *Pa's letters* and *molasses candy*. It is understood, that Mr. N. had departed. He is out of employment and his countenance was very woe before — I am so sorry for him. He can obtain a situation as Day policeman, but will not accept it, as I suppose he considers it as not elevated a position, and prefers to be idle. The duties are not at all arduous, and the remuneration is better than nothing. But it is his business, not mine. Ma consented to let me go out, and I left you yesterday at $4^1/_4$ P.M. on the eve of preparing for the expedition. Finished dressing and to our surprise did not melt. It was however a quite pleasant walk. The streets were deserted; we saw no familiar faces, and every step we took, seemed to reëcho the "Gone to the war". Observations upon the never failing themes of interest, Judo, Beauty, and Major Wheat, occupied our attention, and we promenaded with feelings of no more restraint than if had been "Our Bower".[18] Reached Canal St. and found a little more life and individuals displayed, though not as much as is usually visible on *the* Street. Thought we would take a little stroll on "Rue Chartres" "to see what could be seen". Saw many lovely beings, which were the "particular objects of our admiration": Among them must I class Leopold R. [Rosenfield] whom we had the pleasure of saluting in front of his store?[19] Went to Lyme's and found to our sorrow that they would not furnish us with "Burnett's Cocoaine", having none of the article on hand. The clerk kindly offered to put us up a similar preparation, and that we should call for it in a half of an hour, but this being impossible we specified "to-morrow" (to day). I am so sorry that we are deprived of this excellent article. "Oh thou art the cause of this sorrow Abe Lincoln". I agreed to go for it. We passed "dear Judo's" house, and the thoughts which always arise on beholding it, found utterance on our lips. "In that door, with feelings so varied, and with so many different emotions, she had so often entered. Upon those steps her dear feet, had so often rested. Her snowy hand, so oft had touched that knob". There, at that very door, he has uttered words, which have caused her cheeks to burn, her heart to bound with pleasure. Upon that gallery,

17. "Potato Pone" is baked potatoes.
18. "Our Bower" here means their home.
19. The major shopping street, Canal, also marks the beginning of the French Quarter. "Rue Chartres," or Chartres Street, was the location for numerous stores and offices run by Jewish merchants.

thinking of *him,* and watching for *him* alone, she has often stood, and from *that* door, *she* emerged a *bride,* the bride of "Horatio Sprigg"—Thus thought we, and I trod lightly o'er the hallowed ground. Ma had given us a dime, extra funds, and there was a point to be decided; whether to invest at Blineaus, or ride up. It was a great temptation to pass, to think of the delicacies, for which we so longed, which it contained. The pleasure would be so transient, whereas if we would ride, the effect would be beneficial. After giving all advantages and disadvantages due consideration, we resolved to forego the pleasure presented at Blineaus, and being trés fatigué [very tired], ride up. We seated ourselves, not very comfortably for fear of disarranging our scarfs, in the Omnibus; surveyed all surrounding objects, mused upon the advantages of the other sex, the many pleasant haunts to which they could resort, and wile away the time, the perfect ease with which they could promenade, and a thousand other things. Our eyes turned to the "Louisiana Club Room", to the "middle window in the third story". The 'bus is off, we are "en route" for home. On my arrival there I divested myself of *every* thing superfluous, and subsided into a muslin, minus hoops—I was perfectly exhausted. A. was very tired. It is strange as we did not walk much. Ma says it is from want of exercise, which she is continually telling us about.

After supper Ma and F. went over to Mrs. N. and by 8½ I was asleep. Went to bed before ma came home.

4½ P.M. . . The dreaded time is fast approaching. Kipur eve is at hand.[20] It is a penance for our sins, and were the sacrifice not great, the punishment would not be felt. It is a voluntary punishment for our past sins, to expiate them, and on that day pray for the past, present and future. Last Kipur dear Pa was present. It is a night upon which disunited families, with tears in their eyes, think of the times when a happy mother and Father with a joyous, united band of children, broke fast within their parents' house—

May we, as a happy family, celebrate many returns of this sacred holiday. I have but a few moments more to devote to you. I have before me the duty and pleasant task of braiding A's. hair as we will attend synagogue.[21]

20. The evening service that marks the beginning of the holiday of Yom Kippur (Day of Atonement), called Kol Nidre (All our Vows) in Hebrew, was about to begin. It marks the beginning of the fast associated with the holiday. The meal that breaks the fast the next night was, and continues to be, a joyous event among Jewish families.

21. Jews not accustomed to regular synagogue attendance often attend for the Yom Kippur service.

I went down town to day and obtained the Cocoaine. It is more diminutive than Burnett's, but they say of a superior quality. I doubt it, and prefer "our Cocoaine". A. calls me so "good bye". Thank you for your good wishes for me and family and I reiterate them heartily—

Sunday, September 15th, 1861

1 1/4 P.M. . . . . 'Tis over, and I now hasten to acquaint you with an account of the events since last we met. On leaving you, Friday, I braided A's. hair, and proceeded to dress. I was just in the midst of this important action, when Mrs. N. came up. She staid but a few moments, complained of the heat, and went down. About six, we all assembled to take fast; while at table I learned that Lucy had overheard Mrs. N. telling her husband, that "she came down so soon, because Alice looked like she was angry because she came up". I, as well as all, were struck at the absurdity of the idea, and A. determined to relieve Mrs. N. of her erroneous impression. We took fast on preserves and bread, and I was loth to take the last mouthful. We were then in readiness for Mr. & Mrs. N., and Mr. E. by whom we were accompanied to Synagogue. Miss S. seemed very cold, but no mention of the subject was made, until within a few squares of the Synagogue. A. asked her upon what grounds she made the assertion. She said "you looked so, you looked mad", "and *Clara* too". Alice then *tried* to show her the absurdity of the thought, telling her that it was not *her* house, the visit was not made to her, and it was presumption in her to be displeased with it; and *allowing* that her countenance *was* not very pleasant, why should *she* attribute it to the fact of her presence. I was shocked when *my name* and *appearance* was alluded to; but to my sorrow, the conversation was lost upon me, for being escorted by Mr. E., I compelled to discharge the *duty* due to him, and I had to patiently await to some future period, the hearing. We had arrived at the gate, we went our way, she hers. Mr. E. displayed his gallantry in assisting me to rise, as I tumbled up the steps. I did not find him a very agreeable partner, and in fact for the past time, it seems as though he has not extended to us his accustomed cordiality. It rather perplexed us, but "murder will out", and I have something relative to this subject to communicate. The synagogue was crowded and we were unable to obtain our seats, but were perfectly satisfied with the back ones, which we were lucky enough to get, or at least I, for A. succeeded in squeezing into hers. I had the pleasure of being next to Mrs. M., who informed me that "Harry" had not yet received his bundle; he is sick, and every thing. How beautiful did "Flora" look! In imagination, I was carried back to the time when I had last seen her at night, and then my thoughts turned to Loved "Beauty" — I did not allow myself to look at her long for fear of becoming *jealous*.[22] I had the exquisite felicity of beholding him, Mr. Eisner; who provoked me very much by walking home with Alice, for I would not be one of the party, and not wanting him, and considering it an intrusion, I treated him coldly. Mrs. N's. spirits were not exuberant, and the walk home, was conducted with almost silence. Mr. Eisner left us at the gate, and very earnestly asked "What was the matter with Miss Clara"; I briefly said "nothing", and went in the house. A. and I remained down stairs for some time. She told me that to her great surprise and displeasure, she had found that Mr. da Silva had taken her name off of her seat.[23] This is strange, as he has never presented a bill, and it is not the usual time of the year for the sale of seats. A. felt very much chagrined to think that she had claimed it, having no privilege, and surrounded by so many. She will investigate the matter, and I hope arrive at amicable conclusion, as it is most unpleasant to go without having a seat, particularly always being accustomed to one. It is a very mean act, on the parties concerned, as Pa *once* was a valuable member of the congregation.

We then commented upon all the different persons, but no one claimed so large a share as "Flora", and the dear absent cousin — We doubted the individuality of *such* persons, and refused to give them a separate existence — We thought of the many happy hours they have passed together, and the void that was left in Flora's home, when "Beauty" had left her. What dear friends they must have been! and we pictured many scenes, in which they both were actors. "Were each conscious of the other's charms"?, and a thousand other questions, we vainly demanded answers to. We are both very, very silly on the subject of "pretty girls". Alice then told me of

22. "Beauty" is the daughter of Eugenia and Philip Phillips.

23. Da Silva managed the daily affairs of the Sephardic synagogue. He reported his occupation on the 1860 Census as that of Sexton. Da Silva was born in Holland, his wife Ester in the West Indies, and they lived in England before coming to Louisiana. What emerges here is that until recently Clara's father had been able to afford the annual charges for holiday seats that synagogues to this day assess. Furthermore, the girls sat in the same seats from year to year, indicating that their father indeed had been an active member of the congregation. His name appears in the congregation's records on many occasions after its formal beginnings in 1847.

the conversation, and it is impossible for me to paint it to you, as vividly
as did she to Felicie [the name of Alice's diary book]. She and Mrs. N. had
many words, and Alice *assured* her that she was totally at wrong. She
said "I believe it, but you certainly did look angry". This of course led a
person to think that the impression was not yet wholly removed; it aroused
A. and she said, "I know that you never did like me, and you always attribute everything I do and say to the worst motives". Mrs. N. said "I
thought you were always a person of sense, but I am astonished to hear
you talk in that manner". A. replied "Not more astonished than I am to
hear you". The gate was then reached, and they parted. Oh! what is worse
than an unjust accusation! How wrong, how very wrong to judge hastily
and harshly. And yet, how often do *we* do it. How very far was she from
the right, in thinking that she was unwelcome, and we regarded it as an intrusion. It drew us into a long train of thoughts, and a broad field for conversation. We indulged in them both extensively, and about 10$\frac{1}{2}$, went up
stairs. I went to bed, missed my usual drink; it did not annoy me, and I
soon was asleep. I neglected to tell you that I caught a glimpse of the
"Paragon"; and he does not at all correspond with my ideas of him —[24]
Ludie [sp?] treated us both very friendly and she looked very well. Was
honored with a kiss from Olivia, who told us (Mrs. N.) that old Mr. Marks
was dying.[25] It must be a great consolation to him to see the flourishing
family which he leaves. He is generally liked and respected — Yesterday
morning, I awoke about 7., but coaxed myself again to sleep, and was next
awaken by the noise around me, when I ascertained that they all were
up. It was about 9$\frac{1}{4}$, and as A. and I desired to attend early, we commenced
to dress. I was neither hungry nor thirsty, but I had a headache, which I
felt assured would increase in the course of the day. Sally resolved to
fast, but finding it no agreeable matter, she with much hesitancy (for fear
of being laughed at) consented to partake of her breakfast.[26] Ma provided
us with a bottle of hartshorn [a preparation of ammonia used as smelling

24. Clara used "Paragon" more than once, in this case to refer to the groom of one of the pretty
young women in the congregation.

25. Clara here refers to Alexander Marks, whose family worshiped at the same synagogue. Clara
and her family drew on members of the synagogue for friends, and attendance was for her a social occasion. Alexander Marks, Theodore's father, in fact died on September 14th, the night Clara wrote,
at the age of seventy-four. Alexander's parents had come to South Carolina from England, as had
Clara's grandparents. The Marks family were active members of Congregation of Dispersed Judah
and buried their patriarch in the synagogue's cemetery on the outskirts of New Orleans. Alexander
Marks had been for many years a successful commission merchant in the city.

26. On the day of Yom Kippur, adults are expected to fast. Children of Sallie's age (eight) were not
required to go without food, but she fasted for a short while. Her fast ended with a late breakfast.

salts] which proved of great benefit to us. Accomplished the weary task of dressing and I, at A's. request, went over to see if Mrs. N. was ready. She was but in the first stage, so I told her it was useless to wait, so I left. A. did not go over, not because she was exactly *mad*, but she did not feel like it. I am sorry now that I went, for as A. always accompanies me, it did look very decided and Mrs. N. seemed rather displeased. She told me that it would not take her long to dress, and she would be there, shortly after me. After a hot, disagreeable walk (and pitying those who had so much further than we) we arrived at the Synagogue, and with much trepidation ascended the stairs. "Our seats" were occupied, and we must needs content ourselves with those adjoining Mrs. Marks. I was indifferent where they were, so that we were not separated. I then devoted myself to holy things. To the atonement of my sins, and through the politeness of Mrs. M. who lent me her book, I was able to read the prayers for the day.[27] We interchanged bottles [smelling salts to ease the fast], and the contents of neither fully satisfied me. My headache was intense, but, I did not murmur. There was much running out, which I consider shameful, and A. remarked that "only something of great importance could induce her to go out". It may have been only imagination, but the seats were very uncomfortable, and far inferior to the "front row". Mrs. M. and I were conversing a little, giving our opinions of the pretty girls, etc. I felt like going to Flora, asking her to use of my bottle, and telling her "Though I have never spoken to you, yet I love you dearly". But delicacy forbade it. A. said to me, previous to Mrs. N's. arrival "Maybe Mrs. N is at home, and ma and she are having a dispute". I had already thought the same thing as she was very late and did not come 'till about 12½. About 2½ Sallie came, and I was very much astonished—Josh accompanied her. By degrees some persons went, and my situation became more comfortable, as I was then enabled to recline on the end of the bench. My headaches still continued, and the flavor of something nice was wafted on the winds to my olfactory nerves, but failed to destroy my equanimity. Saw many familiar faces for "Kippur brings together all the Congregation", and all looked very well— Sallie told A. that ma said "To treat Miss S. *as usual*"; and then our suspicions were confirmed—But A. needed no such admonition for she bore no unfriendly feelings towards her. Mr. Eisner was there, and seemed very pious. The day was very warm and fans were in constant use; we would have been lost had it not been for our fine one which Ma had provided

---

27. It is strange that the Solomons did not have prayer books.

us with. Mrs. N. proposed to remain until after the singing of "El Nora", and about 5³/₄ we started for home, Kippur almost over.²⁸ Mr. N. was in Synagogue. His mother is very sick, and he said that it was for her sake he went; as she is unable to attend. The latest letter acquainted him of her illness.²⁹ Mrs. N. left us at the corner, and I was delighted to get home. She would return after she had undressed. Ma then told us that she and Mrs. N. had *had* it, but could not tell us the particulars then. A. and I then disrobed, and feeling very bad descended. Mr. and Mrs. N. and Josh soon came in, and about 6¹/₂ we broke fast on a glass of water, and a few moments after took supper. It was very nice, and I enjoyed it very well. None were sick, and Mrs. N. was *unusually* well; better than she has been for years. After supper Cousin S. came in with his usual hilarity, and greeted the assembly, particularizing no one, for Mrs. N. and he are not yet on speaking terms. He partook of some fish, which he pronounced "excellent". I was again myself, and felt as though nothing had happened. I could not realize that it was over. The longest day *must* end. Cousin S. said that he had received Pa's letter, which did not come by hand, and was detained some time. He promised to bring it up this afternoon for our perusal. They left about 9¹/₂, and we quietly seated down, whilst Ma related to us *the* event of the day. Mrs. N. was offended because A. did not come over in the morning, and said that she had determined to forget it. She said that A. was too haughty and ceremonious, she considered herself offended and Mr. Elburger did also. A. and I bade ma proceed, and we listened with breathless anxiety. "You remember", said ma, "when we were to Mrs. N's. the other night (a week ago) and when Leopold was there, hands were crossed, and Mr. E. said to A. 'I hope Miss Alice that we will celebrate your wedding', and A. said 'I want none of your good wishes, sir'". Mr. E. became offended and considered it disrespectful. Another misconstruction. Words, forgotten with the very breath with which they were uttered, should be construed into an insult. A. was very much grieved, for his superior age and intelligence demanded respect. A. meant that she was obliged to him for his wishes, but she did not wish that they would produce the desired effect. Her words may have appeared abrupt, but the insult was wholly unintentional. He said that he liked A. very much, but found her too haughty. Now then, the cause of his late coldness was explained. Mrs. N. said that A. was too ceremonious and proud, and said "there are many of the

28. "El Nora" is a prayer toward the end of the Yom Kippur liturgy of particular importance in the Sephardic ritual.
29. Sam's mother was in Charleston.

same opinion". "Does she think her proud because she treated Ludie as she did? because she does not speak to Mrs. Harris?" inquired ma. One word brought on another; ma told her of the many slights which were offered us, when she was a little better off in worldly goods, and doubtless awakened feelings in her breast, which for some time have been slumbering. Acts, the unjustness of which, she too well knew. It seemed to hurt her, when ma told her of the many times and circumstances under which Pa had been neglected. Many actions were resorted to, of which possibly Mrs. N. thought we were ignorant. In her heart, she can but acknowledge the truth of what Ma said, for she knows, that when surrounded by other company, into what insignificance ours was, and there is no disputing the fact, that time and again we were slighted. Her conscience was guilty and she felt the rebuke sharply. They had quite an altercation, and I regret my inability to detail the points of it. Perhaps it is better, for all angry feelings or unfriendly ones have been laid bare, and it is wrong to hide them, and have a bitter rancorous feeling at heart.

For myself, I am glad, as I have often wished that a fitting opportunity would present itself, to bring to light all disguised sentiments. Ma told us plenty which astonished us, and it seemed as though it were a never failing theme for subjects for conversation. Ma had forgotten much, but informed as well as her capacities for remembrance allowed. How do the great events of our lives hang upon mere incidents. How much arose from the circumstance of a face's appearing a little graver than usual. Ma went to bed, and A. and I remained some time after, discussing the strange events of the day. We then bolted our mansion and after the fashion of Pauline, in the "Lady of Lyons", went to our couches, but no one to wish that guardian angels would watch over our slumbers. Thanked God, that the day was over.

I read the paper this morning, and was much amused on reading "the resuscitation of Klubs", and a letter from "Artemus Ward".[30] About 11. o'clock James brought us up a letter from Pa. It was of the 10th instant, and very brief. He says, "I will leave in a few hours, for Manassas, accompanied by Capt. Miller, and will write you the day after my arrival". This, with the assurance of his continued good health, comprised the contents.

He was evidently in a great hurry, as it was enclosed in no envelope.

---

30. Artemus Ward is the pen name for Charles Farrar Browne. Browne used the pseudonym to pen letters for newspapers that commented on current affairs in an uneducated version of New England speech.

This morning Alice wrote a note of apology to Mr. Elburger, as her conduct demanded one.

Monday, September 16th, 1861

6 $^1/_4$ A.M. .... Yesterday afternoon Cousin S. brought the letter; it contained nothing at all of any importance. Before he left, Mr. Eisner's unwelcome form was in the house, and of course Cousin S. did not remain much longer. He said that he would probably come back. I did not wish to see Mr. E. so went out of the room—A. called me in and he begged me to tell him in what manner he had offended me, and he said that the visit was for the special purpose of ascertaining—I told him that he had in no manner offended me, but he appeared doubtful, and I did not blame him, for my conduct must indeed have appeared strange. He was unable to account for the manner in which I treated him on Friday night, and said "If I had done anything to hurt your feelings, I would never show my face again"—

I do not like the man; he is an inoffensive creature, and a half hour in his company could be tolerated, but, he stays too long. I will conquer my dislike, and treat him friendly. Ma gave him a letter to mail, which she had written during the day to Pa; and about 8. o'clock the gent took his wished for departure. Mrs. N. had sent word for us to come over, but we declined the pleasure, knowing that her niece [Mrs. Harris?] was there. Cousin S. did not come, and as no one else *could*, we retired early. We were informed that Mr. Marks was dead. I did not state that Pa wrote that Mr. H. [Hitchcock] was sick. I hope nothing serious. Well, my friend, "The dreaded time is fast approaching"—I am going to School this afternoon, and nothing trivial can now be offered as an excuse. I have on repeated occasions expressed my antipathy to the "arrangement", and my wishes that "Mr. Lusher had never been Born", etc., etc.; but "must" is an uncommon word to none.

So to School, I must go. I should be delighted if Alice could go, but it would be too great a tax on her, and too great a neglect towards ma. Being confined *all* day, would be too much. She *once* entertained an idea of joining, but has now totally abandoned it. But she has promised to study with me, and this is a great solace to me. She has *promised*, but will she fulfil it. When my attendance at school shall be an institution will the many pleasant afternoons of late, and the many vows of continued and uninterrupted love and affection be forgotten? Nous verrons—

5 $^1/_2$ *P.M.* . . . . "Dearest and best" of friends, *I have been to school.* About
2$^1/_2$. I began to dress, and how vividly did it recall to my mind my happy
school life of last Winter, and how unfavorably contrasted was *now* with
then. I could not realize that there *was* a time, when the pleasures of Thursday
afternoon would be marred by the thought that "There would be no school
for *me* till Monday". I arrayed myself in my "pink" and was "all done" by
3 o'clock. Eat dinner, and with "a long lingering, look" at A. who was cozily seated writing, I vanished out of the "back gate", à la Mrs. Slocomb,
Moody, etc. The sun was intensely warm, and my headache very bad. As
I drew within sight of the gate my pulse quickened and my emotions could
not have been greater, had I expected to emerge from its portals — a *wife.*
I summoned all my courage, and in a few moments was in my "old room".
No smiles of recognition from familiar and welcoming faces greeted me,
but oh! what a dreary waste. No sweet Mollie Leech, no dignified Ada
Hodges, no — Lizzie Hillman. I prepared myself to confront Mrs. Shaw,
but to my astonishment found Nettie invested with the superiority. She
greeted me cordially, and told me that Mrs. S. was detained home, by the
sickness of her baby.

I then went to Miss Benedict's, ascertained the lessons for the succeeding
afternoon, and to my sorrow, found that they pursued a study in a book
which I do not possess. I wonder how I will get it. Go to Bloomfield and
Steel? She seemed pleased to see me, and after deriving the necessary
information, I bade her "good bye", as I promised A. not to be gone long.
Miss Mitchell came up, kissed me, and said "Oh! I am so glad you have
come back". *That* assurance was not conducive to my happiness. As I was
leaving, I glanced wistfully at the "big room", which was resounding with
the voices of the "Seniors". Ma was surprised to see me back so soon,
but I explained. I was still suffering from my head. Ma allowed me the
privilege to take a plum, which I found to have lost none of their usual
attractions. I went over to Miss S's. She was dressing for the purpose of
going to Mrs. Marks's, a visit of condolence to Theodore [the son]. Josh
said "Cousin Clara, are you going"? I told him, "No, that I once asked
his mother to tell me when she was going but she did not". She contradicted this statement, but I was confident of it. She said, "I went to
spend the day, and I thought it useless to ask you, as I thought you wanted
to pay a visit". I reminded that the first visit paid after my request was
not the one to which she alluded. But I was fearful of another dispute, so
I did not allow it to become an argument, so I said nothing more. She walked
to the corner, and said that if she was home early, she would come over;

and here am I at home. I have something so sad to relate. Ellen mashed her toe so severely this morning, by the falling of *two heavy flag stones* upon it. She received it through her own disobedience and wildness, and has to bear the suffering. She acted quite contrary to ma's orders, by leaving Josie standing and she, playing. It will be a good lesson to her. She pulled off her shoe, and I received a severe shock, by seeing blood on her stocking. Poor child, it was indeed painful. We applied many remedies among them lint, which is excellent. It bled freely. She has been unable to do anything, but has amused J. by playing with her. She must be careful, as the result may be dangerous. I hope that it will soon be well.

Ma and I received another great shock, by the receipt of a dispatch — you can imagine our feelings, being not uneasy at all and not even expecting a letter, to hear the words "a dispatch". Ma tore it open with inhuman haste, and before perusing it, I had not time to think, but only to be alarmed. It was as follows. "Arrived from Manassas. Will send some money in a few days. Particulars by mail". We were soon restored. It was the 16th from Richmond! Up to how late a date, had we received intelligence of him — The news was very cheering, as ma is again out of funds. Pa has money, and *how* he must waste it. In fact, the dispatch was unnecessary. A's salary is not due till Saturday, and Ma asked Mr. N. if he could not get it advanced, but he finds it impossible without a great discount, which Ma is unwilling to lose. He came in a few moments after Ma had received the telegraph. He says that times are awful, and he, being out of employment, is very much distressed. He is unable to know what he will do. I am so sorry for him.

Tuesday, September 17th, 1861

8¼ P.M. . . . We have just repaired from the dining room, where we have been indulging in bread and molasses, and wishing for one of those nice fish suppers, of which nothing but the memory of them, now remains.

Last evening A. and I took our accustomed walk and came in, as the gas light illuminated our parlors. Cousin S. came for a short while. As he stood at the door, previous to entering, I could not for an instant, divine who it was — A thousand images of "Gus Leovies", passed through my mind. The suspense was short-lived, for in a second, I recognized the familiar form. He had the impertinence to say that he was going home to get his supper. We accused him of being heartless, etc. He was relating extravagant things of Little Fanny [his daughter]! I wonder if he thinks we believe him. Before we went to bed Mr. and Mrs. N. honored us. She told us the particulars of Mr. M's. death. Olivia [Marks], and all were in a flourishing condition. They made a very short stay as Mr. N. was sleepy.

This morning I read the paper, and to my discomfort found that *Ellen had not come.* Oh! What a day, what a day before me — Ellen's duties devolved upon me, and they were by no means agreeable. I was uneasy, for E. may have been worse.

Notwithstanding Ma's limited means, she could not withstand the wish of having some shrimps. They were fine, but one objection — the quantity. "Came gentle thoughts, came gentle thoughts of Pa". Miss S. has a quantity of work, (drawers) and Ma took some of them to day. They are not much work, but Ma only made three pair, as Josie was so *very* bad, we found it impossible to sew, but in *ordinary* times we could make about 10 pairs. Josie missed E. and was very troublesome. She is not a good child, nor smart. Mrs. Deegan was here and said that E. was in much pain. Ma proposed for her to come here to-morrow, and Dr B. to be sent for. I hope that she will come. She related to her mother the correct circumstances of her injury. I knew she would, as she is very truthful. About 12. to day Mr. N. stopped in, and said that he mentioned the circumstance to Leopold, who offered to advance the money. Mr. N. made no agreement, but stated the facts to ma, who politely, but decidedly refused to accept of the favor. I think it was presumptuous, Ma regards it in an altogether different light. I would endure much before placing ourselves under any obligation from *him.* Mr. N. evinced his skill in carpentry, by fixing the cistern. A. wrote me a note to day, one of the items of which were "To night will celebrate the nuptials of Dr Packwood and Miss Sarah Hinckley". An invitation was not extended to me. My best wishes attend them for their future lives, and every day serve to strengthen the ties which have bound them together. It is all over, now, and my pretty friend Sarah is hailed by the matronly title of "Mrs. Dr Packwood". Cherish well your prize, you envied man! In the course of time, I may be enabled to acquaint you of the "noble couple's" whereabouts. A. endeavored to gleam as much as possible, but was successful only so far in ascertaining that they would immediately proceed to their mansion on Philip Street. Mrs. Abbott will be present. A. "told to me as twas told to her" that the High and Normal Schools are to give a 'Concert matinée', the proceeds to be devoted to some patriotic purpose. There will be many solos sung; and Belle Harby will take her part in the good work by singing one. May success attend her. Mr. Rogers was the instigator of, (I hope) the grand scheme. It will take place at Lyceum Hall. More anon. I did not go to school this afternoon, as I was sick, in fact, I have been *very* indisposed all day. A fatality, a fatality! I shudder to go, as something always prevents me. This afternoon A. and Ma went to Mrs. N's. When they came home, A. complained of a very severe pain in her shoulder; I was as usual, complaining, and we laughed much at the many ailments to which ma was a patient listener. May our ills never be greater. Ma observed that notwithstanding, *all the bread vanished*. Where did it go? What became of it? "Ellen" is now here. I mean Ellen Blood—A constant unchanging friend. She is gone now, and it is with great difficulty that I now rise from my chair to go to bed.

Wednesday, September 18th, 1861

$8^{1}/_{4}$ P.M. . . . I arrived safe up stairs last night, and after A.'s usual "good night, Clara, must I wake you up in the morning", I retired. Lucy lowered the gas, bade me "good night", & as usual went out. Before the conclusion of my prayers, I was asleep. "Then, in lands of dream did I hear, the voice of him, so very dear". I dreamed that I, in company with Pa, Alice, and Ada Hodges, was on board of a steamboat taking passage for some distant place. I was sitting on a sofa, by a window when some drunken men accosted me. They ran after me, and I fled from their pursuit. I succeeded in evading them, and was so exhausted that I fell down, and the shock woke me. "What sounds were those that fell on my ear"? In a moment, I was out of bed, in Ma's room. I heard strange sounds, which I thought proceeded from Lucy's room. I awoke ma, exclaiming, "ma, I hear some one screaming, I think it is Lucy". Ma, Alice and Fanny turned simultaneously out of bed, an incident which laid the foundation for much subsequent laughter. Ma went to her room, and L. said that she had been suffering all night from cramps, (which I don't believe), and would not come and tell us for fear of frightening us. This was very foolish, as she ought to have known, that she would frighten us more, by the manner in which she acted. Knowing that we could be of no assistance, we remained in our room. Ma administered all available remedies, which afforded some relief. The moon and stars were shining bright, and I was astonished to learn that it was $4^1/_2$ o'clock. I went to bed, and was awakened by the sounds of the 6. o'clock bell. I dressed, went down, and found ma, (who had not been to bed) superintending the affairs of the kitchen. L. was much better, but ma was assisting her. Ellen had not come, so I assumed the responsibility of minding Josie. I appeased her appetite by feeding her with anticipated plate of hominy. I had settled myself for a disagreeable morning when Ellen's welcome face was seen. Her mother was with her. J. seemed glad to see her, and I willingly resigned her to abler and more *patient* hands. Her foot had almost ceased to pain her. Mrs. D. left and went directly to Mr. W.'s, to endeavor to obtain some work. We then eat breakfast which seemed unusually nice, from the fact that it had submitted to Ma's skilful hands. Dr B. came. He pronounced E.'s injury a severe one, and ordered the application only of cold water as a preventive to inflamation. He said that it would not be entirely healed before *two* months. He also prescribed for me. My headache has been intense all day. While the Dr was here, we received a "dispatch", and of course, was the cause of much alarm to us. It was the 17th from Richmond, received N.O. the 18th. The wires were not in working order yesterday. It was briefly as follows, "I am well. Will write to-morrow. All right". He doubtless did it with the idea of dispelling any fears, but how differently did it effect its purpose. It gave rise to many suspicions, the act of telegraphing two days in succession. Ma conjectured that he was sick, but I think the most probable thing is that he has been disappointed in money, and will *not write,* until he can forward some. Our minds would have been much more tranquil, but for its receipt. We must not make "Trifles light as air", foundations for disquietude. I forgot one sentence of the dispatch, "I am very busy" — This , combined with his averseness to writing, would warrant the dispatch. But it is great extravagance. We will put our trust in God. I pray that "all is well", and am anxiously anticipating a letter. Josie has been very peevish. The child is teething. Ellen, though unable to do much is of invaluable assistance in quelling the restlessness of the "little stranger", a pleasure for which I have no decided taste. L. has been quite well. I did not go to school this afternoon, as I was *too sick.* A. told me that Mrs. A. had attended the wedding, and all particulars that were elicited from her were that "the bride looked beautiful". Don't every one? Ma and I applied ourselves assiduously to our work, and with a great exertion, from which I am now suffering, made nine pair, thus completing the dozen. Mrs. N. sent Ma *an-*

other dozen, but she peremptorily refused to take more. It is a perfect imposition to give only a dollar! I won't sew on them. Were they for our "brave soldier boys", I would work unremittingly and with pleasure, but I decline doing them for Mr. Weilman, and him to realize a great profit. Ma says that the women should all rise, and rebel against the *mean* proceeding; but many strive hard and are glad of the small pittance, but it is surely only those, who are necessitated—

God be thanked that we are not. Mrs. N. has a supply of 4 dozen, and says that she only does them from necessity. How Pa would laugh. To toil so unceasingly for *one* dollar, on which *he* places *so* little value. We were sewing this afternoon, so pardon my seeming neglect. To our surprise, we had a drizzly, dreary, dull, drowsy afternoon; and as Mrs. N. remarked "It is raining for Sucot". To-morrow is a holiday. We do not observe it strictly, so the children go to school. It always happens five days after Kippur and there is generally a "Sucot festival". Feast after famine, and on the occasion it is always known to rain. I have never been to one.

I did not dress until dark, and that you must know is at $6^{1}/_{4}$. Yes, friend, at $6^{1}/_{4}$. the gas was lit. Well do I remember the times when I would indite [write at] 7 P.M., and write with perfect ease, without the aid of a light. "The melancholy days have come, the saddest of the year". When at school, the short afternoons are *very* acceptable. Ma has raised sufficient funds to *exist* on 'till Saturday, when A. will surely receive her salary. It will be part in Confederate Notes, but as the banks by order of Gov. Moore have stopped all specie payment, they will be taken at par. In making this recommendation the Governor assumed a high moral and official responsibility, a responsibility much higher morally than officially. These Treasury notes will become the prevailing currency, but one result will be attended with much inconvenience, which is the scarcity of coin of small denominations. This will be certain to invite the remedy of small notes, and nothing is more calculated to obviate the evil than for our banks to issue notes of smaller denominations than $5, on the same conditions as those stipulated by the Governor.

Mrs. N. came in a short while ago—She tells us that she left "Sammy and Mr. E. home, and ran over". Is this in any degree pointed? Did she mean to insinuate that the "honored, offended gent" would not come to see us? It distresses us greatly, and I had given him credit for much more sense. If he considered himself offended, a note of apology ought to cause him to show that all remembrances of it were obliterated—May his shadow never be less. I like him very well; probably he feels ashamed. Mrs. N.

heard from a gentleman who has just returned from the North, *"that they are bent upon coming here. There is nothing to prevent them,* as we *are* not and *can* not be well fortified"*. The height of their ambition is to get N.O.!! Let them try it. All troops, (for some wise purpose) have been ordered to vacate Ship Island. I hear that they have fears of being attacked, and their forces being not of sufficient strength, they may become prisoners.

F. has been entertaining us by the recital of the "Battle of Manassas", a piece possessing many merits. The verdict rendered by Miss Cav. on a previous recitation was "I have never heard anything said better". Quite a compliment, considering "the source from whence it came".

Belle Grant received a letter from Charles H....y. He sends his "kind regards to Miss Alice and Clara Solomon". Much obliged —

Thursday, September 19th, 1861

1¹/₂ P.M. . . . . If we were made responsible in writing for every moment of our lives, what a sinful waste of time, would be laid bare to our sight. With what fearfulness and alarm would our eyes recoil, as we scanned the pages. In a great degree we are responsible for our respective standing and position in society. How many hours are wasted which could be so advantageously employed in the accumulation of useful knowledge. Intelligence and worth are scarcely ever passed unnoticed, and the man whose aim is to rise superior to his fellow creatures is respected. "All men are born free and equal", and endowed with certain faculties, the improvement & cultivation of which, enable one to attain an ascendancy over another. If then every hour can further this noble purpose why neglect the opportunity? Why is not the desire for improvement predominant in every breast? Why does not success crown the efforts of all? Ah! there is a secret. Perseverance, perseverance — Ma was up very early and we breakfasted about 7¹/₂. I did not hear A.'s "get up Clara", and consequently overslept myself. I read the paper, and was rejoiced when E.'s familiar voice was heard, and Alice and I agreed that she was one of the most important personages in the house. We had a nice dish of shrimps for breakfast. Just think, 25 cts. worth! but, as usual Lucy had been imposed upon. A.'s hair was not combed as usual previous to breakfast; but she completed her toilet after; and left for school, with a headache. Oh! mine still clings to me. The Dr's attention was again called to me, and he said that I had a severe cold in my head, and recommended Sedative Water (as if I ain't used out nearly a bottle). He came in ejaculating "Good morning, ma'm, how are all your sick people, cripples included". He is an estimable man, and will not be forgotten by Pa.

The two rooms were cleaned "thoroughly through", and I sustained my part in the noble work. "The new broom swept well". I was on the gallery, and Mr. Elburger passed, and I sympathized with him, for I knew that he *must* have had a stiff neck, as his head was very much inclined in the direction of the opposite side of the street. I suppose he will not *honor* us even with a nod of recognition. What a deplorable state of affairs!! My work was done, and I was very tired; from that period my time has been at my disposal, and it would be difficult for me to say how it has been employed. Wasted, wasted. Mrs. N. stopped in on her way to Synagogue — She was accompanied by Josh, who went with pious object "of getting some sweet bread". He promised if possible to bring some for Rosa. We did not sew to day. Ma has been crying over the "Lady of the Isle", but I was not so fortunate. I have finished "Evelina", and my expectations were not realized — "De gustibus non disputandum". I feasted on some parts of the "Sunny South", a work which in my opinion becomes doubly attractive at every perusal. I can never tire of it. I do love dear "Kate Conyngham". Will our paths ever cross? I wrote A. a note, partly "truth" and partly "fiction". In imagination I was in Paris, seated by Judo, writing to "Mrs. Rothschild", with whom "Beauty" was spending some time — How high can we soar in the realms of fancy — Ma and I retired at 12. "with our usual dignity and partook of a few shrimps". Mrs. N. came from S. and came over. She said that the table was not well supplied, and brought a loaf of bread. It was real bread, and nothing but bread. For a wonder it did not rain, so as to break up the party, but Mrs. N. was obliged to hurry home, as the clouds were very threatening. In a few moments it rained, and has not yet ceased.

5 1/2 P.M. . . . Rain, Rain! I fear another rainy spell has commenced — Beautiful morning and miserable afternoons — A repetition of the programme of the past weeks. It has been raining incessantly — The children got home in good order; before they came, ma was relating to me the principal items of the "Lady of the Isle", as I don't intend reading it.

At dinner A. told me to guess who walked some of the way to school with her. I named many, and ma exclaimed "Mr. Murphy", and was correct. She had a few moments conversation with him, inquired about Pa, and they parted. This is the "homme" for whom A. and I, on repeated occasions, expressed a decided "penchant". Alice and I are side by side, (sitting in a position to which Mr. E. has objected), in our spacious "dining room", and with great forbearance, submit to the combined noise of all the youngsters. I did not go to school this afternoon. The rain has now ceased, but the prospect is not *very* pleasing. My thoughts now turn to Rutledge, and the vivid descriptions which "*loved Julia*" gave of the twilight of a rainy afternoon. Will my evening be spent like hers? A most delightful time with the "beau ideal" of his race. I will not believe that they are but imaginary. Not earthly beings like "Judo, Beauty, and Flora". Where are they now. How widely may their paths sever, and in what different occupations may they *now* be employed. "Would I were with them". To night, two weeks ago, "Capt." and "Gus", were to see us. I wonder where "D" is. How long has the time seemed. "Hospital report". Lucy almost better; Ellen recovering; Clara, the same.

Friday, September 20th, 1861

5. o'clock P.M. . . . Another rainy, rainy afternoon! The children have not been home from School long. Ma, and I was just going to add I, was quite alarmed, thinking that some accident may have befallen them, but I knew that they would remain to the last, and that neither actually had sense to come while it stopped raining — It had ceased from 3 to 3½ and I knew that if they had wished, they could have seized the opportunity, as S. arrived safe. We eat dinner, and ma sent Lucy to ascertain the cause of their detention, as they were provided with "rain protectors". Ma sent Lucy, and she arrived with the intelligence that they were playing the piano, and dancing. Ma was incensed at their thoughtlessness. The ladies soon after made their entrée. I had finished dinner, and a duty was incumbent upon me. Peace was restored when I came in. A. and F. were telling of the fine times they had with Ella Howell, Mary Ames, Annie McLain, who are gifted with fine voices. A. was playing, and merry feet kept time to the music. The gift of song! How priceless a one is it, and yet by some possessed of it, how little appreciated. I would bless *Him,* were I gifted with the power of charming others by the music of my voice, and also for my own gratification and pleasure. I am not so blessed in *any* degree. A. told us that poor little Leonora Levy was dead!! I was much shocked and grieved by the very sad intelligence. She was taken sick on Sunday with the pernicious fever, and at

$12^1/_2$ last night, her little spotless soul, winged its flight to another world. It is a mournful casualty, and it will leave a void which will take years to fill. She was A.'s pupil at one time, and she represents her as a good, lovable child, and one possessed of uncommon intellect. We are not on visiting terms with the family, but they have my heart-felt sympathies. Dear, little Leonora! Thou art far removed from sin and care, and art now with your "sister angels", chanting on strains of divine melody, the praises of Him, who "taketh as well as giveth". Heaven has opened for thee its ever opened gates. The day has been very gloomy, and I have felt worse than ever. Ma and I made six pair of drawers before 12. o'clock. She had nothing to do, and thought she would take them to assist Mrs. N. We then volunteered gratuitously, two pair more, and without *any* inconvenience completed eight pair. This is quite an improvement. I do not know how Mrs. N. has progressed. I did not sew much. My head ached so violently my temples throbbed, and I could find no relief. Will we ever part. Josie has been quite cross and she and I had some few disputes. You may know I was sick as I eat no lunch. I was quite hungry at dinner; at which there was nothing extraordinarily enticing. L. got no meat and we made a shift dinner. As I write the pain almost blinds me, but I won't neglect *you*.

A. and I are in our *imagined* "wing", "the dining room". The rays of the setting sun, for one moment, have gilded the Church steeple. All again is gloom! Last night, Ma went to Mrs. N.'s. We waited for her; she was home at $9^1/_2$. I occupied my time, by glancing over the work of "many short, and unconnected sentences". A. was paying her devoirs to Felicie, and was not remarkably agreeable or conversant. For a short time "Lucy Crofton" fascinated me, but the fascination was short lived. We breakfasted early, and up to the present time, my head has not ceased to ache. I got through with my "work", and contrary to Ma's commands, I persisted in not lying down. Ma has ordered a fresh supply of "Lenna" [sp?] — I dreamed last night that Charlotte B. and her mother came to see us — She said that she had long had the desire, and found it impossible to conquer it, so came. I was delighted to see her, and as I gazed upon her, I thought that she was one of Earth's fairest creatures. How I would wish for the fulfilment of the dream. But alas! they go by contrary — "Shades of evening", etc.

Sunday, September 22nd, 1861

11 o'clock A.M. . . . How are you? I am quite a stranger, but as you see, I am again at my "post". I was awakened this morning by an unusual commotion, but, being very sensible on first awaking, I accounted for it immediately. Ma had determined to go to Market, and she and F. were in a stage of preparation. L.'s services also being in requisition, I volunteered to dress Rosa. After completing the *very agreeable* duty, I prepared to "go and do likewise" to myself. Descended, and found that Ma had departed, and A. was in charge of Josie, E. having not yet come; her welcome form was soon visible, and A. and I read together the paper, which contained no interesting matter. A poem of Randall's, which puzzled both, graced its columns; and this pleasure was soon ended. About $7^1/_2$ Ma came, looked quite fatigued. She doubtless was, as it has that effect upon those unused to the unpleasant. A. and I both declined Ma's invitation to accompany her, as we both knew that we would be "unfit for duty" during the day. Ma is not very well posted in marketing, as during the whole of their wedded life its performance has devolved upon Pa. A. and I have often declared that we would marry no man "who would not go to Market". It is, in point of fact, his duty. The breakfast, which was very nice, was not served up till late, and for some time A. and I have been talking (foolishly) as ever. The fish and shrimps were excellent, as our *once-filled* plates bore testimony. "A change has come o'er the temperature of the weather" since last we met. The dark, sombre clouds are dispelled and the bright rays of the glorious sun illumine the blue vault of Heaven. The cool, embracing winds of Autumn have displaced the warm, sultry air, and we cannot realize the rapid flight of summer. Winter is at the threshold, but its approach is not heralded with bright hopes and joyous anticipations. The day is one calculated for reflection, and our thoughts naturally turn to our present condition. The dreaded war, its incalculable horrors, the privations and suffering to which so many will be subjected, stare us in the face. And with these gloomy forebodings, can thoughts of pleasure and enjoyment intrude themselves. On previous occasions how many hearts have bound with joy at the idea of participating in the enjoyments presented by our "gay city". But now, how different! A deep sorrow is brooding, and "He is gone to the war" is the key to the subdued mirthfulness. At all times I dislike Winter, but under existing circumstances, language fails to express itself.[31]

---

31. New Orleans, known for its frivolity, had in six months become a sad and quiet place.

The subject is a prolific one, and Oh! God! more and more each day do I crave and wish for the gift of speech. It cannot be acquired. I have longings and desires for other blessings, but they all sink into insignificance, and the desire amounts to naught, when compared with the depth of earnestness with which I exclaim, oh! 'the eloquence of Language!' How inestimable a gift.[32] Can I refrain from murmuring when I consider that in no one thing am I perfect; or do I excell in any art. On such lovely dreamy days, are my feelings saddest. When next we greet the Winter, may we be a *united,* happy family. The words last wrote on Friday were in the dark, but I will be no apologist. I dressed *rather* quickly and when I went down, the gas was lit. Ella H. had lent A. a song book, and ma was attempting to play some pieces, and on the grand occasion lit a gas in the front room.[33] *This* suggested to our minds the idea of a *party*—and the transition to a *wedding* was easily accomplished, and A. and I subsided into one of our long talks. The piano had ceased to amuse ma, and she had retired to the sofa, and naturally to sleep, so A. and I were sole participants in the conversation. We wondered if the marriage of any of the Miss Solomons, would ever be celebrated beneath the glare of these lights, and in the self-same rooms. I *said* that *I* would aspire to grander apartments, but I don't *believe* that I *meant* it. For wherever it should be, I would be contented if surrounded by the smiling faces of the loved family. We then mused upon the *impossibility* of any's getting married, considering the limited circle of our acquaintances. We consoled ourselves with the thought that *all* could not be "old maids", and the veil which obscured our future, and the many unexpected events which in a limited space of time, decide our destiny, of which Mrs. Harris' life is a glowing illustration [rags to riches through marriage]. And then, could *any* subject be broached in which Judo, Beauty and Flora, the angelic Triumvirate, did not claim attention. Talked of the priceless jewel, which Mr. S had secured, and the priceless ones which Beauty and Flora's Lords would possess. We then laid many plans, formed many conjectures, made many wishes, the realizations and fulfilments of which would be contrary to the order of Nature. A perfect monomania has seized A. and I, so bear with us willingly for it *may* pass away. It is one of the wishes of our hearts that we may, one day, be on terms of intimacy with our "beau ideals" of feminine loveliness, and I may add virtue, for hearts

32. The irony is that Clara's use of language in the diary is remarkable for someone her age.

33. The front room, housing the piano, was rarely used at night and ordinarily not illuminated. The Solomons used gas sparingly, on this occasion for an unusual moment when Emma was able to put her anxiety and loneliness aside.

and souls, enshrined in such lovely caskets, are worthy of them. It is harassing to think that they, to whom our thoughts so often revert, and about
whom so many speculations are made, are ignorant of our existence. Other
of Earth's fairest creatures, claimed a share, and of course, Mrs. Dr Packwood
was not forgotten. "Mrs. Julian Bartlett", and a host of others, arose before us; and in all probability we would have been talking *now*, had not Ma's
"time to go to bed" — greeted our ears. I suppose we thought so too, as we
went. I had to make great haste with my toilet, in order to arrive in time
for breakfast, for I was a delinquent in rising. Notwithstanding I did not
feel well, I ate very heartily. We did not attend synagogue, as A. had not
seen Mr. da S. [da Silva, the Sexton] and a greater consideration, she had
to go to obtain the long anticipated salary. F. was to accompany her, but
did not, through some misunderstanding in which A. was very much, and
in fact the only one, to blame; she did not: so A. went unattended, as it was
too late for me to dress. She was not gone long. The money consisted of
a $10 on the Bank and two twenties, in Confederate Notes, the first which
I had ever seen. Their appearance is not strikingly different from ordinary
notes, though the paper is of a far inferior nature. It was never more acceptable. After A. had been home for some time, and had related all she
had seen, she thought she would pay Mrs. N. a call, and Ma requested her
to return to her the two (chapters) volumes of the "Lady of the Isle [Lake?]".
My visitor, Headache, still honored me, and I was very dull. Ma sent Mrs.
N. the $10 note to deduct what was owing to her; she had no change and
was unable to obtain any, as people absolutely *refuse* to give specie for
paper. A perfect mania has seized the community, and there is a dearth of
silver money, and those who possess it, will *not* part with it. She sent it back,
and Ma now has it.[34] A. returned about 2 o'clock, played a few tunes and
I then braided her hair. I did not succeed to *my* satisfaction. Something
must be the matter. I can not do it as well as formerly, but I live in hopes.
Anyway that it is fixed, she looks well. She said that Mrs. N. had noticed
that there was a page of the "Lady of the Isle" wanting. *I* was already aware
of this unpleasant fact, and it distressed me greatly, for it was through
my carelessness that it was lost. I had taken it, and put it in my book,
with a view to preserving it carefully, and through my neglect (as I must
confess) it dropped out, and was thus forever lost; the children, I suppose,
immediately destroying it. It would not be of so much consequence,
were it her own. But Mr. E. borrowed it, and lent it to her. Ma scolded me,

34. Metal coins went out of circulation as bad money drove out good. Paper substitutes had not
yet appeared.

and deservedly. She admonished me, always to be doubly careful of borrowed property. I am sure my intention was good, and I can attribute it to thoughtlessness on my part, as my *common sense* should have prompted me to have placed it in a safer spot. But it was done, and it will serve a good lesson to me. I hope that it will elude Mr. E.'s observation, for I know, that with his ideas of *propriety*, he would be very angry. Before I had finished A.'s hair, dinner was announced. My fingers went numbly o'er the fancy work, and we were soon seated at the table. The dinner, though quite nice, was not suited to the taste of all of the fastidious ladies! but Ma said that she could not provide for our likes and dislikes, and that we must eat what is there. My sentiments too, although I am sometimes the sufferer. We have Pa to blame, for the indulgence which he has always shown us. Ma made some molasses candy, and we complimented her on her extraordinary powers. Candy, but *no letter.* The spell is broken. Miss Jo. had arrived in the morning, and A. proposed to pay her a visit, so we started about 5. We thought that our plans would be frustrated as they were on our last attempt, for the clouds were very threatening. Had the pleasure of meeting the handsome Mrs. Sewell, who bowed sweetly to A. What a vision of loveliness!! Our ring at the bell was immediately answered, and to our inquiry "Is Mrs. Hews at home"? the response was "yes". Her pleasant voice was soon heard, and she said "wait a moment". In a few minutes, we were ushered into *her* room, and to our amazement into also the presence of *Mr. Ed.!!* She had stated to him in a letter, the time she intended leaving, and he had arranged his affairs so as to meet her, which he did, to the inexpressible joy of both parties. The reunion took place about 7 o'c. and I suppose it was a happy one. She was charmed with the little Country place, and would have enjoyed herself excessively, had not thoughts of *him* prevented it, but says that she was as contented as she could be, while separated. She does not *look* any *stouter,* although she indulged so extensively in all those nice things. She was delighted with Country life, and painted it in pictures of glowing colors. She made the acquaintance of many persons, and among them were the Fields, whom she represents as being a most unpopular family in those districts. They go to a little secluded place, but are unwilling to conform to the customs. Miss Jo. was a favorite (of course) with them. She thinks that Alice [Fields] is quite pretty, and says that she is the best liked. The conversation, one day, turned upon Charlotte, and A. remarked that C. acknowledged to her, her arrangement with Mr. Eshelman, but *"was* waiting for his pockets to get filled"! C. and A. once met at a watering place, and became quite intimate, and C. ex-

pressed to us a decided liking for her, but Miss Jo. said that their friendship must be at an end, as A. spoke censoriously of her. I know that they
were *once* on visiting terms. She spoke on many subjects and was as conversant as ever. She did not look pretty. Ed. was quite reticent; he was much
fatigued, as his looks plainly showed. He said that he had not been successful in obtaining guns, and was much disgusted with his trip, and is determined not to go again. Miss Jo. was very affectionate, and lavished upon
him a wealth of caresses, which he, without retaliating, seemed to take in
very good part. She worships at his shrine, and almost violates a commandment which says, "Thou shalt make unto thyself no idols, etc." Ed.
spoke in the highest terms of Harry I., and made some astonishing disclosures to us. He clears him altogether from the charge of cowardice, and
says "he is one of the bravest men".[35] Ed. and Jo. seem very cozily situated, and are as happy as though they were the possessors of immense
wealth. Her peace of mind is much disturbed by the thought that he may
have to go away, as she fears the "Artillery" may receive "orders". She asked
us to stay, but we refused. She bade us "good-bye", promising to come soon
with Ed, or alone, to see us. She went back to her room, and now thought
we "for a nice quiet evening"; but — I did not envy them, as he is not the
realization of my ideas of a *man*. Little Mamy was there. She is as devoted
as ever to "Brother". As we were going out of the gate our attention was
arrested by Nellie Gillingham. We stopped, exchanged the usual salutations, and she walked a few squares with us. We talked of nothing but the
Concert. She named some, who are to take parts, but did not know many
particulars. She had taken some tickets to sell, and had disposed of all with
the exception of two, which seemed to annoy her considerably. She entreated us to buy them, but we stated to her the limited state of our finances.
A. however consoled her in some degree, by proposing to take them and
use her endeavors to get their equivalents. Nellie willingly accepted the
proposition. The "Concert" is to be on the 8th of October at "Odd Fellows
Hall". I should *so* much like to go; but it is next to an impossibility. I may
be enabled to go as a scholar, but under no circumstances would without
Alice.[36] N. talked so incoherently and her manner so puzzled me, that the
idea seized possession of me that her mind had lost its balance; and much

35. Harry Isaacson, a captain in the Washington Artillery, had been wounded at Bull Run but
remained in service until his resignation, apparently amid charges of cowardice.
36. The Odd Fellows Hall building, located at Lafayette Square, was often used for civic and musical events. Built in 1852, the attractive building succumbed to fire in 1866. See Leonard V. Huber,
New Orleans: A Pictorial History (New York, 1971), 89.

that she said served to justify my opinion. I told A. and she seemed astonished to think that *I* had noticed anything peculiar, for she had also thought that she was a *very strange* girl; but she attributed it to no cause. Recalling many things that she said, we arrived at the conclusion that she was not as she ought to be. Oh! God! I hope that our suppositions are ill founded, for it is a fearful thing. A young girl deprived of some of her reasoning faculties. I wonder if any one else ever observed it. I should so much like to know. After leaving her we walked quickly home. Arrived there, and ma was relating to us her adventures, how she went to Dohan, succeeded with her money, the articles of flour, soap, sugar, etc. which she purchased, when Cousin S. [Sam Myers] came in. He kissed us all, as a compensation for coming up, and was just taking departure, when Mrs. N. entered, and doubtless her appearance accelerated his movements. She had been seated for but a moment, and was talking when I ejaculated "Why, what's the matter with your tooth"? She laughed, we all flocked to the place, while she told us to our grief and astonishment that she had broken her *front tooth*. We sympathized with her for her loss, as her teeth were her *only* pretty feature. She said that she *almost* cried, I think that *any* amount of tears would have been justifiable. It alters her appearance greatly, and Ma gave her a substitute in the shape of a piece of white wax. She put it in, and it looked "remarkably well", and could not be easily detected. A. knew about it, but Mrs. N. had desired her to be mute on the subject. (By the by, I wonder what has become of the Blind man). We went to supper, and *demanded* of Ma her reasons for not purchasing some edibles at Dohan's. She assured us that he had nothing, and we subsided into bread and molasses. Mrs. N. refused to partake. Mr. N. came and was as *merry* as usual. "If every one's internal cares, etc." A. heard E. her lessons. They left here early, Mr. N. assuring us that he would bring up a letter "sure to-morrow". We perceived the change in the weather. We did not retire immediately, as the events of the afternoon afforded subject for converse. Ma being in funds expressed her determination of going to market. This day, three weeks ago, "Capt." da P. came. The time has seemed neither long or short. I wonder when "Gus" [Leovy] will return, although I must confess, it is of very little concern to *me*. "He may go", etc.

Monday, September 23d, 1861

7¹/₄ P.M. . . . . A. and I were together yesterday until dinner and with the exception of an intermission of some moments in which we talked and acted foolishly, by the performance of a burlesque on "Jo. and Ed"; we were enjoying the society of Felicie and Philomen. After dinner, the principal items of which were tomatoes stew and P.P. [potato pone], A. and I dressed (blue and pink), abandoned you and went over to Mrs. N.'s. Leopold was there, and monopolized as usual, the conversation. Oh! he is so consequential. Were deaf to Mrs. N.'s persuasions to stay, and partly promising to "come back", we left. Nothing occurred worthy of being transmitted to posterity. We eat supper, and after it, by Mrs. N.'s request, Ma paid her a visit. A. and I passed the evening alone. Ma came about 9¹/₂ and ere the lapse of many moments I, shivering, and with feet and hands of icy coldness, was underneath the blanket. Oh! my old complaint! Cold feet and hands! It is so disagreeable.

12³/₄ P.M. . . . . I was unceremoniously called away from the above by Alice's call "to *please* come up and fix my hair". I obeyed the *order* with the *best* imaginable grace. Subsequent to its completion, breakfast was ready, and I adjourned to the "dining room". I enjoyed it much, and *hid* some excellent biscuits, into which Mr. Dohan's flour had, by Lucy's skilful hands, been converted. His mackerel also mysteriously disappeared. The children went to school, and A. looked particularly "jimmy" in a clean muslin. If not for fear of making her *vainer,* I would express myself often, more freely, and as she reads what I write, I know that she would accuse me of flattery, falsehood, etc., so do not imagine that because I do not speak to you of her innumerable charms that she is destitute of them, for your predecessors will bear testimony. I then discharged my every day duties, and with my sewing implements prepared myself to render my feeble assistance towards making A.'s barège dress. It is beautiful, and ma purchased it some time previous, for an incomprehensibly small amount. I wish that I was the "fortunate possessor" of one. About 11 o'clock Ma went to Mrs. N.'s and I am "alone". Were it not for the noise of the children, how easily could I imagine that this was *my* house, and I was impatiently counting the hours that would elapse before *his* return. But strange to say, I have been building *no* air castles. The sewing which ma left me is completed, so I correct the impression which I know you have formed that "while the cat's away, the mice will play". But I am not *so* good, for my actions have often been illustrative of this "saying". Ma is quite uneasy, for she thinks that a letter is due, and the telegraph last received annoys her considerably. And to augment this uneasiness, Rosa woke up last night, crying, and said that she dreamed something had happened to her "Papa". I am not to say *uneasy*, but a letter would be a source of much joy. The day is beautiful! Not a cloud floats on the surface of the blue Heavens. And yet I feel so sad; the effect which such a day *always* has. "The melancholy days have come, the saddest of the year". It tells of nature's decay. The drooping of the flowers, the "yellow, sere" leaves. A calm seems to preside o'er all things. The children's noisy prattle is hushed. Josie wanders far in the "lands of dream"; Dell and Rosa have retired to some sequestered nook, but I know that they are out of harm's way. An inexpressible, and an expressible melancholy broods o'er me. This afternoon is to inaugurate the recommencement of my *"school life"*. "Poor Clara Elvina Solomon, gone to school"! Adieu.

8 1/4 P.M. . . . Oh! I am so tired, I can scarcely write. I have the *Rheumatism* so bad, that I can *scarcely* move.[37] Ma came home about 2 o'clock, and I was very, very lonesome without her, as I had nothing to do. I wandered about, and watched and waited — I had nothing to read or divert me in any manner. Ma found every thing in very good order, and had no complaints to make. My work was satisfactory. L. [Lucy] combed my hair, and I dressed for school. After the expiration of 1/2 hour I was down stairs in full trim. A. soon came home, and dinner presently announced. She informed us of the death of sweet little Blanche Conant, from putrid sore throat. She was a beautiful child, and commanded universal admiration. She was formerly a pupil of Miss Jo., and she stopped at school to day on her way to their house. She was very much affected as she was one of her favorites. She had been sent for, and she was going to attend the Funeral. Poor little angel! Miss Jo. is going to leave Mrs. Calder's, and go to her Ma's for the present. Mrs. C. desires her room for the accomodation of Mrs. Shaw, who is about to break up housekeeping.[38] Mrs. C. is sorry to part with Miss Jo. but of course it is far more pleasant to have her "sweet" daughter with her. She will be much farther from us. Ed is ordered to camp at Greenville, and will be gone for about three weeks! Miss J. is very much distressed, but she will be enabled to see him often — A. says that she has

---

37. Clara's health seemed very poor for someone her age. She was described as frail in testimony during the dispute over her late husband's estate only a few years later.

38. Households could no longer be maintained. Mrs. Calder, from Clara's school, told her boarder, Jo, to give up her room so that Calder's daughter could return to her mother's home to save expenses.

partly promised to spend a night with her, before she leaves her present abode, which will be on Monday. I don't think that Ma will consent to it. If I were she, I would not. A. told us this news at dinner, and as it was quite early A. and I retired to the front room, speculating as usual on the future. The afternoon reminded us very much of one, of which we had a distinct recollection. We spoke of the decrease in our visitors; of the unexpected pleasures of last winter, and pshaw! a lot of nonsense! A. had gone up stairs, and I was just drawing on my gloves when Josh came bounding in with a letter in his uplifted hands. Ma joyfully exclaimed "for me?" and in a second, I was by her side. But I did not recognize the handwriting! *It was not Pa's,* and we were disappointed. The superscription was not familiar, and I pondered "from whom can it be?" It was directed to "Miss Alice Solomon", and postmarked "Pass Christian".[39] I knew no one at "Pass Christian"! It was not from Baby. Thinking that it may have been tidings of Pa, I bade ma open it, and with eager haste tore open the envelope, but before she had seen the contents exclaimed, "I'll tell you; it's from Mr. Levy!!!"[Gus] Stupe that I was, why did I not think of *him.* With it in my hand, I was soon in A's presence. She was much astonished and we perused it together. It was dated Sept. 15th and post-marked Sept. 22nd. Was it a labor of a week? This was the first queer "arrangement". It can scarcely be called a "letter", for it was merely a *note,* in bad pencil, for which he begs pardon and excuses himself by saying "It is written on the beach, late at night, with the aid of no other light than that which the pale moon is shedding". To our surprise it is addressed "Alice". Ma thinks it is impudence, and we all think that it is on terms of great familiarity. It is written in a very sentimental strain, and I suppose he does not wish to destroy the effect by the cold, distant appellation of "Miss". I wonder if he could not have snatched a few moments to have written it carefully, and given it a more *respectful* appearance; for as he *writes* he should have done it properly, and on a *sheet* of paper, and I am sure that he has many leisure moments. But maybe, at that instant a sudden inspiration seized him, and he was compelled to transfer his thoughts to paper. But then when a calm settled over his spirit, he should have copied it with ink. But these are "arrangements" understood only by himself. "In my lonely rambles on the shore of this breezy lake, *Alice* I often think of you". Ain't that cool? The sentence which most puzzles *me* is "I trust that you will overlook its *foolish* sentimentality, and its errors, as you would pardon the errors and

---

39. Pass Christian, Mississippi, is on the Gulf of Mexico coast, about seventy miles northeast of New Orleans.

imperfections of him, who now subscribes himself your sincere friend. G.
. ." If he considered it foolish then why did he write it? Previous to this
he says "As this note is really written by the 'light of the moon' and on top
of my hat, at that, I trust, etc." His "foolish" sentimentality is then attributable to these facts. He entreats a response, and says that "he will not
violate any *confidence* reposed". "With this assurance you ought to trust me,
but you said you would not reply to my letters, I will now see how inexorable are your determinations".

I was much astonished at the receipt of the letter from him, as whenever he spoke of writing, I always thought that he was jesting. We brought
it down to Ma, and she evinced great astonishment at some parts. A. is *perfectly* undecided about answering it. *I* do not know *how* to advise. We did
not have much time for comments, as the clock had already sounded four,
and I must be "off". I put on my bonnet, and very despondingly and unwillingly departed. Oh! how I wished to stay home. I had a pleasant solitary walk; was soon there, and seated beside dear Mrs. Shaw, who
kissed me warmly and said she was glad to see me. The Preparatory
class was reciting, and the recitation was by no means creditable. For such
large girls they did not evince much *ordinary* sense. Mrs. S. has a difficult
post to fill, and still she is always so kind and patient. The Juniors soon
came in, and "there! behold your future class"! The faces were all familiar,
but I noticed some new additions. Miss Mitchell was delighted to think
that I was coming back to school. She greeted me friendly. I *like* her.
Miss Bride (the songstress) looked so pretty, that I could not resist the
temptation of taking a kiss. She is an amiable looking girl. I told her of the
grand accounts I had heard of her singing and she is so modest, that a blush
suffused her face. I remained until the dismissal of school, when I had the
pleasure of seeing many of my former classmates, now the stately "Seniors".
Miss Leech and I exchanged an "unlimited" number of kisses, and she said
that I reminded her of old times. I wonder if there were any pleasant recollections connected with this remembrance. She asked why I had not been
to school. I embraced Ada Hodges tenderly and then Lizzie! the one whom
I was *most* glad to see, my lips but lightly touched hers. I should have greeted
her more affectionately, but I feared that it would not have been agreeable
to her—but I intend to treat her as friendly as of yore. If she will reciprocate this feeling is a question yet to be solved. Maggie said that she preferred the Junior Class. Nettie's worries were as visible as ever. I bade Miss
Leech an individual "good bye", and the others a collective, and at Miss
M.'s urgent request I came. I walked up one or two squares on St. Charles

St., while she told me of the programme for the different afternoons; I then left her and proceeded homeward, "all alone", contrasting the solitary walk with the many pleasant ones, I *had* enjoyed. Found Mrs. N. sitting on the steps, and learned that Ma and Alice were out. I proposed a walk and she was telling me of her purchases of flannel and gloves. She, happening to see "Sammy" go in the gate, went home, I with her. Unexpectedly saw Leopold over there. Her purchases came up for inspection, and some very indelicate remarks (to my notion) were made. She entreated me to tell her from whom A.'s letter was, but I referred her to A. herself. She persisted in my "staying", but I absolutely refused, as I was anxious to get home. She commanded me to come over with Ma and Alice. I related all my adventures, and A. in turn related hers. She had been up by the Market, and Ma had made some purchases, not amounting to much. We eat supper, and here, a few moments after, am I. We did not wish to pay the visit, so Ma declined. Ma is asleep on the sofa and A. and I are alone with "our friends" [their diaries]. Our attention was frequently called away from you by bits of conversation.

4

"The Bonnie Blue Flag":
September 24–October 9, 1861

Tuesday, September 24th, 1861

$10^1/_2$ P.M. . . . . I have been compelled to neglect you to day, and would
have paid my devoirs to you sooner, but for the unexpected visit from
Cousin S. and Mr. Van Oesten.[1] I am now in my night gown, and am writing in my bed-room, as Ma was inexorable and made us come up. I am
writing this by stealth, for I know that Ma would be angry. "Booking it,
booking it all the time"! A. is by me in her night robes, preparatory to taking her departure. She has kissed me, and is gone. Oh! I am so bothered.
This morning I read the paper, and tried to wade through a letter of
"D's" [da Ponte] from Richmond of the 18th date. So he is there. I wonder if he will write to us. Ma was not in a very good humour to day; some
fault was found with my yesterday's work [sewing], and I performed the
unpleasant task of ripping it all, but very graciously to Ma's and my own
satisfaction—I sewed up some skirts for Josie on the machine, and some
other little jobs, and the time passed. I dressed as usual. The children came
home. I was up stairs when A. came. She was soon with me, and showed
me a part of a letter which she had penned in a few leisure moments. They
were directed to "Gus", but she says she did "it for fun", as she has not
the remotest idea of sending it. It is very good diction and worthy of the
lady. No letter to day! I hope *to-morrow*. The gas man "watered" the gas
to day, but I see no improvement. Eat dinner, and I did not depart immediately for school. I indulged in some Molasses candy, and with many regrets at leaving the "rural scene" I took my exit. A walk of five minutes
brought me to the gates of the L.N.S. I lingered some time before entering the room, as I felt somewhat abashed. But after the "Seniors" had re-

1. Van Oesten was a family friend and member of the Sephardic congregation.

tired to their apartments, I summoned courage. Obtained a seat amongst a bevy of strange, unpleasant girls, which did not suit me, so I deliberately got up and walked to the other end of the room, and was finally seated by the side of J. Benedict. We kept up an "incessant chattering" during the "dictation". She is very much like Fanny, but much more pert. After the completion of the lesson, the singing was on the tapis. Oh! how envious was I as I saw "my girls" enter. They passed and were lost to my sight. The detestable Mr. Lusher (whom I see is appointed to be Collector of war taxes of the State) seemed to drink in every note of the sweet music.[2] Miss Mitchell sat in front of me, but I did not speak to her — I don't care for her. Bridget called me to sit by her, and as an inducement said she had something to tell me. I answered by a positive shake of the head. At 6 o'clock we were dismissed. I endeavored to ascertain the lessons, but no one seemed to know anything about them. I went out on the gallery, kissed Bridget and she was just telling me something, when she left. I spoke to Miss L., Ada, and Liz, who when I kissed her, put her arms around my waist. I consented, at her request, to go to the "next corner". She, Miss L. and Net. were in advance, Ada and I, in the rear. She likes her class, but is not particularly pleased with her teacher. She spoke of the Concert, and of the impropriety of girls appearing before the public. She is a sweet girl. We saw that the "advance guard" had halted, and we hastened our steps. Adieux were spoken, and Miss L. and Ada left us, and our party consisted of Net., Liz, and Clara. Liz and I were "arm in arm" as of old. She told me that her mother had been very ill for some time past. She had been attacked with pleurisy a few days after she met me, and said "I did not go out of the house". She said this in a tone which I thought indicated *something,* so I asked her if that was the reason that she did not come to see me, to which she replied, "Precisely, but I think Clara, that you should have come to see me, for you may have imagined that something prevented me". This was foolishness. We then spoke of the past, and resolved to "forget and forgive", and sealed our determination with a kiss. While this conversation was being held, we were standing at the corner of Nayades and Erato, waiting for Net., who had stopped in at her sister's; she came, considerably enriched by the possession of an apple. There was much dispute as to whom should take the first bite, but that being agreed upon we took "turns", and it was soon demolished. On our way home, we met Mag. who joined our party. She and N. composed one company. I walked to the corner of Hercules and

2. Robert M. Lusher was, before the war, a New Orleans school administrator.

Melpomene, and Liz. said that it was not "fair", I should go alone, so escorted me to the next corner. We promised to remain after school for the other. N. said that she was coming to see me, that she had told "Clara" so. Said "good bye" and was off. Saw Mr. Murphy. I went over to Mrs. N.'s, but Sally, who was at the gate, told me that A. had gone down Clio St after me, and I went off in search of her. She had partly promised to come and meet me, but I did not think she would, as it was so late. I went 1 or 2 squares, but did not see her, so returned to Mrs. N.'s. Ma and the children were there. I waited to see the light in our house for then I knew that A. would be home. I saw it, and we came leaving Ma and Sally, and just as I had got seated and was chatting with A. the previously named gentleman made his appearance [Van Oesten]. At the sight of the strange looking gent. our visibilities were excited as they were, when he first paid us a visit last January. How often did our thoughts fly to Pa, in remembrance of that pleasant evening which we all had passed together, and he said "I miss Mr. S. so much". He was very obliging and favored us with many, beautifully sung songs. And oh! what a struggle to restrain our laughter. He sings *well*, but his "ponum" [Yiddish for "face"] assumes so great a variety of expressions. He is such a miserable looking creature. F. went over to Mrs. N.'s and about 8½ she came over with them. On the previous occasion we had wished for her. He had been entertaining us for a long while and he continued the performance for the benefit of the "new comers". Mrs. N. was very much pleased. Much credit is due to Cousin S. for his willingness in accompanying him on the piano. I do love the "Bonnie Blue Flag".[3] Mr. Van O. likes to be charmed by his own voice. Joe [Van Oesten] was then amusing us by accounts of the incomprehensible amount of food which he daily consumes. His average bill a day is $12. Cousin S. has often told us of his wonderful capacities in that line. He is one of the largest of eaters, and yet he is so small. Where does it go to? I do not think that he adheres strictly to the truth, in fact, Cousin S. says so. His veracity is more to be doubted than his voracity. He is very busy now, for this is the *time* for *him* to make money. He sported a fine diamond breast-pin.[4] A. tried to summon courage to buy one of her "tickets", but could not. She had them on her lap, and Cousin S. took one up and said "Here Joe, is a good chance to invest 50cts. for the benefit of the absent soldiers". He gave the money and took the ticket. Cousin S. said that the "Word girls" had al-

3. The "Bonnie Blue Flag" was a favorite Confederate song, the "anthem" before the appearance of "Dixie."

4. Van Oesten was a notorious speculator.

ready roped him in for two.[5] There was some talk about attending, and Joe said, "Sam, let's come around and take them all"! Nothing was done, relative to this proposition. I should like to go with him! I am so anxious to attend. They left about $9\frac{1}{2}$, Joe promising not to make his visits so "few and far between". Mrs. N. stayed a few moments, while we made some comments. We stayed by the gate until she got home, when she gave orders to "go in". We did not go to bed, immediately, for Ma was regaling us with some of the events which had transpired. Mr. N. had struck a "vein of luck" by a speculation in some lead. Leopold suggested the idea, and aided him in the plan, and he considers himself under many obligations. Mr. N. had realized $30 the day previous, and $40 to day! Success crowned all his endeavors, as the Bank gave him three two dollars and half gold pieces in change for a $5 note!!! I hope that this is but the beginning to much good fortune. Speculations are the most profitable employments. Nathan was jubilant, and he prefers it greatly to working hard with no prospects of receiving a remuneration. Mrs. N. told Ma of the reception with which A.'s note to Mr. E. met. He was sorry that anything had been said about it, but his feelings are now the same as ever. He thought that A. was angry with *him*, as in the argument which was held during the evening, A. was opposed to him, and he thought that this incited the remark. He regards her as an inestimable young lady and said "If I were a young man, I would 'buck' up to her". We had finished talking and ma ordered us up. As I expected, "Clara is that you"? "Yes'm". "You ain't in bed"? "No'm". "What are you doing"? "Writing". "You had better go to bed". I do as "Nebachadrazzar, king of the Jews", did.[6] The gas is lowered, and now "good night".

Wednesday, September 25th, 1861

12 $\frac{1}{4}$ P.M. . . . . You wonder at seeing me at so unseasonable an hour, but I have just a moment to stay, as my lessons for this afternoon demand all

5. Clara refers to Nina Word, a classmate and friend, one of the sisters referred to by Sam Myers.
6. "Nebachadrazzar" (or Nebuchadnezzar) refers to the Babylonian king who put down revolts against his authority in Judea and Jerusalem, culminating in the destruction of the Jewish temple there, in 586 B.C.E. A large portion of the Jewish community was then exiled to Babylon. The reason for Clara's reference is obscure.

of my attention. I have just finished fixing the children's lunch, and feeding the hungry ones at home. I arose quite early and copied some portions of my dictation. A. and I were talking of Gus' letter. Alice wishes to answer it, but Ma does object, and *of course* A. would not. She wishes for many reasons to respond, one of which is that she fears if she does not, Gus will think that she viewed the letter in a different light from that in which he intended she should, for she says it is nothing but a friendly letter. Ma was very much vexed with Lucy, whom she again detected in innumerable, unwarranted falsehoods. It is *so* provoking; for in connection with this she is so very impudent, and entirely fearless of Ma. Mr. N. came over and spoke to her. I hope she will do better. Breakfast early and very nice. Oh! I was so disappointed. 250 prisoners of war were announced to arrive here this morning by the J.R.R. Richmond is not large enough to accomodate them all, so they are distributed, and our share is to be 500. Ma, Mrs. N. and I intended to go to the corner to see the grand spectacle, and welcome to N.O. the only Yankees that will see it for *some* time. I rendered myself appearable, and was standing by the gate. The crowds flocked, and ladies and gentlemen were on their way to the depot to greet them. I really feel sorry for them, for many knew nothing what they were about when they took up arms against us. They are torn from their family, and will be incarcerated in the Parish Prison, and no doubt sentenced to very hard labor. The people seemed anxious to show their demonstration, and curiosity was stamped on many faces. Ma dressed and went over for Mrs. N. They stayed some time and when they came, I communicated the intelligence that "the prisoners were not come this morning". I had received my information from Miss Eda Jarreau. I was readily convinced of the correctness of this statement for the mass of people were seen to proceed from that direction, I suppose all as disappointed and as mad as I. Why did they humbug the people by stating the precise day, when they *did not know it*. It is uncertain when they will come, but whenever they do, they will meet with as warm a reception as they would have met this morning. I heard that there were about 5000 people down at the depot, innumerable carriages, etc., etc. After every thing had subsided, we came in. Mrs. N. also, who persisted that Ma should accompany her home. Ma left me some work and went, and I now alone. Mrs. N. extended to me the invitation, but I declined. My sewing is completed, and duty now calls me away. I do not know if the lessons which I intend studying are the correct ones, as it is merely guess work. The day is quite pretty, but *warm*. How changeable is the weather in N.O.

Thursday, September 26th, 1861

6 3/4 A.M. . . . . It is some time since we have been together at this hour, and as I date it the memories of "vieux temps" [old times] steal over me. I awoke last night and heard the splashing of the rain, went to sleep, not knowing if it were imagination or not, but was assured on taking a peep out of my window this morning. The rain has not entirely ceased, but the Sun is striving to gladden the dampened earth. We were not much together yesterday, but it was unavoidable, and now Philomen, I clearly see that I cannot devote as much time to you, as my inclination prompts, so in future I must be more brief in my accounts, and we will look forward to the day when we will be as we once were: when I am no longer a school girl.

I studied yesterday till about $2^1/_2$, when I went to dress. I learned the Rhetoric and Grammar, without any difficulty. Ma came and said that she had waited for Mr. N. but he brought her no letter, and she was determined to telegraph. She had been in but a few instants when the bell rang. I had dared to hope that it was a "letter", but as I heard no ejaculations or expressions of joy, the light went out of my heart; when to my surprise Ma hollered up, "Clara, I have just gotten a letter"!! I could not *possibly* go down, so after ma had read it she brought it up to me. Oh! how glad was I to see again the dear handwriting. It had come by "Adam's Express", and was a valuable letter!!!! as enclosed was two fifty dollar bills! The arrival of the long expected epistle caused ma much agitation, and she could scarcely read it to me. It was dated the 20th from Richmond. He is well, and says that he received our letters by "D", who arrived on the 18th but he says "I was so busy that I did not read them until to day!" He has returned from Manassas, and will stay at Richmond altogether as the purchaser of the goods, paying occasional visits to the headquarters. I know that this must suit him. He regrets very much that Ma was so pushed for money, begs to be forgiven and promises that it shall never again happen, as after the first, he will keep us well supplied. He says that he saw Mr. Grant, and arranged matters satisfactorily. He then mentions the enclosed hundred. It is enough for Ma has no large amounts to pay out. William is a clerk and pa says that Mr. H. likes him very well but "It is more than I do". *Ma* prophesied it.[7] The letter was seemingly written hurriedly as the chirography was very indifferent and the contents very brief. In the P.S. he states that he lost Mr. Marks's bundle, but he saw him, offered him

---

7. Business with his partner Hitchcock was large enough to justify hiring a clerk.

money, and he seemed pleased. It was not Pa's fault, as he gave them up to be delivered, but there were so many thieves about that they got stolen. Mrs. M. [Marks] I presume will be highly indignant. I am sorry that Pa had a hand in it, but I suppose it is of very little consequence to him.

Pa makes no mention of the other favors "D" gave him, but merely says "I will answer all letters Sunday". Oh! what a weight was removed from our hearts. The children came home from school, were apprised of the news and hastily ran up stairs to know the contents. They read the letter, inspected the bills, and we then went down to dinner. So it was quite late, I prepared to depart for school, immediately after. When I left Mr. N. was an attentive listener, while Ma was reading the letter. He was again successful [in his lead speculations]. Arrived there in season and found that I had studied the wrong lessons. I said none. Miss B. was as droll as ever. What a queer little corpuscle she is. I did not see Lizzie. *If* she were there, she did not wait for me. There are no lessons for to day, as the concert seems to interfere. I came directly home, and when at the corner of our house, I saw A. advancing to meet Mrs. N. She went to Ma's and A. and I took a short walk. Found Mrs. N. there when we returned; she did not stay long, but promised to "come over". We eat supper. A. heard E. her lessons, and we were quite surprised by a visit from Maria and Sallie Prothro, who had arrived at 7 o'clock. They are still in their "old house", but I do not know if they intend remaining, or any of the particulars. Their young aunt Elizabeth is with them. Ma will call, and I should like to become intimate, as they are excellent people. In a few moments they went, and Mr. and Mrs. N. and — Leopold, to our great surprise, walked in. Of course, we did not show our astonishment, and greeted him as though he were not a stranger. For some time the conversation was general, but he, A. and I repaired to one end of the apartment. We showed him our accumulation of books, and commented upon journal writing. At my request he wrote his name in my album and agreed to take A.'s to write a piece. I obtained Mr. and Mrs. N.'s autograph as also did A. L. left before the rest, and forgot to take A.'s album. As I looked at him, could I forget the circumstances under which he was last here: but he seems to have forgotten all about it, and I have forgiven. I am neither glad or sorry that he came, but perfectly indifferent if he never does again.

The other guests repaired to their own mansion and ours was soon wrapt in silence. A few moments ago the meeting took place between the "Corner house" and Rosa. She was bewildered, but transported with joy at really seeing them again. I suppose that they will play and quarrel as usual.

8 ³/₄. . . . The wind is fiercely blowing, the doors and windows rattling, and I do not doubt that we will have a *cold* day to-morrow. A. is writing, Ma is sewing on the machine, the others are in bed. Wonderful to relate, I am neither tired nor have I any pains or aches. I departed for school this afternoon in an execrably bad humor. While in sight of the gate, I perceived some girls, and on closer observation I recognized Liz., Mag. and Ada. There was no school, and the High and Normals were practising for the Concert. A walk was then proposed and my company was solicited. Before starting Bridget came, and when informed that there was no school, she expressed the determination of going to see Mrs. N. She walked to the corner and when she told us "good bye", I bade her go and see Alice also. She said she would if she had time. Mag. soon left us, and our party consisted of Ada, Liz. and me. We went to Mrs. Abright's on Apollo St, in order to procure a book which she had promised to Ada. We saw her, but she was very sorry but the book was at school. It is a Philosophy, a book required in the Senior class, but unable to be procured in the City. We then proceeded on our pleasant walk, until we reached the corner of Magazine and Second, when at my suggestion we retraced our footsteps. I was very tired, but Liz. very gallantly supported me, although her own steps were very feeble. She was entertaining us with many incidents of her Vicksburg life.[8] She can talk. I met Maggie with the baby. "I kissed it for its mother" and requested M. to tender also my love. As we were coming home, we stopped at Anna Caswell's, from whom Ada intended to get the book, but she was out. Passing Lou Campbell's house we saw her and Ludy at the gate. Exchanged the woman's salutations, I spoke to Mrs. Hester E., admired little Natty, and we passed on. Ada's time of parting was near, and as we lingered on that spot, how many visions of past days floated before us. Liz. and I were then alone. Found much to talk about. Are we *ever* at a loss for that. She told me that Lou had on several occasions spoken of the visit she *owed* me, and her intentions of paying it. I hope that she will. Liz. said that she would have certainly waited for me on yesterday, but she had thought that I was absent, as when Mrs. Pagand's roll

8. Vicksburg, Mississippi, is situated along the Mississippi River some two hundred miles north from New Orleans. A wealthy antebellum river town, it became the site of a major Confederate capitulation to the troops of General Ulysses S. Grant in July 1863, after Grant laid siege to the town. The Confederate garrison at Port Hudson, Louisiana, south of Vicksburg, capitulated soon after. At that point, the entire Mississippi River fell under Union control. See Samuel Eliot Morison, *The Oxford History of the American People* (New York, 1965), 681–85.

was called, I did not answer to my name. We were very tired, and I insisted on our parting at her corner. I went over to Mrs. N's. She was all alone. Said that B. had been there. When I left she was hearing Josh his lesson. He has been advanced in school, and she is desirous that he shall be perfect. A. had been in but a few moments, when I got there. She and L. had gone out for the purposes of buying a new dress for Felicie [a new notebook], and of paying a visit to Mr. Sewing-machine Davis. She had caused Ma much uneasiness by remaining out so late. L. also had a bad cold, and there was a perceptible change in the weather. We related to each other the adventures of the afternoon. Preparatory to going out she had gone over to Mrs. N.'s to ascertain if she wished her to purchase any machine needles. Bridget was over there, and they left together; B. walking to Camp St. She, *of course*, posted her in many subjects, said that she thought that Ludy and Marion would make a match! I do not think so. Said that Mrs. Dr Packwood was residing with her mother-in-law. I do not envy her, *near* as much as I did. She told A. that she had seen me, and had she not seen *her* she would have "come over". Opinions were given about the Concert, B. condemning the proceeding much. Theodore Marks is sick. A. told me that she then went to Mr. D.'s [Davis], purchased 25 cts. needles for Ma and Mrs. N; paid him $5 on the old account. This is quite a small amount but we must take in to consideration "the times", and let "small favors be thankfully accepted". She had much trouble in procuring a dress for F. as articles of the kind are very scarce in the City, and for those to be found an exorbitant price is demanded.[9] It is a very nice one, and I admire it. It will prove durable. I hope that I will have many similar facts of the above to notice. And what do you think! She is undecided whether to write in pencil or ink. I hope that she will determine upon the former. She said, "Clara, guess whom I met down town". On the second trial I exclaimed, "Gus". They passed each other, but he chanced to be looking in another direction, and A. regrets that she did not have presence of mind to speak, but in her astonishment at so unexpectedly beholding him, her speech took flight, and her silence was pardonable. We both fear that he has taken offense, at the non-replying to his letter, and though we do not appreciate or value his visits, we do not wish that he should be offended, and we know not under what erroneous impressions he may be laboring; but I suppose his visits are now discontinued *forever*, as it is probable that he had been in the City many days. As Ma says, "We drive *every* one away, ei-

---

9. A "dress for F." refers to a notebook for Alice's diary (named Felicity, or Felicie).

ther by an intentional or unintentional insult". "Alas poor Gus". The day of his jesting's o'er, etc. This is merely a synopsis of the news A. imparted, and my memory fails to yield any more, and I hope that *this* is satisfactory. The day has been quite unpleasant; the sun being hidden the greater portion. Rosa and the corner house have been romping, and each seemed to enjoy the society of the other. *"Mary Ann"* requested permission to cook something in our stove, as their utensils have not yet arrived. They all are delighted to get back. It is very cold over there [in the countryside]. I wonder why Baby did not write. Oh! I am so anxious to see her. Mrs. N. has a fresh supply of "drawers", and being desirous of completing them in as short a space of time as compatible with reason, and so she begged Ma to relieve her of a dozen, and Ma consented. Ma has not felt well to day, and we have not made much progress. She was unable to sew on the machine, so *I played* mostly on that instrument. How much work for $1!!! It is shameful, but I do not dislike the occupation; ma has plenty of sewing to do, but as yet no materials. The "rooms" were scrubbed, the last time I suppose for many a day, as our beautiful carpets will soon adorn our pretty parlors. The time seems so short since last I beheld them.[10] Ma wrote to Pa to day. As he mentioned that he would write on Sunday, we are in daily expectation of a letter. I wonder when we will have the inexpressible, unspeakable joy of gazing upon his loved face, and it is *almost* time to anticipate a visit. I hope when it is his intention he will inform us a sufficient length of time, as anticipation is next in sweetness to realization. When A. came home from school, she told me that "sweet Anna McLean" had promised to come and see her to-morrow afternoon. A. has taken a particular fancy to her. I have seen her, and thought that she had a very pleasant face. Mary Ames is going to sing at the Concert. She is bold enough to do it. I do not approve of such publicity being given to a young girl. They can contribute their aid for our "absent soldiers" in some more appropriate manner. But let them do as they like, as it is to be presumed that they are all subjected to the counsel of some one. The paper does not state when the prisoners will arrive, but they say that ten hours notice will be given before they do. A. would be fortunate if they came Saturday. "My work is done, I'll go to bed".

10. The Solomons, like others in a hot and humid climate, stored their carpets for the summer to reduce the heat in the house. At the end of September, the carpets would be returned for use.

Saturday, September 28th, 1861

6 3/4 A.M. Conscious of my neglect, I now hasten to you, and implore your forgiveness, for the circumstance of not seeing you yesterday is, I am assured, a subject of much more grief to me than you. I cannot call it neglect, for my thoughts were often with you, but I could not conveniently take the time to devote to you. A. awoke me. I opened my eyes, made *some* response, but was *so* snugly ensconced in bed, that it was impossible to heed her mandates. A chilly sensation crept over me; I pulled up the blanket, enviously (for I *wanted* to get up) saw her depart to realms below, and I was before aware of my intention, asleep. When my eyes were next unclosed the bright sun was high in the clear heavens. As I predicted, it was the *first cold* day, and I came down shivering and blue. I saw A.'s new [diary] book lying open on the piano. In a moment to my surprise and sorrow, I found *that it was written in ink.* She says "I have continued to conclude our interview through the more respectful medium of pen and ink". She weighed all circumstances, and determined to place the record of their friendship in a more durable form. I tried to dissuade her from it. I laid before her the many inconveniences which would arise, but she resolved to encounter them all willingly.[11]

My principal reasons for urging her not to do it was that we would be no longer alike, and I do feel so estranged. There would be innumerable obstacles towards my pursuing the same course; indeed I *could* not, for the circumstances by which we are surrounded and the different situations in which we are placed render it much easier for her, and precludes the possibility of my doing it. She has requested me, at the completion of this book!!! (when will that be) to abolish lead pencils. But I cannot promise, indeed I have no such ideas. I can write with much more facility with a pencil, and it is attended with so much less trouble, for I know Ma's aversion to having ink in the rooms with the carpets. A. said that when she came down she was so undetermined that she actually wrote the date with a pencil, but it was dull, *I was not down to sharpen it,* so she made a desperate resolve, and penned the lines. Oh! how often since have I regretted those few moments stay in bed, and how dearly were they bought, for I have taken it *very* much to heart; and I think A. was rather selfish, for I asked her not to. She should have continued as we had begun, until I could have *justifiably* changed my course with hers, which I promised to do when

11. Clara used pencil for her diaries which are legible to this day.

I had finished school. But no—she was invulnerable. Upon what little events do our lives turn. "If" I had only got up. Cease your will repining my heart! It is done and the harsh sentence cannot be revoked. Maybe I'm a little *jealous*. I believe I *am*. When I take the book up it looks so unfamiliar, and "unfelicie" like, that I am tempted to throw it down.[12] Mine contrasts so unfavorably, and she is always saying "I wish that your nice book was in ink"! I *wish so too*. A. and I have occasional talks about the length of time that this robe [diary book] will be serviceable. I protest that if I am alive, I will herald the year 1862!! *She* protests that its life will be ended by November 1st. Nous verrons [We'll see]! Yesterday Ma and I worked diligently and without much trouble completed the 12 pair before dinner. I had intended to pay A. a visit [at school], but I wished to stay home and help Ma. For several successive Fridays I have been disappointed. I was very ill-tempered the early part of the day, but I recovered my equilibrium. Sent the children some preserves, the last of the next to the last bottle. Nothing transpired during the day. A. told me that Susie Brown had moved in our neighborhood. I suppose they will be intimate. Oh! Philomen, I committed so rash an act yesterday afternoon. I cut off my curls! and cut them too short, and now they are wholly unmanageable. I am so sorry for *now* they say, "Clara, they were *so* pretty". Of course this only augmented my distress. How blessings brighten as they take their flight. I was unconscious that I had cut so much, and now I wish for them, and think of their beauty. No power on earth would now restore them. A. lamented the fact, as she "always liked them". Ma called me foolish, but commissioned me not to fret. It will be many a long day ere they again adorn my ponum [face, in Yiddish]; maybe—never. What is left is horridly obstinate, and refuse to retain any shape or form. I received the compliment that I looked like a "*stewed rat*". Oh! pity me, ye Gods! I was very disheartened and *may* have written had not Anna McLean come in. A. went in the room, and some time after I dressed and made my appearance. Ma and F. went out with the determination of making some purchases. I bade Ma to procure a pair of gloves for me. By the by, what will we do for Kids [kid gloves, that is]! They are now $1.50. There will not be many in the city. Abe Lincoln! Abe Lincoln! I found A. [Alice's visitor, Anna McLean] to be a very sweet girl. She was very obliging and favored us with many songs. She has a soft, musical voice, and I think that she is not unconscious of it, and *maybe* she overvalues it a little. She is very full grown for her age,

12. Clara used a pun here, as "unfelicie" not only means that her diary is not like "Felicie," the name Alice gave to hers, but in French would mean unhappy.

and quite intelligent. *She* would not take a part in the Concert. She was spending part of summer up at Springfield, and was entertaining us with a description of her life while there. She was there with Miss Jo. and they had splendid times. She was talking of Alice Field, her peculiarities, etc. A. resides at the corner of St. Charles and North [not far from the Solomons]. She has two brothers, both of whom, I think, are at sea. She is motherless, but has a Father whom she dearly loves. "Why shouldn't I", says she, "it is all I have". She left before dark, and as she was going up to her Aunt's we walked up a few squares with her. It was *extremely* cold, and I had on a muslin. Oh! my wardrobe is in a deplorable state. I dread the change of seasons, particularly for this reason. I dislike dresses from one year to another and when they don't fit! A. and I would have gone to Mrs. N.'s, but we just looked over in time to espie Leopold's broad shoulders entering the door, and *then* we changed our minds. We went in the house, A. played the piano, and I was on the sofa amusing Sallie and Rosa. Presently Ma and F. came home. It being so cold they had found it impossible to proceed, so they had spent a quiet afternoon to Mrs. N.'s. L. inquired about my cold, which A. thinks exhibited a very great interest in my welfare, and immediately suggested "a match", etc. Ma did not go back, but after supper, retired to the sofa. A. did not hear E.'s lessons, as it was Friday night.[13] A. was reading to me some portions of her former Journal. We were much amused and interested, and many happy and unhappy incidents were revived. The bell rang, and I went to the door, thinking, almost sure, that it was "Gus". I opened the door, and to my astonishment and fright beheld "Grace Featherston", a young girl whom ma had met at Amite. She attends Webster school [where Alice teaches], and A. had requested her to call. She had on a ridiculously short-waisted dress, and looked very "stag", and to be sure, we all wanted to laugh. She lives on this street with her married sister Mrs. Leonard, with accounts of whom and her baby she was entertaining us. She did not pay a long visit, as she had promised Kate not to be gone long. After she left we had a hearty laugh at her expense. A. was on the piano when the bell again rung. Ellen went to the door, and I heard "*Gus's*" voice. A. went and he handed her a bouquet, but declined coming in, as he said that there was a gentleman at the corner waiting for him, which *I* take the liberty of disbelieving. A. told him that she had seen him the previous afternoon, and he almost immediately as he saw her said "Mrs. da Ponte has come!!" How strange, as though it were the most im-

13. Alice tutored the housekeeper, Ellen.

portant event of his life. It mattered very little to Alice. Doubtless he did it for a joke. He declined to come in, but they had a little parley at the door, much to the discomfiture of the inmates of the room, as the sharp wind penetrated the apartments. He bade "good bye", and said he would be up soon. So he is not mad! I am so glad. I expect he will be up to night. I hope so. We retired about 9¹/₂ for the want of something better to do. I resolved to get up early, and I *did*. But oh! what a great struggle. It is as cold as yesterday.

3 ³/₄ P.M. . . . Dinner over a few moments, and I am now in Ma's room sitting beside the bed upon which she is lying. It is very cold. We expected a letter, but Josh, who has just come in, says that his pa was not home to dinner. But there is no foundation for hope, for had he one, he would certainly have sent it up.

Sunday, September 29th, 1861

6 ³/₄ P.M. . . . . Another cold, beautiful, lovely, Autumnal morning. I have just descended, but A. has been down for some time, and looking over what she has written; I see that she called me a "lazy girl". "It can't be expected", that every one can rise with as little difficulty as she. I left you rather unceremoniously yesterday, but I could not help it, as Sallie's repeated exclamations of "Clara, ain't you coming to dress me"? compelled me to relinquish your society. While at breakfast, Mr. N. came in; he warmed himself by our little fire in the dining room, the first of the year. This suggested the subject of *coal*, the all-absorbing one to house keepers at present, for this article is very high, and with a prospect of getting higher as the season advances. He spoke of purchasing some, and Ma requested him if he did to think of her. He thinks that he can get it at a moderate price from a friend. I wish that we had a supply, for it is so unpleasant to be compelled to be sparing, and we certainly shall have to. Ma, F. and S. went to market, and left A. and I alone. Josh came over to see if we were going to synagogue, as his ma was going. We gave him a negative answer.

We did not know what mischief to get after, so we rolled "Myra" up very carefully, and told Josh to ask his Ma to "accept some 'juju paste', which Cousin Alice had sent her". Josh was excessively amused at the joke. We dusted the rooms, A. fixed her desk, looked over the great accumulation of notes, papers, etc. for she has *every scrap* of paper which she ever received. The note Mr. da P. wrote to Mayor M. [John T. Monroe] was brought to light. I intend when next I see "Gus" to ask him to deliver it, although I anticipate no good results, as *the schools are to close in January.* We reviewed our books, and found *plenty* to talk about. We received a visit from "Mr. Hebe", who wished to see Ma on business; he could not wait so promised to call again.[14]

Lucy came home, and said that Ma would be home shortly. The bell rang; we expected to see Ma, but it was Mrs. L.A. Levy. She spent a half an hour with *us,* for Ma did not come. She is very agreeable, and so often in her manners and conversation reminds us of Mrs. Miller.[15] She is house hunting and asked us if we could tell her of any houses to rent. We directed her to those new buildings on this street, and she intended to go and see them. We inquired about Sarah, and she said that she was living on Philip St. Her child is getting better. She was perfectly disgusted with her summer residence. It was a little desolate place, and they were completely starved. Leah has been very ill, but is now recovering. She has a fine boy who glories in the name of "Sumter Davis". It has not been named. She did not wish that one child should be different to the others.[16] Mrs. L. made us quite envious by accounts of Octavia's great powers in the art of sewing. I wished that I were so blessed. It is instinct with girls, for Fannie H. is as unhandy as O. in a corresponding degree is handy. I wonder if she has stopped her visits in this quarter. We told Mrs. L. to extend to Emma our invitation to spend to day with us. She said that had she no other engagement she would come. We stood by the door, until she got to Mrs. N.'s and we had the fun of seeing her ring the wrong bell. After she left, we partook of some bread and molasses. I should have liked to have had something to [offer] to her. Ma came in very much fatigued. She had been walking to obtain some things, and had made some small purchases of shoes, crockery, etc. She startled us with the high prices of every thing. A higher price is demanded for all articles. And shoes! They are almost impossible to be got. What will we do? They are *now* exorbitantly high. All dry goods will be scarce this winter, and there will not be much dressing. Ma was relating to us her adventures. She bought some paper for the front door. It

14. Clara used the derogatory term "Hebe" for a Jew, a term usually considered anti-Semitic. The "Hebe" most likely was a merchant to whom the Solomons owed money.

15. This Levy family played a prominent role in the Sephardic congregation since its formal organization in 1847.

16. The comment about "naming" refers to the Jewish custom of giving Hebrew names in addition to English ones. It is hard to think of a name to rival "Sumter Davis" for southern patriotism.

is quite pretty. As Ernest, the "d—in statue" stood before us, our thoughts turned to Pa, and the memorable morning when Pa gave him his name. We were then amusing ourselves by reading over portions of my "school journal". The dictation was passable, but the writing was *shocking*, and A. remarked that had she been Miss Perry, she would not have accepted it. It is a slight consolation to feel that I have made some improvement, and as I am so susceptible *now* of it, I may make some change for the better, and I live on hopes, that a time will come when *this* writing will as unfavorably compare with some of my future chirography. "I live in hopes, if I die in despair". Dinner was next on the programme. Pea soup, and beef steak. Ordinarily good. I spoke to you a few moments after the event, and then proceeded to dress.

Now here was a dilemma! Nothing to wear! I finally donned my pink barège, and went down stairs not in a *very* amiable mood. Ma had been out, but when I went by the door, I saw her and Mrs. N. sitting on the steps, A. also; who had on her barège. Mrs. N. said there were very few at synagogue. She went to Mrs. Ellis'. Saw Mrs. B.H. Marks, and her baby, whose cognomen is Sumter Alexander; the latter after his deceased grandfather.[17] She is to spend Wednesday with Mrs. N. F. wished to buy some copy books, and A. accompanied her to Provençals'. They returned shortly with the sought for articles. It was too cold to walk, and as "our bower" is now trespassed upon by noisy children, we adjourned to the house.[18] Mrs. N. and Josh stayed. While at supper Mr. N. made his entrance. He had in his hand a *letter* which proved to be one for Mrs. N. from Columbia [South Carolina]. I left the dining room and repaired to the parlor, where in a short space of time they joined me. I took up my Scholar's Companion, and attempted to study, but before conscious I was asleep. When I awoke I was bewildered to see all the *folks* gone, and it was some time before I came to my senses. Bed was then proposed, and after safely guarding the house against mid-night robbers, etc., we ascended to realms of happiness. There was an account of a shocking accident in yesterday's paper. Fourteen ballet girls were severely burnt at a Philadelphia Theatre. It originated by the clothes of one, catching fire and the others ran to her assistance, and in the haste and confusion of the moment, their clothes became ignited. Many have since died, and amongst the names of the suf-

17. Another baby named after Fort Sumter, in Charleston Harbor, where the Civil War began. He unfortunately died in December, only four months old.

18. Clara refers to the yard in front of the house, using a term meant to describe apartments in a medieval castle.

ferers we recognized those of the attractive and handsome Misses Gale. A late telegraph announces the death of one of them. The description of the casualty was heart-rending, and as I read tears coursed their way down my cheek, and my heart went forth in pity to the unfortunate participators in the scene; and a prayer went up to Heaven for their recovery. It spread a gloom over the City, and a performance is to be given for their benefit.

Monday, September 30th, 1861

6 1/4 A.M. . . . . The last day of the month! How swiftly have the days winged their flight. To-morrow will be the 1st of October, and then Winter should be fairly set in. We are now in the midst of the lovely Indian Summer, and I think that to day will be quite warm. Yesterday at breakfast, some *one* or *thing* annoyed Ma and she continued in an excessably [excessively] bad humour *all* day, and we spent the day quite unpleasantly. Ma scolded and of course all came in for a share, and I do not for a moment declare that some was undeserving for we *are* the most ignorant set of "big girls" in *some* respects that are to be found. One thing suggested another, and *all* of our imperfections were brought to light. I sewed a little and before dinner braided Alice's hair. I did not succeed very well. Before dinner Mr. N. stopped over and told us that he has received a letter from Simon who is in Richmond on furlough. He has been with Pa constantly and says that he is *very* busy, and if the war lasts a year, he will be a rich man.[19] About 4 o'clock A. and I were sitting in the back room, when the bell rang. A. ran up, and I went to the window, peeped and saw *Leopold* — I soon communicated the intelligence to A. and we both agreed that Mr. E. would have been as welcome. A. dressed hurri[e]dly, and lightly tripped down the stairs, and was in the presence of *one* of her former suitors. It was a considerable time before my toilet was completed. I descended & the trio was complete. He shook my hand heartily and inquired about my cold. He looked quite handsome. He brought with him a number of Librettos, for us to read, and was just making a display of his elocutionary powers on the the Pardon of Ploermel, when the bell rang, and the detestable Mr. Eisner

19. Solomon did not emerge from the war a rich man.

darkened the door. L. showed us a letter from Julius. It was from Columbus, Ky., and he writes that he has been very sick, having had an attack of the Measles, but is now convalescent, but is obliged to take extra care of himself. He spoke of the unusual attentions which he had received while an invalid, and of course, he appreciated them highly. Mr. E. and L. were speaking of him, his reasons for joining the army, which L. asserted were not at all from patriotic principles, but says it was a rash, imprudent act, as he is constitutionally unfit for a Soldier's life. The book was the identical one which *I* had used at the Opera. How remarkable a coincidence! Mr. E. was as "rattish" as ever. I don't like him. Ma and F. soon came in. We conversed on a variety of subjects. Mr. E. said that he had reserved some "spool cotton", and I think that Ma and A. intend paying him a visit this afternoon. I was walking up and down with Josie, when L. came out of the gate. I accompanied him to the corner, and he expressed his determination of going to Mrs. N.'s where he, in company with Mr. and Mrs. H. [Harris] had dined. To his inquiry if I, (meaning us) were coming home, I replied a decided "no". Josie and I continued our promenade until "the stars had come out in the blue vault above". I then went in, and found Cousin S. [Sam Myers] the centre of the circle, and as *usual* the star of the company — Mr. E. was still there, and A. and I were looking at each other slyly, as he made remarks which *he* considered witty and sensible. His *nose* participates in all the emotions of his soul. Cousin S. was amusing us by singing hymns, and we imagined that he was a Methodist Preacher. He is the most jocose, entertaining, agreeable specie of the *kind*, that it was ever my fortune to meet. He persisted in Mr. E.'s remaining, and he extended his visit to a disagreeably long period, and about 7½ he, with all due ceremony, took his departure. I was quite friendly to him [Eisner], and I suppose his impression is almost removed. When relieved of him, Cousin S. and I on the sofa, and A. beside us on a chair, enjoyed ourselves excessively. I imagined that he was a handsome young millionaire, and that we were betrothed. He said that it would require a great stretch of the imagination. In the midst of our enjoyment F. foolishly requested the pleasure of our company in the supper room, and we marched to the gay scene in grand style; he, supporting both on his arms, and we were in the realms of fancy in the St. Charles Hotel parlors. As Cousin was hungry he partook heartily of the sumptuous repast. We returned to our places on the sofa, Ma and F. in the back room. A dance was proposed, and we were honored alternately. Mr. Myers was an exquisite dancer and *we* were the belles of the "ball room". This was concluded, and we were again cozily

seated, when there came a "gentle pull at the front door bell". A. admitted "de Gustibus" [Gus]. He bowed generally and subsided into the
sofa. A. and he were conversing, and Cousin S. and I were having a pleasant tête a tête, all to ourselves. He was exceedingly noisy and made me
laugh very much. He invited us to the Concert, and we accepted the invitation—He said that "Jo" anticipated much pleasure from accompanying us to the Concert!! We were astonished that Cousin S. should have
thought that we attached any importance to those words, spoken, as we
thought, in jest on his last visit. We told Cousin S. to tell him that we declined the honor. He remonstrated with us, because we refused to go, but
in vain. I should like to go to so public a place with "Jo Van Oesten"!! I
am quite anxious to be present. You must know that my noble Cousin is
going to receive the nomination for a member of the Legislature, and he is
almost confident of receiving the election. I hope that he will. The "Honorable
Mr. Myers". How aristocratic!! Mrs. N. came in. She was with Ma. Cousin
S. borrowed Rutledge, and seeing the two volumes of the Statesman's
Manual on the table, he asked Ma to give them to him, as they were of
no use to us, but would be a great accession to his *library*. Ma complied
with his request, and he seemed very much pleased. He stayed very long,
considering there were others present, and after taking a kiss, and collecting his books, he left. I bade him beware of the watchman, for he would
think that he had been perpetrating a robbery. *He* had no *fears*. I then joined
A. and Gus, and told them that I sought their society as a dernier [last] resort. G. said that he considered himself insulted. He said that the Pass was
deserted after the evacuation of Ship Island, as the people were fearful
of their safety.[20] He had not paid Mrs. da P. a visit. We doubted him, but
he declared that he hadn't. It *does* seem contrary to nature.[21] Mr. H. J.'s
family arrived in the afternoon. I don't believe that Gus is particularly addicted to the "Madam". We were as ironical as usual; told him how we had
missed him, and how happy his safe return had made us. The conversation turned upon Mr. Jenkins, McKnight, Randall, Henry, Lizzie, Mollie,
and Carrie and—Capt. da Ponte. We told him to go to the Concert, and
he said he would. I did not give him the note, but will on some future oc-

20. Ship Island stands at the head of Mississippi Sound and was considered the major defense
installation guarding the entrance to the harbor of New Orleans through the Sound. Its premature
evacuation by Confederate forces was an omen of things to come. The "Pass" refers to Pass Christian,
Mississippi, the town on the northern side of the Sound that also relied on the Ship Island installation
for military protection.

21. Gus wrote for the newspaper owned by Durant da Ponte, husband of "Mrs. da P.," and
presumably had seen him in Virginia.

casion. Mrs. N. went, but he did not. Ma went to bed. He asked A. if she had received his letter. She replied affirmatively. He then asked if she had answered it. She told him that she had considered it useless, as she expected that he would be home shortly, or something to that effect. He, however, mentioned it incidentally, and said that he would never write again. He stayed a long while, and we talked on a multitude of subjects, an account of which would be as uninteresting as worthless. A. and I talked "our language" which perplexed him greatly, and he called us mysteries, and said that it must have required much study to have arrived at such a perfection. I was very sleepy, and he finally took pity on me, and left. A. and I remained down a short while, and I retired, perfectly ignorant of the time of night.

8 o'clock P.M. . . . Here you are Philomen, ever willing to listen to my joy and sorrows. A. is writing. Ma is sewing, but her thoughts I presume far distant from surrounding objects. F. and S. have just gone to bed, as all other amusements fail. I wonder where our dear Father is to night. A. is sitting on the sofa, reclining in the very spot, where his dear head has so often rested. No letter to day. To-morrow! To-morrow! As the minutes passed on this morning and Ellen did not come, the sad conviction forced itself that she was not coming. This grieved me considerably, and as Lucy handed me Josie, I was loath to leave you. But Dell persisted in amusing her and succeeded, and I took advantage of the opportunity, and hastened to you. Lucy was somewhat retarded [late in appearing], and did not comb A.'s hair as early as usual—breakfast was also rather late. Various surmises were made as to the cause of E.'s non-appearance, the most probable of which, I thought, was the indisposition of her mother. How we do miss her. The children departed for school, and how I envied them!! The work progressed very well, and after finishing my rooms, and subduing J. to a state of somnolenty [somnolence?], I prepared to fix up, for you must know that the intelligence reached us yesterday that "the distinguished warriors of the Lincoln army, who couldn't get away from Bull Run and Manassas fast enough, will positively arrive here on Monday Morning"!! So about 9 o'c. the crowd began to flock. I was stationed by the gate, and it was amusing to watch the "hurrying to and fro" of anxious people. Ladies and gentlemen on foot and in carriages passed the door, and there was a perfect *jam* at the corner. Many escorts went down to meet them, and as they marched on and the band struck up the lively music, persons scampered, and from all sides I heard "Here they come". Mrs. N. came running over and was quite sorry for her trouble, as they were all doomed to disappointment. The train arrived, but no prisoners! It was then rumored that

they would be in at 11, on an Express Train. The crowd remained station[a]ry, but I didn't. At 11½, as the sound of music and the excitement
from the street fell upon my ear, I ran to the door, saw *some* men pass at the
corner, and *this* is all that I saw of the Yankee prisoners. Miss S. promised
to come over and go to the corner, but as she did not I did not wish to go
alone. Six months ago, who would have thought that such a furor would
be caused by the appearance of some Yankees. I sympathized with the
poor creatures. I heard that they were a wretched looking set of men. A
negro woman passed, and I asked "Do they not look like *other* men?", to
which she replied "Zactly, Miss, only they are mighty *small*". Doubtless
she imagined that they were from some distant region of the world. The
crowd departed with them, and quiet again ruled supreme. 250 more are
expected. Josie was as bad as usual, and I accomplished nothing in any
other line than minding her, and not much in that, for I would *never, never*
do for a nurse. Mrs. Deegan was here and said that E.'s *foot* was very
bad. Inflam[m]ation had ensued, but it is attributable to her wildness, for
she was seen jumping rope, and what could be more injurious to it than
this uncalled for exercise. I hope that it will soon be better. As there was
much to be done, I was undecided whether or not to go to school, but finally determined *not* to. When A. came home, she posted me in all the news.
Nettie had moved on Dryades St., a few doors from Erato. All of our friends
live in the immediate neighborhood. Miss Jo. has gone to her mother's.
We are far apart now. She left Mrs. C.'s [Calder's] on Saturday. We contributed our shares this afternoon towards minding J. About 5 o'clock Mr.
Foggine with Minnie and Frank came to see "Miss Solomon". I have been
guilty of a great oversight by not telling you of these children. Mr. F. found
it impossible to keep house, so resolved to board, and his present residence
is on Carondelet St., the Franklin School district to which the children attend. I did not go into the room, but from my position I over-heard the
greater part of the conversation. He is a handsome, intelligent, French *gentleman.* He said that the children were continually talking of A. and had often expressed the desire to come and see her. He asked A. to stop in and
see the children occasionally.[22] A. requested of him their daguerreotypes,
and with a most exquisite, original French bow, he said he would be only
too willing to oblige her.

A. invited him to call, and he said that he would avail himself of the invitation. I should be much pleased, as I am desirous of making his ac-

22. The children were in Alice's class at the Webster School, until they moved to another school
district.

quaintance as A. represents him to be a *most* agreeable personage. He left in about half an hour, and A. and I proceeded to renew ourselves. Went up on the front gallery, talked and laughed upon a variety of subjects, and then suddenly remembered our object in coming up. Were soon prepared to descend, and then took a pleasant walk in the dusty twilight to *Fairex's*, as Ma and "Dr L" have had a slight misunderstanding. Made our purchases, and started for home and of course found much to engage our attention. Passing Mrs. Prothro's house she was sitting by the door, and A. said "good evening". We had gone a few steps when she said "Miss Alice", and we went back. She told A. that she had many messages for her from Baby; she had been expecting A. every day and was much disappointed when she did not come. B. did not know, in time, that Mrs. P. was coming or she would have written.[23] She told Mrs. P. to tell A. "to expect her next month"!! I wonder if Mrs. Stockton is coming. Oh! I am *more* than anxious to see dear Baby. Strange to say, while there talking, Miss Lizzie was sitting in the door and she did not introduce us. It *must* have been thoughtlessness; I hope so. We hastened home for fear that Ma would be alarmed at our long absence, but, thankfully, she wasn't. Divided the cakes, eat supper, and here I am. Ma could not go out this afternoon. We received a visit from "Jacksine". She has just returned from Covington, and brought to Lucy some nuts which were sent her by Solomon. She says he is crazy to see Lucy; he thinks the world of her. I suppose they will make a match. J. did not know until lately that all his thoughts were centered upon her. J. is to hire. It would be *so* pleasant if Ma could take her. She is a finished washer and ironer, and an uncommonly good cook.[24]

Tuesday, October 1st, 1861

8 o'clock P.M. . . . . . From to night the bell rings at eight, and its last note has just died away. Supper is just over. Ma is to Miss Sarah's; Alice, Fanny and

23. "Baby" would have sent a letter with Mrs. Prothro, had she known the latter was returning to New Orleans from some unspecified rural retreat.

24. Covington is not far from New Orleans, on the north side of Lake Pontchartrain. A friend of Lucy, not herself a slave, returned from Covington not only with nuts but more importantly with news of Lucy's admirer, whose name, strangely, was Solomon. Clara expected Lucy and Solomon to marry, and wished that her mother could afford to hire "Jacksine", Lucy's friend. Lucy and her admirer had been separated for some time.

Sallie are with me. The day has been quite warm, the dust is intolerable and we are sadly in want of rain, which I think we will soon have. I was up rather early this morning, and Ellen did not come. I learned that her mother was here this afternoon, and said that she was a little better, but would be unable to be here to-morrow. To my surprise, I found that there was no paper. I should like to know the reason. During the day Ma would say to me, "Clara, are you sure there was no paper? Maybe there is something in it that you don't want me to see". I denied it and laughed at the ridiculous idea. About 10 o'clock A. sent a note to Ma, and before reading it I felt quite uneasy; I don't know why, but my thoughts were with Pa. Ma and I hastily opened it, and read that a pupil in one of the rooms had told her that there was a *roll of money* for her at Adam's Express Office. She had been commissioned to do this by Mr. Lindo, a relative, and a clerk in the office. Of course we were stupefied and agreed with A. that it was "all nonsense", as who could send *her* money. But we determined to ascertain to what it amounted, the particulars of which I will hereafter tell you. J. was bad, and I found it impossible to sew, but studied whenever the opportunity offered, and I am now very much worried, for my lessons to-morrow are difficult and unlearnt, and with so great a weight on my heart, I cannot amuse myself with you. I once attempted to sew on the machine, but was *so* unfortunate as to break a needle so I gave it up in disgust. I succeeded in dressing before dinner, and accelerated my motions in order to get down and hear what A. had to say. She was as mystified as ever about *that,* and could not divine the meaning of it, but Ma and A. intended going down town. We sat down to dinner of which none partook of heartily. A. told me that she had had a few moments' conversation with Miss Dentzel, relative to "Judo". She said that she was a *lovely, selfish, cold-hearted* creature, and loved her husband as well as she *could* love any one. How I love her. She knew nothing of the particulars of the marriage, as it was a very private affair, but *she* unhesitatingly asserts that it was a "money match".[25] I departed for school just as A. was ascending the stairs to prepare to hold herself in readiness to go out. I had a pleasant walk, but was much provoked as I stepped on my petticoat and tore it. It retarded my walking, and I was annoyed to think of to-morrow's *job* [repairing the petticoat]. It was the first afternoon that I answered to my name [at school]. A few moments after I had been there Miss Mitchell came and sat beside me. She looked real pretty and was dressed so becomingly. She is a sweet

25. Claire Dentzel taught "Judo" (Judith Hyams).

little creature. To my astonishment I learned that as the Junior class was so large, six girls had been promoted to the Senior. Those of a mature age were accepted, and I doubt had the promotion been offered to me if I would have accepted it. I do think that there is great partiality shown in some matters. I should have been pleased had I been one of the selected few. Miss M. told me that on Saturday Mr. Lusher had read the schools to which the girls were supernumeraries, but disremembered if my name was on the list. I hope so. The Dictation was quite simple. I saw nothing of the Seniors. I remained to hear the singing which was fine. Miss B. has a beautiful voice. I could sit enchanted for hours. The consciousness of being so gifted would produce on some persons an exalted opinion of themselves, but she always appears so modest and reserved. I should like to have joined in, but couldn't. "The spirit was willing". As Mrs. P. [Pagand] dismissed us she gave as a parting injunction "Wear your bonnets all the way home! I will speak more of the subject on some future occasion". I am anxious to be more informed upon this peculiar "arrangement". I saw Bridget and at her request accompanied her to the corner in company with Miss M. B. talked on different subjects, and said that she was disgusted with school. I am not particularly pleased with it. She requested me to tell Mrs. N. that Mrs. M. would come to-morrow. Miss M. persisted that I should walk a little way with her. I complied with her urgent request. We were witnesses of a little love scene on a gallery of a house on St. Charles St. How I envied them both. Miss M. was telling me of school matters, "etc." She asked me to go home with her, and promised to bring me home, and provide me with a beau. I declined her pressing invitation, but promised for some future period. I liked her very much this afternoon, and she *seems* to like me. I then proceeded home solitarily and alone, and found it impossible to obey Mrs. P.'s command, so quietly deposited my bonnet in my arm. When I got home, I found the house uninhabited, so after relieving myself of books and other unnecessary appendages, I ran over to Mrs. N.'s. Fanny and J., Sally and Leopold were there. Mrs. N. had been quite sick to day, but felt considerably better. F. and the children soon left, and as usual L. was the spokesman of the occasion; it is useless to attempt to talk when he is about — He told us that he heard Cousin Joe Rosenfield was in the City, but had found it to be false. The conversation then branched to Isabel, the entire control which she has over her husband and his unpardonable weakness in submitting to her. "To think", said L., "that *one of the Rosenfields* should be so controlled by a wife". He really considered it a degradation. He said he would have written for him to come on, but knows that it would be an utter impossibility for him to agree with I. [Isabel]. "I would tame her", said he. He thinks it strange that he has received no letters, as many opportunities were offered, mutual friends arriving here from there, so he arrives at the most natural conclusion that they have left St. Louis, have written informing of their intended plans, and the letter failed to reach its destination. I consider this probable. I would like to see them. Came home, and found Ma and A. just returned from their down town expedition. Of course they had much to tell. A. told me that *she had seen Mrs. Chofin.* They were in the omnibus, and she, dressed conspicuously and attracting universal attention, was walking down St. Charles St. Unfortunate, depraved woman. I suppose that every day she is plunged deeper and deeper into crime. Ma went to Dryer's, but the store was closed, and she made no purchases, with the exception of two bottles of Cocoaine. Mr. Ducenge has a small supply of the desired article. It looks to be good. That of Syme's was a "failure".[26] Mr. E. [Eisner] had given the cotton to Leopold, and he brought it up this afternoon. Ma is undecided whether to take it, as the quantity is rather large, four dozens, I believe, and Ma dislikes the idea of giving out so much money for spool cotton. I advised her to take it; as in time it will be very scarce and dearer. Then, they had gone to the Express Office, and had obtained a letter for "Miss Alice Solomon", "Webster School". I was much astonished when it was handed to me and I recognized Pa's handwriting. A $50 note was enclosed, which he accounted for by saying that he had drawn her salary before leaving. He begged her forgiveness and said that it would never happen again! He said you can show it to your ma or not, as you wish. He directed it to the school, thinking that it would be sent there, and as the important news was written on a slip of paper, Ma could read it and not suspect anything, and it was very strange that it was not delivered to her. I was thunderstruck, amazed and confounded. I had hoped that Pa had sent some private funds for me and A. The letter was dated the 24th and was evidently written very hurriedly. He is very, very busy, and says that he did not write on Sunday. Simon was in the room with him, and had been assisting him in his writing. He was well, and said "I have a book full to write, but not *now*". We discussed the letter, pondered over it, and Ma was quite angry at the proceeding. I hope that no difficulty will ensue — Ma is now in funds — We partook of b. & b. [bread & butter]. Ma went to Mrs. N. and you are already acquainted with our respective situa-

26. The Solomons' search for "cocoaine" was unending.

tions. Ma has just come in. I have been writing (and talking) for an hour. She has no news to communicate, but hastens us to bed, and with reluctance, though having recounted to you the principal events of this day, I bid you "good night".

Wednesday, October 2nd, 1861

9 o'clock P.M. . . . . I have not seen you to day, except when I removed the dust from your robe. But I am not to blame, so cease your reproachings. "There is not an hour of day or dreaming night, but *I am with thee*", so you *must* be contented if it *is* only in imagination. I see that you have a tendency to be jealous; this pleases me for it is an indication that you value my society. As the six o'clock bell rang this morning, I took myself from my bed. Came down, scanned the paper, wrote my Dictation, and Ellen being "non est" her duties devolved upon me. Dell came to the rescue, and I have made her quite a little nurse. She performed her services very faithfully, in consideration, I suppose, of her promised reward. I don't like to mind children. Mr. N. came to tell us that our coal would be up in the course of the day. He had ordered 12 barrels apiece for both, at the moderate price of 90 cts. Breakfast late, biscuits not good. While I was arranging the breakfast things, Mrs. D. came in. She took a seat, and we had a pleasant little chat. I wonder what Mr. Elburger would say to that. E. was much better, and she hoped would be able to come to-morrow. I heartily reiterate this sentiment. She was entertaining me with a description of the *one perfectly* lovely creature whom she had *ever* seen. In imagination, I also beheld her with her lustrous orbs and rich brown hair. She last saw her in Ireland, many years ago, and she is now doubtless an *elderly* lady. The morning was cloudy with indications of rain, but they were dispelled, and the day, though warm, was clear. The coal came, and numerous were the applications for the job of bringing it in. It seems to be good quality and measure. Ma wishes that the cold weather would commence; but I do not for there are many other considerations besides *coal.* Josie was as turbulent as usual, and demanded constant attention; she received it through the joint operations of Ma and me. As I left for school I asked A. if she would not about 6 o'c walk down a few squares to meet me; I left not knowing if she promised to comply with my request. Mrs. Pagand said a few words to us. She said that she had heard from good authority that some members of the L.N.S. did not behave with propriety while in the street. This reflected disgrace upon the school, and consequently upon her. Her remarks were particularly addressed to the Preparatory class, among which as a general thing great frivolity of manner pervaded. She remarked that it was mostly composed of children, and their joining the school was a most unwise step, and she would willingly accept the resignation of any. She said that when first instituted it was for the benefit of graduates, and those who could not with propriety attend the High or District Schools; and these girls required the strict discipline to which they in those institutions are subjected. She then forbade all confabs at the door, congregations at corners, and particularly going *home bareheaded*. She said that were any girl pointed out individually, she would not hesitate to suspend her, for no stigma must rest upon the character of the noble institution. She spoke very ably and length[il]y, and in every point advanced I agreed with her. She said "Mr. Lusher will speak to you on the subject, but I presume not as candidly as I". The tap of the bell then dismissed "Juniors No. A" to their room. Mrs. S. was absent, but Miss B. filled her post. "And still I gazed and still my wonder grew that one small head could contain all she knew". She is a well informed personage. I recited Rhetoric correctly. It did not surprise me as I had studied it diligently. The time was so limited that the Grammar was slighted, so we are to take the same lesson for next week. A very agreeable "arrangement". Miss Leech heard "Scholars Companion". I was deficient in it, as I was disappointed in thinking that I would have had an opportunity to study it. Miss M. who sat next to me, helped me however. Miss L. looked beautiful, and I was lost in admiration. She had a good, amiable expression, and honored should the man feel upon whom she will bestow her love. After the class, I kissed her several times. Lizzie was not in school. I have not seen her this week. I joined Miss Mitchell, and we walked together down Nayades St. She was relating to me some of the particulars of the run-away marriage of Miss Mary Harrison, in which *she* figured rather conspicuously. She seemed offended when I refused to go home with her, and persisted in saying that I had promised, of which I had a most indistinct recollection. I do not like the idea of going home, and spending the evening, but would not object paying her a visit. I asked her to come and see me, and she specified Saturday. I have no faith in *that* promise. I had a long walk to take alone, and felt envious when I passed the noble residence of the nobler G.H. Race, Esq. Every one appears to stare at me, when I am walking. I imagine that they take me for a "kept in girl". As I passed the "corner house", I saw some one whom I thought was Mrs. P. [Prothro] I bowed, and a moment's closer investigation sufficed to show me that it was Miss Lizzie. I felt chagrined, as she did not return it. I suppose it was so unexpected. I saw Mrs. N. at the corner, and we went over to her house. I had hoped to obtain a glimpse of Mrs. M., but she had gone. Josh had had some trouble in school. Miss Myers had sent him home, and wrote a note in which she said that he had been misbehaving all day. J. denied this. She makes frequent complaints which annoy Mrs. N. considerably. She is going to see her about it in the morning—Fanny and Josie came over, but did not stay long. A. soon made her appearance. She had been up to Dryades St with Ma, and she was unable to come for me. I did not expect her. Ma had purchased us both a pair of gloves, but Mr. Churchill could not change some money, so they were left there for some future period. When we rose to depart Mrs. N. vetoed the movement, and in consideration of the many invitations we have refused I proposed to stay, and stay we did. While at supper, the Lord and Master entered. Mrs. N. wished for daughters. What good friends we would be! Miss Sarah's children! How strange does it sound. It was our determination to leave at eight o'-clock. Mrs. N. agreed to accompany us home, and a few moments after the "warning bell" had pealed forth the hour, we were in our domicil. Ma was "very happy to see us". Principal topic Miss Myers. Mr. N. came over, and they went a short while ago. A. had some talk with Miss D. As she visits among a great many Jews, she is consequently posted in all their affairs. *Kate Abrams* is going to Savannah, to spend an indefinite length of time with some relatives. She is one of the belles of our congregation, and doubtless will produce a sensation, as a "New Orleans young lady". May her brightest dreams of pleasure be realized. Miss Henrietta Levy brought "Gus'[s] little girl" to see them. She is a beautiful child, and lives with Mrs. E.J. Hart. The Governor has issued a proclamation, wherein he states that the time has arrived for a thorough organization of the Militia, and calls upon every man, between the ages of 18 and 45, who has not joined some company to come forward and enlist. They will all respond to the call. In order to afford time for efficient drill the Banking and Insurance Offices are ordered to be closed at 2 P.M. and other stores at 3 P.M. Many fears are entertained for the safety of our City, as it will be the most important point of attack in the S.C. [Southern Confederacy].

Thursday, October 30, 1861

8 o'clock P.M. . . . . Oh! Philomen, I am such a fool. The texture of your robe is of so fine a quality, that I turned over *two* folds instead of one, but it is not pardonable, as the same accident happened on a previous occasion, and I should have been *more* careful. It disconcerted me considerably. Experience *twice* bought is better than *four* times taught. Ma is over to Mrs. N.'s. She went after supper, by our request, as when writing, we are but little company to her. This morning before going to school, A. went round to Mrs. Deegan's. She subsequently came herself; said E. was improving, and would be here to-morrow. Breakfast aristocratic. Trout and Cream cheeses. Did not spend the day pleasantly and considered myself fortunate in not having any lessons to study, for there was to be merely a rehearsal of the Concert, in the afternoon. Rosa went to school with Alice to day. She was delighted. She behaved very well, but was a little wilful. I was just about leaving for school when some one tapped at the door. A. went to it, a letter was handed, no questions asked, and the bearer silently departed. A. was dumbfounded and "spoke not a word", but delivered *Pa's letter* to Ma, its rightful owner. It was a large double letter, was post-marked Richmond, and consequently came through the mail, and we can account for its mysterious appearance in no other manner than by thinking that it was taken out of the P.O. by some one. This supposition though it *must* be correct *seems* incorrect, for Mr. N. left orders there for our letters to be delivered to no one, but him and Mr. Elburger. Ma tore it open, and divers little pieces of paper dropped out. I learned that he was well. And as it was late, I was apprised of only a part of the contents, so deferred the perusal until 1 should come home, so I will proceed with other events first, and in due course of time make you acquainted with *all* particulars of the loved epistle. I left for school, reluctantly, but the anticipation of the pleasure which I had in store (Pa's letter) cheered me. Before conscious, I was at the "seat of action"; I discovered that our seats were occupied by members of the H. S., and seeing no vacant chair among the N. S. I seated myself in the extreme rear of the room, and, being the only one there, I felt lonely and, no doubt, looked conspicuous, so I resolved that "it wouldn't do". A brilliant idea seized possession of me. I went round through the French Room, took a chair, and seated myself beside Ada. Ever and anon, I congratulated myself upon the wise movement, and its success. Presently Mrs. Fisher came in. She cautioned the young ladies to imagine themselves before an audience, as the programme for the afternoon would be precisely

that of the concert night. Mr. Rogers honored us by his presence, and seemed to drink in the sweet melody. How many memories were awakened by Mr. Wharton's pleasant face and "Good afternoon, Miss Solomon". The singing was excellent, and Nina Word's "Ask me not why" particularly charmed me. She is a beautiful girl. I was surprised to see Sissy Pitkin take so important a part, as I never dreamed that her voice ranked above mediocrity; and the Alto, by which she was accompanied, was so very loud, that her notes were drowned and I am yet ignorant. At the conclusion of each performance Ada and I would comment upon the merits and defects, and the greater part met our decided approval. She had been requested to contribute her aid, but had refused. She left about 5¼. I, knowing how dull it would be to remain without company, followed her example. And I did not wish to hear it all, for in case I should attend the Concert, the pleasure would not be so great. I met Miss Leech on the gallery. We kissed and parted at the gate. Miss Mitchell and Liz. were not there. The final rehearsal is to take place on Saturday. I hope that the Concert will be a success. My appearance at home so early created some astonishment. A. was *amusing* herself with Josie, but shortly delivered her into abler hands, and went to dress. I read Pa's letter, of the contents of which I shall shortly apprise you. When she came down, a walk was proposed, and we forthwith directed our steps to Mrs. N.'s. She went to Miss Myers in the morning, but said "It is useless for me ever to go to her, she '*smooths*' every thing over so nicely". Mrs. N. found it impossible to speak to her otherwise than friendly, and they parted on amicable terms. When Josh came home to day, he told his Ma that Miss M. had told him to say to her that *he had been a very good boy.* Quoth Mrs. N. "What can a person do?" We left as Ma entered. Proceeded to Fairex's, invested in 5 cts. cake at my expense, for you must know that I am in funds, Ma having munificently endowed me with 50 cts. Related to A. the events of the afternoon. I had often wished that she was there, as I know that she would have enjoyed it, being as enthusiastic an admirer of beauty, and as great a lover of singing as I. Nina Word claimed our respectful attention. She has improved wonderfully of late. But, sad to relate, she is very wild and has not escaped the slander of some tongues. How fearful a thing. Cora Jones, Sissie P, Belle H. and numerous others claimed a share of our interesting conversation. I wonder if we'll go. Returned to Mrs. N.'s, Ma still there. She lit the lamp, and we adjourned to the back parlor. Ma was reading portions of the "mysterious document" to attentive listeners. F. came over to see *what* kept us, as we know that she was alone. Arrived home, eat supper, Ma to Mrs N.'s, and *now* for the "letter".

It was a very long one and dated the 26th. He had removed to the "Spotswood House", the most fashionable in Richmond; but he is anxious to leave it for many reasons; the principal one, the price, then his room is on the fourth floor, to which there are many objections, and lastly he can't get anything to eat to *suit him;* he says he would gladly exchange his dinner there for one of *our* "home dishes", and he has inserted an advertisement in the paper for a private boarding place. He received several replies to it, which together with the advertisement he enclosed for our inspection and these constituted those scraps which I before noticed. He had not at the time attended to any of the communications. I hope that he will find a suitable place. He writes that the weather is delightful, and he is enjoying excellent health. He weighs *ten* pounds more than when he left us. He is very busy and says "if you do not hear from me every day, you must not imagine that I am *gone, for I am all right*". He wrote "I may take a trip to Manassas on next Sunday". "Mr. da Ponte dines with me to day; he leaves in a few days for the seat of war". Not a word of remembrance to *us*. Mean thing! He even *promised* to *write.* "Out of sight, out of mind". Pa saw Harry Marks, and told him about the "bundle". He conducted him to Mr. Hector Davis, in whose charge he placed it, and, who forwarded it to its destination, and Harry is satisfied that Pa did all in his power to fulfill the trust reposed in him, and said that he would write and tell his Mother so. He still hopes however, that he may get it, as it *may* have been sent to camp at Gordonsville, while he was sick in the Hospital at Culpeper. Since his sickness, he has not been to camp. He asked Pa to lend him ten dollars which he did, and received a receipt from him. This, he sent to Ma, in the letter with instructions to present it to Mrs. Marks and "if collected, I wish you to give it to *my dear Clara!!!!* This then is the reply to "my little scrap", about whose fate we were so undecided. The question now is "Will she pay it"? I hope so, but she may think it an equivalent for the lost "bundle". What fine dresses will I have!!! $10! Quite a little *fortune, now-a-days*. Simon has been very sick. He is better, and has returned to Camp. Pa has received a letter from Cousin S. He was much pleased with Sallie's letter. Says he will answer it, and attend to her *sister's orders*. And these are all the items of the letter, that would interest you.

Saturday, October 5th, 1861

11 o'clock P.M. . . . . Since last I saw you, how much, how *very* much have I suffered. The pain is now intense, but I will endeavor while in your society to forget it. I have a most excruciating *toothache.* It is a tooth which Dr D. filled some time ago. He killed the nerve, the tooth is consequently dead. I suppose I have cold in it, and when one of this description is so attacked, the pain is most acute. Ma predicted at the time that it would always trouble me, as she has had experience. She advised me to have it extracted, but Dr D. objected and I, also, as it would show, and Ma now tells me to have it out immediately. There is *no* remedy that can be applied, but it will have to run its course. My face will then swell, and I will not be relieved for days. Oh! the pain *now* is unendurable. And I don't know to what Dentist to go. This is a subject which much distresses me, as I have other teeth which require immediate attention. The tooth has been annoying me for some days past, but I thought by not noticing it, it would pass away. I rallied with it bravely up to yesterday, about 12,1 o'clock, when I was compelled to lie down, and since then I have not had a moment's ease. The children came home, and found the tears streaming down my cheeks, and were much alarmed, and when they learned the cause of them, they deeply sympathized with me. My chair was vacant at the dinner table. The remaining 250 Hessians arrived yesterday afternoon. I heard the music, and from the window saw many persons traversing the streets, but my mind was occupied by something else, and the arrival of the strangers was further unheeded by me. I see by to day's paper that they were marched directly to the Parish Prison. I was walking up and down the room, perfectly frantic. A. was down stairs writing to Pa, and about dark she came up, and we both lied on the bed. She was talking, and I suppose trying to divert my attention as I could scarcely open my mouth. Lucy came to fix the bed, and we were compelled to rise. She dressed and went down, after entreating me to do likewise, but I couldn't. Ma had gone over to Mrs. N.'s and up to the present time had not come home, but shortly after her dear voice was heard and also the familiar one of Mrs. N. Ma sent up my dinner, which consisted of some hominy and liver. It was very nice, and I succeeded, with great difficulty, in eating some of it. I was quite hungry as I had tasted nothing since breakfast. I was lying on the sofa, and Lucy had packed the "chicks" in bed. Dell bade me "good night", was gone, and I was alone; for I would not let A. stay with me. She remonstrated, but finally yielded to my wish. My thought wandered to many different persons,

and I lived over many different scenes. Drew from the armoire a long obscured box, and began to view its contents. I came across many relics, of
whose existence I was perfectly unaware, and many papers and letters
which I thought had long since been scattered to the four winds of Heaven.
The associations arising from their perusal were pleasant and unpleasant.
The voices from below grated upon my ear, and I regretted that I could not
join the circle. A person in pain generally has the idea that all around are
similarly afflicted, and I could not realize that they did not have a toothache,
and oft would ask the question. I did not want to go to bed, as I knew I
would be unable to sleep. However I retired about 8½. F. and S. [Fannie
and Sallie] soon came up, both departed to their respective couches, and
to sleep, but I did not. I slept, but at intervals, all night, and when I awoke
this morning, was suffering the same. I am *almost* resigned. E. came yesterday. Her foot *most* better. We had several hard showers, but the weather
still is *very* warm. I thought that the rain would affect a change; but I am
indifferent. If it continues warm, I have nothing to wear, if it gets cold, I
am in the same predicament. Thursday night, while Ma was to Mrs.
N.'s, Alice and I were comfortably seated in our spacious parlors, A. deep
in the Paper, but venturing occasionally to utter a sentence or so, when the
bell rang and our Cousin Sam was with us. He was in the neighborhood
on business, and stepped in for a few moments, for he was anxious to get
home, as Fannie was not very well. He is Captain of a Militia Company to
be organized in a certain district. His duties will be arduous, but the salary,
I *believe*, is liberal. Men, who have not joined Volunteer Companies, are
now prohibited from so doing, and are compelled to enlist in the Militia.
He said that as Pa did not receive his letter, he would write again. He
was silent as to the Concert. "Nary word was said". I don't think that he
has the remotest idea of taking us. He looked very handsome. Gave us a
most cousinly kiss and left. About 9 o'clock Ma came, accompanied by Mr.
Elburger. He apologized for not having been to see us, but said that of late
he had been suffering both physically and mentally. His business is almost
totally suspended on account of the Blockade. Various opinions were advanced as to when it would be removed, and he said that until it was, his
prospects would not be any brighter. Of course, this depresses his spirits.
Had quite a long talk on Politics. I had nothing to say, for I felt a dull aching
pain in my tooth. He left in about a half an hour. After going through the
necessary preliminaries, we marched up stairs, and our mansion was soon
enveloped in darkness.

8¼ P.M. . . . I am up in my room, alone with you. Mrs. N. is down stairs,

and every word of the conversations ascends to my chamber. I am slightly
of the opinion that I am somewhat relieved. Ma sent me up a very nice little supper which I disposed of. She and F. went out this afternoon, and
brought me my gloves, which unfortunately are too large. I would rather
have a larger hand, than to be subjected to the inconveniences arising from
so small a one. I *never* can get a glove to fit properly. F. and S. have just
come to bed. A. was sitting up with me this afternoon when the bell
rang. She went down and it proved to be Miss Jo. I did not see A. again
until dark. She came up, and told me that she had walked around to Susie
B.'s with her, where she was going to spend the night. She did not intend
to be gone so long, but while they were by the door talking Ma passed,
stopped, had a lengthy confab and Ma and F. returned with A. Miss Jo. is
coming to spend one night next week with A., who has agreed to spend
Monday night with her. She goes up to camp very often, and of course is
a general favorite with all the Officers, who unanimously declared that "
Ed. Hews had the handsomest wife of any of them". She wishes A. and I
to accompany her some time. I would like it very much. A. represented her
as looking as pretty as ever. The day has been very warm. About 12½
Octavia and Fannie Harby called to see us. They have not been to see us
for so long a time that I thought they were angry. We found interesting
subject for about two hours conversation. They both looked charming,
and we may with propriety include them in our list of "pretty girls".
They told us to our surprise that Belle was not going to sing at the Concert.
A sudden obstinate freak is the only cause assigned. Comments were made
upon the appearances and capacities of the different performers, and this
subject was exhausted.

Their stock of "news" was very limited. All the "girls'" prospects and
beaus were discussed. They incline to the opinion that Marion M. and
Ludie E. are attached to each other, and yet mysteriously venture to say
that she will never become Mrs. Marion M. though in the course of events
she may claim a right to the title of Mrs. Eddy M. She corresponds with
him!! Are their surmises based upon *this* slight foundation? Is not this a
privilege granted to brother, and sister-in-law? They told us that "Miss
Flora Levy" (just think of it! our dear Flora) was to be married to a Mr.
Denaigre, *so they heard*. I hope that it is false. Mrs. Levy has given up the
idea of moving. She had some trifling objection. Octavia was as loquacious as she always is. I could not recount to you one half of what was said,
and if I could it might fail to interest you. O. has discarded her beautiful
curls, as she persists in saying that they are unbecoming. I, with many oth-

ers, differ with her in this opinion. I wonder when she will get married. I don't believe that she is very much admired by the male specie. Ma predicts that F. will be the first to enter the state of holy wedlock. She is the *prettier.* War, the high prices of goods, "etc., etc." were some of the discussed subjects. They left about 2½. We promised to "come soon". Dinner next; I succeeded in eating. The mosquitoes are so annoying, and the bed looks so tempting that I will now, with the hope of a good night's rest, softly breathe "Good bye".

Sunday, October 6th, 1861

2 ½ P.M. . . . . Sunday again! And every prospect of its being a gloomy one. It is very cloudy, and we have had some rain. With heart elate, 1 now inform you that my pain is almost allayed, and in comparison with yesterday's seems unnoticeable. I am nearly myself again. A. and I have been idling about all the morning, reading the papers, which were perfectly void of interesting matter, and listening to ourselves talk. Ma went to market this morning, and at breakfast a fine fish, and a large dish of shrimps, were placed before us, and a treat is in store for us in the shape of a nice piece of roast. How Pa would enjoy it. I wonder where he now is. Would that some *fairy* would bestow upon me the gift of the Magic glass, into which, at all times, I could look and see the situations of the persons, whom my fancy should dictate. As I now write the rain is pouring, and I expect at its termination, we will have a cold spell. I learned to day that Ma had made some purchases at Dohan's yesterday afternoon. They consisted principally of some salmon, preserved ginger, biscuits, etc. Mr. Isaaks, a sugar merchant, and friend of Mr. N., presented him with a quantity of *splendid molasses,* and Mrs. N. sent Ma a large pitcher full. It is *delicious.* To day, Ma sent her some P.G. I was asleep before she left last night, and subsequently heard that Mr. E. was here. Before coming to you I combed my hair. But am not pleased with its appearance, and I can't look nice in *any* manner. I hope that Cousin S. will come this afternoon and say something about the Concert, I don't care what. To dinner!

8¼ P.M. . . . Ma is asleep on the sofa, A. is with Felicie. The children have gone to bed. After leaving you I went to dinner, which we all enjoyed. The rain continued some time, but finally ceased, and it is now as warm as ever.

After dinner A. and I dressed, neither very elaborately, came down; she wrote, I read everything and anything. A short while before dark Leopold honored us. We were sitting out on the gallery, laughing and talking. He had received a letter from Julius. He is well, and says that it is extremely cold. L. has recently heard that Cousin Joe and family are still in St. Louis. We repaired to the room, and he did not stay long. He went over to Mrs. N.'s and wished us to accompany him, but we did not wish to. We then eat supper. Oh! Philomen, Cousin S. has *not* been *up*. I don't suppose we will see him for weeks; I am crazy to go to the Concert. Solomon, while I was writing the above, came to tell us "good bye", as he leaves with Capt. David Marks to morrow for his Camp on the Opelousas Rail-Road. He is out of situation and adopts this plan as the most beneficial. I told him "good bye" and hoped to see him again soon, and bade him, in case of a battle, to let us hear good accounts of him. As he knocked at the door, my heart bounded. I thought it was — Cousin S. Enough for tonight. *En passant,* what has become of "Gus"?

Monday, October 7th, 1861

$7^1/_2$ A.M. . . . . A damp, disagreeable morning! I have been up some time, and my principal employment has been the studying of my Synonyms. I was absent last Monday, and I studied the lesson at random. A. is dressing. She has been with F. all morning. After the pleasant days of Saturday and Sunday, with some reluctance do I hail Monday. I miss them so. How provoking! Last night A. and I agreed to invest in a creamcheese this morning, and just our luck the Vendor of these delectable delicacies did not pass. Well! we will indulge on some future occasion. Two days of anxious expectation and torturing suspense, and *all will be over.* I have tried to abandon the thought. I feel as though I am going to be unsuccessful. Alice has just descended in her school habiliments. How I envy her. I hope that the rain will not thwart her plans for to night, although I greatly disapprove of girls spending the night away from home. She anticipates great fun. F. and S. are down. Breakfast is ordered. Ma expected!

$7^1/_2$ P.M. . . . . I am alone, with Fannie and Sallie. Ma has just run over to Mrs. N.'s, and Alice has gone to Miss Jo.'s. I am so lonesome without her. According to agreement she stopped at school this afternoon to see me.

Some one came in the room, and said that there was a lady outside who wished to see Miss Solomon. I knew who it was, went out, and found her on the gallery. I would have left and walked a few squares with her, but taking into consideration the disagreeable streets, I resolved not to, but that she would take the 'bus at the corner. This was satisfactory. We remained talking a short while on the portico, I, enlightening her on some of the events of the afternoon. It was quite late, and she was desirous of going, so after telling me of the terrible suspense she would be in until to-morrow, (oh! Cousin S. has not come) and imprinting a heart-felt kiss on my lips, she tripped down the stairs, my parting injunction being "take care of yourself". I returned to my room.

Arrived at school in season [on time]. Mrs. Shaw was not there, as her husband is dangerously ill. Miss B. was tardy, and until she came, I employed myself by studying. Bowed across the room to Liz. and Ada. How I longed to be with them. We were quietly seated in Miss B.'s room, when Mrs. P. entered, and stated that a gentleman, whose little son was a performer on the Accordion, had offered his services to assist at the Concert. He was in the adjoining room, and she allowed us the privilege of going in there, and listening to some of his performances. It created quite a disturbance but finally all was quieted, and he began. He played and sang some simple tunes, and of course there was much giggling. It was doubtless very good, considering his juvenility, but he wants a little more practice, before he can appear in public. I am confident that Mr. Lusher will refuse the offer. How ridiculously do some persons act. They took their departure, and we repaired to our respective places. The lesson was very short, in consequence of the interruption. In fact, it could not be called a lesson. The arithmetic was not recited, as the time specified for it was monopolized by Mr. L. He had made a division of the Junior Class into the Junior and Sophomore, and read the list of names which constituted them. Mine, of course, was included in the Junior. I am offended with him, and feel slighted in not being appointed Supernumerary. I passed him, without recognition, but some time after *he* spoke, and asked how was my sister. I answered him very formally, and passed on. If ever I have the opportunity, I shall speak to him on the subject. Miss B. then devoted the remainder of the hour to informing us of the tasks assigned for each afternoon, but they being so varied from the past programme, I am unable to retain the knowledge but must acquire it gradually. I think from the present, our duties will be much more arduous. Mrs. P. told us that there would be a rehearsal to-morrow, at Odd Fellow's Hall, between the hours of 9

and 11, and she would supply those (not already supplied) with Tickets.
I promised Miss Mitchell that, did I gain Ma's consent, which I have, to
call for her and go together. Ma is distressed because we are so anxious
to go, and without a prospect, and says she would willingly bear any expense. We had considerable fun, this afternoon. Miss M. and I after preliminaries parted at the corner, and she again repeated her wish for me to
accompany her home. With my bonnet on my head, I arrived home safe.
Found Ma at the gate, joined her, and saluted her with a kiss, as I observed
for the first time the new Moon. I amused myself with Josie, came in,
eat supper, Miss Nellie Giradeau being a distinguished guest. Ma, with
my permission, went to Mrs. N. The day has been quite unpleasant;
raining at intervals, but before dinner the sun shone, the clouds dispelled,
and since then the weather has been fine. It has a slight inclination towards
chilliness. The night is most beautiful. The clear Moon and twinkling stars
charm the eye. Ma and I were rather indolent to day. I assisted to sew on
a flounce of A.'s dress, and this is all I accomplished in the sewing line.
Quite a serious accident happened to me. I was leaning back in a chair,
when I lost my balance and chair and I were soon prostrate on the ground.
Regardless of self my first thoughts were of the chair, and to my grand
consternation I ascertained that its injuries were severe, and in dwelling
upon them I *entirely* forgot my own, which were not of so serious a nature.
Ma had declared her intentions of attending to them, but I have determined, and if needed, at my own expense, for it is a precious little chair,
and one to which I am attached, not for its appearance or value, but for
the sake of the old memories connected with it, as it has figured in many
scenes of bygone days. I love it! and, as I gaze upon it, tears start to my
eyes, and my conscience bitterly reproaches me, for my carelessness and
want of consideration in treating it so roughly. It seems to look mournfully
upon me. I entertain the hope that it will soon be restored to its former
beauty and familiarity. Ma was very lenient, for as she said "you may have
broken your back". Nothing else worthy of record transpired, I think.

9$^1/_4$ P.M. . . . F. and S. have gone to bed, and I am down here in the back
room by—myself. A few moments after leaving you, steps were heard on
the gallery (my heart was in my mouth), the bell was pulled (my hopes
went down, *down, down*), the door was opened, and—Gus was ushered in.
Oh! how disappointed was I. (Ah! Philomen *he* has not come, and we can
safely assert that *we are not going*). G. came in, and I arose to greet him.
He took *his* seat on the sofa, and we talked as sarcastically, ironically and
foolishly as usual. He, constantly saying that I was the most interesting

young lady whom he had ever seen, and I not *at all* returning the same compliment as regarded him. Spent last evening with Mrs. da P. Found her as entertaining as ever, and as handsome, but of course, she suffered greatly in comparison with me. He told me a part of something which excited my curiosity very much, but he refused "to make any more disclosures, as he had already been too loquacious on the subject". I entreated, implored, but *all* was unavailing. I offered many inducements, but he said that nothing could serve to alter his determination, for did he comply with my request, he would be compelled to betray confidence. I endeavored to draw him into the lighted room, but could not succeed for more than a few seconds. I wonder why he so shuns the light. He inquired repeatedly for A.; but only so often, in order to annoy me. He is *such* a tease. He remained an uncomfortably long time, and I earnestly asked him to go, but he would not "to oblige" me. But every thing has an end, so did his visit, for about quarter of an hour ago, after strictly commanding me to be at the Concert, he took his leave. F. and S. obtained my permission to retire. *He* has *not* come. There's Ma! Later. She was astonished to find me alone, and called me a "little hero". She is now writing, and I seize this opportunity. She is much provoked, and says that we *shall* go!! It is past 10, and now Philomen with a heavy heart, depressed spirits, and want of confidence in *all mankind*, I leave you.

Tuesday, October 8th, 1861

$7^1/_4$ A.M. . . . I have just come down, but have been up some time, and am dressed with the exception of my dress, etc., etc. Oh! it is such a lovely, *cold* morning. What a beautiful night! How many emotions overpower me as I pencil Tuesday, October 8th!! I have relinquished every idea, and as a substitute will attend the Rehearsal, but "Poor Alice", she will be disappointed. Who will break the sad news to her? I know that hope is not extinct in her bosom, but when the sad intelligence is imparted to her, she will exclaim, "My hopes and fears are at an end. The interesting performance will not be attended by the Miss Solomons". She will come home before she goes to school. The paper lies temptingly on the floor before me. I cannot resist the temptation.

$4^1/_4$ P.M. Cousin S. has just come!!!!!!!!!!!!!!

6³/₄ P.M. We are dressed, and down, waiting for the gentleman. I look *so* ugly, for I prepared in a most disagreeable hurry. I am not joyful. A. has on her Flag dress, I, my organdy. She, looking very nice, I, very indifferent. Ma and F. are going. I am so glad.

Wednesday, October 9th, 1861

6¹/₄ A.M. . . . . Here I am! By great exertions I arose about six. The morning is quite cold. The sun has not yet risen. A. is sitting by me, both engaged in the same pursuit. I will now proceed to acquaint you with the facts of yesterday. Immediately after breakfast I prepared myself to go. Before I left, A. came in. She had learned from the children the sad intelligence and if she had not told me, her face would have plainly indicated the fact. Nine was fast approaching, and as that was my hour of appointment I was obliged to leave, without having scarcely a moment's conversation with her. The morning was fine, and after a pleasant walk, I was soon ringing the bell at Miss M.'s door. The house is at the corner of Camp and Delord.[27] I was ushered up into the parlor, and while sitting there I had an opportunity to inspect surrounding objects. The room was furnished very handsomely, and my impression is that they keep boarders. I was much interested in a book, when she entered. She apologized for keeping me waiting so long, but offered some excuse. We then departed, and walked leisurely along. She is such a queer creature, I found it impossible to understand her. Arrived at Odd Fellow's Hall, entered the door, walked up the steps, and were soon in the midst of a quantity of girls. Kissed many of them, spoke to others, and then endeavored to extricate myself, and for this reason went to the "dressing room", where Mrs. P. was arranging the portion of the songsters. We seated ourselves on the luxurious sofa, and observed the proceedings, as we did not intend taking a part in the performance. Mrs. P. gave us our tickets. The appearance of the room by day awakened in our minds a train of thought. In imagination we beheld the many lovely forms which those glasses had reflected, of the many feet which had tripped lightly over the carpet, and of the many romantic incidents which there had their birth. Our thoughts found expression in

27. Several blocks from the Solomons' home, the corner of Camp and Delord is at the far side of Tivoli (now Lee) Circle.

words, and we carried on a most spell-bound conversation, which was interrupted by orders from headquarters, and we repaired with the girls to the Concert Room, we taking seats among the audience. They marched in, and arranged themselves very orderly. The audience was very small. Mr. R. and Mr. C. were very officious, proposing and adopting various plans. The performance soon commenced, and for some time, I was much entertained, listening attentively, as I thought that it was all I would see of it. Miss M. and I were chiefly speaking of the Words. She lives so near to them, and is well posted in all their actions, which she highly condemns. The subject was a fruitful one to her, and an agreeable one to me, and she willingly replied to all my questions, which, you may be assured, were numerous. She was careful in her manner of speaking and requested me to mention nothing of what she had said, as she did not wish to have the appearance of slander, but undoubtedly all that she said were indisputable facts. The Words are pretty, but what else? At the conclusion of the performance, we left, walked a square up Camp, and then determined to go back for fun, so back we went. The crowd had not dispersed and we *had* fun in watching them. Miss M., Miss McGloin and I held a lengthy confab at the door. Commented upon the appearance of the singers, and wound up with a long dissertation on beauty, and to my joy, I found her as great an enthusiast as myself; this gratifies me, for I sometimes fear that *I* am extravagantly foolish. This congregation soon dispersed, and as there was nothing else to be seen, we agreed to take our leave. Miss M. invited me to her mansion, I refused, we parted, but did not kiss, as she objects to it in the street. I had gone a few steps, when I met, and received a most gracious bow from the stately, handsome Mrs. da P. I feared that Ma would be uneasy at my long absence, so I raced home, and found that she was not. I ate some lunch, related all particulars, and expressed my regrets that we *all* could not attend. Ma was much concerned for us. She made no objections to my paying Alice a visit and forthwith I started. Found her in the discharge of her duties. A place was cleared for me on the platform, and we conversed incessantly. She was quite downhearted, and the Concert was first disposed of. I told her *all* that I had seen, heard or suspected. We mourned over the manners of a certain *man*, and vowed *never* again to speak to him. Oh! you know all that we said. Then Gus' turn was next. What *he* said and did next claimed special attention, and A. and I enjoyed many a laugh at his expense. I believe I told you that "Little Henry" is sick. *I* exhausted and *she* began. She had enjoyed herself excessively, and had had "splendid times". Miss Jo. has partly promised to spend Friday night with us. I hope we will not be disappointed. A. told me many things, but I do not attach sufficient importance to them to honor them by a record, for they amount to nothing. I remained until school was out. She has some dear little children, and one with a perfect hand. It is beautiful. I saw Belle for a second, not long enough to talk. Miss D.'s "beautiful" face I gazed upon, but it flitted past and was lost to my admiring view. When we got home, a consultation was held, and we decided to go over, and ask Mr. N. to accompany us to the Concert, we, defraying all expenses. They were much astonished to see us at so unseasonable a time, but we soon made known the object of our visit, and Mr. N. consented to play the beau. We made arrangements and came home. Eat dinner—Item, Apple Dumpling. Ma was willing to bear the expense of $1, but no more. I had a ticket, so A.'s and Mr. N.'s would amount to that. I was up stairs, when a superiority ring was given to the bell. I had an idea! I ran down! "That voice"!!! "It is"! "thy—Cousin"!!! A. went over to inform Mr. N. that his valuable services could be dispensed with. Ma was amusing him by exposing "our hopes and fears", and he said it would have been a "d—n good joke" if he had not come. We told him our determination. He played the piano, and stayed some time. He was much flurried and excited, as the nomination was to take place in the night.[28] We told him to be up by 6½ and when he left I summoned A. to get her hair combed. Whilst performing the duty, the bell rang, Ma went down, but was soon again with us. The visitor had been Mrs. Marks. She had received a letter from Harry, wherein he stated that he had obtained his *precious*, oft spoken of bundle, and he desired his mother to call on Ma. She said that she would bring up the money. I hope so. She did not remain long, as she did not wish to detain Ma. Finished A.'s hair, called Lucy to do mine. I felt very low spirited, and not like dressing, so was very careless in my toilet. My hair looked remarkably ugly, but I could expect nothing more, as I bestowed *no* pains upon it. Oh! I am so ugly! Our toilets were shortly completed, and I had a few moments' chat with you, prior to our noble Cousin's entrance. He, as usual, accelerated our movements, and after our preparations, and Ma's numerous directions to Lucy, we were on our way. We were arranged in two companies, Ma and F. composing one, Cousin S., A., and I the other. They were in the rear, and we occasionally halted, while the Captain gave his orders for the "second Platoon" to advance more rapidly. He was very entertaining, and spoke chiefly of his expected nomination, and I could easily perceive his anxious frame of mind. His opponents are very popular, but I do pray that *he* will

28. Sam Myers hoped for the nomination to run for a seat in the Louisiana legislature.

receive it; he is then confident of the election. Odd Fellow's Hall was soon reached. At the foot of the stairs we saw Ludy, Bridget and — Marion. Kissed and passed on. The room was almost filled, and we succeeded in obtaining seats very far back. I at first grumbled, but when looking around some time after, and seeing how much better situated I was than many, I became satisfied. The Hall was packed, there was not a vacant chair, and Cousin S. from his extreme politeness vacated *his* for a young lady. A. regretted this, as she anticipated I suppose much pleasure in his society. She told him not to go. "Suppose it were you"? She bade him — go. Ere the lapse of many minutes the performance commenced. I was anxious that A. should see the girls, so I compelled her to use diligently the Opera Glass. I was very much pleased, and they all acquitted themselves creditably. The "Bonnie Blue Flag" was the feature of the evening. It was encored, and at the conclusion called for. Little "Clara Fisher" was the principal attraction, and so persistent were the audience that she tripped to the piano and the dear little creature sang "Comin' thro' the Rye". She has a splendid voice for so young a child, and one of which her elders would be proud. She sang beautifully and met with thundering applause. We were all exceedingly entertained. It was over by 9½ and I could scarcely realize it. How long it had been in preparation, how much it had been thought of, and now 'twas all over. The Concert was *past*. The crowd was *so* immense, that we could, in no manner, obtain an egress, so stationed ourselves in the "supper room", in imagination partaking of the many delicacies which it has so often contained. I was very hungry, but this did not satisfy my appetite. I had an opportunity of observing the people. I saw many familiar faces. As the crowd somewhat thinned we made a bold attempt, succeeded in reaching the stairs and made a safe retreat. The night was beautiful, and the memories of "the times that were" "thickened fast" upon me. The walk was pleasant. Cousin S. left soon after arriving home; he was too excited to sit down. To think, Philomen, his fate was to be decided at 11 o'clock! Was there not some excuse? He left with our good wishes, and orders to come up soon; I am anxious for his sake, but I don't think that it will do him any particular good. We then repaired to the dining room, indulged lightly. I was very tired, and hastily sought my couch. In an unconceivably short space of time I was disrobed, and had stretched my weary limbs down upon my own delightful bed, fully satisfied with the eventful day. Expressed my wish to A. to be awaken early, and she gratified it, for about 5½, I heard her voice and felt her touch. "In a moment" and it grew to many.

That wretched "Cream cheese man". Because we wanted him he did not come.

8 P.M. . . . Here I be! A. is with F., Ma is writing to Pa, from whom we received letters to day, the particulars of which I will acquaint you by and by. The drop light is lit, and we are seated around Alice's table. The mosquitoes are buzzing in my ears but I will submit to them by presuming each to be a whispered tale of love. With the exception of the letters the day has been uneventful, though beautiful and warm. I studied the greater portion, for the lessons for the afternoon were to consist of Rhetoric, Grammar, Geography and History. I knew it would be impossible for all to be heard, so I gave the preference to G. and R., the usual lessons of the afternoon. I had some trouble in getting the books from Fannie, but A. was the only one to censure, as F. put the books in her room, and she neglected sending them. While I was dressing the bell rang, I leaned over and saw that two letters were handed to Ma. With all possible speed I completed my toilet and descended. They were to Ma and Alice and had been delivered by Mr. Elburger. I was standing up, one in hand when A. came to the gate. "Have you got a letter"? said she, as she quickened her pace. After partially devouring them we went to dinner. He is well. Particulars hereafter. After dinner I took a peep at the epistles and was off. How romantic, if *some* handsome gentleman should every afternoon by *chance* happen to cross my path. Mrs. Shaw was in school. I waited for Miss Mitchell and thought how lonely I would be if she did not come. As every form darkened the doorway, I looked anxiously, and hers was presently visible. We had a pleasant talk in the class. She was describing to me her pretty sister. I love her and am desirous of seeing her. She admired my collar, earrings, rings, etc. She looked real pretty. And oh! Philomen, she was trying on my rings, and I forgot to get them, and she went with them. I am so worried! Suppose she should lose my *two diamond rings!* I fear that she will not be in school to-morrow, and then I will not see her until Monday. I am *so* troubled. We parted at the gate, as Liz. wished me to walk with her. We both probably would have remembered it, had we parted at the corner, for there we always enjoy a few moments talk. (Liz. told me that she had received a letter from me, in the day. It was written in July, and she had arrived in the City before it had reached her.)

Miss Leech, Ada, Nettie, Maggie, Lizzie and myself walked together. Miss L. left us at the corner, and we proceeded a few squares up Prytania St. with Ade. Conversation, the Concert. They all looked pretty, but Maggie, in my estimation, bore off the palm. She has improved so much. They wore their bonnets, until they had passed the corner!! Liz. was very affectionate. She accounted for each afternoon, and assigned reasons why we had not seen each other. She said "Wait for me every afternoon, and I will wait for you", and she went up, and I went down. Stepped to Mrs. N.'s but she was not home. Repaired to my domicil, found the children cutting up extensively and Ma and A. out. I silenced them, lit the gas and perused the letter. The absentees were shortly with us. They had gone out for the purpose of purchasing trimming for A.'s Barège. Succeeded and alarmed me by telling of the high price of goods. Former bit calicoes [cheap material] are now twenty and twenty-five cents; and every thing accordingly. What will the people do? After supper A. and I went by the front gate, stood there for some time, admiring the sublime night, the firmament filled with stars in magnificent profusion, struck the imagination with a more powerful grandeur, than when enlightened by the brightest noon-day sun. She echoed my wish for some dear man to enjoy it with us. She was distressing me by her accounts of the beautiful girls she had met. We came in and to you. A flying cockroach occasioned us to perform many evolutions, and a mark of an unexpected movement remains on you. I won't efface it. Cousin S. has not come. It is ominous. I am so sleepy and tired that I am unable to fulfil my promise *now*, but I *will.* Don't be angry.

5

Au Revoir:
October 10–October 20, 1861

Thursday, October 10th, 1861

8 P.M. . . . . Mrs. N. has been here a few moments, and Mr. N. has just come in. Ma and they are chatting, A. is paying her devoirs to F. She is in arrears with her, and is on account much distressed. It is very warm as has been all day. The morning wore on but Ellen did not come. I was sorry for we miss her. Breakfast early. Mrs. Deegan came and said that E. had again complained of her foot. It was not as painful as formerly and she hoped that she would be able to come in the morning. Ma is using her endeavors to obtain Mrs. D. a ticket to the free market, and I think that she will succeed. It will be a great assistance to her. She is entitled to it as her son is a prisoner at Key West.[1] There was a general cleaning up, but I did not help much. Josie was splendid. She sat down, played, and was as "good as sugar". Poor little Sallie was compelled to come home from school, her tooth pained so badly. She has been suffering all day, but Ma could not make it convenient to take her down to the Dentist's, but please God will to-morrow. I could sympathize with her. Olivia's and Mrs. D.H. Marks' babies were over to Mrs. N.'s to day, and she sent them over here. O.'s is a splendid child, but the other is very inferior. They paid but a short visit, as both were hungry. I studied, sewed a little, and that's about all. Before dinner it began to rain, and I was distressed for fear it would prevent Miss M.

1. An announcement in the *Daily True Delta* in November 1861 stated that almost 1,900 tickets for the Market had already been issued. The tickets provided admission to the Market. Additional tickets would not be issued because so many volunteers were in military service, and it was difficult to restrict admission to the truly needy. The city authorities arranged benefits for the Free Market and the funds raised allowed the Market to expand. During March 1862, for example, the Market supplied over 15,000 families, spent $13,000 and raised $15,000 to support its efforts. In the previous month, a Ball took place at Odd Fellows Hall for the benefit of the Free Market. Its praises were also sung in musical form.

from coming to School, for visions of my ring were continually floating through my brain. I was thankful, however, that the shower was but slight, and left immediately after for my institution. I overheard the following remark uttered by a young boy, as I passed him, "I tell you what there are some pretty girls go to the Normal School". I went on, unconscious, who or what occasioned the sentence. It was intentional that I should hear it. A few steps from the school I met Belle H. She walked to the gate with me. The few moments chat was of the Concert. She looked very pretty. Mrs. P. arranged us "more orderly" in our seats. As I saw Miss Mitchell my joy and fear was excited. Joy at seeing her, and fear that she would have bad news to communicate. She sat by me, and I saw "my darlings" glistening on her fingers. My peace of mind was restored. She was dressed sweetly and looked very pretty. Recited first with Miss B. The lesson was short, as she occupied the greater portion of the time in writing. I studied my Grammar as sedulously, and flattered myself that I knew it. As I was reading Mr. Lusher thrust his restless head through the door. According to the new arrangement we then proceeded to Mrs. S. Recited my Rhetoric correctly, and elicited from my sweet teacher "very good". Miss M. and I as usual confabbing. We are never at a loss for something or someone to talk about. She tells me of her beloved home in Kentucky, and her reluctance on leaving it. Of the many dear friends whom she had left and the sorrow and grief of parting from them.[2] Maggie Toby returned to School. Our class was augmented by three young ladies, introduced by Mrs. Matthews. Belle Topping was as beautiful, Olimpia Burei as pleasing, Juanita Del Trigo as obliging, Julia Benedict as meddlesome, as ever. Miss M. and I left, while all were joining in the Bonnie Blue Flag, I suppose, for Mr. L.'s benefit. I did not wait for Liz. Miss M. was going up Nayades [later St. Charles], so I at her request walked a short distance with her. She was entertaining me with an account of her *Lady* loves. What a mysterious creature. As I passed a house a voice from a window exclaimed "Good evening, Clara", and looking to see from whom it proceeded, I espied Fanny Burbank. Her form recalled many pleasant memories. I declare I must go and see her. Miss M. and I bade "good bye". She asked if I wished my ring, and I said "yes", but I knew that she wished to keep it. I, reluctantly, left my little one in her possession, for I was too bashful to ask for it, and she did not offer. From Nayades and Thalia, I proceeded down St. Charles to Clio. Now for a romantic incident. As I was passing

2. Western Kentucky supported the Confederacy; some of its residents moved into the Deep South.

the corner of Apollo and Clio "another voice" exclaimed "good evening, Clara". I was somewhat startled and who do you think it was? Nina Word!!! She kissed me affectionately, nay lovingly. I could not believe my own senses. I was performing in reality what I had so often wished for. She looked beautiful, and I loved her dearly, devotedly. I congratulated her upon her success at the Concert, and she said that the Papers spoke of repeating the Performance, or rather, said that it would bear a repetition. I hope that their suggestion will be acted upon. She asked me why I didn't come to see her, and I put a similar question to her. "I would" said she, "if I knew where you lived". A mutual kiss and hug was then given, I said "you look so sweet"; she said "So do you", and we were separated. I *now* chide myself for being so thoughtless as not to have improved the opportunity, and had a longer talk as we may never meet again — She went on to meet her companions, whom I envied, and I was alone, busied with my own thoughts. Saw Mrs. Prothro, and Miss L. but did not recognize them until they had passed. The afternoon proved to be quite pretty. As I neared home, I observed Mrs. N., F., and S. standing at the corner. S. was crying, still suffering from her tooth. I led her into the house, prepared some Alum and salt, applied it, and it eased the pain. I rocked her, and soothed her by sweet melody. Ma and A. were out. Ma, shortly came. She had been to Churchills. Alice had gone somewheres on a shoe expedition. She was soon present. It was quite late, but she was escorted by Josh, and felt perfectly secure. Supper next, and then you, and *then* to fulfil my promise. First of A.'s. It was dated Sept. 29th and addressed to "my dear Alice and Clara". I was astonished at this as I don't deserve it. A. is displeased, as she thinks her letter merited an individual reply. I have never written to him, and I appreciate his kindness. He furnishes us with an interesting description of Richmond, its public buildings, monuments, etc. He says "the place is getting dull now, there are but few officers here, the others having returned to their respective commands". "Capt. Eshelman is here, walking on crutches. He is stouter than I ever saw him, but suffers yet from his wound". "Capt. da Ponte dines with me the other day. He will leave shortly for Manassas. He is to be an aide to Gen. Van Dorn of Texas notoriety".[3]

3. Earl Van Dorn, a major general from Mississippi, graduated from West Point near the bottom of his class when the Mexican War began. He served with conspicuous bravery there and in the ensuing frontier wars with, among others, Robert E. Lee and Kirby Smith. A close friend of President Davis, Van Dorn served in Texas before coming to Virginia. Later he took command of the Trans-Mississippi region and lost his life, not in battle, but in a duel at the hand of George Peters. Peters claimed his wife was the object of Van Dorn's attentions and shot Van Dorn in May 1862. See Woodworth, *Jefferson Davis and His Generals*, 112–114, 224–225.

Then, Philomen, came words which caused my heart to bound, and my cheek to flush with pleasure. He writes "When I went down to Manassas I made the trip in company with *Col. Wheat, Capt. Miller, and several others. The Col. was very desirous for me to send his kind regards to you all, and says he often thinks of you, and hopes if the Yankees don't kill him to have the pleasure of seeing you again*"!!!! The first words of remembrance from *him*! We are not forgotten!! Those few words furnished food for pleasant thought for many an hour. I wonder if we will *ever* meet again. God bless and shield from harm the noble soldier, the earnest patriot, and the just *man*. *Who* would not be *proud* to be esteemed by Col. Roberdeau C. Wheat? Pa was happy to inform us that he is fast recovering from his wound. Pa was introduced by him to his mother, whom he represents as a "sprightly old lady, full of 'Fuss and Feathers'". Mr. Hitchcock is well now, attending to business. Pa had not yet found a suitable boarding place. Was still at the "Spotswood". He was much pleased with "Sarah's" letter, which he shows to every one. Some items about the weather, etc., his regards to inquiring friends, and an incalculable amount of love to *us*, and the dear epistle is concluded; and *now* for Ma's. It was dated October 3rd. Strange that they should both have arrived the same day. After the usual prelude, he wrote of a narrow escape he had made from death a few days previous, and our blood was chilled as we read of his great danger, and from our hearts, ascended to God a grateful prayer for His watchful love that saved him. He was talking to a merchant about business, and stepped across a *hatchway* to look at some goods. When he was a foot from it the porter, without a word of warning, raised the trap door, and had Pa made a *single* step backwards he would have been dashed to the cellar, thirty feet below!! He assures us that he never enjoyed better health. He rises every morning at 5 o'clock and retires very early. He sees our papers every day. Never received the one A. sent him. He says "We are on the eve of battle. There will be another great fight soon. If our forces are victorious, we will open two stores; one at Centreville, and the other at Fairfax Court House".[4] He intended to send us some Chinguapins, but was told that they would become full of worms before reaching here, so did not carry out his intention. Ma wrote him last night to send *them*, or anything else, for these times all such articles are acceptable. He has made many acquaintances in R. and no doubt some warm friends. "Capt. da P. has gone to Manassas". Nothing more of interest. Mr. and Mrs. N. have gone. I must be "off". Good night.

---

4. Centreville is close to Bull Run; the Fairfax Court House lay in the direction of Washington.

Friday, October 11th, 1861

5 o'clock P.M . . . Alice and I are sitting in the dining room with "closed doors"! Do not imagine that we wish to envelope our actions in the "veil of secrecy". No! for were we so imprudent as to leave them open, the chill air would penetrate the apartment. You gaze in astonishment. The morning was very cloudy, and prognosticated a heavy rain. About 11 we had a slight shower, which effected a great change in the weather, which still continues gloomy. The breath of winter is *now* upon us. E. came this morning. Her foot convalescent. Ma and I have been hard at work on A.'s barège dress, and it is not now completed, for the want of trimming. It is beautiful. I intended to pay her a visit, but as *usual* found it impossible. I have attempted it for about a dozen consecutive Fridays. The wood which Ma ordered yesterday arrived to day, and a poor old man is now depositing it in its place. Ma admonished me not to look at him, for she knew that he would excite my pity to too great an extent. Dear little Sally has been suffering all day, and Ma, immediately after dinner, took her to the dentist's. I doubt whether she will have it out. Before Ma left I instructed her to purchase for me a No. 2 Fabers, *if possible.* I have no hopes though, as they are very scarce in the City. When A. came home she tried on her dress. It looked tres bien. I almost violated a certain commandment, but I anticipate before long one of my own.[5] Two letters, both from Manassas, of "D's" graced the columns of the paper. He has the impudence to say that his trip from R. to M. [Richmond to Manassas] was relieved of its usual monotony, by the society of two amiable, intelligent and beautiful *young ladies.* They are refugees from Baltimore, and were compelled to leave their native State, from their ardent devotion to the South. I will say nothing more of their identity than that they are grand nieces of the illustrious Jefferson. The paper announced the death of Zelia Gale, another victim to that terrible disaster [the Philadelphia fire]. She was betrothed to Mr. Jones. Unfortunate girl! It also contained highly important and interesting news from Pensacola and Mobile. The dispatch is dated Le October 9th and states that 1000 Confederates under Gen. Patton Anderson of Florida, crossed the Bay last night, and landed on Santa Rosa Island at 2 o'clock in the morning. They stormed the Camp of Billy Wilson's regiment of Zouaves, burning and destroying every building except the Hospital. Immense quantities of rations, stores and equipments were consumed by

5. Clara refers to the commandment against coveting what belongs to another.

the fire, and many cannon were spiked. The Camp was *totally* destroyed. Our loss was 40 killed and wounded. That of the enemy, immense. Our forces were Georgians, Mississippians and Alabamians.[6] This is good news for us. I wonder if Miss Jo. will come. It is very doubtful, but I hope that she will — The afternoon is far advancing, and it becomes necessary that I should repair to my chamber, and improve my appearance; A. is preparing to depart. I will soon leave you, but not before again expressing the wish that *Miss* Jo. will come.

Saturday, October 12th, 1861

6 $1/4$ P.M. . . . My wish was gratified. She came! And I now proceed to regale you with an account of the *particulars*. Ma is over to Mrs. N.'s and A. and I are cosily seated around the little table, each communing into her own thoughts, but occasionally giving expression to thoughts, connected with *one* who is dear to our hearts, and ever in our reveries. Well, after leaving you Friday afternoon we ascended to our dressing apartments. I had completed my arrangements, and was on the front gallery, and *had given up all hopes*. I was listlessly gazing around, when, chancing to look up the square, I espied *her* dear form advancing. I ran into A. with the joyful tidings and she was as pleased as I. I hastened down, and in a few moments was encircled by *her* arms, lip to lip, and heart to heart. We went up and we soon relieved her of her bonnet (of her own manufacture, quite pretty) etc., and she seated herself on the sofa, and immediately began to inform us of all her complaints. We reproached her for coming so late, but she offered a thousand and one excuses. We were thus comfortably arranged and talking for some time. Josie was brought in, and her little namesake went to her without much resistance, and by being bribed with candy stayed with her some time. On being informed that Ma had come we went down. She was very glad to see Miss Jo. Sallie did not get her tooth out. It was Ma's intention to go first to Dr McLear, but on passing Dr Smith's she saw a notice of his removal to 180 Canal St. and she determined to pay him the visit. She found that he was not in the City, but a Dr Walker was acting as

6. The Bay to which Clara refers is Pensacola Bay. Santa Rosa Island is a barrier beach that runs east to west in the Gulf of Mexico, below Pensacola. Whoever controlled the island controlled access to the port of Pensacola, an active trading town at this time.

agent. Ma represents him as a very gentlemanly, handsome man, but very inefficient in his profession. S. consented to have the operation performed, but through his mismanagement and inexperience the pain became so great that it was found impossible to proceed. He is not skillful with children, and Ma regrets very much that she allowed him to make the attempt. Mr. Wilcox is yet around the office. He inquired after Ma's "pretty daughters", but *of course* she was unable to reply, as she could not imagine to whom he alluded. Well Ma then went to Dr McL.'s and she is perfectly *in love* with him. He applied something to the tooth, but could not make another trial as the gum was too sore. I am very anxious to see the fascinating Dr. But alas! *he is married*. Ma brought my pencil. I am delighted with it. She says it was the only one in the city. I feel proud of the distinction. Don't you like it? But *pardonnez moi*. I have made quite a distinction, I mean digression. We were all talking, no I mean Miss Jo., Ed's devotion etc., etc. was the subject, when the bell rang, and Mrs. N. and Leopold were ushered in. Philomen, will you believe me when I tell you that I was bad and selfish enough to be displeased at their visit, as I had anticipated a pleasant evening *all alone*. But my displeasure soon vanished, and I became as attentive a *listener* as the rest, while L. and J. monopolized the conversation. Two consequential beings! The only topic discussed was burglars, mid-night robberies, each giving his experience. The conversation was very entertaining, and I was worked up to so great a pitch that I imagined every slight noise to be the attempts of a robber to force an entrance. The bell rang. I went to the door, and wished "good evening" to "Gus". He came in a few steps when he perceived that we had company. I saw that he hesitated about coming in, and A. also did so she foolishly got up and came to meet him. He said "Good evening, I came to see how you all were. I did not see you at the Concert the other night". A. assured him that we *were* there, and asked him to walk in. He said "No, I thank you, there *is a gentleman waiting for me around the corner.* Good evening". And he was gone. *This* confirmed us in the suppositions that we had entertained on a previous occasion, that there was *no* man waiting for him. We all had a hearty laugh, and agreed that he should receive some severe punishment for his extreme bashfullness. They marvelled at his ever making, and continuing our acquaintance, and so did we. It was a phenomenon. The man's conduct was perfectly disgraceful. What a miserable life must he lead. Ashamed to be seen! How undeserving of the appellation of *man*. He was disposed of. Mr. N. came in. He had been to drill and was very fatigued. He is a member of the "Crescent Artillery" [a militia unit].

They left about 10 and we remained down a little while. Before going to bed she [Miss Jo.] felt sick. Mom gave her a dose of Sandanum and Peppermint. She got into bed, was relieved, and it must have had a powerful effect, for she slept immediately, but not before "I wish 'my husband' was with me". I did not wake until the morning, when we had a chat in bed. On first awaking I was confounded. I did not know who was in bed with me. She told us strange things of Anna McL. They may be ill-founded and I think her very wrong to repeat them. We rose about eight. Came down, tried to read the paper, and was summoned to a very nice breakfast. Having partook of it, we repaired to the parlors where we played the piano, sang, danced, and kicked up generally. It was difficult for me to realize that she was not Josephine Pierson [her maiden name]. She has changed but very little either in appearance or manner since she bore that cognomen. About 11 o'clock she expressed her determination of going. We begged her to stay, but "she absolutely couldn't" as her ma had a great quantity of sewing to do, and she considered it her duty to go home and help her, and even sacrificed the pleasure of the Camp. She is desirous for A. and I to accompany her, and requests us to do so on Tuesday, as there is to be a grand dress Parade. She goes up in the morning, but it would be impossible for A. to go then. Her mother is going in the afternoon, so she proposed that we should meet her at three o'clock and go together. This required some deliberation, so she proposed to write a note to Alice on Monday by Georgy and her answer would decide it. This was agreed to. I don't care much about it. She tells us of the times she has up there, of course, being the "Pet of the Camp". Before she left Mrs. N. and Josh stopped in on their way to Synagogue. Two or three "good byes" and promises to come again soon. Mrs. E.S. Hews took her departure — I felt real sad. The pleasure you enjoy while in the society of a person, does not compensate for the pain experienced when they leave. The day has been most beautiful. A. and I have been lounging about. She has been arranging her drawers, etc. and encountered an accumulation of papers and notes of ancient dates, consisting chiefly of foolish notes that I had written to her at School. It was amusing to read them. I was not in excellent spirits to day. I don't know why. Ma and A. went out this afternoon to purchase trimmings for the dress. I remained at home, and amused myself with the children. About dark A. came in but Ma had gone over to Mrs. N.'s. The trimming was obtained, and she was relating to me the principal incidents of her expedition. As she was passing by Mrs. Sam Levy's the Labatts were standing at the door, and Ma and A. stopped and had a long talk. They told them the particulars of little Leonora's [Levy] death. They grieve very much. Another of the children, a boy of 5 years, is very ill with the scarlet fever. Ma thinks that Caroline is *beautiful.* They met Mrs. Miller. She had heard recently from the Capt. In one letter he writes that he is coming home, and in the next, that he has changed his mind, so she is in a very doubtful state, not knowing whether or not to expect him. I do hope that he will *come.* We then adjourned to the supper room, where tempting delicacies in the shape of *Cero* and M. [molasses] bread awaited us.[7] Later . . . Since writing the above, F. and S. have gone to bed, Ma has come home, talked a little while, went up, and A. and I are still writing. Mr. N. apprised Ma of the fact that Mrs. Judy Hyams and Miss Esther H. had arrived in the City. He saw them as they landed, but is ignorant of their destination.[8] My eyes twinkle, my fingers ache, and these are sufficient to warrant me "I'm whispering now, good night".

Sunday, October 13th, 1861

$2 \frac{1}{2}$ *P.M* . . . . What beautiful, Indian Summer, summer weather we are now enjoying. I have but a few moments to devote to you, so I shall improve them. Alice and I have despaired of the cream cheese man's ever passing, so last night, before retiring, I provided Lucy with the necessary funds, with instructions to purchase one in the market. She did as I bade her, and we enjoyed it excessively this morning, and of course had not much appetite for breakfast. My last time! I am again out of funds. Oh! for the inexhaustible purse! The paper was *next* disposed of. It contained rather a surplus of "items". I read that Mr. I.D. Marks was arrested here as a spy and on a charge of embezzlement. He is recently from Cincinnati and Philadelphia and many circumstances justify the belief that he is here as a spy. He had the audacity to go to Gov. Moore, and asked him if he wished him to go North in the capacity of a spy. It is a great disgrace and I am sorry for the afflicted family, but more particularly for his daughter Mrs. Capt. Harry Issacson. The man has participated in *all* kinds of guilt.[9]

7. Cero is a species of fish.

8. Members of the Hyams family, living in Alexandria, Louisiana, would have arrived in New Orleans by steamboat. The steamboat landings were large, open spaces near many of the commercial sections of the city. It was easy for those nearby to see the disembarking passengers.

9. Geography and the low level of military technology made espionage popular. Spies could

I have been sewing on A.'s dress, and it is *done, done.* A short while ago I braided her hair, but I can't divine the cause why. I can't succeed as well as formerly. She is always pleased, but that is not satisfactory. It would be preferable for *both* to be pleased. There was an account of a glorious naval victory which we have achieved at the Passes, under Commodore Hollins. On the night of the 12th he attacked the blockade, and with his little fleet succeeded, after a very short struggle, in driving them all aground on the S.W. Pass bar, except the sloop of war *Preble,* which he sank. He captured a prize from them. No casualties on our side; a complete success. A general exultation and rejoicing pervades the City. Thus have the insolent blockaders and invaders received another most signal rebuke for their insane attempt to subjugate this free and indomitable people. Good bye! To dinner!!

Monday, October 14th, 1861

6 1/4 A.M. . . . . With the rising sun! With eyes half closed I jumped out of bed this morning. Few events worthy of record have transpired since 2 1/2 P.M. yesterday. After dinner I was up stairs, and heard the bell ring. From my point of observation I saw a wagon at the door. I thought it was a letter and sprang nimbly down the steps, and what was my astonishment on beholding a fine, large piece of beef, being conveyed from the parlor. The bearer had a direction upon which was written Mr. S. P. Solomon, 107 [167?] Dryades St. He had succeeded with much difficulty in finding our present habitation.[10] The donor was a Mr. T.D. Miller, a friend (I presume) of Pa's, who was unawares that we had moved. It caused us some merriment, but was very acceptable, and will go towards making a good dinner for to day. Pa would enjoy it!! After dressing Sallie, I indolently performed my own toilet. I was soon down stairs, and in a few moments was joined by A. looking very "sweet and pretty" in her barêge. As she was admiring herself before the glass, the gate was heard to creak, and Mr. Eisner was seen to ascend the steps. It was *his time.* He had been in a short while

---

move about easily in a war where brother fought brother. The number of amateur spies belied their ineffectiveness.

10. Solomon Solomon is listed in the 1859 Directory as having a liquor store at 378 Dryades, near their previous residence.

when our august Cousin unceremoniously entered, kissed us, exclaimed "Two damn pretty girls", and subsided into the sofa. He did all of the talking. The Election will not be decided until Sunday. I think his chances are doubtless. Our neighbor, Mr. Mazareau, has obtained the nomination for Sheriff, and Cousin S. says, will be elected.[11] Mr. M. [Myers] did leave shortly, but promised to "call back" in the course of the evening. Then, we were alone with "dear Jo" [Eisner]. Alice and I were amusing ourselves laughing as he made some queer remark, or his beautiful features assumed varied expressions. Ma came in, and as she was entertaining him *we* took advantage to take a peep into the street. A., from polite scruples, went in, but *I* did not. I was walking and was joined by a group of children and we sang in chorus the Bonnie Blue Flag. Little Rosa acquitted herself creditably, which doubtless she would not have done, had she known that she was listened to by an appreciative audience, for when she had concluded a gentleman, a passer-by, stopped and pronounced it "very good, very good". They one by one disappeared, and I did also into the house. Shortly after Mr. and Mrs. N. and Leopold came. Mr. E. not yet gone. Ma and her company were in the back, Alice and hers in the front room. Mr. E. left and we all formed one company. All partook of supper except L. And now, Philomen, will you credit it, when I tell you that "Gus" came again, walked in as far as the back room, was introduced to L., handed A. some flowers, and "Will he find her"? (which he had borrowed from her), and bade "good evening" and was—gone. L. insists that we should talk to him on the subject, for he may give offense to any person in our parlors by appearing to wish not to be in their company. I shall, for he deserves to be mortified. *A specimen of humanity,* with *no* more confidence in himself. Cousin S. came in, and with the playing of the piano, talking and laughing, the evening passed very pleasantly. L. and S. remained after Mr. and Mrs. N. [had gone] and Mr. and Mrs. H. and their *would-be* or *soi-disant* [so-called] aristocracy was the theme of our converse. I asked Cousin S. to come up Wednesday night, as, nothing preventing, I intend asking Miss M. to spend the evening with me, and I wish him to be her escort home. He promised "to hold himself in readiness". He is acquainted with the family and says they are excellent people. We retired about 10½. Up stairs Lucy told me that Phig[Obed Miller] had told her that his Father was in the City, hav-

11. The neighbor was Adolphe Mazureau, whose family lived with the Jarreau family on Hercules Street. Mazureau won a contested election for the position of sheriff of the First District Court of New Orleans, running as a member of the Southern American Party. *The Daily True Delta* of 31 October 1861 lists the candidates and prints the Notice of Election.

ing arrived in the morning. I considered it veritable, but was indignant to think that he had been a day in the same place with us and not come to see us. I, of course, arrived at the conclusion that he was *angry* about *some-thing*. And thus passed the day.

8:20 P.M. . . . . Oh! Philomen, I am so sad, downhearted, low spirited, and I don't know what else. It is said that a person is never affected with the "blues", unless there is some cause, and that too is my opinion. Well, my principal cause is that I don't like to go to the Normal School. At first it was very pleasant, but now the tasks have become arduous, and the lessons more difficult, but laying that aside, I don't *like to go*. My recitation to Miss Benedict was perfect. The three *new* scholars were present. All are quite good looking but *one* is pretty. They appear to be well educated girls. I wonder if I will ever know them. Mrs. S. said "Miss S. I have a bargain to make with you. Can't you come on Saturday?" I told her decidedly "No", that my mother would have as serious objections as I. I now regret that I did not say more. I wonder if she would come on Sunday! "Of course" she did not wish to influence or force me, but she thought she would ask the question. I was so angry. I don't like her. Mr. Lusher then came in and asked me if I could read music. I replied negatively. He then asked if I wished to learn, and I replied similarly. He then wished to know my reasons. I could give none, so I told him that I would have no objections to learning. But I have, and I don't believe I will. There is to be two divisions of the Singing class: A, to constitute those who are acquainted with Music, B, those who are not. I did not have my Arithmetic, and all these acting in unison tended to put me in an unpleasant frame of mind. Mrs. Shaw said that I would be compelled to bring the Saturday duties on Thursday, which I *don't intend to do*. I was thankful that Miss Mitchell was in School, as *she* is the *only* one whom I care about. We had our usual chat in the Class. She put a ring on my finger, and said "Here is a drop of my heart's blood". I said "I wish that it was, and you gave it to me". I would *love* her if I knew she did. She returned my ring. As I was coming out of the gate, I met Lizzie. She called me and desired my company in taking a walk. I declined and went off with Miss Mitchell. I walked a square with her, and then walked home very thoughtful and overcast. Found Ma and A. out, and Mrs. N. with closed doors, and being too melancholy to sit, I promenaded the moon-lit street, in hopes that the soft, gentle radiance of the moon would have a soothing effect upon the troubled waters of my heart. While I was walking Josh. with his accustomed boisterousness came up behind me, and with a view to frightening me gave a terrific yell.

In my horror and alarm, my hand involuntarily extended, and came in contact with his face, and he received a very hard slap. We laughed over the circumstance, and as he was convinced that it was purely accidental, we became friends, and he accompanied me in my walk. On seeing Ma and A. and Mrs. N. enter his gate, we went over. They had been out on a slight shopping expedition. A. and I were standing by the door, musing upon the loveliness of the night. In her, I found a patient listener to all my troubles. She sympathized with me, but was glad that I do not derive any pleasure from attending the Normal School. She thinks that if no other girls claim my attention, I will *like her* better. As if any *girl* or *boy* could alienate me from *her.* Mr. Elburger came in, and A. and I were *as usual* enjoying ourselves. We came home, Mrs. N. promising to "come over", but she has not yet. Well Philomen, I *have* some *news* to communicate. This morning I was quietly seated, when one of A.'s pupils entered and handed me a letter, which "Miss Solomon" had sent. I recognized *Pa's* handwriting, and read, "Politeness of Capt. O. P. Miller". "Well, thought I, he has arrived, sent the letter by Obed, around to A.'s school, but would not himself come". I handed the unexpectedly received letter to Ma, who after reading it gave it to me. It was very short, as he said that he had written a lengthy one by a Mr. Patterson, which has not yet come to hand. The date is Tuesday, the day previous to Capt. M.'s departure. He is very well, but busy. He had no news to communicate. He spoke of the scarcity and high price of goods and the probability of his sending us something. "I suppose I will be able to *pick up something,* but the most agreeable thing at present would be *myself.* I hope to pay you a flying visit by Christmas". Won't it be delightful! Enclosed was a paragraph from a Richmond paper, headed by a "Gallant officer". It contained an account of a skirmish which had recently taken place between a company of Hessians under Capt. Sponables and a detachment under Capt. O.P. Miller of Wheat's Battalion. The affair resulted in the killing of a number of the Yankees, including their Captain. And so "Our Captain" has earned the reputation of a Gallant Officer. All honor to him!! I had just concluded it, when I observed Ma to give a meaning start and exclaimed "There he is now!!" Before I was conscious the eyes and hands of Clara E. Solomon and Obed P. Miller met. As on *such* occasions I could utter but a few mandible [with lower jaw down] sentences, and asked "How are you". Speech completely deserted me. He took a seat, and I observed him closely. He was the man of yore. He looked very well. His leg is not yet better, and he has a very interesting limp, which I declared was all "put on". Oh! I was so pleased to see him. How many memories were awakened which have for so long been slumbering. He remarked as a singular coincidence that on the very day, four months ago, he had left Camp Moore. I said "I did not expect to see you so soon". "So soon", said he in so reproachful a tone. He had "been to see a little lady round at School". I expected as much. He spoke in his usual *foolish* manner. He had with him the belt of the Capt. Sponables. It is his intention to have it altered for himself. He left Pa well and hearty. He accompanied him to the Depot. He paid a very short visit, and as he went, sly creature, threw me a kiss. The visit so excited me that I did not recover my equilibrium all day. I sent A. the letter, and she forwarded to me a note from Miss Jo. She informed us that the Review was not until Wednesday, and if she was well enough we would make the necessary arrangements to go then. Knowing this, I did not ask Miss Mitchell what I had intended. When A. came home from School we had a long chat, each relating what had passed since last we met. The roast beef at dinner was fine. A perfect treat. When I returned in the afternoon F. told me that "O.P." had called, but no one was home. I have some duties to perform, so must now leave you. I have recounted but briefly the foregoing events, but my time is now so occupied, that I find it impossible (much to my regret) to be more explicit. Aware of your amiability and good temper, I am not fearful of your displeasure.

Tuesday, October 15th, 1861

8½ P.M. . . . . Each performing her vocation. We are seated around the little table. Ma is sewing. F. is studying. A. and I are with "our friends". The day has been cloudy and portended rain, and was quite warm. We are having a long Fall. The *jour* has been characterized by *no* particular event. Ma had a call from a man from Davis and Jackson. He came to remind Ma of the debt. A startling ring was given to the bell, and of all persons Ma least expected to see him. As he was announced an exclamation of horror broke from her lips. I have been quite busy sewing on some *drawers* for myself. The cotton is of a very inferior quality, and none of any better can be obtained for less than twenty-five cents. I stopped at one, and commenced to study. Mrs. N. sent over the Crescent, and I took a few moments recess to scan it. I saw that Mary McStay was married to Mr. Irwin. A letter from Vir. contained an account of the flattering manner in which Maj. Wheat was received into Camp Bienville. It was a perfect ovation. It was as follows, "Maj. W. has formally taken command of his Battalion, which has for several weeks been in charge of Maj. De C. The Maj. looks well, and says that a fight would surely cure him; his reception in camp was a perfect ovation, destitute of pomp and show, but the whole battalion rushed over a mile down the road, and brought him up under hurrahs and shouts." He still suffers from his wound. Bless him. A nobler man *never* lived! I departed for school immediately after dinner. I walked along, looking very intently in the direction of Bacchus St. in hopes of seeing a certain gentleman [Capt. Miller], but I did *not*. After Dictation the division A in music went to Mrs. Fisher, and B to Miss Benedict. By this arrangement Miss M. and I were separated, but she promised to wait for me at the conclusion of the exercises. With Miss B. we read, but the time was so limited that it was impossible for 40 girls to perform a duty. Miss Parker "pretty Neck" was there the whole time. I wonder if she designs joining the School. When I went into the "big room", I looked North, South, East, and West, for Miss M. but she was "non est", and I learned from Lizzie that she had gone. I hope she looked for me. I wished to ask her if she would not come home with me Thursday afternoon. I was sorry that I did not see her. As a substitute I availed myself of Liz.'s invitation and in company with Ada and Nettie walked a few squares. The Dictation contained many difficult words, and as I have no means of ascertaining their spelling, I requested L. to lend me her large quarto Dictionary. I was going home with her to get it, but considering the weight and the drops of rain I resolved to send for it to-morrow. The Dictation is a perfect nuisance. I am so bothered. We have so many lessons for to-morrow. I went to Mrs. N.'s. Found Ma and A. there. A. proposed a walk. Agreed, and she told me that Capt. O.P. had honored her all the afternoon. And what a lot did she have to tell, and how envious was I that *she* had enjoyed him all alone. He was as affectionate as foolish as ever. I wish that he would pay *me* a day visit. He ought to. It is his intention to leave Monday. While here the "Blind man" came!! There's two distinguished visitors to lose. If the N. S. [Normal School] had never been instituted. The "Blind man" paid a visit of but ten minutes, as he was to leave for Tangipaho the same afternoon. O.P. as may be imagined was provoked at the intrusion. A. and I continued our promenade, until the large rain drops warned us of our situation, and going in to inform Ma of the state of affairs, we found her cozily seated, and Mrs. N. said that she was not going, so "my companion" and I made our hasty exit from the mansion of the Nathans. After arriving home it rained quite hard, but the night is now clear. Eat supper and talked of *him* and him *only*. The Golden Syrup is exhausted but Mrs. N. is going to furnish a fresh supply. After the meal, we repaired to the parlor, arranged the drop light, and ourselves comfortably. Steps were heard on the gallery, my thoughts went first to "Gus", whom I am anxious to see; but the door opened, and Ma unexpectedly walked in. She commented upon the bright light we were enjoying at her expense. All in a playful manner. Last evening Cousin S. dropped in. From Mr. I.D. Marks [the alleged spy] the conversation branched to many other subjects, our ancestry, and so forth; a most prolific theme to Ma, and very agreeable hour or so. He is a dear, funny fellow. I have my dictation to write, and with my un-learned lessons staring me in my face and weighing heavily upon my heart, I cannot, with pleasure, indulge in your society. Duty claims the ascendancy, so we must part.

Wednesday, October 16th, 1861

6$\frac{1}{2}$ A.M. . . . . A damp, dismal, sultry morning. The rain is falling, and it promises to be a disagreeable day. In consideration of this fact, I think it wise to relinquish all hopes of a visit to "Camp Lewis" on *this* 16th. of October. I am anxious to go. I, or rather A. overslept herself this morning, which accounts for my tardiness. The paper lies temptingly before me. I will leave *you* for the present.

1$\frac{1}{2}$ P.M. . . . . Since I last saw you, the sun has appeared in all its splendor, and the day is most beautiful. Various messages have been transmitted between A. and I, and diverse notes exchanged. I wrote her if she had heard anything, as I was desirous of knowing if we were going, for if so, I intended to dispense with studying for the day. Ain't I wicked? Her reply was in the *negative*. I thought that Miss J. considered it useless to make any arrangements, for it probably was raining when George left home. I had received the Dictionary from L. and it has afforded me much assistance. I then seated myself despondingly on the sofa, surrounded by Geographies, Grammars, etc. endeavoring to instill into my unwilling head, their useful information. A few moments ago while in the pursuance of this praise-worthy object a little girl of A.'s glided in and handed me a note, the contents of which amounted to this. A. had received a visit from Susie B. She had spent last night with Miss Jo., who told her to tell us to be sure and come, if the day was good. The arrangement is for us to take the cars at Tivoli Circle, and she, with Ed, who is to accompany her, will get in at Jackson St.[12] This is very convenient. After the receipt of this message, I acted upon the "away to books", and as A. writes me to be ready to leave at 2:45 I must depart to make necessary preparations. "With many wishes for your enjoyment, I remain your friend P."

Thursday, October 17th, 1861

6 1/2 A.M. . . . . Again am I an apologist for my late rising. But the morning was so cloudy that it deceived me. The clouds, though are not indicative of rain, for since last evening the wind has changed in the direction of the North. The duty of recounting to you the incidents of yesterday afternoon's expedition lies before me; but I am forced to be very concise, for in the afternoon my time is occupied, in the night I am fatigued, and the mornings are so very short. About quarter past two, while dressing, A. came. She proceeded to don her garments with all possible speed, came down, did not *think* of dining, were provided by Ma with the necessary *funds*, and after many injunctions from her "to take care of ourselves", we left. As the corner was reached the clock struck 3, and as S. [Susie B., Jo's friend] had agreed to wait until 2:45 we hastened to her house, but she had gone. We were perplexed, disappointed, and knew not what course to pursue. We thought that the car had left, but determined to run, and stand our chances. Arrived at the corner of Apollo and Caliope, as the car was entering the Depot. With alacrity we reached it, were politely handed in, and while on the platform, the engine was puffing along. We succeeded in obtaining excellent seats, and a multitude of hopes and fears overpowered us. After reaching Jackson St., we momentarily expected to see Ed, who, of course, we thought would walk through the cars to ascertain if we were aboard. Station after station was passed, we started at every footstep, but our hearts were not gladdened by the sight of him. My fears were lulled to rest, for I thought that he would surely come, and that they must surely have been on the train, for had they changed their minds, we would have been apprised of it. Camp Lewis is in sight. The cars have stopped. The

12. The Solomons could meet the trolley at Tivoli (Lee) Circle for the route going in the direction of the training camp, Camp Lewis.

passengers step off, and amid the vast multitude we wildly gaze for the familiar faces. But *none* are recognized. Oh! how indignant, how mad, how disappointed, were we. It was a base, mean action! The Camp looked so inviting. The pretty white tents, wide spreading trees, and bright sun gave a picturesque appearance. We thought of the pleasant time that we anticipated, and tears arose in our eyes. Not merely from our disappointment, but in consideration of our treatment. How many memories were aroused, and the associations which the scenes would have produced, would have been sufficient enjoyment in itself. What could we do? All the ladies were attended by gentlemen, so we apparently quietly kept our seats. I knew it was foolish, but I had lost power over my actions, but we resolved to employ those dangerous weapons, our tongues, when next we met the party. We went up to Carrollton, got out, and learned that the down train would leave in ten minutes. We procured seats in it, and were soon on our way home. It was our first rail-road traveling since our memorable Jackson R.R. expeditions, and so I suppose you know the subject of a part of our conversation. Our rebellious feelings somewhat subdued, and we enjoyed the ride, for which we were indebted to Hon. Abe. Lincoln. We again passed the Camp, and in a few moments it was gone. Arrived in the city, and walked hastily home, dreading the many questions which would be asked us, and wishing that we were going to an uninhabited house. Happily found Ma out, and with a good grace responded to the queries of the other parties. Of course they were much astonished to see us, but we told them how it happened. I was vexed to think of the money it had cost us, for the attainment of no purpose. Disposed of a loaf of bread, etc., and under the influence of so many emotions we sank into the sofa. We kept our position for about an hour, talking, talking, talking of matters and things, and thinking how pleasant would it be if a *certain* gentleman should chance to drop in. As twilight deepened over the earth, a walk was proposed and our steps naturally went in a certain direction, but to *no avail.* On our return seeing signs of life about our mansion, we resolved to go in. Ma had come. We told her all, and she was indignant as we, and declared that it was a "shameful piece of business". Ma was concerned about our disappointment. A short while after supper, Mrs. N. came over with some sewing which Ma had offered to help her with. A. went into the dining room, to hear E.'s [Ellen's] lesson, and I accompanied them. We remained some time *enjoying* ourselves *alone* in the little cozy room, and picturing ourselves the days, when as two old maids we would occupy a like apartment. We would surely be *happy,* for it would be impossible, while in each other's society to be otherwise. In consideration for Ma's gas we joined the company. We were speaking of Gus, and Mrs. N. had just wished that he would come, when the bell rang, and it *was* he. We invited him into the back room, but he declined, and dropped into the front room sofa. He told us that Henry had moved in Caliope St. I am *sorry.* He showed us his last letter from his "fair correspondent in Mont. [Montgomery],"which contained many mysterious passages, which I believe he elucidated, but I had no idea that *matters* had reached *such* a height. We spoke of his conduct on the occasion of his two last visits, and he explained himself by saying that he came to spend a pleasant evening in *our* family circle, but, seeing company here, he knew it would be impossible, and so left, and he would act similarly at any future time. I do not condemn him for it is a peculiarity, and I am convinced that it is not attributable to bashfulness. I teased him tho', and told him that he should take into consideration appearances, but he said that he placed but *very* little import upon that. He is a queer genius. Cousin S. came up by agreement, but Miss M. not being here, he immediately exited, promising to come up tonight. Mr. N. and Mr. E. honored us. "Gus" left before them. Retired about 10, and thus terminated the eventful day.

Friday, October 18th, 1861

6½ A.M. . . . Lucy has just come to me with the sad intelligence that E. is not coming, and so has given J. to me, but she is now walking around the sofa and wonderful to relate is quiet. The morning is cold and cloudy, the rain *has* been falling. I left you yesterday morning. After breakfast Ma went to the Poydras Market with the view of purchasing some shrimps, and as Capt. O.P. offered to take any bundle, Ma designed to pickle them and send them to *Pa.* I know he will be delighted. While Ma was out I superintended the arrangements of the house, returned L.'s Dictionary, and on her return found everything in order, and prepared for the accomplishment of her plans, succeeded, and the shrimps look as though they will be good. I hope when they reach their destination, they will be in a safe condition. Ma sealed them securely with wax, and intends packing them in a box. You know I told you once that Ma and Alice were using their endeavors to obtain for Mrs. Deegan a ticket to the Free Market, and for this purpose A. spoke to Miss D. [a colleague] requesting her to lay the subject before her brother Mr. Dan Ricardo, Secretary of the Institution. She wrote a note with instructions for her [Deegan] to go down and present it to Mr. D. She went with this intention, but happening to see Mr. Murray, the President, she informed him of her situation, and he told her that it was impossible for her to obtain a ticket, for though convinced that she was a worthy object, he could not grant it, without a certificate of the Capt. of the Company in which her son is a member. This you know is impossible, as surmises *only* are formed as to his whereabouts. Notwithstanding Mr. M. told her that he would assist her, and told her to come on the days previous to Market ones, and he would supply her with provisions. She came yesterday, downhearted, to tell us that she had gone, he had spoken to her roughly, and told her that he could do nothing for her. She is so timid and reserved, and this treatment caused her much grief. I was not all astonished at Murray's conduct, for I well know to what his promises amount. Poor woman! her bark is cast upon a stormy sea, but she has perfect faith and trust in Him above. Ma, by writing, informed A. of this, and bade her to relate to Miss D. the circumstances, and again solicit her influence. I commissioned A. to glean as many particulars relative to our expedition as possible so when she came from School she told me that she had seen Susie. She had been so fortunate as to obtain a seat in the Cars, next to Susie L., and of course were searched for and found by Mr. Hews. She knew that he *started* to look for us. Oh! the *insult*, the *slight*, the *neglect*, which was offered us. A. was very angry and said many things, which in her calmer moments she would not have uttered. Can anyone condemn us for feeling hurt. I wonder what extenuation Mrs. H. can offer. As I was on the eve of departing for School, Capt. M. entered, but I did not see him, and I regarded it useless to breathe "Good evening" and "good bye", in the same moment, so I murmuringly wended my way to the Establishment, which for short I shall call School. Oh! how I envied A. The exercise for the afternoon consisted of Elocution, and I took my first lesson in Music. I do not at all admire the arrangement. I lose much by my absence on Saturday, and consequently can not be expected to be as proficient as the others. Mr. L. said that many of us labored under the false impression that we had *no* voices, and that in all persons it was capable of being developed and improved. Who or what could develop mine. I don't like him. Miss M. and I, by appointment, met at the front door. I asked her to accompany me home, but she refused as she had not come prepared, but promised me the pleasure on Monday. I did not urge her, for I thought that she could look prettier and I wish her to make a good impression. I walked a short distance with her, a short confab at the corner, and we proceeded to our respective habitations. I thought it should be probable that A. would walk to meet me, and looked North, South, East and West for her, but was doomed to disappointment. I know how pleasant a subject would be discussed. Arrived home and found her out, and Ma and F. surprised to see me unattended. I explained. A. presently entered. She had expected to greet Miss M. and an exclamation of disappointment broke from her lips. She had been to pay a few visits in the neighborhood, and entertained us with an account of her adventures. She seized the opportunity while the others went to supper to tell me what he [Capt. Miller] said. He spoke in his *usual style*, and oh Philomen! she told me what I would give worlds to *believe*, that *we* were often the subjects of many pleasant conversations between Roberdeau Wheat and himself, and he assured her that the first named individual had by no means forgotten us. He related to her a romantic incident which occurred one night while they were rooming together. It sounded so improbable that I cannot relate it to you; suffice to say, that *he* the noblest man we ever knew, expressed an earnest desire to be *with us*. Oh! she told me *so so* much, which I cannot *school* my heart to credit. About eight o'clock it began raining, and continued incessantly. We congratulated ourselves that Miss M. had not come and particularly as moment after moment passed and no Cousin Sam.[13]

We talked, laughed, sighed, and the time wore away, and we retired about 9. A. and I disrobed, and seating ourselves on the sofa had a sweet, lengthy, sisterly chat. You know what we talked of. What else could we than of the strange, unexpected communication of the afternoon. I went to bed, but not to sleep, for my mind was too busy, and "the hardest chain to break is made of thought." I *presume* that sleep visited me, for on the next morning, I was awakened.

Saturday, October 19th, 1861

11¹/₂ A.M. . . . . The morning has been dark, dismal, cloudy and rainy, and what do you think, I did not rise until *7 o'clock*, for *A.* overslept *herself.* E. came. Her excuse for her absence of a "*sick headache*", as though she could form any idea of what that is. Mrs. N. and Josh are now here, but A. and

13. Any girl who visited Clara needed a male escort to walk her home. The girls expected Cousin Sam to come by and walk Clara's classmate, Miss Mitchell, home, had she come.

I are closeted in *our* apartment, heedless of all things save *one*.[14] The weather for the past days has been very unpleasant. Yesterday it rained at intervals all day. The sun struggled to gain ascendancy, but was unsuccessful; the clouds would gather and disperse and the rain would fall and cease. *Again* I intended to pay A. a visit, but I was debarred on account of E.'s being "non est". This also prevented me from accomplishing much work, altho' Josie remained in a remarkable state of quietude. Ma was engaged in re-juvenating an old dress of A.'s, which promises to look very well. When A. came home from school, she had in her possession a ticket to the Free Market for Mrs. Deegan, which Miss D. had finally obtained. Oh! I was delighted, it will be a God send to the needy woman. She also had a note which she had received from Mrs. E.L.H. [Jo. Hews] It seems that Susie B. had written her, telling her of the circumstances and Miss Jo. wrote that she was astonished to hear that "Allie" [Alice] was angry or hurt, as Ed walked the cars but did not see her. What nonsensical stuff. She remarked that they *both* were very desirous of her company, and hopes that she will not consider it oversight or neglect on Ed's part. Of *course not.* It was apparent that she could offer no extenuation. A. is ferocious, and is determined *not* to go and see her. I neglected to tell you that yesterday we became the recipients of the expected letter, which Pa entrusted to the care of Mr. Patterson. It was brought by the carrier, and I think that as Mr. P. consented to bring it, he should have delivered it immediately on his arrival. The date was of the 7th and though quite lengthy, it did not contain much matter of *interest*. He is enjoying excellent health, and I dare say looks *remarkably* handsome and *youthful,* for he says that the people will not believe that he is *near fifty,* but maintain that he is not over *thirty-five.* I expect that his vanity is too often flattered, and he will be unmanageable when he returns to us. I don't think that age will ever leave its traces upon *him.* He requests, that when Ma gets money, for us to get our daguerreotypes taken and sent to him, as it will afford him unexpressible happiness. He says that he will ornament his dressing table with them, and exhibit to his incredulous friends his "wife and seven children". Pa's two *Concerns,* one at Centreville and one at Germantown, keep him quite busy. Pa says that from what he can learn there is now no prospect of a fight; Gen. McLellan is on *his* side of the river, and should a fight occur it would be most terrific.[15] He is as disgusted as ever with the fashionable Hotel,

14. Sarah Nathan and Josh stopped by on their way to synagogue. On this occasion neither girl joins the Nathans.

15. Lincoln had given George McClellan command of the Army of the Potomac after Bull

but it is almost impossible to obtain private board. The items amounted to no more than these, with occasional others sent to A. for her perusal. After dinner we were assembled in the front room, Ma was trying on A.'s dress, when a violent jerk was given the bell, and we scampered simultaneously. I saw that O.P. was admitted, and A. and I ran up, fixed up a little, and were soon in his august presence. It was the first *real* time that he and I had been together, and what a pleasant afternoon did we spend. He is a dear, good man. The rain prevented his going and he stayed uncommonly long, but we could *never* tire of *his* society. He left about 5 o'-clock, when A. and I, seated on the sofa, heart with heart and soul with soul communed. She uttered thoughts to *me*, which she would not to *any* one else, and thanked God that He had given her a sister, and *said* she prized the blessing with which she was endowed of a true, loving Sister's deep, unchangeable affection. The children soon entered, and this, together with the bright light which illumined the apartments, broke the magic spell. Eat supper, and pass the evening pleasantly in our own family circle. A. was arranging her desk, and would occasionally read snatches of old letters, papers, etc., and the associations they recalled were of a most pleasant nature. The sight of her letters revived my remembrance of "dear Dolly". The young ladies' [Alice and Clara's] taste inclined in the direction of a previous Journal of mine, and many portions caused to break forth from our lips the merry peals of laughter, as the construction of many sentences were so *peculiarly* queer and mysterious.[16] We giggled enough, you may imagine, as we always do on the *slightest* provocation. A. had concluded her arrangement, Ma had fallen to sleep on the sofa, I with great exertion endeavored to keep my eyes unclosed, when adjournment of the session was proposed and accepted.

Sunday, October 20th, 1861

6¹/₂ A.M. . . . . Wonderful to relate, I was the first to rise this morning, but before I had entirely completed my toilet, A. came sauntering into the room

---

Run, and then made him general of all the northern armies. McClellan used the fall and winter to train a large group of soldiers.

16. They read an old diary written by Clara. A reader can judge for oneself the grammar and sentence structure of these diaries, written by Clara at ages sixteen and seventeen.

lamenting the fact that it "*used* to be as light at *five*". There is no disputing this, as the mornings are perceptibly getting shorter and shorter. I came down, scanned the paper, and *happily* arrived at the conclusion that there was "nothing in it". It is cloudy, and every prospect of another rainy day. I hope so. This weather reminds me so forcibly of last winter. Happening to see Mr. N., Mr. E. and Josh passing down on their way to the Poydras Market, A. in fun told them to bring her something nice, and when they returned, to our astonishment presented us with some persimmons. Mrs. N. and J. lunched with us yesterday. Before dinner, A. and I performed some ablutionary operations, and prepared ourselves with the exception of our over garments, to greet O.P., who promised to call in the afternoon. After dinner A. and I dressed. The rain was falling, and the prospect was gloomy. We descended. Four o'clock, no O.P. Four and a half, no O.P., and we had despaired of seeing him, when *his* welcome and well known ring was heard. I was anxious to see him, for, knowing that he would leave so shortly, I was aware that we would not have many more opportunities of being together. He, A. and I spent a delightful time. And what can I say of his visit? It was characterized by no new circumstance. As he was leaving Mr. N. came in, sporting a Crescent Artillery cap, and looking remarkably handsome. On learning that O.P. would leave for Virginia, he requested him to take a package to Simon, which request he willingly complied with, observing that it would afford him much pleasure, etc. etc. He touched his cap "a la military" and with a "*good evening, Ladies*", was gone. After admiring Mr. N.'s article, and agreeing upon the decided improvement it made, he left. His uniform is in a state of progression. What a handsome soldier will he make! We escorted him to the front door, and we then remained on the front gallery, commenting upon the passers by, and regretting that so many nondescripts passed in the vicinity. The brilliant rainbow which spanned the Heavens in the afternoon, could not have been indicative of a cessation of rain, for up to this time the drops were still pattering down. A. and I executed a *brilliant* duet on the piano, which contributed to the amusement of the others as well as ourselves. I profanely said that I would give "my birthright in Heaven" if I could play; but I am consoled by the hope that, please God, in the "better time coming" my desire will be gratified.[17] We took our accustomed seats, talked, were silent, laughed, were sad, and thus the few hours imperceptibly glided away and departed, leaving no traces of their existence.

17. Clara alludes to the biblical story of Esau and Jacob, in which Esau casually gives up his birthright as Isaac's first son.

9 o'clock ..... *P.M.* .... Oh! Philomen, I am so disappointed! "I have watched and waited hourly for that Cousin Sam to come", and he *has* not, and *will* not, make his appearance. I invited Miss M. to morrow, thinking *surely* that I would see him to day, as he is generally regular in his Sunday attendance. I wonder what keeps him. I am in such a predicament. I am anxious for her to come, and I dislike to tell her of the circumstances, as I *know* that she will come prepared. Oh! Myers! how many moments of anxiety and suspense hast thou caused me! I was momentarily expecting him, and for this reason delayed writing. There is no possible chance of seeing him to morrow. Ma is asleep on the sofa, A. and I are seated around the little table. She has on her "rejuvenated dress", which looks extraordinarily handsome, and as Fannie philosophically remarked "*What* cannot hands accomplish?" Its charms are heightened by thoughts of what it *was*. About 5 o'clock, while dressing, this afternoon (quite late, wasn't it!) Leopold called. We, however, soon went down, and were much astonished to see him in his *uniform*. Oh! he looked splendid! And we paid him the greatest compliment which we could pay anyone by telling him that he looked like *our* Major Wheat, and indeed the resemblance is very striking, and we remarked it on our first sight of our distinguished friend. He ought to have felt flattered, for he *well* knows the opinions we entertain of the Major. L. is first Lieutenant of his company, the Pelican Guards, and as he had been parading most of the day, the Flag having been consecrated, he was much fatigued. He said that he had heard rumors of the company's being called into active service. After due inspection of his regimentals, and ordering him to turn round and round, assume different positions, in order to view him closely, we allowed him the privilege of sitting. Our conversation turned upon Maj. W. with whom he is not *personally* acquainted, but I doubt not knows him by the *many, vivid* descriptions which we, at different times, have furnished. L. received the same flattering reception from each member, and I expect, felt an inch or so taller than when he entered. If he only *were*, what a fine looking man he would be. He left about dark, and A. and I accompanied him to the corner. He was going to the N.'s, and invited us to come over, which pleasure we most respectfully declined, as we were aware that Mrs. H. was there. It *would* be quite agreeable, if we were on friendly terms. A. and I walked a short while. The night was beautiful. Went in, and to supper, which I did not partake of heartily; probably I was excited fearing Cousin S. would not come. I repaired to the room, and expected him up to the time that I came to you, when *all* hope was extinct. I have disposed of the latter part of the day, and now to the earlier.

There was quite a struggle between the Clouds and the Sun, and the contest was finally decided in favor of the latter, and the Earth was gladdened by its rays. I was not particularly pleased, as the rain would have been as acceptable. I think that its final visit for some time was paid yesterday. My companion and self were as jubilant as usual, and giggled and "cut up" to as great an extent. Ma is thankful that we are together but two *days* for she *knows* that if it were otherwise, she would go distracted. We are ridiculing, imitating, and laughing at persons, and Ma says that she never hears us utter a single sensible remark. *When* it *isn't* O.P. that we are *praising*, it is some one else we are condemning. We excuse ourselves by reminding Ma of our youth, etc. etc. We all contributed our aid to A.'s dress, and about 12, while we were sewing diligently, dear O.P. came. Away with work! He looked so well, and informed us that he would not leave to morrow as *he* had *expected*, and *I* had *hoped*. He has changed his mind, and cannot state the precise day of his departure. I am sorry, as I wish him to go and be done with it. He did look so handsome. I declare, *next* to *Pa, he* is the dearest man on Earth. He asked us if we had seen his acknowledgment in the Picayune of the receipt of 21 pairs of socks presented to him for his Company by Miss Tillie S. Todd, with whom he says he is not acquainted. We borrowed the paper from Mrs. N., and had the felicity of reading it. It is a shame A. and I have contributed in no manner to the comfort of our volunteers. A. has resolved to *learn* how to do something, and when that *something* is decided upon, you shall know. The moments, as when in his society, passed heedlessly by, and after a visit of about $3/4$ of an hour, he went. It is strange that *we so* unimpressible should have taken *so* great a fancy to a person on *so* short an acquaintance. About one and a half I "put up" sewing, and went up stairs to inspect one of my Winter dresses, and after ascertaining that it required some alteration, I arrived at the conclusion that a barège would not be unseasonable for the afternoon. I showed F. some sums, and was soon joined by Alice. Our place of rendezvous was the "little room on the gallery", and while there Ellen conveyed to us the cheering intelligence that *Ma* had received a letter. We expedited our downward movements, and found that it was really *so*. Greeted Mr. N., its deliverer, learned that the letter was to A. and became attentive listeners while Ma read it aloud to the assembly. The date is the 13th. He assures us that his health still continues excellent, and then proceeds to inform us how he passes the days. He is very busy, buying and shipping goods. Thank God, this agrees with him. In A.'s letter she asked him to give her some of the particulars of his connection with the

18th Mississippi Regiment, and in reply he stated that they had not connected themselves with *any* Regiment, but supplied 20,000 men from a number of Regiments that were *sutlerless*. He sells a great deal for *cash*, and this suits him very well, as they need much ready money. On his resigning the 18th. Louisiana, he concluded to dissolve all business relations with *Mr. Hardy*, whom, it appears, he *never* liked, and his actions in the "closing scene" served to convince Pa his unfavorable feelings were not *unjustly* entertained.[18] Pa says he left some time ago for this City. The letter, although commenced on the 13th, was not concluded until the 14th as he was interrupted while writing by the arrival of several gentlemen, whom he had invited to dine with him. He has sent us some chestnuts by Express. This pleased us all. He said that he would, in a few days, send some Butter. This pleased us more, as it is difficult to obtain a good quality of this article. Five dollars were enclosed, and it is his wish that Ma shall devote it entirely to his "boy and girl".[19] Mr. N. left, and we proceeded to dinner, the principal items of which were a nice dish of tomatoes Stew, and P.P. [potato pone]. How many dear memories did the *first* awaken.

18. Hardy had been Solomon's partner in the first sutlership with the 18th Louisiana ("Polish") Regiment.

19. Solomon refers to Rosa as his "boy."

6

Letters from Pa:
October 21–November 10, 1861

Monday, October 21st, 1861

9 o'clock P.M. . . . . After leaving you last night we went up stairs. A. and I dis-robed, and comfortably seated ourselves under the gas light, her thoughts with Felicie, mine, with an elaborate composition on "Memory". About 11 we retired. Today has been beautiful, and I think that a term of fine weather is now inaugurated, not cold, but pleasant. I devoted the two hours pre-vious to breakfast, this morning, to the performance of some sums, and af-ter some difficulty I succeeded in solving them all. I sewed until one, when my lessons demanded my strict attention. I studied my Geography and History, and at $2^1/_4$ prepared myself for School. When A. came from School, she had a pair of India Rubber shoes, which she had commissioned Belle G. to purchase for her. After dinner I was standing by the window, drawing on my gloves, preparatory to starting when a horseman alighted from his horse, rang the bell; I opened the door, Mrs. S. was asked for. She appeared, and the precious document, a letter by Express, containing *$100* was handed to her. She signed her name and the gallant knight departed. The letter was very short. He was well. Said he had sent *more* Chestnuts (the others have not yet arrived) and gave Ma particular injunctions, to restrict the children in eating them, and advised to boil them. I walked along, framing 100 different expressions by which to break the intelligence to Miss M. I felt a delicacy as so many things have prevented her paying *that* long-anticipated visit. I thought how pleasant if a certain person should happen to emerge from his door, and we "should meet by chance". "Oh! never till life with memory perish", "can I forget" his [Capt. Miller's] ex-pressive countenance. When I arrived at School I found the room deserted, and the hands of the clock pointing at $3^3/_4$, so I immediately surmised that the hour for commencing had been changed to $3^1/_2$. I was correct. When I entered "my apartment", the History lesson was in a state of progression. I, however, had an opportunity of displaying my knowledge of the subject. Miss M. had not yet come, and as she is a regular attendant, I was astonished when she did not make her appearance. I congratulated myself on my good luck, and thought how opportune was her absence. I was contentedly seated by Miss Del. Trigo, when a young lady came in the room, and announced that there was some one outside who wished to see "*Miss Solomon*". A 100 suppositions as to who it could be rushed through my mind. I went out, saw a strange girl, who handed me a note, which I immediately recognized to be written in Miss M.'s handwriting. I was much excited, and tremblingly perused it. She requested me to excuse her absence, as she had been indisposed for the past few days. She could not have imagined how willingly I accepted her excuse. I wrote in reply a few lines, and furnished her with the lessons for the succeeding days, which favor she asked. I then intrusted it to the care of the domestic, and returned to the room, not totally restored to my equanimity. I handed in my Composition, and as School was over, I started directly for home. Arrived there, found Ma and A. out, and Mrs. N. seated on the steps. I joined her and she left about dark. Went into the house, lit the gas, awaited the return of the absentees. They soon entered; had been down town. A. was considerably enriched by the possession of two pairs of shoes. 3 pair in a day! Quite a sudden accession to her stock. Mine are beginning to look rustified. I must notify Ma. They spoke as usual of the high price, and, indeed, scarcity of goods. Eat supper, and I was entertained with the *little* particulars of the expedition. Afterwards Ma went to Mrs. N.'s, where she now is. F. and S. have retired. A. is still writing. C. — I hear Ma bidding Mr. E. "good night". There she is. Adieu.

Tuesday, October 22nd, 1861

8 ³/₄ o'clock P.M. . . . . I have a slight pain in my tooth, and in fact, do not feel very well. I returned from school quite fatigued, assumed a recumbent posture on the sofa, and was informed that O.P. had called. Ma and A. who had been out, shortly made their appearance. They had been to see about the daguerreotypes; and if Ma determines to have them taken, she intends to patronize the daguerrean saloon at Dryades St. to which she is recommended. Judging from their specimens that I have seen, I daresay their work will prove satisfactory; it will also be much more convenient than going down town.[1] If Ma decides, they are to be taken tomorrow afternoon, but had I a voice in the matter I would object to this, as I *know* the hurry which will be attendant. I dislike to have my picture taken to send away, particularly to a place where it will be seen by so many. Oh! on such occasions is my desire to be handsome, more earnest if possible. How *gratifying* would it be, for as each person to whom it was shown to, involuntarily exclaim, "How beautiful a face"! Alice then told me that O.P. remained but a few minutes, and is going Thursday, consequently immediate preparations for the pictures must be made. And now I have something to tell you. O.P. told her that yesterday afternoon I *passed him and his wife, and by not recognizing either seemed to treat them both with contempt.* His indignation was not awakened by the slight offered to himself, but the insult to his *wife* aroused him. Did you ever hear of anything more preposterous. To think that I, thinking of him and looking for him, should knowingly pass and not *speak.* Why, *nothing* would have afforded me more pleasure. Oh! the idea is ridiculous, and I am certain that there *is* some mistake. I am almost certain that they mistook some one else for me, for I am noted for my recognition of persons at a distance, and it does not sound probable, that coming into contact with them, as he said, I should have failed to observe a *soldier,* and *Mrs. M.* would not have failed to excite my attention. Oh! I am enraged with O.P. that he should have imagined me guilty of such a *breach of politeness,* and as in their sight my conduct must require an apology, I intend going there and offer it as soon as is convenient. I felt like going as soon as I heard of it. Of course, A. made all excuses in my favor, and O.P. requested her not to mention the circumstance to me. It annoyed me considerably, for it was my first *like* accusation. If it was *I*, how *could* I have been so *foolish.* This little incident threw a shade over my spirits. After supper, Ma sent the box containing the shrimps around to O.P.'s by E. She returned. A. heard her lessons, she went home. Ma sought the sofa, embraced slumber, and A. and I, taking advantage of this (for Ma thinks us selfish if we prefer your society to hers), came to *you.* I would like to see Obed Plummer. He is mad with me. I feel it. Condemned, accused *unjustly.* The day has been beautiful. According to instructions

1. The recently developed art of photography was already popular. The daguerreotype was an early form of photography named after its French inventor, Louis-Jacques-Mandé Daguerre, that involved use of a silver-coated copper plate treated with iodine vapor. New Orleans boasted several portrait studios using this process. The Civil War gave the new art form ample opportunity for experimentation and development. The photographs taken by Matthew Brady, among many others, have given us an indelible record not available for prior wars.

Mrs. Deegan called between the hours of 8 and 9 this morning to procure her Ticket to the F.M. [Free Market]. When Ma handed it to her she was as astonished as pleased, and returned many grateful thanks. Ma requested her to take an order to a Grocery store for her, and about 11 o'-clock the articles consisting of rice, sugar, molasses, etc. arrived. Ma was satisfied with them. Ma aided me in making some alterations on my Solferino dress, and it now fits very well. It is a handsome material, and every body says, becoming to its wearer. Before dinner Mrs. D. returned to show us the contents of her basket. It was sufficient for her wants, and I see that wood and coal are also to be provided. She amazed us when she said that she had been there the *whole* day, for as the crowd was so immense it was an utter impossibility to get served, although great regularity prevails. I should like to be present on "market days". The children came from School, and dinner was immediately announced, as I find it difficult to be in school at the appointed hour. A. was entertaining me with an account of all the particulars which she could glean of the marriage which was to take place in the night of James McConnell, Esq. and Miss Delphine Blanc. The ceremony was to be performed at Christ Church, and had that Cousin of ours [Sam Myers] shown himself, I intended to ask him to attend us there. I suppose ere now the noble couple are united. He is a paragon, she a beauty. I departed hurriedly for my academy, and was in time. Miss M. was present, but I again could not extend to her my invitation. She proposed to walk home with me, and return before dark, but to this I raised serious objections, the most weighty of which was that I knew A., who is desirous of seeing her, would not be at home. So I resolved to make no more appointments. We spoke of the fatality attending her visit. I have a presentiment that she *never* will come. We sat on the steps of an unoccupied house on Nayades St. while I read to her the Dictation, which she did not have. I walked a few squares down with her. She is an interesting little "creature". I like her *very* well. I met Fanny Burbank, stopped for a moment, kissed her, apologized for my neglect, and reprimanded her for being so ceremonious. She said that she *was* coming several times, but something had always prevented her. I must go and see her. I declare A. and I owe visits to *every* one of our acquaintances. I hope soon to pay them all. I had the *pleasure and pain* of walking behind the lovely, queenly Mrs. Caulfield. How I envied the noble looking man by her side. I quickened my pace through unattractive Clio St., and was soon in the door of my unpretending domicile. All safe! I learned that Olivia was over to Mrs. N.'s. I would have gone there, but I don't know why, I didn't feel like it, although

I should like to have seen her. Perverseness of human nature! Ma has awakened and recommends that we retire.

Thursday, October 24th, 1861

1 o'clock P.M. . . . . As my lessons for this afternoon are quite simple, I will devote this, *my time* to you for the purpose of telling you of the events of yesterday, which duty I was unable to perform on the last named period, for reasons, Deo volente [God willing], I will hereafter assign. The morning was quite cold and very gloomy looking, and was quite a contrast to the preceding, and I thought it inexplicable how one sky could be so clear, and the next so o'er cast. Before breakfast I studied, for you must know that on Wednesday our lessons are most difficult and numerous. I instilled the History into my mind, fixed A.'s hair, and breakfasted. As the clouds of the morning were dispelled, and the sun shone over the Earth, Ma determined to take Rosa and get their daguerreotypes taken. After performing various domestic duties, writing my Dictation, etc, then I summoned Rosa to have her toilet made. I was compensated for my trouble for she did look so sweet in her little pink barêge. I then assisted Ma. When she had finished she came down, left me with some orders, fixed the lunch, lamenting all the while that she was unable to intrust that duty to me, and then prepared to go. She told me that it was her intention to pay A. a visit. After she left, I partook of some bread, and dispatched the mid-day repast to Dell. She returned and told me that "Missis was at Miss Alice's School". I had been expecting O.P. all the morning, but had *now* given up the hope of seeing him, and was reproving myself for having been so foolish, as to have imagined for a moment that he would come, and his absence confirmed me in my opinion that he was angry with me. I *had* been awaiting him, yet all the while the thought would occur, that I would not see him. At 12 I began to study, had become familiar with the maps of Mexico and Central America, with the English discoveries in America, with the nature and properties of Verbs, and was on the eve of acquainting myself with the "Elements of Beauty" when from the bell overhead there sounded a deafening, startling peal. I jumped to my feet, and for fear of being disappointed, I determined to think of *no* one, but I *couldn't*. I heard the heavy, manlike step of O.P. and in his own characteristic voice ask, "Is Clara home"? He was replied in the affirmative, and soon *fully convinced* that *she was*. I told him that I thought he was angry with me, but he appeared astonished when I told him how he had unjustly accused me. He was confident that I did not recognize them, etc, etc. and assured me that Mrs. M. was not offended. This passed over. He was as handsome as ever, but his face bore a saddened expression, which *I* think looked too natural to be assumed. He spoke of his departure, the probability of our never again meeting, and *asked* me to *sometimes* think of *him*. I wished to make him a present and a few days previous had gained Ma's consent. Knowing that he had lost his little diary book I thought that one would be acceptable to him, so without ceremony or superfluous words, I presented to him a handsome one of mine, and expressed only the wish that he would, at times, write my name in "sweet remembrance" on its pages. He thanked me, and said he would *forever* keep it. A. intends giving him her "traveling cup" which Pa gave her. *That* will be a more worthy gift, and I know that he will prize it more for *its* sake as well as the *donor's*. He asked me to tell A. that he would be unable to come in the afternoon, but would pay his farewell visit in the evening. I invited him to stop in the morning as he was going to the Depot, but he urged that it would be impossible. After a stay of about 45 minutes, he expressed his determination of —*going*. Oh! Philomen, I felt *so so* sad, as I gazed upon him and thought that in all probability we should *never* meet again. I know that if I saw him before his departure it would be only for a few moments, so I bade the final "good bye". As I looked upon that proud, manly form, an earnest prayer ascended from my *soul* that a Yankee bullet would never pierce his noble, generous heart. He took my hand and said, "Clara, I have one favor which I wish you to grant. Think of me sometimes with kindness". You know my reply. He held my hand, and as I almost inaudibly breathed "God be with you", he relinquished his hold, and in a moment more had *gone*. I felt so bad, but it was consolation to know that the last interview was of so pleasant a nature. I went to dress, and as I came down Ma, Alice and Rosa entered. Ma had been to A.'s school. She had the daguerreotypes, and Rosa's! it was life like. I never saw anything more perfect, and I thought of the happiness it would afford Pa to have so exact a copy of his "boy". Oh! it was beautiful! and bore the same expression as did her dear little face when she used to bestow upon Pa those epithets he so loved to hear her say. Ma and she were taken together, but Ma's was not as well. It was an excellent likeness, but could have been improved, and we intended to request the Artist to make a few alterations.[2] Ma had made an appointment for us at 4 o'clock, so we immediately disposed of dinner, and proceeded to equip ourselves for the grand event. I dressed Sallie very sweetly in her yellow merino, F. donned her blue muslin, and they, with Ma, left, leaving A. and I to follow, as serious objections were made to such a crowd. A. was for some time undecided what to wear, but finally decided in favor of her "Flag" and I of my "Solferino". Thus robed we departed, and soon reached the Saloon on the classic Dryades St. We were much astonished by the appearance of E., but much more so when she handed to Ma a *letter,* which Mr. N. had given to her. It was from "my Father" (Bless him). I made several attempts to read it, but being continually interrupted, I resolved to wait until a more favorable opportunity. We sat in our turn, and took but a casual glance at them when we arose. As it would take some time for him to color, etc. etc. Ma, who had some articles to purchase from Churchill's, left and promised to return and meet A. and me. We employed the time by perusing the letter. It was as dear and lengthy as his former ones, and bore the date of the 17th. He is enjoying his usual health, but his absence from us often caused him to be morose and appear insulting, and he writes that a few days previous he apologized to a gentleman who accused him of treating him *impolitely.* Pa excused himself and explained that his thoughts were with us, and his bad humor and seeming rudeness was attributable to the fact that he was compelled to be separated from us. The gentleman accepted the apology. Pa says that he would have been with us before now were the intervening distance not so great, but *if* he is confident that the war will be of long duration, *we will join him at Richmond!* Wouldn't that be glorious. But I know that it would not meet Ma's approval. He asked Ma if she would prefer for him to write "six lines" *every* day or as he does now. Why, of *course,* as he does *now.* Capt. da P. is at R. [Richmond] but will return to M. [Manassas] in a few days. Pa chanced to be sitting at the same table with Capt. Eshleman. He inquired about us, and in the presence of *many* passed compliments upon his "*daughters*", much to their astonishment, being surprised on learning that "Mr. Solomon" had *grown children,* as his *youthful appearance* seemed to contradict the fact. Oh! what would I not give to see him! Virginia air must agree with him. Capt. E. requested Pa to tender to us his kind regards. More than the *Owl* ever does. When we had finished the letter, we talked of its writer, and I declare, I had no idea how much I wanted to see him. To-night two months is Christmas

---

2. Much can be done to alter a daguerreotype after it is made.

eve. If God is willing I hope that *he* will complete our family circle.³ Ma
then arrived with a parcel containing some flannel which she had purchased. She laid it upon the sofa, for the gentleman announced that he had
completed his work. Night had spread her mantle o'er the Earth, and many
were our regrets that we would be unable to see them in the daylight. He
has regretted that the time was so limited for he thought that he could em-
bellish them more. Well, he showed them to us, and they were perfect, A.'s,
F.'s, and S.'s, and they said mine; but I was not satisfied with mine, and
complained to Ma that it was not *pretty*. "Well", said she, "did you expect
to make a *pretty picture? Do ugly* people generally." Wasn't that cruel. We
then expressed our satisfaction to the Artiste. I would not hesitate to rec-
ommend him to anyone. He is not only skilled in his profession, but is so
kind and obliging. To be sure we traced resemblances between him and
other people, but, laying joke aside, his likeness to Mr. da P. was most striking, and we have concluded that he is an *exile brother*.⁴ Ma recompensed
him, and promised to solicit patronage. He thanked her and gallantly held
the light while we tripped down the stairs. I could not realize that it was
over. On our way home, we stopped at Mrs. N.'s; Leopold shortly came
in, and both pronounced them splendid, exact, etc. L. was astonished to
hear that Jacobs had not taken them. How much genius lies hidden
from the world. While there, E. entered with the news that "Capt. Miller
was over at the house". A short while after the receipt of this intelligence
we were starting in that direction. He seemed very merry, and I *think* I
know why he was so. It was his last visit, and he informed us that he had
but a *moment* to stay, as he had visits to pay, trunks to pack, and 100
other things to do. He told us to send all our bundles and things around to
his mansion in the night. During one of the moments A. presented to
him the "cup". He appeared to be dumbfounded, and looked as though he
could *not* believe that it was really intended for him. He thanked her gracefully and gentlemanly for it, and said he prized it highly, and appreciated
the goodness and thoughtfulness that prompted it. I knew that he would
like it for it is a most convenient little article. Every moment lessened the
time that he was to be with us and at last the one arrived in which we were
to part. We bade him go to Pa, talk with him, kiss him, and deliver in

3. The Christian holiday had taken on some familial meaning for Jews who in so many ways
had assimilated into life in New Orleans.
4. Without pursuing the matter with the photographer, the Solomons decide that he is Jewish.
Of the photographers doing business in New Orleans at the time, several were Jewish, and when they
later show the photographs to their friend Leopold, he is surprised that Edward Jacobs, a famous
Jewish photographer, was not chosen to do the work.

perfect safety the valuable treasures we would commit to his care. He was pleased with them, and rendered the same verdict as did the others. He said that Pa would be the possessor of all, with the exception of A.'s and mine, which would by some accident have been lost and he would tell Pa to expect *them* by *Express*. He shook hands, hoped to see us again; we followed him to the door, and I see him now as he then stood by the gate and said "Ladies I have spent many hours with you. I can say no more now." He touched his cap, walked on, and as we, for the tenth time, uttered "God bless you", his "Thank you" were the last words of *his* that fell on our ears. We went to supper and while there "Gus" called. A few moments after Louisa Grant brought a letter to Charles Hurly to be delivered to him through the "politeness of Capt. M." She did not stay. Gus as usual. Ma, in order to bring him into the back room, requested him to arrange the drop light; of course, he could but comply, and we had an excellent look at him by the glare of the gas. After the performance he noiselessly *slid* back to *his* seat on the sofa. We showed him the daguerreotypes, and by him they were styled "handsome", and he protested again and again that it was shameful to send them to Virginia, when there were others who could prize them so much more. We told him that he was using insulting language, but he cared but little. We talked as great a pack of nonsense as we always do. He left about 8. Ma was writing to Pa. We joined her around the little table, and our thoughts went to Virginia and next to Pa, *you* know with whom they lingered. Having gained Ma's consent we determined to do what we have for some time been deliberating about. I did not tell you of it before, for we were so perfectly undecided. Well, we had some beautifully pressed roses and the brilliant idea struck us to arrange them properly, enclose them in an envelope, the superscription which was to be *Col. C.R. Wheat,* and to intrust it to O.P.'s care. Having no suitable envelope we went over to Mrs. N.'s to procure one. Succeeded, returned home. Ma was still writing, and A. and I pondered and thought, thought and pondered for many moments as to appropriate accompanying words. Finally I suggested "Tokens of remembrance from Alice and Clara". It was accepted and the deed done. Submitted to Ma's inspection, and then sealed. Ma then prepared to pack the pictures, and when in a state of progression Mr. N. came in. He regretted being unable to see them, and left presently. We then dispatched the package and letters round to O.P.'s by Lucy. Don't you wonder what will be the destiny of *our* letter. Is it not unparalleled impudence? Will he view it in that light? Nous verrons. We then stayed up some time discussing the events of the day, and as important were they that the memory of them caused a languor to steal over us, and we retired. I must go and dress. I would be satisfied to be always with you.

8¹/₄ P.M. . . . Philomen, we are all seated around the fire in the back room, for the day has been really cold. Ma and F. are asleep, and this is the scene which I picture to myself for many a winter night. This morning we were up quite early, the wind was whistling around the house, the cold air had penetrated the rooms, and A. and I stood shivering. This together with our uncertain state of mind, prevented our usual morning chat. I confidently expected that O.P. would stop to see us, but 7 o'clock came and he did not come. I was quite disappointed, but made due allowances for him, and particularly as the mornings are so short, that it is only with much difficulty that necessary preparations can be made. I heard the whistle of the train which bore him from the Crescent City. Ma and I have been sitting in the dining room, the machine has been transplanted from its "accustomed place" to a nook in the sitting room, and every action, every movement, recalled the unpleasant last Winter. We were engaged in the duty of renovating, altering and making Flannels for the children. Flannel is exorbitantly high. Before leaving for School A. and I agreed to meet at Mrs. Millers. I was late as usual, but passed a pleasant afternoon with Miss B. and Mrs F., as the exercise consisted chiefly of singing, and I learned that another concert was "on foot". Bad news for us. I walked a short distance with Miss M. She told me of a compliment she had heard passed upon me, and delivered to me from Nina Word, her love and 1000 kisses. I bade her return them to her in a double ratio. I stopped at Mrs. M.'s. She was out, and Obed told me that Miss Alice had been there. I met her and we walked home together. As usual found plenty to talk about. Arrived at the door and went in. Eat supper, talked, and here I am. I do not feel very well, and as the kettle is steaming on the fire, and I have in anticipation a nice warm foot-bath, I will go. I have been very brief, but as it so seldom happens you will excuse me.

Saturday, October 26th, 1861

10¹/₂ A.M. . . . Oh! Philomen, it grieves me so, when I think of the time that has elapsed since we were together; but it was unavoidable, totally. Friday afternoon, I was so fatigued after my excursion, that I was unfit for service. You look inquiring. Well, I will explain; but first let me relate the facts

of the morning. It was *warm* in comparison with the preceding one. I did
not arise till very late; came down, *eat* the paper, and *read* breakfast. The
children had gone to School, and I was sitting in the rocking chair with
my charge, Josie, when Ellen came bounding into the room, an envelope in her hand, which I immediately recognized from the color, so, taking it from her, I went to Ma, quietly saying "Ma here's a dispatch". She
hastily tore it open, and we read "I received your last letter. Will write in a
few days. All well". It was very thoughtful in Pa, as it would have caused
us much uneasiness had we not heard from him. Ma then made up her
mind to go down town on a shopping expedition, and, about 11 o'clock,
we were in the bus on our way. Paid our first visit of about $2^1/_2$ hours to
Danzinger's. Made some purchases, and among them a dress for Ma and
me, both very pretty and cheap. Then proceeded to Eisner's, but as he had
very few of the desired articles, we made but a short stay. He was minus
belts, buckles, bracelets, etc. Invested in some stockings, handkerchiefs
and a net for Fannie. Then directed our steps to Meunier's. Their stock
was very small, and we invested in some cheap belts. Then tired and warm,
we made rapid movements towards Canal Street, and after investing at
Blineau's were in the public conveyance. Arrived home about $3^1/_4$. The children were waiting for us, and cries of "Give me some, give me some" greeted
us. Shortly after the bell rang, and the "Chestnuts" were announced. Eat
dinner and then opened them. They were very safe and sound and splendid. We were feasting upon them all the afternoon. I was worn out and the
greater part of the time was lying down on the bed, relating to A. the adventures of the day. As A. put on her barêge she said "Clara, I am going to
see Leopold", and when we came down the named gentleman was seated
in the room. He partook of some chestnuts, and left at $7^1/_2$. Supper was
then disposed of, and Ma left immediately after for bed, and A. and I went
over to Mrs. N.'s. Spent a very pleasant evening in the society of the host
and hostess, Mr. E., Mr. Benjamin C. a new acquaintance, and Leopold.
As the clock struck nine, we arose to depart and were escorted home by
L. Entered the house by burglarious means, and after arranging the fas-
tenings securely, we were "en route" for up stairs. Were soon looking very
interesting in our "night robes", and then, more so with our youthful heads
upon our snowy pillows. To day is quite pleasant, but not at all cold. A. has
gone to Synagogue, but I did not feel like accompanying her. I braided her
hair, but not elaborately, after breakfast, and assisted her in making her
toilet. I have not been with Ma much this morning, and for fear that she
will think me exclusive, I will now join her.

Sunday, October 27th, 1861

10 ½ A.M. On descending this morning I first applied myself to writing a note to Nettie P. . ., requesting her to ascertain for me in School the lessons for the Arithmetic, on the following Monday. Dispatched Ellen, who returned with a complying reply. I intend asking of her this favor each week and I hope that it will not inconvenience her.[5] The miserable Paper then claimed my attention, but only for a short while, as no interesting matter graced its columns. Ma did not come down to breakfast this morning as she was not feeling very well, but I am thankful that she feels better, and is now in the dining room, where I, in company with her and the others, have just had the pleasure in participating in the concealment of some monstrous shrimps, which after L. [Lucy] brought them from market were submitted to a boiling operation. But I have not yet disposed of yesterday. The day continued fine, and on A.'s return she told me that she said that Mrs. Rosly Marks had spoken to her, and A. assured me that, from what she said respecting my money, that it was forthcoming and I would by the first of the month become its possessor. Good news for Clara!!! I assisted Ma in fixing her Armoir, admiring our dresses, and the time passed. Before dinner, I dressed Sallie and myself, and repaired to the lower regions where I had the pleasure of greeting Mr. and Mrs. N. and Josh. Subsequent to their exit the noon repast was announced. Ma then prepared to go out, as she and Mrs. N. had agreed to call on Mrs. Marks. They left, both looking very pretty. A. and I went round to Mrs. Miller's, and "mirabile dictu!" [wonderful to relate] found her at home. She was as lively, as vivacious as ever, and did not seem to grieve over the departure of her Lord [Capt. Obed Miller]. As I expected, he left in a great hurry, and Mrs. M. is confident that she will see him again. She is blessed in being possessed of so cheerful a disposition. I think that she could dispel any attack of the blues, and the cares that would weigh on her heart or depress her spirits would indeed be great ones. I love to be in her company. She showed us a daguerreotype which O.P. had brought. It was picked up on the plains of Manassas after the battle. How highly was it prized by its owner, and what a tale of misery does it tell. It was the picture of quite a pretty Yankee girl. She also had a pair of *ladies drawers*. Another trophy which O.P. obtained. A party of Yankees crossed the river in order to have a marriage performed, but they were pursued by a scouting party of ours, and in their

---

5. Clara needed the assignments given out on Saturdays.

flight left all their wardrobe, and this was *his* share of the victory — Mrs. Ripley, the mother of one of our Camp acquaintances, called while we were there. She is a very pleasant lady. Mrs. M. was so fascinating that it was impossible to get away, and "shades of evening" had for some time closed over us ere we were on our way home, escorted by the manly Obed. Met Ellen on the way, and thanking our little beau, bade him "good night". Oh! how I long for a brother like him. Ma reproved us slightly for remaining late, but we explained how unavoidable it was. Mrs. N. was there. Eat supper, and then *passed round* Chestnuts. I laid on the sofa, fully determined not to close my eyes; heard Mr. N. come in, but was totally unconscious when our guests took their departure.

$2^{1}/_{2}$ P.M. . . . I have but a few moments. I have just finished braiding one side of A.'s hair, but will not commence on the other, as I know that I can not complete it before dinner. I have written a lengthy epistle to Pa, which *something* tells me he will never receive. I hope that I will be mistaken. To day one week ago O.P. was in our midst, now, how far, far away is he from us. He is nearing his destination, and I presume he will reach it tomorrow night. There's dinner! I am hungry!!

$8^{1}/_{4}$ P.M. . . . I shall devote but a short while to you, as I am determined to study. I am sitting up in my room, *all alone.* After dinner F. received a visit from Julia Colton, an acquaintance of hers. A. and I helped to entertain her a little while, and then ascended to dress. Came down, and were in momentary expectation of Eisner, but he did not come. What can be the matter? It was his *time.* I hope he is not offended. Leopold's delicate proportions were soon seated in a chair by us. Shortly after our noble Cousin, with his usual pomposity, strutted in. He looked so handsome, and met from each the same reproaches and abuses for his long absence. Philomen, he was defeated in the nomination. I was amused at seeing him and L. together, as I know how jealous he is of him. L. staid until almost dark, and I walked to the corner with him, and he faithfully promised to come up Tuesday night, when I will *ask* Miss M., but I have not the slightest idea that she will *come.* Mr. and Mrs. N. stopped on their way home. They had been riding in the cars. We promised them to go over. L. adjourned with us to the supper room, broke slightly through his rules, and eat a few shrimps.[6] Then Ma, he and A. went to Mrs. N., but I declined accompanying them, and thus do I explain how I am *solitaire.* My History lies before me. I feel like studying, so "good night."

---

6. Shrimp are prohibited food under traditional Jewish dietary laws.

Monday, October 28th, 1861

9 o'clock P.M. . . . With depressed spirits, I again come to you. Ma has been in an execrably bad humour all day, and I, being the only member home, have it all vented upon me. I declare Ma is at some time unreasonable. I am now though, calmer than heretofore. The drop light is lit, Ma is writing to Mr. Wall, A. is with F. F. [R.?] and S. have retired. The weather is yet warm. This morning I performed my sums, in Discount, and though not difficult they were very long. I wished Mr. N. to mail my letter, so sent over word requesting him to stop in on his way down town, but, to my sorrow and disappointment I was informed that he had gone out and so my letter will have to wait until tomorrow. I have just finished directing it, and I suppose when Pa receives it he will be a little puzzled, as my hand writing is not familiar to him. Maybe he is now gazing upon our Ambratypes. I hope so. The day has passed very disagreeably and I was glad when $2^{1}/_{2}$ arrived. I arrived at School, sooner than usual. Nothing notable happened. Miss M. and I feasting our eyes on the few beauties of our class. I love to look at Olympia Burie. I did not have an opportunity to ask Miss M. to come tomorrow, as she walked off with Mrs. Shaw. As I was coming home, I looked in all directions for A. as she had promised to meet me, and as I was going *in* the door, she was coming out of it, and was quite surprised at seeing me so soon, for I must inform you that School is dismissed at $5^{1}/_{2}$. I was mad and sad so I remained in the house; presently the gas was lit, and the usual programme was enacted. Ma and A. have finished their writing, and I must follow their example.

Tuesday, October 29th, 1861

$7^{1}/_{2}$ P.M. . . . Here we are again seated around the little table, performing our various duties by the aid of the soft radiance of our drop light. Ma is manufacturing her newly purchased dress which promises to be very pretty. I am in want of *mine.* — I was out of my bed this morning as six o'clock bell rang — I deserve much credit for this, as it is almost dark. How perceptibly shorter have the mornings got. I studied until breakfast; and after disposing of the dishes, putting Josie to sleep, I made a complete wash of the gas fixtures, which was by no means a task destitute of difficulty. Ma

was not restored to her usual good temper, nor was I. I did not accomplish much sewing, and commenced today to dress Rosa, a duty which I do not like, particularly as it detracts from the short time that is allotted to me for study. When A. came home from School she had on her hair a very pretty worsted "fly trap", the handiwork of Mary Ames. It is a great ornament to the back hair. A. furnished the material the color of which is blue. I left home perfectly undecided whether Miss M. would come, but notwithstanding I bade A. to prepare for the occasion. As I was seated at my desk, the rustle of every gown and the sound of every footstep caused me to turn my head in expectation of seeing her, but she did not come, and I knew that Cousin S. will be here, and again accuse me of "humbugging" him. I wonder why she was not in school. Well, just my luck, and I do believe that there is a fatality attending the visit. I don't think that I shall ask her again. I was lonesome without her, although Miss Del Trigo was as entertaining as usual. Dictation and Reading constituted the exercises of the afternoon, the latter of which is very amusing, particularly when Miss Benedict indulges in her "Theatrical propensities" of which she is well aware, but protests that she does not care a cent for the opinion of the girls. She is an intelligent, eccentric little being — No notable incident attended my homeward walk. At the corner I met A., whose face assumed a downcast, disappointed expression as she exclaimed "all alone"; for you must know she is anxious to behold my companion. I then accompanied A. to Provensal's for the purpose of purchasing some worsted braid, as Ma is desirous of having one of the "concerns". They had the desired article, but as it had increased in price, we refused to take it, fearing that it would not meet Ma's approval. We then went to Fairex's with the intention of investing, but principally for the purpose of getting change for a *one* dollar bill, which Ma has without success endeavored to get changed. The obliging gent. could not furnish us, but politely gave us the privilege of retaining our purchase, and "call in some other time". It is difficult to obtain specie, and they will sooner refuse the sale of goods than give it.[7] A. and I *tasted* the rusks, and a la Marx, we eat nearly all before our arrival home. Ma protested that she would give no more for the braid and we were glad that we did not buy it. I sent my letter this morning by Mr. Elburger. I trust that it will reach its post. Mrs. N. and family have gone to the Crescent Artillery Concert. I wish that I could have gone. I wonder if O.P. is in Richmond. The omnibus stops. The bell rings — There's Cousin Sam. *Later*

7. By October 1861 the currency situation in New Orleans had become intolerable. Confederate money had lost value, and coins disappeared.

... He has gone, and I am happy to say, was not a particle angry about his disappointment, for I know that he is desirous of making the young ladies [sic] acquaintance, as he has often spoke of the beauty of *her* and her sister. I have been laughing immoderately as I generally do when he is about, and relating his inexhaustible anecdotes. He was much perplexed and undecided how to act in a certain affair. Mrs. Williams [his landlord] is going to move up town, and he does not know whether to follow her, knowing as he does how inconvenient it will be to him. Ma advised him to remain with Mrs. W. His financial affairs are not in as flourishing a state as formerly as his profession in *these* times, *his* profession is one that does not *pay*.[8] I would like to have asked him to come up again for a similar purpose, but I could not. He accepted Ma's invitation to dine with us on Sunday.

Thursday, October 31st, 1861

6¹/₂ A.M. .... The last day of October! With what startling earnestness do I write these words, and so rapidly has the month winged its flight that I can scarcely force the conviction upon my mind. Tomorrow is All Saints day, and A. and I wish to visit the Graveyards, but will not from the want of suitable companions as Ma and Mrs. N. both object to such "proceedings". It is generally a very pretty sight, but one which everyone is not inclined to enjoy. Since we last parted, a great change in the atmospherical regions has occurred; and I was quite surprised yesterday morning on perceiving it. I arose about six, and studied until breakfast, and found my blue dress, which I altered without any assistance, to be very comfortable, and also an excellent robe for in doors. It is very pretty, and I regret exceedingly that it is unfit for street wear. It was considered no bargain *last* year for *15* cents. Compare the *times*. I do find it utterly impossible to accomplish any sewing of importance in the day and particularly on Wednesday. So at 11¹/₂, after assisting Ma but very little with her dress, I bade farewell to thimble, needle, scissors, etc. and was soon deep in the discoveries of the 16th century. I studied assiduously as Wednesday is *the* afternoon in School. Olivia's baby was to see Mrs N. and she sent it over

---

8. Sam Myers specialized in commercial law, a field that suffered during wartime.

by Maggie to see us. It is a beautiful child. I learned that Gudie was spending the day with Mrs. N. While dressing, E. came up to me with the intelligence that the "deaf and dumb man" was down stairs.[9] I was quite
astonished and accelerated my movements and was shortly down. Ma was
on the sofa writing to him, and I complied with her earnest request and relieved her. She said that she was tired of it. I sat and talked with him for
some time. He had been in the city for but one day and came for the purpose of purchasing some instruments which he had with him, and he
was going away on the six o'clock train. He spoke to me of his profession,
the success which had attended him, and the pleasure it had afforded him.
He maintained that it was superior to that of a Lawyer, Doctor, or of a
Major, Captain or *Colonel.* I ventured to disagree with him, but the wild
look in his eyes, his variety of expressions, and his meaning gestures, convinced me of my error in saying what I did, and I must confess slightly
alarmed me, and after calling the children in the room to ensure my
safety, I determined to speak no more on the subject of his "profession". I
then said "You do not ask for Miss Solomon", altho' I knew to the contrary
for Ma told me that he had been inquiring for her, and the many queer
things he had been writing. She told him that she would be in at 3, and I
believe he resolved to remain. *I* wished to *draw him out.* He began by remarking that Miss S. was a very charming young lady, and asked me if I
thought there was *any chance for him.* I pretended to not understand him
and he went on to say that he wished to marry her and was *determined*
and wished to know if in the accomplishment of his purpose, he would
meet with many trials. He said plenty which I, *fortunately,* disremember,
and to all his inquiries or affirmations, I laughed, as though at the absurdity of what he said. Of course I discouraged him in all he said. Told him
that Miss S. had refused many wealthy offers, and I thought that it was
her determination not to marry for some time. I said much more, which I
desired to have the effect of showing him how hopeless was his case. He
told me that he could get plenty, and extended his two hands, meaning all
over the world. I told him that I was glad of it, and suggested that he should
avail himself of the fact. He stated that he had written a letter to A., and
he was furiously indignant and enraged when he learned that she had not
received it, and vowed that he would have the Post Master and Clerks arrested for non-performance of their duty. He told Ma that it was a letter
that she would like to see. A. came home, but wisely did not come into the

9. The "Blind Man," from Clara's first visit to the military camp at the beginning of the diary.

room. I saw the look of astonishment on her face, as she entered and saw me engaged in earnest conversation with a man. She looked inquiringly and as the truth flashed upon her mind it amused me to note the varying expressions imparted to her face. The gent. demanded the hour; I gave it to him; he wrote, "I must go; I will see you in 2 weeks", and without another inquiry concerning "Miss S." he had gathered up his packages, bade adieux, and was gone. How glad was I. My first act was to wash my hands, for his slate was in a disgusting condition, and himself no better. Dinner was then announced, and he was the subject under consideration, and many a burst of laughter did the memory of his words cause. We all agreed that he was *insane,* and were indignant "to think of his presumptions too, the *dirty, nasty mute.*" Can he be in his right mind? Does he imagine that A. would *marry him!!* We unanimously voted to excuse ourselves to him on his next visit. If the man's mind has not lost its balance, I think that his conduct surpasses in impudence, anything of which I have ever heard; and yet if I were A., I would feel *flattered* by the consciousness of possessing the power of inspiring love within the heart of such a being. I daresay he has often felt it, as he is a great admirer of woman and — beauty. I presume that it was A.'s *uncommon beauty* that first attracted him to her. Poor, isolated creature! If "*love* is akin to pity", oh! ye powers! guard *my* heart, for I am fearful that I shall lose it; for *he* awakened in my breast the feelings of sympathy and pity to a greater extent than ever any object ever has. The hands of the clock pointed to $3\frac{1}{2}$ and I was forced to leave the party, and after a rapid walk under the shady trees of Clio St., I was occupying my seat in the Junior apartment of the L.N.S., and was fully recompensed for the time and study I had bestowed on my lessons, when I recited them to *my* gratification. I was pleased to see Miss M., who informed me that indisposition occasioned her non-appearance at School on the preceding afternoon. I expressed my regrets at her absence, as I told her that I was again deprived of her company. We enjoyed our stolen chat, which was chiefly on the price of wearables, such as dresses, gloves, bonnets, etc. The bell for the dismissal of school fell joyfully upon my ear. After making my preparations for the street, and impressing a real kiss upon the beautiful lips of my pretty Belle, I, and my chum, were on our way, the old school house behind us. We parted at the corner; it was the very same, where evenings before we had parted without breathing each other's name. It seems as though I like her more each time that I see her. On my arrival home, I found Ma and A. out, so I ran over to Mrs. N.'s. She and Josh were seated by the table, and I joined them, and completed the trio. She apologized to me for

the light, and I patiently listened to all her complaints of the newly purchased oil, which was recommended by the venders, and which is now sold
for $4.00 per gallon, its former price being $1.25! Oh! what a blessing is
Gas! At *all* times, but particularly at *this* crisis. The Lord of the mansion
soon entered. He was not at dinner, and had nothing to eat, so demanded
something, declaring that he *"was* starved". His spouse made preparations
for supper, and while so doing, Ma and A. came in *just for a moment*. Mrs
N. insisted that we should remain to sup with her. I complied and Ma
and A. also, after much begging. I ate heartily, for I was hungry, as I could
not dispose of all of my dinner. Ma and A. had been on a "bonnet excursion" which was unsuccessful. Ma was "star" in her new dress, which looked
very pretty and was very much admired. Mrs. N. purposes, if possible,
to purchase a similar one. Ma and A. left shortly, but I remained, Mrs.
N. promising to accompany me home. I instructed Josh in his lesson, at
his request, "skipped him in his Tables", talked, etc., and about 8 was on
my way home, escorted by my host and hostess. Was saluted by "Gus".
The elders adjourned to the back room, the "youngers" to the front. "Gus",
well what can I say about him? He was as *peculiar* as ever, as complimen-
tary, and we, as *trustless*. We were conversing some of the time upon the
idiom of the language, the correctness and incorrectness of many of its expressions, and the few persons to whom it is understood. "Gus" is *right
smart*. Mrs. Da P. was, to be sure, introduced and pronounced for about
the 10,000th time interesting, charming, etc., etc. All our mutual friends
were discussed. I soon observed that he was initiated into the secrets of the
distinguished "Mr. Cavanagh", and afforded him much sport, declaring
that so fine an offer is not presented to every one, and reproved A. for
being so hasty. I am always so sleepy while in his society, and after several
unsuccessful attempts to keep awake, I sought the sofa, went to sleep, was
conscious only for the moment when Gus shook my head to say "good
night". When *again* conscious, all the guests had departed. I did not tell
you that Mrs. N. and co. were charmed with the Concert. She was invited
by Mr. E. and regretted that we were not there. The singing was fine, and
she gave such glowing descriptions that I almost imagined that I had been
one of the audience. The amount realized is not yet known. Several others are in preparation, the proceeds to be devoted to various purposes. O.P.
has been gone a week! Bless him. Has Major Wheat our "token"? Nous
verrons, nous verrons!!!

Friday, November 1st, 1861

6 $\frac{1}{4}$ A.M. . . . The morning is bleak and dreary, the wind is whistling from
without, thick clouds are drifting through the sky, and from all appearance the day will be a most disagreeable one for the observance of the
old time custom of visiting the resting places of the dead, and decorating
the tombs afresh, within which repose the ashes of loved ones gone before.
I have vacated my ancient seat by the front window, and am seated before
a cozy, comfortable dining-room fire. "Miss S." has not yet descended, and
I suppose that old Boreas' breath keeps fast her eyelids close.[10] I left you
yesterday morning, and nothing extraordinary characterized the early part
of the day. Studied, sewed, eat, as usual. Departed for school in as great
a hurry, and Ma has issued orders for dinner to be on the table at *three o'-
clock.* Arrived at school in season and was much entertained by the exhibition of Miss Benedict's elocutionary powers. Miss M. and I, together in
the class, but separated as I proceeded to Singing, choosing as a substitute, pleasant Miss Del Trigo. Miss M. and I met at the dismissal, and left
together. I requested her to walk a few squares down with *me,* and she complied. A. had promised to walk to meet me, and hoping and expecting to
see her, I made the above request. We had gone a short distance, Nina
Word being the subject of our conversation, when, at the corner of Clio
and Apollo, I perceived two ladies approaching, and imparted to my friend
that my *mother* and *sister* were coming. She naturally felt a little diffident,
in the expectation of being in the presence of persons who had so often
heard her spoken of. In a moment it was over. Miss Mitchell, my Sister,
Miss Mitchell, my Mother. Her bashful feelings vanished, and we halted
a short while and talked. A. told her that she had heard me speak of her
accompanying me home, and extended to her the invitation to call. I asked
A. to join us, but she and Ma had some few purchases to make. I had
promised Miss M. to go *back* with her, so we parted. Oh! how anxious was
I to know their opinion of her. She expressed hers of them. Thought A.
was *very* pretty, sweet-looking, etc., etc., but could not give hers accurately
of Ma, as *"she had looked at A. all the time".* I escorted her a short distance,
and she almost promised to come home with me Monday. I suppose I
will see Cousin S. After leaving her, I accelerated my movements for the

---

10. Clara followed the Christian custom of whitewashing tombs on All Saints Day, for which
there is no Jewish counterpart. "Boreas' breath" refers to Eos, the Greek goddess of dawn, who awoke
early each morning to precede her brother into the heavens. One of her children is Boreas, the north
wind, that keeps Alice's eyes closed. Clara's knowledge of Greek mythology was extensive.

stars were beginning to peep out in the "blue vault above". I could not restrain the feeling which prompted me to stop, and, like a "*Vulgarian*", look
through the open windows into the spacious parlors of G.H. Race, Esq!
What an appearance of ease and comfort was exhibited. Busied with other
thoughts "Little Clara" was turning Clio St. Ma and A. were not at home
on my arrival. I waited some time expecting them, but as they did not come,
I sent E. to see if they were at Mrs. N.'s. She returned, saying that they
were, and delivered the message for me and F. to come over after supper.
We partook of the repast, and as F. did not want to go I went alone. I *should*
have remained with you. Leopold was there and presently Mr. E. entered.
They too had been informed of the "blind man", and much merriment from
talking of him ensued. A game of "Keno" was proposed and joyfully accepted, and A., L., and I came over to procure the box, which fortunately we possess.[11] Succeeded and were soon seated around the table prepared to gamble. The party consisted of all the persons present. Mr. E. was
very unlucky, and after losing $1 he stopped. About $9^1/_2$ the rain was heard,
but we heeded it not, and about $10^1/_2$ we arose from the table, I *ninety cents*
richer than when I was seated. The rain had not yet abated, but was raging with increased violence. We could not get home, and L. was at first
very restless, *knowing* that he *could* not get off, and thinking that we
would leave, and he would compel his hostess or host to remain up. But
it continued with startling furiousness, the lightning streamed through the
window, the thunder shook the house. Ma was uneasy about home, but
we were obliged to take it cool. A, L. and F. retired into the front room, I,
on the sofa, the others ensconced in arm-chairs. We chatted, laughed,
expressed many regrets for the "poor graveyards", and the moments passed —
I slept for some time, A. also, but it was only a nap. We insisted upon Mrs.
N.'s retiring, but she would not. Mr. N. and E. had complied with our requests, and were then in the "Land of dreams". The rain continued, the
streets were overflowed. Here was a dilemma. We submitted to our fate.
Took a look out, the water was flowing off, and the prospect was better,
so we determined to make a bold venture. Mrs. N. had a lot of Mr. N.'s
shoes, and L. looked particularly interesting as he performed the duties of
a shoeman. Wrapped up carefully and thus shielded from the inclemency
of the weather, we bade Mrs. N. "good morning" at $1^1/_2$ A.M. and with a
bound were safe and sound within our own mansion. L. bade us "good
day", and no doubt, envied us. Mrs N. can never complain, for I think that

---

11. Keno is a card game in use today.

we spent with her a *very* long evening, and please God, when, next year, we are endeavoring to recall the incidents of the *last* 31st of October, no great effort will be required, for it will be marked by an event of *not* an *every day* occurrence. All was right at home, and after ridding ourselves of all superfluous articles, we were in our bed chambers, soon undressed, and soon asleep, and I have not suffered any from the grand frolic in which, I must confess, I enjoyed myself. The "King of Day" will not be visible. The 1st of November, 1861, will be ushered in gloomily, and yet, I suppose the Cemeteries will be well-attended. They intend collecting subscription for the relief of the families of the absent volunteers. A praiseworthy object. We were anxiously expecting a letter yesterday, but were disappointed. I hope that it will arrive to day. There is one advertised for Alice, but I am positive that it is the "Blind man's".[12] I am desirous of beholding it. A. wrote to Baby yesterday, requesting and begging her to come and spend some time with us. I do hope that she will come, or at any rate respond to the letter. I do want to see her so much. I must leave for breakfast.

Saturday, November 2nd, 1861

10 1/2 A.M. Oh! it is a splendid day, a decided contrast to yesterday. The sun is gaily shining and nature is decked in a new robe. My pious sister A. in company with S. has gone to attend Divine Service. I did not attend. The day yesterday continued as gloomy as the morning indicated, and I would much rather prefer a stormy day. I was engaged the earlier part in mending, renovating, etc., for last year's garments are in requisition. Things are daily increasing in price. Soap which formerly was 20 cts. a bar, is now $1.00! Coffee $1. per pound, and Ma has notified us that we must soon say "good bye" to it. She tried the experiment of mixing it with *rye*, but we were dissatisfied with it. Change is impossible to be obtained, and some devising individual has introduced as a substitute omnibus tickets! What are we coming to? The Blockade must be raised. About 12 o'clock, Mary came over, and in her hand, two letters, both for Alice; one from Mr. Cavanagh, the other from my dearly beloved Father. Ma hurriedly tore open the seal of the last-named one, and eagerly perused its contents. The dear one

12. The Express office put notices in the newspaper for items that had arrived.

was in the enjoyment of perfect health, and tendered many apologies for his silence, and sufficiently convinced us that it was not from neglect. He has much company, and this, with his business keeps him occupied, and he was often on the eve of writing when a "batch of friends" would drop in. "I should have written", said he, "but six lines; but no; when I write I must write a long letter".[13] We freely forgave him, and appreciated the consideration which prompted the Telegram dispatch. He replied to A.'s inquiries as to the manner in which she should act as regards Mr. da Silva, etc., etc. Told her to demand the bill, and he would send the money.[14] Capt. da P. occupied a *considerable* portion of the epistle. During his stay in R. he was much with Pa, and, I would venture to say, often the subject of his hospitality. He showed Pa a note which he had received from Gen. B. [Beauregard], who complimented him upon his report of the Battle of Manassas, in which he expressed his surprise that a civilian could be so well informed upon the science of War, and a hope that he would live to write a history of the battle. Capt. da P. felt very much flattered, and desired Pa to write it to us. He is a volunteer aid of Van Dorn's, and receives no pay from Government.[15] Pa has bestowed upon him many favors, for which he was very grateful. I will speak no more upon this subject only that Pa concludes by saying "I do not dislike him". The welcome intelligence is imparted to A. that she "will before long receive a present", but "Miss Clara need not expect one, till she writes me a letter". I don't suppose that my favor has come to hands. I wonder what the "present" will be. Maybe his dear Ambrotype. And mine! He stated that he would write Ma "to morrow", and the date of his was the 27th. He asked "What has become of your friend Miss Josephine? you never speak of her". His remembrance of her dear friend pleased her excessively. Dear, kind, considerate Father. He knew that it would gratify her. Did his *equal ever* live?? He sends his love to all inquiring friends, and then concludes the loved epistle by saying "It is now 1:30, and as we dine at 2, I *must go and commence my toilet for dinner*". As though he had a valet de chambre, and his toilet was an important ceremony. My handsome Father. I hope that the Virginia ladies have not spoiled him. Oh! I am so anxious to receive a letter, an-

13. Solomon appears as a gregarious person, with friends in Richmond from the military and business worlds. At this stage the fighting was not continuous. Between battles Richmond was a social haven for many who were far from their homes.

14. The Solomons did not have their usual reserved seats during the Holidays because they had not been paid for. Da Silva, the Sexton, was in charge of such matters. Solomon replied from Virginia that he would pay any bill offered by the synagogue.

15. See n. 3 in Chapter 5 above.

nouncing the receipt of our presents. Ma sent the other to A., presuming too much to open it. When she had finished reading it, she returned it to us. It was a very short letter, in fact a *note*, composed of very short detached sentences, and I did really expect a more brilliant piece of composition from him. He addresses her as "My beloved Lady". The idea of its being a "letter which Ma would like to see". We forwarded to her the other document, which, I presume, afforded more pleasure. When she returned from School dinner was disposed of. We then discussed the *loved* messenger, read and reread it. Then played our duet with fingers "cold as ice". A. was reading to me portions of very interesting articles from a paper. I did not improve my appearance any, and A. *hardly* any, as the afternoon was so cloudy. Came down and ran over to Mrs. N., the wind guiding the way. Found her and Josh cozily seated around a blazing fire, engaged in the romantic occupation of endeavoring to demolish some Molasses candy which she had manufactured, but unfortunately had allowed it to remain too long on the fire, and it was consequently burnt. We however lent our assistance and our mouths were busily at work. We had been thus comfortably arranged for about a half an hour, when the door opened, and the rustle of silks, etc., always attendant upon the approach of Mrs. Harris was heard. It was a very unpleasant situation, but we could not get up immediately and go, so we were compelled to remain. She announced the intelligence of the arrival of Mr. Mordecai Hyams. Mr. Harris is very deaf, and the loud manner in which persons are forced to speak to him rendered it impossible for A. and I to restrain our laughter. Her husband is *getting old*. We took our departure in about ¼ hour, and it seemed strange to leave the room without bidding "good night" to all the occupants. On our arrival home a cheerful fire was in the hearth, and a bright light was in the burner, but the apartment was unoccupied. Proceeding farther we beheld the party assembled in the dining room, having just partook of the evening meal. Ma was a *little* angry at our being gone so long, as I suppose she considered it a *slight* to her. This feeling soon vanished and we repaired to the back room. Found no lack of subjects for conversation. Recalled the incidents of the last 31st, compared the past with the present, and thanked God that the comparison was so favorable. Nobody came, and we were soon asleep. What a somnolenic effect is produced by the fire. I must go.

Sunday, November 3rd, 1861

2 P.M. . . . . A succession of beautiful weather, but I do not enjoy it, as I am a very great "home body", and in fact, have not many opportunities for "gadding". I have been sewing on my new dress, which was cut out to day. I do earnestly wish that it was completed. Sewing is a nuisance. I have finished braiding A.'s hair. We had a few *words* preparatory to the act. I was again unsuccessful. Her hair was not done well. She has been writing to Pa all day, and is not yet done — I wonder if Cousin S. will come. I have not forgotten to day, so *many weeks* ago. I would like to know where *he* is, and what *he* is doing. I have not yet discharged the duty of posting you in the affairs of yesterday. A. returned about 12 from Synagogue. She had paid a visit to the Lyceum Hall previous to her arrival, and had obtained her month's compensation. According to agreement Ma was prepared to go out as [soon as] she came, and a few moments after they took their departure for a down town shopping expedition. I did not envy them. I provided A. with 25 cts., with orders to purchase for me 3 of White's copy books. After they had left, I was sitting up in Ma's room, when my attention was attracted to a woman on the Viennes' gallery apparently arranging the awnings. I paid no further heed to her until, on happening to look again, I thought I saw her attempting to climb or descend the post, but on closer investigation I perceived it to be an attempt to hang herself. I threw up the window, and ran on the gallery. The alarm was soon given, and crowds soon flocked to the place, and she was timely rescued. She is an old woman; numerous rumours are afloat as to the cause of this desperate act. Some attribute it to the ill-treatment of her *devilish* master, others to intemperance. I was much affected by the sight. It perfectly overcame me. I was compelled to lie down. Ma returned about four, and had scarcely made any purchases. A. brought my copy-books, and Ma, a quantity of cakes and candies. A. bought the worsted, and I must now tell you of the plan in view. She is going to knit two comforters; one, for Mr. Hitchcock, and the other, for *Major C.R. Wheat.* Yes, really for him. Were two girls ever more daring. Mrs. Grant has kindly offered to do one, and A. has accepted it. Isn't it glorious! We know that a comforter would be useless to *Pa,* so intend sending him something suitable. I wish that they had them. Dear Roberdeau!! Ma and A. had paid a visit to Mitchell's, and made a few purchases, which were brought up while we were at dinner, which was not over till 4³/₄. A. was smitten with Mr. W.C. Mitchell, my friend's handsome brother. Ma went over to Mrs. N.'s, and at dark A. and I descended, and like Ladies of State seated ourselves in our regal robes before the roaring fire, imagining that it was my house, her house, and all sorts of things. The noise and stamping from without, announced the family, who marched in, augmented by Mrs. N. She said that Leopold had partly promised to come up and have a game of Keno. We eat supper, and when eight o'clock came and he did not, we prepared to play without him. I was alternatively winner and loser. Each succeeding game for about a half of an hour was declared to be the last, but so fascinated were we that it was after *11* before we arose from the gaming table. I can *almost* forgive, and can heartily pity gamblers. Mrs. N. ran home, and we remained by the door until she was safe within her gate; she said "good night", which was a signal that we could enter. Paid the dining room a visit previous to retiring, for Keno makes demands upon your stomach as well as your purse. Tomorrow is the election. The only office in which I am interested is the Sheriffalty, which will be spiritedly contested between Mr. G.W. Mullen, Pa's friend, and Mr. Mazareau, our neighbor. I would wish that Mr. M. would be successful, for his goodness to Pa, and Mr. M., for I know that he is in need of it. Who will be the lucky candidate? Cousin Joe S. is a candidate for the Legislature.

Monday, November 4th, 1861

6 1/4 A.M. I hesitated before penciling this date, for it is so familiar to me that I feared I had already written it. How long has it been talked of and now here it is, and before to morrow's sun the fate of the candidates will be decided. The morning is pleasant, but not at all cold. In fact, Saturday was the last cold day, for yesterday the fire was allowed to die out. We waited until about 3½ for Cousin S., but he did not come and we dined without him. I would like to know what detained him for as a general thing, he keeps his word. We had his favorites, Tomato stew, and Potato Pone, and I know that he would have enjoyed them. I will be generous and think that his absence was unavoidable. After dinner, we were in the front room, eating some delectable molasses candy, Ma's manufacture, and engaged in a game of Keno, Ma too, when the bell rang. Cards and every thing were dropped and the scampering was instantaneous and universal. A. and I ran up, and soon learned that the visitor was Fanny Burbank. I at first thought it a very unseasonable hour for a call, but remembered that on

Sundays people generally dine at 2, and at 4 or $4^1/_2$, the afternoon is far advanced. We invited her up stairs, in consideration of the time that it would take us to dress. She complied with our request. She kissed me warmly, and I was very glad to see her. She looked as pretty and interesting as usual. We talked and laughed, and then A. proceeded to dress. Before she had finished Olivia and Mrs. N. were announced. She made all possible haste and went down accompanied by Fanny. I was much surprised on hearing that O. had come to see us, for we owe her a visit, and really neglected her. I was glad that she came, as I like her. Ma prepared herself and descended, and I bade her tell O. not to go before I saw her. Oh! I felt so little like dressing. *I* was so unwilling it seemed as though my hands would not perform their duties. While in a state of progression, I heard a gentle tap of the bell, which I knew was caused by Eisner's *fairy* fingers. My toilet completed, and I can assure you that there was nothing elaborate about it. In a few moments, I was by Olivia. She looked so pretty. She is in black for old Mr. Marks, and it is very becoming. I was informed that she had been spending the day with "Aunt Sarah" [Nathan]. Poor A. was in the front room, entertaining Mr. E. I sympathized with, but did not join, her. We chatted upon varied and numerous subjects. Regaled them with some molasses candy, which they pronounced "excellent". Mrs. N. said "I must go, as I left Rebecca home, but I won't tell you 'good bye', for you must be certain and come over". I did not say "good bye", but I thought it doubtful that I should see them again. I then joined Mr. E., whom I found to be as apologetic, as humble as ever. I neglected to say that Fanny had gone. She left "good bye" for me. I will positively go and see her. Probably one afternoon from school, and spend the evening with her. I requested F. to go around to Nettie's and ascertain the lesson, which she did. I was standing by the gate, when to my utter astonishment who should enter but *Ludie* and Bridget. They came down to Mrs. N.'s to spend the evening. I did not think that L. would have come to see us, but I think more of her for it. I escorted them into the house, introduced them to Mr. E. The gas was then lit. Presently Leopold entered. *They* had heard of him, but had never been in his society. There was talking, giggling, as always when L. is about. She is a pretty girl, also. Josie was standing up on the floor, leaning against F. when she performed an act not usually done in *parlors*. The suppressed laughter *could* not be restrained. But the male portion never "cracked a smile". And to improve matters E. [Ellen] comes in with a rag and wipes it up; and as it disappeared so did our mirth vanish. How little does it take to provoke a laugh among girls. L. left and to our satisfaction induced Mr. E. to accompany him. Ludie then insisted upon our going over, saying that she *only nodded* to Mrs. H. [Harris]. Well, in consideration of this we consented. Ma took the Keno box, I some change, and we started on the tour. We entered the room as though unconscious of Mrs. Harris. A few moments after we were summoned to supper; while eating L. came. He, as usual, refused to partake. L. and A. and I were sitting together, enjoying ourselves, when Mrs. N. proposed Keno. It was accepted, and all, with the exception of Mr. and Mrs. H. and Mr. E., joined in the game. I was very unlucky, winning only *one* game. The pool was an item consisting of 45 cts., and Theodore Marks, was the chief winner. About 9 o'clock he expressed a desire to go, as they "had already left the baby too long". We insisted upon their staying, and, after much "umming and awing", and considerations of the distance they lived, it was decided that they *should* go; they prepared themselves for their departure, and subsequent to much kissing, hugging, "come up soon", "come down soon", they had gone and we were alone, Mr. and Mrs. H. having previously exited. I wonder if we will ever pay L. *another* visit. We, gamblers, again proceeded to the gambling table, the pool considerably diminished, but still better than nothing. L. agreed to play *one* game more, as he did not wish to encourage the bad propensity which is beginning to develop itself, but of course he could not resist the ladies' entreaties, and we roped him in for about a dozen; when he arose; declared that he'd *go*, and with reluctance, we accompanied him. In the afternoon Cousin S. came, and said that he was detained by business. Ma had saved him some dinner, and I was told that he enjoyed it. He came in while O. and Mrs. N. were there, and acted very impolitely by not bowing to either. I did not see him but commissioned A. to tell him to come back, as I wished to request his company for the following night, which she did, and on our arrival home, we found that he had come and was angry that we were out.

Again, again, Miss M. cannot come. A. thinks she is quite pretty, and traced, as I did, a decided resemblance between her and Alice Myers. Well, I have been guilty of quite a digression, but I presume that it is understood that we went to bed and thus ended the eventful day. A letter is due us to day. I hope that it will arrive.

Tuesday, November 5th, 1861

6 $1/4$ A.M. On descending this morning I first proceeded in the direction of the front window, with a view of obtaining the paper, being very anxious to know the result of the election, but to my surprise and sorrow it was not in its accustomed place. On Sunday the erratic carrier had failed to deliver it, but I thought that it was merely accidental, but now am convinced that he intends discontinuing his visits. Saturday he called and received his pay for the last three months with injunctions from Ma to come again at the expiration of six months, and the foolish man must certainly have misunderstood Ma in some manner. If the news boys pass I shall purchase one. The morning is beautiful. I arose this morning and was compelled to dress by gas light. Appreciate my devotion. The "corner house" moved yesterday. I miss them very much. We never called on them — Ma cut out my dress, and I sewed a little on it. She and Mrs. N. had made an appointment to go out, and about 12 o'clock they left. I immediately commenced to study, and while so doing a violent pull was given to the bell, and the summons was answered, and *what* do you think it was? Why, a barrel of Chestnuts by the Express! I signed my name in the book, rolled the barrel in, and through the combined exertions of Lucy and me, it was opened.[16] They were very fine, but I would rather have had a letter, as I am quite uneasy. I locked them up for fear the children would partake too freely. They must have been very long on their way, as long ago, Pa wrote that he had sent some. I, as usual, dressed Rosa and myself. A. did not come from school until after three, as she had remained with Belle, to wind the worsted. Louisa had been in the day, and A. sent some to Mrs. G. who intended commencing it immediately. Ma did not come before 3 $1/2$. Mrs. N. had purchased one of those dresses, similar to, but prettier than, Ma's — They had paid Leopold a visit, and Ma had made quite a large bill, and L. was going to bring the articles up in the afternoon or evening. The first words that ma heard were chestnuts, and she was disappointed when informed that there was no letter. Ma brought up some small articles, among them a beautiful shell comb for A. and several round ones for the children, and a pair of knitting needles for A. Ma had been to see about her bonnet, but I am ignorant of the result. While at dinner the hands of the clock pointed to 3 $3/4$ and I was undecided whether to go to school, I determined to go and left after filling my pocket with chestnuts. When I

---

16. Clara's father was able to send more expensive gifts now.

arrived there the History lesson was concluded, and I was provoked that
after studying it I was compelled to lose my credits. Was perfect in my
Rhetoric and Geography. My chum, Miss M., was present. After School,
I told her of the state of affairs, and she wished me to accompany *her* home.
I refused and she parted quite angry. I walked home with Miss Earhart, a
school-mate. On my arrival, I was accosted by Leopold, eating *chestnuts*.
He had conveyed the purchases from his store to our mansion. Ma exhibited to my admiring gaze a beautiful blue fan, spangled with silver stars,
which she told me was *mine,* and a like red one, which was Alice's. I thanked
her for the thoughtful present, and she regretted that she had not reserved
A.'s together with her comb for her birthday, which is on the first of next
month. Among the things was a pair of jet bracelets, but as they do not suit
us, we intend exchanging them. Hdkfs., stockings, etc., etc. were included
in the outlay. Ma went over to Mrs. N., L. remained with us. The gas
was lit. A. played the piano, L. and I being the audience, imagining we
were seated at the Opera. Ma came over alone. Mrs. N. was unable to
accompany her, but sent strict injunctions for all to "come over". Supper
was next on the programme, and while indulging in the bread and molasses there came a "gentle pull at the front door bell". We readily formed
an *idea* as to who it was, and as we expected Ellen announced "Mr. Loevy".
We were glad that L., the apparently formidable gent, was present, so A.
and I formed the brilliant scheme of going in, and letting L. appear in a
few moments knowing how disconcerted "Gus" would be at the unexpected appearance. We saluted "G" and his first words were "Miss Alice,
I brought you some music". She thanked him and I inspected them.
They were the "Colson Schottishe", a part from the "Pardon de Ploermel",
and "Our Triumph at Manassas".[17] He took *his* seat on the sofa, and appeared very comfortable, when L. made his entrance. I perceived a sudden start, restless movement, and he said rather low, "*It's a fact, I* must go
now". We introduced the two gents, who cordially shook each other's
hands. L. took a seat and joined in our conversation. "Gus", not leaving,
but appearing remarkably brilliant. We gave him some chestnuts, which
he seemed to like. Ma left for Mrs. N.s, and L. some time after. When he
bade us "good bye", he said "I am going this week to Baton Rouge, and
probably to Frankfort, Ky., and I do not think I will see you before I go".
I *know* that *he* has *no idea of going.* "Gus" was himself again, and of course,
accused him of being a beau, etc. I was very sleepy, and despite my en-

17. The Confederate victories at Bull Run earlier in the year were already celebrated in music.

deavors, I could not keep awake. I reclined on the sofa, and before aware of it, was far away from Earth. A knock at the door aroused me, and I jumped up. Ma approached and a voice from without, which I immediately recognized as L. exclaimed "Good night, 'Lady of Lyons'". This is the only name by which he calls me. I don't know why, but he protests that I am the laziest girl that he ever saw. Is she symbolical of laziness? He says that I am always in the rocking chair, and no doubt this comfortable position suggests to his mind the idea of Royalty. I again fell asleep, and heard "Gus" as he shut the gate. A. presented him with a bouquet. I reluctantly arose from the sofa, mechanically did my duties, and without being very conversant, retired to my couch, admonishing L. to "wake and call me very early". Later: Since writing the above I have procured the Paper and read that "Mr. A. Mazareau is elected to the Sheriffalty". This intelligence has caused joy to some hearts, and sorrow to others. No letter yesterday!!

Wednesday, November 6th, 1861

6½ A.M. No paper delivered again this morning, but I have purchased one, but not yet perused it. Thick clouds are drifting through the sky, which are indicative either of rain or a change in the weather. The past few days have been quite warm, and it is an impossibility in New Orleans to have a succession of cold days. We were again disappointed yesterday in receiving no letter. I hope to God he is well. I left yesterday at 7 o'clock. Well, I anxiously waited for 10½, the time for the arrival of the train, hoping that it would bear tidings to us of the lord. Mr. N. had promised, if it arrived, to send it up immediately, and as the hours wore away, and no one came I knew that there was none. I try to think that he is safe. I am uneasy, for in his last he said, "I will write to-morrow without fail". That cheering "to-morrow" lights up many dark paths of our life. I sewed on my dress, but accomplished *very, very* little. Little Rosa paid Alice a visit and she did look so sweet and pretty in her pink delaine. Her spirits were most exuberant in consequence of the anticipation of her pleasure. I studied assiduously until 2¼, when I prepared myself for *my* matrilineal visit. As usual, dispatched dinner. My orders have not yet taken effect, for the children generally remain in School until after three — The fare was not very epicurean, for I believe that the *cow* had reached a mature age. L. is not an adept in marketing. (I want something nice to eat). I departed with a few nuts in my handkerchief, my dress being minus the necessary appendage of a pocket. I disposed of them in a short time, and on Nayades St. met Mr. N. I asked him if he had a letter. He replied "Yes, two", and I joyfully exclaimed "Let me see them", when to my sorrow, he showed me his open hands, walked on, and I knew that it was but a joke. I arrived at School in season, and was soon writing of "An Overland Journey to California", Miss M. and I mutually assisting each other in the orthographical [spelling] line. We parted, she to go to singing, I to reading, but met after the dismissal of the Institution. She walked a few squares with me, and I, with her, when we separated for the day. I like her very much, but would still more, if I were confident that she liked me, for I would feel flattered as I know that she is not very easily attracted towards *every* one, or very impressible. At the corner of Dryades and Clio I met A. approaching. She requested me to accompany her to Mrs. Miller's; I complied, and on the way met the lady in question. The unexpected encounter astonished both parties. She looked very well, her spirits as buoyant as ever. She had not yet heard from O.P., but promised on the receipt of one to inform us. We stood talking for some time at the corner of her mansion, declining her invitation to go with her. We left her and walked hastily home. Found Mr. and Mrs. N. there and Josh, indulging in chestnuts. They went, but intended coming back. As we were eating supper, they did. Mr. N. devoured an inconceivable quantity of nuts, and we all joined with him in wishing that they were gone, for it is impossible to *stop* eating them once you *commence*. The "Lady of Lyons" began to get sleepy at about $8\frac{1}{2}$; she sought the sofa, and didn't arise until after the departure of the guests. The clouds were but transient, they have disappeared, and the bright sun is peeping out. Today one year ago Abe Lincoln was elected President of the United States. How many changes since then have transpired. How much has been accomplished.

Thursday, November 7th, 1861

$6\frac{1}{2}$ A.M. I arose as early as usual this morning, descended, purchased the paper, scanned it, and read a distressing account of the drowning of two brothers, one, 13, the other, 20 years, of age. They were on a visit to their uncle on his plantation, one, I think, fell into a ditch, and the other immediately plunged in to rescue him, and neither arose until life was extinct. It filled my heart with sadness. Their bodies were conveyed to this City, and their funeral took place on yesterday. Two healthy, promising youths, without a moment's warning, were thus snatched from a home, which was enlivened and brightened by their presence. How much romance and tragedy is there in one half of the world, of which the other half never dream. But to return to yesterday — No event characterized the early part of the day. Twelve o'clock came, and no letter, and to day we *must* get one. I would start at every ring of the bell, expecting surely to receive a dispatch. Ma was uneasy, but for her sake, *I* pretended not to be — My dress is progressing rapidly. The waist is almost finished and it fits beautiful. I did not do much to it, for a person can not accomplish much sewing from $9\frac{1}{2}$ to 12. Wednesday again, and with it the difficult lessons, and before I left them, I felt satisfied that I knew them. A. now never gleans any bits of news from the Webster Academy, and never imparts to me any intelligence. Her comforter is rapidly improving. B. intended to commence A.'s, but the knitting needles proved to be too large. Eat dinner, filled my pocket with nuts, and at $3\frac{1}{2}$ was pursuing my path in the direction of Nayades St. As I appear at such regular hours on the different streets it is strange that I do not meet the same individuals each afternoon. I recited my lessons well, and during the intervals I with Miss M. enjoyed ourselves by feasting our eyes on the rare beauty of Belle and Olympia. Maggie Toby is a very pleasant girl. I used to go to school with her and we had many mutual friends. The Misses Logan, I am not yet acquainted with. They seem to be such sweet girls. I should like so much to know them. I scarcely ever see dear Lizzie. We cannot *always* be together, then why some time. Miss Leech, Ada, Nettie, etc., are strangers to me — Miss M. walked to the corner of Bacchus and Clio, and insisted that I should go home with her, and offering to escort me to my house in order that I could gain Ma's permission. I positively refused, and told her that I would not pay the first visit, so she promised to come the following evening, and leave instructions for the servant to come after her, her brother being too busy. This was agreed upon, as I did not intend asking Cousin S. again. I supplied her with chestnuts, which she was very fond of. She faithfully promised to come, and I think that she will. On my arrival home, Ma and A. were to Mrs N. and I went over. A. was just waiting for me as she wished me to accompany her to Provensals, for the purpose of attempting to exchange her needles for a finer pair. We did but they did not have the desired articles.

It was quite dark and we walked very rapidly—Met Mary Haughton, stopped and had a few moments talk with her. She now attends the Normal School. She is a sweet girl. A few moments after we arrive Ma and Mrs. N. came. (Coffee is $1.25 a pound, and Ma and Mrs N. have both determined not to have it, and for the first time in many years, coffee will not be on our breakfast table. Ma is going to get some Cocoa. I shall miss it very much.) We eat supper, and then a game of Keno was proposed and accepted. No one had money and the pool never exceeded a dime. That was not much fun. Mr. N. came in about 9, and we stopped. Ma wrote a Telegraph to Pa, as follows, "I am very uneasy. Why don't you write?" and commissioned Mr. N. to inquire at the P.O. and if there was no letter, to send it. They all laughed at Ma and said she was foolish. They left, and we retired.

Friday, November 8th, 1861

6 1/2 A.M. I see by this morning's paper that Gen. Scott[18] has resigned, and is going to Europe, and that one of the rooms of the *White House* will soon be fitted up for a *nursery*, but I have more glorious news than that to tell you. I was quietly sitting down and thinking of Pa, when the bell rang, and I threw down my work, ran to the door, and was handed two letters, from the Adams Express Company. I immediately apprised Ma of the fact and we were soon inspecting the letters. One was valuable, containing $60, and the bearer said "That one has been here since the 2nd of the month"!! It is shameful that an Express Company should have been so negligent in the delivery of their articles. We told the boy so, but he said he had nothing to do with it, as they were just handed to him. They would have arrived much quicker by mail. I think that it was a perfect outrage. Ma and I were very sorry to think that the Telegraph had gone, as a "dispatch from home" would cause Pa much alarm. But it was done and could not be helped. The carrier departed, and Ma and I proceeded to devour them. The one containing the money was first written and bore date of the 29th inst. He is in

18. Winfield Scott had remained loyal to the Union despite his Virginia background. As commander of the U.S. Army, he made preparations for the defense of Washington until he retired (he did not resign) at age seventy-five.

the enjoyment of excellent health and as busy as he cares to be. Ma wrote to him about Mr. Davis' visit, and Pa says that it will soon be settled. He wrote him a letter, thanking him for his former acts of kindness, and requesting him to wait a little longer, for they have the promise from the officers of Col. W. battalion, that everything will be right, as they owe a great deal, and Pa says "we are making a fortune as fast as men generally do, but just now it keeps us tight up, for on every dollar's worth of goods we make a dollar. Just hold on a little while and every thing will be right. Send for Mr. D., and tell him what I say, also that he will never see me again until I am an independent man. I shall *never* be able to pay him for his acts towards us." Pa enclosed a list of goods, purchased since last Saturday, merely as a "matter of curiosity". It comprises an immense quantity of goods. The enclosed $60 was for a certain purpose, and he said that he would send money for the house in the early part of the month. Speaking of that piece of "roast beef", he said that he did not think it was intended for us, as he was not acquainted with a man by the name of Miller. The weather is quite cold, and he wished to know how we are "getting along about coal". He writes "I wish you were all here with me. Do you *think you* could come on for a trip? I am frightened that it will be a little too cold; but no matter, I will have you on next Summer. Now, that is some consolation for I do not know how we will be able to make it any otherwise, as it is nearly impossible for *me* to come on, and I never will return, until I can an independent man". Oh! haven't we something splendid in anticipation. A visit to Richmond! He is still at the Spotswood, which he dislikes as much as formerly but he has not time to hunt up a private house, but he is determined to leave. He writes that he was suffering from a severe headache, and of the kind attention which he received from an old German lady, the wife of a man from whom he made some purchases — She applied some remedy, and kindly offered her services in case he should be sick. I hope that he will not require them. I thank the kind hearted woman, and beseech God to favor all who favor him. He said that he was looking at some dresses for "Alice and Clara", but he did not think that they were fashionable; although the man said that people could not be particular now. Pa told him "No, not in this *one horse town,* (God bless him, I think I hear him), but where I am from". Presents in that shape would be most acceptable. He sends his regards to all his friends. The letter was enclosed in a beautiful "Spotswood Hotel" envelope, with our new postage stamps bearing the likeness of "Davis, our loved President". His expressive, characteristic features will thus be familiar to all. The other letter was

of the 31st, and he announces the arrival of O.P. [Miller] and his receipt
of the packages. "What can I say or what language can I use to express
to you my pleasure on the receipt of your ambrotypes — I was delighted
and they are now before me. I must say (and I regret it) that they do not
come up to my fancy — I think they are very badly done, especially your
own which looks to me as if you were in great distress — It is very badly
taken and does not look like you. Alice is passable. Clara has her mouth
on one side, and makes a very *ugly looking* picture. Fanny is passable and
natural. Sarah is very good, but all of you must have been in dull spirits.
My son [Rosa] looks very well. I will not show your pictures to any one.
They are got up coarse. I wanted them got up as well as possible, but
with all I thank you 1000 times for your kind attention, and although they
do not come up to my taste, still I see you and them in them, and I feel as
if I was now on the sofa with you all around me". Oh! Philomen, how
astonished, how sorry were we when we read this description of them. We
were surprised, as all who saw them pronounced them "excellent". I
have no doubt that they were not fine, and I suppose that they did not look
as well in the day. We were totally unprepared for it. And he won't show
them to any one. I suppose he will put them away in his trunk — Oh! it is
too bad! too bad! The shrimps came safe to hand but he had not opened
them, and expressed his determination to *"get even with us one of these days."*
He thanked us kindly for them — He enclosed us a letter from Mr. H.
wherein we perceived that they had an extensive business and realizing a
profit of 6 or 7000 a month. The letter was quite brief. He said that he
would write again on Sunday. Oh! Philomen! To think of the daguerreotypes. Nothing yet, respecting our "tokens of remembrance". Maybe *he* is
offended. I expect *never* to hear of them. Ma then sent them to A. knowing how overjoyed she would be on receiving them. On her return from
school we talked about them and she was as disappointed about the pictures as we. I went off immediately after dinner, as I dislike to be late, for
I dread Mrs. P.'s ill humored looks and snappish words. During the hour
with Miss B suffixes and prefixes received due consideration, and we spent
the remainder of the afternoon with Mrs. Fisher. She is so kind. I like
her very much. I am improving in my musical department. I distributed
some nuts between Olympia and Maggie, and they considered them, as do
others, a rarity. Miss M. informed me that she was really going with me,
and we proceeded down Clio St. towards my home, as in imagination we
often had. Long planned, at length effected! We arrived at my residence,
and found Ma and A. out. She divested herself of bonnet, etc., I introduced

her to my sisters, and she particularly fascinated with Sallie, whom she considered the prettiest—At her request we sat by the front door a few moments, and then the gas being lit, we repaired to the parlor, where she entertained me with a few tunes. I showed her my handsome Father, whom she was anxious to behold. We then fooled around, did various things, inspected books, talked, laughed and were quiet. Ma and A. came, Ma appearing in a new, pretty, becoming bonnet, manufactured by Mme. Fabio, the material of which is black and white straw, with trimmings, etc. I learned that A.'s and mine were ordered, both to be alike. They welcomed Miss M. and joined us. Leopold called. We played Snake, the piano, and enjoyed ourselves. Ma was not with us much as she was writing to Pa, desirous that it should leave in the morning. About 8 o'clock Miss M.'s domestics came, but it was very early, so I asked L if he would not escort her home, he willingly complied, and I bade Miss M. dismiss her attendants which she did. About 9 o'clock we left. The night was beautiful and we had a pleasant walk. She gave me my ring, and we conveyed her safely to her mansion. I don't think Ma or A. was much attracted towards her, but she is one who improves upon acquaintance. And *that* visit has been paid. The "Lady of Lyons", though her companions were quite agreeable, became inexplicably sleepy on her homeward journey, and it was with some exertion that she wended her way. When a short distance from home, the sound of sweet music was wafted on the evening wind. On proceeding a *little* further the sounds appeared in our direction, and on proceeding a *little* further, we perceived a great crowd surrounding Mazareau's domicile, and we readily imagined that the Sheriff was being complimented by a serenade. We were correct, for Ma informed us of the "grand doings" since our departure. He had invited them in to a well spread table, and the flavor of tasty dishes and the cracking and splashing of tumblers, plainly told us that the guests were enjoying themselves. Cousin S. had paid Ma a flying visit. He occupied a conspicuous position in the ceremonies, being Grand Marshal. L. remained some time. The band struck up, the inspiring "Marseillaise", "three cheers for Mazareau" rend the air, and they were off to the favorite air of Dixie. I wish that my Father occupied the position. L. shortly left. We proceeded to the "supper room", Ma painting to us in glowing descriptions the events that had happened. Her letter was prepared to go. Miss M. for the next moments was the theme under consideration. After all our planning with Cousin S., L. should accidentally drop in and perform the duty of the wished-for escort. And now do I leave you with a much lighter heart than yesterday. The folks have come down.

Breakfast will soon be ready. No coffee! no coffee! "How happy are they who have coffee." For the past few mornings tea has usurped its place.

Saturday, November 9th, 1861

11 A.M. . . . When I came down this morning and went to the front window, I was fully confident of seeing our paper in *its* place, when to my astonishment beheld a blank, dreary space. Why haven't the individuals around the Delta Office more sense. I read the paper, and it contained news of importance of which I shall hereafter tell you. A. has gone to Synagogue, but my dress is too warm for the day. Alice has not much more, except her barège, which is called into requisition on such days. I will not go out to get my bonnet. Dear little Rosa went over to Mrs. N.'s and she has just come home, dressed in Josh's uniform (which Mrs. N. pinned up to fit) and looking exquisitely lovely. What would Pa give to see her. If she only were a boy. But it is better as it is, for if she were, she would be spoiled beyond endurance. I feel *rather* lonespirited. To day two months ago, this present robe of yours was brought into active service, when *its* career is ended, I am perplexed what to do for the City is minus such articles. Will our friendship have to end? Yesterday according to agreement, the man came to put down our carpets; our usual man Nelson, failing to come. The job was accomplished and the two parlors and Ma's room were carpeted. Our carpets are beautiful and it seems, as though each flower, recalled a train of remembrances, some pleasant, and unpleasant. I love to look at them. This will be their third winter, but their appearance would indicate but the first. I was so provoked by Ma; but I will not expand upon the subject, but suffice to say that the few words spoken served to put me in a most miserable frame of mind. I paid the farewell devoirs to my dress, hemmed the skirt, sewed on the flounce, bound it, sewed in the sleeves, on the buttons, and laid it away in the armoir, perfectly indifferent as to whether I shall *live* to wear it — If I had my choice, I would wish to die, for at present *I am miserable.* When the children came home they were pleased with the carpets, and it does seem so natural to see them. A. said that she had heard in school the announcement by the news boys of "Extra Delta", and she could gain but a few items. We were so anxious to know. After dinner, A. and I assisted in arranging the parlors, and admiring the great

improvement. We talked upon various subjects and 5 o'clock quickly arrived. We then dressed. When we came down, Mrs. M. was there, and she
had the extra, which is published in to day's paper. The Telegraph is
from "near Columbus, Nov. 8th 10 A.M." and is as follows. "At 9 o'clock
yesterday morning, 10,000 Lincoln troops under Gen. Oglesby, landed on
the Missouri shore, above Columbus, and engaged Pillow's Tennessee
Brigade, and Bethel's Louisiana company. The enemy captured and spiked
our battery. Being reinforced we recaptured the battery and took 2 of the
enemy's guns. The battle was desperately fought and did not end till dark.
The enemy's loss is 400 killed and several hundred wounded — Ours,
200 killed and wounded, 80 prisoners — Maj. E.G.W. Butler was killed and
we lost many other gallant officers. Another battle may be expected soon.
Every officer behaved most gallantly, and did prodigies of valor. It was a
bloody battle, but a brilliant victory." It is glorious that victory was with
us still. A. and I went to Mrs. Millers, and found her home. The lamp
was shining brightly, and the room was so cozy and sociable, as is every
one where *she* is. She had received a few lines from O.P. He had arrived,
and was on the eve of starting for Manassas. Pa's name was not mentioned.
We asked her if she had noticed among the letters we sent, one directed to
Wheat. She said that she had, and told us that O.P. picked it up from the
table, and in angry tone said "I wonder what they are writing to *him* about" —
Ah! he was jealous! We remained until after dark, and were escorted home
by dear Obed. He is such a fine boy. Arrived home, eat supper, and were
assembled in the back room when "Gus" was announced. He had the
Evening paper, containing an account of the Battle, and an Extra, issued
since its publication, and conveying us sad news. It was from Savannah,
Nov. 8th, "Fort Walker and the Bay Point batteries were evacuated yesterday afternoon, after a terrible contest — Our loss is 12 killed, 40 wounded.
We lost no prisoners. All the guns in the forts were abandoned and the
Federal flag was flying over the works at last accounts. The enemy have
taken possession of our batteries at Bay Point and Hilton Head; also the
town of Port Royal — They are now within 10 miles of the R.R. connecting Charleston and Savannah." This is sad, and the Northern papers will
be teeming with accounts of their *great* victory. They know that we are con-
centrating a great force *here* which intimidates them, and I think that
Charleston will be their point of attack. We are prepared for them. The
Extras were talked about and "Gus" entreated us to cease upon politics, as
he was surfeited with them. We complied, knowing that he is always in the
midst of dispatches, etc. Naturally the subject changed to the da Pontes

and Brookes [da Ponte's in-laws]. He has made Charlotte's acquaintance and was charmed with her. He told us that her affections were bestowed upon Capt. E. [Eshleman], but not reciprocated by him, for he is shortly to be married to a Virginian lady. I am astonished for I am certain that he did love her with all the ardor of his affectionate nature. Mystery! mystery! All is mystery!! How I would like to unravel the mysteries of many hearts. "Gus'" appearance was extraordinarily *imposing*. Mrs. N. called, and she and Ma enjoyed themselves in the back parlor, we, in the front. I did not go to sleep. Mrs N. left and Ma joined us—I became sleepy and repaired to the rocking chair. I went to sleep, "and woke to hear his parting words good night, good night". He told us that he was shortly going to Tampico, for the purpose of establishing a mail route between it and other places. He does not know how long he will be gone. It was about 10, and the meeting adjourned for the night. *2 P.M.* I have just finished dressing my Sallie, and must hasten to perform ablutionary operations upon myself. The rain has for some time been falling, but now has ceased, and the sun is peeping out. Ma and A. planned going down town, but the rain has frustrated it. A. returned from Synagogue. She had seen Mrs. Marks, but had not spoken to her. I don't think that she intends discharging that little debt. It has the appearance of meanness. I could very well dispose of the money. I must go.

Sunday, November 10th, 1861

8 1/2 A.M. When I arose the drops were pattering down upon the roof of the house, and the morning was dark; I came down, looked and found no paper, notwithstanding that Mr. L. had promised "to see to the matter". With great difficulty and many struggles I obtained an edition, and the first production which greeted my eyes was "Kentucky" by "Plumas", a very inferior article. The paper was particularly interesting. It contained a eulogy on brave Major Butler. As I write the clouds are passing away. I wish that it would continue raining. Yesterday cleared off, and the remainder of the day was beautiful. We had "chestnuts raw and boiled and roasted". I did not dress until late in the afternoon, as I was assisting Lucy to extricate from the dish some molasses candy, which persistingly adhered to it. We succeeded admirably. Ma and F. went out, and A. and I dressed, descended, took a short stroll with the children and then proceeded to Mrs. N.'s — She was remarkably well, and happy to see us. Ma and F. shortly joined us. *We* returned home, Ma and Mrs. N. promising to follow. I was reading with Sallie, a beautiful story entitled Truth, and the tears blinded my eyes, it was so affecting. The elders arrived, and at supper observed that my nose shone remarkably, which fact was attributable to my recent tears — After supper, seated ourselves around the "gaming table", wished that L. would come, *only* to increase the company, and wondering if he had gone to Baton Rouge, as he had intended — We played a few games when our party was augmented by Mr. Elburger. Game succeeded game "kitty", "kitty", and it was 11 o'clock before we arose from the table. I was signally unsuccessful, and was the loser of 55 cts. which I could ill afford. After they left, Ma, A. and I "settled" and I ran up to escape the confusion and disorder of the room, and dispatched Lucy down to arrange. I wish that A. slept with me. We have so few opportunities of talking together. Not that we have anything private to say, but merely our foolish thoughts and saying. As she *comes from school, I leave for* it. "Ah! is it right to sever two fond, trusting hearts", etc. Don't I love *her!* Strong, indeed, must be the counter charm that can rival hers. She is the dearest, the best of sisters. There she comes now, looking prettier than ever, in her robe de chambre. We will digest the paper together. I know she will exclaim when she sees "Gus"'s piece. I am right — Her eyes have rested upon it — I will reread it with her.

2 1/4 P.M. I have just finished braiding A.'s hair and dressing Sallie, and should rightfully devote this time before dinner to the arrangement of *my* silken braids. The day is quite pretty. Mr. N. is down stairs, eating chestnuts, and only occasionally stopping to wish that they were gone, and then devouring them as unremittingly as ever. He is attentively listening while Ma is reading to him, portions of a newly received letter from dearest Father. About 12 the bell rang violently, and Ellen returned with a "letter". It came by Express, and was dated Nov. 3rd!! It had been 7 days on the way, and I think it would be advisable to entrust them all to mail, for this should have come to hand a day or two ago. It is addressed to A. and is a dear, sweet letter. He is well, and again returns thanks to Ma for her present, "the most palatable and delicious thing I have tasted since I left my home". He then tells us how he indulged too freely one night and suffered for it the next day by partaking too heartily of the shrimps. I cannot forbear to quote the following lines, "Yesterday it was raining and boisterous, and kept me confined to my Hotel the greater part of the day. About

10 o'clock I had the honour to be introduced to Gen. Wigfall, Major Fisher, Col. Christy, and Col. Jones, the owner of the property upon which the battle of Manassas was fought. Having a good glass of whisky in my room, we all adjourned to take a drink. I asked the party if they would wish to try a few shrimps which my kind wife had sent me from N.O., and there was not a dissenting voice. I ordered bread and butter, had the lunch spread out, and they all decided that they were delightful. Gen. W. filled his glass and 'Gentlemen let us drink to the health of Mrs. S. and family', which was done with great gusto — Your pictures were introduced, scanned and admired (for they improve by *keeping*)" — A page is then devoted to politics, and he sent us enclosed small photographs of Gens. Davis, Beauregard, Johnson, and Bartow. All noble, trustful faces. I was most charmed with brave Bartow, who fell in the battle of M. at the head of his command — Davis and B. though their faces *may* indicate all the good qualities of mind and heart, are not very attractive. Pa writes "Capt. Eshleman is to be married in a few days to a beautiful girl of this city, at whose house he was carried after his wound received at M. (What will Miss Charlotte say to this?)" What *will* she say? And so it is really true. How romantic. Mystery, mystery! Pa says "I will send my photograph one of these days". "Hug my boy and girl for me; every lady says what a fine head my boy has; and in fact, they all say that you all have good heads." He then says that he wants us to get him a bottle of snuff like Mr. Harris uses, and if not possible to send it any other way, forward it by Express. It was his intention to write for it a month ago, but always forgot it. His regards to all friends, and his letter is concluded. I am anxiously waiting for a response to mine. I hope not to be disappointed. I have written more than I intended, and must now devote the next moments to the appeasing of my appetite. Au revoir.

7

The Home Guard Begins:
November 11–November 30, 1861

Monday, November 11th, 1861

6 1/2 A.M. Here I be! The morning is cloudy, and rain will visit us to day. I arose with great reluctance this morning — After dinner, yesterday, A. and I had several games of Keno, and I became the winner of 30 cts., but *not* in *cash*. We then proceeded to dress, and descended after the conclusion of the disagreeable operation. We were standing by the gate when Mrs. Miller approached, and at last paid *the* visit. We entered the house, announced to Ma of the visitor, and she soon appeared. While they were busily chatting, A. and I went to the gate to see what could be seen. While there, who should come up almost simultaneously, but Alex. Kelly and Gus. Leovy. We stood up for a short time talking, and as A. was in a hurry, he could not come in. He looked very handsome in his "soldier clothes". All were well at his house, and he reproved us for not keeping our promises — We made many excuses, and told him that we would surely come down soon. I should like to see Annie. How many remembrances did Alex. awaken — Dryades St., its associates, etc. He left and G., A., and I took seats on the steps. He had some beautiful flowers, which had been plucked from the flourishing garden of E.J. Hart, Esq. Conversation turned upon the usual topics including Capt. E., Mr. Randall, Mollie and Carrie Hart, his two beautiful *nieces*. We do have fun with him, correcting each other, and being corrected — And we made an agreement to talk as the words came, each being aware that the other could speak better with a little trouble. A very convenient "arrangement" — Mrs M. went, and he proposed a walk to which we, after gaining Ma's consent, consented. We wended our steps in the direction of "way up town". Enjoyed ourselves exceedingly, and I returned home quite fatigued. Found that all the folks had retired — Gus staid some time, and deplored my infirmity — sleepiness.

But it was excusable considering the exercise. I so wished for him to go, and he did about 9½. Quite a long visit—He was here 3 times during the week—I think that he is very agreeable and entertaining. A. and I both very tired, retired with our usual dignity, after partaking of some bread and butter. Leo, did not come—He must be gone. I wonder what that "Cousin of ours" has done with himself—He failed to discharge his usual Sunday visit—The sun is shining, but not very brilliantly—A. calls me to "smooth her hair". *Ain't* she helpless. I must go.

Tuesday, November 12th, 1861

6 ¼ A.M. No paper again this morning, though "Gus" *had* attended to the matter, and said that he would again see about it. I have just purchased one, and handed it to A., and she tells me there is a very interesting letter from "D"—When I came down this morning, I could scarcely see to write. I threw open the window and then could scarcely discern the lines on the paper. It is again cloudy, and we shall certainly have rain. The sun peeped in and out yesterday, and the day was not very pleasant, as occasional showers would descend. I was employed in altering a dress of mine, and "ending" some hdkfs. after Ma had hemmed them on the machine— The day was uneventful. In consequence of the weather, I was undecided whether to go to school, and finally decided *to go.* Had a very disagreeable walk, and was happy to arrive at the mansion—and—in time. I knew my lessons. Miss M. and I, as usual, together. I know that she will ask me to go home with her, and I don't want to. She told me of the sudden attachment between "Gen. Loviggo" and "Nina Word". She is constantly with him. Maybe there is a *wedding* in prospect—Miss M. left me, and walked quite hurriedly for fear of not meeting her "sweetheart". I stopped at Mrs. M.'s for a few moments. As fascinating as ever. On my arrival home found Ma and A. both out, but shortly returned—Ma had been to make some purchases on Rue de Dryades, A. had gone down town for the purpose of changing knitting needles, and had succeeded. She had met "Gus" on Camp St. and he had accompanied her to the corner of the house. They had no doubt a pleasant walk. A. met many Normal girls, and either by intuition, or my descriptions, recognized the "oft spoken of" Miss Leech. I know that it was she, as A.'s description of her dress, corresponded with mine. A. had gone to Werleins, and left orders for the piano to be tuned. Ma had bought some coffee, as she finds it impossible to do without it, but *we* were all satisfied with the pleasant substitute of Chocolate. After supper I, with my book in hand, laid down on the sofa to study, A. in a chair beside me. Some strange sounds proceeded from her direction, and on looking up, I found that she was asleep. I determined to remain awake, but a few moments after was startled by the fall of the book from my hand, and I know I made no attempt to recover it. At about 9 o'clock we were snug in bed. Where's Cousin S!

Wednesday, November 13th, 1861

6 $^1/_4$ *A.M.* The mornings are so disagreeable, when I arise the fog is so thick that all surrounding objects were invisible, and the water is rolling off of the gallery. The wretched paper man has not brought the paper, and I have not yet purchased one. I don't believe that "Gus" ever attended to it. Yesterday's contained an interesting letter from "D", which in course of time I perused. By the by a letter is due us — I so love to receive them — It did not rain yesterday. The man came and tuned the piano. The sounds fall much sweeter on the ear — I was up stairs studying when the bell rang. A hope that it was Mrs. Marks for a moment lifted my soul — Dell came up and told me that it was the French young lady from next door, who wished to see me. I was a little alarmed, as I could not imagine what she could want, as we were not on terms of intimacy. I was soon in the room, she spoke cordially, calling me by my name, Miss Clara, which I did not think she knew. She made known the object of her visit. She had heard that I was a member of the L.N.S. and as she was desirous of joining she wished me to give her the necessary information how to act. I told her that I would be much pleased if she would accompany me in the afternoon, and I would introduce her to the teacher. She said that she would do so. We then had a little chat, and I easily discerned that she was quite intelligent, speaking English remarkably well. She is very pleasant and agreeable, though not pretty. I would like to know her. She remained about 20 minutes, and when she left, I went to make my toilet. A. was not home to dinner, as she was in school, as Belle was teaching her how to knit. She is now sitting by me, going very slowly, but surely. Mrs. G.'s is in a state of

rapid progression. Well, I met A. as I was emerging from the gate, saluted each other, and passed on. Arrived at school, before the Dictation had commenced. At its conclusion Miss M. and I parted, and I proceeded to Reading Exercises with my Tuesday Friend, Miss Del. Trigo. Miss M. and I again met, and in company left the Institution, and "good bye" at the corner. I walked leisurely along, meeting with no romantic or unromantic adventure. Found Ma and Mrs. N. sitting on the steps, and A. out. I gladdened the children's heart by presenting them all with some chalk. As I was walking I perceived the queenly form of Miss Solomon approaching. "A moment more and we had met." She had started with the intention of going down to see about the bonnets, but on reaching Canal St. she saw that it was too late to continue, so retraced her steps. She divested herself of bonnet, etc., and we took our *now usual* promenade, and for them memory of "vieux temps", sat on the "corner house" steps. She of course had heard of my visit, and I furnished her with all particulars. Seeing Mrs. N. and Ma at the corner we joined them, stood up talking, Mrs. N. went over, but promised to come back. When we went in we were very agreeably entertained by Emma Fairex, one of Sallie's companions, who was playing the piano and singing, and she succeeded admirably for so small a child. Her voice is excellent. She left and we adjourned to the supper room, and indulged freely. Mrs. N. came, and the evening passed very pleasantly. Laughing, (of course when she's about), talking (when a number of females are). F. and S., for the amusement of the company, favored us with some poetical recitations, which reflected great credit upon them. Wonderful to relate, I did not go to sleep—She exited about 10¼. I must leave you now, as I wish to study. Remember to day is Wednesday.

Thursday, November 14th, 1861

6 o'clock A.M. I am now writing, and can scarcely see as it is almost dark. Lucy woke me and I jumped out not knowing how soon it was. I don't regret it though, as I can always find something with which to employ my time—By the paper I see that Beaufort, S.C. is virtually deserted and in possession of the enemy. Something to this effect was hinted at yesterday, and Mrs. D. is quite uneasy, as she has relatives there; but I suppose they are safe. The early part of yesterday was very cloudy and unpleasant, but as it advanced affairs assumed a more cheering aspect. It was marked by no uncommon occurrence. I sewed, studied, eat dinner hurriedly, and left for school. Knew my lessons with the exception of Geography, which was so difficult that I did not pretend to study it, so I lost my perfect mark. But misery loves company and I had enough of that. I wonder if Belle knows that she is so beautiful—I wish that you could see her, in order to join me in my enthusiasm. As I was standing at the corner with Miss M. a handsome, very handsome soldier passed, touched his hat most politely, and would you believe it, until he had passed, I did not recognize Mr. N. Oh! he looks splendid in his uniform. I should certainly have fallen in love with him. Miss M. walked some distance with me, and asked me to accompany her home. I, of course, declined. I wonder if I will ever go—I wish I had the pleasant walk that she has every afternoon. I charged her with love and kisses to Nina to which she seriously objected, declaring that it was too great a portion of hers. I would like her to love me for she is very impressible. I wish, like her, that I could meet my sweetheart every afternoon. She is enamored with some individual. I saw Miss Jarreau on the banquette, stopped, kissed her. She told me that she would wait until Monday, as her sister also wished to go.

I should have spoken longer had not I seen Leopold at the door. He was glad to see the "Lady of Lyons"—He had returned in the afternoon, and had brought some butter for Ma and Mrs. N., which was over to Mrs. N.'s. We sat on the steps for some time, Ma and A. having gone out, and taken Ellen with them, to get the bonnets and bring mine up—The gas being lit, we adjourned to the parlor. I read to him portions of Pa's letter, and showed him the pictures, and he also, as do many others, traced a striking resemblance between Jeff. Davis and Abe. Lincoln. Mary brought over the butter. It was excellent. I thanked L. for the acceptable present as the article is very, very scarce, and what is to be had is a much inferior article. He had other things for us, but he left in a hurry, and was unable to bring them. Ma and A. arrived. A. had her bonnet on and it looked beautiful. Ours are exactly alike. I am delighted with mine. They are black hair, with white dots, and trimmed with crimson. A.'s is most becoming. What *ain't* to her? I hope that mine will be. When I see new bonnets, and particularly with red ribbon, do my thoughts turn to Baby. I wish she would come. L. could not stay, as it was drilling night. Ma thanked him for the butter, and he left no doubt in the happy consciousness of having done a good deed. It was very thoughtful of him. He admired our bonnets. We eat supper, and the unusual quantity and quality of the indispensable article was very agreeable. We had some molasses candy, which was very nice. We had finished supper, when the bell rang. I went to the door, and with much surprise welcomed Cousin S., Mrs. Williams and little Fanny. Cousin S. left for some meeting. Mrs. W. came in, and we spent a pleasant evening. Mrs. W. is a very nice lady, but better visiting has been done on either side. She has now moved in our vicinity. F. is a smart, pretty child, and is devoted to her "Father" and her Father to her. She entertained the company by her interesting conversations and various songs. Oh! Cousin S. is so proud of her. Unfortunately the chestnuts are "out", and some candy was offered to the company, of which they slightly partook. About 9 Mr. Myers came and in a few moments they went. To be sure he does not lengthen his stay where Mrs. N. is. Yes, Philomen, they are not yet on speaking terms. Mrs. N. staid a short while, and then departed for her mansion. She admired our bonnets very much. Soon our house was wrapped in darkness, and we, in slumber. I am sleepy by 7½ P.M. No letter yesterday.

Friday, November 15th, 1861

6 ¼ A.M. Today is set apart by our president, Jeff. Davis, as a day of fasting and prayer, and consequently there will be no school. A. is quietly sitting by me, happy in the consciousness that she will not be disturbed by Lucy's, "Ready, Miss Alice". She is now standing by the gate, her sparkling eyes wandering up and down in search of a "paper-boy". She is unable to write as she has a sore finger. She has hailed a boy, and he has informed her that the Delta was "short" this morning, and none of them obtained any. I wonder the reason. Today is 3 months that our dear Father has been gone. How cruel in this short life thus to be separated from those we love. I don't believe that it ever will be cold. I wish that it would. Yesterday was quite pleasant. Ma and A. had a slight altercation of words, and A. left for school, *not* in a *very good* humor. Ma was not very agreeable during the day, but not *stormy*. I assisted to make a dress for Josie, and studied as usual. Dinner quite early. When A. came home she told me that Belle had taken her work home and would knit on it during all her spare time. The other is almost done. Charles Hurley is coming home. I had the provoking pleasure of walking over to school with Miss Parker, alias "white neck", but unfortunately I do not know her. Miss M. was not in school. I never have an opportunity of conversing with any of the Seniors. Miss B. paid me a compliment by saying that I always knew my lessons. Mrs. Fisher did not come, so we were dismissed at $4^1/_2$. I was not glad as school was preferable to home. I had no place to go so came immediately home. Found Ma and A. and was informed that a telegraph had been received from Pa, which was as follows, "I am well. Will write Sunday. Business all right". His last letter was the 5th. We will not receive one now for a week. Pa has not written for 2 weeks. I assisted A. to make her toilet, and then went by the door. Spoke to Miss Jarreau, asked her to accompany us to a walk, but she excused herself on the plea that she was not dressed. We proceeded alone. Had not got around the corner when, whom should I see approaching, but— Miss Mitchell, and Nina Word. I ran to meet them and kissed pretty Nina again and again. They walked home with us. We entered the house, talked, laughed, etc. Miss M. said that as she did not see me at school, she could not resist the temptation of coming to my house. I was much obliged to her, and also that she had brought Nina. I was much surprised to see her, and when I look at the sofa, I can scarcely believe that Nina W. was the last who sat there, and how strange that I was so anxious to become acquainted with her. She was just singing when Leopold came in. He was introduced and she continued. He was pleased and pronounced her voice excellent. I was anxious for them to stay, but did not wish to ask L. to see them home. So I unwillingly let them depart. I walked a short distance with them, and it was quite night. Miss M. asked me to go home with her Monday evening, and I partly promised. After an incredible amount of kissing and hugging we parted and I was very sorry. I ran back home, found them assembled in the parlor, and learned that Ma was spending the evening with Mrs. N. for which L. soon started. He had asked us to go with him on Sunday aboard the Floating Battery, and became quite angry because we did not give him a decided answer. We eat supper, and were comfortably disposed of, I of course, in a rocking chair, when L. came over with orders to get the Keno box, and us. We did not feel like going, but could not resist his earnest entreating, so with reluctance we went. L. left about 10. He is so regular in his habits, and he received the name of old maid. We played till $10^1/_2$, and I won 60 cts., I mean lost. I am so very unlucky at the game. Our party consisted of Mr. and Mrs. N., L., Mr. E. Pool 35 cts. Quite an item. Were escorted home by Mr. N. Nothing more in connection with yesterday. I cannot divest myself of the idea that today is Saturday. It reminds me so of the past summer to see A. sitting beside me on the little sofa. She has become quite lazy of late, and does not rise early. Breakfast is ready. "To the dining room in the house, let me go, let me go."

Saturday, November 16th, 1861

6¹/₂ A.M. Sleep visited my eyelids this morning for a longer time than it generally does, but it would be useless for me to rise any earlier, as it is so very dark, and continues so so much longer on account of the fog. The sun does not rise until 6½. I have just hailed a little "news-boy" who imparted to me the ridiculous intelligence that the "Delta had busted", and there were no editions to be had so I purchased from him the Crescent, which I have not yet perused. A larger member of that corps has just told me that there will be no numbers issued before this afternoon. It is quite chilly this morning; probably it will turn cold without rain. A., lazy thing, has not descended. S. has just come in to ask me which I prefer for breakfast beefsteak or cream cheese; to be sure I decided in favor of the latter. I sewed yesterday till about 11 o'clock and finished a dress for Josie, who by the by walks very well now. She is, though, very backward. Ma had made up her mind to spend the day with Mrs. N., but as she was on the eve of starting, when Mr. N. came up with a letter to me, which he had obtained from the Delta office, and kindly brought it up immediately. After she had finished its perusal, she met with another detention, a visit from Mrs. Marks, who brought the $10; after this Ma went, and A. and I sat down to enjoy our dear letter. It was dated the 9th, and had been a week on its way. He freely forgave me for my long silence, and says that he is again well, after another very narrow escape. A cask of ice fell against him, knocked him down, and hurt his leg and foot, but he made a most providential escape from being injured for life. He received much attention from his friends, and was enabled to ride out the following day. Oh! I am now so anxious that he has not been prudent enough. I want to hear from him. Maybe he is sick, and consequently telegraphed the other day. I am so uneasy. I wish that he would never write us of such things. He says that he is almost well. I wonder if he is. He says "I am making money as fast as men generally do, and one of these days won't we have a big party"! God bless him. He received an early visit from Capt. da P. yesterday, as he left for Manassas.

He begged to be remembered to us. He said that if he saw Col. Wheat he would tender my regards. He acknowledges the receipt of Ma's telegraph, but said that he was confident that Ma would receive a letter as soon as his answer. He again spoke of the shrimps, and the pleasure they afford him, and says that we must send him some more if possible. He speaks nothing more of Capt. Eshleman. Sends his love to all inquiring friends and his dear, sweet, letter was concluded. I can not tell you all he says. I was delighted in the receipt of it. I answered it, and finished by dinner time. We eat dinner alone, all the children being over the way. After it I read my letter to A. and entertained both her and Fanny by exercises in Elocution. We laughed, talked, and did not dress until about 5 o'clock. F. went over to Mrs. N. I soon followed her, and was joined by A. We walked up and down conversing upon matters in general. We returned home with the exception of Ma. Mrs. N. commanded us to come back, and insisted on our remaining. Eat supper, dispatched E. for some cake, adjourned to the parlors, began talking of Pa, his kindness, and many little remembrances which caused our tears to flow in unison. F. went over to Mrs. N. and A. and I cried ourselves to sleep, and resolved to go to bed at 8 o'clock, when the bell rang and F. and Gus entered. F. had come over for my letter to give to Mr. N. and they had met at the door. I gave her the letter and she left; Gus was very agreeable. I did not go to sleep for some time. Ma came over, went to bed, and sleep at last overcame me. When he went, A. said that he thought that he was angry from some trivial thing which she had said, and at which, she thinks, he took offense, but it was a matter of little difference to us. He said that he had again ordered the paper to be sent. There must be great irregularity about the office. A. and I remained down a short while, talking, soon up stairs. I was very sleepy, and in an inconceivably short time I was outwing on my pillow. I didn't tell you that Alice sleeps with me now . . . .

Sunday, November 17th, 1861

6 ¹/₂ A.M. I don't believe that I'll tell you that I have just purchased a Delta, scanned it, and came to you to account for myself of yesterday. After breakfast A. and I went up to dress for Synagogue. As it was cold, I had made up my mind to go. It was quite late, and we resolved that if we were not

ready by 10 o'clock that we would not go, but we were and went over to
Mrs. N.'s for her. I had on my new bonnet and dress, A., her new bonnet,
and both looked very nice. About 15 minutes after our arrival Mrs. N.
tripped down the steps, looking "as pretty as a pink" in her new bonnet.
She admires ours more each time. After a very windy walk we reached the
Holy Place of God, entered, and thankfully A. and I obtained our old seats.
Divine angelic Flora engrossed the greater part of my attention. If ever a
mortal created in my breast a feeling of envy, she does. I *love* her now as
devotedly, as earnestly as she ever can be. Her figure equals that of "Venus
de Medici". I fear that our darling beauty is on her way here. I am so sorry,
for when she is absent I forget her. A. and I devoted a few moments in commenting on the appearance of the Jews in general, and the beauty of the
respective girls. There was to be a grand review in the afternoon, and Mrs.
N. said that if she went she would let us know, and we would go together. After Synagogue, A. and I walked down town to see what could
be seen. Gazed upon the former residence of angelic Gods. Went to see if
Dr. Lonith had returned. Had the exquisite felicity of beholding B.B.L.,
and catching a glimpse of the handsome Dr. Walker, Capt., I mean. Dr. L.
was still absent. We then promenaded up Canal St. and indulged at Blineau's.
Saw the beautiful, stately Mrs. Violet, and two of her lovely children. As
we emerged from G.'s whom (and I nearly approached them) should I see
but Carrie and Mollie, H. and Gus L., but unfortunately there was
something very attractive in the window in which they were looking,
and as we passed, their eyes were intently looking in that direction, and he
did not see us. Mollie did and I suppose told him of it. I presume they went
to B.'s and we regretted the unlucky circumstance of coming out so
soon, for had we been a moment sooner, or later we should have met,
and probably honored with an introduction to the beautiful girls. But so
it was. This encounter furnished food for many a square's talk. We are peculiarly unfortunate. In some matters a moment is of great importance.
Passed the heavenly Mrs. Canefield, and on our homeward way were smil-
ingly saluted by the queenly Mrs. da P., and A. and I are going to see her
one of these days. Met Mr. N. who stopped a moment and handed us a letter, which he requested us to give to his wife. As we passed Henry Levy's
house a little darkey was standing by the gate and for mischief we called
her, and told her to tell Mr. Henry that two ladies sent their love to him,
and threatened to report her to Miss Betty if she did not. I wonder if she
will. Won't he be puzzled. Went to Mrs. N.'s and gave her the letter. It was
from her sister Leah. She was in great distress about Beaufort, and their

relatives of which they have heard nothing. Lolly P. went there with his company, and no intelligence has been received of them. I suppose they are safe. We staid over there some time. She was going, and immediately after dinner Mr. N. was going to turn out. When I came home, I dressed Sallie, fixed myself, and about 3 ate dinner; Ma refused to accompany us. Ma went to the market, and we had a nice dinner, the first cabbages of the season, but I did not enjoy it as I ate it so hurriedly. Mr. N. came over to show himself in his soldier clothes. We left about 3½. The streets were thronged with people, and we reached Canal St. in safety. Made applications to Hyde and Goodrich to go on their gallery, but they refused, and we gained admittance to Moody's and luckily after some time obtained very excellent standing places. I was shielded from the sun by a parasol of a lady next to me and was entertained by the interesting conversation of two interesting pretty girls on the other side of me. There was an immense concourse and I recognized many, many familiar faces. They did not move until about 5, and we had a fine view of the Gen. and staff, who were immediately beneath us. Canal St. presented a magnificent spectacle, and they were about 10,000 braves in line, and which is about ¼ of what we can bring out in 2 hours, a guarantee that, although the Crescent City has contributed so largely to the Army, we *still* have enough to keep the invader from her soil. The militia reflected great credit upon their officer, and we saw our noble Cousin at the head of his command, and screaming at the height of his voice, "Forward March"!! It was a splendid turnout. How I would like to see them all "pitch" into the Yankees and give them a sound thrashing; I love to see the brave boys who keep time to their martial music. I had the pleasure of hearing for the first time, by a brass band, our "Bonnie Blue Flag". What a quantity of handsome beings did I behold, and if such a thing as love at first sight is felt, I may safely say that I experienced, for I was fascinated by a gentleman in a splendid carriage, and *not* a soldier. The carriage was beneath us during the whole time, and I was spell bound, I could not but look at him. I liked his face so much and when he drove off, and was lost to my view, oh! I felt so, so lonely and unhappy, and I know that we shall never meet again. In the crowd I searched in vain for him. His image is indelibly impressed on my mind. We did not see Mr. N.'s company and strange to say, while we were so anxiously looking for it, it passed unobserved. We saw some vacated places on Tyler's gallery, and we crossed over and came in Moody's and went out to Tyler's. I was delighted with the soldiers, and with our fun. I like "wild goose chases". Stepped into Blineau's; and indulged freely, bought some soda, paid a dime, they giving the cake for "glanjuppe" [free]. It was quite night and we were very tired, and there was a rush for the "omnibuses". We at last succeeded in getting one and were comfortably seated on its luxuriant, relict cushions. A very agreeable gentleman, of considerable dimensions, "procked up" a talk with Josh. We got out, and Mrs. N. went her way, promising to come over. I got home, took off my dress, and was soon lying on the sofa. Mrs. N. came over, we eat supper. Had some fried fish, which all enjoyed. After it Mr. E. came over and we played Keno. Pool 35 cts. Had some nice molasses candy. We played till 10. I was particularly fortunate, and sleepy. I won 50 cts. They left, and we retired, fully satisfied with the adventures of the day. A. and I had a fire "bath", and after a few seconds talk in bed silence reigned supreme. This morning is quite cold. I must go and see about the breakfast.

Monday, November 18th, 1861

6 $^1/_4$ A.M. I have but a few moments to devote to you, as I have a quantity of sums to perform and have never an opportunity in the day, so I must briefly recount to you the principal items of yesterday. The day was fine, but warm, and Ma was in a remarkably bad, disagreeable humour. I sewed till 12 and the conversations and words were anything but agreeable. Ma, at times, is so very unreasonable. I then wrote a thesis for Saturday, braided A.'s hair, and then ate dinner. Did not enjoy it, altho' it consisted of fine piece of roast. After dinner I dressed my Sallie, but not myself until quite late. A few moments after I came down, we were joined by Cousin S., and while he was entertaining us, our party was augmented by dear Joseph, Leopold. Cousin S. left shortly after, and I bade him to come up through the week, which action he declared himself impossible of performing. I left A. alone with J. and was by the door with Josie when Alice Jarreau came in and spoke to me. I gave Josie up, and we walked for a long while. She is so agreeable, I like her very much. How unexpectedly do things transpire. I little imagined that we would ever walk together. She told me that she would go with me the following day to school. We talked upon various subjects. I wish that she would introduce me to her handsome brother. When I entered the house, "S" was still there; I took a seat on the sofa, and was very comfortable, when Mr. N. came, and said that we must go to

his house as Mrs. N. could not come over, her domestic being out. Of course the Keno box was to accompany us and on asking Mr. E. he also consented. We had a pleasant little party and quite a large pool. We had played 2 or three games when Lieut. Rosenfield darkened the door way. He was dressed in his uniform and looked very handsome. L. had been on duty all day, and tho' very tired, he increased our gaming party. I won 25 cts., A., $1.30. We played until after 10. Refreshments were handed round which were very acceptable. We were escorted home by Leopold and Eisner. My slate, pencil, and Arithmetic lie pleadingly before me; to them I go.

Tuesday, November 19th, 1861

6 1/4 A.M. Here I am in my old place on the sofa, and A. on hers. She is writing, altho' her finger is not yet well. We arose together this morning, both with much reluctance. Nothing can convince me that December is most at hand for the morning is quite warm. We have just purchased a paper. Wretched Gus! I have not yet read it. Yesterday was a perfect Spring day. Nothing of importance transpired. Ma unusually disagreeable. At 12½, while I was studying, I was interrupted by a visit from Alice Jarreau. She came to tell me that she would not go in the afternoon, but would inform me when she would. She is so talkative. When she left I wrote my Analysis, dressed Rosa, and finished my lessons. Dinner quite early and I left a few moments after, regretting my inability to talk with [Ma?]. She had her work, which is progressing finely. I had given up the idea of going to Miss M.'s and had on my old pink barége. I arrived at school in time. Sarah Chappell has rejoined our class. I believe I told you that she has lost her mother. She is now an orphan. Miss M. was in school. I told her I could not accompany her. Nina was well; they had had grand times. Maggie L. told me that Miss Belle had lost her cousin, a young man now in Vir. She was not in school. I knew my lessons, handed in my thesis and Analysis. Miss M. and I parted at the corner. I don't think that I will ever go home with her. I declare she is the most undemonstrative being that I ever met with, too much so, it be lovable. I don't know how she must feel. Walked slowly home, for the later I got there, the better. Found Ma out and I went up to A., who was dressing. She informed me of all the school news. Mrs. Dentzel had made a real declaration of love and friendship to her, offering it to A. and she accepted it. It was very unexpected, as A. never imagined she liked her. Quite a distraction to be loved by " — ". Maggie Myers has been promoted to the 2nd assistancy in the Paulding School. She is, of course, delighted. A. finished her toilet, and after walking up and down for some time, we came in, and I read a note, which she had received from Miss D. A. very sorry at learning that Ma was to Mrs. N.'s, we (dined) supped without her on molasses, Mrs. N.'s gift. She has received a fresh supply. After supper A. wrote and I studied, and when 8½ struck, we were disrobing for bed. I was partly asleep when I heard Ma ring the bell. I cannot study at night. I am too tired and sleepy. Haven't I been brief? But I know you'll excuse me. It is going to be warm today, and I have "nothing to wear". Pity me. A. has gone to have her hair dressed. I wish I were she, to go to school. I despise to stay home.

Thursday, November 21st, 1861

6½ A.M. I was deaf to Lucy's commands which continued for about 10 successive minutes to get up, and finally came to my senses, as the last stroke of the bell pealed forth. A. arose simultaneously and is now by me writing, though slowly on account of her disabled finger. The prospect is very dismal. It has been raining. I had so beautiful a dream last night about Henry Myers. I could not come to you yesterday, as my lessons were very present and monopolized my whole attention; but I won't fail to give you a synopsis of Tuesday. The sun and clouds both strove for ascendancy, and it is difficult to say which gained it, for the sun would occasionally shine forth. Ma was in an execrable bad humor, and about 12 o'clock Ma and Rosa went to Miss Sarah's and I was left alone. I studied my lessons, and received a visit from Mrs. Deegan's honored self. She remained for about 15 minutes. Ma returned to dinner, A. did not come until after 3½, which, of course, made me quite angry, as I was obliged to wait for her bonnet. I was very angry, and when she came, I took it and left without saying a word. Oh! Philomen, I can say this morning that my heart is filled with grief and sorrow. I am unhappy. The signification of that theorem was never more deeply felt. I am unhappy, yes miserable. I proceeded to school, and it sprinkled a little, but I heeded it not, as any place or thing is preferable to home. I arrived *just* in time for the Dictation, and obtained my usual seat between Misses M. and D. Miss M. and I parted at its conclusion, and met no more that afternoon. Miss B. complimented me on my reading. It seemed like old times, to sit by Sarah Chappell. After school the seniors being dismissed and having no one there that I wished to see, I left immediately. On Clio St. met A. and F. They were going to get some laces that were at the Blanchiseusse [the laundress]. I passed on and went home, found Ma out. I took Josie, walked up and down. Delivered her up. Ma came in, went in. A. came, and went to Mrs. N.'s. We met at the corner, and spoke as usual. Came in, eat supper; Mrs. N. came over. We played Keno till after 10. I won nothing, A. 13 cts. Mr. N. went to drill, and came for his spouse just a little too late. Mrs. N. gave the signal that she was safe in her house and we entered ours to reduce the chaos to order. This being accomplished, we extinguished the light and were en route for upper regions. A. and I had a pleasant little chat while in bed. The intimacy between her and Miss D. is daily increasing. Miss D. has expressed a passionate earnest love for her, "as instantaneous as it is pure", writes she in one of her notes, all of which A. shows to me. I should feel flattered to be liked by one, who like her has so wide a circle of acquaintances, and who has conceived no particular attachment for any. It is a very unexpected event. Nothing of importance happened yesterday. I commenced to sew on some drawers, but accomplished scarcely anything. It did not rain and in fact I don't believe that it ever will. I'd like to know when we will be favored with a change in the weather, which at present is very warm. Ma was in no better humor. If an act of the others occasions her annoyance, her wrath all descends on my head. I thankfully left to study. The lessons were quite difficult and I put my whole mind to them. A. did not come home till very late, and I was compelled to wait. I was very angry. She and Miss D. had been courting. I almost forgave her for detaining me. On my arrival at school the Geography lesson had been recited, so I lost it. Knew the others to my satisfaction. Sweet Belle has not been to school since the death of poor Eldridge. Maggie T. and I are "quite thick". Olympia is as attractive. I like the L.N.S. very much. After school an opportunity offered to speak to my old friends, Liz, Ada, and Miss Leach. I seized it, kissed them so tenderly, fashioned so slenderly. It seemed just like old times to be with them; Lizzie and the others were going to Mr. Lusher's to obtain his permission for Holiday on Saturday. You know there is to be a grand review on that day, when our entire force is to be reviewed by the Governor. All business is suspended and I think it but right that ours should. It will be a splendid sight, and it is suggested to charge 25 cts.

to all who occupy a position on galleries, the proceeds to be devoted to the Free Market. I don't suppose that it will be adopted. Well, I have made quite a digression. Miss M. was in school, but I lost sight of her. Well, I had partly consented to go with L. We were standing at the corner when some one from behind put their arms around me, and kissed me. I looked around, and to my astonishment beheld Nina Word. I was glad of a pretext to go, and bade them "good bye", and left with Nina. She told me that Miss M. was waiting at the corner. We met, and they walked a few squares with me. Nina looked very nice, but is not near as pretty as I once thought her. I promised to go and see her, and probably shall. We embraced affectionately and parted. As I passed the Mazareau's, Alice [Jarreau] was standing by the gate. I stopped and asked her to come into my house. She consented. A. shortly came in. She had been to Blanchiseusse. We were chatting for a long time. She is very agreeable. Ma came in; she had been out. Where, I don't know. When Alice left we ate supper, and at 8 o'-clock I went to bed and the others, with the exception of A., followed. I was asleep when she came to bed, and she played an excellent joke on me. About 10 o'clock she woke me and told me to get up that it was after six. I was very sleepy, but jumped up. I heard A. and S. laughing, saw the moon not far in the heavens, and was too sleepy to deduce any conclusions. I was bewildered, and six or no six I determined to go back to bed, which I did and knew nothing of the joke until this morning. A. wrote a note to "Gus" about the paper, and sent it this morning by Mr. N. Today is the 20th anniversary of Ma's wedding year. May we all live to celebrate many, many more happy ones. I hope that we will get a letter today. I am so anxious to hear from my precious Father.

Friday, November 22nd, 1861

6 A.M. Excuse chirography, as I can scarcely see to write. It is yet dark. The mornings are so very short. There is no rain in the clouds, as I see the bright reflection of the sun. A. is by me. Today is the anniversary of Ma's birthday. May we as one united family enjoy many happy returns of the day. I wonder if Pa thinks of it. I do hope that we will receive a letter today. I am really uneasy. Tomorrow is the grand review, but there will be much suffering in that rank, occasioned by the oppressive heat. It will be a grand sight, but difficult matter to obtain a good view of it. Gus has not been. He must be angry. Mr N. delivered the note, but he seems not to have noticed it, as the paper is not left. He will go away in a few days, or probably has gone, and A. just said a few trifling words in jest. Pshaw! he is too sensible to be angry. Here's Mr Burckett. I see him every morning, going to market with his newsman behind him. What Miss Bougniennes missed. Ma was exceedingly more pleasant yesterday. Told me that she had been to see Miss Josephine and Mrs. Pierson, the previous afternoon [Miss Josephine is "Miss Jo" Pierson, wife of Ed Hews]. They are going to move on Clio, at Nayades and Apollo. Won't that be glorious. I will pass the house every afternoon [on the way to school]. Miss J. is not well. She has promised for some time to work a little sacque for Josie, so Ma took it to her. A., during the day, sent home the scarf which Mrs. G. had been doing. It is finished and is quite pretty. Remember Philomen, whose swan-like neck it is destined to cover. Will it ever? I did not see A. before I left for school. She sent me her bonnet so I thought it unlikely that she and Miss D. would remain to court. I, as usual, was late at school. Miss M. was not there, but I was entertained *as well* by Maggie and Olympia. During the music lesson we enjoyed ourselves admirably, gossiping, scandalizing, etc. Mrs. P. said that she would dismiss school on Saturday on her own responsibility. I waited a little while after, and proceeded home alone. Found no one home, but A. She was up stairs, and I joined her. She told me of her love affairs with "Imo" [Imogene Dentzel], etc., and we remained up until voices below announced the arrival of the folks, when we descended. A. and I were arranging her desk when martial music was heard. We threw down everything and ran out. It was that splendid corps, the Continentals. When a little further up the street halted in front of the residence of Col. Thos. Murray, which is immediately opposite to Mrs. N.'s, and Mr. N. was thoughtful enough to come over for us. We went and had a fine view. We are so angry at the idea of the bountiful collation [literally, a light meal] with which he would entertain them. We saw them enter, and emerge and remained until the last spectator had departed. I love to see soldiers. Mrs. N. came over with us and of course we passed the evening with Keno. I wonder where Leo. is. He angry too? I won 35 cts. A. lost. Ma won. Pool 25 cts.

Saturday, November 23rd, 1861

6 1/2 A.M. How incredible, but as I write my fingers shake, my teeth chatter. The wind is whistling from without, and I am enveloped in a shawl. How providential for the review. I could not get up as early as usual and A., lazy thing, is not yet down. I am glad of the change. Yesterday A. sent Ma a very pretty cup, a birthday present. I was offended to think that she did not ask me to contribute. It is very pretty. I believe Ma is going to have a little something tonight. It continued warm and sultry until about 9 o'clock when the rain began to fall. It continued quite hard and ceased about 4 o'clock, when it was quite cold. The children arrived home safe, but Miss A. not till after 4. She had been courting, and the whole afternoon she devoted to "Imo", and herself. I sewed considerably in the day. Ma very good. Dinner very good. About dark A. and I laid on the bed. Ma was in her room. F. to Mrs. N.'s. A. having an extra [coin?] went down to buy it [a newspaper]. Did so and found that she had been cheated. The boy had given her half of concept. F. remained to Mrs. N.'s. Ma did not come down. A. and I retired about 9. Performed ablutionary exercises. She is worthy one and we amusing ourselves by watching our brave volunteers as they pass on their downward way. Grand doings today. I am undecided whether or not to go. The paper lies before me. I must scan it.

Sunday, November 24th, 1861

6 1/2 A.M. Think how great a compliment I pay you, by rising so early this cold morning. It was but the struggle of a moment and I was on the sofa, putting shoes and stockings in their usual place. A. is by me! We have just purchased a paper, which contains a description of the Review of yesterday, of which, by the by, I must relate the particulars. Mrs. N., A., Josh., and myself first went to synagogue, Ma promising to meet us on Carondelet St. The attendance was very small. As we were walking down, we met Ma, and we proceeded together with difficulty. There was a total suspension of business, not a store was opened, and it seemed to be a more general holiday than Sunday, but this was to be expected, in order that all men should be in the ranks. When, at Canal St., the prospect was discouraging. Every gallery, every window, and every available or unavailable place was black with crowds of human beings. The town buildings were a perfect spectacle, as far as the eye could reach, masses of persons were presented. The day was as beautiful as ever dawned, and many thanks ascended to God for his manifest goodness, for had it been warm, it would, in so large a concourse, have been unfavorable. We despaired of obtaining a place on any balcony, so contented ourselves with one on the banquette. Ma had been standing a few moments when she declared her inability to do so any longer, and contrary to our persuasions left. We then resolved to endeavor to better our conditions, and ascended the steps of the Merchants Hotel, and made necessary inquiries of the gentleman who informed us that we could have a *window* for $5!!! This is the advantage they take on such occasions. We remarked that it was *very cheap*, and descended. A few moments after Mr. Mordecai Hyams stopped, spoke to Mrs. N. and was introduced to us. He is a very pleasant man and quite handsome. We then resumed our positions on the side walk, envying. Oh! how much those favored ones on the gallery, but we consoled ourselves by the thought that we were safer than they, as I should consider all such places hazardous. I saw lots of familiar faces. Bowed to "Little Henry", and earnestly wished that Gus would cross our paths, as he may have been of service. But many were in the same condition as we, and nothing more could have been expected from coming down so late. The first familiar soldier face that we recognized was Leopold's, from whom we obtained a deferential bow. He was at the head of his company, and quickly passed from our sight. We then took a stroll up and down and stopped right in front of his command, which was halting. We remained some time, and by steadfastly gazing upon him, hoped to attract his attention. Finally he cast his eyes around and they rested upon us. He smiled and a short while after was with us. He considered our places excellent and maintained that we would have a better view. He looked remarkably handsome. He said that the line extended from the Lake to the levee, and as many beautiful faces greeted them through the entire route. Sad to say Blineau's was closed and we were very hungry. L. left and procured us some cakes, which we speedily devoured. He gave us water from the tin cups, and best of all introduced his Captain, Mr. Mader, to us. He is a very agreeable gentleman, and very intelligent. His sister, Azilie was a schoolmate of mine. This little encounter was most fortunate, as these moments passed quickly. We passed a most pleasant half hour, and it was with regretful feelings that we beheld them "Forward March". I am half in love with the handsome Capt. M. About 1 o'clock the procession commenced to pass and oh! the multitude of handsome, determined faces, and manly forms. I lost my heart over and over again, and as one fascinating creature would pass on, another would immediately fill his place. Conspicuous among the companies was a newly organized one, bearing "a Black Flag" upon which was written "We gave no quarters and we ask none" it being their determination to have every Yankee, whom they obtain and retain as prisoners. They are a fearless looking set of men, and of course attracted universal attention. We saw Cousin S. and the Militia made a fine appearance and how fine would it be if each man had a gun. They are very poorly armed. I had no idea that we had so many soldiers. How can we have any beaus! Our brave boys with half their numbers will put to flight, the invaders of our soil.[1] We met with no other adventures and remained standing until 5 o'clock, when the splendid display was over. A display, the equal of which has never been seen on this continent. I forgot to say that we saw Mr. N. Mrs. N. left us and went to Mrs. Harris, but said she would be up soon. Met Lizzie Hillman. She had been out since early in the morning. Told of the fun she had had. Happenings most on Todd's gallery, man of her acquaintance. She spoke of Mollie and Carrie Hart's being there. Oh! ruthless Fate, why did you not direct our steps there. L. was with some friends, otherwise would have come up with us. We arrived home safe, and as may be imagined Ma was quite uneasy. She was sitting before a cozy fire, our dinner was next ordered, which we enjoyed, being very, very hungry. We then rested ourselves, and talked over the events of the day. Mr. and Mrs. N. came over, Leopold also honored us and the principal talk was the Review. Both gentlemen were quite exhausted, so Keno was dispensed with. Gus came and A. and he, no doubt, enjoyed themselves in the front room. Very complimentary to her other company. He was mad, but could not remain away, as he leaves Tuesday morning. The guests went, but he did not. I joined them, and spent a very agreeable few moments. Review, Mrs. da P., Henry, Aunt Bettie, etc. etc, discussed. I regret his departure. It's enough we know him. His assertion in the cause of the paper had so far been productive of no good results. He left about $10^{1}/_{2}$, and asked when he should come up again. We told him whenever "his heart dictates", and he was gone. He is a queer genius. A. and I staid down a short while, talking, talking. Then gathered together our bonnets, gloves, etc. and were soon in bed. Big thing on Alice, and so ended the eventful day. There Josh comes running in the door. It is his birthday, and in his uplifted hands is

---

1. A lack of weapons was a serious problem throughout the Confederate Army.

a gold pencil case, a present from his good Mother. I must give him a kiss. Today he is nine years old. How few persons ever dreamt that he would ever live to celebrate it. On the returns of many more ones be he blessed as he now is, and as each successive year rolls by, may the fragile vine expand in the sturdy oak. Josh! you have my best wishes!

Monday, November 25th, 1861

6 ¹/₂ A.M. Another week, dear Philomen, do we usher in. How quickly do they pass. To day 3 months I will be 17! Where shall I be. The morning is clear and cold. The sun does not now rise until very late. A. is on my left, writing a note to her dear, newly found friend "Imo". A.'s finger is not yet well, and it, in a great degree, retards her writing — I wish I was with my dear Pa this morning — Yesterday was a beautiful day. We did not break-fast until very late, and after it the time speedily passed. Josh received diverse little presents from us, which he seemed to prize highly. He and S. commenced a new term at Sunday School. They may make a match. (Stranger things than that have happened.) I did not sew, altho' I should have, as I had several things to mend. But I, of my own accord, would never do anything. Ma commanded Mr. N. to bring her up a letter, and he consented to obey commands. I did the greater portion of my sums, and yet have some to perform. About 2 I was just in the first stages of braid-ing A.'s hair, when a messenger came up to us with the glad intelligence that Ma had received a letter. Quicker than thought we scampered down, A. with hair "wildly flowing", and with breathless suspense listened while Ma read the precious document, which was dated the 17th, and had been a week on the journey. He is quite well and has almost totally re-covered from his injury, but says that with the aid of a carriage ride and a stick he is doing first rate, and that he was able to wear his shoe. He says, "You will perceive that I am no longer Lieut. but Capt. and that has been my title ever since I have been in Vir." But this is not satisfactory as he does not tell us how he became entitled to it.[2] This business is prosperous and if they continue lucky they should make by the first of May, from $60 to

2. There is no record in the Confederate Service Records at the National Archives that Solomon had a military rank with any Louisiana, Mississippi, or Virginia unit.

$80,000. He furnishes us with a diary of his days, which was very interesting.[3] He acknowledges the receipt of F.'s letter, and will answer it next week. He said that he would write on Wed. so a letter is almost due. He concludes by his respects to all inquiring friends. Oh! how much joy and hope did the dear letter infuse our hearts. He was well. Thank God. Mr. N. received our most heartfelt thanks. I then proceeded to do A.'s hair. She had the letter, and read it over and over to me. I could read one until the next comes. When I had done, dinner was announced, which was very excellent. Mrs. N. sent word to us that we must come over and sup with her. A. and I played several games of Keno, then went up stairs, and seated before the window in Ma's room chatted some time; in fact too long, for it was quite late when we arose to dress. While so doing Cousin S. was heard below, and his inquiry "If anybody was home", ascended to the upper regions. A. went down but I had not done. I had on my dress which I altered and which looked very nice. When I went down, he was gone and Mr. Eisner was occupying a seat. Oh! thought I, too much encouragement was given on last Sunday. A., however, joined them. Ma went over to Mrs. N.'s with F. When F. returned Mr. E. was yet there and she delivered the message to come right over. Mr. E. took it and left. Shortly after L. came for us. We were undecided whether or not to go, as we learned that the *Harrises* were over there, and while deliberating, Mary entered with orders from headquarters, and we went and were shortly in the august presence, and seated around the supper table. At the termination Keno was introduced, and it seemed strange to play with those with whom we are not on friendly terms. I won considerably, the pool being quite an item, 50 cts. L. left at 10, but the others not till 11. We spent a very pleasant evening. How agreeable would it be if we and Mrs. H. spoke. We were escorted home by Mr. N. And before we sought our couches the clock struck 12. I have some sums to perform, and must now breathe "good bye".

Tuesday, November 26th, 1861

6 1/2 A.M. I have spent the past $1/4$ of an hour in reading some of A.'s notes

---

3. More than "interesting", the father's diary would have given us a capsule of the work of a sutler, or provisioner, during the war. The expected profits of $60,000–80,000 were not as large as they look, given the continuing depreciation of the Confederate currency.

from "Imo", and in perusing the paper, which was obtained from a news-boy. I know that it is useless to attempt to get a carrier. What changeable weather. The morning is not at all cold, in fact yesterday was quite warm. I dislike Monday of all the days, for the children, after 2 days hol-iday, return to school, and I miss them, particularly A. "Alas, by some degree of woe we every bliss must gain". I spent the day with drawers, which, thank gracious, are almost completed. Alice J. [Jarreau] came to tell me that she would accompany me in the afternoon. Mrs N. was spend-ing the morning with us, and about 12½ a loud report was heard which caused us all to start, and which we imagined to be the shutting of a door, or some noise in an adjoining house. Prescutt E. came in with the in-telligence that the Nayades St. steam car had exploded, and asked us if we had not heard the noise. I was slow in crediting it, knowing how very lo-quacious he is, so we went by the door, and to our sorrow learned that it was actually so, and heard exaggerated reports of the injuries and dam-ages which ensued, but I see by the paper that 1 man was killed and 4 wounded. A large 10 pound piece entered a house on Bacchus St., smash-ing all the contents, but fortunately the lady of the house, Mrs. Lindo, hap-pened to be out, and thus made a providential escape. The occurrence pro-duced much excitement, and the streets were thronged with anxious and curious persons. A. had said that she would probably go and see if Miss J. was in her new house, so fearing that she had gone, and been there at the time of the casualty, Ma sent to school to see if she were there. The mes-senger staid a torturing length, and returned with the glad tidings that Miss Alice was in her room. It is the first accident of the kind that has happened for some time, and I presume that it was attributable to the oversight of the engineer, who was killed on the spot. I studied as usual. Mrs. N. went about 2½ taking Sally with her. Mr. N.'s Company is ordered to Columbus, but Mrs. N. does not feel the least uneasy as "Sammy knows better than to go". To my astonishment in yesterday's paper, I saw that Mr. Rosenfield's store was partly consumed by fire on the previous night. While he [Leopold] was quietly sitting, and playing Keno his property was burn-ing. But I am confident that his loss is nothing, as he was fully insured. Tuesday and Wednesdays are his drill nights, so we will not hear the particulars till Thursday. The children came home from school, remark-ably early, and dinner was in accordance. Alice and I met at the door, and proceeded together. Mr. Mazareau is acquainted with Miss Leech and A. requested an introduction, which I granted at the door of the school. We went in, A. was introduced to Mrs. Pagand and took a seat on the platform. I saw nothing more of her until after school. Miss M. was not in school, so we left together. We walked leisurely along and she told me that she was in the School of Practice and was much pleased with everything. We met A. coming to meet us. When we arrived home Alice came in on the steps, and staid some time, finding much to talk about, as she is an incessant chatterer. She promised to lend me the "Volunteers Friend". Ma was out, but came in presently. Alice left, we went to supper. Adjourned to the drawing room. Gus came to pay his farewell visit, but he does not leave until tomorrow. Mrs. N. came. G. was particularly agreeable, joining the conversation and not occupying his place on the sofa. Mrs. N. left and strange to say G. did so about $8^1/_2$. He shook hands as usual and the only difference being the remarking of the cold, meaning "good bye" instead of "good night". He is a heartless being. He contemplates a visit to N.Y. and he may be gone for years, and he may be gone forever from me.[4] We gave him our best wishes, bade him give our love to Pa, if he *should*, in his journeyings, pass through Vir. He promised to and was gone, gone, gone. May prosperity attend the footsteps of my eccentric friend Gus. Ma went to bed, A. and I remained a short while, talked over the events of the day and then followed her.

Wednesday, November 27th, 1861

$6^1/_2$ A.M. Philomen, do you ever tire of my society? Say no, even if you don't mean it, for I shall then be in happy ignorance. Day followeth day, and each succeeding one finds me in my place on the sofa, sometimes joined by A. and sometimes alone. Who can tell how long it shall last. Can I ever forget this period of my existence? When I came down I left A. safely ensconced away in a corner of the bed, but I hear her up stairs, and I presume she will soon be down. Gus leaves this morning, the very atmosphere seems to breathe it. Yesterday continued warm. After breakfast Ma and Mrs. N. went to market and made extensive purchases in the beef line. Ma complained of a headache, but thought it was slight and would pass away, but it was no easier at 12, and she was compelled to lie down. With great trouble, I succeeded in quieting the house, but it was useless.

---

4. There were transportation routes from South to North that allowed for such a trip.

Ma could not sleep. I studied as usual. After finishing dressing I came down, and found Mrs. Ellis and the baby there. She was spending the day with Mrs. N. The baby bears a most striking resemblance to its poor mother. She went home quite early, and when she left, dinner was announced. Ma felt too sick so we dined without her, enjoying but very little the fine piece of roast. I was late at school, but the Dictation had not begun. Miss M. and I did not meet after it. Reading was the next feature, and I was with my friends. Alice and I met after school, and walked home together. Exchanged kisses with Liz., Net., Ada, Miss Leech. Alice lent me the "Volunteers Friend". I was anxious to see how Ma was so walked hurriedly home and entered immediately. Ma was in bed, but was somewhat relieved and as it was best for her to remain quiet we left her, and she slept. Eat supper. I then perused the paper, which is very creditable to the young ladies of the 4th. D.H.S. and they will realize a considerable amount.[5] Among the pieces I recognized one of Josie Guion's. I must go and see dear Clara. Mrs. N.'s domestic was sick so she did not come over. I studied my history, and knew it before I went to bed. A. was asleep by 8 o'clock. She and Miss D. had a disagreement, and she showed me all the notes, and repeated the principal conversations that had passed between them. "The course of true love", etc. etc. We retired early. A. has come down, and as she has some important things to tell me about "Imo", and as I have my lessons to get (remember, Wednesday), I will depart with the hope that ere the day closes we will have received tidings of the loved one.

Thursday, November 28th, 1861

6 1/4 A.M. Light has just spread her mantle o'er the darkened earth, and I am writing, scarcely able to trace the lines. The noble mansion of the Vienne's is wrapped in silence, and the general appearance is indicative that it is morning. There are some whom I see each successive day. There comes the milk boy, as regular as the morning, swinging his pail upon his arm, and seemingly as happy and contented as possible. The morning is very warm. Nothing of import happened yesterday. Alice and I went to school together. Arrived there just in time. I knew my lessons. Miss. M. was not in

5. A concert to aid the war effort was being prepared by a New Orleans high school.

school. Maggie and I enjoyed ourselves commenting upon the different girls, and pitying in particular poor Emma Lewis, who is so ugly. After the dismissal Alice and I came home, I stopping a few moments to chat with my senior friends. Alice [Jarreau] has her books, which she had much difficulty in getting. I think that she should be in the Sophomore class. When home found Mrs. N. there and A. out. Took Josie, and promenaded for some time, and brought A. home. We went in, she had been to Miss Jo's and she was out. Then to Mrs. N. who gave her a most explicit account of the particulars of the explosion, and the damage to Mrs. Lindo's house who is her particular friend. She then told me that she and "Imo" had "made up", and all sorts of stuff. Mrs. N. went home and Josh was out with Mr. E. and she was quite uneasy, so thought that he may have come. Ma went with her and after the lapse of an hour and no tidings were received I went over, and to my astonishment they had not come. Mrs. N. was in an uncredable state of suspense and anxiety. They had gone to Gretna[6] and imagination was busy in picturing the most horrible accidents. This state continued about $1/2$ hour longer, when I heard Mrs. N. joyfully and tearfully exclaim "Here they come" and in a few moments they entered. Mr. E. laughed at Mrs. N.'s uneasiness, but it would be as useless to command the water to stand still, as a person to suppress their anxious fears. We went and Mr. and Mrs. N. promised to come over, which they did and we had a pleasant game of Keno, but sad to say I was the loser of 30 cts., A of 40 cts. Too expensive, these times. Returned about 10. I hope that we will get a letter to day.

Friday, November 29th, 1861

6 $1/4$ A.M. I have not yet quite recovered from the effects of a most startling dream, which I had just before awakening. My nerves are shattered. Little Rosa came down with me, and is now standing by me asking numerous and curious questions relative to my writing. The morning is warm, and summer like. I have now the joyful news to communicate that we were yesterday the recipients of a letter from dear Pa by Express. He was well and he can without difficulty wear his shoe. Regretfully, in consequence of lim-

---

6. Now a New Orleans suburb, in 1861 Gretna was considerable travel time from the Solomons' neighborhood.

ited space, I can enter into no particulars, save that Capt. E. is not married. Oh! Philomen, what am I to do when this robe has performed its services. How fortunate if its donor should just make his appearance.[7] I met Alice at the gate, and we walked to school. Miss M. was not there. Probably she is not coming back. I excused myself to Alice and accepted Liz.'s invitation to walk a different route. How vividly were we reminded of our walks of last spring. L. is as pretty as ever. I am sorry that we cannot be more together. L. escorted me to the corner, and I hastened home for fear Ma would be uneasy, but fortunately she *was out*. A. and I sat on the front steps, relating to each other the events of the day. While thus seated the bus stopped and Lieut. R. [Rosenfield] emerged from it and soon joined us. We sojourned to the house and had been there a few moments when Mr. N. came over, commissioned to bring us with him. We went, although not feeling like it, and honored the Keno box. We played but a few games as the majority was in favor of it. Sunday is A.'s birthday, and Ma proposes to have a little something and requested S. to send up the Champagne. We will have none but ourselves, as we have no intimate friends, and could not ask one without giving offense to another, so we will just have ourselves. Just a little something to celebrate the 19th anniversary of dear Alice's birth. S. accompanied us home. A. brought home the other comforter. It is finished and all we want is Pa's slippers. I hope that we will be able to get some shrimps.

Saturday, November 30th, 1861

7 *P.M.* Oh! I have just had such a fright. Sue came in and handed me a letter, which I immediately recognized as a dispatch. Mr. Barnes' negro had brought it. I ran up with it, and A. and I opened it before telling Ma, who still was quite alarmed before we could tell her what it was. Oh! my hand is trembling. I can scarcely write. It was as follows, "I will write to Fannie Sunday. I am well. Butter by Express yesterday". It rained very hard last night and it is now quite cool. This has been the programme for the past few weeks. And now, Philomen, I must continue this account to

7. Clara was finishing another diary book. At this point she wrote on the frontispiece and leaves of her book, to use every inch of space. She was not able to muster the funds for a diary book on her own, despite her occasional allowance and earnings as a substitute teacher.

your successor. 'Tis useless to attempt to express my regrets on our parting. But rest assured that it could be no greater than were it a friend. I love
you dearly, and *no* one knows with what reluctance. I breathe my last words
in the ear of my most highly prized and favored Philomen . . .

[There are no entries from December 1, 1861, through March 12, 1862.]

8

"*Tents Beneath the Moonlight*":
March 13–April 24, 1862

Thursday, March 13th, 1862

In presenting you with this new robe, dear Philomen, do I bind more closely
to my heart the link of our friendship, our cherished friendship, which has
braved the storms of a year, and appears now more purified, more refined,
for our joys are they not more appreciated, if, in obtaining them, we encounter sorrows? I never dreamed that our *acquaintance* would further expand, and that you would have bound yourself so firmly around the tendrils of my heart, that *your* existence *now* seems essential to my *own*. May
each succeeding month strengthen the ties. You know to whom you are indebted for your present garb, and to be candid with you, I am not at all
pleased with it, and shall take the first opportunity to effect a change.
My reception has not been very cordial, but it is on occasions like this that
my want of knowledge is most strikingly presented to me. One of the greatest gifts bestowed upon man, that of words or language, has been denied
me, and oh! I agree with Quintillian, "*Luxuriance* can *easily* be cured, but
for barrenness there is *no* remedy". How trying is my situation, surrounded
by one whose every thought, every wish can be expressed in most adequate terms. Our defects are never so apparent as when contrasted with
almost perfection. Well, I am almost tempted to hide my diminhedd [?],
and I am almost inclined to feel myself entitled to the punishment of a de-
serter, but I have returned to my post and know you will overlook my
absence. Circumstances were such that I could not conveniently attend to
you, so I will now endeavor to make the reparation that is in my power.[1]
Up to Saturday night no account of events have been transmitted to
you. Ma requested L. to call at the P.O. and to forward to her any letter,

---

1. This diary book is inferior in size and quality to the earlier ones.

which should there be found, directed to her, and bright and early, Sunday about 10 o'clock, he came up and delivered one into her hands, for which he received our many thanks. He remained some time and we had fun, Baby, of course, participating more, perhaps, than ever. Pa was well, and would you believe it said, "I have not forgotten your presents". The remainder of the morning we laughed and talked, always finding something, so much did we have to relate. Showed Baby our new things, which, of course, occasioned much surprise to the "country lady". She and A. dressed before dinner, B. expressing many regrets that her silk was double-skirt, etc., etc. After dinner, I was making my toilette, when from the voices below I distinguished Cousin Sam's, the tyrant, and Leopold. I hastened down, and was in ready demand to complete a set for a quadrille, and a refreshing little dance did we have, L. left with a promise to return, and we extorted from Cousin S. his promise to bring up his accordion and "Jo", the following night. When they went, we were left to our own resources for amusement, and you may depend that we have many. We played on the piano, and sang, much to the discomfort, I dare say of the passers-by. Baby was just beginning to look like herself, and wore a very becoming net of A.'s, to which she had taken a fancy. We were standing by the gate, resolving upon a walk, when the form of Mr. E. was espied in the distance. When he stopped, there was a general titter among us, attributable only to our foolishness. We came in and it was well that he did not perceive any of the sly glances that were aimed at him. He stuck, and stuck, until shades of evening had closed over us. He presented me with a gold tooth pick and ear-picker attached, for which I thanked him, but I think in future years whenever it should be spoken of in Baby's presence it will create a laughter. I appreciate very much the kind remembrance of my "birse day", but he might have given a more appropriate present, for they all declare that a close observation of my organs of hearing induced him to give me a useful gift. But I know to the contrary. I suffered very much with my shoe which I was compelled to abandon. S. came over. He is in great demand, and is regarded in a very favorable light by Baby. Our company was augmented by "D", who, as usual, was not very loquacious.[2] S. went, but there Mr. E. staid as though he were glued to the spot. "D" and I had a little miff, and he made his exit not very pleased. Baby told us the most extravagant things of his and "Caffie's" conduct at the Bay. Mr. E. was immovable. I yawned, Ma yawned, but to no effect.

---

2. Some new "initials" appear in this diary book. "D" is unknown.

Conversation lagged, and then the happy moment arrived when he arose
from his seat, fifteen minutes extra was allowed him, and at its expiration we had the extreme felicity of observing his departure. We had
made an appointment with S. for $4^3/_4$ the following afternoon to pay a visit
to the Free Market, intending to improve our opportunity, as the Crescent
Regiment to which he and Mr. N. belong was to leave for Camp Benjamin
on Tuesday morning. We partook of some supper, and reviewed the events
of the day, and proceeded up stairs, anticipating much pleasure on the morrow. Ma and Baby intended to go shopping. It was some time before we
went to sleep, as we had so much to talk about, Leo. to discuss, and Baby's
regrets to listen to that he was a "Jew". She was *very* much attracted to him.
Unconsciously we fell asleep, visions of Free Markets dancing thro' our
busy brains. The morning dawned very uncertain, but we still entertained
hopes that it would not rain. Ma and B. prepared to go, when a heavy
fall of rain deluged the earth.[3] It ceased and hope had again revived, when
another succeeded. Ma and B. gave up their expedition, and it was
amusing to see us by the window, as intently gazing into the sky, as though
our lives depended upon some circumstance connected with it. Mr Monet
[Baby's father] paid us a visit. He is a dear old man. I love him. He spoke
of Baby's returning, but we as I thought completely overruled him. He said
he would be up on the following day, and would signify his intention. When
I conducted him to the door, the sun was peeping from the clouds and
the old man encouraged us in our hopes. But a short time after the
leaden clouds again o'erspread the heavens, and the rain fell as hard, as
would our tears had we been less sensible girls. During the cessations, occasional notes from A. to the effect of "No Free Market", etc. would indicate that her thoughts were flowing in the same channel. As a parent feels
when he witnesses the downfall of a precious child, and sees that his teach-
ings have proved of small avail, so did we, when we contemplated that the
rain would frustrate all of our plans, not only for the afternoon, but for the
evening. No sky was ever watched so closely, and none ever evinced such
symptoms of rain; but with the spirit of youth there was much hope in our
hearts. To beguile away the moments we played the piano, sang, dance,
talked, during which period the rain fell in torrents, and all hope was abandoned. I deemed it useless to study, as I thought it would be an impossibility to attend school. The heavy shower was succeeded by a calm, and
when A. came home we determined to go. Dressed immediately after din-

3. "B" refers to "Baby" Monet.

ner, and were just in the act of putting on our bonnets when the intelligence was received that it was raining. We quietly replaced them in their receptacles, convinced that the fates were opposed to our going and we lamented the circumstance which had deprived us of so much unforeseen fun. It was the hardest rain of the disagreeable day. At its cessation we went to Mrs. N. where we were greeted by Mr. N. in "tears", as he was going to the camp on the morrow. There is no funnier man when he is in the humor, and he excited Baby's visibilities unusually. Mrs. N. was much grieved concerning his intended departure, and expressed many times that Gen. Lovell had never been born.[4] We girls left Ma and went to take a little stroll on Dryades St. where we halted at "Dr. T.'s", and indulged. Returned home where Ma soon joined us. L. was expected but he did not come to say "good bye". We laid many plans for our amusement, hoping that they would not be doomed to destruction. We retired quite early, imagining how refreshing an influence the "ice cream" would have exercised. Ma and B. went out the following day about $10\frac{1}{2}$ and I devoted the remainder of the morning to sewing after which my books claimed my attention. F. arrived from school and assisted me. Poor child! Her fate is yet unknown. I hope that she is admitted. I ate my dinner, and left before they came, but after Dictation I obtained permission from Miss B. to be dismissed, and hastily wended my steps homeward. Mr. Monet was there, and I received the information that Baby was to leave on the morrow at 5 o'clock. Mr. M. was obdurate. He would have allowed her to remain would there be any regular communication, but Gen. L. had ordered a removal of the troops from the Bay, and there would be no boat. Oh! Gen. L. why were you ushered into this terrestrial sphere.[5] It was so unexpected to me, for we had always been so sanguine, so certain of her remaining. We had gone no place, seen nothing, done nothing; the days she had been with us seemed so quickly to have flown. A. and she were up stairs preparing to go out, as Baby had a visit to pay to one of her dear friends with whom, instead of saying a few parting words, she had anticipated spending more time. Mr. M. left with them. F. and I went out, and she treated me generously. Mrs. N. very lowspirited was at our house. "Sammy" had gone. Before A. came there was a heavy shower which alarmed Ma considerably, but they arrived uninjured. They had seen whom they had wished. The last evening was highly prized, and B. [Baby] was certain

---

4. General Mansfield Lovell, another West Point graduate, came from New York to New Orleans to head the Confederate garrison there.

    5. General Lovell ordered the ship channels cleared of civilian craft.

that we would meet before long. The morning was quite rainy, but I presume you know that if it rains before seven it will clear up before eleven. And it certainly did. B. was compelled to go out as she had deferred the purchase of many requisite articles. I wished that it would rain, in order that I could have an acceptable excuse for absenting myself from school, but despite all my wishes it would not, and I had to study. At 2 o'c. while so doing B. in a sad plight with the mud, made her appearance. We escorted her up stairs, assisted her to unrobe and made an examination of her purchases. She had seen "dear Colon", spoken to him. What fun we would have had going down together to see him. I dressed, and assisted B. in packing her trunk. A. came soon and I was not in a hurry for my dinner, as I resolved to see her go. At 4½ the bell rang, and the carriage which was to convey her away was at the door. I went down to entertain Mr. M. who extended to me a kind invitation to visit them in company with A. in the summer. B. is determined upon it. She came down, equipped to go. The adieus were made, the tears dried, and the carriage rolled away. I went to school, excused myself to Mrs C. Ernest paid us a visit and detained us too long. When I got home Ma and A. were to Mrs N. Capt. S. was over there. I have an indistinct remembrance of him, and he is connected with my recollections of Villere St. A. informed me of the visit of the afternoon, Mr. and Mrs. da Ponte. I was much surprised. They made but a short visit. A. is impressed with the idea that she is affected, and consequently does not admire her as much as formerly. Mrs. N. supped with us, and B. was not missed as much as I had expected. "D" came, and we had a game of Keno, he and I nearly restored to our former relations. He had gone to see Mr. P. but he was out, and "D" reliably informed us that the Confederate Regiment would return in a few days. I won nothing. F. had been to school, but was yet ignorant of her fate. Baby is nearing her home. In a few days shall she forget about us?

Saturday, March 15th, 1862

7 A.M. Here am I again called upon to record a change in fickle weather. Will the time ever come when we shall have an [un]interrupted succession of similar atmosphere! It is cold! and I suppose this circumstance is sufficient to indicate a cessation of rain. I feel so very downhearted! And do you know why? because Mary [the Nathans' domestic] is going to leave us to-day. She is compelled to thro' the interposition of her thousand and one aunts, uncles, and cousins who desire her services at home. She is an estimable girl, and I deeply regret her departure. All our plans for the future have vanished into air. I so dislike to have anyone part from me, whom I am accustomed to see daily, especially when I entertain for them friendly feelings. But these Irish girls, their most fault is in having such a quantity of relations. "Sic transit gloria mundi". Thursday I was just in the act of subduing the youngest member of the Solomons into a state of somnolency, when a ring of the bell startled both of us. It was announced that my services were requested at the Webster Academy. I discarded my charge and proceeded to prepare myself for the pleasant duty. Was soon in readiness and on my way to the horrid Institution, where after being apprised that Miss Cornelius' room was waiting for me, I departed thereto. Everything passed on smoothly and I had no complaints to make. The girls were very obedient and extremely studious. My S. and E. recited admirably, much to my satisfaction. The room is composed, as all are, of some sweet pleasant girls, whom I like excessively. Often would I wish that the apartment [appointment?] was mine. Recess I devoted to my lunch and Scholar's Companion, and the solving of a sum for one of the misses. It is the shortest of half hours, and before I was aware of it the bell had rung. In company with A. and Miss Calder I paid a visit to the lower regions, which falls far from partaking of a pleasant nature. I then repaired to my control, and the two hours passed astonishingly rapid. I dismissed immediately as I was anxious to get home. Did not see Miss D. and as A. was not prepared to go, I went without her. When I got home, can you imagine what an unpleasant communication was made to me? Ma said, "*Fannie is rejected*"! Oh! Philomen, I was so shocked, so grieved! and I did not till then know how disappointed. I previously had some fears but reasoned to myself that they were groundless; but then I felt as tho' an arrow had pierced my heart. I knew that the disgrace would be more keenly felt by us, for she has not the thought to even feel in the matter. She is one of the five of Miss C.'s girls who were rejected. A. and I passed through the High School with so much honor, and it is to be deplored that a stigma should now fall upon the reputation of the remaining daughters. Oh! I felt so badly, worse I know than she did. Her exercises must have been very ordinary in order to class them with those of the others who were rejected, as they are comparatively ignorant girls. F. is smart, but too indolent and dependent to cultivate her knowledge. As badly as I felt, I expected A. to feel worse as the unpleasant task would fall upon her of telling it in School. And when the report becomes so universal, Ma is undecided what course to take, or where to send her as she objects going back to Miss C.'s. How will Pa feel. I, of course, had but little appetite for my dinner, which we ate without Alice. F. was smiling, but I know that her feelings were deeper than they appeared to be, and that she was too much ashamed to give expression to them. "Where are all the hopes she cherished"? All our plans of late seem to have been dashed to pieces. My walk to school was not disagreeable, as my shoes did not hurt, but had they I should scarcely have known, so engrossed was my mind with its all-absorbing topic. I was in season, and had the pleasure of a seat next to Kate, where we kept up quite a spirited conversation. I knew my lessons. Teacher in the day, and pupil in the afternoon. The hour spent with Mrs. F. was very entertaining, especially as dear Belle's arm encircled my waist. We were dismissed early, and after an impressing kiss on her rosy lips, I left the place of my joy and sorrows, and on my path, occasionally hearing "she taught me today", etc. No one was home, but F. and S. Ma and A. had gone out, and R. with Mrs. N. Sallie's little chum, Emma, a dear child, was studying with her, and as a mark, I hope, of her affection, she presented me with a nice piece of cake, which was very acceptable. F. was as usual. The subject was not broached. Yes it was. She said to me, "Clara, what is the disgrace of it?" You can judge for yourself her extent of human knowledge. She is too thoughtless to know. Mr. Foggine paid A. a visit, but unfortunately she was out. Mimi is again her pupil. Mrs N. conveyed Rosa safely home, and shortly after the absentees appeared. They had been to Miss Jo's. She is going on Saturday and A. promised to spend the following night with her. After supper we went to Mrs. N.'s, where we unexpectedly saw Mr. and Mrs. H. The old Captain was there. He is so funny. I believe that he could entertain me for hours. We spoke of many incidents of the past time, and he last remembered me as a little girl of 9, "whom he was prepared to see developed into the young woman of 17". He spoke of the miraculous change that had been effected in Emily. He joined us in our game of Keno, at which I was as usual, not winner. Mr. H. was uncommonly agreeable, and he being my companion, I enjoyed myself. I never think so much of Pa, as in his company. We got home about 11, A. and I with a consciousness of right performed ablutionary exercises. Yesterday, before going to school, A. went to see Mrs. O. as we intend making every possible investigation into the matter. By a note from her, I was informed that my services were indispensable, and mean Miss C. was there. The strongest wind blew all day that I had ever seen, but no rain accompanied it. I sewed, Ma sewed, F. sewed. E. did not come. She was sick. A. returned from school at 2. Miss C., fearful of a storm, dismissed them. Miss C. was shocked, when A. told her and all of her other friends offered their sympathy in the unpleasant matter. A. borrowed "Great Expectations" [the Charles Dickens classic was first published in 1861], and from a circumstance connected with it I feel as though I ought to read it. But pray, where is the time in which to do so? The wind was lulled to rest, and about 4, we had a tremendous rain which ceased before dark, and the clear moon sailed thro' a starry sky. A. did not go to Miss Jo. Another plan frustrated. Dear Rosa was not very well, so Ma bathed her feet; when I came down this morning, she was sleeping. I hope that she may be better today. "Mary leaves today"!!

Sunday, March 16th, 1862

10 1/4 A.M. But a few moments have elapsed since I partook of my breakfast, unabled as I was, feeling so bad to arise from my bed, where dear little Rosa kept my company, for she has indisputably the measles, a disease which is not dangerous, but very contagious and apt to attack those in a house, who have not had it. None of the younger children have had it, and it is Ma's desire to prevent it, if possible, as she does not believe in forcing children to be sick. As they have to have the measles, a few years older is a more pleasant age. Dear Rosa is so patient and enduring. She slept with me last night, and with her restlessness and my sufferings, I passed a wakeful period, and awoke to find myself no better this morning, but since I have risen, I feel considerably relieved. The sun rose upon as lovely a morning as ever dawned, and thousands of people will be wending their way this Sabbath day to the camp of instruction on the Gentilly road, to visit their friends among the Confederate Regiment. How changed we are in this goodly city today from the circumstances of a March Sabbath two years ago! Then, our thoughts mainly involved within the circumscribed boundaries of trade and money-making, how joyfully the day of rest from worldly cares was welcomed on its weekly approach; but now, with fathers, sons and brothers, husbands and lovers away from home, this day is principally featured as the occasion for visiting Camp Benjamin, where so many of our citizens are fitting themselves as soldiers to fight out the sturdy contest that shall decide the mastery of the key of the Mississippi. Many a picnic dinner will be eaten among the tents with a pleasure that can only be appreciated after separation from home, its ties and its comforts, and, Philomen, A. and I expect participating in one of them. Mrs. N. was to go with us, but she has accepted the invitation of Mr. M. and in company with L. etc., will be conveyed there in carriage, while A. and I will avail ourselves of Mr. E.'s invitation, and we shall all meet there. Ma would have too, but for the circumstance of R.'s sickness. A. and I also object going, but Ma will overrule our objections. Mrs. N. has received several letters from her "Sammy" in which he expresses himself delighted with the locality and everything appertaining to it, and represents camp life as pleasant as city, (rainy and windy days excepted, when they are obliged to clutch their tents to prevent them from being scattered to the four winds of heaven). On Friday last my thoughts were often with them, as *I* have had experience of a rainy day in *camp.* It is the general opinion that they will not long remain there. Kind Dr. B. has just gone, and in connection with us, expressed his thanks that it was not the prevalent destroyer, scarlet fever. In tones of gratitude do my thoughts ascend to the Almighty for his kind dispensations, and watchful care of our flock. Yesterday, 7 months ago [15 August 1861], our loved Father took leave of us, and thanks to Him, who dwells above, the physician's services have not been needed. I have perused the paper, and the principal topic is that of — Martial Law. The announcement yesterday of Martial Law being proclaimed startled the timid, but when the people got time for reflection, and seeing the names of the Provost Marshals, confidence was at once restored, and a general feeling of security prevailed the community. One of the many directions which must be immediately complied with is that all places for the sale of liquor will be closed at 8 o'clock P.M. This will be productive of many beneficial effects to our population. Notwithstanding that yesterday was very disagreeable, A., I, and Mrs. N. repaired to our "House of Worship", where very few were in attendance, and the service very short, Mr. Da Silva officiating. To my infinite satisfaction Flora and Beauty occupied seats behind me, so I was spared the necessity of looking at them.[6] After Synagogue, A. went to Jo's, but I felt too ill to accompany her, so came home. It was very cold, and I was partially frozen. Ma was nursing Rosa, who had taken [ill] since morning. Mary had taken her departure, without one fond embrace, one word of adieu. Short lived indeed was her glory. A few moments

---

6. In the absence of Rabbi Gutheim, Mr. Da Silva, the sexton, officiated. There were few formally trained rabbis in the United States at this time.

after who occupied a seat in our dining room but Leopold, who was on a furlough to the city. I did not feel very talkative, so I was glad that he did not remain long. Mrs. N. came over, but went before dinner. I did not arise from the sofa the whole afternoon, and would frequently fall into a doze. At night Ma doctored Rosa, in hopes that she would be well today. Leo. came and was very devoted, and *anxious* to know the cause of my *unusual* laziness. Did I gratify him? An extra was purchased which contained an account of the evacuation of Centreville and Manassas, etc., etc.[7]

Tuesday, March 18th, 1862

7 1/2 A.M. How astonished was I on awakening this morning to perceive the rays of the bright sun peeping thro' the window and gilding all objects in the apartments. My first impulse was to look at Rosa, whose fever is not as high as it was, and who seems, thanks to God, to be in a state of convalescence. Her little face is as speckled as is the sky on a starlight night. My next impulse was to arise and demand from S. her reasons for noncompliance with my request. She asserted that she had made several attempts to arouse me, but as I saw, all had proved fruitless, and I suppose that my sleepfulness is attributable to my wakefulness during the night. Oh! I neglected to inform you that I am safe and sound at home, as from foregoing remarks you had every reason to take for granted. Mrs N. came over and remained some time. A. and I made preparations and with S.'s, were completed at 1 o'clock. Mrs. N. had gone a little in advance as the carriage had come. With many injunctions from Ma to take care of ourselves and each other, and a kiss from her and F. we hailed the 'bus, and were rattling down to Canal St. S. extremely jubilant. After getting there, we were detained a short while for the other 'bus, which fortunately was not much occupied. With the exception of closed stores, the streets had no appearance of Sunday, as there were crowds of persons, the destination of many, I *presume*, being the same as ours. After a pleasant ride, we arrived at the Depot, where we alighted from *our* carriage. We emerged from the crowd and selected solitary standing places, which we did not long retain, as the locomotive came steaming along. We mounted steps,

---

7. These movements must have disrupted her father's business.

and with our escort [Eisner] were comfortably ensconced in its inviting seats; but oh! my thoughts went back to our Jackson Rail Road, and despite my efforts, I *could not* be cheerful. The ride was short and not extremely agreeable, at any rate, to me, as I did not feel quite well. At the station we looked around for Leopold, as he had promised to meet us, but it was certain that he was not there. Mr. E. was acquainted with the road, so we allowed ourselves to be guided by him, and after a tiresome, hilly, marshy, disagreeable unpleasant walk of half a mile, we got to seeing distance of the Camp, and the first familiar form of L. came to greet us. He inquired the cause of our delay, and said that the other party had been down an hour. It was unaccountable, as we had met with no noticeable detentions. He said he had been to the Depot *so often* that they had refused to allow him again to pass the line. He escorted us to his "Island No. 10", assembled wherein was Mrs. N., Mrs. Levy, Olivia, Ludie, Octavia, Mr. and Mrs. Barnett, numerous Jakes, etc., so you can imagine that it could not easily accommodate any more. After saluting the party we proceeded to take off our bonnets, being excessively warm. Oh! everything reminded me so of our beloved camp, that my tears I could hardly restrain. I looked for our dear Major, "O.P.", Capt. White, Dickinson, etc., but in vain, and when they did not appear, I began to realize where I was. On that occasion we were the guests of a Major, and Captains, now of *privates*, but had it been Colonels, we could not have been more hospitably or sumptuously entertained. They invited us to dine, and before the unpretending board, we seated ourselves, where we partook of the delicacies of city life. How little can that Regiment, composed as it is of the wealthiest men of our city, surrounded by every luxury that money can procure, judge of *Camp* life, its privations and its hardships. Leo. introduced us to Mr. Maurice Rice, a young man of handsome appearance, and a most gentlemanly bearing, who with our host contributed largely to our enjoyment. Mr. N. looked well, and is, I think, *too well* pleased with his present life. L. is the kindest most thoughtful of men, and in his endeavors to entertain discarded altogether ideas of self, and devoted himself to us. Dr. Palmer was to speak and about 4 o'clock a vast crowd assembled in front of the rudely constructed pulpit, where the eloquent soon made his appearance.[8] To our comfortable plank supported on 2 stools were we indebted to the thoughtfulness of Mr. R. who carried his design into execution by carrying the

8. A fiery speaker, Reverend Benjamin Palmer was the Presbyterian minister who delivered a famous sermon in support of secession shortly after Lincoln's election. He became a chaplain in the Confederate Army.

board with him. The sun's rays were very intense, and in the absence of parasols we were compelled to resort to our cloaks to hide the glare from our eyes. The service commenced by the chanting of a Psalm, and situated as I was between two such noted gigglers as O. and L. you can well imagine my difficulty in suppressing for a time *my* laughter, and not astonished when I tell you that I did not succeed *very* well at *first*, but when the words of eloquence flowed from his lips, I became intensely interested and would cast reproachful glances at all who were so impious as to appear indifferent. It could scarcely be called a sermon, as it was an address, and not sectional, but well adapted to all classes of religion, which he intimated was his object. He did not speak as much of the present state of the country as was expected, and did not speak much to the Confederates [Home Guard] of an engagement, as I presume, with the majority, he imagines that they will not be in one. In about an hour he had finished, when we repaired to our tent, partook of some refreshments and prepared ourselves to go and witness the Parade, which was to take place at 6 o'clock. And at that parade, did I see represented all the beauty and fashion of our "Crescent City". How can I express to you the many feelings which reigned in my bosom, as I perceived angelic Judo at a short distance from me, in company with her husband who seemed to regard her with a devotedness she could well inspire. Oh! that I could have overleaped the bars of ceremony, flown to her and impressed upon those ruby lips a "kiss". But no! I could but stand and gaze at her lovely countenance, and that privilege for but a few moments was allowed, as I was hurried away by the remainder of the party, who would not have done it had they appreciated my feelings. "Judo" was dressed handsomely, but oh! so so conspicuous. Her fair brow was partly concealed by a white spangled veil, which was to impress a person of her spirituality, for really she looks like an angel, and in my ideas of those heavenly beings, I never conceived of one more lovely. I saw every one that I know or ever did know and earnestly hope that the report about "Dibbie" is unfounded; but I fear not. "Kate Marks" as beautiful as ever attracted my gaze. Amiability beams in every feature, in her soft, dark eyes, and pleading mouth. The handsome Mrs. V. I espied at a distance; oh! should I proceed enumerating all whom I saw, I fear I should never cease, suffice to say, I was content with the array of beauty presented to my eyes. Again we went to our tent to make preparations for our departure. Bade adieu to all of our friends, and promised to see Mrs. N. on our return. L. and Mr. R. accompanied us to the Depot in addition with our original escort. Had I not been so fatigued, I should have enjoyed the walk, as the moon was gliding thro' the heavens, the night was beautiful and I had *so* agreeable a companion. When we got to the Depot we were obliged to wait an unconscionable length of time for the cars, and when they came we almost despaired of getting in and I am confident never should have, but for the indefatigable efforts of Mr. R.'s. Mr. E. not being of any more service than a *stick*. L. left us, and we were soon on our way, and such a jam as it was. I was so fearful of an accident, and just then wondered at Ma's consenting to our going, as she is so averse to any excursions of the kind. My companion was a well grown son of the Emerald Isl., and where the others were was more than I could ascertain, but I know that I should not be forgotten, nor was I, for when arriving at our destination they stood before me. We waited for the rush to subside, and then forced our way out. The 'bus was crowded so we deemed it prudent to take the cars, which were in the same condition as were the 'buses, so in order to arrive at Canal St. what did we do but hail one on its downward course, and remain in it. It occupied some time and I was uneasy for I feared that Ma would be uneasy, and I was right, for she was much distressed particularly as Mrs. N. had been home so long. Ma vetoed our ever going on a similar trip without her. Mr. R. accompanied us home, where was Mr. "D". Since Mrs. N. had gone, some thief had entered her mansion, and stolen from her locked bureau drawer, Mr. E.'s gold watch and chain, which had been put there for safe keeping. It is evidently some one well acquainted with them, who seized the opportunity when all were out, and made no attempts to get possession of anything else, but who the guilty person is will, in my opinion, be a mystery which will never be solved. Mr. E. takes the loss of it very calmly. Well, we related to Ma the leading events of the day, and expressed our indebtedness to Mr. R. for I do believe that had it not been for him we should not have been home *now*. "D" left, and Mr. R. a short time after and we extended to him an earnest invitation to call again, which I hope he will, as I like him very much. We then went up, and I was soon in my bed, and did not know until then how tired I was. Made a fruitless attempt to sleep with Josie, in order that Ma could be with Rosa, "but it wouldn't pay". My excessive fatigue rendered it impossible for me to arise early, and it was fast approaching eight ere I took myself from my couch, and the time until breakfast I devoted to my books, but did not accomplish much, as the intervening space was but a few moments. The day in beauty could well compare with its predecessor, and how great a contrast did it present to the preceding Monday, when Baby and I were so anxiously watching the sky. We have almost forgotten about her. The day,

I passed in R.'s room sewing. Mrs. N. had been over but a few moments, when a message was received that some one wished to see her at home. I studied, and when I had finished did not know my lessons. I did not feel like applying myself to them. Ate dinner with the rest, A. excepted, who is never home, and on my way to school met Mrs. N. who had been out. I knew my lessons, but oh! I feel so discouraged when I think how much I lose by being absent on Saturday. "Ernest Linwood" did us the displeasure to pay us a visit, as he inevitably detains us very late. Returned from school and joined Ma and A. in Rosa's room. In the evening we spoke of our visit; no one came, and we retired early.

Thursday, March 20th, 1862

6 ¹/₂ A.M. When I leave you for a day or two, what changes or what events can not have transpired? But do not be alarmed, I have nothing important to relate, as the thought was only induced by the variable weather. The morning now is bright and beautiful; not a dark cloud is visible in the blue sky, and it resembles the smile which radiates a face after a shower of tears. Tuesday was a very fine day, but quite windy, but *rain,* why I never dreamed of the *possibility* of *such* a thing. As usual sewed. F. is also exercising on doll clothes. In the morning Ma sent her around to Mr. da S. with the order for the Motsoes, for you must know that Pasaic is fast approaching, and Philomen, our butter, our precious butter is almost gone, gone, gone, and what *shall* we do if Pa does not send us more!!⁹ Mr. N. was in the city on furlough, and paid us a visit. To be sure, we asked him "how long was his furlough", and he replied until the following morning, so yesterday he repaired to his "camp of instruction", I should say "amusement". Mrs. Ellis is spending the day with Mrs. N. and came over to see us in company with Mrs. N. She is *very* patriotic, but as the majority very despondent, and thinks that we are gone.¹⁰ I could not control myself when she began to talk; she does render herself so ridiculous, and I am sure that Miss B. would have no difficulty with her, if she was required to read a piece in the aspirate voice.¹¹ When she was upstairs, it was about 2¹/₂ and I was

9. Today the English spellings would be "matzah" [unleavened bread] and "Pesach" [Passover].
10. The war was less than a year old, and New Orleans was not yet in Union hands.
11. The "aspirate" voice refers to pronunciation of a word with an accompanying *h* sound.

sitting down stairs, "otium cum dignitate" with my book in my hand, when the bell rang. S. answered it, and I perceived a female figure, which for a moment I did not recognize; it was for *the* moment *only*, for in the next, I was in dear Lizzie Mix's arms, her lips to mine. It was so unexpected that the emotions of pleasure were not felt. She looked beautiful but as usual was in a hurry. I owed her a visit and she came to see what was the matter with me, and "if I was in the land of the living". She also delivered to me Althea's message that she was coming to see me. I wonder if she will. Lizzie did not remain long, but it was too late for me to wait for dinner when she went, so taking up a piece of potato, I made my exit, much to Ma's displeasure, who wished me to wait for dinner. But no! Normal School girls must submit to sacrifices. In school, Tuesday evenings are the most pleasant, because I have the least to do, and am *out* a little earlier. When I arrived home was informed that Mrs. N. had invited us to spend the evening with her, it being the *16*th anniversary of her marriage. I was undecided about accepting, but no one but Mr. and Mrs. H. would be there. The "Orleans Guards" had gone off in the afternoon, and A. and I were standing by the gate, watching the crowds of people which emerged from that direction when to our astonishment it began to rain, and it was as hard a one as I ever saw. I had made up my mind to go, but then abandoned all idea. A. was not going. Uncongenial company. When it ceased F. came over and said that "if Mrs. H. could come way from down town, we could come just from across the street". Ma and F. went over, and I intended to follow after fixing the suppers, and with my precious shoes encased in india-rubber ones, I skipped over there. I enjoyed her supper very much being quite hungry. Of course played Keno, and while so doing down poured the rain in torrents, to use a common expression it rained "pitchforks", and when it was time to go home, the question was, "how are we to get there"? We waited our opportunity until it slacked and then ran over, but on arriving at our house it poured down again. Mrs. H. took off her dress, left it here, put on our india-rubbers, my shawl, and took our umbrella and started. Of course we examined her garments, and it would have been a wonder had I not wished that I *had* a spencer like hers. The night reminded me of the 31st of Oct. when we remained with Mrs. N. until 2 o'clock A.M. A. was asleep, and R. too, and C. also very soon. You know it is an old saying "Rain before 7, it will clear up before 11", and I most heartily wished that it would do so the following morning in order that my services would be needed at the school, but it did not, anyhow the city is indebted to me for the sum of $2. Nettie has a permanent situation for the

Paulding School, and Lizzie H. fills the vacancy for those months in the Jefferson caused by Nettie's removal. My only hope, faint as it is is the "Garden District".[12] We had frequent showers thro' the day yesterday, and a very heavy one about 2 o'c. which I thought would render it impossible for me to attend School, but it was of short duration and when it had ceased, the sun came out, so I had to prepare myself for the Institution. Ate my dinner, but had no appetite, as the search for a few moments previous for my locket had deprived me of it. As I hoped A. had taken it with her by mistake, and when I beheld again what I had never expected to, I pressed it to my heart in all fullness of joy. At school, Maggie imparted to me the sad intelligence that the present would be her last week at the N.S., as she was going up the country to teach. Miss M. has not been in School for some time past. I wonder what has become of her. Probably I shall pay her a visit. We were as usual detained long on Wednesday, and Mrs. S. gave some curious passing from a book, which I am desirous that "D" shall procure for me. Came home, went to Mrs. N.'s, very much depressed. Her "Sammy" gone. The Capt. was over there but did not remain, as he was certain that it was going to rain. Mrs. N. came home with us. Ate supper, and after, A. made a pretty exposition of her temper. With my eyes partly opened and closed I attempted to study my "Companion". When Mrs. N. left, contrary to the Capt.'s opinions it was a beautiful star-light, chilly enough to indicate that this day would be cold.

Saturday, March 22nd, 1862

7 A.M. I cannot realize that the month of March has so far advanced. I remember in past months when the idea of Ma's going was at its height, this month was selected as suitable one for which to begin to make rations; but now it has come and almost gone, and nothing of the event is spoken or thought of. Oh! I shall be so pleased if these coming three months will pass so rapidly as did the past three, for in the coming time what an ordeal have I to pass through, an examination. The morning is quite cold, and I fear that the day will be cloudy, and no doubt it is preparing for a rain. A. and I shall, in all probability, attend Synagogue, perhaps in company with Mrs.

---

12. Normal School students filled in as substitute teachers.

N. and the Captain. Well, nothing of importance has characterized the latter days. Thursday was beautiful. Mrs N. came over early and spent the greater part of the day with us. I commenced a letter to Pa. It is quite time for us to receive one from him. We had a meatless dinner, as L. was unable to procure any. It is very scarce and dear. But that does not annoy me, as I like shift dinners. Thursday afternoons are the only ones when I enjoy the society of the Miss L. Kate is a sweet girl. I received a *silent*, but very gratifying compliment from Miss Benedict. She regards *me* as an excellent scholar. I know it for she said so. I hope that I may always render myself worthy of her good opinion. The hour spent with Mrs. F. was unusually agreeable, being as I was by the side of "pretty Belle". I was almost ashamed to exhibit to my teacher my limited knowledge of music. I must really try to improve myself in that important accomplishment. I was home very early, and found that A. was out. I reclined with Ma on the bed by the side of Rosa, until, unconsciously the "shades of evening closed over us", when A. returned. She had been to see Fanny B. and had returned her Album, which has been in our possession for some number of months. Sally returned also from her friend, Emma, with her little pocket stored well with the good things of this life. It is a never failing source of speculation how Emma has the privilege of at any time helping herself to the contents of the store. How often in my childish days (and even now) have I wished that my Father was the master of a confectionery. Perfect bliss, must it be. A little book of A.'s on "Love" amused me for a length of time. A. was reading [aloud] the "Missing Bride", and despite all my efforts, her mellifluous [voice] did not possess the power to prevent me from going to sleep. Yesterday was another lovely day. Leopold paid us a visit, being on a furlough until the afternoon. He went to School to see A.; F. at Mrs. N.'s request went over to her house. When I had finished sewing, I read to Ma until dinner was announced. Dear Rosa is very well, but we are obliged to be careful, as they are so susceptible to cold. After dinner, I finished my letter which was quite lengthy. A. had a visit from Eva, and near dark we walked partly home with her. Stopped at Mrs. M.'s, but she was out. Went to Mrs. N.'s and found her *so* jubilant, caused by an almost perfectly reliable report that the "Confederates" [Home Guard] would be up to day, and if so she is going to give a large party, dinner, and if not they are going down there on Sunday. Mr. E. was very disconsolate, probably at the fate of his watch; but his grief is silent as he never mentions it. Mrs. N. asked me if Jim delivered to me a message when he returned the things. I answered affirmatively and repeated it, whereupon she said, "the stupid boy, I thought so". Rebecca told him to say that she would thank her when she came to see her, and of course she was astonished when he delivered no reply. Some negroes can never deliver a correct message. As we were leaving, the lady in question and her husband came in. Got home and found "D" there. I was not astonished when he said he had been sick, as it was easily perceptible in his face. He had made three unsuccessful expeditions to Mr. Parham, and intended to make another (successful) one today. I requested him to procure for me a Grammar, and he said he would comply with my request with all pleasure. He left about nine, and after he had gone, Mrs. N. sent over for Mrs. S. and the young ladies to come over, and if not, we would incur her eternal displeasure. Ma did not wish to go, A. and I either, but to be obliging we went, and I took my letter. Mrs. N.'s spirits were still effervescent, and we had considerable fun. They are going to make extensive preparations for their Camp visit, but could not complete them without Ma; but I think that they will be obliged to, as I consider it doubtful if Ma will go, as she will not leave Rosa, and objects to her going and us staying home, and we will not go without her, or one without the other, as I presume Fanny will represent our party. But we are calculating too hastily. They may be up today. We did not leave until near 11, and were escorted home by R. and her husband. Ma had not yet retired, but had adjourned to the upper regions and we joined her before the pleasant fire and related to her the particular event of the evening.

Sunday, March 23rd, 1862

$7^{1}/_{2}$ A.M. How swiftly the past week has flown, and do we offer up our thanks to God for his watchful care of our darling Rosa, and for her speedy recovery. The morning is beautiful, and the day promised to be a fac-simile of last Sunday, but I am certain that we shall not pass it in the same manner. Yesterday, after breakfast, A. and I prepared ourselves for Synagogue. We had just begun, when a message from Mrs. N. arrived that she was ready. This was a most unusual occurrence, as we always are the waiting party; but we could only account for it from the fact that our clock had stopped, and our idea of the time was erroneous. We commissioned her "to wait", and with all imaginable expeditiousness finished our toilette. It was very cold, and the wind resisted our most earnest efforts, and almost frozen, we entered the "House of God". The bride was there looking as do all of that class, "very sweet", and Sarah N. related to me a very curious circumstance in connection with her, one which I was astonished to find was as universally known as S. represented it. Mr. G.'s [Rabbi Gutheim's] discourse possessed no interesting points, and seemed to fail of its intended object. I am not at all pleased with him. [Neither] Beauty, nor Flora was there, but representations of both; of Beauty, her beautiful little sister. Lina has gone away, to Georgia, her husband's residence. Had a few moments to talk with Mrs. N. and obtained from her funds to the amount of $1. She was going home, we down town. O. and F. being a few steps in advance of us, we hailed them, and walked down to Canal St. with them. When I saw O. was it to be supposed that *I* could suppress my laughter, as the correct representation of *her* laugh arose before me. We parted at Canal St. they going one direction and we that of the Smiths, to whom we intended to pay a visit. While at Blineau's, who should come in but F. just returned from there. We found E. by the door and she was very glad to see us, but reproved us for our long absence. We went up, and as her Ma and Pa were both out we cut up generally. I have arrived at the definite conclusion that E. is much prettier than Ida, and that both are very sweet girls. Little G. as attractive as ever. We remained about two hours, and left there about two, and on our way home could not summon courage to purchase a nut cake. I did not see $1/_2$ the number of ladies on promenade as I am accustomed; there is a visible diminution in them. Our walk home was characterized by no important event, save the meeting of one of Mrs. L.'s negroes, thro' whom we transmitted a message to Henry, which I hope, for the sake of tormenting she has delivered. Then "came gentle thoughts, came gentle thought of Gus". I wonder where he is. On arriving at our mansion, whom to our astonishment did we behold sitting in the room! Why—Rebecca!! How often in sportive imagination had she been there, that I could scarcely credit the correctness of my vision. I kissed her and *was* very happy to see her. A. greeted her cordially, as all her ill feelings have vanished. We had determined to charter a 'bus for the purpose of going to camp, and Mr. H. had done so for the sum of $8, which on consideration, we resolved to be too exorbitant, so she said that if possible she would have the order countermanded, and would send word of the result in the afternoon. She was on the eve of going when we entered, and when she left extended to each *individually* an invitation to come and see her. Who in the course of human events would have ever predicted such a thing. What will Cousin S. say? What will Leopold say? We were then informed that Cousin C. and Emily had been here during the day, and had spent the greater part of it with Ma. I was not, for diverse reasons, sorry that I was out. In the afternoon, Ma went to Mrs. N.'s, and A. and I remained with Rosa. At dark, when Ma came, she apprised us that the omnibus had been countermanded, so we were not home. In the night went over to Mrs. N.'s. Nevertheless she was going on the morrow in the cars, and she and Ma were laboring to think what she should take with her in the form of edibles. I do not know at what decision they arrived, as I went to sleep, and have never since inquired. I would not go today, for I know how disagreeable and cold it must be there, and without a party we could have no fun. F. is going with Mrs. N. and I can assure you that I do not envy her.

Tuesday, March 25th, 1862

7 A.M. It is only by the greatest resolution and strength of mind imaginable that I have not allowed myself to be in a bad humor this morning, for I had a most tantalizing dream last night in which I lavished upon "Judo" the fondest caresses and kisses, and then awoke to find it but—a dream. But how I enjoyed them. Had they been genuine, my joy could not have been more intense. Will wonders ever cease. Here we have had more than a week's succession of cold weather, the coldest of the season; but it will not be of long duration, as the white frost of yesterday predicts rain in three days, so adieu to all fine weather. Today, two weeks ago, Baby was with us. It was the day before her departure. Well, Sunday, Mrs. N., F. started about 9½! It was a bitter cold day, but the sun was brightly shining. 9½ ! A.M! is plenty of time.[13] Mrs N. was slightly displeased at none of us accompanying her. I was quite busy in the morning washing up the gas things, and cleaning up in general. I did no regular sewing, but mended various things, crouched down before the fire, which I regret I cannot transport with me. Rosa has not yet descended, and for her little ladyship are we indebted for the bright fire which blazes in *our* fireplace; but the cold is out on a visit. A. dressed before dinner, but not I. The "principal meal of the day" was enjoyed by all, particularly the "afterclapps", as dear Pa used

---

13. Sarah Nathan, in the company of Fannie Solomon, went to visit her husband at his camp.

to say. I do hope that we shall receive a letter today. To our surprise F. was home by 4$^1/_2$. She had not much to say, but from what she did, the deduction was that she was glad to leave the place, it being so very cold. Into particulars I did not inquire, as I did not care. Later, I was dressed and A. was reading to me "Great Expectations" when the bell rang, and "D" was ushered in. He gave me a book, for which I returned him my thanks, but I do wish that it had never come under his observation, as I know I shall find it difficult to learn. He was considerably better, but not quite well. We had a jolly time with conundrums, riddles, grammars, etc. until Ma implored us to cease with our cases, words, tenses, etc. But he is so well-informed that when he is in the disposition, it is a pleasure to converse with him. He knows everything. His other effort to see Mr. P. was also fruitless. Try, try again!. F. came over with Mrs. N.'s command for us to come over, whereon we returned the answer that we had company, whereupon F. returned with a command to bring the company with us, but we did not act upon this suggestion, and I know when he went that he was not very well pleased, as we had almost given offense, by not asking him if he would go. But I do not admire taking "married men" out with us. If he were single, oh! if! if! if! A small world, but how much is contained therein. R. and Mr. H. were over there, and a short while after the "game" began. As usual I won nix, although I claimed many games. But it is an indisputable fact that the more games you win the less money you do, and a little success at the end counterbalances much ill luck at the beginning. We did not leave until 11! I was very hungry, so helped myself to a piece of bread. When we go to our gate, R. said "Let us have a game of keno at my house tomorrow night; won't you all come down? Aunt Sarah is coming, so be sure and come". To be sure we felt a little embarrassed, but thanked her, and as we were but creatures of circumstances, would avail ourselves of her invitation if Mrs. N. would, as we were destitute of escorts. A. once said "When she invites us to her house, my opinion will be changed". The eventful period had arrived. What strange things happen, and in how many tragedies and comedies are we actors. R. said "Come to see me". The wide bridge had been overleaped. How often when Mrs. N. is going there I would say, "I shall go with you", feeling that should I ever, it would be a fit of insanity. But calculating mortals! How closely is the future veiled. We staid before the fire, talking, and aided Ma in giving orders what to have for dinner. Doubtless in my sleep visions of Customhouse St. and its attractions were before me, but I disremember. Yesterday morning was the coldest that I had ever felt, and during the day

I was uncapacitated for my duties, but was bending over the fire, no doubt in every point resembling the witches of which we read. I began to sew up the seams of my dress. When *will* it be finished? I studied, while so doing M. came, for the purpose of telling us to come down in the night. She had been to Mrs. N. and she had given no definite answer. She [Sarah Nathan] was very low-spirited as the Regiment are in town, and encamped in the Lafayette and Annunciation Squares, and it is thought that they will be there for some months, so she said that if she did not see Sammy she would not go, consequently we sent word to R. that our actions depended upon hers. After dinner, I went to School, and received the intelligence that the hour of commencement was changed to 4! I am delighted. I had plenty of time. Went to see L. in her seat. Miss S. has gone up the country to teach, and L. misses her very sadly. M. was in School. I knew my lessons, and after a kiss from the *pretty* ones, I was on my way home, a few moments after its dismissal. At home, found Ma and A. in a blissful state of ignorance about going. I went to Mrs N. and she was not going, consequently we were not. She was crying about "Sammy", as if she expected him to be up the first day. He is up town, and she declares she will move up there. I staid but a short while, and then told the result to Ma. In consideration of it being our first invitation, she should have exerted herself to go. I hope that R. did not prepare and was not disappointed. After supper, we went over there [to the Nathans']. The Capt. entertained us by himself. I have *heard* of people being unabled to get in a word edgewise, but never saw it verified before then. He talks, talks, all the while and amuses you very well. A. and I laughed. Mr. E. took it to himself, and I know was offended, as he did not offer to see us home. *Probably* Mrs N. will go down to night, *probably we will* accompany her.

Thursday, March 27th, 1862

$6\,3/_4$ A.M. I sometimes think that the 6 o'clock bell will never ring. I wait an interminable length of time and then arrive at the conclusion that it is not going to ring; but my deductions are wrong, for I must remember that 6 does not come as soon at it is accustomed to in the winter months. It is quite cloudy, and I consider it quite possible that it will rain. Can we enjoy a succession of good weather? I suppose it is useless to inform you that it is warm again. At any rate, it will not surprise you. There is nothing of interest in the paper. Gen. B.'s call for bells has been promptly responded to. The planters have sent them plantation ones, and people have donated copper to melt for the purpose of cannons, and I see that he already had sufficient for his purpose. The idea was inspiring to some one, and the poetical effusion, "Melt the bells" did justice to the subject.[14] Tuesday, why let me think. I have no recollection of any important event. I know that it was quite cold, and what else, I disremember. I [remember] also, that I studied very diligently and committed to memory a great large page of the Geography. I am delighted beyond expression that School does not begin before four. It allows me so much time, and I need not be so anxious about dinner. Mrs. N. hinted the probability of going to R.'s, but in consequence of her drooping spirits changed her mind and went to the camp to see her Sammy. I am desirous of beholding their [the soldiers'] new habitation. It was a wise movement to locate them there, as it insures the safety of the city. As I was coming home from School, little Clara F. informed me that if I went home, I would not see my sister, as she and another lady had gone to Mrs. P.'s. I was glad of the information and determined to join them. I was ushered up into Jo's room where was Ma, and A. and little Josie, on a visit to her namesake. Jo returned to the city a few days previous, in anticipation of the impending battle she wishes to be here in order that she shall receive her dispatches more expeditiously; but if it does not occur at the expiration of the week she will return to Mrs. B. who was very loth to part with her. J. looked very bad, and as usual traces of tears were on her face; but in my opinion, she bears up very well, for I, I could not stand it at all. Ed writes every day, and is in the enjoyment of his good health; and this knowledge is a great satisfaction to her. Mrs. P. was very busy packing up, as there is to be an important change in their domestic affairs. Sister C. is going to join her husband in Texas, and Mrs. P. is going to take charge of her house during her temporary absence. As Jo objects to emigrating so far into the woods, she is going to remain with a friend. I am sorry that they are going to move. But what else is to be expected. It is enough that we know them. Jo thinks that there is a prospect of her becoming in the course of *9* or *10* months, a *mother.* Were Ed only

14. General Pierre Gustave Toutant Beauregard, son of a Creole sugar planter, was a West Point graduate and a favorite in his home state. After being successful at Bull Run, Beauregard irritated President Davis to the point where Davis removed him from command in June 1862. His call for bells was heeded, but the bells never left New Orleans. They were found by the Union occupying forces, sent north, and sold for $30,000.

with her, her joy would be intense. But in such a *condition* and he away from her. Away from her at the time when of all, he wished to be with her. The thought distracts her. We got home before dark. Emma and Sally, as usual, together. I hope that the intimacy will be of long duration, as E. is a sweet child. After supper, Ma and F. went to Mrs. N.'s. A. passed the evening in reading, I studying my Rhetoric which was very difficult. I had no idea that in the "Formation of the English language" so many obstacles had to be encountered. We remained up until Ma's return. Mrs. N. went to camp. There was a great crowd as is daily. To think of soldiers, real soldiers camping in our squares, the places devoted to the gathering of our children. Tents, real tents scattered around. Who, a few years back, would have imagined such a thing. Yesterday morning I wrote my History, which was not very lengthy. We are all complaining of our loss of appetite. My breakfast, which I once enjoyed can scarcely tempt me, only when there is cream-cheese, for to that am I devotedly attached. Little Josie was unwell, and had every symptoms of the measles, but is now better. I hope that she is not going to get it. She seems better this morning. About 10 o'c. Mr. and Mrs. N. paid us a visit. He was on furlough until 3 o'c. and they stopped on their way to R.'s. He looked very well, and is much pleased with his new life. Since Mrs. N. sees how satisfied *he* is she had made up *her* mind to be likewise, and is not going to fret a particle more. She will be lonesome, but one of us will be with her the greater part of the time. I have promised to sleep with her tonight. She told us that Mr. E. was going to go away from them, but entered into no particulars then as she was in a hurry. Ma is very uneasy about Pa, and as she was going to see Miss E. about F. she intended to go down to the Express Office. She left home after 12, and returned about $2^1/_2$, very much fatigued as it was very warm. At A.'s room she had met Mr. and Mrs. N. on their return home. She said that she would, would send word in the afternoon. Ma also told me that Mr. E. was much offended with A. and me, and that was one of the excuses he offered for his departure. He is the most foolish "big Indian" that I ever saw. There was nothing for Ma at the office, but there had been no mail for a week. When A. came home and I told her about Mr. E. she was as dumbfounded as I when the intelligence was communicated to me, and joined with me in declaring him a fool. Ma is angry about it, but I am sure we did not *mean* to laugh at *him*. It was general. I went to School, and had the satisfaction of knowing my lessons. Mrs. S. had some performances in the Diagrams for which I was very grateful, as I am deprived of the instruction received on Saturday. Amanda, Kate and M. were present. It was quite late when I got home, and I found Ma and A. dressing, so it did not require much thought to guess for what, so I "pitched in" with all my might. When I began, A. had almost finished, and tho' *I* had my hair to comb and everything to do, I had finished before her. But how I was done, I don't know, as I did most in the dark. Often I would say to A. "for what are you dressing"? and she would as often reply "to go to Rebecca's", in imitation of a mother who when her daughter was dressing for her wedding said "My child, why are you getting your hair combed"? "To get *married*, Mother". But laying *that* aside, who could have foreseen that hour. Yes, "going to Rebecca's" [Harris, in the French Quarter], and I did not know how anxious I was to go. The Capt. was to be our escort. We hailed an omnibus which proved to be full, so we had patiently to await another which in due course of time arrived and in we stepped on the "*way to Rebecca's*". Canal St. was reached and every step brought us nearer to her mansion. At the corner A. whispered "Cease thy wild beatings, my heart", and I reiterated her words. A moment more we were ascending *her* steps, a moment more at her door, a moment more kissed by her, a moment more ushered into her brilliantly lighted hall, a moment more and *it all was over*. We went up into her room, took off our things, and surrounded by such royalty, I never was. Her spacious apartment was handsomely furnished and I could not refrain contrasting it with hers, "when first she came out here". Maggie was sitting in the room studying, and when we went down, she did not join us. We descended to the illuminated parlors, and I felt no embarrassment. I could not realize it. She was mistress of a mansion like that, and the contrast between it and Gabrilla's home was marked, and the Lord [Rebecca's husband?] why he would suit very well. He was not in, but presently arrived. Our destinies, our destinies! By whom can they be revealed. Never in her girlhood fancies did her aspirations reach higher than her present attainments; and not only with every comfort that wealth can bestow, but with a model of a husband, on whose fortune it is but for few girls. I was so full of thoughts and meditations that I was almost inanimate. Everything that I had heard recurred to my mind; her dinner parties, Cousin S., Isabell G; her grand party etc., etc. things which when related I had not the most distant conception of seeing the place of their occurrence. She had her Keno table fixed and said that she had been waiting an hour, so to make reparations, we immediately began operations. We were soon joined by the Master and I never saw him so lively, so agreeable (I presume because I had never been entertained by him as a guest). He was very glad to see, and seemed to spare no pains to render the coming pleasant. There was only one interruption in our game and that was when summoned to supper. They said that they had a nice supper Monday night for us, but now we would have to take what we could get. Their dining room! What a contrast to ours! I ate plenty as I was very hungry. Oh! mentally, ejaculated I, this is the way to live, and I believe if I went often to aristocratic houses, I would be unmanageable at home, I would be so dissatisfied. Whenever I turned at the table, there was a negro at my elbow to administer to my every want. Silver in profusion; *everything* of the finest quality. Only once A. and I were tempted to laugh, and that was when the toothpicks and finger bowls were handed, but to suppress our mirth, we suggested that the meeting should adjourn. On our return to the parlor R. favored us with a few tunes, and then we resumed the game uninterruptedly until 11$\frac{1}{2}$, when I stopped no better off than when I began, and A. the fortunate possessor of $1.50 more. After a short discussion prepared for our departure. Jim was ordered up and descended with our trappings, which we donned. Bade the lady good-bye and were told to come again soon. Mr. H. insisted on accompanying us home which he did to Triton Walk. The walk was very pleasant and seemingly short. The Capt. slept to Mrs. N.'s. We did not go to bed immediately, but conversed on one of the epochs (!!!!) of our lives.

Saturday, March 29th, 1862

7 A.M. Oh! Philomen, do I usher in this morning with a heavy heart, heavy with my own individual sorrows, which I shall not weary you with recounting. But I do feel so *bad*. Thursday morning there was a little muss relative to Keno, and inseparable with it here, and a remark Ma took unwarranted offence and has been very unreasonable and chilling; since Thurs. she was an ice berg and for nothing. If punishment is to be inflicted I far rather prefer that it should be merited. I sewed down stairs by myself, and continued so until 1, when I willingly relinquished it for my companions, my books, but Ma was so selfish in my allotted time that I had scarcely time to master my lessons. Dear little Rosa made her debut down stairs, Josie is not yet sick but has the symptoms, I think, of the measles. I left for School, before A. came. Kate was not there, but Amanda supplied her place. I knew my lessons, and then came the "pleasantest" hour of

School, the singing one, when I could be next to Belle. It is the first time that I was ever on speaking terms with a really pretty person, and I so earnestly asked B. if she were aware of her extraordinary personal charms, if she did not know that her eyes were surpassingly lovely, as liquid and soft in their radiance as any which had ever inspired a writer; if she did not know that her complexion was like alabaster without its paleness and that her mouth was perfect. She bade me hush, and called me a "silly child". But I gazed upon those cherry lips and with all the passion of *my* heart pressed mine to them. When I see her beautiful hair, I think "how lovely", and when I behold those orbs of "blue serene" I think "oh! nothing can be lovelier", and when I see that mouth, as ripe and delicious as the fruit just plucked, I say "oh!" for a lovelier sight do I care not. She knows that she is pretty, but let me tell you a secret, *she places no value upon its possession.* I encircled her waist with my own arm, and thought, "Oh, if her heart could only reciprocate the love which mine *could* yield to her". I arrived home not in a very excellent humor, (as the green-eyed monster took possession of me when I saw her and M. walk home together) and found Fannie B. there. I don't know why, but I felt so fatigued and left A. to continue as the host. F. did not remain much longer, and when she left, we walked a short distance with her. I then returned to my mansion, and joined the children in their occupation of picking lint to be sent to various depots in view of the impending conflict.[15] Shades of evening closed over us and we remained out doors, when a form darkened the gateway and we told Leo. [Leopold] that he just came in season to see what *we were doing for him.* He was out on furlough, as he always is. He is rather tired of his camp life. Ma and Mrs. N. came. They had been to camp. Crowds were there, and many girls promenading without their bonnets, thereby rendering themselves very conspicuous. If all the girls go there I hope that A. and I will be exceptions. We amassed a quantity of lint, and L. was very affectionate, I went home with Mrs. N. to sleep with her; L. accompanied us there and remained a short while. He was very solicitous that A. and I should pay a visit to his camp, but I hope that we will prove an exception to the girls.[16] The momentous question of marketing being settled, Mrs. N. and I retired. Had a short talk in bed, and I was soothed to sleep by the sweet voice of Mrs. Plowell. I have no remembrance of the night as I did not awake, but remember being very astonished when I woke in the morn-

15. The lint, to be used for dressing for wounds, went to various locations in the city in preparation for a Battle of New Orleans that never took place.

16. Visits to a military camp were no longer of interest to Alice and Clara.

ing and found where I was. Mrs. N. got up before me to write a note and to dispatch F. with some things to Mr. N. I named the bed posts, but who I dreamed about I have an indistinct recollection. Descended, read the paper, and then partook of breakfast. F. returned with the message that he [Sammy Nathan] would probably be home. They are allowed the privilege of 3 days furlough each week. About 10 he came, staid a few moments with us as he was anxious to go on the Levee. When he left Mrs. N. made up her mind to go out, her principal object to get him a flannel shirt, and I made up my mind to go with her. I went home to dress, but as the morning was cloudy, we decided upon not making *very* elaborate toilettes, and I again joined her in a short time. (Elburger has gone). The 'bus deposited us at Canal St. Our attempts in several stores were unsuccessful in procuring the required article, so we were compelled to resort to the common expedient of buying a shawl, and cutting it to suit the purpose, and we were troubled at the thought that he would not be pleased with our selection. We made several other purchases of minor importance. Went to R.'s, but as it was late and Mrs. N. feared her spouse would be home, we did not remain long. Went to Blineau's, and found that the soda had raised to a dime. We were soon in the 'bus rolling o'er the stony street. Passed the Camp which more resembles a picture than an incident of real life. Mr. N. was home, and delighted with our purchase. I did not dine with them as *Ma* had willed it otherwise. I was very mad and ate no dinner home. A. did not come from School until 4¹/₂. Ma went out and A. and I had a long chat. She and Miss D. are now on speaking terms. I could not record all their disagreements and reconciliations. She showed me a sweet note she had received from "Beautiful Annie". It was to this effect "Sweet Alice, come and see me, a world of love and happiness waits to greet you". A. intends going to see her today. They are indebted to Miss D. for their acquaintanceship. Mrs. C. is so love[ly]. A living representation of wax work. If she only loved me. We remained talking until most dark, when I went by the door to turn rope for the children. After supper, Ma went to Mrs. N. and before 9 o'clock A. and your humble servant was in bed and I would not have been the least astonished had our dreams been of Ernest Linwood.

Sunday, March 30th, 1862

7 *P.M.* We have had a whole week of delicious spring weather. Not a cloud, not a cold blast, not a drop of rain has there been to interrupt the reign of constant sunshine and balmy airs. The thousands of flowers with their myriad colors and profusions of scents, the blossoming and bearing fruit trees, the springing grass and sprouting harvests make our garden district never more delightfully attractive than it is at present. Our city is now a camp; up town and down town. The Home Guards are bestowed conveniently for use at a minute's warning. The past week has seemed so long. Was it only last Sunday that the excursion to Camp Caroline was on foot? And what a change in the weather. Then how cold, now how hot. We have no letter from Pa, and I am real uneasy. Since his departure, so long a time has never elapsed between any two. But I hope there is one for us today. No inquiries were made yesterday for us at the P.O. I see in the morning's paper the marriage of Dr. Folwell, "Envied" "Nina". With *that* exception there is very little matter of interest. Had I the necessary funds I should have procured the Delta. I wonder what has become of "D". Ma and Mrs. N. anticipate going to market after breakfast, which I presume will be sewed up soon. Dell is not very well, I have not the slightest doubt she is getting the measles, *then* it will go all through. Josie is not well. Yesterday A. attended Synagogue without me as I did not feel like going. Emma came to spend the day with S. and brought some cakes etc. with her. F. went to Dr. S.'s but he was out of the city, so back she came. A. and Mrs. N. returned home about 1½ and I gleaned from them the events of the synagogue. Beauty, looking angelic, was there and after that I cared for none besides. Oh! to be the object of her love, for her to press her lips to mine and say "Clara, I love you". Will the yearnings of my heart ever be satisfied? Will I ever find that congenial spirit? I dressed S. before dinner. I miss Mary then, for were she here that duty would devolve on Lucy. After dinner, as A. was preparing to go out, Mrs. N. sent over to know if we would go with her to see the Confederates drill. I did not want to, but I knew that if both returned negative replies that she would be angry, so nothing was left to me but to accept her invitation. I assisted A. to dress, for as she was going to "Annie's" she wished to look her best. She escorted me to the corner and then our paths diverged; she east, I west. Mrs. N. was not quite ready, but was before the lapse of many minutes. The walk was very unpleasant, as we selected a disagreeable street, through which we ultimately arrived at the Levee where were collected crowds of ladies wit-

nessing the maneuvers of the "crack Regiment". We obtained standing places, which we retained the whole time. Mr. N. and L. were fortunate to stand before us and in the intermission between battalion and dress parade they came and spoke to us. It was a beautiful sight, as pretty a one as I ever saw, and the men should have felt honored at the gathering of so many fair ones. The dress parade did not end until dark and was seven ere the Exhibition had concluded. We were very fatigued from standing and blessed him who invented 'buses when we were comfortably seated in one of them. Arrived home safe, disrobed. A. soon returned. Had been to "Annie's"; glorious accounts of her! I retired early.

Tuesday, April 1st, 1862

7 A.M. April, with its sunshine and its flowers, do we usher in today and my own conceptions seem to deceive me when I write April 1st! Oh! how sinful but I cannot refrain from expressing the wish that the succeeding 4 months had passed. Oh! I am so tired, so weary! so sick of school. I was up before six, and here I have been penning, ciphering, until my brain is dizzy and every nerve seems to be deprived of its strength. I can imagine no life so happy as that one which is "schoolless". I am tired, yes heartily tired of studying. In fact it is too much for me. I shall sink under my many trials.

Notwithstanding the "state of our country", I shall venture to say that there will be many jokes perpetrated today. It is a great pleasure. As with love, far better to give than to receive. How many years ago it is that poor Rachel sent Ma those delicious batter cakes stuffed with—cotton! I cannot pay as much attention to you, as I would like for I already have a dull pain in my breast from continual stooping. Sunday we perceived that Dell and Josie were peppered with the measles, but both are now doing very well. Nelly's turn will next come. It is excellent weather for it. The greater part of the day I devoted to sewing. Ma was occupied with J. who, as may be expected, is extremely cross. The most important event was the race between A. and me but in a few moments after we were on amicable terms. After dinner we dressed. I combed my hair "Marie Stuart", but it is impossible in any style to make me look presentable. Mr. and Mrs. N. were our first visitors, and they were succeeded by Mr. Eisner, whom we were quite glad to see. He had been sick which accounted for his absence. He remained until dark and left a few moments before Mr. and Mrs. N. who gave us strict injunctions to come over to their house. We considered it doubtful, as we did not wish to go without Ma. A. and I took a short walk and when we returned the gas was light, Sally was entertaining her company and F. was to Mrs. N. E. favored us with a few songs. She had a very fine voice. "D" did not come. Oh! I am so fearful that he is offended, for Ma will have more to talk about. I was astonished at his non-appearance. He may be sick, but I consider that doubtful. Oh! I [am] certain we offended him. But I am sure unintentionally. F. came about 8½ with the startling intelligence that R. was not to Mrs. N. "Surely", thought we, "Something of great importance must keep her from Keno". I went to sleep with "Ernest L." in my hand, and thought that then was fit time to retire for the night. Yesterday Ma remained home until 11, in expectation of a letter, when, as none came, she dressed to go down town to see something about one. During her absence I studied diligently. Of all school days, Mondays do I *most* dislike. I was very anxious for her return but when it came we were in possession of nothing more. L. had gone to the P.O., but—. He bade her to suppress all anxious fears, as the mail was very irregular. Ate dinner without A. but she came before I left. Nothing interesting transpired in the Institution. When Mrs. S. asked me for my exercises, my heart sickened within me. Old L. paid us a visit. I hate him. I walked home with Liz. and Alice, the first time for many months. In school Maggie informed me that R. was sick in bed, which news I transmitted to Mrs. N. whom I found at our house. A. and I went to walk, and indulged in a most romantic treat, *"very cheap"*. Mrs. N. spent the evening with us. "D", non est. He is certainly mad. I am sorry. Leopold honored us. He had considerable fun about "Shyster Myers" an appellation given to *our* Cousin by the True Delta.[17]

Thursday, April 3rd, 1862

6 ½ P.M. In the midst of a most pleasant dream, one relative to Pa, I felt a tremendous shaking at my shoulder, which on arousing to perfect con-

17. See introduction, n. 8

sciousness I perceived emanated from L. I jumped up, dressed myself, came down, and here I am. Well, I do think it the strangest thing in the world that we do not hear from Pa. I fear that his luck has been so ill that he dislikes to inform us of it. I am very uneasy. There are no letters in the P.O. as Mr. N. and L. inquire each day, their furloughs not being at the same time. I hope that our hearts will be *gladdened* today by the receipt of one. And now, how sad a thing have I to relate. *Our butter is gone!* Gone! how that sound falls upon the ear, and our only hope of enduring future existence is in the prospect of getting more. How earnestly do I hope that our wishes may be gratified. Our patients are doing very well. J. is so very cross, and her screams and Ma's slaps awoke me last night. My *heart* is so much lighter this morning. I did not get fooled once on Tuesday, and in fact I heard so little about it that until evening I totally forgot about it. Mrs. N. stopped in on her way down to R.'s; quite jubilant because her lord was with her. No important event marked the day. I walked to school with Alice, the first time for many a month. Was there quite early, and until Miss D. came, amused myself watching the entries of the different young ladies, some pretty, some otherwise. When Miss D. came I prepared some exercises for Mrs. Shaw, which occupied my time until Miss B. came. "Dictation" was the programme until 5 when we repaired to our "Reading room", where I received many compliments from the teacher for my fine clear voice and excellent elocution, and chid[ed] me, so endowed, with saying "I can't" in some branch of reading. "As if", said she, "a person as gifted as you could not accomplish *anything*". I thanked her in looks, if not in words. At six, we were dismissed. I walked home with A. and partly with Liz. She is not teaching now. When last heard from Miss L. she was very well. I had expected to see Mrs. C. home, but was disappointed and found Mrs. N. in her stead. A. and I took a walk and coming home had a little spat which resulted in our pursuing different paths to arrive at our destination. E. came in with super abundance of cakes, which were quickly disposed of. I did not feel very well in the evening so found it impossible to study. I, however, made up for it yesterday morning. I expected rain, but it did not come and there is no prospect now of it. I sewed on my pink silk. Oh! there is so much sewing that I am almost discouraged when I commence. I had every occasion to remember that it was Wednesday as our lessons were extremely difficult and I devoted my whole mind to them and then had the satisfaction of but knowing them imperfectly. A. entered as I was going. I can't imagine why she will remain so long in that room after school is dismissed. I was quite early in School, and after succeeding in borrowing a

Geography, I studied it. I like to watch the entry of the different girls and observe how each one serves to swell the number. My friend, Miss D., soon arrived. I find her so pleasant. Well, happily to say, I did not fail in my recitations, but I was almost worn out before the dismissal, and should have been completely so but for Maggie, and we mutually contrived to keep up each other's strength and spirits. I had inspired her with a sense of right in the cultivation of her nails and she was much honored to see the progress they had made, as she had not bitten them for 3 days. I tried to encourage her in the accomplishment of the noble work, for *I* know by experience that it is *one* of the greatest victories which a person can achieve, and I often wonder at myself ever having attained it, but I can attribute it to nothing else than a feeling of pride which maturer age served to develop. In school (high) it was the lament of my companions that "*such a dear little hand*" should be abused. M. and I conversed upon a variety of topics, Belle included (oh! how beautiful she looked), and I am confident that our inattention did not escape Mrs. Shaw. In a few moments conversation with Nina, she informed me that Miss M. had left school. She never mentioned a word to me. I do so dislike such sly-handed movements. It was quite late before we were free and then with the impress of dear Belle's lips upon mine and sallied forth, as usual, alone, but so absorbed in thought that I was unconscious that I was at the corner of my home. Went up to see Josie, and went over to Mrs. N. where was A. As we were seated on the steps, a fine looking soldier turned at the corner, stopped at our gate and who but did not recognize him as "D". I went over alone, A. not wishing to leave Mrs. N. alone. He acted so strangely that he alarmed me, and I feared that he was really offended. But on further examination I found out that he just had a little attack of the blues, occasioned no doubt by his recent indisposition, which had interfered with his arrangements of going away. He was grieved that we were uneasy about Pa, and expressed himself willing to do anything for us and said that he would send to the P.O. the following. He explained to us very definitely the significance of the perplexing word, at which R. was very much surprised and could not refrain from saying, "Ain't you ashamed of yourself". Having an engagement at $7\frac{1}{2}$, he left a few moments before that time and bade "Good bye" with a — —. I said not a word to him or he to me, respecting Mr. P. As A. had returned I went to Mrs. N. knowing that she would be lonely. Took my book with me but did not accomplish much. I staid until about 9, and she expressed her thanks to me for my company. I was just in time home, as they were preparing to go to bed.

Saturday, April 5th, 1862

6 1/2 A.M. A balmy, Spring morning! And oh! the lightness of my heart capacitates me to enjoy it. The circumstance which tended to produce this change I shall in time relate to you. Summer is indisputably approaching. Its warm breath is already felt. Oh! how I should like to leave the hot, dusty city & repair to some sequestered vale where rumors of war & crime would never be wafted to my ear. I presume that there will be many "can't get aways", & in fact people would be alarmed for their safety to go to our watering places; but we are going to attempt (I pray) to better our condition by removal to a more pleasant house, if we can be so successful as to find one in the searches which Ma & Mrs. N. intend making in quest of suitable mansions. Now, there is very little prospects of Ma's leaving the city, so she protests that remain in this "hot house" she will not. I recommence operations on our barêges last Thursday with the vain hope that they will be finished by the holy days, which are fast approaching.[18] Next to the difficulty of *getting* a dress is the decision of how it is to be made — White spencers are all the rage, of course I am captivated with them. Allow me to express the hope that I may have as many as I desire. F. & R. went down to Dr. S.'s but returned shortly, he being unable to lend his professional services. Before 12 I received by beautiful Minnie a note from A. informing me that my services would be required at 12½, as Miss D. was going out, & I was to officiate in her place. This tiding was not pleasing to me as it interfered with *my* arrangements, so with not a very good grace I prepared myself & when my toilette was completed my usual equanimity was restored & by 12½ I presented myself before the gate of the School. The few remaining moments of the recess I spent with "Sacquez" & A. & at their conclusion was at my post. Imagine me at the head of 60 children. I was almost inadequate to the task. As I expected, the children were quite unruly in the absence of their teacher & it resisted my efforts to reduce them to a state of quietude. Miss D.'s order is not good, but I presume that it must be a difficult matter to subdue so many young, restless spirits. I felt sorry myself for the little things, but in a School-room order must be preserved. Some were very refractory, but I did not feel inclined to fulfill her injunctions by inflicting such punishment as I thought proper. Judge Brice paid me a visit, but fearing to make a passage thro' the mass

18. Clara refers here to Passover, the weeklong holiday commemorating the exodus of the Jewish people from Egypt.

of little ones, he contented himself & (me too) at a very respectable distance. The continual buzz in which I was surrounded had a powerful effect upon me for at the dismissal of school I was worn out. If I were a teacher
some of those little dears would twine themselves around the tendrils of
my heart. I studied before I came home, & when I arrived there the delightful intelligence greeted me that Ma had received a letter, & with tears
of joy, did I gaze upon the hand-writing of one so enshrined in the portals
of my heart. My pleasure was soon abated when I became conscious of
the contents. It was dated from Lynchburg & had been many a day on
its journey — Pa says that when Manassas was evacuated, & they were
compelled to remove that he can safely estimate his losses at $30,000! To
think, says he, that we should lose all for which we have been so striving
for, for months, in a day — Their handsome building was completed on the
very day that orders were received to abandon the place & before night
they applied the torch to it, & now in its stead is a mass of ruins — It was
a very hazardous enterprise & most injudicious move, which is a matter of
surprise to us as Mr. H. is very farsighted. But fortune is as fickle as war
& we should thank God that he is in the possession of his health but I hope
that he may soon rally from his despondency, & though very trying, apply
himself with renewed vigor.[19] The letter was very brief & contained
$200. With lighter hearts than for many days did we gather around the
dinner table — He was well! No accident had befallen him! God be praised.
I went to School, & knew my lessons as well as if I had studied as diligently
as I had intended; but my peace of mind for fear that I *should* miss was not
as great. Kate & I sat together & aided each other. Oh! I can't divine
how people can be cold & undemonstrative. If I like a person, at first sight,
I must tell them so & *kiss* them. Amanda & I are very good friends & the
hour spent with Miss B. is very pleasant, much more so than the anticipated one with Mrs F. promised to be, as I feared to display my ignorance
in the musical line. But Belle & I assisted each other, & I braved the storm
much better than I had expected. Oh! P., she is so pretty. When our lesson was finished little Clara F. favored us with a few songs — I lingered near
Belle & for fear of stealing the 6th kiss, stole myself away. Josie was doing well. I did not feel so weary until I got home. I laid on the sofa from
which I was unable to rise, except to partake of some supper & then to ascend to the upper regions. Before going to bed, I decided to comply with
A.'s request & pen Miss D. a few lines, & ever since, I have been regret-

---

19. The amount of the loss, $30,000, was their expected profit, as the building itself would not
be worth that amount.

ting the idle waste of time, I employed in doing it yesterday morning, & when it was completed, I was undecided whether to send it fearing that its ironical tone might offend her, as I spoke in flattering terms of her apartment—After A. was in School she wrote me word that Miss D. had learned from some girls the behavior of the majority & A. had heard unmistakable signs of castigation with all its "concomitant melodies", so she decided not to dispatch the missive, as considering her state of mind it would but serve to increase her anger & I agreed with her. She was desirous of knowing if I had left any record. But intending to be lenient, I hadn't. I sewed diligently *all* day, but cannot see what I have accomplished. I do wish that our dresses were in a condition to be worn today as "I have nothing to wear". Josie was very cross! Poor child, she misses the street. Dell has not left her apartment. When A. came home, she apprised me of the fact that Mrs. C. was coming to see her in the afternoon, so after dinner, we made additional changes in the rooms in order to make them look "bon ton" [clean and comfortable]— While redressing, the bell rang & it was *she*. A. went down in rapturous glee, Ma soon joined her, but I, foolish I, was too diffident to go into the room, but I remained outside listening to the sweet music of her voice, & I am sure I should never have summoned the courage, but for the circumstance of the ringing of the bell & the entrance of "D" when I made a bold movement & joined them too—You may know how I devoured her with my eyes, & yet she is not as beautiful as I had expected; her features are not regular, but the tout ensemble is decidedly handsome. She is so lively, so girlish & seemingly so unaffected. The glances which "D" cast upon her convinced me that his views concurred with mine. We had a mutual friend in Major Wheat, & our encomiums passed upon him I know would have been flattering to him. She spent a day at Camp Moore, & seemed to be as delighted as were we. I think she is beautiful & yet how much more attracted I am towards a blonde. She staid until dark & we passed a most pleasant evening & I was very glad that I was prevented from accompanying her & A. as I know that they wanted to court, & I did not want to intrude, so with a passionate kiss, I bade her "good bye", & thanked her for her kind invitation extended to me—A. returned shortly, & Mrs. N. honored us. Leo. came & a few seconds after "D" took his departure. Mrs. N. had been to R.'s. She is convalescent. About $8^1/_4$, while we were quietly seated chatting the bell rang which quite startled us. When the door was opened, I heard the inquiry "Is this Capt. Solomon's house", & the emotions which agitated me, oh! how numerous & torturing. I so feared that some revelation was to be made that I resorted to my usual habit of stopping my ears & watching the countenances of the party, thus being able to judge of the character of the disclosures. Their faces assumed quite a placid expression, & seeing the stranger walk in, I felt a little curiosity to know what it was about. I was soon satisfied as the gent introduced himself as Mr. Duncan & delivered to Ma a letter from Pa. Pa has often spoken of him in his letters & represented him to be one of his intimate friends. We were so glad to see him. To see some one directly from Pa, some one whom he esteemed. Ma had written to Pa in the day, so she added a few lines & Mr. D. volunteered to bear it to its destination. The letter, I think, was from Gordonsville — It was quite brief, & he seemed to be reconciled to his great loss. Mr. H. is going to remain at G. & Pa is going to camp. He says "this letter will be handed to you by Mr. D., a perfect gentleman". Pa's recommendation is sufficient. He is a very intelligent & agreeable man & Pa's selection of him for a friend will vouch for this. Pa & him became acquainted thro' his children, two little boys to whom Pa took a great fancy. He staid an unconscionable length of time & Mrs. N. & L. left before him. We charged him with numerous messages to Pa & he was kind enough to answer our various questions.

Sunday, April 6th, 1862

7 *P.M.* Oh! Philomen, I had a most tantalizing dream just before waking. I dreamed that my dear Father had returned & my lips were pressed to his in all the fullness & joy of daughter's love — All dreams are unpleasant. During the period of bad dreams our sufferings are so intense & when we awake from a pleasant dream, our sorrow is intense to think that it was but a dream; so I'd rather not dream at all. The morning, contrary to my expectations, is bright & sunshiny, but if the day will so continue is another question.

Yesterday A. & I did not attend Synagogue as a shopping expedition was planned & we feared to be too tired. We began quite early to dress, but with occasional delays & stoppages did not finish until after 12, when minus a single protector from the Sun's rays, Mrs. S. & her two interesting daughters sallied forth. Ma could not resist A.'s earnest entreaties so consented to go to Washburn's & have her daguerreotype taken opposite to Pa's in her locket. After considerable waiting we were attended upon,

& while Ma was undergoing the operation A. & I were amusing ourselves by watching a lady, whose beautiful expressive countenance struck us both, & as she descended, we expressed the regret that in all possibility we should never again behold her. We then took a close scrutiny of the different pictures of the apartment & gazed with admiration on one which we are confident was intended to represent "Marian Mayfield". Three & four attempts the genius made "to take Ma", but they all proved unsuccessful, & deploring the waste of time, we bade him adieu promising to come another day — Our expeditions to the stores were as fruitless — Everything very scarce & prices inordinate — Met the Smiths, looking very pretty, who informed us of the death of Miss Canter, Ida's sister & a teacher in one of our Schools — Harry must lament her loss — We purchased a very few articles & returned home about four, "almost dead". Disposed of the dinner & A. & I were preparing to go to Mr. Davis' for Ma, when the bell rang, & Ellen came up & presented to us two cards bearing the names of *Mrs. M.E. Abbrams* & *Miss Imogene A. Dentzel;* so all ideas were abandoned & hastily A. proceeded down. Ma, & I in due course of time, following. Bertha was also with them, & the mark of her recent fall was quite visible. Miss D. looked very well & was radiant with *diamonds*. A diamond bracelet decked her arm, a diamond pin rested upon her fair bosom & ear rings graced her ears, the tout ensemble being very imposing. They remained quite a long while. Mrs. A. is such a sweet lady. I am almost in love with her. The visit was quite unexpected, & the afternoon was passed agreeably. A short time after they left, Maggie came, with an invitation from Mrs. H. to come & spend the evening with her. We had expected to have the pleasure of her company at our house, but we returned an acceptance of the invite, should no unforeseen circumstance occur, & Mrs N. will accompany us. We went over there & I spent the evening with her. Mr N. was home, but suffering much from a bad cold. Something, quite ominous, I hope, happened. Her cat received an increase to her family, the only occasion in which a similar event has transpired in her house. Let us hope that the next will be an addition to *her* family. Went to bed, as I came home, as I had a severe pain in my limb from which I am not now quite relieved. I must now stop, as I see Ma & I know she wishes breakfast as it is her intention to go to Market to day.

Tuesday, April 8th, 1862

7 A.M. The morning is *growling* & I would almost venture to assert that the long-expected rain will visit us to day! & we are very much in want of it, for we would be suffocated with the dust were it not for the efficient waterings by the Viennes [neighbors], in which noble work the man is now engaged. If it is compelled to rain, I should choose any other day but this day, as Tuesdays are the easiest ones in *School*, (that detestable combination of letters). After Breakfast, on Sunday, Ma went to market, & during her absence, A. & I perused the papers of modern as well as ancient states, & discerned indisputable evidences of merit in Pontchatrain's effort of "Too late" addressed to J — — L. Fearing Ma's displeasure if she should return & find the apartment in a state of disorder we forthwith proceeded to arrange them & Ma returned after its completion. Naturally she was very tired as marketing, I presume, is most fatiguing. Doubtless a weight was removed from her heart as she had been to Mr. D. & presented him $200, the sum sent by Pa for our expenses. But in order to effect the payment of that debt, we would willingly submit to sacrifices. A large amount is still due. How unjust a debt & oh! God how much suffering has it caused us. For how many months had Mr. D. been the skeleton in our *house*. Can we ever forget our gratitude to the noble man?[20] After Ma had rested she cut out our cambric skirts, & I prepared to sew them, but I did not accomplish much, as strange to say, I laid down a moment & slept until I was aroused to go to dinner. We had the pleasure of Josh's company & also of some green pea stew, the first of the city season, & one of blackberry dumpling to which we all did ample justice. In the afternoon, while dressing Leo. came & A. playfully sent the message to him that she would be down in the course of an hour, & to our astonishment, a few moments after, we ascertained that he had gone. Oh! Heaven pity *us*, if he is offended, which I can scarcely think he is, as he is possessed of too much good sense. I paid extra attention to my toilette, as we were going to R.'s, & it is particularly when I am going outside of my own circle that the fact of my limited wardrobe is forcibly presented to my mind. I decided upon my silk & when finished had the impression that I was looking my worst. When I came down A. was to Mrs. N. so as in every leisure moment I devoted myself to those bugheous [?] of my existence — my books. Before dark, A. returned & bade us get ready early, as we were to have no es-

---

20. Having paid part of the bill to Mr. Davis, Emma was able to resume purchases on credit.

cort. We were unfortunate enough to see a crowded 'bus pass us, so resolved to go to Apollo St. where, with difficulty, we succeeded in procuring seats in one of the vehicles. I am *confident* that the individual next to me
was no *gent*, but I hope that he was convinced that *I* was a lady. Passed the
Camp & "the tents beneath the moonlight" presented a truly picturesque
appearance. When at the corner of her house, a gent, whom at first we did
not recognize as Mr. H., stopped. R. *had* just sent him after us, & she was
very glad to see us, as she expected that we would disappoint. She
looked very pretty, & no indications of her previous indisposition were visible. We had a few moments talk before Keno, in which, as usual, Mr. H.
rendered himself agreeable. I like to be in his society, because he reminds
me so vividly of dearest Pa. Keno was interrupted by the announcement
of supper, which to be candid was "a very poor affair". Maggie partook of
it, but disappeared at its conclusion. We played until 11, & I won two games
& had the satisfaction of losing my entire salary for the past month. A. was
the winner. Mr. H. insisted upon our seeing his garden & it did not present
a very romantic aspect by candle light. They have a fine house. He presented A. & I with two beautiful roses of his own growth. Mrs. H.'s calls
awakened us & we prepared to depart, Mr. H. accompanying us home.
The walk was very pleasant. Could it have been otherwise? & we arrived home safe; it was after 12 before we retired & I was up in the morning by $5\frac{1}{2}$. While sitting down here on the sofa, writing my history, the
sounds of "Extra Delta", "True Delta", & "Picayune" fell upon my ears.
Simultaneously must it have fallen upon that of many others, for such a
slashing & crashing of windows, slamming of doors, whistlings & "hur-
ryings to & fro" convinced me of the fact. The boys were in great demand & I succeeded in obtaining one of the desired articles. It was 5 miles
from Monterey & dated April 5th, & read as follows: "Our army is advanced to within 5 miles of the enemy's line—Skirmishing has taken place
all the morning—There is no probability of a fight to day as the enemy
shows no disposition to advance. But the battle must certainly take place
tomorrow by the advancing of one or the other party. P.S.—Sunday, April
6th A.M.—Fighting has commenced!" This left us in great suspense & we
momentarily expected to hear something thro' the day & I was so very nervous. Nothing was heard until 2 when A. sent home an Extra which Mrs.
G. had bought down town & which did not reach up here as they were all
disposed of before reaching this section. Hark to the soul-stirring news it
contains. "Battle of Monterey. Glorious victory—Corinth, Apr. 6th—The
great battle for some days anticipated commenced at sunrise this morning

by our attacking the enemy all along the line. We have captured a large
number of pieces of artillery, & killed great numbers of men. The battle is
still raging with tremendous violence & everything indicates a glorious
victory. The enemy was surprised. Let all rejoice. 4 P.M. The battle commenced at 6 this morning. We have taken camp after camp, & battery after battery. The slaughter was immense on both sides — The battle is still
raging furiously. Cheer after cheer rending the air as our men advanced —
Later — The battle is still raging. The enemy has been driven back to within
3 miles of the Tenn. river. Many prisoners have been taken. The slaughter is immense. Beauregard, God bless him, is wherever the fight is hottest
& hardest. He says *he has the enemy, & will make a sure thing of it.* Our loss in
killed & wounded will be heavy, but the men are fighting bravely & gloriously. We shall capture the entire army of the enemy. 5 P.M. — The enemy
are in full flight — We have thousands of prisoners. It is a glorious &
complete victory — Beau. says it is better than Manassas. He calls it the
battle of Shiloh from a place on the river, near the engagement. *Gen. A.
Sidney Johnston, I deeply regret to say, is among the slain.* Prentiss has been taken
prisoner. 'The W.A. in the fight'. Your noble W.A. [Washington Artillery]
were in the engagement & fought bravely. Two are among the slain & others wounded. N.O. should rejoice over this victory as it has been won by
her generals & *her* men". This was sufficient tidings to awaken feelings of
the most intense joy even in the hearts of those in whom the flame of patriotism is not brightly kindled. We had achieved a glorious victory over
the vandal hosts, one which probably will do much to decide our destiny, for can you imagine the sentiment which would have pervaded our
city had it proved a defeat. The despondent would have grilled entirely
& we would have been constrained to discern truth in the assertion of
the croakers that "we were gone". Beauregard will live forever in the hearts
of his countrymen & future generations will be taught his right to their
love & gratitude. He will arise the second Washington, the second pre-
server of his country. If I were a man his reputation would produce within
me feelings of enviousness, to think that he, but a man, could be so exalted
above myself. Over & over again I read the document in my hand, alarmed
lest it should be the delusion of my brain, & when A. came home we had
ample food for conversation. Ate dinner & went to School. Employed
my time in working my sums. The joy felt on the reception of the news of
the battle was accompanied by sorrow almost as intense. For how many
brave & noble sons had been sacrificed upon the altar of liberty. But
does not our cause demand it. My heart ached as I looked around & saw

the many occupied seats. Many awaiting either to hear the confirmations of the fears respecting dear relatives & friends, while to others the suspense was ended, the sad tidings had been communicated. I felt as though I ought to have had some one in the fight, that my victory was too easily gained, & then I wished to be with some to console them in their time of woe. Every face bore as sorrowful an expression & then did I realize this slaughter of human lives—this, this is war; war, with all its horrors. My thoughts went to poor Jo, & the conflict that was raging in her bosom. I was satisfied that Ed was safe, for were he not & being an officer, the news would have been received. No private telegraphs are allowed to be sent, as the lines are appropriated by the government. Mrs. S. was very tearful & Mr. L. gave permission for the early dismissal of School. I was informed that there would be no graduation of the Seniors this year, but the six girls who had passed the most creditable examinations would be promoted from the Jr. to the Sr. Oh! Philomen, that Examination is the spectre which haunts me "in my sleeping or my waking, my pleasure or my pain". I will not be one of the lucky ones —I walked home with Alice—She is a warm-hearted Southerner, & rejoiced over our achievements. She informed me that "Mimi" was to be married, & entered into some of the particulars—Met Ma & A. going out. I went over to Mrs. N. Mr. N. was very tired as the entire Confederate Reg. had been marched a distance of 20 miles to suppress a mutiny among some soldiers. I supped with her, & about 8 was on the eve of coming home when Ma & A. came over. We departed about 9. This morning the paper states "The day is ours. We have achieved a glorious victory. Our loss is supposed to be 1500 killed, enemy's 3 times that number—It was the hardest fought battle ever on this continent. Gen. Johnston's remains are expected to arrive in this city to morrow morning."[21] Capt. Wheat fell in the engagement. The dear Major's brother! With his wealth of affection & love, how ardent must have been his for a brother. It was but the other evening that Mrs. C. was talking to us of him, & describing his beautiful eye. Alas! the long silken lashes forever droop over the magic blue eye of the noble son of Louisiana.

21. The Battle of Shiloh, which took place in southern Tennessee near the northern border of Mississippi, began with a Confederate surprise attack on 6 April, but was the culmination of attempts on both sides to concentrate forces in the area. Initial Confederate successes gave way to Union strikes the next day, and Confederate troops retreated afterward. The battle was the largest to date, with both sides suffering huge losses. At Shiloh, Confederate forces suffered over 10,000 casualties, about one-fourth of the troops deployed there; the Union Army at Shiloh suffered over 13,000 casualties, approximately twenty percent of the Union soldiers engaged in the battle.

Thursday, April 10th, 1862

$7^1/_4$ A.M. The temptations to remain in bed were so great that I could not resist them, & notwithstanding L.'s repeated calls & violent shakes there I remained. A. & I arose at the same time & both marveled at the long mornings & the difference between $6^1/_2$ in summer & $6^1/_2$ in winter. The morning is beautiful & *cold* the particulars of which change, I shall hereafter inform you. My prophecy on Tuesday was fulfilled. The day was cloudy, & partly rainy. Ma, amid grumblings, etc., was putting the flounces on *those* barège dresses & after considerable exertion succeeded admirably. Oh! how I wish that I knew how to sew; possessed of the talent of putting parts together & constituting a whole. Oh what use is the little knowledge of sewing, I have, to me, when I am only able to sew an article when it is fixed for me. Oh! I despair of ever attaining this height of my ambition. Dell made her appearance up stairs & is looking very well. Josie is quite better, but we have another patient, little Nellie. The measles has gone "thoroughly through". We were eagerly listening for Extras, but none came, & we were very much alarmed lest it portended bad news, for I felt so uncertain, knowing the fickle nature of war—one moment victors, the next retreaters. In our glorious battle of Manassas, news was first received that we had retreated, & a subsequent dispatch, that we had completely routed the enemy. Before dinner we had quite a hard shower, but I was determined that it should not interfere with my School arrangements, & anticipating another rain, I left a few moments after dinner & a short confab with A. The afternoon resembled one in October, one of the so many impressed in my memory. After going some distance I heard a voice behind me, & turning, I espied Alice panting & puffing having been attempting she said to attract my attention for some time. I was in School extraordinarily soon & having nothing to do I employed myself in making observations. I was pleased to see the Misses L. as their absence on the previous evening had impressed me with the idea that they had sustained some loss. I learned from them that as yet they had received no sad tidings of their friends or relatives.

Mr. L. was there during the Dictation & was no doubt much edified. Miss B. wishing to drill her own class was willing & generous enough to dismiss us —As I walked home a few drops of rain were falling, but as I was neither sugar & salt, I did not accelerate my steps. Reaching home I saw "C.L." on the table, & so absorbed was I in it that I became dead to

surrounding objects, & a ring of the bell revived me. It was "D", & a few
moments after the 6 o'c. bell rang, & I was astonished to think that I had
been home over $^1/_2$ hour. "D" was blue, hungry, & in a few words disgusting, ridiculous. He is sometimes so affected. With great labor, he succeeded in uttering a few words. Said that a storm had interrupted the work-
ings of the wires. That Mr. D. had left in the morning & would not
return to Virginia. The clouds became very lowering, & anxious for his
own safety he left. We had a tremendous shower. Leo. came, & I really
thought that he would *never* go. It was not raining when he left but was unprepared for the great change in the morning. Yes, it was cold, real cold,
but knowing that it was Spring, I could not feel the same sensation as tho'
it had been Winter. You cannot imagine how we miss our butter, as though
a friend had departed. At an early hour, crowds gathered around the
corner of Caliope St & this vicinity in order to witness the remains of our
"gallant Gen. Johnston", who fell in the thickest of the fight. Mrs. N. & F.
went, but I have no predilection for such things. Stand there a length of
time to see what? Soldiers, & a hearse! No, my heart was aching while at
home, & why should I stand among the eager, unfeeling crowd, whose
sympathies would not be awakened as the car which contained the rem-
nants of a nice noble man rode by. I often wish that I were not sympathetic.
No one enters into my joys & sorrow, as I do into theirs. As the sound of
the sad music & muffled drums fell upon my ear, prayers for the future
happiness of the great patriot, he who had died for us, ascended to the
throne of the Most High. "He fills an honored grave". What a balm to a
crushed heart. But the sacrifice of human lives is war, & many as noble as
he have fallen. Ma & I tried on the dresses & mine fit beautifully, & Sammy
is desirous of witnessing the operations of our wedding dresses. I studied quite diligently & when I went to School, took a beautiful rose, but
as *Amanda* was not present, I presented it to no one. Mrs. S. was absent
& Miss C. officiated in her place. I walked home with Alice. Found A.
out—She soon returned—Had been to Jo.'s. She was in excellent spirits,
having received a telegraph from Ed, & he was well. When I saw S. she
told me that Miss C. was to be absent today & desired me to fill her
place. "Bully for Miss C." Strange coincidence, I have never taught but
on Thursdays. There was an Extra published in the afternoon which contained further news from the battle field. It says "The 2nd day's fight
(Monday) has been the bloodiest conflict ever known on this continent &
was illustrated by deeds of heroism & valor never exceeded. Lieut. J. Levy
is among the killed. He is the son of Mrs. J.L. Levy & the report is that his

grief-stricken parents are inconsolable". In the evening, I studied a little. Nobody came. There is Te Deum to be chanted in several churches to-day for our late successes.

Saturday, April 12th, 1862

7 A.M. It was a moment before I could bring to mind the day of the month, but what true Southerner can ever fail to remember that on the 12th of April 1861, the first collision of the Con. & Fed. forces took place. It was at 4¹/₂ in the morning that the bombardment of Fort Sumter, Charleston Harbor, commenced. On the same day Gov. Moore issued orders to the volunteers organized throughout La. to hold themselves in readiness for active service at a moment's call. Who has more nobly responded to the call than our own native state. The 12th of April is the anniversary of the birth of one of America's most illustrious statesmen & noble patriots, Henry Clay. It is 2 years since the grand inauguration of the Clay Statue. Oh! Philomen, my sleep was so disturbed last night that I feel utterly exhausted. Suppress your anxiety & I shall tell you why in a few moments. Ma sent for the Dr. thinking Nellie's symptoms very alarming as there is no sign of measles. The Dr. himself was non-plussed & said that until the measles showed itself, he could not assert what it was. He ordered some medicine & we patiently waited for the measles to appear, but as they did not we are very much alarmed. The Dr. said that had there not been measles in the house, he should never have treated her for such. No measles this morning & we are again to be disappointed. Ma has the impression that she is quite sick. She is such a good dear little thing & I pray to God that nothing serious is the matter with her. Mrs. N. went to see about the "Motsas" & after much difficulty succeeded in obtaining hers & ours. They are of a very inferior quality & I agree with her in thinking that it is a mere *farce* surrounded as they are by bread & biscuits. But for form sake we must have them.[22] Ma & I sewed steadily all day. It was very cloudy & momentarily threatening rain. Sally returned from School at about 2¹/₂ & from

22. The Jewish festival of Passover approached, and the Solomons were fulfilling one of the festival's requirements, to eat matzah, unleavened bread, instead of regular bread during the week-long religious festival. During ordinary times matzah would be baked separately and not come into contact with leavened bread. The war made that procedure impossible.

then until 4 there was no rain & Ma resolved not to send the shoes for A. as she should have had the sense to come home. Ma & I were sewing & had the heaviest succession of showers that I ever saw. The dresses are not finished. About $5^1/_2$ & she did not come, Ma sent Ellen after her & imagine our consternation when she returned & said *she was not there*. We were startled, bewildered & a thousand fancies ran thro' my brain. No place was as accessible as home & where *could* she be. She would not voluntarily go away from the School, for she knows how easily excited we are. The most effective plan thought of was sending E. to Mrs. G. to obtain information from her. Ma, in the pouring rain went over to Mrs. N. to see if Mr. N. was there, as the one idea seized possession of me that she had been locked in [school]. Mrs. N. also sent F. & such torturing moments of suspense I never experienced — It was impossible to imagine where she could be & to add to my fears night was fast approaching & the rain was increasing. I had to appear calm in order to assuage S. who was crying & going on. In & out the room I was, looking up & down the streets, but no vestige, no sign — By many occasional inquiries to Ma I perceived by the tone of her voice her state of mind. Oh! thought I, if A. were only here I would beat her, I would have no compassion on her. On the gallery I perceived 2 females approaching whom I recognized as Miss D. & she. I did not go down, I did not see her. E. returned dripping & said Mrs. G. was out. I went to Mrs. N., but Ma had seen them. I did not feel as some persons would, "Oh! if she would come, I would forgive all"; for the more incensed I became when I knew her to be home. I asked no questions, but learned from her that the gate was not locked as they had just left the School. Ma gave her a deserved scolding. The fright so debilitated me that I felt as though I had a spell of sickness. She complained of a headache & went to bed. Which had the most cause for a headache. Mr. & Mrs. N. came over, & she & Ma were mostly with Nellie. It rained very hard, but I presume they got home safe. I was sleeping quietly in bed, when I was awakened by A. & I heard the rain pouring in torrents & the light penetrating every crevice of the room, the thunder roared, & it was a dreadful night. Ma came in our bed & then school, etc. was all drowned in our fears. Such deafening claps of thunder, I never heard, & I was more alarmed in consequence of the present state of affairs. It seemed to be a visitation of God's wrath upon the wicked world & I so dreaded some dreadful termination. A. was much shocked when we told her of the death of J.B. Joseph. We had been awake several hours, & upon getting up after the rain had ceased, to our astonishment, we perceived the moon shining "in all her glory", & we chose to accept it as a good omen — The old year had passed away [the Jewish calendar begins with the month of Passover]. Many times did our thoughts revert to Pa, & prayers for his safety in Camp arose to our lips. If he were only with us, & each heart echoed the wish. Much to my pleasure, I went to sleep & was not again disturbed. This morning I did not feel as refreshed as usual. The sun is shining brightly & there is every prospect of a good day. I succeeded admirably in School on Thursday. The girls were very obedient & studious. Dear little S. in particular, whose recitations reflected great credit upon herself. She is so smart & good. She & E. acquitted themselves honorably in a Dialogue — How I wish that the room were mine. At recess I received the lunch which is daily intended for Miss C. One of the items was my favorite — cream cheese. Miss D. disposed of a cup of tea. After recess we paid a visit to those "delightful retreats which exhale upon the air such odoriferous perfumes". I resumed my duties & at their completion was quite fatigued. Came home, ate my dinner & was just departing *this* life when A. came. Invariably she keeps those children (I was just about using a harsher term) in after hours. I delivered to Mag. a bundle for Miss R. which I had been requested to do. The Misses L. were not in School. I do hope that they have sustained no loss in the recent engagement. I know my lessons, music included & had a pleasant time with "beautiful Belle". When I got home, found Ma & F. had gone to Dr. S.'s & A. was alone, waiting for me. Being in charge of the children we could not leave the house — Did we wish to with "Ernest Linwood" for a companion? Continued in our underlining of the beautiful sentiments, that is the exceedingly beautiful ones, for of noble sentiments is the book composed. It may truly be called a book of poetry, for language was never before employed as the vehicle of such thoughts. Ma & F. returned — The girls had sent to us their love. In the evening Mr. & Mrs. N. & Leopold honored us.

Sunday, April 13th, 1862

7 A.M. I think that Mrs. N.'s prophecy will be fulfilled as the morning does not appear as clear as yesterday & we have already had a few drops of rain. But, you know the old saying "Rain before seven, clear up before eleven". A few moments ago my paper-boy brought me the Delta, with the infor-

mation that the Picayune Press had broken down & editions were not
yet issued. It contains beautiful obituaries to C.H. Hartnett & J.B. Joseph.[23]
I have not perused it attentively. How overjoyed am I to inform you to use
one of L.'s expressions that "Nellie is peppered with the — measles" — Poor
little thing. She has been most sick. I was some time yesterday in deliberating whether or not to attend Synagogue & finally made up my mind to
go. Accordingly prepared myself & in due time with A. Mrs. N. & J.
[the Nathans' son Josh] was treading the old familiar path. There was
scarcely any indication in the street of the recent rain, & I am asserting the
truth when I say that there was a little dust afloat. Caught a glimpse of Dr.
J.N.F. Very unsatisfactory. Pshaw, he is *married*. There was not a very full
attendance & everyone's face wore an expression of sadness — Beauty's little sister was there. My eyes were riveted upon her. Such glorious eyes!
Such heavenly lips! Such an angelic smile! Such pearly teeth! Such a transparent complexion! Do not these justify a person in directing their gaze
upon her — Mr. G. [Rabbi Gutheim] was unusually eloquent. Probably
our recent victory has stirred the water of his soul, & eloquence comes
gushing out. After service we had a short talk with Mr. D. or rather listening to everybody's complaints about Motsas. No one has them. Always
a confusion. Rebecca walked home with us, & we left them, they promising to come over. At our gate we met L. with, what do you think? Why —
a letter. What more acceptable could he have brought than tidings from
that absent loved one. We thanked him heartily & declining our invitation
to come in we hastened up to Ma with the precious missive. How good
of L. to bring it up immediately & most possibly incommode himself.
The letter bore date of the 31st & wafted to us the gladsome intelligence
that he was in the full enjoyment of his usual health. The letter was brief.
His terminating line was "I am on the eve of departure for Camp — There
sounds the whistle, I must go". He admonished us not to be imagining 1000
things about him while he is there, as he is well & intends to remain so, &
I add "deo volente" [God willing] — But how can we suppress our anxious
fears for his safety when he will be so much more exposed. But as "God
is on the waters, just the same as on the land", will he not o'erspread *him*
with his guardian wings whether in city or in camp? He could but allot
to Mr. H. the position in town, as he has undergone camp life during its
most trying season, for now it will be very pleasant. He does not speak of

23. Joseph, a member of the Crescent Regiment, died at Shiloh at age twenty-two. He was, like
many of Clara's circle of Jewish friends, a native of South Carolina, having moved to New Orleans
with his family some six years earlier.

paying us a visit, but oh! I pray how fervently that the day is not far distant which will be characterized by that event. He acknowledged the receipt of my "welcome" letter, but declared his inability to assert when he would have occasion to reply, as his future life will not admit of many opportunities. I fear that our letters will be very few & like angel's visits, far between. R. & Mrs. N. came over, & remained until quite a late hour — A. went to see Mrs. C. but when she returned, I was apprised that the said dame was out. I dressed S. before dinner. After it Ma went to Mrs. N. & I was so foolish as to shed tears over A.'s reading of E.L. I am so weak. While A. & I were dressing, "Victoria H." was announced. Oh! I was so glad to see her, as I thought she had forgotten us, but her visit clearly indicated that she had not. We owed a visit & for 10,000 times have been going to pay it, but one thing & another has deterred us from it. She looked very well. Had no news to communicate. Sue had not been very well. In her allusions to "Frank", I recognized G. the Col. of Conf. Reg. He is her brother-in-law — When she went, we walked a short distance with her & left a few articles at "Bombergs" — On our return stopped at Mrs. N. & envied her a locality on the "sunny side of the moon". Went home & promised to return, but did not. I went to sleep early. Were I to assign the reason you would know me to be more wicked than you now imagine. Who can calm the storm but him who made it, & who can quell the innate feelings in our breast. God helps those who help themselves. Why does *he* not extend to me His aid — Since penciling the above, the sun has emerged from his hiding place & is shedding his refulgent rays o'er the city —

Monday, April 14th, 1862

$5^3/_4$ P.M. I have returned from School a few moments ago being very solicitous about Nellie whom I am sorry to say has taken quite a change, but I am inexpressibly happy to say that she is not worse. This morning to our astonishment & dismay every vestige of measles was off of her little body, & this alarmed us, it being the danger in measles for it to strike in — We sent for the Dr. & by various applications succeeded in drawing it out. The poor little darling has been very sick, but I hope to God will continue to do well. Measles, though a simple disease, is sometimes dangerous & oftentimes fatal. It is so painful to see a little innocent so sick; & yet she seems unconscious of pain—Mrs. N. is here & brought with her some Yankee trophies from the Plains of Shiloh, the property of a friend. A beautiful flag with the stripes, & envelopes bearing flags & inscriptions of "The union forever", etc., etc. To day we had a general cleaning up preparing for Passover, which commences this evening[24]—Mrs. N. has left to go to Synagogue, but we did not accompany her. I was very uneasy about my lessons, but to my pleasure found that there was no History—I recited my history & then gained permission to come home. Yesterday, being in attendance on Nell, we did little else. Our dresses are finished—In the afternoon Mr. E. came—The children went with Mrs. N. to Camp, & as they had not returned by dark, I became quite uneasy & went over to see if they had come. None were there & on my way home I met Mr. & Mrs. H. who insisted I should go back with them which I did—A serious accident had happened to Mrs. N. The dog had pulled the table cloth off the table & deposited the lamp & contents on the carpet, producing grease thereon, & reducing the lamp shade to atoms. Mr. H. lit the new one, & a short while after the lady of the mansion arrived. We ate supper, & after repeatingly sending for Ma & A., they came. We played Keno, but not very late. All unfortunate, with the exception of Mr. H. Came home & found N. sleeping quietly. Gen. Gladden has died of wounds received at the battle of Shiloh; also Major Monroe, brother of Mrs. Leovy. *Shades* of evening are fast closing o'er me, so I must be closing.

Thursday, April 17th, 1862

7 A.M. Well, Philomen, here I am again & not feeling well at all, as I was quite sick yesterday & have not quite recovered. Oh! I feel miserably now & were I in the right place it would be bed. I left you Monday afternoon. That night we did not go to bed until very late, giving N. her medicines, etc. The next morning she seemed better, & A. & I prepared for Synagogue. Donned our new dresses which looked very pretty & repaired to Mrs. N. when we were soon on our way. Thankfully our seats are not occupied. There were a great many there, all in their holiday clothes & new bonnets, but did that matter to us; but I must confess that I devoted some of my time

24. Part of the preparation for the week of Passover is to clean the house to remove all vestiges of leavened bread.

to general observations. Kate M. looked as radiant as the Sun, & my thoughts were with Mr. N. when I looked at her. Flora & Beauty & Emma were there, & such loveliness I dislike to behold. I was near to them, so near, but for them it was as though I was yards, even *miles* away. Could Beauty have looked into my heart. Could she have seen its longings to break the fetters of ceremony & bestow upon her every tender epithet embraced in the vocabulary of words. Did she but know with what fidelity I would devote this heart to her, she would not, she could not reject the offering. There I sat casting occasional shy glances at the stranger, who when absent for months was never forgotten. Mr. G. spoke quite pathetically of the death of our two members, & all shed the pitying tear. My feelings were more touched, seeing Mr. J. [Joseph], an old man, shedding such tears of bitterness, so completely bowed down with grief. All were affected with the exception of a few whom I now regard as cold & hard-hearted. After Synagogue spoke to Ludy, Marion, Mrs. M. etc., left Mrs. N. who was to dine with R. & walked to the corner with Olivia, who looked very sweet. Came directly home, & found N. no better, Dr. B. had been in the morning, but seemed to evince no interest in the case. Ma was not satisfied & it is torture to have a physician in whom you have no confidence, so we concluded to send for Dr. Folwell. He arrived with the messenger. Ma was compelled to tell him the state of affairs, & to promise to inform Dr. B. of the case, before he would prescribe. He said that he found the child very sick, but with proper care & attention he had hopes of her recovery — A. & I caught a glimpse of him from behind the curtain. He is so elegant looking & destined to be one of our first physicians — She was no better or worse in the afternoon. M.E.M. came to see A. Mrs. N. came, staid some time & promised to come back, which she did & remained quite late. We did not retire for some time. Yesterday Mrs. N. was over very early. Dr. F. came & found N. very sick. The measles is no more. They have had a tendency to inflame the brain, & *brain* fever is the result. We became very much alarmed, but he is very comforting. His directions were immediately attended to. I imagined her to be doing well, she looked so knowingly; but it is one of the deceptions of the disease. She looked too lively. The dear little thing tosses on her bed, but seems to be in no pain. Dr. B. did not come. Ma wrote acquainting him with *false* circumstances, for as he has been so kind we would not have him know that want of confidence in his skill prompted us to the deed (which *was* the case) & said "You may call if agreeable to you". He did not & we fear that he is angry. Ma has often been in this situation, & I think it advisable to have a discontinuance of Dr. B.'s visit, as thanks be to God they are not often requisite. Mrs. N. remained most of the day & she & Ma were constantly nursing her. I was quite sick all day & was delighted that there was no sewing, as I should have been utterly unable to do it. Feeling relieved, about 1, I began to study, but did not accomplish much. A. was home quite early, but dinner was rather late. School was not in until late, in consequence of Mrs. P.'s absence, which has extended thro' the week in consequence of indisposition. Mrs. S. took charge of the Seniors & Mrs. L. of us. I did not know my lesson as well as I ought to have known it. Took advantage of Mrs. S.'s absence & had quite sociable chats with Julia, Maggie, & Olympia. Came home hurriedly — N. was the same. I joined Ma & Mrs. N. on the gallery & was stationary until receiving the intelligence that Mrs. Miller was down stairs. I went down, soon followed by A. The lady was in her usual health, & presented the same restless, pleasing appearance. She had not heard from the Capt. for some time, & there are rumors of the mail bags having been seized, the connecting bridges burned, etc. which I hope are without foundation as we are all very anxious to hear from darling Pa. He has been gone 8 months. Mrs. M. as gay, as lively as ever. She paid quite a long visit. During it Dr. F. with one of his most elegant bows entered. He said that the child's symptoms were much better, & she was doing very well. How I thanked him — He is so handsome, so elegant, so — Ernest Linwood like; that speaks for itself. Mrs. N. came over at evening, no one else. I expect "D" has gone "without one fond embrace, one last farewell"!!! I slept all night & was ignorant until this morning of the fact that Ma did not go to bed at all.

Saturday, April 19th, 1862

7 A.M. Well Philomen, here I am again & very much bothered, as Nellie seems no better, in fact, not as well, as she did a few days ago. Thursday Dr. F. found her to be improving & ordered a discontinuance of the medicines. I had the pleasure of escorting him to the door & receiving one of his most profound bows. I remained in the room with N. She was very restless, but I attributed it to her knowledge of her sickness & her disinclination to be in bed. Mrs. N. was here in the morning, accompanied by Mr. N. on his way down town. I helped Ma to pack a basket of things to send

to School. They were raising a box to send to the Hospital at Corinth, composed of the contributions from each scholar, & Ma sent Sallie's share. It is an excellent idea, & I hope that the children's mite will be appreciated. I did not study as usual, but as a substitution wrote. What do you think? Mrs. S. requires us to write a history of the war from its commencement to the present day. It is, as you may imagine, a *slight* task. Miss Del T. has kindly lent me hers from which I copy. Were I compelled to search for the events myself, it would take me a life time. In fact, I could never do it. Before dinner, I went round to A.'s School. Everything is bustle & confusion. Lints, bandages, bottles, etc. in the greatest profusion. Miss C. though not well was busily engaged in helping, assisted by her pupils & teachers. I did not stay long, knowing Ma was waiting for dinner, so left with A. Ma had decided upon getting no dinner of any importance, but as it was it was suited far better to my taste than our usual dinners. Everything is so dear. It is an utter impossibility to obtain *bread*. The bakers have suspended baking, & flour is selling at enormous rates. Our "motzoes" are so miserably sour that I don't think I have eaten a whole one. A little bit of corn-bread suffices me.[25] I expect before long we shall all starve. I met Alice going to School, & we trod together the old familiar path. Mrs. P. was not in School. Scholar's Companion with Miss B. passed very pleasantly & I have discovered that I know my lesson as well without much study. But I suppose Miss B. would think anything right that *I* say. "Is not that vanity"? I can almost interpret the smile that illumines her countenance when I recite. Oh! I derive no pleasure from School. There is no one there for whom I have a particular affection. Oh! how often do I sigh for my old friend, Clara Gascion. She was so sweet, so *affectionate*, (every fault is drowned in this one *virtue*. I hate "cold" people. Let them be as far removed from me, as the poles are from each other). There are Misses L. Very nice girls to be sure, but what does that mean. What does it express. A smile of recognition when seen, a touching of lips. Then Maggie, she says she likes me, but do I believe it? Were she never to see me, she would never think of me. Oh! for some congenial spirit! Some one to love me, & I shall certainly love them. In singing class sat next to Olympia. A very nice girl; quite pretty. What more. After School I came directly home. Ma was down stairs sewing, A. up dressing, F. out. I resumed my writing for a short time then went to take Josie. Resisted my efforts to quiet her. F. came. Dr. S. was out. Had seen the girls. The pretty ladies F. had seen had made her

25. Clara did not abstain from bread entirely for the week of Passover, as is the custom. The matzah was inedible.

quite envious particularly of their toilettes & she cautioned *me* not to go on Canal St. for I would see too much *grand* dressing for my own comfort. Innocent child! How often have I returned home almost downhearted at the remembrance of the pretty dresses & faces I had seen. I put the chicks to bed. N. seemed to me, better. No one came. Was asleep at 8, & in bed at 9. "D" Must be angry. I am sorry. I imagine he has gone & I would not wish him to depart angry, "but it's all the same in 100 years". Yesterday, being "Good Friday", there was no School, but the previous afternoon it was agreed that the teachers should meet at School the following day to superintend the arranging & packing. A. went about 10, but as I had some little work to do, I promised to follow ere the lapse of much time. I was faithful to my word for it was not an hour after that I was on my way to the institution *"which for briefness"* (where is Dolly?), we shall call W.S. [Webster School]. Everything was very orderly & as only a few suitable large girls had received permission to come. A. was stationed in the yard, receiving & disposing of the articles as they were sent down by Miss Cornelius. I gave a helping hand & in a time they were all conveyed to the proper place. Went up where some were busy doing everything, labeling goods, sewing up bags, etc. All the teachers were there with the exception of Miss D. who had gone home sick the preceding day & Miss C. who was doubtless too fatigued after the excitement of the night, as allow me to inform you that Miss Nellie Gillingham & Mr. Walter Couple were united in the holy bonds of wedlock. I should have liked to know the particulars of the event. Well, pardon the digression. We all descended to the lower region in expectation of our packer. A gentleman friend of Miss C. kindly volunteered to furnish us with boxes & a packer, who in course of time made his appearance. He was welcomed by us all, who had begun to despair of his coming. A most powerful rain somewhat interfered with our arrangements as there were many errands to perform, many outgoings to do. Such a collection of things! It was perfectly astonishing how it amasses. But from such a quantity of individuals everything swells the number. There was everything necessary for Man's comfort & well-being. Every variety of everything, & it seemed as tho' each thoughtful parent had contributed some useful thing unthought of by another. There were over 1000 bandages, ranging from 1 to 20 yds. in length, clothes & lint! why a blanket full. Crockery, medicines, & I can't begin to tell you. But I can say that not a needy thing was missing, & I was almost envious when I saw the delicious things consigned to the box. But with everyone went our blessing & the hope that every drop of the contents of the bottles would infuse new life into the dear wounded soldiers. We received a visit from Mr. C. the gentleman to whose care the box was to be intrusted. He was perfectly delighted with everything & said he would tell them all how the children neglected their studies & the teachers devoted their energies for the promotion of their comfort. We told him that we designed them for the wounded soldiers, *privates* in the hospital. He promised to comply with all our wishes & insured us that they would reach their destination in good order. After considerable time was occupied in the tight, close packing of one box, we all took a farewell glance at it, speculating by whom it would be opened, how received, etc.; the gentleman covered it up & then left to obtain another one, saying he would be back in $1/2$ hour. We began to feel the necessity of refreshing the inner man, so we concluded to dispose of a bottle of preserves, conscious that the one bottle would in no degree detract from the soldier's share. The tempting biscuits before me, I refused. But there is not sacrifice in keeping a fast, if temptations are not placed before us. Many a half hour elapsed & the man did not come, when we began to think that the man's life would be longer than a person would imagine from the present indications, if all of his $1/2$ hours would be of considerable length. We were all seated down stairs on benches, when we were joined by Miss Cor. who regretted the absence of a Daguerreotypist to sketch the romantic group & surroundings. We did not, for I can assure the picture would not have been one upon which a lover of beauty would admire to dwell. With Miss Cor.'s head resting upon my bosom I transformed her hair into the dearest ringlets, imitation of mine, so much admired. Mrs. F. has a characteristic face, & to me very sweet. Miss Tobin, I can't do justice to her, nor Miss Grant. At three o'clock A. & I deemed it advisable to go, which we did, promising to return. Dinner soon was ready, & subsequent to its disposition we left for School. The other box was packed, the cardiverous[?] individual having returned, actually & really. With pride we gazed upon them both. Two such full boxes, exclusive of Miss Cor.'s room, whose girls disdained the idea of sending theirs with ours, but finally succumbed & when Miss C. went she left the management to us, & four well filled boxes was the result of the collection. No School has excelled us. On top of one was some fans & we earnestly wished that our hands would, with them, cool some fevered brow, & all lamenting our inability to accompany them. I should like to administer the things myself. May every wound, to which the lint, picked by the fingers of old & young, with warm Southern hearts devoted to their country, be applied, heal. May they all perform the missions for which they were intended. We remunerated the "gent" & a smile of satisfaction beamed over his pallid features. It was quite late before we left the building after the performance of one day's devotion to the brave defenders of our homes. Ma was quite anxious about Nellie as her symptoms did not appear favorable. I resumed my writing & Ma sent over for Mrs. N. who came, with R. & L. who were at her house. She was not alarmed about N. & I hope she is better this morning. We are undecided until the Dr. comes. I went down. Our company remained until dark, & then the evening passed as usual.

Sephoahttdllimemocshtignerneigdanchsirtnanhtmim. "Be silent"!!!

Tuesday, April 22nd, 1862

7 A.M. I am almost ashamed of myself to think that so long a space has intervened since last I was with you, but I know you will acquit me of intentional slight; for yesterday being holy day, I was prevented from communicating with you through our only medium.[26] Saturday, we did not go to Synagogue, not wishing to leave Ma & being anxious about Nellie, who, thanks be to God, is slowly recovering. The Dr. continues his daily visits & never omits his "Oh, she'll get better, *mum*". I loitered about the greater part of the day, & I know I will be unable to account for all those precious moments I have wasted. I dressed S. before dinner. Mrs. E. was spending the day with Mrs. N. & the two named ladies paid us a lengthy visit. After dinner we dressed & went down. Mr. N. was on his way to drill, stopped in for a few moments. Nobody came & the whole afternoon I passed in sitting on the steps & observing the passers-by of the "Goblin District", (dear Charlotte). My little pupil, Miriam, was with me, & with her & my S. I promenaded "our banquette". At night put the chick to bed, & when I descended to the lower regions Ma had gone to Mrs. N.'s While eating supper, the door slowly opens, & this acting is followed by terrific shrieks from each party, & I believe I should have fainted had I not so quickly recognized Ma, who had stealthily entered from the front door with the intention of giving us a slight fright. To use F.'s words, "it unstrung all my nerves", & of course what was I to do but lie on the sofa & go to

26. Of the prohibitions imposed by traditional Judaism, Clara followed one that forbids writing on holidays. There are other prohibitions, all derived from the biblical injunction against doing work of any kind on the Sabbath or holidays, that the Solomon family ignored.

sleep. In the night I was awakened by a tremendous shower, but was not again conscious until the morning, when I awoke with a peculiar sensation of coldness, & I learned from L. that it was very cold. Imagine what a change, from summer weather, hot, to winter weather, cold. It is too sudden. I did not rise until late & was unprepared for the miraculous change in the atmosphere. Ma, having the Picayune, I purchased a Delta, which contained much interesting prose matter, but no poetry. "The Victory & spoils of the battle of Shiloh" was an ably written article, & I perused it with intense pleasure. Daily we see an obituary notice to those who fell on that glorious field & the battle would be more talked of did not more important subjects engross the mind. After breakfast & the disposition of those things, I devoted myself more attentively to the reading of the papers, & then went up to request Ma to cut off my dress, which she did. I then proceeded to sewing it, feeling very grateful for the cold weather, it being a dispensation of Providence to those who have no spring clothes. Mrs. N. was to spend the day with us, & she came over in tears, because "Sammy" had sent up for some clothes & things, as they had been ordered to pack their knapsacks to be in readiness at a moments warning to go — they know not where. She was of course certain that they were to go to the Forts, but we convinced her that any but Artillerists would be useless there. She was very uneasy, & in a miserable state of suspense, doubly increased by the reticences of the negro man, whom she knew had been ordered to keep silent.[27] It was a most disagreeable, murky, cloudy, cold day, & served but to heighten the depressed spirits of any one. The idea of Mr N.'s going away is the "skeleton in her house", the one thing that robs her of her quietude & happiness, & she declares that if he went he would never gaze upon her as the living. According to this "Conscription Act", he is free from *some* duty being over 35, but he is very patriotic & is determined to follow his company to h—l, should it be there sent, & I am sure if Mrs. N.'s wishes were to be gratified the whole Regiment would be there long ere this. We were just going to dinner when Leo. came in & all ran to see him, eager to hear the news. He succeeded in composing her by saying that they were ordered no place & most undoubtedly would not be, but the orders that were given were just for effect. He declined to join us in dinner, & when we returned to the room, he was asleep on the sofa, He was very fatigued being on duty the previous night. He remained a long while & promised before he left to send word up if there was any news at the Camp.

27. Lincoln had not yet issued the Emancipation Proclamation, at which point the freeing of all slaves became a stated war aim.

I dressed & came by the door, where it was freezing cold. Repaired to the house, & were all packed up together on the sofa, Mrs. N. much livelier, & in pleasant conversation; the afternoon passed away but before evening spread her mantle o'er the Earth, our hearts were gladdened by the sight of Mr. Eisner. He staid & staid & to our amazement accepted our invitation to go to supper. It was the first meal that he had ever eaten in our house & he seemed to enjoy it. After it he was also immovable. A. was to sleep with Mrs. N. & I suppose he would never have gone had not Mrs. N. showed the first disposition. S. & R. were my little bed fellows, & my prayer was granted. I did not wake up until the morning, & knowing I could do nothing I did not get up. Before breakfast I devoured the Crescent, so had not much appetite for the meal. Oh! there were so many beautiful letters. The Dr. came soon, & found N. much better. A. came over & for the first time they met. She was as much impressed by his elegance as was I. She had spent a very pleasant night & had an interrupted sleep. It was quite late & again donning our winter clothes were prepared for departure to Synagogue. Met Mrs. N. at the corner & proceeded together. The day was lovely & today promises to be a fac-simile. But it was cold & I was, during the whole service from the position of my seat. Poor Mrs. Katz was there, looking like a skeleton of her former self. My heart went out in pity of her. There was a very full attendance, but what were all to me, when my *"Beauty"* was not present. K.M. was as radiant as ever. Amid all the jabbering & confusion afterward, A. & I pass silently out, scarcely stopping to speak to a person. Walked a short distance with Mrs. E. & strange to say, she did not discourse on the state of affairs. When we left them, Mrs. N., A. & I ran home, it was so cold. She went home with us, staid some time & I went home with her. A. stopped in on her way to Mrs. Caulfield's. During Mrs. N.'s stay in the kitchen, I was very well entertained by the books, I was reading. Mr. N. came home, & at our earnest solicitations counted his money before he called for dinner, as we were not hungry. He finished & the repast was partaken of. Upon eating an artichoke, the first of the season, I made a wish which I hope may be granted. The "gentleman" immediately left for his "beloved camp". Mrs. N. & I had considerable fun. I declined accompanying her to Mr. *Krails*, so went home promising to be to her home before her return. A. was alone, & glad that I came. Mrs. C. was home, & sent me her love & a kiss. During my absence Miss C. had sent A. some of Nellie's wedding cake, which of course we could not eat. Ma & S. were out, F. to Dr. Smith's, A. & I were standing by the door, when we espied the soldier form of "Capt. D. da P." approaching. Unobserved by him we went in, & in a few moments he was in the house. He had been *very sick*, so all my suppositions were false. He was then suffering with a headache & was with his "Hartshorn". E. endeavored to make a fire, but when Ma came all that was visible was "the last expiring gleam of a baleful flame", & we were all "nigh" frozen. F. came. Mr "D" notwithstanding his condition was unusually agreeable. He gave Ma some good advice to lay up provisions for some months, as it is possible that N.O. will soon be in the hands of the cussed Yankees, & it will be an impossibility to obtain provisions. He is very sanguine & will not listen to the idea of the city's being taken, but in such times as these, people must make precautionary measures. There has been firing at Fort Jackson [at the entrance to the harbor] for the past week, & he is one among the few who think that we will be able to withstand their fires much longer. Then there are two ends to a river, & should they come here, we could but quietly surrender, for it would be folly to oppose their force. Then what a miserable state of existence to be governed by Yankee devils. Oh! God! it is too terrible to contemplate. It is from this that the rumors of the C.R. [Confederate Regiment] being sent away originated, for in that case every man would be sent away in preference to be taken prisoners. And the women — they will have to protect themselves. Oh! we are in the midst of dangerous times. Will it ever come, when the Federal flag will be waving in our city. Oh! God, avert such a calamity. "In you is our trust". "D" staid a long while. His "Too late, too late" was discussed. It is so beautiful. Then followed a short discussion on its lovely, angelic dedicatee, whom I am never so fortunate as to see her, although she resides in this city. Mr. "D" left about 8½.

Thursday, April 24th, 1862

7 A.M. My prediction has been realized. This week, notwithstanding Monday, was a holiday, has been one of the longest I ever knew. And it invariably happens so, & my reply to A.'s remark "Will not this week seem short", was "no, it will be longer than any other", & I am anxious to solve the mystery. *My* day [to substitute as teacher] has again arrived, but I am not anxious to be sent for today as I have some sewing on hand which I am desirous of completing. My last experience was two weeks since, & probably my next will not be for many more to come. There is a visible change in the state of the atmosphere. It is not as cold & I presume that this is our farewell visit of winter. The paper states that there was continual & vigorous firing at the forts, but no damage done, & they are confident of ultimate success & propound the question "why is the city so despondent"? Already they have consumed $400,000 worth of powder, & what have they effected? The killing of a few men. My heart aches as I daily read the long lists of death. "Died from wounds received at the battle of Shiloh".[28] I had the pleasure of seeing the notice of Nellie's marriage, & directly beneath it a most unusual occurrence, that of a birth. We shall view it as ominous, friend Nellie, hoping "George" has no objections! May you realize all & more than you have ever imagined of wedded bliss & may *he* prove faithful to the charge which he has sworn to love, cherish, & protect. Tuesday was as frigid as its predecessor. A most beautiful day, one fitted for a delightful promenade. I wrote some of that ever-lasting History & about 11 began to sew, Ma & I concluding that it was no sin.[29] Mrs. N. stopped in on her way to Mrs. E. where she was going to spend the day. I did not make much progress with the dresses, as I had so short a time to sew. My studying hour I devoted to the "Second American Revolution", & then did not near complete it. A. came in while we were at dinner & a few moments later I was off with some of her choicest flowers. Arrived there quite soon enough, considering my great lack of associates. Miss D. came & then I was a *little* better satisfied. She is a most agreeable Mlle. Mrs. P. was in school, looking very bad. Miss B. soon there & then began the interesting Dictation which consumed the hour until "Company B." were ordered to their private room. A kiss from A. & off I was. Could a person exist destitute of a congenial spirit? We had been seated a short time when the intelligence was received that the "Juniors can be dismissed, as I wish to devote this afternoon to the Sophomores". Donned my requisite articles & in the twinkling of an eye, little Clara, alone & solitary, was wending her path up Clio Street. My early appearance at home created a little surprise. Joined Ma & A. & had been seated a short while when the Misses Smith were announced. I went down. Was glad to see them & be seen. A. descended. Visitors as flowering as ever. Quite pretty girls, but not very sound in the higher locality. Indo [?] introduced Laura, decided to be the prettier of the two. Had just seen her on horseback, & she looked too lovely to be de-

28. What looked at first like an overwhelming Confederate victory became an inconclusive slaughter.

29. The question was whether Jewish law forbids sewing on a Holiday because it is work. Clara and her mother decided for themselves that they could sew.

scribed. How becoming must the costume be to her! Be silent! the girls were as loquacious as usual, & would you believe it? After a few moments observation I distinguished *between the two.* They are going to Mandeville in all probability, next week. Enough we know them. An *inexpressible* sadness was brooding o'er me, which was noticed by them & despite my efforts I could not dispel it. When I am *inclined* to be sad, if it is noticed by *any* one, it is only increased. They paid a lengthy visit & left with the injunction to come down soon. To be sure. Will six o'clock one morning do? A. & I traversed "our grounds". We dispersed, I expect she not finding me very agreeable. I concur with her that no one has the *blues* without *some* cause, however trifling it may be. In the evening I wrote History & finished when F. took the ink away & insisted upon my retiring. Paid a visit to Nellie, who thanks to God is fast recovering. Yesterday was a very fine day & I went to my sewing early. Mag. brought O.'s baby to see us. It is so beautiful. She informed us that O. & Mrs. M. were spending the day at Mrs. N.'s. I was reluctant to go to my studies & leave my unfinished dress, but "it had to be did" & during those few hours, I tell you, I studied. Wrote abstracts, etc., etc. I overtask myself. When I had finished, Mrs. N.'s F. came & what do you think she had? A *letter* from my darling Father. I conveyed it to Ma who was overjoyed at its receipt. Opened it eagerly & read it carefully, but I must confess that I can't tell where he is. The letter is from Gordonsville, having left the Camp which was considered insecure, & he intends commencing business at some other point. He was well & cautioned us not to be uneasy about him. Not a word of coming home. Listen to this—"A company being short of officers, I volunteered to accept the place of Lieut. & the other day in a *little expedition* where several Yanks were killed, I thought of home"!! Now, is not this consummate impudence. It annoys me considerably, & I wish he would not write us such things. He mentioned Major W.'s name, so I know that he is with him. The letter was brief but very welcome. We ate dinner without A. As I went out of the gate, I met Alice, & we had proceeded to the corner when we met A. Arrived in School, & had much to occupy my time. There was a new admittant to our class, & there being a vacant seat beside me, Mrs. P. conducted her to me & introduced her to me.

[There are no entries for April 25 through May 3, 1862.]

Clara's parents

Emma Solomon Solomon (1824–1913)   Solomon P. Solomon (1815–1874)

Clara's sisters
Clockwise from upper right: Alice (1842–1880), Frances (Fanny) (1847–1881),
Rosa (1857–1948), Sarah (Sallie) (1853–1931), Josephine (Josie)
(1860–1945)

Clara Solomon

Cover of sheet music for "Free Market"
   Courtesy Louisiana and Lower Mississippi Valley Collections, LSU Libraries, Louisiana State University

Sutler's store on a Union army base. Solomon's store for the Confederate forces around Manassas, Virginia, would have looked much like this store.
Courtesy National Archives

Canal Street, *ca.* 1866, showing the trolley tracks that so excited the Solomons
From George Mugnier Stereographs, Louisiana and Lower Mississippi Valley Collections,
LSU Libraries, Louisiana State University

Congregation Dispersed of Judah, Carondelet Street
Courtesy Library of Congress

Duncan and Company, Canal Street, mentioned often by Clara
Courtesy National Archives

9

The Yanks Arrive:
April 25–May 29, 1862

Sunday, May 4th, 1862

6 ¹/₂ A.M. Who can penetrate into that unknown future? Who can remove the veil in which a kind Providence has enfolded it? And would anyone have the desire to do so? Do we desire to prepare ourselves for coming events? I answer "no", for it is not for whose purpose that it is hidden from our eyes & why should we endeavor to solve the mystery. I little imagined when last I conversed with you that days would elapse ere I again performed the pleasant duty. Did I dream of the inauspiciousness of this present moment. Oh! from the depths of my heart my gratitude ascends to God for so veiling the "coming time". Oh! Philomen, a gloom has settled o'er my spirit, a gloom envelopes our dearly-beloved city. My breaking heart but aches the more, when I am prepared to record events, which can never fade from my memory, & did I not consider it a duty, I should spare myself the unpleasant task.[1] Nevertheless I promise to go into no minutiae, but to record merely *facts*, devoid of their accompanying incidents or circumstances of the past week impressed upon that most lasting page, the mind. I am not myself, so pardon any digression. Oh! how I dread to begin the narration! But why linger? Why shrink from duties, which we are compelled to perform, & yet to be candid, I have deferred it from day to day & this is my last available opportunity. Last Thursday [24 April], Ma, F. & I were seated up stairs in the pursuance of our vocations, when Mrs. N. came in. Ma & F. went out, & my curiosity being excited by hearing F. remark, "They will think you foolish", I went out & learned that it was her determination to send for Josh, as rumor had said that the *Yankees*

---

1. New Orleans had been occupied by Union troops during the gap of a few days in the diary.

had past our forts, & were on their way to the city. We scorned the idea, but simultaneously in came Sallie, quaking with terror, & informed us that the whole School was alarmed & about to be dismissed. Oh! my God! our fears were then awakened. We went by the door & the excitement & commotion was an indication that something was the matter. Uniformed men were hurrying to & fro, & we gained from them that the whole military was ordered out. Oh! my God! Imagine my feelings as the Idea of a battle arose before me, but I immediately abandoned such ideas for what resistance could we offer to them on the water. Mrs. N. was frantic with terror, for the safety of her husband. Oh! never have I experienced such emotions as in those moments, never did my heart sink so deep within me. I would not permit myself to dwell upon the subject, but went up to arrange my sewing. A. came, school being dismissed, & the expression on her countenance assured me of her feelings. It was true, oh! Father, too true. We knew not what line of action was to be pursued. Ma was to Mrs. N.'s & after I dressed A. & I joined her. The Capt. was very sick, & this to Mrs. N. was a source of trouble. She & Ma determined to go down town at any risk to hear, to know something, & A. & I volunteered to remain with the Capt. The bustle in the street had died away, & a calm had succeeded. Oh! how long & weary were the hours before their return. About 4 o'c. we came over to dinner, & Ma shortly came, very much excited & fatigued. I went to Mrs. N. & gained particulars. You can imagine the state of down town. They had seen different people, went different places, & had been advised differently, by some to remain in, by others to leave the city, "D" [newspaper publisher da Ponte] giving the latter advice. They went up to the camp & there held conversation with Mr. N. thro' the railings, none being permitted to enter. He advised her to do as she thought best. He would not remain in the city, as the military would be sent out of it. We did not know what to do, how to act, no one to come up to us, alone, alone we were. Mrs. N. grieving very much. In the afternoon we were all with her, but we ourselves needing consolation. Oh! I cannot attempt to describe our feelings, to dwell upon the subject. Mrs. N. had asked me to stay with her & I had accepted. In the night we were coming over & we met Mr. da P. He accompanied us into the house & handed to Ma her transport, which he had obtained with much difficulty. He advised us to go to Pa, for how could we live here cut off from all communication with him. He remained a long while & informed us on many subjects. Beyond doubt, the Yankees had passed our forts & were on their way to our city, it having been decided to be the most daring naval exploit ever attempted, as they passed under our fires, our brave men, fighting to the last.[2] Mr. "D" left with a promise to see us again at an early period. We went home. But little sleep that night visited our eyes. At every sound we would startle & jump up & were patiently waiting for the dawn of the morning. It came, & our first impulse was to get the paper, which contained no news. Friday, we decided upon going out. Mr. N. came up on an hour's furlough when the alarm bell rang before he had been up 10 minutes, & off he ran, screaming "Do as you like". It was cloudy, but we hastily made our toilettes, & were on our way down town, the omnibuses having ceased to run, the stores closed, & everything betoking the calamity which was to befall us. Ma having sent a telegraph to Pa, we went to the Office, but no answer had been received, & they expected momentarily to close. But certainly Pa knew of it. It had been telegraphed. By appointment we met "D", & proceeded to his office in company with Mr. Duncan. Remained there some time & decided to seize the first opportunity to go away, *as it was thought probable that the cars would soon cease to run. He walked a short distance with us &* then was summoned by some one who said the Major wished to see him. He was unwilling to leave us, we insisted & when he left us, it was our intention to leave in the afternoon; how, when, & where we knew not, but Mr. Duncan was also going. To add to our gloom, the rain began to fall, & in the midst of it were we. We stopped at Mrs. D., borrowed umbrellas, & in the mean time there was a general stampede & hundreds of persons running & exclaiming "They are coming"!!! We joined in the crowd, but soon extricating ourselves, made our way through the pouring rain. The tents were all removed from the Square & we were informed that the Confederates had gone some place up the road. Mrs. N. was distracted. Standing at a corner we saw one of our finest boats, of our own accord committed to the flames.[3] Oh! *never* shall I forget the 25th of Apr. 1862. Such expressions of woe as were on the faces of every one, & such sadness as reigned in every heart. Oh! that that day should ever come! We reached home, very wet, changed our clothes, & then began *to pack*. I was of little assistance being so excited, & I sat by the window, watching the rain which was pouring in torrents, for the heavens indeed were in tears. We sent for A. & she came,

2. The forts, Jackson and St. Philip, withstood severe Union shelling for several days, beginning 18 April. Union forces then decided to make a run past the forts before dawn on 24 April. In a daring operation, the squadron led by Commodore [later Admiral] David G. Farragut succeeded and captured the city. See Stephen R. Wise, *Lifeline of the Confederacy* (Columbia, S.C., 1988), 79–80; Terry L. Jones, ed., *The Civil War Memoirs of Captain William J. Seymour,* 1–40.

3. There was no way to defend the city against naval forces once the forts protecting the harbor were passed. The river meanders through the city.

& remained home. After dinner went to Mrs. N.'s who did not know what
to do. The rain ceased & Mr. D. came up. No train left & it was not known
when we would & we were again undetermined about going. He remained
some time & promised to come up again, he, not knowing what he was going to do, & telling us that Pa would come over. In the afternoon went to
Mrs. N.'s where was O.L. & Mrs. M. [Octavia Leovy and Mrs. Miller?].
Supped at home, but left early. The Capt. was no better. Did not sleep well.
In the paper there was the correspondence between the Mayor & Com.
Farragut. The Mayor's document was ably written. All our chief men had
left, Gov., Lieut. Gov., etc. & everything devolved upon the Mayor [Monroe],
& *his* conduct will ever be remembered. He surrendered the city to a
more powerful force without resistance, but would not consent to our lowering the flag which waved so proudly from the dome of our City Hall.
They wished to humiliate us, but could not. We had fallen, but not disgraced. Mrs. N. & Ma were out the greater part of the day. Mr. Eisner
came up. I did not remain home, as I promised Mrs. N. to mind her
house & the Capt. L. & O. came in & remained to dinner. Mrs. N. brought
no news with the exception of our determination not to take down our flag,
to die first. Oh! how glorious. They are content with our submission. There
is not a man in our midst whose hand would not be palsied in the act. Dinner
very light, as it is impossible to purchase anything, stores all closed. What
are we to do for provisions. In the afternoon R.[Rebecca Harris] came up.
What an attentive niece. Left early. Ma & A. came over in the night, "D"
having been to the house, & I think we had given up ideas of going. Mrs.
N. heard nothing of Mr. N. Sunday brought no tidings. Correspondence
between the authorities was in the papers; late in the day Ma came over.
Said Mr. D. & "D" [da Ponte and Duncan] had left after a long visit. O.
& B. came in the afternoon, & seeing no one at night, with heavy & aching
hearts we retired to bed. Oh! how terrible to think of. I awake in the morning & imagine it to be all a dream, but too soon the illusion was dispelled.
Mrs. N. had been assured that Mr. N. was safe & would be back, but she
could not be consoled. We were hopeful on Monday, when Ma came in
with the tidings that "D" had just communicated to her. Com. F. [Farragut]
had allowed the women & children 48 hours to leave the city, as it was to
be shelled, we refusing to haul down our flag. I cannot refrain from quot-
ing some parts of the letters. "Major M. [Moore], I deeply regret to see,
both by their contents & continued display of the flag of Lou. in the Court
House, a determination on the part of the city authorities not to haul it
down. Moreover when my officers & men were sent on shore to commu-

nicate, & to hoist the U.S. flag on the Custom House, they were insulted in the grossest manner & the flag which had been hoisted by *my* order on the Mint was pulled down & dragged thro' the streets. All of which go to show that *the fire of* this *fleet* may be drawn upon the city at any moment, & an amount of distress ensue to the innocent population which I have heretofore endeavored to assure you I desired to avoid. The election is therefore with you. But it becomes my duty to notify you to remove the women & children from the city within 48 hours if I have rightly understood your determination. Your obd. serv. D.G. Farragut". His reply, or portions was as follows, "Sir, you now renew the demand made in your former communication, & you insist on their being complied with, unconditionally under a threat of bombardment, & you notify me to remove wom. & chil. that they may be protected from your shells. Sir, you cannot but know that there is no possible exit from this city for a population which still exceeds in number 150,000 & you must therefore be aware of the utter insanity of such a notification. Our women & children cannot escape from your shells if it be your pleasure to murder them on a mere question of mere etiquette. You are not satisfied with the peaceful surrender of an unoffended city, opposing no resistance to your guns, because of its bearing down with some manliness & dignity, & you wish to humble & disgrace us by the performance of an act against which our nature rebels. This satisfaction you cannot expect to obtain at our hands. We will stand your bombardment unarmed & undefended as we are. The evil world will consign to indelible infamy the heart that will conceive the deed & the hand that will *dare* to consummate it"!! Now, in what a predicament were we. No male around to assist & protect. Mr. da P. advised Carrolton [that the Solomons leave their home and go to Carrolton, just north of the city], & promised us the protection of Duncan, who would be up in the afternoon. Immediately we went to work, & converted the raw materials into edibles. I had great hopes that the worst would not come to pass, but still we had to prepare for the emergency. We intended to take but a few clothes with us & were willing to make any sacrifice to behold our prided city reduced to ruins rather than it should fall into the hands of the barbarous invaders. Ma packed each a bundle, but with my commands nothing of mine was molested, & I went to my temporary abode. Mrs. N. was all excitement & terrified at the idea of being further separated from Mr. N. whom we knew not where, & knew not for how long no communication could be received. Mrs. N.'s wish was to go to Charleston [her birthplace], ours to Virginia , but it was impossible for either to be gratified. In the afternoon Mr. E. came up & told us not to be alarmed, as they would not dare to shell in consequence of the many foreign subjects. But it was probable that the City Hall, over which our flag floats would be shelled. Mr. B. came up on the night & was of the [same] opinion. In the night Mr. & Mrs. H. came & there was a little quarrel arising from their unparalleled attention. Mr. D. did not come, which gave us some foundation for hope. But the time was occupied in vague surmises as to where we might be in a few days. In the morning no wiser were we, until about 11 o'clock when we heard that Forts Jackson & St. Philip had surrendered & the enemy had consented *themselves* to lower our flag. The news was reliable, read the following, "Gent. The Forts St.P. & J. having surrendered, & all the military defenses of the city being either capitulated or abandoned, you are required as the sole representative of any supposed authority in the city to suppress every ensign & symbol of government whether state or Con. I am now about to raise the flag of U.S. upon the Custom-house & you will see that it is respected with all the civil power of the city." Now it was at an end. We had maintained our dignity to the last, & though humiliated were not disgraced. In the night I was eating supper when E. came for me, saying that Mr. da P. wished to see me. I went & he informed me that he was going to leave the city probably on the morrow. He was so despondent, so sad. He gave us an account of the events of the day & the tears in the eyes of men, as our flag was lowered. He held the consultation with the Fed. officers. I pitied him for I knew his feelings. Mr. D. was with him, his intention being to leave. The next morning *Mr. N. came.* What does it not express! He had been since Saturday on his way home, & had come by the way of Baton Rouge, leaving L. [Leopold] there. The Reg. had disbanded.[4] Oh! how happy was Mrs. N. He gave us an account of his adventures, his fears & uneasiness for his family & he was as delighted to see us as we were to see him. Mrs. N.'s troubles were at an end. I remained with her that day, which she employed partly in writing to her friends, the letters to be forwarded by our kind friend Mr. da P. Mr. E. came up to inform her of what he had heard respecting the Confederates, & was pleased to see her husband safe at home. Mrs. E. came to see her, very much fatigued. They had the greater part of their things removed to Carrolton, & it required some labor to again restore order. That day with what less heavy hearts we dined, at least she, for my every thought was with dear

4. The Home Guard Regiment simply disappeared as an entity, its members reverting, so it seems, to civilian status.

Father! When, oh! when, shall we meet again. The rolling stock of the R.R. has been removed, but if he wishes, he can effect a passage someway. Olivia, safe in the possession of her husband, came up with him in the afternoon & we passed a short while in the Captain's room, who does not seem to be recovering. He is very grateful to me for my kind society but little did he imagine when I was sitting apparently listening to what he said, how distant were my thoughts from himself. I supped with Mrs. N., she being determined to make me have it out, & I then left my house, bed & board for one week past, a week which seemed as though seasons had passed, instead of days. I was so sad all day, & was reproved more than once by her, but I bade her not to molest me, for my spirits I could not revive. She accompanied me home & delivered me to other hands. Mr. da P. was there. He was going on the morrow, & sadness, disappointment & regret was impressed upon his face & visible in his manner. The following day Fed. transports arrived, & have been continually, Gen. Picayune [petty] Butler being in command, a gentleman with whom "D" was at one time on terms of the closest intimacy. "D" did not wish to remain after a Yankee foot had polluted our soil. In the morning he & M.A.B. stepped out of a carriage & ascended our steps & entered. Mr. Duncan was to remain, to be in the office [of the newspaper]. The publication of the paper [the *Delta*] will continue, but it will be but a chronicler of city items, cut off as we are from all the world. Affairs in Tennessee, & Vir. we will never know. Ma gave "D" the letters, & he promised to stop in again before he left in the afternoon. M.A.B. is to accompany him. When they went I sewed (not feeling like it) on the very dresses which I was sewing on a week before. One o'clock, or so, "D" came. We went down to see him. I must not here fail to express our thanks to him for his kind attention during our late struggles. But for his kindness we would have been isolated, deserted, & we appreciate it. Oh! so highly, & hope at some future time to repay it but under more pleasant circumstances. He was going to Pres. Davis, but said "God only knew his after movements as he had no idea of them". He was going out of the City. He promised to prevail upon Pa to come for us, & if not to pay us a visit. He did not know when *he* would return here, but had a presentiment that it was some distant day. Being so enthusiastic a Confederate, & his paper being one of its first advocates, his life would be in danger. Ma gave him a "traveling cup" with which he was highly pleased & promised to keep it forever. He dreaded to enact the last feature of the performance, the "good bye" (so did we) & he said he would stop in on his way to the Depot. I resumed my sewing. I ate nothing all day. He did not come in the afternoon. I know he was prevented. Well, he is far on his way & may success attend him. I sewed in the afternoon, with a heavy heart. Oh! to think we are in a captured city. But how disappointed are they! Not a bale of cotton fell into their hands for $2,000,000 worth was consigned to the flames.[5] Nothing Friday. Finished our dresses. In the humor for anything but dressing. Never intend to again. Spent the evening with Mrs. N. Mr. N. very depressed & "ready to die". Saturday's paper contained an account of the seizure of the True Delta Office. A detachment of U.S. soldiers went to the office & took possession because its proprietor refused to print a proclamation. They solicited printers from their own forces who will print it with the material of the Office, & interrupted no further in its affairs. They informed the proprietor of the St. Charles [hotel] that if he did not open it, Gen. B. & staff would occupy it any hour. It is now their headquarters. They are quartering at Odd Fellows Hall, & have seized a private house on Poydras St. which they have converted into a hospital. In the heart of the city! They seized the Telegraph Offices, but happily all the implements had been removed. The supply of this large population with the necessaries of life is a question of the greatest moment to our people. The land forces of U.S. have occupied Opelousas R.R. & forbid communication by that, our principal means of transportation of fresh supplies. We have since learned that they have made arrangements for us to receive provisions, so ideas of starvation are now abandoned. They are camping in Lafayette Square! What a contrast to its late occupants! The papers speak in equivocal terms of a visit from "yellow Jack" [Yellow Fever, a frequent visitor to New Orleans]. His appetite will be whetted by abstinence, & how many subjects will he fix upon.[6] Why N.O. won't be large enough to bury them. The times justify profanity. Already some have died from the effects of the sun! How can they stand it in the days to come! Oh! I am incapable to recount to you $1/2$ of what I feel or know, so pray be satisfied. Saturday, we attended Synagogue.

Mr. G. [Rabbi Gutheim] prayed earnestly for the S. Confederacy! I suppose they will interfere with the Churches. I wonder with the School? I pray, for the Normal. Oh! I hate to go. When I am in the street I do not seem to breathe a free atmosphere. It is not free. Laden with the breath of

---

5. Any cotton that could be sold during the war commanded extremely high prices. Confederate policy everywhere in the South, when retreating, was to destroy all cotton that could be found, so as to keep the potential revenue out of the hands of the Union troops.

6. There had not been an epidemic for some time.

those invaders. I am sick at heart. What a victory. The taking of N.O. The Fed. flag over our Custom House. They have the valley of the Mississippi at their command. I am alarmed to walk the street & would not be out after dark. In fact, all citizens are requested to be in doors by 9. We are conquered but not subdued; & our independence *will yet* be recognized by the leading powers of the world.[7] Poor Beauregard. What a blow it was to him. On my return from Syn. I dressed S. & went to Mrs. N. where I dined. She got in some provisions for herself & Ma. Beef is 40 cts. a pound. Everything in proportion. No bread at all. There is no flour. Gen. B.'s Proclamation [Butler at first allowed the mayor to exercise civil power] appeared in the evening paper. It was not very arbitrary, but we must remember that it is his first. Mrs. Miller, I deeply regret to say, has left the city & gone up to her relatives in Mississippi & in a short time I presume that she will join her husband. May we meet again. The Smiths have also evacuated this place, & I suppose upon inquiries for many of our friends, we shall find that they have acted likewise. Many left precipitately, & now regret it. I would not like to desert my native city in this, her hour of trial, but feel it the duty of every native to stand or fall with the fortunes of their own Louisiana. We feared so much from the enemies in our midst, but thanks to God, none with the exception of Mr. Summers, who is now with them at the St. Charles, have been found. It was anticipated that when their flag was hoisted there would be cheers for "Lincoln", but instead, when they had accomplished the act, there arose upon the air, one deafening, rousing cheer for Jeff. Davis, & the Southern Confederacy, which was represented to be by a witness a "truly sublime spectacle". And now, how inadequate a conception have I given you of our trials & adventures of the past, never to be forgotten week. But remember that the fullest heart is that which does not admit of expression & this, with your knowledge of my want of command of language, will, I know, acquit me in your eyes. How ignorant are we as to what will be the contents of each succeeding page, for never did the idea once present itself to me that I should ever relate the particulars of New Orleans, the Queen City of the South.

---

7. One vital measure for success of southern secession was the extent to which members of the international community recognized the Confederate States of America as a legitimate government.

Tuesday, May 6th, 1862

6 ³/₄ A.M. One sixth of the month has gone, & as each succeeding day is numbered with the past, how happy am I. I know such feelings are wicked, but so long as I cannot suppress them I do not imagine that it is injurious to give expression to them. I long for the time to pass, for some termination to arrive, & I have the hope that each moment, in some manner, brings us nearer to the "idol of our hearts". We are sometimes weak enough to *believe* that he is on his way, but whether or no, I have a sweet presentiment that we shall soon meet, & I hope it will be in Vir. for how little will our craving hearts be satisfied with a flying visit from *him*. But our trust is in God & the Future will determine *all* things. The morning is lovely, to us, but with what concomitant horrors must the unacclimated regard it, for such cool, late Spring always precedes a most unhealthy summer. In spirits I am no better, & I fear I never shall be. I have individual troubles; that wretched L.N.S. where my footsteps will be this evening tending, is staring me in face, & a dose of emetic [something to cause vomiting] would be far preferable. One consolation. Lusher is not here. Sunday there was a dearth of news in the paper. The day I employed in sewing, & completed a pretty little spencer for Sallie. Donned my new dress in the afternoon. Mr. E. came up. Oh! he is a foreigner & cannot sympathize with us.[8] Ellen Blood paid us a visit. I envy her, her residence. One of the cannons of the gunboats points into her middle window. Had a short talk with Alice, who was engaged in the manufacture of Secession flags; she is so patriotic. Ma spent the evening over the way & we retired early, contrary to A.'s wishes, but alias Farragut, she had to submit.[9] The wretch is so often quoted. He has left these abodes, never daring to land as he was once a staunch friend of the South, & a short time ago was received here with great hospitality. His mother is a resident of the city.[10] The Crescent of yesterday speaks as follows, "Our readers need no apology from us for the dearth of uninteresting matter in our columns. In the absence of mails, & the 'rather binding' proclamation of Gen. B. 'staring us stark in

8. Eisner was a "foreigner" in the sense that he emigrated recently from Europe and was not native-born like Clara. A new immigrant would have more difficulty adopting the cause of the Confederacy.

9. There was a 9:30 curfew in force.

10. David G. Farragut was the adopted son of David Porter, Commander of the New Orleans naval station. Although raised in New Orleans, Farragut served in the U.S. Navy throughout his adult life and remained in the U.S. Navy at the outbreak of the Civil War. With roots in New Orleans, Farragut was regarded with special contempt by the Confederate population.

the face', it is not wonderful that a 'pent up Utica' contracts our powers'', considering that this "mighty continent is not ours". Speaking of the scarcity of beef it says, "salt pork & muddy Mississippi water, in warm weather, are not exactly *suited* to the constitutions of the unacclimated, & if persisted on would consign more to the dark shadows of the Metaire Ridge [cemetery area] than did the cholera in '32". But this will be obviated as we are to receive beef. Mrs. N. came running in yesterday, exclaiming "good news", & then proceeded to relate it to us. "Washington is taken. The Confederate flag is waving over the Capitol. We have taken 40,000 prisoners, Macgruder is killed, & our Johnson & Lee, mortally wounded". Oh! my God! my heart bounds with delight at the mere idea! But oh! it seems to be too good to be true. How it would compensate us for our loss! Oh! I begin to be so hopeful. The darkest hour is just before dawn & I feel so confident that those Yankees cannot remain here long. It is *probable* that there has been a terrific battle, but for the authenticity of the other, we cannot vouch. Is it not heart rending that we can receive no intelligence, no news can be published. We should send in a messenger, anything to relieve our minds of suspense. We were all elated at the prospect. How "old the"[?] will be marched in triumph thro' our streets. During the day I felt more cheerful than for a long while & was oh! so busy building air castles, & picturing to myself "old Butler picking up his traps to be off". Hope to God that we may be better informed today. I prevailed upon Ma to let me remain home, & she did. But why delay it. Commenced & finished a dress for Rosa. Had a heavy rain in the afternoon & our sighs for Emma G. was useless as the night was beautiful. Mrs. N. honored us in the afternoon. I had a short talk with Alice & she gave me the particulars of the advent of Mrs. V.'s twins. One of them died, but the other is a fine, healthy boy. While we were standing talking we were joined by Father Monghan & our conversation was interrupted by the appearance of an inebriate gent who came in close proximity to us, when we unceremoniously ascended the steps of the Mazareaus; were invited in & only remained until the visitor had departed. Mr. & Mrs. N. spent the evening with us. I think that Mr. Duncan could call to see us. He cannot be gone away.

Thursday, May 8th, 1862[11]

6 1/2 A.M. Two weeks have elapsed since the intelligence was first received
that the Federal gun-boats had passed our forts. The time has seemed like
months, but I am confident that when years shall elapse my recollection
of that memorable time will be as vivid. And now I ask myself the question "what are we going to do?" Is not Pa coming home, or he is going to
send for us. Can we live in this isolated condition, cut off from all communication with him. And yet I am hopeful, oh! so hopeful that all will *yet*
be well. The morning is cloudy, & I presume we shall have rain. We have
had our share of good weather. It is quite pleasant yet & we are thankful
for this prolonged Spring. Tuesday was characterized by no important
event. Sewed all day, my favorite occupation, & almost finished a dress for
Fannie. *Seven* dresses is but one apiece. I have completely got out of the
humour to study, so determined not to, but too brisk the storm of not knowing them. Remained sewing until 2½ when I proceeded to adorn my person. Wore my new dress with which I am in love. Eat dinner & then departed on my loathsome way. With what different feeling had I last trod
that path. Then I breathed the air of a free city, now I breathed the air
tainted by the breath of 3,000 Federals & trod a soil polluted by their touch.
My thoughts & feelings I can assure you were none of the pleasantest, &
assumed no better a nature when I entered the Institution. The 10 min. before the commencement I spent with A. Mrs. P. expressed her pleasure at
seeing so large an attendance, the best for many days. Some so excited my
displeasure by wearing upon their shoulders black crepe bows. How silly!
All know that our hearts are in mourning, but why make any outward
demonstration. Do we go in black for a very sick person? Our *cause* is not
dead, it is only *sick*. The Yankees are here on a *visit*. I also disapprove of
Confederate flags about the persons for they are well aware of the feelings
& sentiments of Southern women.[12] Miss D. was there for the first time.
I passed a very disagreeable evening & was glad when the release time
came. I hear that Mr. Lusher is not in the city. Walked home with Alice.
At our corner met beautiful Mrs. C. who informed me that she was on the
way to our house, so she accompanied me. Happily A. was home &

11. Clara's handwriting became very small at this point, to save paper. She was again writing
on the endpapers of her diary book.

12. Girls and women throughout New Orleans, not only at Clara's school, adopted the practice
of wearing black mourning bands to express their displeasure with the occupation, and some wore
clothing with the Confederate flag as the pattern.

much pleased to see her friend. We spent a very pleasant time; she is as agreeable as handsome. She exacted from A. a promise to spend a night with her during her husband's absence. We walked a short distance with her home, she kissed me very affectionately & gave me a most pressing invitation to come & see her. Ma was quite angry with us for being out doors at so late an hour, & I was astonished at myself. I regret to say that our good news is regarded by many as a hoax. After supper we went to Mrs. N.'s. The Capt. is much better & Mr. N.'s spirits somewhat rising. Mrs. N. told us that she heard from a reliable source that Butler had opened the prison & allowed all the negroes to be released. It is this fear which alarms me. I fear more from the negroes than Yankees & an insurrection is my continual horror.[13] But oh! so many rumors are afloat. We should make up our minds to believe *nothing.* Yesterday was a fine day & being desirous of seeing something & of getting out, she concluded to go down town, & I & S. was to accompany her. Our toilettes being made we stepped into the bus, a little after 12. Passed the scene of action the City Hall, & all flashed across me. The Square is still occupied by some & there are a few remaining tents there. But the St. Charles! My heart sank within me when I beheld it. *Never* in connection with the Yankees have I experienced such sensations. It looks to be a perfect wreck. They are loitering around it, lying down, playing cards, & their clothes hanging around. Oh! it was a loathsome sight, & I wondered how men could submit to it. I *couldn't.* Saw stragglers on my way to Canal St. & there saw more, who are strutting along with such an air of defiance as I never saw, so scornful, so unassuming. Their looks being, "We have conquered you". They were sporting uniforms with any quantity of brass buttons. Oh! that our streets should be ever disgraced. But few stores are opened & in some that we went Con. money was *refused.* This is to be ordinated as the Safety Committee are about issuing a currency, shin plasters being one of our greatest nuisances.[14] Canal St. did not present the same spectacle as in former times. There was a dearth of ladies, & everything reminded me of a ruin. For the benefit of R.'s [Rosa's] —we took a ride in the cars, & frequently would spy a Yankee. One tore my dress. A live Yankee stepped on it. They are subjected to every silent insult by the ladies. A car on Camp St. containing a number of the

13. Many in the South had feared a slave insurrection, even before the Civil War. Planters in rural Louisiana, the principal slaveowners, were the most concerned; Clara, an urbanite from a mercantile family, had the same fears.

14. Shinplasters were private currency notes issued by private individuals in response to the inadequate Confederate currency system.

last named articles was hailed by some Fed. officers & as they walked in the ladies walked out. As some officers came into their pews in Church they vacated them, & it is said that they seemed to feel the insult. We had a pleasant though solitary ride in the cars, which R. enjoyed excessively. On our arriving at Canal St. sought our own omnibus & I was wishing that the driver would be more dilatory than usual in coming to his post, as I had a most formidable opportunity to see what was going out. There were throngs of men, & contrary to commands I oftentimes saw more than six conversing together at the corners, which "no commander" forbids. Had the good fortune to come up on the 'bus with Emile Jarreau! He is so handsome, & the circumstance of his having fought in the battle of Manassas tends to render him doubly attractive. He still wears a W.A. badge. I wonder if "he isn't skeered of the Yankees". Repassed the wreck [the St. Charles Hotel], & as I gazed upon it tears voluntarily sufficed my eyes at the thought that one of our noblest institutions should be so disgraced as to be the abode of the invaders of our soil. Was assisted from "our carriage" by "Emile" & the pressure of his hand upon my "kidded" one was felt for many moments after! Pshaw! Don't mind my foolishness. I am only in a jocular mood, so pardon all extravagances. I perceived an unusual excitement around the Powells' house & was soon made wise of the fact from my own *sense* that the Yankees were at the door. I was all curiosity & subsequently learned that they, knowing that the house contained government stores, had come to take possession of them; the family left the city on the first day of the excitement. I took off my clothes, donned another dress, & went to the corner. Mrs. N. & Olivia were standing at theirs, & by their invitation I joined them, & they insisted on my remaining to dinner, which I did. Mr. M. informed us concerning news. Gen. Butler has allowed the Mayor & c. to resume their authorities, promising not to interfere with civil powers, but no confidence is placed in his word, & it is anticipated that he may at any moment violate it. Mr. N. however is charged with looking on the dark side of the picture & he prophecies that there are bad times in store for us. *Nous verrons.* "A new" broom sweeps clean. O. went early disliking to be out in the street at a late hour. The excitement at the corner increased & the tumult & confusion was great. I never dreamed that the quiet precincts of Hercules St. would they penetrate. Never imagined when looking at the house that it would be guarded by "*Yankee sentinels*". They laughed with the children, & seemed to be pleased & at their composure. I do not feel so vindictive towards the poor privates, but their wretched leaders are the ones for whom the gallows are awaiting. The juveniles including ours screamed the "Bonnie Blue Flag" & some daring ones waved the flag in their faces. They seemed to appreciate. What a novel sight they seem to be. A crowd will be following a single one, & yet I hear that their deportment has always been most gentlemanly & I also heard that there were many handsome ones. Take care of my heart, I must. The street was crowded until at a late hour when they continued their watch. Our square guarded by Federals. I supped with Mrs. N. & we promised Ma to come over. Mr. N. came home with the news that we were guarding "Arlington Heights" but I don't believe it. When we went home, found Mr. D. [Duncan] there. His excuse for not coming before was the pressure of business, which as secretary to the Mayor devolves upon him. He entertained us, oh! so agreeably with accounts of the meeting between the Mayor & Gen. Butler, & descriptions of the last named individual. He had heard from "D", from Jackson. In Mr. D. Mr. N. recognized an old acquaintance. He remained for some time & left, leaving no doubt impressed with the idea of his intellect. He does not altogether discredit implicit confidence. And now, my Philomen, my cherished darling of two months, the time has come when we must separate. No longer shall I pour into your willing ear my thoughts & hopes, my fears & wishes. How faithful you have been in your mission, none can know. But the pain, that parting inflicts, is known only to me & could you penetrate beneath the surface & see the emotions of my heart, could you desire a more conclusive proof?

Saturday, May 10th, 1862

6 ³/₄ A.M. Again, dear Philomen, do I invest you with a new robe, & by so doing increase, if possible, the love which days, weeks, months & years have matured. When your mission is fulfilled, another volume will be added to these so sacred now to my sight & prized by me next to earthly things. While you are decked in this garment, may the thoughts which I confide to you be of a pleasant nature, & the hopes & wishes, I express be realized; my sorrows be not anticipated, & the angel of happiness hover over our intercourse. Need I again give utterance to the oft-repeated expressions of my affection? Need I say how dear you are to my heart, how essential to my existence? I once disagreed with a friend who said that the most fervent love was that which did not admit of expression, whose fervor & depth

was too deep for words. I there agree. "T'would be vain to tell thee *all* I feel", then tell me a part of it, & if a person loves me, to convince me of it, each day must I be told of it, & then I will be content to *think,* that "their sweetest melody could never tell *one half* their love for me". I am an exacting body, & in matters of the heart would be so to a fault. I act on the principle of "love *me forever* & love *me alone*", & fearing that you have inherited my disposition I will tell you how I love you, how in the tumultuous past time the thought of being separated from you was madness, & the joy when I again communed with you was overwhelming. My wish has been granted, for each succeeding month *has* strengthened the ties which bind me to you & like wedded love, I find that I love you more each day. Is your little heart now satisfied or is there longing in it yet unsatisfied? Your donor is probably now at his destination, & anticipating your wish, I hope, that success may attend him & that we may all meet again, when our city is again the "home of the free". His kindness we honor with a grateful remembrance. And the other wanderer! When shall tidings be wafted to us of our idolized Father, when shall that joyful reunion occur. "Day succeeds day", & no wiser are we concerning him, but our trust is in God, & let us hope & pray that he *is* well, & that "all may yet be well". There is no news in the paper & can we blame them for the dearth of it, for where are they to obtain this delightful article, I never read them, but my thoughts wing themselves to Pa, aware as I am of his partiality for that kind of reading, & now during its scarcity in his section, I wonder how he compensates for it. Old Butler has issued no proclamations, further, but in his dealings with us has been very lenient, & his allowing the Mayor to retain his position was an unlooked for piece of generosity. In the paper appeared a notice to this effect; "In order to *disappoint* the *hopes* of the *wicked* & to allay the *fears* of the weak & timid, I will make the intelligence that since the capture of the fort, every means have been adopted to prevent *any* epidemic from making its appearance in the city"!! He knows how anxious we are for "Yellow Jack" to pay us a visit. A recruiting officer writes all those who are loyal to the U.S. government to come to him, as he is going to raise a regiment, in order to insure their protection. I hear, but do not vouch for its veracity, that some of our citizens have flocked to the standard. It would not astonish me, for I know there is much union sentiment which is suppressed, but which on a favorable opportunity would be expressed without hesitancy. There is a stand-still in affairs at the present & I am patiently waiting for some communications. The programme of each day is unvaried. Get up, eat breakfast, sew, go to School, come home

& go to bed. I made a great omission; forgot dinner, that important epoch. Contrary to my expectations, Thursday proved to be a very good day. Nothing of moment transpired. Went to School in the afternoon. Knew my lesson, although I had not devoted a moment's study to it. This grieved me, for I fear I shall be tempted to practice the game again. Miss B. is easily satisfied, at any rate with me. Belle looked beautiful. I had but a few moments talk with her, as I was not in a very lively humor. Sat by Miss D. & my voice did not join in the beautiful melody. Singing lesson was concluded with the "Bonnie Blue Flag". Walked home alone, my thoughts being companions, tho' not very pleasant ones. A. & I went to Mrs. N.'s. The Yanks were yet at the corner & there was no diminution in the crowd or confusion. Such an excitement was never before known on unpretending Hercules Street. All day they had been employed in removing the stores. Ma came to Mrs. N.'s, & A. & I took a short walk. Aroused Alice's curiosity by showing her name in the letter list. Nothing is more harassing than this, particularly when you are not expecting a letter & I can't imagine from whom it is. Alice left us to go to Mrs. V. who is improving. Oh! I am in love with her Doctor. He is a perfect Mr. Rutledge, but unfortunately married & his wife is the loveliest creature upon whom my eyes ever rested. I know they are happy. "Mimi" is as beautiful, as graceful as ever in my sight. She is to be married. Her betrothed is at Corinth.[15] No one came in the evening. As usual, I resorted to one of your predecessors to acquaint myself with my movements "this time last year". I was then in an awful state of mind respecting the "Examination", & that is now the spectre which haunts me day & night. Would that it were over. I dare not anticipate promotion, for fear of disappointment—Retired early. No diversion. *Mr. D. calls & then a blank until his next visit.* Yesterday was a pleasant day & employed by me, as usual, profitably. In the afternoon the heavens began to lower, but nothing more was effected. I was spell-bound by the children's singing of our popular national air, & almost forgot to dress. They attract a great deal of attention & are occasionally cheered by enthusiastic passers by. It now possesses double attractions. Went "over the way". Mrs. N. is tied home on account of the Capt. who does not seem to improve. Came home, but to fulfill my promise went back, on conditions that Ma would return at 9, which she did. Lucy shampooed my hair & it was some time before I sought my bed. My bed-fellow was A. & I deem it a useless waste of words to assert that she was in the "land of dreams".

15. Confederate forces remained around Corinth, Mississippi, at this time, following the Battle of Shiloh.

Sunday, May 11th, 1862

7 A.M. Yes, this morning, so many weeks ago, we were rapidly rolling over the dear old Jackson Rail Road. Pardon the allusion, but the morning in some manner *particularly* reminds me of that epoch of our lives, for thinking of it, I always am. No more such pleasant excursions in anticipation, for the cars do not now run regularly & rumor says they will certainly cease. How different an aspect does Camp Moore now wear. I have been engaged for some moments past in the perusal of the paper, which is quite interesting. There is some reading matter, a *little* poetry, & taking into consideration "the times in which we live", it is a very excellent journal. There is a notice from the Gen. commanding the Department of the Gulf in which he promises protection to our unprotected & starving population, "even altho' some of the food will go to supply the starving wants of the wives & children of those now herding at Camp, & elsewhere in arms against the U.S. Ready only for war, we had not prepared ourselves to feed the hungry & relieve the distressed with provisions. But to the extent possible within the power of the Com. Gen. it *shall be done.*" What unparalleled instance of generosity. What is his object. Surely his motives are disinterested. We shall see. I dislike Sundays — Oh! I wish it was this time two months. Who know where I may be, or who cares? I am sure, I don't. Yesterday A. attended Synagogue without me, as I did not feel disposed to accompany her. Saw a most wonderful sight. A Yankee officer attended by six or seven of his men passed on the other side of our street. I was astonished that he was not accompanied by some cannons, as this seems to be their principal article of defense. I glanced over my Geography, but to be honest, I passed the morning in shameful idleness, & I could have employed it most profitably. How can I ever account for this disgraceful waste of the precious sands of life. I must be more cautious in future else kind Butler will furnish me with some employment as he has signified his intention to employ all those according to his own pleasure, who are at present unemployed, his object being, doubtless, to endeavor to promote business, as its suspension seems to be to him a source of great annoyance. The Delta gives him a good "hit" by expression of their pleasure at the future prospects of our merchants & traders, lawyers & judges, in the delightful occupation of street cleaning, etc. etc. It is a wonder that it was not afraid to speak so openly when such stringent restrictions are placed upon them. Oh! I have digressed from my subject, but my heart & head is so full of these dear Yanks & their movements that I cannot refrain from giving

expression to them. I was quite sorry at not having attended Synagogue, when A. returned & communicated to me the unwelcome intelligence that the bride had honored it with her presence. Now I have a peculiar penchant for seeing brides on these occasions, & it is not to be wondered at that my regrets were numerous. I may not have an opportunity of seeing her for some time, as I hear she is to make, shortly, a bridal tour of Europe. I have no particular regard for the lady, but after becoming a bride, there is an unaccountable attraction in them. The man whom she has chosen is prophesied to make a good husband. Rebecca has not been to her aunt's, since their slight disagreement. She is doubtless angry, but I hope there will soon be a reconciliation. These are not angry times. While I was performing ablutionary exercises Octavia & Fannie were announced, & in short while I was prepared to join A. to entertain them, or rather to be entertained. As usual where O. is, there is no want for food for conversation & our tongues flowed as rapidly as the stream. She has plenty to tell & less to hear. She is, in my eyes, quite pretty, but this does not seem to be the general opinion. She is 19 today. I wonder whom she will marry? And F. too. She is a sweet pretty girl, resembling both Leah & Sarah. They paid a long visit, & when they left it was after three, but I know they were ignorant of the time. I hope that we will return their visit before *six months*, the period which she declares took place before her last one & *our return*. While at dinner, the bell rang & imagine our dismay, & particularly Ma's, when made aware that the ringer was Mr. Davis. Ma went in to see him, I followed. His wife & child were with him, so I was satisfied that it was but a friendly visit. We were foolish to be alarmed, as Ma, a short while ago, discharged a part of the debt, & "the times" do not justify payments. But his is a debt of honor, which shall be paid at all sacrifices. As I looked at him, how I thought of the debt of gratitude which we owe to him; one, which we can never forget, & for which we can never cease to bless his name. He is good. Enshrined is his goodness in the hearts of the humble recipient of his great favor. Mrs D. seems to be a very nice lady & we shall be happy to return her visit, which she earnestly requested us to do. She was dressed very handsomely. Does not his means admit of it? When they left I went to Mrs. N.'s, & judge my astonishment when in her mansion I was introduced to a — piano. Mr. N. had made an investment. A very good one, as it will be valuable, when Confederate money may be useless. It was cheap & he will dispose of it if he can obtain a reasonable price. It is not an A 1, but with a little operating upon can be rendered better. Each member were as amazed. A. played on it much to the satisfaction of the Capt. who declared that it made him feel (I forget how many years) younger. At dark we came home & joined the children in the ring & chanted with them our "Bonnie Blue Flag". Mrs. N. came over in the night, & the conversation which was carried on was extremely interesting, but despite "Sleepy Heads" efforts, she could not keep awake. Ma summoned me to breakfast, so with a kind "good bye" I must leave you.

Tuesday, May 13th, 1862

6 ³/₄ A.M. Oh! I fear that A.'s sleepiness must be contagious for I could not this morning arouse myself, until the hour above designated. But when I do fairly awake, & see the bright sun from without, my exit from bed is not very slow. Well, sleep is one of the greatest of pleasures, & bed is a poor person's paradise, especially when they lay their heads on their pillows with light hearts. I think we have all inherited this failing of dearest Pa. No tidings have we as yet received. Today, a month ago, was the date of his last letter. Can such a state of things be long endured? The morning is a lovely one, & realizes all that has been said of May, flowers, birds, etc., etc. The paper asks "What has become of the merry month of May"? It has not been seen in this latitude. We do not know where to look for an answer to our inquiry; certainly it would be folly to expect one from "down East" or the cotton manufacturing districts of England & France.[16] There are no signs of a revival of business, & I cannot ever recollect the time when we saw a perambulating musician grinding out the tunes of a dulcet hand organ. Where have they gone to. I see that Friday by "Davis" orders will be a day of fasting & prayer. The name of our new P.M. [Provost Marshal], Mr Parker, appears & we are notified that mails for "loyal states" are made up, & also for Europe Well, nothing of moment has transpired since last I saw you. On Sunday every paper was at my disposal. The poor True Delta "got in good". In a previous edition they spoke of the burning of our cotton as an act of unexampled patriotism which shall never be forgotten. Butler disagreed with him & said "Your remarks are inadmissible. Wanton & criminal acts of destruction of property are not acts of patrio-

16. Expected support for the Confederacy from the cotton mills of Europe and New England did not appear.

tism, but Vandal incendiarism which will be punished. You will not receive further caution but punishment for like offense. Publish this conspicuously". Now, how degrading that men have to submit to such insolence. But what can they do? Suspend the publication of their paper, from which so many derive their support? The burning of that cotton is an act which Thorg never can forget & forgive.[17] I discharged my debt to A. by mending her long promised petticoat. Performed other jobs including the ripping of my barège to renovate, for in these times people must devise all sorts of means. Had a meat dinner. Meat, which in former times we would consign to the Mississippi, now sells for 40 & 50 cts. per lb. Mr. E. came in the afternoon. I just saw him a short while & he left before dark. A. & I went to Mrs. N. & the piano was made to sound, A. favoring us with all she knew. We had no idea of staying, but she *insisted* on it. After supper, Ma, F., S. & Dell augmented the party, & I tell you we had fun, dancing gigs, quadrilles & polkas, singing, etc. & Mr. N. was gratified that the piano could contribute so wholly to our enjoyment, & we often charged him with "enjoying his things". We sent in for "Mrs. Kerr", but "Edmund" was so cross, she could not leave him. Our fun ended about 9, when we retired to our abode. A piano changes the aspect of a house, & like a baby "it is a well-spring of joy". How harassing to know that your fingers cannot draw music from the "silent keys", & so another Sunday was added to the Past. How many happy ones have I enjoyed. Yesterday, we had a little foretaste of the "heated term" [summer] in which we are entering. Old Sol's beams, tho' far from being so fiery as they will become ere the long, enduring summer begins to wane, were sufficiently ardent to make any but light clothing uncomfortable & the shady side of the street very desirable. I see that Camp & Canal had quite a gay appearance, so large was the turn out of fair ladies & damsels, surely I did not swell the list, for I was enjoying myself. I am, as Ma says, a "little enthusiast", & now I am in the view of sewing. I fixed my dress very nicely, & put on my first flounce, which I hope will not be my last. Ma was engaged on a white body for me, a prevailing & pretty fashion. With many regrets, I left to study, but my mind being on something else, & my lessons being at random I returned to my work. Studying is a bore, & the L.N.S. ditto. Dreaded $2\frac{1}{2}$ came, when I had to prepare myself. Quite a catastrophe happened. E. [Ellen, the domestic] broke a beautiful pitcher. I do so dislike for anything valuable to get broken, but always endeavor to suppress my anger, knowing it

17. Clara may have meant Thor, the Norse god of thunder, often regarded as the God of War. The *True Delta* refrained from publishing reports antagonistic to the occupation forces after this threat.

to be an accident, & doing as I should like to be done by. After a light repast, I left, & was soon in School. Got my sums, studied my lesson, & was much gratified when my recitations were perfect, minus much labor. The Misses Logan have gone away. I am sorry. Mag. & I had a pleasant time, talking; she gave me Miss Mitchell's love which had been sent to me. In these emergencies we are out early, & I was almost home before six o'clock. Repaired upstairs where I resumed my occupation & my dress is almost finished. Continued until it was too dark for me to thread my needle. (Ma & A. were out.) My thoughts were going as fast as my fingers, & I was contrasting the present events with those of a year ago. We went to "Camp Walker", & as A. says "her life then began, for she first saw — Robert". Oh! what a delightful time we had. Saw O.P. for the first time & made him (I thought) a vain promise to visit him at Camp Moore. In the night we went to the lake, had a fine supper, & when I say that Pa was with us, it is "*superfluous*" to say "we enjoyed ourselves". A. had signified her intention of celebrating the occasion which doubtless was her reason for going out. She declared she could not remain at home. Mrs. N. came over & was relating to me her troubles with the Capt. He is so cross. As she was gone, Ma & A. came. They had been to Rebecca's & had had a pleasant time. She seems angry with Mrs. N. but I hope they will make it up. Mr. & Mrs. N. honored us in the night & then followed a long dissertation. In what a different locality were we May 13th, 1861. Did O.P. & C.R.W. think of it. Never! Never!

Thursday, May 15th, 1862

6 1/2 A.M. I am so often undetermined what course to pursue: whether to commune with you each day & relate to you the events, no matter how few & insignificant they may be, or do as I now do, visit you every other day, & by an accumulation of the incidents of the days make the recital more agreeable, but even now I am often at a loss to know what to say, & in this dilemma, I naturally seize upon trivial objects. But I must abandon ideas of *now* changing my course, as other duties interfere to influence my actions, as there are some times which it is requisite that I should devote to my studies, & in the early part of the day. When I am undisturbed, & my brain clear is the most favorable opportunity. But looms there in the distance "the better time coming" so "cheer! oh! cheer! away with idle sorrow"! This morning *nine* months ago, we accompanied our darling Father, a short distance up the road, & when I stood on the steps of the Magnolia Hotel, & saw the car which bore him from me, saw his dear hand waving a farewell until it could no more be seen, I little dreamed how many days would elapse ere I should again behold that angel countenance. How much more bitter would have been my tears, but an all-wise Providence have veiled from us the future. I know well now that the grief of separation is far greater after the lapse of time, for at first it is novelty, & that engages the minds, but when that wears off, we awake to reality, to the stern reality that he has gone. My tears blind me. Oh! God! answer our prayers, & waft to us tidings of him whom our hearts adore. We are now enjoying lovely weather. Tuesday was a glorious day; quite *warm*, but remarkably *cool* to those to the "manor born". Surely if the papers give us no news, what can you expect from me. There is a deplorable want of this article almost as much so as the necessaries of life. The doings of the Yanks alone occupy the public mind & so completely fill it, that there is no space for aught besides. So many rumors are afloat, some so extravagant & absurd that I am determined to give credence to those only, which I consider as emanating from good authority. By these reports a person is plunged into a continual state of excitement & for nothing some one will tell you that a certain place has been seized. You will relate it to another party only to receive from them a decided contradiction. But it is a fact beyond doubt that they have taken possession of our elegant & commodious St. James for a Hospital. As so many places are put to this purpose it is obvious, though they deny it, that there must be much sickness among them.[18] In the afternoon, I attended School, & requested Maggie to deliver to R. Ma's message, inviting her to come & spend the following evening with her. Miss B. was unusually cross. But she is excusable, as her duties are very arduous & fatiguing, as she also teaches in the morning. After a display of our elocutionary powers & the reading of Shakespeare's Cassius & Brutus, that amiable lady dismissed her obedient class. Walked home hurriedly. Found Ma out, & A. in the first stages of her toilette, so I enjoyed myself sewing on the machine. Then escorted by A. & Josie took a promenade. Met Ma, who had made an unsuccessful pilgrimage to Dryades St. in search of some dry goods, being unable to finish our bodices until we had some suitable trimming. I have not seen "Mr. da Ponte, Jr." as frequently since the visit of the Yanks to his abode. He has probably selected

18. Clara and others expected Union soldiers to succumb to all the tropical diseases, particularly Yellow Fever, to which the local population had developed some immunity.

a more desirable residence. In the evening we were honored by a visit from Mr. Duncan. As a general thing they are very lengthy, but none the less agreeable. He is of the opinion that Pa is on his way home. Marion Baker is expected this month, & we anticipate some news by him.[19] Mr. D. had none to communicate. He is a sort of croaker & predicts bad times coming. He is not pleased with our leading men in government & Pres. Davis has received much censure, & all are of the opinion that things would have been different had our "brave Beauregard" been in his stead.[20] While they were deliberating for two months what color & devices to have for a flag, the Feds. were busily engaged in building gun-boats. It is passed & we must try to make amends for the future. He left about 10. Took his exit in a Gus Leovian manner. By the way, what has become of our old friend Gus. Let us give him a passing thought. Yesterday was another beautiful day. More sunny, glorious weather. "Although *far* from being as hot as it no doubt will be ere long, the weather in the middle of the day was much warmer than we fancy was necessary to promote the comfort of the *many* among us". So says the Picayune which offers no consolation to our visitors, whose visit has induced so many to become profane by wishing evil upon them. So many endeavor to believe that so many things prognosticate a most unhealthy, "yellow Jackish" season. Old But. has taken his headquarters at Pass Christian, as though "Bronze John" cannot attack him there as readily as here. By his orders, the "Crescent" has been suppressed. The reason being that its Proprietor, I.O. Nixon, is a Rebel now in arms against the U.S. government. But why not do likewise to the other papers whose proprietors are likewise engaged, for instance, the Delta & Bulletin. He also says "It having come to the knowledge of the commanding Gen. that Friday next is to be observed as a day of fasting & prayer, in obedience to some *supposed* proclamation of *one Jefferson Davis*, it is ordered that no such observance be had". Now is this not stinging, humiliating. I do not understand how men can endure, but in this city they accommodate themselves to circumstances, *too readily.* I sewed but was compelled to leave early, as Wednesday is a detestable day. Eat dinner without A. I scarcely ever see her from morning until evening. Arrived in School in season & was informed by M. that a previous engagement prevented R. from accepting Ma's invite. I did not know my lesson very well,

19. Marion Baker was the mayor's secretary before occupation.
20. There was much criticism of Jefferson Davis and the men he chose for his cabinet. Judah Benjamin was not popular, but had the confidence of President Davis. Beauregard was always a favorite in his home state, but not a serious replacement for Davis.

& as misery loves company I was glad not to be alone in my misfortune. Mag. was absent & I missed her. Our class is very small, & before you are aware of it a question comes around again. Oh! what a nuisance! Came home & informed Ma that she need expect no company, & she was much pleased that she had made no preparation. I sewed a little, but soon put up, not feeling in the disposition. As the children were singing the Bonnie Blue Flag, they had the satisfaction, while at the part "Rather than take down our flag to die we would prefer", of seeing three Yanks on the opposite side, who looked over & laughed, seemingly enjoying it. Ma, A. & I went round to Bombergs, but as she was unable to change a bill, we could not procure the desired article. When will the City Treasurer be prepared to issue the promised small note currency? Its appearance is eagerly looked for & it would greatly facilitate small business operations besides ridding the public of that host of shin-plasters. Saw Mrs. da [Ponte]. but was unobserved by her. I was much fatigued on arriving home. I do not take sufficient exercise. Partook heartily of the evening meal, indulging in my favorite of favorites—cream cheese. Mr. & Mrs. N. honored us. They were both in excellent spirits, doubtless occasioned by the circumstance of gas being introduced into their mansion. A short time ago, I heard them express their intention of moving. Today is three weeks since that awful day & two weeks since the departure of "D". It seems like years. But one half of this month has gone.

Saturday, May 17th, 1862

6 3/4 A.M. I have been up for some time, & in obedience to A.'s orders, the Paper was brought to her, & the general orders No. 29 & 30 were so unexpected & startling that they completely unnerved me, & I was unable to continue my toilette. I was not quite right in saying that they were unexpected for do we place any reliance on the word of that unprincipled Butler? Order No. 29, "On the 27th day of May, all circulation of or trade in Con. notes & bills will cease within this department, & all sales or transfers made on that day will be void, & the property confiscated to the U.S."!! Now, how terrible a blow is this. The greater part of the money now in circulation is the Con. notes, & the loss to many will be enormous. None, I presume, will now be received in payment & what substitute are we to have. The "Wretch" said in his proclamation that he would allow them as a legal tender, & see how he has violated his word. I have no doubt but it will produce a great commotion in the city & why shouldn't it, when it will involve the ruin of thousands. General order No. 30. The *N.O. Delta* having published in today's issue, an article discussing the cotton question in a manner which violates the terms of the Proclamation, from these headquarters, *the office of that paper will be taken possession of & its business conducted under direction of the U.S. authorities.* They knew that it would eventually come to this & they should have suspended it. How indignant will Sophie [Mrs. da Ponte] be, how enraged, "D". I am so sorry. A paper which it takes years to establish, in the prime of its life to be so cut down & the unemployed devised [deprived] now of their employment. This dark day I foresaw. Oh! had they been more cautious. Upon Mr. W., I suppose, falls the blame. The continuation of the order is, "The N.O. Bee, having published an elaborate though covert article in favor of the burning of the cotton & the mob, is hereby suppressed. No publication of any kind will issue from that paper until further orders". Now the old driver is beginning to draw his reins. For a while he was quite willing that the papers should continue, but now his object is accomplished & paper after paper will depart. The taking of this city & the burning of our cotton will be the making of our Confederacy, for it will show the foreign nations that we are in *earnest* & willing to make any sacrifices, that we are a brave determined people imbued with the same spirit as were those 13 little colonies who triumphed over the greatest nation on earth. There were gloomier days than this during the Revolution, for says a London paper, "the capture of Charleston or N.O. itself would, if the Southerners intend to hold out, be but the commencement of the war. Let it be remembered that we took all these cities & Boston & N.Y. besides during the war of Independence. We had nothing to conquer but the Atlantic coast & we found after a fair trial that it was impossible. It was not so much the volunteers as the *country* which beat us. We had a much more desperate battle & a much more glorious success at Bunker Hill, than the Fed. had at Fort Donelson but it had little value towards the conquest of Massachusetts".[21] This seems as though they were decidedly in our favor. That cotton is But.'s tender point, & may it often be assailed. Oh! my head is so filled with them that every other topic sinks into insignificance. The weather is at present fine, but yesterday we had a touch of summer & we again realize that this house is not adopted to that season. It is a very unpleasant summer residence & had

21. The writer refers to the important Union victory at Fort Donelson in northern Tennessee earlier in 1862.

things been different it was Ma's intention to move, but can we now think of such a thing, unsettled as we feel. I declare I, & in fact we, are so foolish. When the bell rings all kind of antics are practised, & I dread to ask who it is, fearing that the response will not be "Pa". Oh! ye minds! waft to us some tidings of him. Our bodies are not finished, but some others were on hand of a finer material & by hard labor we completed them yesterday, it being a very good job. They are beautiful & I believe mine to be the prettier. A very happy belief. Some Yankees passed & being alarmed that they were going to School, we dispatched L. to see, & they didn't. In the afternoon A. & I made up our minds to go to Mrs. Caulfield, so we made our most elaborate toilettes for that purpose & by 6¼ left our abode. A pleasant walk of a few minutes brought us in sight of her residence, & we espied the "venus" standing on her gallery. She ran down to greet us, & said that she was *so happy to see us*. She looked very pretty & as I gazed upon her I did not wonder that the title of the "prettiest lady in N.O." had been awarded to her. But—she is not *my style*. Oh! for the "golden hair & eyes of heaven's own blue"! She had a great deal to say as all have at these times & you can imagine the general topic. The house next to her is unoccupied & cheap & she is so desirous for Ma to take it. I don't know if I should be pleased, for you know "Too much familiarity", etc. Several of the d—m wretches passed, some in carriages & some on horseback. Oh! that—I could have had [at] them. Ma's strict orders were that we should be home before dark & for fear of being prohibited in the street, *at all*, we left early, & she walked some distance with us. She & Vic. are going to pay some visits today in a carriage, & she said she would stop in & see us. What beautiful sisters!! Arrived home safe. Mrs. N. was there. Left shortly. Mary has left her. In the night Ma & F. went over, A. & I preferring home, & we managed to keep awake until their arrival. I declare I had almost forgotten to make any observations of Thursday, & with the exception of one item, it would have made no material difference had it entirely escaped my memory. When I arrived in School, I noticed an unusual stir & commotion & when I inquired the cause, there was some astonishment expressed that I had not heard the news, the General order, No. 28. I was informed of it & when Miss B. came she read it. "Be silent that you may hear. As the soldiers of the U.S. have been subject to insults offered to them by the women (calling themselves ladies) of N.O., I hereby order that should any female treat with contempt, or insult in word, gesture or movement any officer & private under my command, she shall be liable to be treated as a woman of the town, plying her avocation". Oh! Philomen, I cannot express to you the indignation this thing awakened, my feelings are akin to a lady, who speaking of the subject, said "I cannot tell you how I feel or what I think". I hear that the men were perfectly exasperated for you know the insult offered to us is also to them. The cowardly wretches! to notice the insults of ladies! But the news will get abroad & then we shall be praised for our actions. They will see the spirit of our women, aged, even children, but they *dare* not notice their insults. And how did they expect to be treated. Can a woman, a Southern woman, come in contact with one of them & allow her countenance to retain its wonted composure. Will not the scornful feelings in our hearts there find utterance. They may control our actions, but looks, they never can. Nothing was thought of in school, but it, & there was also some unusual excitement, as it is rumored that it is their intention to pay a visit to the School, & they are daily looked for. The High School was to be closed on the morrow [Jefferson Davis had ordered a fast day], but I think it is injudicious to so totally disregard But.'s orders. True, Davis is superior to him, but we, *we* are the captured in a captive city & as servile to them as is the slave to his master. Oh! how long will, *can* this state of things exist? We were dismissed early & a few moments after I got home Fanny B. came in. She is very patriotic & still wears a flag, which I greatly disapprove of, as we should not lay ourselves open to insult for is there any law to protect us? She did not stay very long & we walked a few squares with her & observed "D" Jr. emerging from his mansion. Went over to Mrs. N., Mr. N. very much enraged, so much so, that he determined to say nothing. A long argument & discussion was kept up, upon patriotism, the different ways of showing it, etc., etc. Truly, I would have made any sacrifice rather than those — should have had possession of our city. Shall it? yes to the ground. For it would be of as much use as it now is to us. But they should never have been allowed to enter. The report of Gen. Lovell's death is untrue. Many rejoiced at the mere mention of it. I do not doubt his loyalty to us, but I do doubt his competency to fill the position he held. His character as a military man is ruined. No one came at night & after the usual programme retired. Endeavored to kill as few mosquitoes as possible. For two reasons, the first being that we should be polluted by being touched by "Yankee blood", & secondly each one increases the number & aids in biting & tormenting them. I wonder how they like them! Oh! ever & anon come thoughts, come gentle thoughts of the poor Delta.

Sunday, May 18th, 1862

6 1/4 P.M. I am sitting on the "back steps" not a very romantic position, indeed, as the view which surrounds me consists principally of cisterns, clotheslines, etc. But it is solitary & quite pleasant & the gentle breezes as they fan my cheeks waft to me thoughts of my dear Father who so often has sat in the selfsame place & enjoyed the refreshing coolness of the "pleasantest place in the house". But it is not requisite that I should be here, to think of him, for with every spot is connected some association of his dear self, & every thought of mine is entertwined with one for him. "There is not an hour or day of dreaming hour, but I am with him". Oh! when & where shall we meet again. Has "D" seen him & given him all the particulars or do fears for our safety ever distress his mind. It is quite an unusual hour for me to be with you, but as it presented itself, I thought I would seize it. Ma & I have been busy today on two dresses for S. & R. We finished them & I decked "my pretty child" in hers & felt well repaid for any labor. Dear little Rosa has the hooping cough & is not looking very well. I have been employed in ripping a flounce off of last summer's dress, & I intend to convert it into two diminutive ones. Necessity & *war* is the mother of invention. My toilette I hastily made as appearance is now a matter of no importance. Alice is down stairs, Ma & F. too & I am here alone. The day I have passed, not idly. The early portion I devoted to the arranging & putting away of the winter clothes as I suppose their reign for the season is over. Then the papers claimed my attention, the Picayune & True Delta (how my heart longed for the Delta). There was *some* reading matter but I looked in vain for General order, No. 31. My curiosity was much aroused by their statement that they had become acquainted with some matters of importance, but fearing their publication to be contraband they had decided not to publish them. I should have disposed of these journals before breakfast, but was quite tardy in rising. L. called me before she went to market & on her return was astonished to find me still reclining. I am in such sleepy humours these mornings. I must be the conqueror to-morrow morning as I have detestable School duties to perform. (By the by the L.N.S. would be an excellent locality for a hospital!!) There was a change in our "bills of fare" which occasions us much merriment. Vegetables are plentiful, but the all absorbing question is "with what are we to purchase things"? There is a gloomy future. A. & I did not attend Synagogue yesterday, the principal reason being, I *believe* that we had no new bonnets. We dressed in expectation of our promised visit nor were we disappointed.

About one o'clock, the bell rang. I answered it & was presented by the footman of the carriage with cards bearing the names of Mrs. I. Caulfield & Mrs. B. Searrell. I look out, saw them. They stepped from their carriage & entered & two creatures of wondrous, dazzling beauty stood before me. Vic. & I were old schoolmates & we greeted each other as we had of yore. They were dressed mostly alike & by the occasional glances, Ma & A. cast at me, I knew their *"opinion of the subject"*. It is difficult to decide which is the handsomest, but we have all decided in favor of Vic. She is the finer size & a nobler looking woman & in my eyes more beautiful, but Annie's manners are more fascinating & herself more simple. When I looked into the surpassingly lovely eyes of Vic., I wondered if any womanly feelings ever occasioned their glaring light to be less tender, for she does seem so cold; but probably the flattery of the world has enacted a part in this. Oh! were I but capable of awakening in her breast the emotion of love. For those sweet eyes to beam on me with love & tenderness, & their cold beams wilt into those of affection. Altho' she is not my style, I could lavish upon her all that love which such a resplendent beauty as hers inspires. And can she be blamed for being vain? Probably she has been so surfeited with compliments that she is indifferent & callous towards them. And her husband! He is a perfect Apollo! She resides at the Florence House surrounded by officers, whom she manages at every opportunity to "cut up". And "Annie"! She is so sweet, so childish! There is much disagreement respecting their beauty & I have always heard her called the handsomest. But it admits of no dispute that they are two as handsome sisters as can be found. In imagination I compared myself with them. They paid a long visit, the principal subject of conversation being the Yanks. They both reminded us of our turn to call. I should like very much to go & see Vic. but I do not admire the locality of her residence, *these times*. Oh! they do kiss so feelingly & when their beautiful lips rested upon mine, it was the realization of one of those moments of which I had so often dreamed. They had gone & but the remembrance of their beautiful selves had they left. Talked a short while about them & then summoned my S. to be performed upon with ablutionary exercises. She not very cheerfully consented & when her turn was ended mine began. I read a little. Ma was to Mrs. N. but returned in time for 3 o'clock dinner. Devoted some of the afternoon to A.'s hoop. Had an idea of going to Mrs. da P.'s but abandoned it, deferring it to another period. Made up our minds to go to Miss Calders. Donned our barêges & in due course of time arrived at the mansion of that most estimable lady, & had the extreme felicity of finding her home. We did not remain long, as the clouds looked very threatening. When we came home Alice informed us that the morning had witnessed the advent of a little nephew of hers, the first boy born in the Mazareau family. It is quite a populous neighborhood, the births in it since our residence being very large. As it is in the male line, maybe Ma would be so lucky. But fortunately there will be no little baby *this year at any rate.* We had a hard shower in the evening & my fears of a storm were, happily not realized. I prophesied a rainy day, but a la contraire, it is a most beautiful one. I feel guilty for being so selfish, so must hasten down & proffer my company to my sister Alice.

Tuesday, May 20th, 1862

6 1/2 A.M. I am very late in descending, but my excuse — "not feeling very well" — is an excellent one, & I can assure you that I would feel much more comfortable in my bed. But I cannot give up to such indolence. The morning is beautiful & a continuance of such fine weather is quite novel. We are now enjoying the cool mornings & evenings for which our "Sunny South" is so famed. Dear little Josie, with her sweet prattle & endearing epithet of "Tita" is by me. "Our darling" is two years old today. "Our little sis, just two years old is worth her weight in *gold*". Now this is a bold assertion, considering the demand for, & the value of the last named article!! How well do I remember the events of this day two years ago, when I was first ushered into the presence of the "little stranger". She is such a fine child! so smart & promises to be the prettiest of the family. But alas! Ma says that we all gave promises of so being. How we have disappointed them. The time that has elapsed seems very long & it has been fraught with many important changes for us. I am so delighted when Monday is over. Yesterday I was up at five, studying & writing & when 8 came, I was weary, oh! so weary. I wish they would abolish the school. Can you enter into my feelings. I want to leave & yet I do not *want to.* Paradoxical. Had "D" 's attempts been crowned with success!!! Ma & Mrs. N. went out to endeavor to make a disposition of their money, as in this section it is valueless.[22] I was sewing on my muslin & succeeded in gathering a flounce & putting it on, my 1st

22. Some merchants accepted confederate money, but none in the Solomons' neighborhood.

endeavor. I was loath to leave it at 12, but "necessity knows no law". About 2 Ma came, fatigued, as may be imagined. She amused me with relating the prices of goods, which had not the source been so reliable, I should have doubted. $10 linen is $50, 12½ cts. muslin, $1.00!! & every thing in proportion. It reminds me of the times of the Revolution, when $75 in Continental money was given for $1 in silver. It will not be here so, for all trade in it will cease in a week, & the all absorbing question is what will be done. Indisputably some expedient will have to be adopted but while the "grass is growing, the horse is starving". Some of the stores refused to take the money, but all who did not, will sell to the amount of a bill, but deliver no change. They succeeded in making a few purchases, & Ma did not even change her bill. There were many ladies out. Met Rebecca & she & Mrs. N. were as friendly as of yore. Jim has again gone & is attending an officer. The streets are crowded with them. Oh! that we could strike them out as one man. But our time will come, & soon enough they will see the folly of their attempts to restore the Union on the basis of the consti- tution. A. & I are determined *not* to go back, notwithstanding the course taken by all beside. But what a waste of words! *Can we ever be subdued?* Allowing that, can we ever be united in the sacred ties of brotherhood with those for whom we entertain the most rancorous hatred. For a time it *may* endure. But the proud spirit cannot always be claimed, it will break the fetters at any peril & then again there will be a devastation of another civil war.[23] We do not ask for a cessation of hostilities. No! we wish to gain our independence by a mighty struggle & convince them of our power, & though they have the "right of might", have we not the right of justice? & "thrice is he armed, who hath his quarrel just". Ma had heard a great deal, but I will not give credence to it. The report is that the *Mayor* is under arrest & is to be sent to *Fort Jackson*, for remonstrating with "But" [Butler]. on Gen. Order No. 28! I do not believe it, & yet it is not impossible for what dare not he do? We ate dinner without A. & I proceeded to School, not in a very enviable humour. Met Olympia & Ann, & progressed with them. I hear that the Yanks have offered some insults to ladies, who have violated the Gen. Order. I cannot sympathize with them. I knew all my lessons, but I must not omit to mention that we recited *one*. Learned with much regret that Miss Del Trigo had left. "Girl after girl departs"! Hurried home as I did not feel very well. Finished my dress which looks very well. Went over to Mrs. N.'s. The Capt. is down & is fast recovering. Mr. N. was as gloomy,

---

23. Clara felt that defeat would not bring the North and South together because of the hatred in the hearts of southerners. Another civil war would inevitably break out, she thought.

as reticent, vengeful as ever. Mrs. N. has succeeded in procuring a domestic. We left before dark, & did not fulfil our promise of going back. (Nobody came. What a superfluity) & we retired early. I wonder what has become of our attentive cousin Sam! He does not know if we are in the city & he does not care. Could anyone imagine the intimacy which once existed? And our Bayou cousins. Knowing we are here alone would it injure them to come & see *how* we were, & *where* we were?[24]

Thursday, May 22nd, 1862

6 A.M. How great a change does a few moments make in the morning. It is so quiet that one could easily imagine herself in some rural district, but presently the confusion of every day life will be heard, the hum of busy voices & the pattering of anxious steps. Each one, as he passes, has his own thoughts to occupy his mind, unknown to any beside. How great a privilege is thought. To wander, unresisted where'er our fancy may dictate. We can visit the abode of a king, or the herds of the poor; can lay plans for the future, & how noiselessly does it perform its operations & yet how mighty are its accomplishments. In fact all things in nature are carried on in silence. No noise indicates the rising of the sun, no noise attends it when it sinks into the West. The Earth revolves upon her axis! There is no jostling of machinery, the little bud expands into the flower, & oh! how noiselessly, thought performs its duties under head. Oh! when all else is denied us, when freedom of speech becomes a crime, oh! happiness it is to know that no one can exercise authority over the realms of thought. My paper has not come, & I am anxiously waiting for it as it is to contain the list of letters remaining in the P.O. & hope whispers "there may be one for us". I am confident that Pa has written & entrusted it to some one's care, but there are many instances in which the bearer of letters, fearing for their own security, have destroyed them. There has been much excitement of late in the city & it astonishes me how each day there is something new to speculate upon. It is really true that our Mayor has been sent to Fort Jackson, for how long a space of time, no one can tell. He wrote a letter to "But." [General Butler] remonstrating with him on his order No. 28 [the

24. The "Bayou cousins" were the family of Joseph Solomon.

"Woman" order] & upon this pretense he arrested him. How faithfully he has not interfered with the city government! It is his object to imprison all of our office holders & all our prominent men, many of whom have already been sent. Mr. Duncan is keeping the Mayor's company. A nice predicament he is in. Better had he left the city. On Tuesday the carpets were to be taken up, but in consequence of "Mr. Nelson" failing to make his appearance the job was not performed. The day was *hot,* but I have felt many *hotter!* I donned a muslin dress for the first time this year. Accompanied by Alice went to School. Had a great deal of fun there with Belle & Maggie, during Dictation, & it continued during Elocution. Miss B. dismissed us unusually early & we remained a short while to hear the girls sing, & ourselves joined in. I, rather too loud, so made a precipitate flight from the room. I gave Belle her Album, & received her thanks. I was determined that she should have it, for after I got to School, I found that I had left it home & went back after it. A. & I took a short walk, & on our return at A.'s invitation sat down on their steps & staid there for some time. "Tots" is such a lovely child that I was loath to leave her. She has no mother [her father Emile Mazareau was a widower], but they more than fulfill her place. In the night a Proclamation of Gen. Shepley made its appearance. "During the Mayor's absence", he fills his place, until a loyal citizen of the U.S. shall be elected. I hope that we will find no disloyal citizens seeking for office. His article was very presuming & I regret not having it at my command. There is a letter from Summers, in which he endeavors to exculpate himself from blame, says "I am no traitor".[25] Mrs. N. came over for a few moments. I have seen the list of letters. Our name is not among them. Nothing of import happened yesterday. Rosa was quite unwell, but we attributed it to her cough. I sewed as usual. Ma was very low-spirited. I don't presume that M.A.B. will come back. I went to School unattended, & to my surprise I saw reposing upon the bosom of a young lady there a breast-pin, which F. lost about a year ago, or to be more lenient its fac-simile. I politely asked if the pin she wore was a found one, & being answered in the negative, left her, & went to my seat "maiden meditation, *fancy free*". I knew my lessons & never & anon would my thoughts stray to the "lost sheep". M. & I enjoyed ourselves excessively & are very fearless. Mrs. N.'s sweet face attracted my attention. I came home with O. The Feds. have

25. Summers was a New Orleans judge who spied for the Union. He was escorted safely to Union headquarters at the St. Charles Hotel, and from there to the safer Customshouse. That Summers could be publicly led from the Hotel without harm has been considered crucial to Butler's ability to govern the city without fear of mob rebellion.

taken up their quarters in Tivoli Circle, & a most revolting spectacle was presented to me, in the shape of the U.S. flag, floating from the centre of the ground. Oh! that I could "trail its stars on the ground". Today, four weeks ago, we were all panic stricken on account of the wretches. "D", 3 weeks. I found A. in the first stages of her toilette, & went down, & was soon on the front steps interested in the Lamplighter when a carriage stopping at the Mazareaus attracted my attention & double so when 2 Yankee devils stepped from it & rang the bell. A few seconds more they entered it *with Mr. Mazareau.* I was in a state of doubt & conjecture & Alice could give no information as she knew nothing. Mrs. Gray, to our surprise came round & brought the pin, related the circumstance, & said it was her daughter-in-law's but she wished us to see if we could detect any difference between hers & ours. To be sure, we could not, for they are identical. But I am wrong for being so harsh. But the fact of F.'s losing it in school, & its appearing on the Porteress's daughter is very convincing. But we assured her we were satisfied & expressed the possibility of there being two alike (which I do not believe). I am content to know its fate. I was playing with my angel "Tots" & with pleasure was hearing her lisping in French, & when to your questions the sweet replies of "Oui" was given, I was fairly tempted to eat her up. It is strange, how peculiar a propensity some people have to inflict pain upon the object of their love. "I know a gentleman", who when he loves you the most invariably pinches & slaps you the hardest, & this is the way with me. About 7 the carriage again rolled to the door, containing the two detestable Yankees, one of whom got out & inquired something of Mrs. M. & then went. A. left us to make inquiries & returned & said that they just asked "if Mr. Mazareau had a sick daughter", & departed, leaving our minds in a state of suspense & conjecture. The most plausible of which was that Mr. M. had so told them, but they, so mistrustful, had come to ascertain its truthfulness. They were very anxious & bothered, & we sympathized with them. After supper when we went to Mrs. N. we stopped there, but they had heard nothing more. Mrs. N.'s parlors were illuminated with gas light. It is a great improvement in a house; she has ideas of moving & I hope that no considerations of us will influence her actions to the contrary as we are not dependent upon them for our well-being. If their friendly feelings are not such as to sacrifice in a small degree their pleasure & comfort, why they can move. We left at an early hour. We were up stairs & undressed, when horror of horrors! our bell rang. Oh! who could it be at such an hour, was the question which our reason failed to answer. L. looked & saw a gentleman, & went down to open the door. Our thoughts were of Pa, & I was confident that we were to receive bad tidings of him. With trembling hands we dressed & went down, oh! so unprepared for anything & I am sure that had my fears been confirmed, I should have died. Ma & A. went in, but I, too fearful to venture, peeped in & in a moment recognized the gentleman as Alice's brother, Emile. Oh! God! what a relief, & with a prayer of thankfulness on my lips, I entered the apartment. He came to inform us that Mr. Mazareau was a prisoner, but was present at his house on his parole of honor. He can only form surmises, but upon the slightest pretense, our officials will be arrested [Mazareau had been elected Sheriff]. He was only allowed to return home on account of his sick daughter & our supposition relative to the affair was correct. He staid a long while. Oh! he is such a dear man, so handsome, & so polite & has such a lovely child, which in my eyes enhances his attraction. I am in love with him, & *would* have him *for the baby, if nothing else. He thanked us for the interest we had evinced in the matter,* & I hope he will avail himself of our invitation of "call again". Mr. M. is to have a hearing tomorrow, & has made up his mind to go to Fort Jackson; but it may not be as bad, & we should endeavor to look on the bright side of the picture. With what different emotions did I ascend the stairs. Sometimes I am almost glad that Pa is not here, for fear of his being involved in difficulties. When shall we hear from him?

Saturday, May 24th, 1862

6 $^1/_4$ A.M. Well, I am glad that the morning gives indication of its being a good day, for I am not always in the humour for it to rain. It is delightfully pleasant & no doubt our Northern visitors regard our cool mornings & hot days with no little degree of wonder. Oh! Philomen, where is it natural that my thoughts should stray this morning? Will the events of today, one year ago, ever fade from my memory? Can I ever forget my visit to camp Moore, fraught as it was with so much pleasure as to be classed as one of the epochs of my life. This morning 52 weeks ago, we were steaming along, ignorant of the enjoyment in store for us. Imagination pictures every scene of the eventful days before me. The sumptuous dinner around Capt. White's table, & it is a consolation to know that all the brave men who were gathered there, tho' they have borne part in many a conflict since, have escaped

danger or death. Today was not so remarkable as to-morrow, for it was then that our acquaintance with *that noble man began*. It is happiness to be able thus to revert to scenes of past pleasure, though the thoughts may be intermingled with transient feelings of sorrow, but do not joy & sorrow always go hand in hand, & oh! "rather than be one bliss forgot, be all our pains remembered". The paper announces the fact that Provost French commenced his duties as Chief of Police, on Thursday. He visited the police stations, & said that the oath of allegiance must be taken by all, who would henceforth serve in the police force. At the 2nd station, the men being drawn up in a line, a call was made for such as were willing to take the required oath, when one, only one, an old man, stepped forth & when the question was put "are any more willing", the reply was, "None, none, none". At the 3rd, only 2 of the immense number took it, & at the 4th, 6, all old men. How gratifying to see the display of such feelings in our poor men, men whose situations were their only dependence, & yet they were willing to sacrifice anything in preference to their honor & their country. Our city will now be guarded by Federals. The paper contains an account of the evacuation of Portsmouth, & — Norfolk, our strongest forthold. Everything seems to favor our enemies, but we shall not despond. Thursday, old Sol was out in all his glory, & his beams were as ardent as we ever experienced so early in the "heated term". About noon the storm burst upon the city, & soon the rain fell heavily & the temperature was sensibly decreased. We were thankful that Nelson had finished shaking the carpets (so you know they are up), & bare floors are not to me, as to many, an unpleasant sight, particularly this morning, as they were cleaned yesterday. I was spared the bustle & confusion consequent upon their being removed. About 1 Rebecca & Maggie came in (they had been to Mrs. N.'s also). R. had a great deal to say & monopolized the conversation; a person to be agreeable should be willing to listen as to talk, but evidently she is not of that opinion. She gave us an account of the Mayor's arrest & the escape Mr. H. [Harris] made from accompanying him. They remained a long while & she said she would be up one morning next week, as Mr. H. objected going out at night. I hastily prepared my toilette for L.N.S. Eat dinner without A. I had gone a few steps, when hearing my name, I turned back & was greeted by Alice, & together we proceeded. "Pretty Belle" sat with me, & as usual we laughed. I knew my lesson, altho' I had not bestowed 10 minutes study upon it. Learned that the Schools are to have no vacation, for if they do so, they will be occupied by the Yanks. I cannot vouch for its veracity. Singing lesson passed off very well, & R.'s "Life in the Old Land Yet" was rendered very well. Saw Liz., Ada, Mag. in the distance & memory was busy with the "happy day of yore". Was dismissed at six, & alone I trod the old familiar path. On arriving home, found Mrs. N. there. We sat on the steps & were joined by Ma & A. & I took a stroll around the corner & relate to each other the events & news of the day. Nobody came at night, & we retired early. We were visited by a shower yesterday, but this was not by far the most important visitor, for imagine our surprise when the bell rang & *Leopold* was announced. His feelings of gladness on beholding us was reciprocated. He was looking very well, I told him, & his opinion of me was similar. He said I had grown stout! On what? Cornbread!!! He came on a skiff & brought us some butter! A most acceptable article & had it been possible he would have brought more things. He signified his intention never again to go soldiering! Never! Never! He often thought of us & wished he was here & declared himself willing to do our bidding. I am glad he has come, for Mr. N. (so obliging)!! is of no assistance to us. Ma wrote to Pa, as one of Miss D.'s friends was going, & was willing to take letters; but I doubt if he will receive it. The one entrusted to Mr. H. [Hitchcock] was destroyed. In the afternoon Mr. & Mrs. N. honored us. She brought a letter from Charleston of Apr. 7th containing an account of the finding of a body of a man, in the woods in Georgia, & from what information they have received respecting it, they believe themselves to be correct in asserting it to be Mr. Myers; & now there will be great suspense until further news is received. It will not be a matter of much concern to Mrs. H. In the afternoon while talking to Alice & Miss Eda, & holding "sweet Tots", who should pass but Miss Del. T., her sister & several others. What they were doing up in this part of the world, I cannot imagine. In the evening Ma & F. went "over the way", but I, interested with the "Lamplighter" & A. with "My Novel" preferred remaining at home. (Doubtless you accuse me of inconstancy towards "E.L.", but I must inform you that it is in the possession of Miss D.). How unexpected had a handsome stranger (say Emile) have stopped in. To be sure we never imagined of such a thing. Not once! Not once!

Sunday, May 25th, 1862

6 1/4 A.M. We will have today, what has been denied us for some time, a rainy Sunday, an occurrence, which is of such a former date, that it has en-

tirely escaped my memory, & I should not have regretted it had the present morning not served to impress the circumstance on my mind. Well, do I remember today, a year ago. We were sitting in the parlor by the window, (I think I see it) surrounded by Capt. White, Lieut. Adrian, Capt. Miller, Mrs. White, Mrs. Chaffin, & then "Toody" committed an act for which she was severely reprimanded by her mother. Oh! the pleasure of the day, the fine dinner at which "our host" presided, & the *sad, though sweet ride home*. How long since have *they ceased to think of it. For forget it, they could not, at once*. There is nothing in the True Delta, a paper which I am beginning to despise, for I do believe that it was unfavorable to us. Only a scarcity of the Picayune, compelled me to take it. Oh! Philomen, in what terms can I express my feelings of humiliation, of sorrow, of revenge, as I perused the "Delta" of yesterday, whose touch polluted me. It is a Yankee paper, has exactly the same type & in defiance retains the name of our "Delta"; is so similar to it in appearance that no difference can be observed. My boy handed it to me before breakfast & a feeling of such deathly sickness came over me, as I read the motto, "The Union—it *must* & *shall be* preserved". My heart sank within me, & it seemed as though every nerve had ceased to perform its functions, so sensibly was I weakened. It was curiosity which prompted me to read it, but no honorable person should contaminate themselves by a contact with it. There was a lengthy article, descriptive of the Mayor's excursion to Fort Jackson in which Mr. Duncan figured most conspicuously. But I shall not so insult you as to repeat anything from the infamous lying Journal; suffice it to say that when I came down this morning & saw the "Sunday Delta" under the window, I left it there & when my boy came commanded him to take it away. He told me that they compelled them to sell them; "oh", said he, "those fellows have ruined our business". He is so patriotic. I regard the True Delta with scarce more favor. They have a spite against the Delta, its being the first & strongest Secession paper. How mortified must *one* of its proprietors feel. I handed it to Ma, saying "Ain't you glad that the Delta is restored to us"? She was as delighted as surprised, & prepared herself to read it. The first thing her eyes fell upon was its motto, & she sprang to her feet as though a reptile had bitten her, & thrust it from her as though it were the offender. A paleness suffused her face & she exclaimed, "The wretches". I did not get over the effects for some time & it diminished my appetite for breakfast. After it, I went over to Mrs. N.'s & saw her prepare for Synagogue. After which I came home & assisted Ma & A. to make their toilettes & about 11 they started on their expedition. During their absence I employed myself variously, & occasionally "1861" would be present to my gaze. I dressed S. & about 2½ they returned. Had met Mrs. da P. & Baker, & they both fell in love with the latter [Sallie]. They had been attempting to procure passports, but none would be granted. Mrs. B. is "crazy" to go to her husband, *who will not return*. Ma made some purchases & entered into no definite arrangements about our bonnets. Confederate Money is taken so they cannot believe it to be wholly worthless.[26] After dinner Alice came in to deliver a message to us from Miss Rosa, that we must come in & see her in the afternoon. She remained a long while & while she was here, L. [Leopold] came in & had it not been for him, we should have gone with her when she went. I saw by the paper the death of Mr. T.R. Wharton, whom I remember with much pleasure as one of our most efficient directors during Miss Perry's term. When L. went, we went next door. Were entertained by Mr. M. [Mazareau] until summoned to see Miss R. She is very well & has a fine boy, the "image of its grandfather". We did not remain long with her for fear of wearying her & she told us not to wait to come in, until she had another baby. We repaired to the parlor & were engaged in conversation for some time. Mr. M. was very down hearted & if possible hates them more, the intruders. He is on his parole of honor, his trial to take place on Tuesday & he imagines that they will be very severe with him. The charge against him is his being President of the S.I. Association.[27] He is very intelligent man, & he has my good wishes. F. spent the evening with Mrs. N. We retired early. There comes A. Good bye.

Monday, May 26th, 1862

2 P.M. As the length & difficulty of my lessons render it impossible for me to know them, in disgust I have thrown them aside, & as a comforting angel have sought your sweet society; but even while enjoying it the cares & troubles of life intrude & detract from the pleasure it *would* afford. A constant source of annoyance to me is the coming Examination, when I am

26. Confederate banknotes continued to circulate among certain merchants, as they were still allowed to do.

27. The S. I. Association was an organization of sheriffs.

confident that I shall not acquit myself honorably, & the fear that promotion may be denied me. Mingled with this feeling is one of reproach, for often times is the thought presented to me, "You have not been studious enough". And then we have received no tidings of that loved Father & husband. Know not if he is well or sick, but only that his separation from us, is a source of much anguish to him as it is to those who every moment think of & sigh for him. In my dreams last night, I saw him, but oh! so sad he was! Happy is the thought of the contrariety of dreams & life. Ma, to dispel the blues, & partly to endeavor to dispose of her Confederate money, as to day is the last allowed for its circulation, had gone out & I hope that she may be successful in procuring those now imaginary articles, cheap things.[28] I wonder when provisions will be plentiful! There is now a scarcity of bread, flour being so exorbitant, while at "Old But.'s Shop", [a Union store] it is selling for $7 per barrel. Ma has an idea of making an investment there, & I do not countenance it, for indirectly we will have to be fed from their hands. The city is invested with them; new arrivals daily & this weather is no less astonishing to them than to us, as to day is *really cold*, warm clothing being not uncomfortable. Doubtless they think the reports of the warmth of the city to be exaggerated I should not wonder, did we have an uncommonly cool summer, & an intelligent friend of mine is of the opinion that everything seemed favoring them, that there will not be a *case of fever*. With so many subjects, I imagine it to be absurd in a high degree. And if it does not visit us, "God is just" & let this be our motto "In Him is our trust". Oh! tis not the fault of the people, our present calamity; our government is inefficient, & Jeff. Davis is to blame for the deplorable state of our loved Crescent City. Too late alas! we find that *he* is not the "right man in the right place".[29] Mr. Soule, when speaking most eloquently of *him*, his *dear* friend, uplifted his hands & exclaimed "If Jeff. Davis would only die!!" Physically & mentally he is unfit for the position he holds. "Too late, alas!" we discover our error. But without expressing regrets for the past, we should endeavor to make amends for the future. God spare to us, our noble, chivalrous, beloved Beauregard. Dear little Rosa is asleep on the sofa by me. She daily indulges in her naps & awakes much refreshed.

28. Butler had set 27 May 1862 as the day on which Confederate currency would cease official circulation, and he planned it in a way so that the banks, not the depositors, would suffer the loss. See Capers, *Occupied City*, 85.

29. Clara echoed widespread disillusionment with Jefferson Davis as president of the Confederacy. Many historians think he managed the war effort very badly. See Beringer et al., *Why the South Lost the Civil War* (Athens, Ga., 1986).

Josie is being subdued into a state of somnolency. It is a time of rest to her, as she has the hooping cough very badly. Dell, for some trivial offense has been consigned to the corner, but is now beside me, & with much admiration, watching me write. Fanny is "out doors" with Lucy. Ma is quite troubled about her, as so many (her acquaintances some) have run away & sought the protection of the Yankees. They say they do not intend to interfere with slavery, then why do they encourage them to come to them?[30] They allow a master to take his slave, *if he be willing to go.* But is not that harboring them? They should drive them away. I hear the Custom house & boats are being crowded with daily arrivals. There are many instances in which house-servants, those who have been raised by people, have deserted them, though they have received the kindest treatment at their hands; but they imagine no sacrifice too great with which to purchase freedom. L. is very weak-minded, & is as a tool in the hands of anyone & yet I sometimes think that she would not act so, yet — the most *faithful* have betrayed. Should one of mine, I would inflict severe punishment, & should discard them for ever. Yesterday was dull & cloudy & reminded me of the Sunday before the Yankees came. Maybe it will be last Sunday before they leave. I was up stairs fixing my dress & Ma & A. were considerably busied down, & when I descended I observed the result of their labor. The furniture had been changed (in position), curtains were shading the windows, which heightened the effect of the shades, the gas fixtures were enveloped in prim tarleton, & all spoke the favorable change which had occurred, to which I can scarcely adapt myself, imagining that I am in a strange house. In that respect I resemble an amiable "cousin of mine", who, when things had been in a position for some time, was opposed to their being removed. L. was unable to procure meat, so we had a light dinner. Dressed after it & came down. A. was poor company as she was scribbling something — mysterious & oh! I felt so lazy altho' I had so much to do, & such a weight oppressed me, so to drown my cares, I perused "Lucy Crofton" & was interested in it when the bell rang & I admitted "Old Eisner". While he was here, who should pay us a visit but Mary Ratican, so I enjoyed but little of his *dear society.* M. was astonished at the change which a few years had made in all of *us,* particularly me, who (do not believe me vain) she declared had grown *pretty.* How far from the truth she fell, how depraved is her taste. Me pretty! Did such an idea ever present itself to any one else? Ah! yes! *I remember one, whose taste was as vitiated.* Could I see with

30. The Solomons feared that Lucy would leave and ask for Union protection, as slaves from all over Louisiana had already done. Lincoln had yet to issue the Emancipation Proclamation.

their eyes. She is the "Mary of old" & promised to pay us frequent visits. She inquired about Aunt Sarah, Isabel & all of them. There are means of communicating now. Mr. E. left before dark, & A. & I after a talk with Alice, took a walk. L. came in the evening. Remained very long, was quite a bore, & thus closed the day of May, 26th 1862.

Tuesday, May 27th, 1862

6 1/4 A.M. I have been told that a cloudy or rainy Monday prognosticated a similar week, but the falsity of this assertion is visible in the morning, which is so bright & sunshiny. I could believe it to be October, so cool & bracing is the air. There is *nothing* in the paper. Poor Confederate Money is deceased, but there will be much secret trafficking in it. It will be good, for why is *Gen. Butler buying it up*? His lady is at the St. Charles, & quite disappointed with the ladies of N.O., who, *with some exceptions*, have so visibly slighted her. But my thoughts stray from her far away. The dreaded period is approaching. My class is to be examined in Geog. on Saturday, & I on Thursday. Oh! horror of horror! What a spectre haunts me. I carry my Geog. around with me, in hopes by so doing to instill it into my brain. Oh! Luckless man! who laid the foundation of the L.N.S. Just as I had finished yesterday, Mrs. N. came over. I was glad when she went as I was impatient to dress, it being after 2½. Ma shortly came, & had made no purchases. Many people out & stores crowded. Upon A.'s arrival had dinner, & I departed immediately after, as I had several duties to perform. Arrived there & found several like myself, in "a stew", & many were the wishes expressed that there was no School, that the Yankees would take it, etc., etc. all of which had unanimity been required would have carried the point. With great exertion I accomplished what I wanted to & to my surprise with the assistance of a few echoes did not miss. The Examination in Gram. & Arith. is to be postponed until Mr. L. & R. come. The latter I hear is very sick & the former does not wish to return as long as those miscreants are here. The city sustains no loss in his absence. Came home, Mrs. N. was there. A. & I went by the door & joined by Alice took rather a long walk. Enjoyed ourselves. Returned, found Mr. N. Josh was sent to bed by him, I being the direct, unintentional cause of it. Mrs. N. doubtless blessed me. They left & we did not fulfill our promise to return. I could not concentrate my mind upon the Geog. & heartily wished there had been no discoveries in the world. Even in sleep my peace was disturbed & every spare moment must now be devoted to it. My hands tremble, my heart sinks!

Thursday, May 29th, 1862

6 A.M. Well, the day has arrived & I am in a delightful state of uncertainty, now knowing if I am to be examined this afternoon or not, Mrs. Shaw being unable to tell me so undecided are they as to what course to pursue, left as they are almost to themselves to act. But I must, not withstanding, prepare myself. I dreamed last night that the school was to be suspended. Oh! unlucky fate! Dreams go by contrary! But do we ever, in this state of things, expect to be teachers? It is a wonder that they do not interfere with the schools, by compelling the teachers to take the oath, as this is one of the requirements, to hold any public office. I hear that our Governor, Gen. Banks, will shortly arrive & "But." is going to give a ball in honor of him. There I committed myself! Did I not say that I would not repeat the idle rumors.[31] The morning is fine, but I do not feel so, as I have a bad cold, & a peculiar rawness in my throat, which I suggest to have cooked! "My boy" has not come, but I will be no better informed after I have read the paper. Tuesday, my services were required at the Webster Academy [where Alice teaches]. I went & found that Miss Cavidaly in consequence of the crevasse was unable to get down, so I was requested to command Miss Cornelius' room, while she fills the place of the absentee. I commenced my duties with Dictation, & could then realize Miss Benedict's arduous duties. The girls behaved admirably & I determined to be strict & maintain that order which is one of the first requisites. I had finished with the first class, & while engaged with the 2nd Miss C. made her appearance with the unpleasant intelligence that Miss Cav. had come. By means of a skiff she had reached the cars & then the city. Miss Cav. thanked me for my trouble, & said I was doubtless glad to be relieved. How wrong was she, for I was very contented & had made up my mind for a pleasant day. I remained a short while with her, & regretted very much her presence, &

31. Lincoln did replace Butler with Nathaniel Banks, an indifferent military leader but a politically important one. There was concern from all sides, including the European diplomatic community in the city, about the dictatorial behavior of "Beast" Butler.

seeing her occupy my place which I looked upon as a usurpation. After giving one the trouble to come, *she* should have retired. Her room is a very pleasant one, & oh! how delighted should I be were I its mistress. I came down, & spent some time with Belle who was much excited over the "Delta". It seems to circulate largely altho' no one buys it. It is the only journal from which any information can be obtained. Oh! I never feel so patriotic & warm, as when after reading it. Yes we will keep the papers & how glorious when our independence is acknowledged to read of "crushing the rebellion", etc. After leaving her, I went to Miss D. who was as talkative as ever. Had a great deal to say & detained me longer than I expected. I should have liked to accept her invitation to spend the recess with her, but I had pressing business at home, for which I departed about $11^3/_4$. Ma was much surprised, & of course, frightened, to see me, but I made necessary explanations. I had intended to study, but seeing an unmade dress of Jo's on the table I could not resist the temptation to do "just a little" on it. But so fascinating was it, that I did not abandon it till $1^1/_2$, when it was most completed. I then had before me the study of the world, & I am sure I did not devote enough time to it to perfect myself in it. I did not have to dress, so that was a little saving of time. A. dined with us, & I retired immediately after, accompanied by A. She gave me some cheering news which I have since heard to be reliable. We have taken the Hartford [Farragut's flagship] & — Farragut is our prisoner. We are fixing up it for our own use. Oh! revenge! thou art sweet! But this is our commencement only. After arriving in school, Alice & I promenaded upon our spacious balconies until the bell summoned us to the "big room". Mrs. P. had received a letter from Lusher, portions of which she read to the school. After expressing many wishes that the N.S. would survive these struggles & c. & c; he recommended that we should forgo a formal written examination, if it met the approval of the teachers, & that our accounts for the year should entitle us to promotion. God bless him, for once! But Mrs. S. does not approve of it & is very much in favor of an Ex. so here arises the doubt. There are no directors here who are willing or — capable to correct our exercises, but I hope Mr. L.'s advice will rule the day. Dictation was short in consequence of much time being consumed in talking, & our spirits rose high at the prospect of no Ex.; but something whispers that we'll not be so lucky. Miss B. dismissed us early & Belle, Maggie, Olympia, Julia & myself spent some time in talking, when, fearing of detection, we separated; I one way, they the other.[32] Came home, disrobed & donned another dress.

---

32. A small crowd on the street might attract the attention of the occupation forces.

Ma & A. went out & I joined F. & the other children by the door. Had the pleasure of hearing them shout for Davis & Beauregard, as three officers rode by & I could not help myself from turning my back upon them, & I was in fear for some time after that a file of men would be up for me, but they did not come. Alice & I with dear little "Tots" went for a walk, & when we came back, Ma & A. had returned. In the evening before going to supper, the bell rang, & guess who it was, why—*handsome Emile* [Mazareau]. *He had come to pay a friendly visit.* We talked about many subjects & found him very interesting. He gave us an account of his sojourn in Vir. & the part he acted in the battles of Manassas & Bull Run. Ill health compelled his return to the city. Oh! I have made up my mind to quietly resign him to A. He is our style &—a *widower.* Be quiet, my heart! Emile's heart is another's. He staid very long, until 11 & *most* gentlemen's company is a bore after 10. I hope that our acquaintance will continue, but as we never become acquainted until a short time before one of the parties move, we are in fear of it & upon our expressing this to him, he said that if we did not move from the city that he should be most happy always to come & see us. Bully for Emile! We repaired to the dining room where we partook of some corn-bread & molasses, after which we retired to dream of Emile. His spectacles render him so attractive but he dispenses with them in the night. I was in hopes of being sent for yesterday, but Miss C. came & I understand that the water is subsiding. Nothing of import transpired during the day. I sewed, Ma sewed & F. sewed. Josie's wardrobe is being daily replenished. We still have much sewing to do, but it is only dresses & such things as Ma is entirely out of cotton & linen. Beer making is the fashion, & our attempts have proved successful. In the absence of ice, it is an excellent substitute for a drink. I did not study much. Dined. A., she came in as I was leaving. Item —I had on a clean muslin! Saw Alice [Mazareau] before me, but at too great a distance to attract her attention, so we did not meet until in School. *I like her so much.* I knew my lessons very well. I am quite afraid, for Mr. L. requires deportment *perfect,* for promotion & I wonder what he would call the incessant chatting which M. & I carry on. Mrs. S. never corrects us. Oh! there is such a diminution in the School. The School of Practice is reduced to 7, the Sophomores to about 18, the Juniors 12, & the Seniors 14. I remember when the room used to be crowded & each class full. I have ceased to bestow one thought upon Amanda or Kate. "How like a dream they passed away". I believe I must go & see Mary Mitchell. I hear that my friend Clara G. is married. I neglected her shamefully. Mr. McC. had a conference with Mrs. S. I do not know the result. I did not walk home with Alice, as she had business up town. I had "Tots" by the door & she was contented tho' in the presence of Leonie. The child possesses *new* attractions. Don't mind me, am I not silly. But you know it is only my foolishness. When Alice returned she & I promenaded & she was telling me of her former school-life. I wish I spoke French as well as she does English. We were by the gate when we were joined by A. & Miss Eda, & as usual there was no end to our conversation. Ma was to Mrs. N.'s & after supper A. & I went there. L. was there & all very indignant about an article in the paper. Spent an agreeable evening, but dull in comparison with the previous one. How well I remember this day *five* & *four* weeks ago.

10

No Letters from Pa:
May 31–June 15, 1862

Saturday, May 31st, 1862

11¹/₂ A.M. Tempus fugit! The last day of May! Oh! how happy am I, that unconsciously the time has slipped. The time, in November, which we used to anticipate, as the long dreary months of March, April & May, has come & has gone, & much to the joy of all parties has gone quietly. The fact can be readily accounted for. So many important events have transpired to claim our attention that we had taken "no note of time, but from its loss". And yet strange to say the past month has seemed very long & surely no week was ever longer than that *most eventful one of our lives*. How vividly, every scene, can memory recall. Today, five weeks ago, how miserable were we. Miserable in the prospect of a bombardment of our city, & yet how preferable should it have been to its occupation by the U.S. troops. Affairs have no reason to look brighter & yet I feel so much more hopeful, so confident that by some unexpected fortune, they will be compelled to evacuate "our city" & that it will soon be the "home of the free". We shall soon enter upon the month of June. Oh! God! ere its "course is run" gladden our hearts by "good news from Pa". There are daily arrivals from Vir. of gentlemen, who are probably acquainted with *him*, & were there any one sufficiently interested in our affairs to make inquiries of them, we might be so successful as to obtain some information; even the agreeable company of Mr. Duncan is denied us. How miserable must he be at Fort Jackson. There are so many rumors, respecting their treatment there, & we will accept the most plausible & imagine them to be treated as prisoners of war, as gentlemen.[1] Upon the length of their confinement, people are as ignorant. I did not rise this morning until 8 o'clock. I feel quite bad

---

1. Butler had converted one of the forts guarding the entrance to the city into a prison for Confederate sympathizers.

having a most disagreeable cold, but I earnestly hope I am not getting the hooping cough. I did not, as usual, have my Saturday morning converse, & though it is postponed a few hours later, I hope it will not prove the less entertaining. You cannot imagine how worried it makes me to hear *so so* much, & not relate it all to you. But I not the time, & — I must remember that your robe must serve as long as possible, for where am I to procure another one; & again my judgment dictates to me the impropriety of repeating all the rumors that are afloat & though I may sometimes be injudicious in my selection, *remember my youth*. After breakfast I made a general "clearing out" & "cleaning up" of my safe, & while in the pursuance of these praiseworthy actions was *so* unfortunate as to break a long nail which I have been cultivating for a number of months. I would never yield to the solicitations of my friends to cut it, & yet when its death came I bore it with "Christian fortitude" & "Jewish resignation". I have arranged it & shall be patient until it reattains its former growth. I like to be eccentric. Ma went to market; came home disgusted with the world. She is now to Mrs. N.'s, J. being rather sick. Poor child! He commands one's pity. He is so delicate. That cough alarms me. And yet have we any foundation to hope that "the fatal malady" will not at some period of existence attack him? Born when his mother was in a decline. How noble a part has Mrs. N. acted towards him. She devotes to him more than a mother's love & more than a mother's solicitude & love she bestows upon him. He is very *bad*, & when I am tempted to be angry with him, his extreme delicate health & the many sufferings he has endured pleads for him, & *not* in vain. It is to be expected that he should be spoiled; & he is, too much for his *own* happiness. Little Fanny has grown rapidly & is a sweet amiable child. Mrs. N. sends her to school & it would be cruel to neglect to cultivate the intellect of which she is possessed. With the exception of a few respects, she is as one of the family & is in as much favor with Leo. as formerly.[2] A. implored & entreated me for a succession of minutes to accompany her to Syn., but while I convinced her of the unpleasant duty of refusing to comply with a person's request, I returned a peremptory refusal, when she is resolved — to go by herself. Since her departure, I have been perusing the "Delta" obtained from Mrs. N. It contains an extract from a Northern paper of the Capture of N.O. written by an eye witness. As I read, my Southern blood was fired up, & the blush of indignation glowed on my

2. Josh and Fanny do not appear to have been the natural children of Sarah Nathan. Whether they had any family connection to the Nathans is unclear. Josh's mother may have died in childbirth, or shortly thereafter, and was someone Clara knew.

cheeks, & my pulse throbbed high, when I contemplated our fall, which, at all times, I cannot realize. Tears suffused my cheeks & I felt how strong was my love for my beloved country. They were but joking when they said "We were confident of success, for our faith was in our leaders & that Providence who favors the cause of right & justice." Yes, that same righteous God says "Vengeance is *mine* & I will repay". A new flag was raised on the Customhouse & saluted by Butler & his staff, uncovered. Not long may they enjoy their glory. Thursday morning on taking up the paper, what was my *horror* & amazement to see the following, "The old journal, the Bee, made its appearance today, upon what conditions, the following note will show. 'Gen. B. Sir We never did, & never intended to advocate the burning of cotton & destruction of anything else. We consider it a wanton waste of property, one not to be tolerated by the civilized world'". Oh! how my spirit rebelled at such conduct. Underneath was the following, "Upon the publication of the forgoing, the Bee may resume its publication". You know the reason of its suppression & how men can be so debased for the sake of a few paltry dollars to which poverty would be preferable. To be sure, the public highly condemn the proceeding & all the merchants have resolved to withdraw their subscriptions. Were not the editors clear sighted enough to see this. And Dr. Harly's conduct does not astonish those who know him, for his miserly propensities impress everyone. No true Southerner should step upon his threshold. As I now feel, I am determined that *I never shall*. I did not study as much as the occasion demanded, for I had a faint hope that we would be spared the trying ordeal of an examination. Alice [Mazareau] was absent, it being in her religion, a very important holiday. When Miss B. came in with delight she communicated to us some cheering intelligence of our successes at Virginia & Corinth, but while it suffuse a little hope, I did not & do not, as I have had no confirmation, dare to give credence to it.[3] She regarded her source as most reliable & her spirits were so exuberant that she most neglected our lesson. The news seemed to have the same effect upon the temper of all. Singing with Mrs. F. passed off pleasantly, I dorsaling [looking from the rear] more attentively upon the beautiful face of Belle, than the notes which emerged from the throats of 9 maidens. I heard nothing of the Ex. & all I know, was that I was not tested. Arrived home & received from A. the welcome tidings that Miss Cor. had requested her to tell me that my

3. Stonewall Jackson had been pushing Union forces back across the Potomac River in the Shenandoah Valley of Virginia. Fighting had continued around Corinth, Mississippi, since the Battle of Shiloh in April.

services would be required in her department on the following day, as she would be absent. Knowing, I would be unable to sew, I resumed it, wishing to complete pointing a body for A. Leo. came in & I did not quite succeed. Alice, to our sorrow, informed us that Mr. Mazareau's sentence was—*Fort Jackson* & he is to take up his abode there on Monday. But he does not seem to care. It is the best spirit in which to take it, & when the Yanks bare [leave], these men, who have acted so unselfish will be remanded by the city, while such renegades as Dr. Harly & Crew will have to follow the fortunes of the Feds. for they will never be allowed to remain here. I went over to Mrs. N.'s, supped with her & she & her spouse came over & spent the evening. I finished the body & A. is much pleased with it. Friday, I came down as usual, & about $7^{3}/_{4}$ repaired up stairs to dress for School, & during the process expressed many regrets that I was not called upon to perform the pleasant duty each morning. Wouldn't it be a dream of happiness realized for A. & I to be teachers in the same school. We endeavored to come as "near to nature" as possible & our toilettes were exactly alike. Eat breakfast & left the room "like a lady", F. generously absolving me from "*dish duties*". A. & I departed for the Institution & arrived there but a few moments before the ringing of the bell, after which there was a teacher's meeting in the hall in which Miss D. & Tiny Winy held conspicuous positions & while our voices were almost drowned by the screeches of the B.B.F. [Bonnie Blue Flag] & other melodies, from the various rooms. After some minutes confab when we separated to the discharge of our duties. My girls behaved exemplary & everything passed smoothly. They seem to like me & yet I am very strict. Sallie [younger sister] recited beautifully, & is the "gem" of her class. I should like to command such a company. Having some spare time I made out A.'s report for her. Passed the recess with Misses C. D. & Solomon & at its expiration descended to the realms of odoriferous fragrance, & then returned to our rooms. The time passed very quickly & before aware of it the "first bell" rang. I was quite sorry when the day was over. The finale was the singing of the patriotic songs which they rendered with much feeling & then *my room* was dismissed. A., of course, was keeping in, & I went to Miss D. where we had a "goodly chat", & then joined A. who shortly dismissed her interesting charges & it was $3^{3}/_{4}$ before our arrival home, when we partook of dinner. I did not feel well in the afternoon. Took a sleep on the sofa, but was disturbed by frightful visions. I changed my dress, & later in the afternoon Ma, A., & I took a walk, & on our return, Alice joined us. I retired early & this morning feel much better.

June 3rd, 1862, Tuesday

6 1/4 A.M. I declare I am getting so absent minded, I really forgot to put the day of the week, until I had written the month & noted there was a peculiar look about it. But it is no wonder. Suspense & anxiety tend to make people forgetful. Well, the "merry, merry month of May" has flown, & Philomen, can you imagine that vacation is but 3 weeks off. I hear many vague rumors of there being no vacation this year, for fear that the vacant schools may be occupied by our "visitors". If it has any foundation, I do not know. The morning is pleasant & unusually cool. There is not a particle of news in the paper, but oh! we have been the victims of such a deceit. It was confidently asserted & universally rejoiced in, that the Hartford was taken, & Farragut our prisoner, but the "lying Delta" announces that F. is in the city, "in the enjoyment of his usual health" & his vessel is safe; yet I sometimes doubt it. We make up our minds to believe nothing, yet so willing are we to credit good news, that we forget our resolution. It is too bad! Major Strong, I *hear,* died with the Pernicious fever (a type of the yellow). Saturday afternoon, Miss C. & a friend of hers paid us a visit. Miss C. brought A.'s compensation for the past month & "amount due Miss C.E.S. for supernumerary duties," $2!!! Every one shares in common the regretful feelings respecting the fate of Farragut. They remained a long while & we walked a short distance with them on their homeward path. F. & I have a good joke respecting Miss C. Tho' silly, it invariably creates a laugh, between her & me, *if* no one else. In the evening Mrs. N. came over. While standing by the gate, Emile passed, & bowed, oh! so politely. *I wonder why he isn't more sociable.* A rattling wind & rain storm visited the city early on Sunday morning. The storm was of brief duration & had a delightful effect in cooling the temperature. No vestige of its visit was visible when I arose at 7 1/2! June opens beautifully with sunshine, showers & refreshing breeze. F. had the miserable complaint, toothache, & went round to Dr. Nelson & on her return, her pain was alleviated, & I hope that her heart suffered no pain. Ma was in one of her "former Sunday humors", but her ill temper vanished as the day advanced. Our white dresses are cut off & I am so anxious to have them worked. If I were only gifted myself. R. partly promised A. to do hers. I did little "odd jobs", but accomplished not much sewing. The "Delta" asserted that the "season for the fever is over & a most healthy summer may be anticipated". Deluded fools. Murray, of the Free Market, is [a prisoner] at Fort Jackson. In the afternoon, Leo. came & while here, we were visited by a hard rain, which after lasting some time, entirely ceased. L. was very restless until safely lodged in Mrs. N.'s house. During the rain, Dr. Smith came in. The very man that Ma wanted to see. He is an agent for schooners, & transacts business with Butler, with whom I think he is on terms of too much intimacy, but the patriotism of our men extends only as far as their interests are concerned.[4] He thinks of going up the road & promised faithfully to write to Pa. His family are at Mandeville [in unoccupied Louisiana], very comfortable. He regretted his inability to perform any dental operations for us (as F. & I both stand in need of it, Dr. D. leaving my teeth in a very unfinished state) but said he would introduce us to any dentist & if necessary sustain the charges. I like to see him conscious of his obligations to darling Pa. When he left A. & I walked round to Nettie's to ascertain the lesson, but she was not home. Encountered Eisner going, unobserved by him, but had the delightful anticipation of meeting him home, but luckily we did not, as we learned that he was to Mrs. N.'s A new feature on the programme. Sent E. & obtained the lesson. F. spent the evening over the way; but we preferred home. L. stopped in as he escorted F. [Fanny Nathan] to her residence. I have just fathomed the attraction at Mrs. N.'s for Leo. It must be "little Fanny". I do not admire to go there, when Mr. N. is there, as he is so cross & disobliging & takes no more interest in us than if we were strangers. On hearing that a gentleman of Pa's acquaintance & *his too* had returned from Vir. he suggested to Ma, for *her* to *go* & see him while he the greater part of the time is unemployed. It is disgustful. How unmindful is he of favors once bestowed. Monday morning was ushered in by delicious showers, that had the effect of washing the face of nature, making the skies so blue, & the earth so green & of cooling the atmosphere to a most bracing & healthful temperature. I was up quite early in pursuit of my wretched studies. How they do harass me! The day was fine. A number of Yankees were parading up & down the street on their canons & in presence of many I called L. out & said "Don't they look like they've got the yellow fever".[5] Such looks as were cast at me! Ma, to my pleasure, fixed one of my dresses for me, & I donned it for the afternoon. In school, to my great surprise, I learned that Miss Del Trigo was to be married on the 10th. Her leaving school can be accounted for. We are to be examined tomorrow & the only class, as it is the will of the "Aub Mouth". When I came home, A. & I went round to Fanny B.'s. She was out but we were agreeably entertained by her sweet mother, who was very sorry F. was out, as she "loved us girls so much".

4. Many of the city's residents accommodated themselves to the occupation.
5. If by "L." Clara meant their slave Lucy, Clara did act impetuously.

She is a sweet girl & we will endeavor to be more intimate. On our return, Alice was standing by the gate & we *had to go* in. Conversed with Mrs. M. who can speak but little English. Mr. M. is prepared to go, but his friends neglected him, by not coming for him. Miss Rosa is about, looking very well. "Jarreau", too, was there. The first time that we have been in his society. They are so hospitable to us & I like them very much.

Thursday, June 5th, 1862

6 1/4 A.M. Fine weather! Oh! how delightful must it be to walk these beautiful mornings. How well I remember our morning walks when Alice Myers was with us. How long ago is it. I know *I* was a little girl. There is nothing new in the political world. Lafayette Square is evacuated by U.S. soldiers & open to the public. The little children are gamboling under the welcome shade of the trees, as in other & happier days. The six soldiers condemned by But. to be shot were reprieved, & sentenced to hard work at the forts. How long this week seems. I am getting quite lazy. Tuesday I did scarcely any sewing, but I was so bothered, so worried, so harassed that I could apply myself to nothing but the hated Geography. I wandered listlessly about, only caressing it. I departed from home, before my venerable sister arrived. *All* the girls, which is but few, were present & Miss B. so kindly occupied so much time in talking that we had but little for Dictation. Repaired to Reading, where O. & I had a pleasant time. I did not have the opportunity of displaying my elocutionary powers & I lost my energy, as sweet Belle's face was not before me. I walked home alone, & at many times prefer my thoughts to company. Found Ma. & F. about going to Dr. N.'s & A. in the first stages of her toilette, so I took a book, & seated myself on the steps, but, how often my eyes wandered from it, as I pictured to myself the trials & hardships of a school-life. How I wish I could quit it. A. joined me & dispelled gloomy thoughts & we took quite a long walk. As I passed a Yank, I turned my back & "cut up" various tantrums, for which I was much alarmed, fearing to be insulted. But I cannot pass one quickly—cannot. A. was telling me, that while they were drilling in front of the school, the B.B.F. [Bonnie Blue Flag] resounded from every apartment & they were requested by one of them to cease it, & of course were obliged to comply, particularly as the directors disapprove of it. When we returned, Alice was by her door, & she & I promenaded on our grounds. She spoke quite confidentially to me, & her request of "not to mention it" was useless, as I never betray another's secrets. She promised to show me an ambrotype of a "dear friend". I excused myself & went in to study, but did not succeed. Ma went to Mrs. N. & I was sympathizing with "Lucy Crofton" & occasionally thinking of the dread tomorrow. Yesterday was a holiday. We did not sew, but the children went to school, of which, I also had a faint prospect, but Miss C. came, unfortunately. I must confess that I studied scarcely any, but was loitering about, laughing & talking & watching Ma make some "arrangements". Mrs. N. came over. I think they have decided to move. I felt, when I was dressing, as tho' I were going to be executed. I knew that the *time had* to come, & oh! how earnestly did I wish it was over. I ate scarcely any dinner & after providing myself with pen, inks, & papers, was on my way to the Institution to pass the ordeal which for months has been a "grim spectre" haunting me. Found my girls as excited & frightened as myself & faintly endeavoring to pound the Lat. & Long. into their unwilling brains. I watched the clock, & when the hands pointed to four, & the bell tapped, I never experienced such feeling; & when Mrs. S. came, I expected my heart to burst from its prison place. Maggie shared my feelings, & we sat with locked hands, hers as warm, as fire, mine, as cold as ice. When Mrs. S. began to read, my feeling defy description, but so trembling was I, that a few, faint marks were all I made, but I summoned courage & knew the worst had passed. We were allowed to sit together & the examination was different, but with a few promptings which I retaliated, I succeeded admirably & I fear that "a good beginning will make a bad end" may be verified in my case. I was much discomposed, & feel now like I could answer better. There was congratulation & rejoicing when it was over, but for me, it was short-lived, as I thought of the coming afternoons. But it is over, Geography is passed & the idea of entering Mrs. P.'s class is more hateful than Examinations. If Fortune should only so favor me as to compel me to leave! I was quite late, when I got home, & was just in time to see Rebecca for a few moments. She was standing by the gate waiting for the 'bus. I related my experience to A. Ma was out. Leo. came & remained a long while. Ma returned, having been to Mrs. D.'s. She had received no communication from *her husband*. In the evening we went to Mrs. N.'s. I wonder what has become of "Blue Eyes". He must be angry.

Sunday, June 8th, 1862

6 A.M. I can scarcely believe it is June, so delightfully refreshing is the breeze, & were I to wake up after a protracted sleep, I should certainly pronounce the morning to be October. But our sunny South "is noted for its gentle winds". How well I remember the events of this day a year ago; but as the other participants of our pleasure have ceased to think of it, I will make up my mind to forget it. Yet, how can I. I have not been with you since Thursday, in which I felt like a released prisoner & had the vain hope that the coming Examinations would not take place. But it is inevitable. The day passed as all do & I proceeded to School with different emotions than on the previous day. Found the general topic to be the Examination. Oh! I had such a fright! Surely a "guilty conscience needs no accuser". I thought that I should never again recover. Knew my lessons, & had a pleasant time in Singing Class with Maggie & Belle. As I was coming home, met Ma & the children on a riding expedition. A. & I went walking & on our return, by 100 invitations were induced to go into Alice's. Miss Rosa was there, as well as usual. Her boy is 3 weeks old. I like very much the whole family. Ma & the chicks returned, & Ma spent the evening with Mrs. N. & we did not "go over" as requested, but enjoyed ourselves much more, by reading to each other, "L.E.L.'s" fascinating words, "The Venetian Bracelet" charmed us the works. All her writings breathe a sorrowful tone & I should imagine she has been very much disappointed in love. I little dreamed that Friday would be so eventful a day. The earlier part passed very quietly, I sewing on a waist for F. & Ma not in a very enviable mood. Things continued so till about 1 o'clock when Alice Jar. rang the bell. I thought she came to tell us that Mr. M. had gone, for strange to say, he has heard no further from the Yanks. I came down & she greeted me with "Good news! Good news". I saw that she was excited & I became very nervous while she was telling me that Mr. Ogden, a friend of Mr. M. had arrived from Beauregard with dispatches to Gen. Butler, which *I understood her to say* were made public. He came under a flag of truce & one of the dispatches was to the effect that we had gained signal victors. in Tenn. & Vir., had 10,000 prisoners & cautioned B. not to molest one of our men, for triply shall theirs be re-paid. Oh! I was delighted & felt so confident of its truth. I wrote it to A. & when the children returned, I heard that there was the greatest excitement in School, a total suspension of business. My note was handed from teacher to teacher, the dispatch was copied by all, & in fact such a commotion was never before known. Cheer upon cheer rent the air for Beauregard,

& the pent-up feelings of the heart was poured forth in song. Teachers & pupils were mad with joy, so confident did they all feel that the news was reliable. The report was the news had come from Mr. Solomon, & when Josh came home, Mrs. N. came bounding over & such scenes transpired as do not occur every day. A. came home wild with delight & yet I feared to believe it. The excitement continued & several people came to make inquiries of us. In the afternoon Lizzie came to see me, she of course, had heard it from her brother. She & I took a very long walk, & passed lovely Mrs. H. L. is a "peck of trouble", as the valedictory is still undecided there being a tie between Addie & her. Neither will relinquish it to the other & I think it should be decided by luck. When we returned, Alice & A. were engaged in close conversation & to my horror, I heard that I had not understood her rightly. She said that the dispatches were sealed & that what she told me was only surmises. I was laughingly reproached by A. for raising the mind without a foundation; but we are confident that they contained some good news. What will the School say to me! Many persons had gone to Mr. M. hearing the news had come from him. We walked home with L. & all advised her *not* "to give up the ship". Confabbed with A. Mrs. N. spent the evening with us. I had on my new body which looked very well. There is an account of Ogden's visit in the lying Delta, which purports to be the truth, but I shall not repeat it, so assured am I that they could not state it correctly & their very dearth of news is an indication that there is some good for us. We did not go to Syn. Some altercation between Ma & A. is the reason. We have not our bonnets. The U.S. flag "at the request of many citizens" was raised upon the City Hall, & a salute of 34 guns was fired the noise of which we attempted to drown by singing Bonnie B.F. There is an account in today's Delta & of course the cheers at again beholding the flag was deafening. A vast concourse of people were assembled & joy was upon every countenance. What a loathsome sight to see the hated stars & stripes over the City Hall. Everyone is fired with indignation at the atrocious *wonder* of yesterday, the hanging of Mumford for tearing down the U.S. flag from the mint. It is atrocious & oh! God, help us to revenge it.[6] I am astonished to see among the Union meeting the names of some of my acquaintances, one being Mr. Torrey. I studied yesterday considerably. F. had an engagement with Dr. N. for 12 but he called to ask her to change it to $5^1/_2$, when she & Ma went. Ever & anon the events of yesterday would break upon us; yet I believe it, & A. is more willing "to meet

6. See introduction, above.

the foe". In the afternoon we dressed with the intention of paying several visits. Ma came before we left. Donned our spencers which looked remarkably well, & proceeded on our way to Octavia. Had a pleasant walk, but the displeasure of finding her out. Went up Magazine & in our walk met Rebecca & Mr. H. Principal topic, political affairs. He believes like us, that Mr. O.'s visit was of much import & it is not to be expected that the Feds. would state his true mission. We are confident that we have gained glorious victories in Vir. & Ten. & beyond doubt McClellan's army is ours, & we are within a few miles of Washington. Oh! how glorious when the Con. flag shall wave o'er the Capitol. Then shall the capture of N.O. be revenged. Talked some while & then after commands to "come up early" & "come down early", parted. Proceeded whither our footsteps & the gentle wind bore us until we found ourselves in the "Garden District". Had the misfortune of seeing a group of lovely girls, including Kate A. & M. & oh! how great the temptation not to kiss them. I disapproved going to several places mentioned by A. & proposed to stop at Mrs. C. & if nothing else, inquire how she is, as she has been too sick to receive visitors. She acquiesced & we were shortly at her domicile. Were greeted by the lovely, queenly Victoria (who is now living with her) & after sending up our cards, were informed "to come up quickly". She looked beautiful in her deshabille & said of course she *would* see us. She *has* been quite ill. We regretted that evening was approaching & our visit would have to be limited. But we promised to come round often, & I, one morning. The parting was over, when Vic., who had company, joined us & insisted on our coming back & speaking to her a little while. We did & were *compensated* by delicious refreshment. The 2nd parting o'er & Vic. walked some distance. How my heart goes out to a lovely woman, & I could scarcely resist from saying "How beautiful you are"! But how often has she heard it. She kisses so sweetly. I can almost imagine I feel the pressure now, of her beautiful lips upon mine. We walked hurriedly home, & encountered none of the "animals" [Union soldiers]. Found Ma talking to Alice & Eda, joined her a few moments & all retired into the house. Quite a romantic event transpired in the evening. Did nobody come? Did we retire very early. What has become of *Emile*! He must be offended, & I am confident, with me.

Tuesday, June 10th, 1862

6 1/4 A.M. Oh! dear! Again a dilemma! Wednesday is approaching, & we are to be examined in wretched History. I feel as tho' I were robbing myself of time, in being now with you, & in fact, I reproach myself for extending my conversation to such a degree, as in fact, I do not have time to *think* of anything but my lessons. I cannot refrain from a brief mention of the weather, which is the most extraordinary ever known. It is actually so cool, that I am compelled to close the window & should do likewise to the door, did it not prevent an egress for the mosquitoes. Now what shall I say in the *briefest possible* words? The account of the execution [see text at n. 6, above] in Sunday's paper was enough to cast a gloom over the spirits of all, & I cannot think of the atrocious, inhuman crime, & suppress my tears. Universal sorrow seemed to pervade our community. The haste with which it was done, serves to convince us that "good news is on the way". I am sure that N.O. is the only dark spot in the S.C. I did not sew much & A. & I sympathized with the poor widow & orphans. God will protect them, & tho' it is hard for them to bear, his murder will contribute to our good. A. received a visit from one of her pupils which occupied us for some time. I devoted a time to the renovation of my hoops, which I am anxious to make as diminutive as possible. Succeeded, not to my satisfaction. Dined early & then A. & I were trying our skill upon chain & thorn stitch. Got along admirably considering we have never been pupils. I am determined to do me a dress. After dressing S. I did likewise to myself, & joined A. in the parlor. I am so trifling. I *should* have studied, but passed the time more agreeably by reading to A. When the sun had almost sunk to rest, when accompanied by Alice, we went to walk. We seemed to attract attention, & it was either because we were dressed *alike* & so *prettily.* On our return stopped at Nettie's, where I obtained the lessons. The Valed. is not decided. In these times it is impossible for people to meet & part quickly, as there is so much to talk. N. is very sanguine & is disposed to credit the good news. Refused to go in as it was contrary to the rules of etiquette, she having received the last visit from us. We did not detain her long from her company. Found Leo. home. In the evening Mr. & Mrs. N. came over, & we did not retire early. When I went to bed, I laughed for about an hour, as the events of Friday came upon me with all their earnestness. A. was averse to going to school as I had made myself so ridiculous by *my* dispatch, *so characteristic of Beauregard.* It is the funniest thing I ever heard, & I laughed myself to school. In all respects yesterday did not seem like Monday. I knew not why. I was up early & my head swam, after I had extracted from my brain an abstract, & I don't know what else. It was so light, I am sure it would have floated. I was soon out by breakfast. Oh! to be a member of the graduating class! Mrs. Gard. called to see Ma; she is going some place where she can communicate with her son, & as it is impossible for Ma to *accompany* her, she intends to give her a dispatch to forward to Pa. Not a word have we heard. I received a note from A. showing me that she was alive, & had passed *thro' the ordeal like a hero*, all the teachers *supported* her & added *their* testimony to hers, & all was satisfied to be true with the exception of that dispatch & when A. spoke of it as *the joke of the war*, my visibilities were again excited. I can never think of it with composure.[7] I felt so lazy. I could not sew & did not study. I am so indolent. A. did not come from school before I left. Walked leisurely to school, as it was early. Every one much excited in consequence of the news. When I came home what was my astonishment to hear that Mr. N.'s house had been besieged & himself arrested, no one knew for what. Mr. K. being in the house was also arrested. Mrs. N. had immediately gone down to the Provost Indgis [?] office, but she returned, having gained no satisfaction. A few moments after up comes Mr. K. & fancy her feelings, when no "Sammy". He was in the Customhouse, & the charge against him was — murder. Instantly I was reassured that it was a mistake, but Mrs. N. was wrought to the highest pitch of fear, knowing they were so cruel as to punish him unjustly, & Fort Jackson & its concomitant horrors rose before her. Leo. was dispatched down with a bar [barrister?], & so visible were the events of that dreaded Friday before me that I felt a feeling of sickness creep over me. A. & I went home, leaving Ma & F. there. After supper we intended to go, but changed our minds. After being in bed some time they came; I was not surprised when I heard he had come; they were mistaken in the person. Mrs. N. was jubilant. Oh! that Examination!

Friday, June 13th, 1862

6 ¹/₄ A.M. I was about to say that I am ashamed of myself, as our intercourse has been so interrupted; but I am not, as I feel myself perfectly innocent,

---

7. The spreading of erroneous information regarding battle victories through Alice's school was a matter of concern.

& tis only the contingencies of the times that is to blame; for you know I would not willingly neglect you. I must acknowledge that my absence yesterday was occasioned by the peculiar fascinations possessed by my couch. We are still enjoying fine weather, with the breath of Summer, but I fear its life will soon be ended, as it has been of so long a duration. Well, I shall begin methodically. I left off Tuesday; well, that day passed very pleasantly. I was engaged in flouncing, an occupation to me most agreeable, & so desirous was I to finish it that I worked steadily until $2^1/_4$.[8] F. went to Mrs. G., but she is unable to tell when she can leave. Ma wrote a letter to Pa, dear Pa (old times) in order to have it ready for any time. The city is alive with excitement. The Yanks confess to be slightly defeated in Vir. & there has been a terrific battle & Mrs G. is anxious to know the fate of her sons. Oh! if I *wished*, I could not tell the rumors what are afloat. All are sanguine, & many entertain the thought that the flag is, or soon will *be*, flying over the capitol, & Baltimore is ours. We are confident of our success, & the news boys are screeching of B.'s march to Washington. The lying Delta says if he has not lost his life, he has his regard for truth. What deluded animals. Old But. called on Mrs. Gen. B. & like a lady (some think) she entertained him politely. He spoke of her husband's bravery & talent, but regretted that it was so misdirected. I should not have listened to it. Ever & anon I was thinking of Miss D. her bridal evening. Did she think of us? It was my intention to go to Mrs. C.'s, but I was "out rather late". Ludy & Olivia were to Mrs. N. & I did not wish to go there, as I felt angry at not being sent for in the day; Ros. was there, happy. I started out with the intention of going to A.'s; went as far as Mag. street, & seeing how far it was resolved that it was "too late", so postponed it for another afternoon. What was my grief & indignation, when Alice told me that Mr. M. had just received orders to be at the Ocean Queen at 10 o'ck. in the morning as he was to go *North*, & not to Ft. J. as anticipated. How cruel! & so short a notice. He is sheriff no longer. His fine situation gone! They all seemed very despondent & well might they be. Ma & A. came home, & were shocked when they heard it. They had been to see about bonnets, which I think will be ready today. Mrs. Ellis came over, & staid a long while & of course had plenty to say. B. brought back my note & we had great fun over it. Mr. Mead, Yankee, says the origination of the news is to be found out, & apartments are being prepared at Ft. J. for her. I'll take you with me & won't we have fun. A. & I had plenty to communicate as so many

---

8. Clara attached a ruffle to a skirt, to make an old skirt look different.

events transpire before we see each other, each day. I was quite sorry to inform her that the Valed. was decided in favor of—Ada, & my heart went out to poor Lizzie, whose tears could not be restrained—she *should* be satisfied with the honor allotted to her. Mrs. N. sent over for us, & not wishing to be "strange" we went (after supper). Marion was there & we had "very good fun". I must tell you that they have a house "way up town" by the Ellis', & that it was their intention to move soon. We could not overlook so unfriendly an act, as to leave us here alone & unprotected, so for the past few days we have been rather cool, & no allusions have been made to her house & anything pertaining thereto; for really it is a slight, & I know that were we placed in a similar condition we should have shown more consideration. But—friends! What a misnomer. A charm which lulls to sleep! Well, oh! well. Wednesday the dreaded day arrive, & I was up by times, participating in the Revolution, War of 1812, glorying in the defeat of Cornwallis, & contrasting these with those times. The carriage was at Mr. M.'s [Mazareau] at an early hour, & after breakfast I took my position at the window, seeing but unseen. It was a sorrowful sight as the carriage bearing him drove away [to prison]. This is war! this is the result when a barbarous enemy have possession of a once happy city. The separation of loved members of a family, to meet, when again, no one can tell. But we will hope soon, & our prisoners will one day enjoy their triumph. Be patient! Rome was not built in a day, neither can our independence be accom. in a day, a week, a month, or a year! After his departure, I turned to my books, & did not unturn from them the remainder of the day. How often the vain wish was expressed, that the day was over; but well, I knew how severe a struggle, I should pass thro' ere its course was run. A. kindly assisted me in some of my Exercises & Ma amused herself by reading my Confederate History. At the last moment I was in a hurry, & so excited that I went without giving one thought to dinner. Wended my weary steps along the path which for *four* years I have daily traversed, & I thought to myself with what varied emotions & feelings. Some times how despondent when wondering if Miss P. *would* give me the Salutatory, & then, how happy, when I cried Eureka! The prize is mine. I have passed thro' many examinations, but that does not serve to diminish the fears on each separate occasion. Oh! the terror, the agony of the moment, preceding the delivery of the questions. My heart goes pit a pat, my head swims, & the operations continue until the close, when I proceed to write my knowledge on the blank sheet; I know the answer to part of the questions & in the midst of my fear I was amused at the whispers which passed from one to the other.

"Maggie, when was peace signed"? With mutual acts of kindness we succeeded admirably & delighted was I when six came, & we had not finished. What a weight off my heart, when the performance was concluded. Then was held a consultation, congratulations followed & it was quite late before I got home. Found Ma & A. out. Ate my dinner, & then joined the children by the door. When they returned we had as usual much to communicate. The General Order, No. 41 by which it said no one should be in the employ of the City, or perform any calling, was the principal topic, in as much as it is by many thought to be applicable to *teachers* & many entertain the opinion that the Schools will be suspended, while others think that women will not be required to take the oath, as Gen. B. said that the women of the N. & S. took too much part in political affairs. I am of the opinion that it extends particularly to teachers as it is not their wish that Secession principles shall be instilled into the minds of the rising generation, & in the possibility of the present teachers' places being supplied by Unionists Law earnestly do I hope that but few will send their children. But I fear that many regard with more value, a paltry sum of money. It has thrown the teachers into great consternation, for to many, their salary is their chief & *only* support. The schools may continue until the 27th but after that —
—. The order goes into effect on the 15th & deprives all of practising their profession. To obtain a passport, the oath is required. Some console themselves by saying they would not value it, as an oath at the point of the sword is not binding; & now that nothing binds us here, I do not know if I would hesitate to take it in order to get away, for we cannot remain here; *we will go to Pa.* In consequence of the excitement of the day previous, I did not arise until a late hour yesterday, & did not feel the Incubus [an evil spirit that affects sleeping persons] of the morning on my heart. We understood it was a day set apart for the removal of the Nathans. Ma, not wishing to be present at the parting, determined to go out. She went to market after breakfast & then went to A.'s "house", & I should forward a "dispatch" for Ma to return, when the interview, which *she* had so designed to shun, should have been over. The day advanced, & as no message was received, Ma thinking that she would not come during the morning, deemed it expedient to come home. During this time, I was very zealously engaged on a dress for A. The fates were against Ma, for no sooner had she arrived, when in comes Mrs. N. I could not but act as my "heart dictated", & she noticed my coolness. One thing after another was divulged, until everything was "out". We accused Mr. N. of slighting us, of being little concerned in our affairs, & of making but few endeavors to be of any assistance. She ac-

quitted him of blame, etc. It is an impossibility to trace a quarrel; it rages like a fire, & the senses of each, like water, is requisite to extinguish the flame. She noticed our coldness, & our few inquiries respecting her house. Did she not engage it without one word to us? Did *she* express one regret, or ask *us* to move by her? The thought of many things added fuel to the flame, & in the course of it, Ma went over there, & I regretted not being a listener. I resumed my work, but from my extreme nervousness was a long while at it. About 2½ Ma came & a few moments after Mr. N. He accused of being *proud, putting on airs*, A. & me & suffice it to say; it will be many a day before we, & I hope Ma, will go to see her. They parted quite amicably but the same feelings can never again exist. If people do not show their friendship in actions, in what can they? & these are people who profess to be our friends, who once told Pa that they could never forget his kindness & "that him & his family were bound to them by ties dearer than friendship". What a mockery of words. Pa was *rich* then. There is a sequel. *Times have changed;* but we trust they will again be bright, *then Mr. N.* will endeavor to show his friendship. I wish we could go from here. It is no doubt we will miss them much. But— —. Went to school. All excited with the news. In the absence of Miss B. Mrs. L. was the presiding genius. Mrs. F. as talkative as usual & when she dismissed us, Mrs. P. requested us to remain a few moments. M. was absent, but I was content with "beautiful Belle". Mr. R. & Mr. C. made their appearance & told us that in present contingency of the times they deemed it prudent to award the diplomas to the girls at an early period, so designated this afternoon. Our class was the only one invited & we were requested to bring no friends with us. When I came home found A. had gone to Mrs. C. & had left orders for me to join her, but I did not wish to. Took a walk with Ma, & saw Miss M. Spent some time with Alice, & while walking met A. In the evening had lots to talk about, & occasional glances at the deserted mansion [of the Nathans, or the Mazareaus perhaps] increased the quantity. Where is Emile?!!!

Sunday, June 15th, 1862

3 ¼ A.M. Dinner, I have just concluded, & have sought the only retired place in this furnace, our room, & could you see the drops of perspiration on my face, you would imagine I had been "earning my bread by the sweat of my brow". The thermometer stands 90, in a cool place (remember there is no such situation in this mansion) & in consideration, you will be lenient to excuse all digressions, mistakes, *brevities*, & c. & c. I left A. in a listless state on the sofa, *attempting*, no doubt, to read. Ma, fanning vigorously, as usual. The children never feel hot, & Josie is happy with "sweet sis", & I presume the feeling is reciprocal on "sweet sis" (side) part. These days remind me so forcibly of Pa, & particularly so did today, as dinner we enjoyed for the first time, the *luxury* of *ice*. Would that the pleasant work of preparing *his* glass of water now devolved upon me. Is he well!! Oh! God! I sometimes grow frantic as I imagine that he may be ill. When! oh! when! shall our hearts be gladdened by the sight of his dear, good, handsome face. With tears of joy, dear "Absent Father" do I gaze upon your image, & press on those speechless lips the warm kisses of everlasting love, invoke God's blessing on you, & pray that the dear original may soon be near our hearts, either in La. & Virg. Smile again upon us as one unbroken family! Hope whispers "All will yet be well"!! I have been quite lazy today. But the weather is so enervating & we feel a great deprivation of our energy. I did not rise until late this morning. Devoted much time to the perusal of the papers. Ma went to market & to that fact is attributed the circumstance of an unusually *fine* dinner. There is no news afloat, & everything is seemingly as noiseless as the passing Zephyr [a gentle wind]. On Friday, I performed my daily routine until 12 o'c. when gaining Ma's permission to pay A. a visit, I prepared myself for the event, & arrived there before recess was over. Found Misses D. & C. with A. in her room & all three in a state of lassitude, but I think I conduced to cheer them up a little. Probably the Gen. Order No. 41 & its probable effects was productive of the state of their minds; but really it is no joking subject. When the recreation was passed, we repaired to the lower regions, where in view of the times, we had a little fun. Miss Car. joined our company for the short while. The teachers' consciences reproached them for being absent so long from their apartments, & one of the most honest, proposed adjourning to them, but I can safely say that but little duties were performed by Misses C., D. & S. among whom I distributed my time, giving to D. the larger share. A. & I were in there until the closing of school conversing on a multitude of subjects. She is so strange. She seems to like me, but I am confident that she is not sincere, but I may be mistaken. She is very agreeable. We did not remain long after 3, as I was going to the "show", & after writing a few severe sentences on the board, (hoping they would meet the eyes of some Yankee) & having a short confab at the gate, she & I separated for a while, as she was to be present at the "ceremony". After dinner, I began making preparations, & after much thought decided on my pretty barège skirt, & ditto white body, & was some time in making my toilette, & when I had finished did not look quite as well as would have *Judo & Beauty.* How discouraging! (At the mention of these names the "old feeling" returns to my heart). *Will it ever die?* I was anxious very, for A. to accompany me, but she was obliged to go down town to see about her bonnet, & she regretted it as much as I. At 4¹⁄₂ I started, sun bonnet on head, & was one of the first there; but soon they came, all. Our class was the only one invited & the ex-graduates were privileged to attend. The graduates were dressed so tastefully & with a few exceptions all looked pretty. It commenced with a recitation & was dispersed with a few compositions, songs, remarks from Mr. McC. & Campbell, & then came the awarding of the diplomas, which some acknowledged by a graceful bow, & others a nod, in proportion as they valued or not the piece of parchment. I knew I wished that I were to be possessed of one, & then I remembered the "Patience worketh wonder" which was the response to a similar wish, some years ago expressed. It was announced that the Valedictorian was Miss Hodges, & the exercises considering the haste with which they were prepared, I was not of the opinion of my friend who thought they were "tame". At the conclusion congratulated my friends on the "honor" they had achieved, & had a talk with Miss D. who looked *particularly handsome.* I enjoyed myself considerably & was quite late before I started for home, in company with Liz. & Mag. who looked very pretty. Had the misfortune of having my dress torn in several places, the mending of which has cost me much trouble today. Ma & A. were out. L. was there, & I excused myself for a few moments, to change my dress. Ma. & co. had been to Rebecca's & had a lot to say. Had told them particulars of the Nathans, & Mr. H. volunteered to do anything for Ma. Probably they will be up tonight. L. spent the evening & the Nathan topic was again discussed. I *think* they will come here first. I gave A. particulars of my adventures & she, me of hers. L. remained quite late. We did not attend Synagogue yesterday for diverse reasons. The teachers were requested to meet at the Washington School, for what, they could only speculate. A. dressed & patiently waited for her bonnet, which was promised, but it did not come & much against her will, was compelled to wear F.'s, *which* I consider quite becoming. During the day, I arranged my drawers & things, & then went into a room, shut the doors, determining to devote my time to thought; but unconsciously my thinking faculties were suspended, & I was in the land of dreams until 2 o'c. when I was awakened by A. who informed that they were remunerated for the $\frac{1}{2}$ month, as the Directors were to resign & what course of action was to be pursued is not known, but I am of the opinion that the oath will not be required of female teachers; I do hope it *will* be, of those of L.N.S. I performed ablutionary exercises on S. & subsequently on myself, read a little of "Night & Morning", was summoned to dinner, where I made a hearty meal. In the afternoon, A. & I resolved to go & see about our bonnets, but as we were on the eve of starting, they came. We were much pleased with them, but suggested some improvements so determined to wear them down to have it made. I think they are quite becoming. Hailed the 'bus. Passed flocks of the wretches in Lafa. [Lafayette] Square, & City Hall, but on our arrival at Canal encountered not many of them. Informed Mrs. F. of the reason of our visit, but as it was quite late, she promised to send up for them. Did not meet Rebecca on her daily promenade. Had a pleasant walk home & encountered no adventures. When I arrived there, disrobed & made myself comfortable. Nobody came. Every one is much grieved at the death of Dr. Harby. He leaves an interesting family, but fortunately in fine circumstances. I am melting, so think it is time to cease. Where is Emile?

11

"Fairies of Ancient Times": June 17–July 11, 1862

Tuesday, June 17th, 1862

6 1/2 A.M. From the present aspect of the skies I think we will be favored today with that scarce article rain, & much in need of it do we stand. We either have a dry or rainy spell, & when the latter is inaugurated, I expect it will be of long duration. There is no news afloat. The excitement of Vir. has died away, but there is always something to engross the public mind, & I presume it is now the correspondence between Mr. Coppell & Old But.[1] A short while after leaving you, on Sunday, the bell rang, & guess who it was! You never can, so I may as well tell you, Mr. D.G. Duncan. We all dressed hastily & went down to see him, & expressed our unbounded astonishment thinking he was safely incarcerated at Fort. J. He informed us that he was unconditionally released, for nothing, as he had been imprisoned for nothing. He told us a great deal, & talked as beautifully as ever. He was at hard work down there—keeping off the mosquitoes. The Mayor is still there. Mr. D. has a passport to leave the city & I do hope he will see Pa. When he gets out of But.'s lines won't he give him the devil, & won't he show him up thro' the columns of many a paper. Mr. D. heard all the news & rumors down there & so we had naught to tell him new. While he was here, it amused me so much to see that the entire conversation was of the Yanks & state of the country. What did people use to talk about. Picayune inquired for Mr. da P. & was told that he had left the city. "D" used to know that "wretch". Mr. D. promised to call again before his departure. When he left, Mr. E. came in. He left after dark, & the remainder of the evening was left to our disposal. I heard that Emile

---

1. Clara here refers to protest from George Coppell, the acting British consul in New Orleans, regarding Butler's extension of General Order No. 41, the oath of loyalty requirement for New Orleans residents, to foreign nationals.

was sick, but it must be recently. Why don't he come. I was up very early yesterday, & studied very diligently wrote a horrid abstract in Philosophy. Oh! I despise school. I wish it would smash. But no such good luck. After breakfast F. went down town to get the sampling & when she returned it was sent to A. Mrs. F. sent for our bonnets. I did not sew until 1, as I had lessons to study. What shall I do, when I enter the Senior? Study! study! study! I did not go to school, very early, but was there in time. Knew my lessons. Those grateful showers we anticipated yesterday did not come. There was a feeble effort of a few scattering clouds to let fall some "gracious drops" but it amounted to nothing. When I came home found Mr. E. there, & was anxious to know the cause of his visit, but for the sake of politeness was compelled to repress my curiosity, until I subsequently learned that he came up for the purpose of telling Ma that he thought he could be able to send a letter off for her, as one of his friends leaves the city. Ma intrusted one to his care, but we have not the slightest idea of its reaching its destination. Sometimes I think it very strange that we do not hear from Pa. He has so many friends, & some coming here, surely they would be bearers of messages; & yet I am certain that he has written & the promises to deliver his letters have not been fulfilled. At any rate we cannot live this way much longer & if I were Ma, I would resolve to go on this summer. For two long months we have received no tidings of him, & imagine how uneasy we were when expecting a letter, a few days elapsed, & it did not come to hand. Mr. E. left before dark, & previous to his departure, Leo. darkened the doorway. I produced quite an excitement by the intelligence that a Yank was at the Viennes, & seemingly entertained as a visitor, the windows of the parlor being open, quite an unusual event. When L. saw him, he dispelled the illusion, by pronouncing him to be the French Consul, quite a different aspect on things.[2] I fell in love with him he was so handsome & had on so beautiful a uniform. L., A., & I took a short walk, in hopes of obtaining a few breaths of air; on our return supped, after which the evening passed in conversation, no mention being made of the Nathans. I wonder how they are getting along in their new quarters. Mr. N. has been very attentive & protects admirably at a distance. How faithfully he discharges his promises to Pa. To be sure, he protected us, & does still. All right!!!!!

2. Many residents of New Orleans, Jewish and non-Jewish, were citizens of France, and a discussion beween a French national and the French consul would not be unusual. Numerous French nationals, residents of New Orleans, had left for France to await the outcome of the war.

Thursday, June 19th, 1862

6¼ A.M. Last Tuesday, I prophesied from the appearance of the skies that we would have rain, & the prophecy was fulfilled, & now tho' the same indications are visible, I shall refrain from saying anything, as I do not wish it to rain, but I am confident that my wish will not be gratified. There is nothing of much interest in the Paper with the exception of the spicy correspondence between But. & the foreign Consuls, who raised objections to his Gen. Order No. 41. Oh! he cuts them up awfully, advising them to take down their flags & go home, for as no one has invited them here, no one would be regretful at their departure. The "brute" is very insulting in his remarks. By a new order of Gen. Shipley [Shepley], all men who have ever been in Con. services are required to report themselves to Ldg. & I dare say be compelled to take the oath, & if they fail to report they will be treated as spies. This is very stringent. Nothing further relative to School has been heard, & I venture to say that the oath will not be required of the ladies (Onhcusdoogkcul). We had some delicious showers on Tuesday Mor. & the air in consequence was deliciously cool & invigorating; but as the sun's rays gained sway the indications of another hot day were unmistakable. I did not sew as late as usual having lessons to attend to. Enjoyed my dinner, & departed after it. My most thoughtful time is when I am walking to school. Miss B. affected us very much (!!!) by hinting that our Dictation lesson would be the last with her. I do not entertain any serious fears about not being promoted, but still I am a little skeered. I do lose so much by my absence on Saturdays. In reading class we had considerable fun, particularly when our teacher exercised her elocutionary powers. Belle is so pretty. At 5½ we were informed that the Juniors were dismissed. Remained a little while to talk & then I trudged on my solitary way. No nice girls go my way, few exceptions, & I envy those who have "sweet" Belle's company. A. was busy with her work, which is very pretty. I was reading & yet found the afternoon so long. As Josie was in my arms by the door a Yank passed, when of her own accord she said "Hurrah! for Depp Dabis & Beauregard", when he turned & bestowed such a sweet smile & his face bore such an expression of surprise that my heart warmed towards him. Unvaried programme at night. A recapitulation of the events of the day. Nothing transpired yesterday. I devoted a great deal of time to the Philosophy & then to my sorrow, it was not recited. You know Mrs. S. has abandoned, to our joy, Examinations. During the day A. sent me a copy of a letter, the original of which was rec. by Mrs. Nelson from her

Father in Cor. [Corinth] & contained accounts of glorious victory. The excitement it produced was equal to that by my Dispatch. I saw A. for a few moments but not sufficient time to have any conversation. Mrs. S. read to the School, the same letter, which Miss C. had brought to her. After School, I went to Mrs. C.'s & had the pleasure of seeing her, the first time since her illness that she had been down; she was looking quite bad. Miss D. & Mrs. A. dropped in & we had considerable fun, tho' I expressed my satisfaction to them when they were about to take their departure. A. & I were to meet there, & I was about to leave, when the lady, having been unavoidably detained, made her appearance & consequently lengthened my visit. Vic. has left & is again boarding. Annie looked beautiful & promised to make up in her visits what she has so lost by her illness. She is going to visit the Spanish ships, & said when she did, she would send for us, hoping it would be agreeable for us to accompany her. I should be very pleased as I hear glowing descriptions of them.[3] We remained quite late, & necessarily hurried home. Ma, not uneasy. After we had got up stairs, about 10 o'c. the bell rang, & of such a moment of suspense. The thought foremost in our hearts was "Pa", & it found expression on our lips. Oh! I was so excited, & when in answer to my inquiry L. answered Mr. Duncan, I then considered it a hoax, & flew down, when to my disappointment I beheld the above-named gent. He had called in the afternoon & Ma had told him about the news, & he had been making investigations. He is very skeptical as he says many frauds have been practiced, & it was probably sent to school, knowing what an excellent medium that is for circulation. He is anxious to see Mrs. N., as he is desirous of asking her if she is confident that the handwriting is that of her Father's.[4] Mr. D. is waiting his opportunity to go. Ma gave him a letter which he is to *get to* Pa. After his visit we were much enervated after the excitement, & it was a long while before sleep visited us.

3. Spanish warships were in New Orleans harbor, providing a social diversion. The city and its harbor were in Union hands. Spanish warships were in the area as part of a multinational force created to force the Mexican government to pay its foreign debts. The force fell apart, and the Spanish ships were taking advantage of a break in their duties. Spanish ties to New Orleans were strong, dating from Louisiana's colonial period.

4. Sarah's father described a Confederate victory at Corinth in a letter from Charleston. Duncan was skeptical of the truth of the letter, one of several fraudulent documents that appeared in Confederate circles in New Orleans around this time.

Saturday, June 21st, 1862

11 A.M. Today being the longest in the year, I have deferred paying my devoirs to you, as "I have plenty of time". It is invariably the case that the longer space of time we have, the more dilatory we are. I can still plead another excuse. Ma & A. went out this morning at 8 o'c. on business, the importance of which I shall, in the course of time, acquaint you with. It was agreed when A. returned that she & I would go to execute a mission. A few moments ago they returned having completed it without me. I was inclined to be angry, but my better nature conquered, & I was not, so received accounts which you shall know in consideration if you display that virtue of patience. The day is very warm, & I adopt Ma's opinion that "we will pay for our past delightful weather". Oh! Philomen, I am so happy!! So in the excitement consequent upon this uncommon state of mankind you must overlook everything. And yet I am in an awful state of suspense. The transfers are to be made today, & suppose I am not promoted. Oh! the disgrace would kill me. It is very near Vacation, yet I suppose they wish us to be Seniors, in case that School will not re-open, (and this is my earnest wish). Nothing further is heard of the oath, but up to this late day there are some rumors of the continuance of School during the Summer! I doubt it. I slept very late this morning; but I can easily account for my late sleepiness. I read "When the mind is weary, sleep", & surely is mine from such continued excitement. So many subjects engross the mind that I am totally incapable of directing my mind to one object, & I often fear that I do not portray to you a faithful delineation of events; & yet I console myself by the thought "that it cannot be expected" & I am often tempted to throw down the pencil, & refrain altogether. And yet I knew my friend's leniency & feel content that if she is not made acquainted with certain events, I am cognizant of them & according to an axiom "Things which are equal to the same thing are equal to each other", & is not my knowledge equivalent to yours? Contrary to my expectations Thursday was a most bright, sunshiny day. The morning clouds dispelled & the face of nature never looked more radiant; but it was intensely hot. It was 8 weeks since the "fatal day" [surrender], & one, since the Nathans & Solomons were belligerents. We do not miss them as much as we expected, but in "these times" all objects not in connection with the one sink into insignificance. Ma was quite low-spirited, & in fact so was I, so the conversation of the morning was not very lively. I wrote my "Dictation" & experienced a mingled feeling of pleasure & pain, at the thought that it may be the last one required of me. If I only were a graduate. Oh! hopeless schoolgirls. After dinner, preparatory to leaving home, I took a look in the glass, & opened the door for the purpose of allowing a better light to fall on the love (!!!!) face therein reflected, when a step was heard on the gallery, & glancing back, I saw the diminutive form of "D.G.D." I entertained him till Ma came, & then aided for many minutes after. He announced his intention of going down to the Lake, & embracing the first opportunity to go. (Would *I were an opportunity!*) He had the evening paper, in which was reference made to a "mysterious letter of the 11th which is going the rounds". It is the identical letter of Mrs. N.'s & Mr. D. says it is the principal talk on "flags". Many discredit it, for our past experience has taught us to be *very* skeptical, credulity now being a thing of the past; & yet who can doubt this. Many have seen papers of a late date, having no mention of it, persons from Camp Moore who know nothing of it & in fact in the midst of those conflicting rumors it is difficult to *decide what to believe.* A. came in, & as usual had news from the "Depot". Mrs. N.'s sister had received a letter from her fiancé in Corinth containing a most *graphic description of the engagement in which he played an important part, "being in the thickest of the fight".* It containing personal matters she refused to give it to the public, but allowed Mrs. N. to take extracts, & the copies which were struck off of them were innumerable. A. had one, she read it & when had finished Mr. D. said, *"It is a genuine letter".* There were the names of the killed & wounded, & oh! who would practice such a hoax. It is a beautiful letter, & I have read & reread it. It is a most affecting account of the battle. He was writing it on the field, the following day. Mrs. N.'s inquiries amused me excessively. He was so anxious to give it circulation as coming from a reliable source as he was confident of the beneficial effects it would have on our people, so at his request, A. gave it to him. Oh! this is the evil which we foresaw. Barricaded in this city, receiving torturing accounts of a fierce, bloody & terrific contest, yet unable to obtain any news, any intelligence of those who have sacrificed their life blood on the Altar of Liberty. I left without bidding him "good bye" & what was my astonishment on arriving in School to behold the hands of the clock pointing to 4:35 & the exercises of the evening not begun. I learned that the hour had been changed to 4:30 to suit Mrs. P. & the cars. Mrs. S. was reading the extracts which I had just perused, & many seemed unwilling to admit them as truths. Belle & I were very good friends. Mrs. F. thanked us for our efforts on the Friday evening previous. I arrived home quite apropos as A. & Ma were dressed to go out on business of import, & Fanny B. had just come in. My presence warranted them excusing themselves, & I was left to entertain F.; she is a sweet girl & were we sociable girls, I do not doubt but we would be very good friends. She too refers to the "Camp" as some of the pleasant days of her life. Are we forgotten by our "Camp friends" of last Summer? While F. was there Bertha A. came to deliver a letter which A. had promised her Aunt to entrust to the care of Mr. D. She did not remain quite long. I sent my love to her Ma, & "respects" to her "Aunt". The 'bus halted in front of the door & the "slender" form of Leo. alighted therefrom. F. left a few moments after as she was about to pay a second visit. Shortly Miss Calder came. She had received a letter from her brother in Vir. & it was delivered by a gentleman who had arrived in the city. She intended to go & see him & make inquiries of Pa, & promised to come & tell A. the results. Her mother being very impatient did not wait for her but went alone & forgot a great many things, dates particularly; but he knew Pa, had seen him, & said he was making a fortune. She had scarcely told us this when a boy knocked at the door. I answered it imagining it to be no unusual a circumstance, but still the one thought of "Pa" ever present, was awakened & when to his inquiry "if Mrs. S. lived here", I replied in the affirmative, & he pulled a letter from his pocket & handed it to me, & I recognized that handwriting for which my soul was yearning, the scream of joy which escaped my lips was the only intimation that my friends had of the joyful event. Words fail to describe the emotions, the life-inspiring emotions which infilled my bosom. I could have kneeled at the feet of the boy, & poured forth my thanks to the faithful deliverer. Good or bad, cheering or desponding, it was tidings of our idolized father, & in the fullness of my joy, I pressed it again & again to my lips thinking only of him whose hand had traced the letters upon which my cheek rested. It was from him. Did I care thro' how many hands it had passed? It was from him! Tears of joy arose in my eyes, & I did not fear that my company would consider my filial love a weakness, for who could not love such a noble man? I felt so doubting; so alarmed lest it was only a deception, a vision of my busy brain! So I clutched it with a firmer grasp, confident that a letter was in my possession. It was no forgery for where could I not distinguish that writing? Among a thousand & in what ever form, with pride, I would point to it as the chirography of my Earthly Father, my love for whom is typical in its strength & majesty for that borne to my Heavenly One. It was a "trying moment". It was directed to Ma, & I would not unseal it in the presence of strangers, but oh! could have flown to a spot alone, & read, while each word would have sunk into the depths of my heart, words penned by that hand, that hand of him, from whom no news for many a weary day had reached us. They deemed me foolish not to open it. But did they imagine how I longed to see it! A sense of duty prevailed. To Ma sh'd be the honor, the privilege of breaking the seal, of being the first to peruse the precious document. How impatiently I awaited their return & how pleased was I at the pleasure in store for them. But I had to disguise my feelings in order to accommodate myself to my company, but they did not dream how far away my thoughts were. How I was in the Old Dominion state, gazing upon a face, one of the dearest in the world, my heart beating next to one, for which I would have coined my life blood? Oh! thought I what may not the letter contain? Time passed. They came & with womanly thoughtfulness, I broke it to them gently. Both gazed at Miss C. as if to thank her for her kindness; but all was explained. Need I dwell on their rapture? With trembling hands did Ma open it & she & I together read. It was of date of May 11th. Just think only 10 days after the arrival of the Yanks. I was a little disappointed & yet content. He spoke of their possession of the city & said had he advised us it would have been to remain in the city as he was confident the city would not be shelled. He did not dwell long on this lamentable subject & in fact on any as the letter was quite short, he having no hope of its reaching us, & as we had anticipated he had sent several, embracing every opportunity. He said, "Camp life" was "rather hard" but he was again in the enjoyment of his usual good health; but in an awful state of mind as he feared we were wanting for money. He told us to borrow of Mr. Maz. [Mazareau, who had been sent out of New Orleans as a prisoner] & the check for it he would deposit in S.E.Co. He knows not of his destination. "I would send some in this letter, but it is so uncertain" says he. His business is again prosperous, & he realizes from $1000 to $1500 a day. If we could only enjoy it together. He hoped that the "black child" was better & said he would not write much as he dared not hope that it would come to hand.[5] Oh! what pleasure the few lines afforded & if we could receive them regularly. Our friends were much gratified to hear of the good news it contained & rejoiced with us. Miss C. remained a good while, but could not spend the evening. L., A., & I accompanied her to her domicile, & oh! with a lighter heart than for many a day did my feet traverse the ground. When we got home, nothing was talked of but the letter. The discontent of human beings! If we should only hear from him of

5. Lucy's daughter Dell had had the measles the previous April. Solomon was selling goods at the front in an inflated currency at this point. Success in selling to soldiers was a day-to-day matter, not always achieved.

a later date. If he would only send for us! His coming I regard as very improbable. While at supper, Mr. D. called & in pleasant conversation the evening passed away. The last words of the Mayor to Mr. D. were "Tell them I will never take the oath, as long as there's an army in the field". The letter "of the 11th" was spoken of. "Dare." had shown it to his friends, & many had pronounced it "genuine". L. being anxious to see it & we having no copy home, he agreed to go to the School, the following day to procure one. He & "D.G." left together. With a prayer of gratitude on my lips did my spirit pass into dreamlands. In our joy & grief do our thoughts turn more forcibly to the Giver! But each day have we not much to be grateful for! Does not the "Angel of Health" preside over our dear family, & surely amid any trouble, this is a blessing. Oh! God! how weak, how sinful, & at times how forgetful of thy mercies, am I. Watch over my darling absent Parent! Shield him from danger! Yesterday, after breakfast, Ma & A. called on Mr. Larelle, but were so unfortunate as to find him out. I would have paid A. a visit but was quite busy. She brought home no news. A calm has succeeded the storm. Resolved to go out, & by six, Ma, A. & I were equipped in our holiday garments ready for the expedition. Our dresses were pretty, our scarfs graceful & our bonnets becoming; altogether we cut a "sorell", & you would also have been of this opinion had you seen the glances cast on us in the street. Resolved to go to the Harby's. Visits of this description are very unpleasant. (Saw Miss D.) It is not often, to my pleasure, that I am required to pay visits of condolence. As we went in, who should be there, on the eve of departure, but Mrs. N., Ludie & Olivia. We kissed all, with the exception of her, & then I reproached myself very much by offering her such a pointed insult. For I was only avenging the insults & slights to all. I was very sorry & I saw by her face, the feelings which reigned within. O. was very cool, & if she comes with her tantrums to me, I will give her a piece of mind. They walked out without a word, a look. How unfortunate that we should have met; B. conducted us upstairs; there were some visitors, & I was unprepared for what I saw. I may be harsh, but O. & F. had not the appearance of just losing a kind & affectionate Father. They spoke with nonchalance on a variety of subjects. Mrs. H. [Harby] only seemed to feel the loss she had sustained. I will be generous & think that the feelings of the girls were restrained. A sickening feeling crept over me as I entered the room, wherein he so often had been, & thought that he would never return. B. was as lively as ever. Sarah H. was there but we did not speak. I wish we did. First cousins![6] Our visit was short.

6. The Harby family also came from South Carolina.

We will go soon. Walked down Camp Street & reaching St. Joseph proposed going to Mrs. da P. only for a few minutes as it was quite late. As I approached her house, I perceived a female, & when I entered behold! there in all her radiant beauty & splendor sat — — Charlotte Brooke [a relative of Mrs. da Ponte]. We did not kiss, as our long separation has produced an estrangement. She accused us of neglecting her shamefully, & we have, but it will be a long while before we will visit her; & yet it is such a temptation, she is so beautiful, so fascinating!!! The summer of '58 passed before me, & the many happy hours we had passed in her dear society. So many happy scenes did her sweet face & voice recall. The time unconsciously skipped by & when we parted at the corner it was very late & the "stars were out in the blue vault above". Sop. [Sophie da Ponte] has not heard of her husband. Walked hurriedly home & from excitement & heat were much fatigued. Were honored with no visitors & departed early to our respective couches, while beautiful angels with dark, lustrous orbs, & rare curls flitted around. Ma & A. went to Mr. L.'s this day. They were unable to see him, he being sick, but he conveyed to Ma the intelligence that "Mr. S. was the last person to whom he bid good bye to"; that was at Camp. He went to Richmond & left 3 weeks after.

Sunday, June 22nd, 1862

4 P.M. Such continued excitement. So many subjects engross the mind that I am totally incapable of directing my mind to one object, & I often fear that I do not portray to you a faithful delineation of events; & yet I console myself by the thought "that it cannot be expected" & I am often tempted to throw down the pencil, & refrain altogether. And yet I know my friend's leniency & feel content if she is. Altho' we had a delightful shower today, its beneficial effects are not now felt as it is excessively hot. A. is by me grumbling as she is "devoting her whole energy to her hoop"; but these indispensable articles have become much reduced in price, as there had been an influx from Yankee Land, & it is useless to say you will not purchase Yankee importations when the majority of individuals do. And poor deluded creatures! They will not much longer offer their goods for sale to the citizens of the Crescent City. Old Butler! If he could only have as many ropes around his neck as there are ladies in the city & each have a pull! Or if we could fry him! Or give him many salt things to eat, & have water in sight, & he unable to obtain it! Oh! You dear Angel! You have our good wishes! I have concluded a hearty meal of Okra Soup, the first of the season, & while we were enjoying it our thoughts winged themselves to Pa. Josie is entertaining us with her shouts for "Jepp Dabis & Beaudegard", & while listening to that name is it surprising that my mind should be abstracted? God bless him. Ma is attempting to sleep, but I know she will have the same complaints to lodge as she did yesterday; but we cannot prevent the chicks from indulging in their antics. There comes Lucy to comb me; I will go, but it is not necessary that it will interrupt our chat. How dependent I am. Unable to look nice, if L. does not "have a hand" in my toilette. My hair is coming out sadly, & my efforts to prevent it have been futile. Ma has the finest head of hair of the family, & is in fact, the best looking. F. still wears hers short, & we wonder when she will ever "put it up". She is so childish for her years. I have not been industrious today. This morning Mrs. G., Ma & A. went to Mr. L. but again were unable to see him. Tomorrow is the last day for the men to take their parole, & I fear the wished for conversation will never take place. The Delta of today was very interesting, that is full of reading matter. Yesterday afternoon A. & I went out in our "suits". At the gate I met Alice; I feared to approach her, but she said "Clara, you are promoted". I wished no more. I asked no more; for being absent on Saturdays I did not expect to be high. My trepidation was at an end! And yet I was far from to be happy. We went to Ludie's & —*found* her *out*. Then deliberated for some time about going to Mrs. N.'s & after weighing every consideration, decided to go, but to stay a few minutes. Without any difficulty found the house. It is a very nice place. Were greeted *very* cordially by Mr. N. who escorted us into the house & *wanted* to insist on our divesting ourselves of our bonnets.

Mrs. N. was showing her house to a visitor & presently joined us. Greeted her with the usual style. Leo had told them of our letter. We remained about *10* min. & she said "This is a very formal visit. You must come soon & stay long". Ah! it is exactly what we intended it to be. As to the latter part of the sentence —she desired us to give her love to Ma. We were as "cool as cucumbers", & would have given a piece of our minds had an opportunity presented itself. We went to see them, for a variety of reasons; but I do not know *when* I will record a similar event. Stopped at Amie's, & passed a pleasant $1/2$ hour with her. She is almost well. Paid the penalty of remaining with her so long, by being obliged to *trot* home. Found A. & E. Jarreau there, & would have wished them any place else, being very hot & fatigued.

A. is rejoiced at her promotion. They staid unusually long, & on their grateful departure we disrobed & *then* partook of supper. "Dear Dave" came to bid us "good bye" yesterday. Of course there are many *funny* associations connected with him, & during our acquaintance many events transpired, which when reverted to excite our laughter. He went by the way of Madisonville, how or where I do not know. He entirely discredits the letters, & believes with me that had so important events happened we would have received confirmation of them. So, all our hopes are dashed to the Earth, & everyone is resolved to believe nothing *even what they see.* A. is teasing me to come & dress, & you know with *our* circle of acquaintances, we should be in readiness to receive them.

Wednesday, June 25th, 1862

6 1/2 A.M. Here am I, Philomen, with a variety of feelings in my bosom; sorrow, because I have to go to School this afternoon, & *joy* because there are only two more, & oh! how earnestly do I hope there will be no reopening, for I do despise it. I seize upon the least event, & try to make it a foundation for believing or hoping. I wish Mr. L. had never been born, then *probably* the idea of a Normal School would not have originated in another's brain. Oh! had it only *originated* in his!! Well, I am a Senior, & can assure you that consciousness is hailed with no delight, for I am sure I will kill myself studying. And for what? I do not feel like I could devote this time to you with my books lying around & unlearned lessons staring me in the face. But, thank God! Twice more & I hope for ever! But "Shep! come to my relief". I would rather — than go to the — & yet I do not want to leave. I am not studious, & do not appreciate study. If "D" had only succeeded! Sunday L. came. Towards dark we went to take a walk, & returned home like two old women — tired. Partook of refreshments. Oh! he staid so unreasonably long! I think men on such occasions ought to be drummed out of houses, as they do soldiers out of camp. I went to sleep, & A. came as *near* it as possible. How *boring some* people become after certain hours. At last he rose to go, & then I became a little more awake. I had on my new body, which was very becoming. I had so beautiful a dream last night & my sorrow in awakening & finding it "but a dream" can account now for my depression of spirits. How sad is the realization of life after a delightful dream. *I was with Althea,* as in the "days gone by", her arms encircling my waist, & each whispering our oft-repeated tales of love, & everlasting constancy. Oh! how transparent are school-girl's promises. Yet I have never forgotten one, & would prefer being now with her to *any female* on the Earth. How I do love her! If she would only come to see me! Unobserved I caught a glimpse of her the other day, & so many "old feelings" crept over me that I really felt *ill.* Could my companions penetrate my heart, when I said in a careless tone "Althea Bright" lives there? I studied very diligently on Monday, & yet seemed to learn nothing. We had dinner early, & as school does not begin till $4^1/_2$, I went to A.'s school. She & Miss D. were chatting but the company soon dispersed. When I got to school, I found the girls as excited as myself & all in dread & fear of the "coming time" (which I hope will *never* come). Imagine our feelings when our future mistress appeared! I had to shut my mouth in order to prevent my *hearts* escape, & when she said "seniors, go to your places", I thought I was a "gone case". To be sure, we felt a little proud of the station to which we were advanced, but oh! — Before commencing the lesson, she made a few remarks, with her sweetest smiles which always intimidated me. "Hoped the year would be a pleasant one to all". She would be very strict, & in after years we would thank her for it. (precious bit). The girls had sent some of their books to the class, & Addis fell to me. As she handed it she said, "Miss S. I hope the mantle will fall over you". (No chance). The lesson began, & I was more confused than ever, but amused to see the girls change color as they rose to recite. I could almost hear the beating of Belle's heart, & I am sure she heard mine. To be sure "a new broom sweeps clean", & she was very kind & gave moderate lessons, but if you could hear some account of the length of them from former pupils, you would be dumbfounded. It required constant study. Oh! I dread the future, more than I would hanging. The time slowly passed, & our first trial in the Senior class was over. If it had not been for Lusher, I would have been one of the graduates. Miss H.'s books were given me, but I presume to buy, which I don't intend to. The girls are raising a subscription to give Mrs. S. a present. I signed my name & annexed $1, but where it is to come from I don't know, as Ma is averse to such proceedings. Walked home very melancholy, & as Ma & A. were out applied myself to the Physical Geography of which I have heard such *horrid* accounts, & I must say it is *very* difficult. Became sick & tired of books. (Wished there had never been a school one) & amused myself with the children. Afternoon passed, evening came & to the — Geog. again. Was up by times yesterday studying it, but did not accomplish much. Began again at 12, & studied till three. Went to the despised School. Girls as frightened, girls as excited, girls as disgusted. Reviewed it, & when the awful moment came was nonplussed. I shall not dwell upon details. They are too unpleasant. I inwardly laughed, as I heard Miss B. screeching the Dictation & reproached myself for not *enjoying those days*. Sweet Belle walked to the corner of this street, as she was going further. Both blue. When I arrived A. insisted on my taking a walk. Endeavored to get some thread, but was unsuccessful. Walked past Mrs. H. but no lovely form greeted our vision & we retraced our steps. Saw Mrs. G. but "is it possible" had not the pleasure of speaking to her. Alice is quite despondent, & has made up her mind to quit *until the next session*. They have heard of Joe. I do not like those people as well for I think they have prejudiced *Emile* against us! I *tried* to study at night. Oh! Greene! had you never compiled an "Analysis"!

Friday, June 27th, 1862

6 3/4 A.M. Well, has this day, the *last one* of *school*, really arrived. How quickly has the time passed. How well I remember when we used to say, "long March, April, May & June", & now, they are with the past, the never-to-be forgotten past. It is my usual habit on such a day to pay a visit to A.'s school, but for diverse reasons I do not think I will today. A. is down in her deshabille, *doing her work*! I feel very warm, & may be prepared for a "swinging day". I don't care so long as the *Yanks* suffer. I have a headache, & in fact do not feel like myself. I am worried, & do believe that in the ensuing summer I will waste away. (I hope so). There is no news in the paper. The old Yankee Picayune is as dull as ever. I declare I am disgusted with all the papers, & prefer the Delta to them, for it openly expresses its views, while the others do it covertly. I am glad of the fate of our Delta, for it *may* have disgraced itself. *I have suffered so much since Wednesday* (mentally). That day I studied hard, & when on my way to S. felt as tho' I would prefer to be hung. But you understand me. *I don't want to leave* & yet I would give worlds if I could. The "paper list" was presented to me, & I promised (à la Pa) to bring it "tomorrow". I do not care what they get. I am not interested. I disliked the school *more than ever.* When I got home, I was so depressed that in the fullness of my grief, I gave way to tears. A. rallied me, & I went down, where was Leo. a National Advocate in his hand, containing the

joyful news of *our recognition by France.* Leo. said there was much rejoicing in town, but many were doubtful, & I am included in the latter. Oh!
wouldn't it be glorious for us! England would follow in her footsteps, &
who then knows how soon the insolent invaders may be driven from our
soil!! It revived my drooping spirits, yet there was a sadness brooding over
me, which but few things could have dispelled. Josie had her hair cropped,
& looks like an "orderly Sergeant", "Little Patrick", etc. I think she is the
ugliest of the flock. Sallie is the "Beauty". L. was very agreeable, particularly after asking us to take a ride the following afternoon, in the down
town cars, to which we acceded. We tease him about "Mrs. Williams". I
did not rise until late yesterday, as I made up my mind to abandon school
until September. I had a most annoying dream. Beautiful while under its influence; aggravating when not. A circumstance happened at breakfast,
which soiled my temper for the greater part of the day. I cannot tolerate
injustice & inhumanity. Oh! if A.B. [Althea Bright] would only come. I
know she would if— —. I shan't say what, for *fear other eyes may* rest upon
this. I was glad to be able to sew *all day.* After a great struggle I asked Ma
for $1 & sent it around by Ellen. About $5^1/_4$ Leo. came but we were not
ready until 6. Were conveyed to Canal by the 'bus, which was cutting up
some antics. "Made faces" at the Yanks I saw, & were safely deposited by
the car, in which we seated ourselves, & were soon enjoying our ride. I
looked in vain at Judo's house, A. for her *"Adonis".* It is always my misfortune in cars, to sit opposite some handsome lady or interesting gent.
in which my gaze is riveted. Amused Leo. by the resemblances we traced
between the passengers. One was Gen. Lovell, one, Duncan, one, catfish,
& each one looked like some one, & Leo. could but acknowledge the resemblance *tho' slight.* The ride was delightful & long to the "Alfway Ouse"!
Strolled in the gardens, imbibed a refreshing drink & went up in the same
cars, & it contained our same passengers with a *few* more. *It was a jam* &
Mr. O.'s feet came often in collision with mine. I was next the "Gen." &
oh! I pity him, for I do not think he is happy. The pretty lady was on my
other side, but I saw little of her. The "Gen." got out. I watched him to the
last. He had such ferocious light moustaches, (my style). I was sorry when
we came to the termination of our ride, but my sorrow soon vanished before the glass of ice-cream (a delicacy seldom indulged in) at Vincents. It
was so delicious. I ate as slowly as possible, but alas! "Ever thus from child-
hood's hour", etc. Waited at the corner for the 'bus, but failing to make
its appearance, we proposed walking to meet it. Did not succeed, & the
walk was so pleasant that thoughts of the 'bus escaped our mind. A. & I

gave it to the Yanks. I lifted up my dress, put my kerchief to my nose, & when we passed the sentinel on his watch, made some vague allusions to the night air & yellow fever. I was a *leetle scared*. After we passed the "city" I became quite fatigued, but was not excessively so on my arrival home. Was much pleased with the entertainment of the evening. L. staid a little while, & we made arrangements to go to the Bayou on Sunday, (deo volente), & L. accepted our invitation to dine with us. Oh! Emile! "Friend after friend".

Sunday, June 29th, 1862

6 ³/₄ A.M. It is such a *delightfully* beautiful morning, & so many sweet associations, I know not how, does it recall. Oftentimes a word, a look, a wind recalls memories of the past. A. & I both rose early this morning, A. earlier. I have been reading the papers, & A. is by me, with her work. I declare I was affected on reading accounts of the death of poor de Kay, away from his friends & home! But why was he? How many more Sundays will elapse ere we are *with* dear Pa, or *hear* from him The past week has been one of the *longest* I *ever* knew. Each day seems "to drag its slow length along". I *went* to School Friday! And such a confusion, collecting the books & arranging them. Then thoughts of who would displace them would arise. All seemed to catch the spirit & everything was excitement. I spent my time with B., Miss D. & A. School never closed under such gloomy auspices & none seemed to entertain an idea of ever again resuming their duties. *I* felt sad at the solemnity of the occasion. A. was loath to dismiss her charges, for who knew if they would ever meet again! And they were affected too. We had quite a little treat thro' the kindness of Mrs. C. School was dismissed at 12, & such kisses & promises "to go & see". A. took down her flags which have been proudly waving since Examination, & which were only lowered for fear of their being disgraced. Miss D. & I were enjoying ourselves being spectators & listeners. She is quite agreeable. The last farewells were spoken & all gone except A., J. & myself. I soon left being considerate enough to think that they might wish to have a private conference, probably for the last time. They are such good *acquaintances*. Miss D. reminded me to come & see her. At home, set to marking some stockings for Ma with "chain stitch", & succeeded admirably. Contrary to my

expectations A. was home before 2. Mrs. G.'s intention to close the school caused their early separation. I was quite provoked when A. told me that they did not give to each other "those sweet pledges of affection". A. occupied herself with her work, & I sat on the sofa by her, but found it impossible to sew & talk, so resigned myself to the latter, having plenty to say. After dinner it was excessively warm. I indulged in a pleasant siesta, tho' I fell to sleep with tears on my eyelids, & was awaken by one of my wild vagaries. Our toilettes being made, we proposed paying some visits. The first to Miss Julia C. an acquaintance A. made at the Bay, & heard was in the city. She was out. Met Mary N. I was so glad to see her, & her presence convinced me of the truthfulness of Mr. McC.'s statements. I plead guilty to the charge of "treating her shamefully" & do really intend to go & see her. Went round to Annies, & she was out. Society should be remodelled & every one have reception days. I am glad she is "going out"; & we may soon expect a visit. We will wait for one. Passed F.B.'s house, but it had the appearance of the inmates not being in it. We were really unfortunate, & but one event marked the evening. It was meeting Susie C. who informed us that Gen. Shepley said the schools would re-open under different auspices & with different rulers, & the teachers were not to be compensated during Vacation. Am I to believe it? Is it to be expected? Ma was inclined to discredit it!! Old Butler has taken Twigg's house for his summer quarters, & Shepley, the one adjoining; Mr. Race's house is to be occupied by officers of the army. Yesterday, Mrs. G. came to inform us that a schooner was to leave in the afternoon & she intended to take passage on it, & then go to Madisonville & from there to Canton & probably further. She offered to take a letter for Ma, provided it be unsealed. Had quite a welcome shower, but it was not of long duration. We were watching for some time Z.V. [Zulma Vienne] & a gent. who from appearances we presumed to be her lover, & whose dress indicated he was a Naval officer of the Span. vessel. It was very refreshing. The rain seemed to render the air more oppressive. A. & I laid on the bed, & while I was reading L.E.L. to her, the wicked girl went to sleep. Took a walk, & seeing F.B. at her door, stopped & remained some time. She walked some distance with us, & when we passed Race's gave the Yanks "fits". Coming back here from Nayades seem[ed like] going into the woods. Had a chat with Alice. She had also been engaged in the interesting occupation of watching the neighbors. Z. became acquainted with the handsome Span. by going on board the vessel, & they are now engaged. It is very sudden. The vessels are crowded with daily visitors, & I am so anxious to go. *I may make a conquest.* "Emile"! what is the matter. I shall never speak to you again! Never! Never! Never!!

Tuesday, July 1st, 1862

5/4 A.M. Welcome July! When your "course is run" may I be happier than I am! It is a bright, pleasant morning, but I never intend to calculate my proceedings for the day by the appearance of the morning. Sunday morning I said "It is a delightfully beautiful morning"; it merged into the day & still continued. We added some touches to our toilettes before dinner in order to be ready soon after. About 2 Leo. came & a few moments later, dark clouds were spread over the heavens. We regarded them as but transient but while at dinner the drops began to fall, & continued for so long a time, that we were compelled to give up our promised expedition! Alas! "The best laid plans of mice & man", etc. We postponed it to some future occasion, when I hope we will be more lucky. We will hope that we have now entered upon one of those gladdening seasons, when a shower a day is a thing, *of course,* for a succession of weeks. There was much excitement at the Viennes' in consequence of the arrival of the Span. Officer & other visits, whom we immediately recognized as going to dine there. I amuse Leo. much by my earnest desires & strenuous exertions to see everything that was to be seen. About 5, I went up to complete my toilette, did so, & then sat at the window to observe the lovers, who were courting out *on the gallery.* He is so handsome, & if ever I felt envious it was when I looked at them. How devotedly he regarded her, & how affectionate were his caresses. Oh! how my lonely heart craved for love, some one to love. Will its cravings ever be satisfied? How often I wish I had not been cursed with capacities for loving, & no one on whom to exercise them. Would I were as coldhearted as the majority of individuals; or that I were only blessed with the love, so essential to my existence. And yet I live without it. The clock struck 7. I started. "If the time has passed so quickly to me, watching, with what rapidity has it passed to them"!! I left the scene of happiness, & went down. Leo. had gone, & Mr. E. was there, on the eve of leaving, but my presence delayed him for a few moments. The rain had ceased, the eve was fair, & when he left A. & I went to walk. Were joined by Alice. Topic, the courting; & she agreed with me, it was too public.

He is of noble birth, is 1st Lieut. in the command, has been twice presented with medals by the Queen, & it is considered eligible match. He seemed to love her with the ardor of Spanish, & she, him, with the ardor of her French heart. If they do be one, may they be happy. Envied Zulma! Envied Antonio Terio! Passed some Yanks & to Alice's fear, gave them *some of our tongue*. She came home with us & remained some time. No one to come, & as usual the evening wore away. Yesterday vacation commenced, & not under very auspicious circumstances. E. did not come, having a sore finger. Ma was in a bad humor, which I fear she communicated to others. We did not do much sewing, in fact, it seemed like a holy day. There is no bread to be had as there is no flour in the city. Truly the people have not the "staff of life" to lean on. The wants of the "inner man" were not well satisfied, & à la Pussy, we were not very merry. A. was amusing me by playing on the Piano. I resolved to write daily, for my improvement, & selected meet L.E.L. A. immediately followed in my footsteps, & we alternately wrote & dictated. Ma made agreements to go & ride in the cars with all the "chicks". But before Ma & they were ready, & all fusses over, you may imagine the state of mind of the former. She was in an excessively bad humor with all ere her departure, & left many *orders* which if they had not been so given would have been executed. Dell, A. & R. behaved admirably. It was so very warm, that A. & I dressed with great exertion. It was any place, imagine our room. With difficulty we prevented the powder on our faces from assuming a *cakey form* & when we had finished went on the back steps to "cool". Oh! some houses are so delightful & yet some who possess them desert them & prefer to summer at a crowded watering hotel. Ascertained the where abouts of D., R. & A. When the sun set, a delicious breeze sprang up & prevailed during the evening most refreshingly. Cancer, the crab, went out in a glow, & Leo enters today. We hope he will abate somewhat of his usual rage, in consideration of his predecessor's reign. The city is most healthy for this time of the year. May it continue so. As A. & I were standing by the door, a woman passed & said to us "are you not sisters"? We replied in the — & she said "Excuse me; I asked you because you looked so much alike". Did you ever hear the beat? We had no trouble with Robert Wheat's namesake, D. having subdued him into a state of somnolency. N. made occasional requests for "Mama Lulu", & altogether A. & I passed a pleasant afternoon. About 8½ they returned but we invariably make it a point — "To ask no questions".

Thursday, July 3rd, 1862

7 1/4 A.M. Do not be skeptical, but believe me when I tell you that I did not rise until a few moments ago, & then I was awakened from so sweet a dream in which "two *dear persons* (males) *figured so conspicuously*", how sad I was to wake & contrary to my thoughts find myself in my own bed. Oh! dreams are unpleasant in whatever aspect we near them. It is a beautiful morning; for the day none can answer. The glorious 4th will be celebrated in the city tomorrow; but oh! how differently from former years. Salutes are to be fired & national airs to be played sound the "Sage of Ashland" & the "Hero of N.O.". God grant that the day is not far distant when we the people of N.O. can celebrate our independence. My feelings accord with the state of my beloved country. A cloud dark as that which hovers over her is above me. In these terrible times who can feel otherwise? Beauregard, God bless him, is in Vir. where his command has been removed. To him is assigned the most difficult & perilous stations, for success always has crowned his effort, "Our second Washington", the future "Father of his country". My heart burns in all ovation before him. How joyous will be his return here, when with hearts overflowing with gratitude, we will stream flowers in his path for him to walk upon, as was done a man in many years past. Earl Van Dorn has succeeded Lovell, & a proclamation of Gov. Moore has created much excitement. He says the country shall send no provisions here & thus we are doubly blockaded, & it is a question of much moment, "What is to become of us"! We are willing to make sacrifices. With corn meal we can never starve.[7] Vacation began very inauspiciously. Tuesday Ma was very bad, having not recovered from the excitement incident to the ride. When Ma is in one of those humors you may imagine how unpleasant is home. We had a heavy rain, which saturated the needy earth, gave fresh verdure to the gardens, & renewed vigor & elasticity of spirits to man. I had quite an annoying toothache which but heightened my bad spirits. I did little sewing, as usual, when Ma is so ill disposed. In the afternoon did my usual writing, but it was passed no more pleasant than the morning. By the evening paper we saw that Mrs. Phillips (Beauty's Ma) has been sentence to *Ship* [Island]. Is to be *there confined;* with one servant; soldiers rations; & to have no communication, verbal or written, will be allowed her. The charge against her is "she is found on the balcony of her

---

7. Lovell had been criticized for the loss of New Orleans, then under his command, and Davis gave him a subordinate position under Van Dorn in Mississippi.

house during the passage of the funeral of De Kay, laughing & mocking at his remains, & upon being inquired of by Com. Gen. if this fact were so, contemptuously replies, 'I was in good spirits that day'".[8] This is one of *the outrages* of But. command separating this woman from her family & keeping her in confinement in that miserable place, no one knows how long. And what anyway could a woman's taunts do them! How much more manly to pass them by with silent contempt. The P.'s have cause to hate them with a deadly hatred, for their sufferings in Washington are kept fresh in their memory.[9] As the Delta says "It will create a hullabaloo in certain circles". When we were dressed, A. & I went to walk. Saw the Yanks & made no demonstrations, as A.J. [Alice Jarreau] is very timid. Had a long argument on religion & our views were materially different, she being Catholic, & we — I was —. After getting home we stood up for about an hour talking. The argument became quite fierce, but we parted good friends. Were surprised to see Leo. in the house when we entered & apologized for our absence, as he had seen us, & doubtless that we had seen him. While at supper it began to rain, & pour in torrents. He remained very long & when he left, there was a cessation. I abstracted his hdkcf. from his pocket & will keep it as a memento, if he does not inquire about it. Ma's temper was a little improved yesterday. A. & I resolved to go down town to get some shopping done, & about 11½ departed very joyfully for that purpose. Had a pleasant walk down, as the sun was peeping from behind a cloud. Met Mr. H. & bowed *very coldly;* they should have been up here ere now. But I can imagine why they haven't! While at Deters, Rosella M. came in & we spoke to her. Of course, she enlightened us on the life & adventures of Antonio Terio. She is acquainted with the officers as she pays frequent visits to the vessel, her father being friends to many from his own country. Romantic *meetings* between us & Mr. Overall. I wonder if he recognizes us. I doubt it. Having fulfilled our mission we walked in Chartres some, with a hope of seeing Leo., when visions of ice-cream danced thro' our brains. Oh! the frailty of human hopes! A. yielded to my entreaties & walked on Canal Street. She has such old-maidish notions & is fearful of rendering herself *"conspicuous"* Resolved to walk up, as we wished to be economical with the trip, & tho' *half starved* resisted all temptations. It may have been too unbending, but — —. How often were our tho'ts with Alicia

8. Eugenia Levy Phillips was mother of one of Clara's idols and wife of Philip Phillips, a well-known Jewish lawyer from New Orleans.

9. As an attorney and friend of Judah Benjamin in Washington, Phillips had argued the cause of the South.

& the extensive preparations going on in a certain mansion in the "Jew district".[10] The visions of the garlic & sausages together with the Yankees afforded us food for amusement & diverted our attention from the state of our stomachs. Passed Twiggs, & sighted around his beautiful door were the handsome officers of Butler's staff. I walked on the extremity of the pavement & insulted them in every way but — — —, in which A. did, making allusions to the "stolen paper" they were reading, & tell you both were a little alarmed, particularly when we heard hasty steps behind us. Visions of a lone desolate isle passed before me, but we were unmolested. Stopped at Mrs. Deegan's. Ellen's finger is quite bad, & she has not yet been. Very *weak* when we arrived home; I disrobed & laid down, fell into a sleep, & was unceremoniously aroused from it to go to dinner, which I wished in Halifax, my appetite having passed away. In indignation [dreaming] A. & I were in the Goldsmiths' house; we counted the hours as they passed & saw A. [Alicia] in the different stages of her toilette, & were in the midst of the excitement. In the afternoon on our way to Miss C. passed the house. The street was "alive" & any number of "You Gents" on the gallery, among whom was Leo. who honored us with a bow. How we envied the fair bride, or in fact, any of the company, & how wistfully were our glances directed to that story, wherein report said was laid the table. What does it not call to mind! Found Miss C. home; she told us of Mrs. S.'s interview with Shepley, in which the 1st named was much abused. Saw the "Beautiful". Miss C. walked some distance with us, & accompanied us up Nayades in order to get another peep. Passing Miss Cor.'s house, we were joined by her. Our view was very unsatisfactory, as we only caught glimpses of flowing robes, etc. etc. But the supper. That were my feelings were enlisted. Parted with our corner. Bread & molasses, which A. & I imagined to be delicacies. The luxury bread is not now indulged in & cornbread which A. so once loathed is in demand by her. Something to it. In the night A. & I were "tripping it on the light fantastic toe" with Jalohs [?], Altman, Bhrur, Levi, [wedding guests] while sweet issuance of garlic & onions was wafted in the "evening wind". Oh! Imagination. How wide are they roaming! They are calling me to breakfast. Adios.

10. Clara passed the "Jew District" on her way home from the French Quarter, along St. Charles Avenue. There is a photograph of the Goldsmith home in my *The Business of Jews in Louisiana, 1840–1875* (Tuscaloosa, 1988).

Sunday, July 6th, 1862

6 1/2 A.M. Oh! Philomen, a weight of despair is on my poor heart! Despair, anguish & grief! Attentively have I scanned the papers, but nothing further have I ascertained. I dread to tell you. I refrain from saying it. Yesterday there was an "extra Delta" published about 11 1/2, & the sound of that "old tune" produced much excitement, & were immediately purchased. They were accounts of the late Rebel victories taken from the Mobile Advertiser. There has been some terrific fighting at Richmond & the substance is that McClellan has been badly whipped, & he is expected to capitulate. The Delta says, "While we reproduce them, we say emphatically that we do not believe them". In the battle of Richmond, June 28th, the following paragraph arrested our attention, "*The gallant Major Wheat of the Louisiana Tigers is killed*". Oh! It seems profanity to repeat the words, the awful words. It was not as great a shock as it might have been, for Fanny B. had told us she had heard a rumour to that effect. The paper dropped from my hand, & together A. & I shed those bitter tears of grief, bitter only to those who have had the sad experience. *Our* dear Major! No! no! it could not be. Hope whispered reports are so false. There may be an error & then despair would seize us, & hope vanish, & the thought that it was too true. He is so brave, so impetuous, I know he would himself be in the thickest of the fight. That noble man. Maybe he died with his affectionate heart praying for his dear Mother. Perhaps no man's gentle soothing & care was with him, & oh! God! how miserable to think that his life may have passed away in the arms of a man. How hopeful one year ago did he leave us; so hopeful of a joyful return. If it would say *wounded*, for see how providential was his recovery from the wounds at Manassas. He has enough scars, he should come home. My heart sickens when I talk of him. We may never hear a confirmation, a contradiction, but oh! how blessed is hope. In the battle of Fort Republic June 8th his dear name is among the wounded & is there not a probability that he was unable to be in that of the 28th. Have wishes against hope! But it is blessed. There was an account of the wounded & among them was Ripley, all others of the wounded whom I know are not mentioned. I hope O.P. is safe.[11] A. & I

11. Obed Miller's military career turned out to be a sad one, ending with his death in Virginia in the summer of 1863. Having enlisted as a captain in Major Wheat's Special Battalion in June 1861, he was severely wounded at Manassas in July of that year. Returning to the front after some home leave, Miller was again in a military hospital in Lynchburg, Virginia, in June 1862. While there he sought, in letters to Jefferson Davis, a transfer to a regular army unit. He was not transferred, but,

were going out but we abandoned all ideas. Every word of his, every look from those beautiful eyes arose to my memory & to arrest my attention I read, I talked, but would not believe. I tried to be gay. Oh! God! how dearly bought are all our victories. I did not know how bright a future I had been picturing till I tho't my hopes dashed to the ground! Oh! why must people love. Why have an affection! Is it not one day to be severed. I was so despondent the remainder of the day, but A. & I cheered the others. In the afternoon Miss C. & her mother came. Miss C bro't A.'s money. They were paid for two weeks. She was very gay, & spoke of our late successes; she had passed idly by that name. She spoke of victory, spoke of him, but these are words idly spoken to the childless one, the orphan's ear, or to the widow's heart that's broken. I had a very severe toothache, from which I am now suffering & I retired early. God grant my prayers!

Tuesday, July 8th, 1862

7 A.M. Oh! I fear our worst fears are confirmed! I do not think that there is a shadow of a hope remaining. I am miserable! My whole life seems to be departed. I have no energy, no spirit for anything! It is so painfully, acute a subject, that I refrain from mentioning it to you & prefer to think, think! think. No greater sacrifices have been offered than those *two* of Earth's noblemen. *Two* young men cut down in the prime of their lives! Oh! Robert! That noble governing heart stilled forever! Oh! God! How uncertain is life. After his terrible wound at Manassas, I deemed him guarded! And yet it is a pride to think that he *died fighting* gallantly.

---

with Wheat dead, his battalion fell into disarray. Miller tried to form his own unit with soldiers from Wheat's Battalion in Virginia, called Capt. Miller's Independent Mounted Rifles, with the nickname "Wild Cats" (Major Wheat's unit had been dubbed the "Tigers"). Miller officially tendered his resignation from Wheat's Special Battalion, but he had already left camp and was fighting on his own. His own unit was called a "disgrace to C.S.A.," a "lawless company" that had the worst elements of Wheat's original unit in it. Part of the 9th Virginia Infantry, Miller's unit was disbanded and Miller's resignation approved, being preferable to a court-martial proceeding. In August, 1863 Miller's widow filed a claim in Virginia for back pay due her. The course of events was very strange indeed. Confederate Service Records, Louisiana, Wheat's Special Battalion, RG 109, National Archives.

Died! Can I ever realize it! How distinctly do I remember every event of those happy days, which have been followed by such anguish. Had I never known him! I can speak of nothing! To every subject am I indifferent. Everything we love is doomed to destruction. And yet there is a ray of sunshine in the prospect of our loved Father's return! How I wished for it to ask of him. Oh! every thought seems connected with him. Every hope of the future! We have no friends! Even the Nathans have deserted us! We are blessed with health. Well, every cloud has a silver trimming. And now, the omnibuses, our old friends, have *ceased* to run. Oh! I miss them so much. They were such pleasant companions, so agreeable to watch. It seems like the country, & in fact I would as leave be in the back woods! And then the inconvenience to which we are subjected, the nearest line being Nayades Street. A. is by me, working. Poor child!! The morning is bright! But what do I care. Let all be gloomy, as is my heart. Sunday I had a wretched toothache & in conjunction with other things I was very sad. Ma's temper has improved considerably. Nobody came. I did not dress & remained up stairs all the time. Of all pains that in the tooth is the most painful. Yesterday morning I went to Dr. N.'s & he put an application which relieved one. I am in such a peculiar position having no dentist to whom to go & I have not confidence enough in Dr. N. to entrust my teeth to him. Feeling so much better, we stopped at School, where Mrs. Fred. has some scholars. Arriving home we determined to take advantage of the last day of the 'bus to go down town. Ma, S. & R. accompanied us, & we were in readiness by 11½. After getting out of the 'bus whom should we meet but "sweet Annie". She told us that Mr. P. had received dispatches, & it was an undeniable fact. Oh! I did not know how much I hoped until this blow was struck. Annie was very sad, & we parted at the corner. Ma proposed going to the Bayou, & of course we assented, but how little did we feel like it. How preferable to have left the jostling crowd, & go home in solitude to weep. I so much wished I had not met A. for it is sweet to hope. I felt miserable in the cars. Everything reminds me of him. I so often imagine the joy of riding with him in the cars, & yet I felt more for A. for I know her heart warmed to him. His manly form! How well I see him. Every future hope was blended with him. My heart goes forth to that childless mother, whose sons were the pride of her life. He has rid us of his love for his mother. How she pets him as tho' he were again a child. But why must I think of him. Cease, cease thy wild beatings, my heart! Broad St. was soon reached, & after a hot walk of 4 squares we were at the gate of the Solomons. Our ring was answered by Mathilde, who informed us that they were out. We went in & were there some time when Cousin J. came in, having been in the garden & just apprised of our visit. We had no idea of it but he insisted on our taking off our bonnets; persisted in it & we had to obey. He looks well, but traces of his sorrow are still visible. He is not the same man as of yore. How terrible an affliction was theirs.[12] We spoke of going, but he laughed at it, & we consented to wait, & in a few moments E. & Cousin C. came, so we knew it was an unusual occurrence for them to go down town & it was unfortunate that we should both have selected the same day. Some time after we rose to go, but they would listen to no excuse, completely overruled it, & would not allow us to get our bonnets. We remonstrated that we had no idea of remaining, but they would accept nothing, so we had to stay. I was so sad, but my feature had to wear the seeming of a smile. They were kind & hospitable. Emily looked beautiful. She is the style I most & so admire, blonde. Her hair curls in beautiful curls over her graceful shoulders. Her complexion is lovely, her mouth & teeth beautiful, but—her eyes—ugly. She plays beautifully on the piano & the time passed very agreeably. Dinner was not a great item. The fruit is not ripe on account of the dry weather. Made promises to come up soon, & pay our visit, & about $6^1/_2$ we prepared to depart. They walked to Esplanade St. with us. I wish I had men relations. I am sure I would love them for I love those people, & would more so, were they not so mean. Were deposited in the cars, & the last farewell spoken. Were soon at Canal St. & I shrunk from the wide crowd & sought an omnibus. I was so selfish I could look at no man. I begrudge them their lives. Why should they live & Robert so noble, so superior to them, *die.* How insignificant they all appeared. I was glad to get home, where I speedily disrobed. F. was not alarmed. Mr. N. had been. How considerate to call after the lapse of a month! Glad we were out. Leo. had been. When I came down deshabille, A.J. was there & remained until 9. Emile passed, &—broad. If I could only solve the mystery! How strange! But any insult was not intentional. A. & I disposed of some corn-bread & then laid our weary heads upon our pillows, but *not to sleep.* Oh! *Robert,* two hearts mourn for thee! It *is a* dream! *He is not dead.*

---

12. Joseph and Caroline Solomon had recently lost a young son.

Friday, July 11th, 1862

7. A.M. How do you do, Philomen! I am frightfully alarmed at the late habits of indolence & indifference which have of late seized possession of me, & affairs have reached a crisis, when I neglect you, *but* to be candid I did not feel like enjoying your society, yesterday, so postponed the visit today, & yet I am constrained to be very brief, as I cannot allow you to don your robe, for too long a time, as it is fast wearing out, as alas are my shoes whose 4th month birthday was celebrated the other day. Oh! how I dislike getting new ones, tho' they together with most other things, are very moderate, a reduction which is wonderful. Two weeks of the vacation has passed, & I can say that in future times I can never revert to them with any happiness. I can't derive the cause, but the day has passed without a contest. Well, we will hope for a "better time" when we can smile & wonder at this. Mrs. G. has returned, for I know Ma has been there, but the particulars of the visit I do not know. I should like to see Mrs. G., but for the present her house is *forbidden ground*. The Nasty Delta has daring dispatches announcing the "Fall of Richmond"! 50,000 prisoners taken!! etc. As if they themselves believe it! Another victim to the late battle was Col. I. Seymour. His countrymen mourn his loss. Something of Col. Aubon I read. He says that But. was right to stop his paper as it was indeed a rebel sheet. He is a true patriot. I had a dream last night! Alas! It will be but a dream. A.B. will not come. We are used to the omnibuses not running, but on Tuesday it was quite novel. In imagination we were in our "Country seat", & I really tho't it true. It is the woods! It will depreciate property in this section & I think some line should be started. Saw a Spaniard take a note to Zulma. Began to sew the flounce on A.'s dress with the pleasant prospect of two more. Ma purchased 5 hoops, but some was for me, as I am not quite in need of one. In the afternoon Ma went out, & A. & I remained home. Was with A.J. & while walking met Justin & Miss E. & how much I would have liked an introduction. But nary one. Ma bro't home some nice things & was generally smiling. While standing by the door, Emile passed & bowed very politely. How provoking! F. has formed some new acquaintances & together with Major, her afternoons & evenings are passed agreeably. Wednesday was very cloudy, but in the morning there was no rain. Ma scolded us for appearing so sad, but I could not help it. My feelings I could not disguise. I was engaged in the flounces & finished one & was very well satisfied with the general appearance. Just before dinner a note came from Annie inviting us to accompany her in a

visit to the Spanish vessel. We have been long anticipating it & the prospect
was hailed with delight & after gaining Ma's consent A. replied to her sweet
note, accepting the invitation. A short time after dinner we began to dress,
as we were to be at A.'s at 6. I feared it would rain, but my fears were groundless. The cloudy weather was most favorable to us, as it did not render our
toilet room so hot, the sun being obscured. We were at A.'s house in time
& were ushered right up stairs where the little darling, blazing in diamonds,
was a perfect vision of loveliness. Her toilet was not completed & it was
amusing to watch her; she was so interesting, so sweet! so beautiful!! She
said our escort was to be a Mr. Dugne & when he was announced how
frantically was the last bit of powder applied & how angelic she looked!
We were soon before him & introduced. I was not at first very favorably
impressed tho' he was quite handsome. We walked to the horse station,
but there was no sitting room in the cars, so we were content to stand. The
car was crowded with ladies on their way up, & among them I recognized
one whom I had met & fell in love with in the down town cars. After a pleasant ride, & a walk of a few squares we reached our destination. And the
time we had to get to the ship, I never shall forget it, & I could not believe it when I was safely deposited. Annie was so bothered about the powder, etc., but I assured her it was all right. Our escort was very gallant &
being on such a huge monster of the deep, the first man of war I ever visited, & yet I am told it is small in comparison with some other of Spain's
navy. The commander's suite of rooms is perfect. His parlor is a perfect little bijou [jewel] & taking up in it a pen & piece of paper, we wrote a few
words to the commander & signed our names. We had the misfortune to
find all the officers out, & the afternoon was not passed very agreeably;
agreeably it must have been with Annie as a companion, but towards dark,
when the other visitors had left, we went down in the parlor to have a little fun; were playing the piano when 3 midshipmen, the only officers on
board, joined us. They were known to Mr. Dugne, his cousin being engaged to one of the officers, & oh! the time passed so pleasantly, probably
more so with the Middies than any others. They were very hospitable,
offering us cake & wine. They wrote their names & gave them to us, & we
returned the compliment. Little José de la Puente is such a dear creature, only 15 years old, & it was too provoking that we could only speak
thro' our interpreter. We sang the B.B.F. at which they were highly pleased,
questioned them about "Zulma" & "Natalia", & I believe could have remained till now. We found it difficult to get away, & when we did reach
the upper part of the vessel they insisted on our going up on deck & we

obliged. It was delightful, the night was so lovely. They handed us cigarritos which we accepted & will keep as mementos. They promised to come & see us, & after such a getting down stairs we were on land. Rode to Annie's house, where we rested & were refreshed & she walked him, A. & she. Mr. D. & I—I found him very agreeable & like him very well, particularly as A. says he is rich. He is Dreux's cousin, & it was in his arms that Shorty fell, when shot. He was entertaining me with particulars. Met Leon coming from Z.'s. Annie came in for a short time & then we parted. I was satisfied. Yesterday I finished the 3 flounces & it looks beautiful. A. intends to present it as my chef a'—I am quite proud of it. It will be beautiful when finished. In the afternoon A. & I were walking when we met Leo. who joined us, & escorted us to Romberg. Passed some more Yanks of whom A.J. is very frightened. L. spent the evening with us. And now, Philomen, we have to part & with how many regrets! Move on, parting from me, for the four months' intercourse binds me so closely to you. I did not imagine how sad would be my thoughts in parting, and how mournfully I would be thinking of him who is sleeping in Virginia, one whose acquaintance was one of the most joyful things in our intercourse. Oh! Robert! [Col. Wheat] May we meet in the Heaven to which your soul has winged its flight! Every man is insignificant when compared with you, & from the depths of my heart springs the wish had I never known you. The perplexing question is how shall I procure for you a robe. D. is not here, Pa is not. Ma's funds are low!! Oh! ye fairies of ancient times, come to my assistance. Good bye, my love!!

Afterword

Efforts over the years to trace the fate of Clara Solomon and the rest of her family were, initially, not very successful. Much information surfaced quickly about younger sister Rosa, who became a celebrated Victorian hostess in New Orleans after her marriage many years later to Durant da Ponte, an important figure in Clara's diary. But the fate of the rest of the family, especially of the diary's author, remained a mystery for some time.

More recent research, started by genealogist Patricia Ann Fenerty of New Orleans (see Acknowledgments), has yielded much new information on the family's history, and led to contact with grandchildren of Sarah (Sallie) Solomon, another of the younger sisters. The Census records provided the basic data from which information on the current generation of descendents followed. Mr. E. Spencer Lazarus, Jr., and Mrs. Alice Dale Cohan, herself named after Alice Solomon, remember all the sisters and have kindly supplied photographs and genealogical material, filling many gaps in the record, so it is now possible to look at the Solomon girls in later life and put together an outline, if not a complete picture, of the Solomons' fate after 1862.

The family remained in New Orleans through the war and afterward. Clara's older sister Alice married Alexander Dalsheimer in 1866. He was a native of Baton Rouge and no doubt related to the Jewish mercantile family of Leopold and Nathan Dalsheimer, both of whom had successful clothing and dry goods businesses before and after the war. The Dalsheimers were most likely of Germanic origin, not Sephardic Jews. Alexander Dalsheimer died in 1878, leaving behind Alice and one child, Sarah. Alice herself died unexpectedly in 1880, at age thirty-seven. References on her tombstone indicate that she was very much admired and respected in the community. The inscription also mentions the "increasing sorrow" of the Solomon family, referring to the loss of her husband and to other family tragedies about this time.

One recent tragedy concerned Clara's father, Solomon Solomon, who died in 1874 at age fifty-eight, at which time the family was living on Magazine Street in New Orleans. An earlier family loss concerned Clara herself, whose first husband Julius Lilienthal, twenty years her senior, died in 1867, less than two years after their marriage and without children. From the probate proceedings we find that Julius, a jeweler, was known and respected within the Jewish mercantile community, although he had been beset by major financial reverses in 1867. Clara's father knew of Julius Lilienthal's excellent business reputation, although he had not known Lilienthal intimately. During 1866 and 1867, Solomon Solomon acted as a kind of guard at the Lilienthals' jewelry store, staying there from dark until 10 or 11 P.M. while Julius's brother Ed took care of the inventory. Clara's father also borrowed money from his son-in-law's business, but in small amounts.

At the hearings on the disposition of the estate of Julius Lilienthal, Clara's father stated that Clara had no means of her own and was living with her parents after her husband died. Solomon had been working since roughly November 1868 at the U.S. Customshouse, but had been unemployed for a year before then. He said he had been "speculating all around" since his return from the war in 1865. Before the war Solomon had described himself as a wholesaler. In other words, the Solomon family did not fare well economically between 1865 and 1869. Certainly the Solomons did not revert to what appeared to have been a comfortable standard of living in antebellum times.

Clara's mother Emma lived on almost forty years after her husband died. She died in Atlanta, Georgia, in February 1913, but had remained in New Orleans until sometime in the 1890s, living with her unmarried daughters, Sarah (Sallie) and her husband Henry Lazarus, and her orphaned granddaughter Sarah Dalsheimer under one roof. Emma and granddaughter Sarah moved to Savannah, Georgia, to live with daughter Josephine and her husband, Eugene Hinton. By the time of the 1910 Census, the Hintons had moved to Atlanta with their own children, along with Emma and granddaughter Sarah. Sarah Dalsheimer was already widowed by this time.

Alice and her parents are buried at the cemetery of their Congregation

Dispersed of Judah. The Congregation's records note that Solomon Solomon had remained a member until his death. Also buried in the Congregation's cemetery is Fanny Solomon Rubel, wife of Charles Rubel. The family's records show that Fanny married in December 1879 and died less than two years later in February 1881, when she would have been thirty-four. Her remains had been moved from Tennessee for burial.

The cemetery also has the graves of Clara's infant and toddler siblings who did not survive. Eveline, whose name Clara also carried as a middle name, died in 1853, age two. Chapman Solomon, the only son born to Emma and Solomon, died shortly after birth in August 1850.

We know quite a bit more about Sallie, eight years old at the time Clara wrote. Public records of the New Orleans Clerk of Court and private records in the hands of Sallie's grandchildren show that Sallie (1853–1931) married Henry Lawrence Lazarus of New Orleans in 1875. This couple remained in New Orleans, and a grandson lives there today. Henry Lazarus practiced law in the city and for a time was a local judge. Henry and Sallie had six children who survived into adulthood, several of whom moved to the New York area. Among them was Alice Dale Lazarus, named for Clara's older sister Alice, who used Sylvia (or Salvia) Dale as a pen name for her poetry. Alice Lazarus named her own daughter Alice Dale as well, and this granddaughter of Sallie Solomon, living in a New York suburb, has been extremely helpful to me in collecting information, and is responsible for the family photographs reproduced in this edition. Eldon Spencer Lazarus, Sallie's grandson, has remained in New Orleans in his father's house on Octavia Street, and has been equally cooperative, particularly in sending me a copy of Sallie Solomon's high-school diary.

Josie, an infant in 1861, is mentioned above. Her given names were Josephine Pierson, the same given name and surname as a family friend prominent in Clara's diary, Josephine Pierson Hews. (I am not sure of the connection, or if it is more than fortuitous.) Josephine (1860–1945) married Eugene Hinton of Mississippi when she was twenty-five. Their first child, Allan Francis, was born in New Orleans shortly thereafter, followed by Lawrence and Fanny. Their last child, Eugene, was born in Savannah, Georgia, in 1899, a few years after the Hintons moved there and took Sarah Dalsheimer, Alice Solomon's orphaned daughter, with them. The 1910 Census of Atlanta shows that the Hintons' eldest child, Allan Francis, no longer lived in his parent's home, but that Emma Solomon had come to live with them. By this time Sarah Dalsheimer, Emma's granddaughter, was herself a widow at age forty-two, having married someone named Halley.

We have interesting information on Rosa Solomon, born 22 July 1857. Rosa died in New York City in 1948, having lived more than ninety years. Rosa, who came to be regarded as one of the most beautiful women of late Victorian New Orleans, married a gentleman often mentioned in Clara's diary, Durant da Ponte, publisher and owner of the *Delta* newspaper. It was the second marriage for da Ponte who, at fifty, was about twice Rosa's age when they married in June 1882.

Da Ponte was a grandson of Lorenzo da Ponte, the librettist for many of Mozart's operas. He was quite wealthy and lived with Rosa on St. Charles Avenue at Roselawn, in which she had built a Little Theater for performances and charity events, with herself as lead actress. Durant was so taken with her that he donated some of his land along St. Charles for a park to be called Rosa Park, which to this day is one of the most beautiful nooks of New Orleans. The couple had one son, Serrill, but Durant took ill in 1894 while in California and died that year. Rosa retired from the eventful and public life she had been living with da Ponte, and moved to New York City with her child.

The decade or so of the marriage between Rosa and da Ponte was an exciting one. The da Pontes hosted numerous charitable and theatrical events in New Orleans, with the husband providing the financial backing and Rosa the grace and beauty. The photographs of Rosa from this period justify the mounds of admiration heaped upon her by the "society" of nineteenth-century New Orleans. There is a fascinating story, reported in the 1930s, of a trip to Europe and the Middle East taken by Rosa and Durant shortly after their marriage. Rosa was supposedly kidnapped by an Egyptian pasha while in Cairo, and it took the intervention of the American consul there to secure her release.

As for Clara, we cannot really tell how she fared in the postbellum world. What she wrote while seventeen years old and living under Union occupation in 1862 gives some indication of a feisty soul, but one frustrated again and again by the inability of the Confederacy to resist Union forces. The surrender of New Orleans, which undoubtedly saved numerous lives and gave the Solomons and others an opportunity to reestablish themselves in some fashion after the war, embarrassed and confused Clara. Her father's dreams of becoming rich from selling clothing and equipment in Virginia did not come to pass; nor did his hope of moving to California with Emma and the six girls. In retrospect, one feels that California was a distant dreamland for these Confederate diehards, but such hindsight would be an unfair judge of the participants in 1861 and 1862.

Clara, as stated above, married Julius Lilienthal shortly after the war's end, in April 1866, several months before the wedding of her older sister Alice. On the surface, then, Clara's concerns about living in the shadow of Alice and perhaps not marrying at all were unfounded. Clara's marriage to Lilienthal, however, was an odd one. He was about twenty years her senior and a respectable merchant in New Orleans at a time when Clara's father was trying to get back on his feet after being away from the city during the war. Solomon himself had said that he could not readily find work in 1865 and 1866, and Clara's marriage may have been one of convenience for economic benefit. Julius, furthermore, was known to have been a very sick man at the time of the marriage, although his family tried to blame his physical deterioration and subsequent death on Clara when contesting her inheritance claims.

Clara and Julius made two trips to the Hot Springs spa in Arkansas for medical purposes during their marriage, and Julius died there in December 1867 while under the care of Dr. George Lawrence, a Baltimore native and doctor in the Confederate forces, who worked at the spa during its "season." In antebellum times Lawrence had been a medical officer in the United States Navy. While the Lilienthal family questioned Lawrence's medical treatment of Julius, Clara herself thought enough of Dr. Lawrence to marry him in 1872. They married in Memphis, and there is no indication that Lawrence was Jewish. The couple lived first in New Orleans and then in Hot Springs, where two of their four girls (Alice Rosa and Elizabeth Elvina) were born. Clara continued her parents' propensity toward producing daughters. The older daughters, Ida Mary and Sally Emma, were born in New Orleans. There is record in New Orleans of only one marriage, that of Sally Emma, which apparently produced no children. Further information on Clara's descendants will have to await research in other states.

We know little of the Lawrences' life during their marriage, but we know that the doctor died in 1889. Clara lived until 1907, a New Orleans resident at her death. In the 1900 Census, Clara and her four girls were living on Eighth Street, near Chestnut. There is a telling comment in an obituary for Clara, indicating a strong devotion to her children. The obituary in the *Picayune* read as follows:

> Mrs. Clara E. Lawrence of this city, died Saturday last, leaving a legion of grief-stricken friends and four inconsolable daughters to mourn an irreparable loss. Mrs. Lawrence, though ill for the past

two years, gave promise of better health because of the new-found joy in the convalescence of one of her daughters who had been ill for several months, when she passed away in an acute attack of heart trouble. Her friends, who will forever cherish the memory of her brilliant mind and her gentle heart, will, however, find their sweetest consolation in the almost unparalleled devotion to her daughters, which has been the increasing inspiration in which they have learned all those qualities of mind and soul that have never failed to endear them, as they did their beloved mother, to the hearts of all.

Clara not only came to live a life that at the least equaled in sentiment that of her revered older sister, Alice. She also succeeded in adapting to the postbellum world in the South by devoting herself to her family, as her own mother had done.

Publication of these diaries will allow many more people to peek through the gallery of the Solomons' home on Hercules (now Rampart) Street and watch the early stages of the Civil War unfold in New Orleans as presented by a civilian, a very young one at that. The reader will then enjoy the drama as much as this editor has while preparing the diaries of Clara Solomon for publication.

Index